J. Fitch

D0140372

Readings in Clinical Spectrography of Speech

C. Frith.

Readings in Clinical Spectrography of Speech

Edited by

Ronald J. Baken, Ph.D.
and
Raymond G. Daniloff, Ph.D.

A Joint Publication From

 Singular Publishing Group, Inc. and 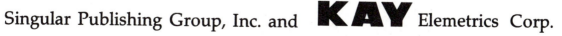 KAY Elemetrics Corp.

A Joint Publication From:
Singular Publishing Group, Inc.
4284 41st Street
San Diego, California 92105

and

Kay Elemetrics, Inc.
12 Maple Avenue
Pine Brook, New Jersey 07058

© 1991 by Singular Publishing Group, Inc.

All rights, including that of translation, reserved. No part of this publication may be reproduced, stored in a retrieval system, or transmitted in any form or by any means, electronic, mechanical, recording, or otherwise, without the prior written permission of the publisher. The additional copyright information listed on page 563 of this volume shall be considered a continuation of this page.

ISBN: 1-879105-04-7

Printed in the United States of America

Contents

Foreword

Only quite recently has the sound spectrograph, as a stand-alone unit, been eclipsed as the most productive analysis equipment in the speech laboratory. For years, the spectrograph was the centerpiece of many laboratories, and it enabled the development of the field that has come to be known as acoustic phonetics. Even today, with the proliferation of powerful computer systems, the spectrogram remains a valuable tool for the study of speech. Indeed, the spectrogram may be more useful than ever. The contemporary student of speech does not have to generate spectrograms in the tedious and noisome fashion of the old machines that burned traces onto sheets of facsimile paper. Computer-generated spectrograms appear easily and quickly on a video terminal. The more powerful computers can display a spectrogram in a matter of seconds — a fraction of the time required to produce a spectrogram with the workhorse instrument used for the better part of the last half-century.

The spectrogram's importance derives largely from its ability to display the rapidly changing spectral properties of speech. Because it is a compact representation of the remarkably complex patterns of speech, the spectrogram is unique in its overall utility in speech analysis. Learning the spectrographic correlates of speech sounds is still a fundamental step in understanding speech.

The collection of papers in *Readings in Clinical Spectrography of Speech* is a dual record of spectrographic analysis and acoustic phonetics. The temporal span of the papers gives the collection a historic value in the best sense of the term: the older papers in the volume possess a current importance that validates their designation as classic. Reading through the papers gives one a sense of the development of the science of speech analysis. Laboratory science is partly tools, theory, data, and hard work. The papers collected in this volume are the products of several investigators who have labored to understand speech with the aid of the sound spectrograph.

A particularly welcome feature of *Readings* is the inclusion of papers in the area of speech sound development and clinical application. Acoustic analysis in these areas is a relatively recent phenomenon, and the early results hold promise for a productive future. Work should be facilitated by the current availability of low-cost computer systems for speech analysis. These systems may usher in a new era in which spectrography and other forms of analysis are increasingly — perhaps even routinely — applied to the study of speech development and speech disorders.

The primary focus of acoustic analysis in the last four decades has been on the normal male talker. The result of this effort has been the accumulation of a large amount of data on the patterns of men's speech. Attention is now being directed to comparable studies of the speech of children, women, and persons with communication disorders. This expansion of acoustic phonetics will enhance its vitality and utility.

Sound spectrography should play an important and continuing role in this evolution of acoustic phonetics. Applications of sound spectrography are far from exhausted, and it will be interesting to observe the new domains of its application. *Readings* is both a record of the spectrographic analysis of speech and an introduction to the future of spectrographic analysis. In this future, the spectrogram likely will be one of several types of acoustic analysis afforded by ever faster and more powerful computers.

Baken and Daniloff's *Readings* is a volume that should be eagerly received by the researcher, educator, clinician, and student. It brings together a set of papers that define the clinical spectrography of speech, beginning with discussions of the spectrograph itself, proceeding to the spectrographic characteristics of normal speech, continuing with considerations of speech sound development, and concluding with applications to evaluation and therapy. The publication of *Readings in Clinical Spectrography of Speech* signals the maturation of spectrography and its specialty offspring, clinical spectrography.

Raymond D. Kent

Preface

It is unlikely that anyone realized it at the time, but Friday, November 9, 1945 marked the beginning of an era. On that day, issue number 2654 of the weekly journal *Science* was published, and it carried, along with discussion of "race differences" and the sexual maturity of hamsters, an article called "Visible Patterns of Sound" by Ralph K. Potter. In it, Potter and his coworkers at Bell Telephone Laboratories unveiled a "new instrument that we have called the sound spectrograph," developed during the war but kept secret because of its military importance. The report provided nothing in the way of a technical description of the device (that came later, in the first article included in this volume), but it contained the first modern sound spectrograms to appear in print: a few words of running speech, single utterances by speakers of different dialects, musical tones, environmental noises, bird calls, and barking dogs. For those of us who deal with speech communication, it foretold a professional world that would never be the same.

There were, of course, already ways of visualizing speech signals. Oscillograms — tracings of the speech sound pressure waveform — were already common, and the spectra of a few brief moments of speech had been derived (by hand) and published. But such methods had very serious limitations. In those pre-computer days, calculating the spectra of successive instants of speech required massive effort. Oscillograms, as Potter pointed out, really contained too much information. Because of differing phase relationships among the spectral components, the waveforms of repetitions of the very same utterance by the same speaker could look completely different, masking critical similarities. "To portray sound in a form that the eye can encompass in a glance," said Potter in the article's introduction, "requires that means be provided for selecting the information and displaying it in an orderly fashion." The sound spectrograph gave anyone the means of obtaining, *automatically*, a display of the changing content of a sound in a form that the eye could, indeed, "encompass at a glance."

A prime motivation for Potter and his colleagues was improved communication for the deaf. The sound spectrograph, he said in this report,

> opens the prospect of some day enabling totally deaf or severely deafened persons to use the telephone and the radio or to carry on direct conversation by visual hearing.... Most immediately, and from humane considerations most importantly, it opens a new avenue of help ... to learn to speak, and for those who already speak, help to improve their speech.

At the very outset, then, the sound spectrograph was seen as a clinical device.

Reading sound spectrograms for communication purposes proved to be impractical for a host of reasons. The undertaking involved intensive exploitation of the sound spectrograph in the examination of speech sounds and the nature of their interactions. The results of these investigations were documented in *Visible Speech,* the classic work that Potter, George Kopp, and Harriet Green (later Harriett Kopp) published in 1947. In that publication, the authors presented hundreds of spectrograms of speech sounds, syllables, and sentences, which were spoken, sung, and chanted in English, French, Ojibway, Danish, Arabic, Chinese, Russian, and other languages. The spectrograms showed the acoustic components of speech, its *content* — not in the more common sense of signification, import, or meaning — but in the physical sense of its acoustic structure: its molecules and atoms, and their constantly changing assortments and combinations.

It was not that theories of the physiological bases of speech production had not existed before, or that there was any paucity of views about the foundations of speech perception, but rather that suddenly there was a mine of information, available to any prospector, for theoretical construction, refinement, and validation. This wealth of quantitative and qualitative data shouted for attention, demanded explanation, and tested the power of models and hypotheses. The expansion of our understanding of normal speech proceded in quantum leaps and our insight into the nature of speech disorders increased apace.

During recent years, speech sound spectrography has become easier, cheaper, and potentially more useful than ever. The power of microcomputers has largely replaced the old analog methods, resulting in the ability to perform more sophisticated analyses in close to "real-time" and in a more "user-friendly" environment. Nonetheless, clinical utility rests primarily on the vastly improved theoretical underpinning that relates the acoustic product to the physiological behavior. With the wonderful circularity that typifies much of good science, good spectrographic interpretation is founded on good scientific theory and solid theory has been developed out of better spectrographic interpretation.

For this volume we have selected several articles — a very small sample of what the literature holds — that serve as enduring landmarks and guides. Their import is suggested in the introductions to the four sections of the book. We trust that this collection will prove useful as an instructional tool for the neophyte and valuable as a resource for the experienced. We also hope that it will be recognized as a salute and token of gratitude to our antecedents and colleagues whose talents have brought our profession to where it is today.

R. J. Baken
R. G. Daniloff

PART I
Sound Spectrography: Basics and Beginnings

There was speech-sound spectrography before there was a sound spectrograph. As far back as the 19th century a kind of spectral evaluation was done by Helmholtz, who used resonating bottles to find out what frequencies were present in the speech signal. In a feat of considerable persistence and diligence, Steinberg (1934) actually calculated the spectrum of the vocal tract for every fundamental period in a single sentence *by hand* — a task that, without even a simple electronic calculator, must have entailed untold hours of drudgery. The work, he said, was an illustration of "a method of approach to studies of speech production and measurement." The value of the method was indisputable, but the labor involved ruled out its routine application.

That changed in 1946 when Koenig, Dunn, and Lacy described an electronic sound spectrograph that had been developed at Bell Telephone Laboratories during the war and showed how it could be used to evaluate speech and other acoustic data. This was a genuine landmark in the phonetic sciences, a birth announcement of a new era. For the first time quick and easy sound spectrography was possible in any laboratory or clinic.

The modern sound spectrograph has improved on the original design in many ways: integrated circuits have replaced vacuum tubes, magnetic tape recording has given way to digital storage of the sampled signal. But, under the surface, the evolution of the Sonagraph has left the basic analytical method intact. Despite the changes in the instrument, Koenig, Dunn, and Lacey's description of how the spectrograph works remains essentially valid and very useful. It is also as clear and succinct an explanation as one is likely to find. Along with it, we have selected a few articles (Peterson, 1952; Lindblom, 1962), Fant, 1962) that guided early users of the Sonagraph and that, with equal effectiveness, can initiate the newcomer today.

Readings

Koenig, W., Dunn, H. K., and Lacy, L. Y. (1946). The sound spectrograph. *Journal of the Acoustical Society of America, 18,* 19–49.

Lindblom, B. E. F. (1962). Accuracy and limitations of sonograph measurement. *Proceedings of the Fourth International Congress of Phonetic Sciences* (pp. 188–202). The Hague: Mouton.

Fant, G. (1962). Sound spectrography. *Proceedings of the Fourth International Congress of Phonetic Sciences* (pp. 14–33). The Hague: Mouton.

Peterson, G. E. (1952). Parameter relationships in the portrayal of signals with sound spectrograph techniques. *Journal of Speech and Hearing Disorders, 17,* 427–432.

The Sound Spectrograph*

W. Koenig, H. K. Dunn, and L. Y. Lacy

Bell Telephone Laboratories, Inc., New York, New York

(Received May 4, 1946)

The sound spectrograph is a wave analyzer which produces a permanent visual record showing the distribution of energy in both frequency and time. This paper describes the operation of this device, and shows the mechanical arrangements and the electrical circuits in a particular model. Some of the problems encountered in this type of analysis are discussed, particularly those arising from the necessity for handling and portraying a wide range of component levels in a complex wave such as speech. Spectrograms are shown for a wide variety of sounds, including voice sounds, animal and bird sounds, music, frequency modulations, and miscellaneous familiar sounds.

I. GENERAL

IN many fields of research it is necessary to analyze complex waves. If these waves are steady in time, the analysis presents no particular difficulties. If, however, the wave is complex in its frequency composition and also varies rapidly in time, the problem is very difficult. Numerous methods have been employed in the past to try to show changing energy-frequency distribution; several examples have appeared in the pages of this journal. Figure 1, for instance, shows a series of harmonic analyses of the successive periods of a vowel sound.[1] The dotted lines mark the regions of resonance which change continuously throughout the production of the sound. By performing this operation on a whole sentence, an effort was made, as shown in Fig. 2 taken from the same paper, to represent the time variations in the energy-frequency distributions. Here the frequencies of the various resonant regions are represented by the solid lines and their relative amplitudes are roughly indicated by the widths of the lines. The generation of this graph represented a formidable amount of time and labor.

Figure 3 shows another representation of a changing wave form.[2] This is an oscillogram of a series of 11 steady tones sent over a radio channel and received through a bank of narrow band filters whose outputs were commutated at the rate of $12\frac{1}{2}$ times per second. A slight gap was left between cycles, as marked at the bottom of

Fig. 3. The successive cycles show varying profiles, due to the fact that the frequency response of the radio channel was continually changed by selective fading. Similar pictures would have been obtained if a varying signal such as speech had been impressed on the bank of filters without

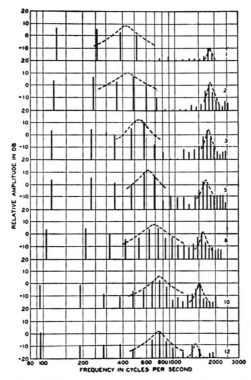

FIG. 1. Illustrating one method which has been used in the past to show how vocal resonances change with time. This is a series of harmonic analyses of successive periods of the vowel in the word "out."

* Paper presented before the meeting of the Acoustical Society of America, May 10, 1946, New York, New York.

[1] J. C. Steinberg, J. Acous. Soc. Am. 6, 16–24 (1934).
[2] R. K. Potter, Proc. I.R.E. 18, 581–648 (1930).

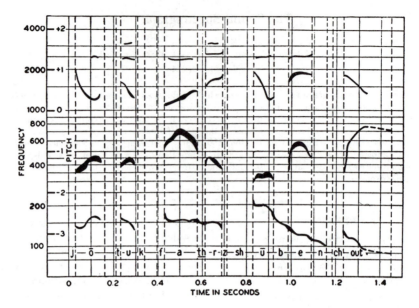

FIG. 2. A plot of the time variations of the vocal resonances in a short sentence, compiled from a series of analyses like those in Fig. 1.

the radio link. Instead of making oscillograms, however, the output was at that time displayed on a cathode-ray tube. The changing profiles of these patterns portrayed the changing energy frequency distribution in speech. An attempt was made to learn to recognize these word patterns, but with little success.

Figure 4 shows another device for portraying a complex wave.[3] Here a kind of three-dimensional model was developed by analyzing the amplitude of each harmonic component of a piano note as a function of time, plotting the results on cards, and cutting out the profiles.

Still another method is illustrated in Fig. 5. Here the frequency range was divided into ten bands[4] by means of band filters. The output of each band was rectified and recorded with a string oscillograph, so that each oscillogram shows the variation of amplitude with time. Despite the rather small number of bands, a kind of speech pattern can be discerned in this array of oscillograms.

Figure 6 shows this process carried further.

These are solid models built up of oscillograms of about 200 overlapping frequency bands, cut out in profile and stacked side by side. In the upper model only the high peaks in the speech are prominent. In the lower model the level differences among the various regions have been equalized by electrical compression which will be explained subsequently. Of particular interest in these models is the sharpness of the wave front which appears at the beginning of some of the words. It can be seen from these models that in speech the energy-frequency distribution is very complex and changes form rapidly with time.

The production of solid models, while useful for particular purposes, is hardly a practical method for everyday needs. Furthermore, it is difficult to portray the results usefully in a two-dimensional picture. If, however, we substitute for the third dimension in these models a system of varying shades of gray or black with the highest amplitudes represented by dark areas and the lowest amplitudes by light areas on a flat surface, then we have a method which can be rapid and convenient. This is the method of the sound spectrograph.

[3] O. H. Schuck and R. W. Young, J. Acous. Soc. Am. 15, 1–11 (1943).
[4] Homer Dudley, J. Acous. Soc. Am. 11, 169–177 (1939).

II. GENERAL PLAN AND FIRST MODEL OF THE SOUND SPECTROGRAPH

Figure 7 shows in highly schematic fashion the basic method of the sound spectrograph, as originally proposed by Mr. R. K. Potter.[5] It is necessary, first, to have a means of recording the sound in such a form that it can be reproduced over and over. The means shown here is a magnetic tape, mounted on a rotating disk. In recording, some predistortion of the signal may be desirable and is therefore indicated in connection with the recording amplifier. With speech, for example, it has been found advantageous to raise the amplitude of the higher frequencies by about 6 db per octave in order to equalize the representation of the different energy regions.

Second, a means of analyzing must be provided. Most convenient is the heterodyne type of analyzer employing a fixed band pass filter, with a variable oscillator and modulator system by which any portion of the sound spectrum can be brought within the frequency range of the filter.

Finally, the output of the analyzer must be recorded in synchronism with the reproduced sound. The simplest method is by means of a drum, on the same shaft with the magnetic tape, carrying a recording medium which should be capable of showing gradations of density depending on the intensity of the analyzer output. Each time the drum revolves, the stylus which marks the paper is moved laterally a small distance, and the oscillator frequency is changed slightly. Thus a picture is built up which has time as one coordinate and frequency as the other, with intensity shown by the density or darkness of the record. It may be necessary or desirable to distort the amplitudes in the analyzer output, depending on the recording medium used and the use to be made of the spectrograms. This function is indicated in the figure by the compression in the last amplifier.

The first spectrograph set up in the laboratory differed in some particulars from the arrangement shown in Fig. 7. Instead of a recording drum on the same shaft with the magnetic tape, use was made of a machine built for radio fac-

[5] See introductory paper of this series.

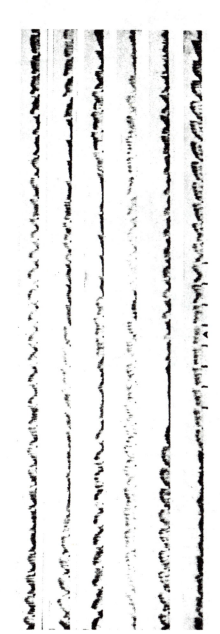

Fig. 3. Oscillogram of a series of 11 tones transmitted over a radio channel and received through narrow band filters whose outputs were repeatedly scanned with a commutator. A single cycle is included in the section marked A; here the circuit was momentarily almost flat; the other cycles show changing profiles due to the changing response of the circuit through selective fading.

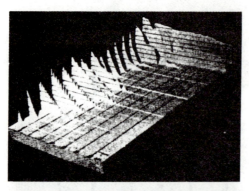

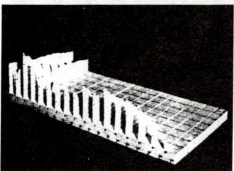

FIG. 4. Three-dimensional models portraying the amplitudes of the several harmonics of a piano note as functions of time.

simile reception, which happened to be available. This device had a cam-driven arm sweeping a stylus across a strip of conducting paper. The paper had a light-colored surface which became progressively darker as the current passing through it increased. Each sweep of the arm was started by a synchronizing signal which in this case came from a contact connected to the disk carrying the magnetic tape. The paper was automatically advanced 0.01 inch between sweeps. The machine had to be modified to the extent of slowing down the motion and providing a new cam to make the motion more uniform.

For the analyzing portion of the system, use was made of another piece of available equipment, namely an ERPI heterodyne analyzer. No mechanical connection was provided between the analyzer and the magnetic tape or the recording system, so the frequency had to be shifted by hand after each sweep of the recording arm. In the beginning, the output of the analyzer was rectified and a thyratron threshold arrangement was employed ahead of the recorder, so that it printed only when the analyzer output rose above a predetermined level, and there were no gradations in density. When it was found that intensity could be shown by the density or blackness of the record, the threshold was dispensed with; but because of the small range of currents required for printing the full density range of the paper, it was necessary to compress the sig-

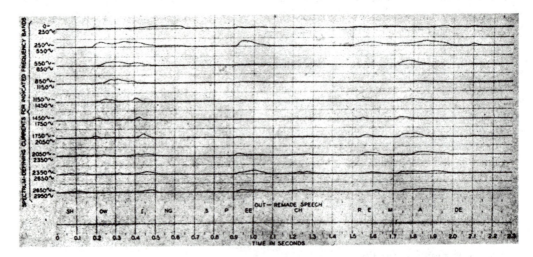

FIG. 5. Another method of illustrating the energy-frequency-time distribution in speech: a series of oscillograms of the rectified outputs of 10 band filters.

FIG. 6. A solid model built up of oscillograms, similar to those of Fig. 5, for 200 overlapping frequency bands. The words are "visual telephony for the deaf." The two models differ in the amount of amplitude compression.

nal. This was done with a sort of partial automatic volume control arrangement, and adjustments were made until a 35-db signal level range was covered, with what looked to the eye like even density steps on the paper for even db changes of level.

A sample spectrogram of speech made with this arrangement is shown in Fig. 8. The coordinates of time and frequency are indicated. The analyzing band width was 200 cycles, with the band being shifted (by hand) 50 cycles for each new sweep of the recording arm. The sentence shown is a familiar one, containing most of the vowel sounds. The most gratifying feature of these early spectrograms was the clear indication

of the almost continual shifting in frequency of the dark bars which represent the vocal resonances. It would take weeks or months of harmonic analysis from oscillograms to obtain the same information. Considerable consonant detail may be seen as well. Predistortion, to the extent of raising the higher frequencies by 6 db per octave, was used in making this spectrogram.

While pitch inflection is not shown in Fig. 8, it may be brought out by two methods. If the analyzing band is made narrow enough, the separate voice harmonics appear and their rise and fall with pitch can be seen. The other method is to permit the beats between harmonics in a wide band to register. producing characteristic

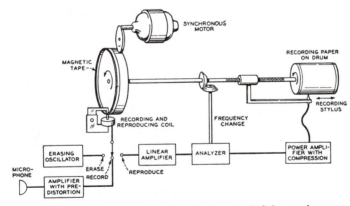

FIG. 7. Schematic representation of the basic method of the sound spectrograph. The sound is recorded on the loop of magnetic tape, and analyzed while repeatedly reproduced. The fluctuating analyzer output builds up a pattern of light and dark areas on the electrically sensitive paper.

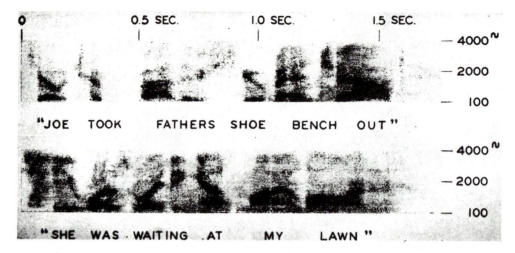

Fig. 8. Spectrograms made with the first laboratory model assembled from available equipment. The vocal resonances are clearly indicated. Further description of the features of spectrograms will be given in connection with subsequent illustrations.

striations vertically across the pattern. Both of these effects will be illustrated subsequently.

The work with this experimental equipment was carried out before our entry into the war. Because of its military interest it was given official rating as a war project and a self-contained model was developed which is described in the next section.

III. PRESENT MODEL

A photograph of the present model portable sound spectrograph is shown in Fig. 9 with the equipment set up as in operation. The recorder unit is at the right, the amplifier-analyzer is at the left with associated control circuits mounted on a panel attached above it, and the power supply is on the lower shelf of the table. The units are interconnected by means of flexible cords and connectors so they can be transported separately. This spectrograph, although basically the same as the early model described above, differs considerably in mechanical and operational details.

The recorder unit, which serves as the magnetic tape recorder as well as the spectrograph pattern recorder, is built around a modified commercial two-speed turntable of the type used for disk recording. The signals to be analyzed are recorded on a length of vicalloy magnetic tape ¼ inch wide and between 2 and 3 mils thick,

mounted against a shoulder in a step turned on the lower edge of the 13″ turntable platter. About

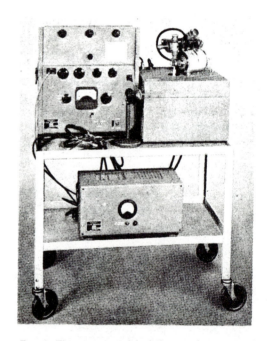

Fig. 9. The present model of the sound spectrograph, built in three parts for portability. The magnetic tape unit is in the right hand box, whose superstructure also carries the paper drum and stylus. The amplifiers, analyzer, etc., are in the left-hand box. The lower unit houses the regulated power supply.

one-third of the tape projects below the platter rim. Precise machining of the step is necessary to prevent eccentricity or wrinkling of the tape. The ends of the tape are sheared diagonally at about 45°, to a length which will provide a 2- or 3-mil butt joint when the tape is mounted. The joint is slanted so that the overhanging sharp pointed edge of the tape trails as the turntable rotates. When the tape is cut and mounted carefully, the joint is hardly noticeable in the patterns. The tape is held to the platter rim by a serving of heavy linen thread wrapped around the upper two-thirds of the tape and cemented in place by several coats of clear lacquer. The turntable is rim-driven by a synchronous motor through friction drive idlers at 25 r.p.m. for recording and 78 r.p.m. for analysis.

Two sets of magnetic pole pieces, one for recording (or reproducing) and another for erasing, are mounted on the bed of the machine so that the overhanging edge of the tape passes between their faces. The recording pole faces are about 40 mils square and are mounted with a pivot and spring so that their inside edges will just pass in a shearing fashion when the tape is removed. In order to insure good contact with the tape at the shearing edges, the pole faces are initially machined at a slight angle (2 or 3 degrees to the tape) to reduce the time for "running in" to a good fit. Very small misalignments of the pole

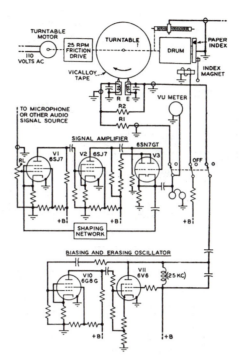

Fig. 11. Schematic diagram showing the spectrograph components arranged for recording a sample on the tape. The erasing and recording processes are continuous until stopped by the switch; the last 2.4 seconds of signal are then on the tape.

RECORDING-REPRODUCING POLE PIECE, 40 MIL FACE   ERASING POLE PIECE 50 MIL FACE

Fig. 10. View with cover removed, showing the magnetic tape and the pole pieces. The butt joint in the tape is exaggerated in this picture.

faces may cause a decided loss of high frequency response. As shown in Fig. 10, the erasing pole pieces are placed about one inch ahead of the recording pole pieces; their pole faces are slightly wider than the recording pole faces so that erasing will be effective even if there is a small relative misalignment of the two sets of pole pieces. Between the two sets of pole pieces may be seen a spreader with which they may be lifted out of contact with the tape for safety during shipment or handling of the turntable. An oil-saturated wick placed ahead of the pole pieces serves to clean and lubricate the tape as it rotates.

The superstructure mounted above the turntable (Fig. 9) serves as the spectrogram pattern recorder. In addition to the conventional cutting head carriage and lead screw, a 4″ diameter metal drum, mounted on a shaft parallel to and below the lead screw, is driven through 1:1 spiral gears from a vertical extension of the turntable shaft. A flexible stainless steel stylus about

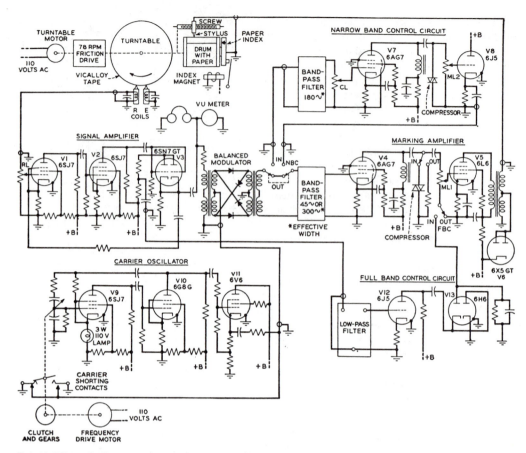

FIG. 12. Schematic diagram showing the spectrograph components arranged for reproducing and analyzing the recorded signal. The carrier oscillator is slowly swept through the frequency range while the signal is repeatedly reproduced and impressed on the modulator. The output of the band pass filter is amplified and marks the paper with a density corresponding to the instantaneous level. The control circuits govern the amplitude compression.

10 mils in diameter is mounted on an insulating block fastened to the cutting head carriage, which can be lowered to or raised from the recording position manually. An automatic paper index mounted on the drum shaft indicates the position for placing the lap in the facsimile paper so that the beginning of the sound sample recorded on the tape will coincide with the leading edge of the paper.

The schematic diagram in Fig. 11 shows the various elements of the spectrograph used in the recording condition. The signal amplifier and the biasing and erasing oscillator are in the amplifier-analyzer unit. The signal amplifier is used also for reproducing and the oscillator forms a part of the carrier oscillator for analysis of the recorded signals. Switch contacts for making the change from the "record" to the "reproduce" condition, however, are left out of the schematics to make them more straightforward.

A microphone or other signal source is connected to the amplifier input, and the recording level, which can be read on the VU meter, is adjusted by means of the RL potentiometer. Shaping networks are provided in the feedback circuit so that the relative levels of high and low frequencies in the signal may be changed if desired. The low impedance output of the amplifier is connected to the recording coil R through a high resistance $R1$ which gives essentially constant recording current for equal voltages over the frequency range of the input signal. Erasing current of 25 kc is supplied to the erase coil E by the biasing and erasing oscillator. Some of this current is also applied as a bias to the recording coil R through the resistor $R2$. Small tuning condensers across the recording and erasing coils raise the effective coil impedance at 25 kc but have little effect in the voice frequency range. These condensers also serve to reduce oscillator switching transients which otherwise tend to magnetize the tape so strongly that complete erasure is difficult.

The turntable and tape are driven at 25 r.p.m. which permits recording a sample of 2.4-second duration at a linear tape speed of approximately 16 inches per second. Continuous recording and erasing are effected as long as the switch is in the recording position. The erasing coil, since it is just ahead of the recording coil, erases signals which were recorded 2.4 seconds earlier. When the "record-reproduce" switch is thrown to the right, erasing and recording are simultaneously stopped, thereby capturing the last 2.4 seconds of signal on the loop of tape, after which it may be reproduced over and over.

The paper index magnet is energized in the recording position, and the paper index rotates frictionally with the drum until the index magnet armature engages a pin projecting on the side of the paper index, causing it to remain in a fixed position. When the index magnet is released at the end of a recorded sample, the paper index is free to rotate with the drum again. The paper index then indicates the position on the drum corresponding to the end of the sample recorded on the tape. Since the drum is directly geared to the turntable on which the tape is mounted, the above relationship will remain fixed and the facsimile paper can be placed on the drum so that the end of the paper coincides exactly with the end of the recorded sample. After a desired sample has been recorded, the turntable is stopped and a pre-cut sheet of electrically sensitive paper is secured to the drum by means of rolling springs.

The turntable is then speeded up to 78 r.p.m. by shifting idler pulleys in the friction drive. It should be pointed out that, although the signal sounds unnatural when speeded up approxi-

mately 3 to 1 by this shift, its wave form is unaltered. The effect is merely to divide the reproducing time approximately by 3 and multiply all of the frequency components of the recorded signal by the same factor. This operation converts the original frequency range of approximately 100 to 3500 cycles to about 300 to 10,500 cycles. Since it is very difficult to vary a narrow band-pass filter over this range for analysis, a heterodyning process is used with a fixed band filter.

Figure 12 shows the various circuits of the spectrograph in the reproducing condition. Starting at the upper left of the diagram, the signal is picked up from the magnetic tape by the reproducing coil R. A small equalizing condenser in shunt resonates the coil at about 12,000 cycles to keep the high frequency response from falling off. This provides an over-all frequency response which is essentially flat when the sample has been recorded without pre-equalization.

The reproducing coil works into the RL potentiometer which is used to adjust the level of the reproduced signal to a suitable value. The three-stage feedback signal amplifier has a resistive feedback network to provide a flat frequency response with a voltage gain of about 100 times while reproducing.

The output of the signal amplifier is impressed on the balanced copper oxide modulator. Carrier is supplied to the modulator by the R-C carrier oscillator through the cathode follower amplifier stage $V11$. As the carrier frequency is slowly

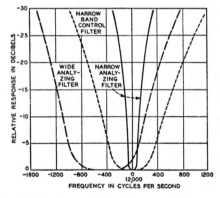

Fig. 13. The characteristics of the several filters used in the spectrograph. The effective band widths are less than those shown by a factor of 3:1, which is the speed-up ratio of reproducing vs. recording.

shifted by the frequency drive motor from approximately 22,500 cycles to 12,000 cycles, the lower sideband output of the modulator is swept slowly across the fixed band filter connected to its output. The normal sweep rate is such that the turntable makes approximately two hundred revolutions in the time required for the frequency to change from the highest to the lowest value. Since the stylus advances about 10 mils for each revolution of the turntable, the resulting spectrogram is approximately 2 inches wide for the 3500-cycle frequency range. The carrier shorting contacts, which are operated from a cam on the condenser drive shaft, switch the carrier current on and off to define the high and low frequency boundaries of the spectrograms.

Either of two filter widths may be slected by a switch which selects one of two values of mutual capacity between the anti-resonant sections of the band-pass filter. The characteristics of the two filters are shown in Fig. 13. It will be noted that the mid band frequency of the wide analyzing filter is lower than that of the narrow filter. With this particular filter structure, changing the pass band is accomplished by shifting the lower cut-off; the upper (theoretical) cut-off remains the same. These curves show the actual pass bands of the filters; the effective widths are about one third of the indicated widths, because the frequencies of the speeded-up reproduced signal are spread apart by a factor equal to the speed-up ratio, namely about 3:1. As pointed out previously this does not alter the wave shape of the signal but spreads out frequencies and reduces time, with a net effect of speeding up the analysis by a factor of three.

The output of the analyzing filter is impressed directly on a two-stage amplifier which has enough gain to raise the rather low voltage to a value sufficiently high to mark the facsimile paper. The output of the amplifier is not rectified, but is connected to the stylus through a step-up transformer having a turns ratio of about 1:2. Under some conditions a very high signal may reach the grid of the final marking amplifier stage. If the stylus is not lowered to load the amplifier, very high positive peak voltages tend to appear across the output transformer secondary. The biased diode (V6) is shunted across a portion of the high winding to limit the peak voltage to a value which will not damage the transformer insulation. When the stylus is on the paper, the normal range of marking voltages does not exceed the bias voltage and the diode has no effect. A rather small transformer with ordinary insulation will safely withstand the voltages with the diode protection.

In this connection it may be noted that the process of recording on the paper generates a considerable amount of smoke. A blower is therefore incorporated in the recorder unit to draw the smoke through a charcoal filter. The hinged plastic shield which may be seen in Fig. 9 directs the smoke into a slot in the top of the recorder box.

The marking range of the paper is limited to about 12 db. A 70-volt signal on the stylus will make a barely visible mark and about 300 volts will mark the paper full black at the linear paper speed of approximately 16 inches per second. Since for some applications it is desirable to show components of speech which cover a range of 30 or 40 db, it is necessary to apply a compressing action to the marking amplifier to reduce the signal range to the limited range of the facsimile paper. One kind of compressing action is secured by shunting across a high impedance point a non-linear compressing resistor (thyrite) whose voltage varies as the 3rd or 4th root of the current through it. This form of compression operates directly on the wave shape, and there is no time constant involved. It produces a rather uniform gradation of blackness on the recording paper over a 35 or 40 db range of signal intensity and brings out low level detail in the signal being analyzed. However, the compressing action when secured in this manner tends to degrade the frequency resolution of the filter. Better definition has been secured by the use of control circuits which accomplish compression in a different manner.

Two control circuits are provided as shown in Fig. 12. The narrow band control circuit is used with the narrow (45-cycle) analyzing filter and the full band control circuit is used ordinarily with the wide (300-cycle) filter. The narrow band control circuit is a series arrangement which may be switched in ahead of the 45-cycle analyzing filter. It includes a control filter whose characteristic is shown in Fig. 13. Its pass-band is

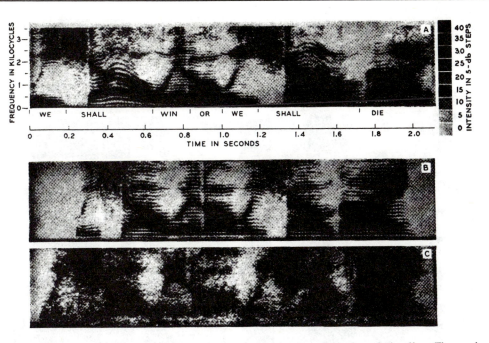

FIG. 14. Spectrograms of speech made on the present model, using a 45-cycle analyzing filter. These and subsequent illustrations have been trimmed and reduced. The originals are 12.5 inches long (for 2.4 seconds) and 2 inches high, recorded on pre-cut sheets 4.5 inches wide. Section (A) normal speech. (B) monotone. (C) whisper.

about 180 cycles (effective) surrounding the pass-band of the narrow analyzing filter. A compressor having the same characteristics as the one described above is inserted in the control circuit amplifier. Since the compressing action takes place ahead of the analyzing filter, the frequency resolution of the analyzing filter is not impaired as it is when the compressing action is placed after it. Compression at this point is permissible because the control filter passes such a narrow band that no important modulation products generated by the compressor fall in the pass-band of the analyzing filter. Various degrees of control can be obtained by changing the working level of the compressor by means of the gain controls provided.

The full band control circuit ordinarily but not necessarily used with the 300-cycle analyzing filter, is a shunt arrangement. The low pass filter passes the entire frequency spectrum of the signal which is then amplified and rectified with a time constant of 2 milliseconds. The filtered or smoothed d.c. output of the rectifier is applied as a bias to the marking amplifier grid thereby controlling its gain. This arrangement serves to control the gain after the analyzing filter by the spectrum ahead of the filter. The direction of control is to reduce gain for higher spectrum energy.

The effect of these control circuits on the spectrograms will be illustrated in the next section.

Returning to the photograph Fig. 9, the location of the various items mentioned above is as follows. The panel attached above the amplifier-analyzer unit houses the control circuits, which were added relatively recently. The two left-hand dials regulate the degree of narrow band control, and the right-hand dial the degree of full band control. The switch on this panel selects the type of control—"full band," "narrow band," "compressor (in the marking amplifier) in" and "compressor out."

The main panel has two attenuators at the upper left, one for controlling the recording level, the other for the reproducing level, both levels

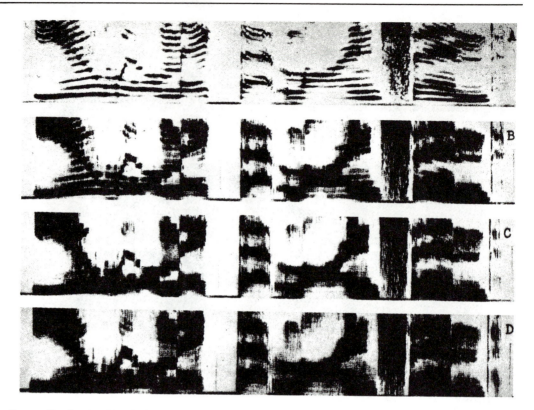

FIG. 15. Showing the effect of widening the analyzing filter, with a high pitched voice. The widths are 90, 180, 300, and 475 cycles in Sections (A) to (D), respectively. The words are "you will make that line send."

being read on the VU meter in the center. The next knob is the recording-reproducing switch, and the next the filter selecting switch. To the left of the VU meter is the predistortion selector, and to the right is the dial for resetting the carrier oscillator at the beginning of each pattern. This dial returns the rotating condenser plates to their starting position; a small motor inside the panel then drives them slowly back through a friction clutch.

Just below the VU meter is a gear shift lever by means of which the rate of frequency sweep can be changed so as to make the patterns 4 inches high instead of 2 inches. The two buttons at the bottom permit reading the carrier and marking voltages, respectively, on the meter.

The power supply unit provides filament and plate voltages to the rest of the equipment. It is highly regulated and operates at 280 volts from 110-volt a.c. power.

IV. SPECTROGRAMS OF SPEECH

Figure 14A shows one kind of spectrogram produced by the later models of the sound spectrograph. The well-known sentence which appears in this spectrogram has been used for testing and illustrative purposes because it contains monosyllabic words with a variety of resonance patterns. The frequency scale of the spectrogram is linear and covers 3500 cycles as shown by the scale at the left. The time scale is also linear and covers 2.4 seconds (in the illustrations the spectrograms have been trimmed at the ends). They have also been photographically reduced; in the originals the vertical height is 2 inches and the length is 12.5 inches, making the time scale slightly over 5 inches per second.

This spectrogram shows a great deal more detail than the ones in Fig. 8; it was made with a much narrower analyzing filter—about 45 cycles wide at the 3-db points. With this filter the

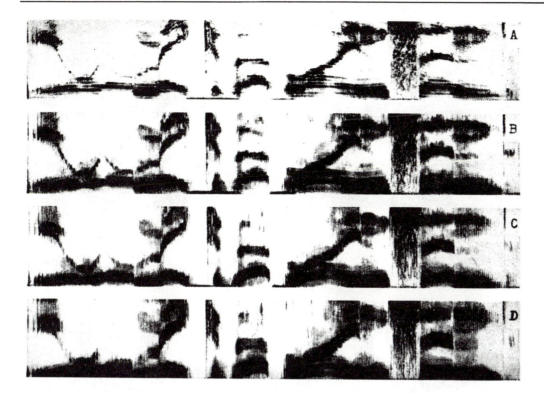

FIG. 16. Same as Fig. 15, but with low pitched voice.

individual harmonics of the voiced sounds can be clearly distinguished. The traces curve up and down as the pitch of the voice is varied in normal speech. The wider the spacing between harmonics, the higher the pitch at any particular instant. In the word "shall" for instance, the pitch first rose and then fell. If the words are spoken in a monotone, the harmonic traces remain level and equi-distant as shown in Section B of Fig. 14. If the words are spoken in a whisper, the spectrogram appears as in Section C. It will be noted that the distribution of dark and light areas is closely similar in all three spectrograms. These dark areas indicate the regions of maximum energy—in other words the vocal resonances. In the whispered words the vowels and consonants all have the same fuzzy texture with no harmonics present. The same texture appears in normal speech in unvoiced sounds such as the "sh" sounds in Section A.

These spectrograms were made with the compressor in the marking amplifier. The gradations of black produced by various signal intensities are shown in the upper right-hand corner. Since the last two steps are nearly alike in blackness, the range is somewhere between 35 and 40 db.

The effect of widening the analyzing filter can be seen in Fig. 15. These are spectrograms of a rather high pitched female voice. The filter used in Section A of Fig. 15 was twice as wide as that in the previous illustration, that is, 90 cycles. In Section B the filter width was 180 cycles, and the harmonics of this high pitched voice are still clearly resolved. In Sections C and D the filter widths were 300 and 475 cycles, respectively; with these wide filters the individual harmonics tend to merge and only the resonant areas can be clearly resolved. The first word in these illustrations shows clearly that the trend of the resonant areas may be opposite from that of the voice pitch. It is evident that the pitch is rising in this first word but the frequency of resonance is rapidly falling so that each harmonic in turn is reinforced momentarily,

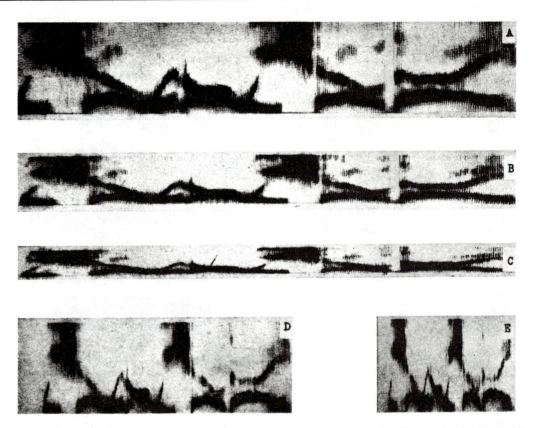

FIG. 17. Spectrograms illustrating various aspect ratios, using the 300-cycle analyzing filter. Section (A) "normal." (B) and (C) frequency dimension reduced by 2 and 4, respectively. (D) and (E) time dimension reduced by 2 and 4, respectively. The words are "We shall win or we shall die," identical sample in all spectrograms.

producing a step effect which is somewhat undesirable for visible speech purposes. With a lower pitched voice such as is illustrated in Fig. 16, the resonance areas tend to form smooth dark bands as soon as the filter becomes wide enough so as not to resolve the individual harmonics. The filter widths in this figure are the same as in Fig. 15. With most male voices a filter about 200 cycles wide would be adequate to smooth the resonance bands. A 300-cycle width has been adopted as a compromise, and is adequate for most voices.

In Fig. 16 it will be noted that there is a distinct pattern of vertical striations in the voiced sounds. This pattern is caused by the fact that more than one harmonic is passed by the analyzing filter. It is well known that two or more frequencies separated by equal intervals will produce beats at the interval frequency. In the case of speech, this frequency of course is the voice pitch. Each vertical striation represents the crest of a beat, and the separation between crests can be seen to vary as the pitch changes. In Fig. 15, where the pitch is very high, the vertical striations are so close together as to be barely distinguishable. Incidentally these vertical striations sometimes persist unbroken across the whole frequency range, which is probably due to the particular kind of phase relations resulting from the mechanism of phonation. Sometimes there are phase reversals in the striations, however; this subject would make an interesting study in itself and probably throw light on the voicing mechanism.

The time and frequency dimensions of spectrograms were originally chosen so as to give ade-

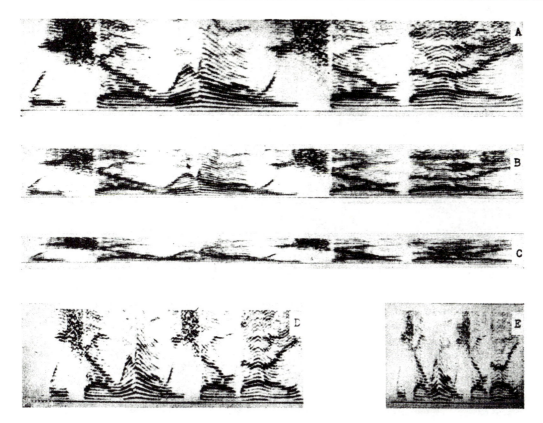

FIG. 18. Same as Fig. 17, but with 45-cycle analyzing filter.

quate resolution for a particular purpose. When the spectrograph was applied to visible speech, the question naturally arose whether some other choice of dimensions might not be more suitable. Figure 17 shows some spectrograms made to explore this question. The upper one (A) has the original aspect ratio, that is, the ratio of the frequency to the time dimensions. In (B) the frequency dimension has been cut in half by increasing the speed of the carrier oscillator sweep, leaving the time dimension the same as before. In (C) it has been reduced by a factor of 4. Changing the aspect ratio in this direction apparently does not contribute to the appearance or legibility of the patterns; rather, it tends to reduce the curvatures of the resonant traces and thereby make the different sounds less easily distinguishable. Spectrogram (D) was made with the opposite kind of change. Here the time dimension was cut in half by decreasing the di-

ameter of the paper drum, while the frequency dimension was left normal. In (E) the time dimension was reduced by a factor of 4. After a study of these and other samples, it was felt that while the aspect ratio originally chosen might not be an optimum, at least there would be no very great advantage in changing it.

Figure 18 shows the same series of spectrograms and the same speech material analyzed with the narrow filter. Here again there appears to be no particular virtue in changing the aspect ratio. In addition there is a distinct loss of detail when the frequency scale is reduced. The "normal" spectrogram is made up of 200 horizontal lines so close together that the frequency is shifted only about $\frac{1}{3}$ the width of the filter. Spectrograms (B) of Figs. 17 and 18 were made with only 100 lines and (C) with only 50. It is apparent from these illustrations that when the narrow analyzing filter is used the number of

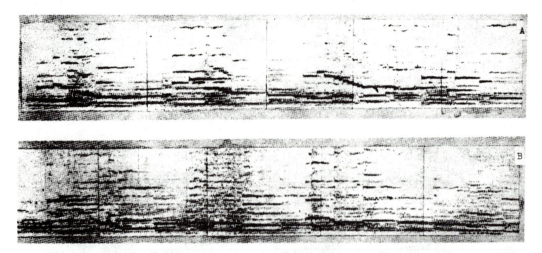

FIG. 19. A passage of piano music with reduced time dimension as in 18(E). This aspect ratio seems quite appropriate for music, though not for speech.

lines cannot be materially reduced, at least with low pitched voices, without loss of frequency detail.

In this connection it may be mentioned that while the normal aspect ratio appears to be nearly optimum for speech, it is not necessarily so for other applications. Figure 19, for instance, portrays a passage of piano music with the time dimension reduced by a factor of 4. With this aspect ratio the musical action is clearly indicated while speech, as shown in the previous illustrations, appears much too crowded in the time dimension. For other applications it has been found desirable to lengthen rather than shorten the time dimension.

Figure 20 illustrates in a somewhat different fashion the effect of changing the amount of frequency overlap in successive lines. Section (A) shows a normal spectrogram with the narrow filter and (B) shows the same sample with the same time and frequency scales; however in making spectrogram (B) three successive lines were made alike, and the frequency was then shifted by three times the normal amount. The effect is the same as though a stylus three times as wide as normal had been used with the lateral shift and the frequency shift also three times normal. The harmonics now appear to rise and fall stepwise rather than smoothly. With the wide filter, however, this process can be carried much further. Section (C) for instance shows the same material analyzed with the wide filter. Here each line has been repeated 4 times and it requires close inspection to distinguish this from a normal spectrogram. In Section (D) each line has been repeated 12 times. Obviously this has carried the process too far, but these illustrations show that if only a wide analyzing filter is of interest, considerable time could be saved by reducing the number of lines in the spectrograms and hence reducing the number of times the sample must be reproduced in the process of analyzing it. In the present spectrograph of course the analyzing time has been set by the requirements of the narrowest analyzing filter rather than the widest.

Figure 21 shows the need for some kind of compression in portraying speech sounds and illustrates the action of the full band control circuit mentioned in Section III. Spectrogram A shows the words "one, two, three, four, five, six" made without any compression except a certain amount of limiting action in the last power stage of the marking amplifier. The strongest consonants such as the "t" in "two" and the "s" in "six" can be seen in the spectrogram, but the weaker consonants such as the "f" in "four" and "five" are completely missing. Section B was made with the thyrite compressor in the marking amplifier. This spectrogram shows all the

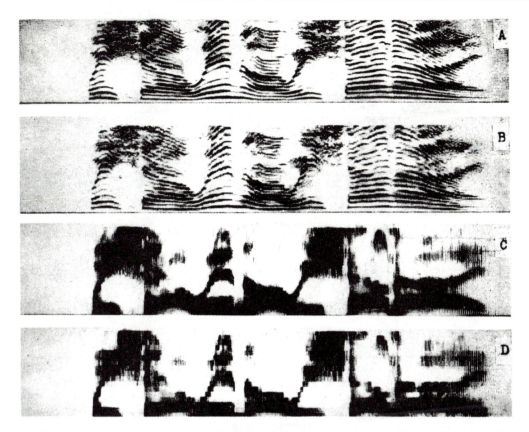

FIG. 20. Showing the effect of degrading the frequency resolution by laying down several identical lines, then shifting the frequency by a correspondingly greater amount to keep the normal frequency dimension. Section (A) normal spectrogram, (B), (C), and (D) 3, 4, and 12 repetitions, respectively.

consonants clearly. However, the low level portions of the vowel sounds are also brought out and the resonance bars are made fuzzy. For visible speech purposes it was desired that the consonants should show as clearly as they do in (B), and at the same time that the vowels should be portrayed as they are in (A). The full band control circuit accomplishes these purposes as illustrated in Section (C). Here the consonants show at least as clearly as they do in (B) and the vowel bars are resolved about as they are in A, with the low level material suppressed. The action of the full band control circuit, as discussed in the previous section, is to adjust the gain of the marking amplifier not according to the momentary output of the analyzing filter, but according to the energy in frequency bands other than the one being scanned at the moment. With

this arrangement sounds in which the energy is weak in all portions of the frequency range are amplified, but the low level portions of vowel sounds are suppressed.

Figure 22 illustrates the action of the narrow band control circuit, using the same words as Fig. 21. Again Section (A) was made without any compression except the limiting action of the last marking stage. Section (B) was made with the thyrite compressor. It is clear that a wider range of levels is covered in (B), which is desirable; however, the harmonics have become fuzzier and tend to merge together. Section (C) was made with the narrow band control circuit with a setting such as to show the same range of levels as appears in (B), but here the harmonic traces are much more clear-cut than in (B). The control can be set to bring out an even wider

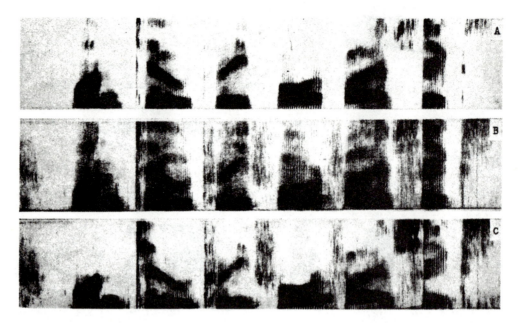

Fig. 21. Illustrating the need for amplitude compression and the action of the full band control circuit. The words are "one, two, three, four, five, six." Section (A) no compression. (B) compressor in the marking amplifier. (C) full band control.

range of levels, if desired, still leaving the harmonics clearly resolved. The action of this circuit is to adjust the over-all gain depending on the energy in the frequency regions immediately adjacent to the one being scanned. The gain is not raised when the analyzing filter happens to pass between two harmonics, but it is raised when the energy level is generally low.

V. OTHER APPLICATIONS

Thus far attention has been concentrated on spectrograms of speech. Other types of signals can be handled as well. The spectrograph is a useful laboratory tool for determining the nature of the time and frequency distributions of energy in sounds other than speech, or in complex waves of any kind whether they exist as sounds or not. Some applications of this type will be illustrated in this section.

Figure 23 shows in Sections (A), (B), and (C) some samples of thermal noise. In Section (A) it was reproduced at a very high level and it shows almost uniform darkness except for occasional light patches randomly spaced. In Section (B) it was reproduced at a lower level and the

characteristic pattern of this type of wave can be clearly seen. Since in thermal noise the energy is concentrated in different frequency regions in different instants of time, the spectrogram shows randomly spaced vertical spindles whose length corresponds roughly to the width of the analyzing filter, which in this case was 300 cycles. In Section (C) the 45-cycle filter was used and the spectrogram shows fuzzier patches due to the slower response of the narrow filter. Many familiar sounds contain such random components. Section (D) for instance shows the sound of striking a match. The dark area at the left portrays the sound generated by the abrasive, the longer portion the roar of the flame. Both of these areas contain random noise as previously illustrated. In addition, sharp vertical lines may be discerned across the whole frequency range. Sharp lines of this type represent clicks or crackling sounds which are characterized by a wide frequency distribution of energy and short duration.

Section (E) shows the sound of filing on a metal plate. Three file strokes are included in the picture, and the actual sound of the file

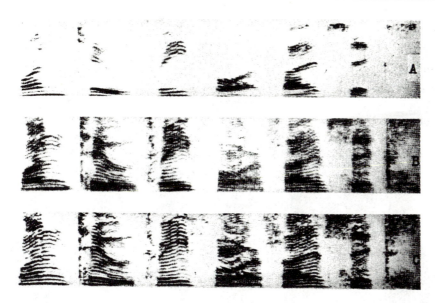

FIG. 22. Illustrating the need for amplitude compression and the action of the narrow band control circuit. Section (A) no compression. (B) compressor in the marking amplifier. (C) narrow band control.

teeth can be seen dimly as rising and falling bands in the lower part of the spectrogram. The dark regions in the upper part of the spectrogram represent resonances in the metal plate which of course remain substantially constant in frequency but vary in amplitude. The definite components can be distinguished from the random components by their more uniform texture. Section (F) shows some machinery noise. There is a low frequency periodicity in the random components, and a dark band across the middle which indicates some discrete components. The small section at the right was made with the narrow filter and shows the four discrete components more plainly.

Whether the wide or narrow analyzing filter should be used depends on the nature of the sound and how far apart in frequency the components are. Figure 24 presents two sounds analyzed with both filters, showing that in some cases the two sets of information from the wide and narrow filters complement each other. Sections (A) and (B) represent the sound of an infant crying. Each cry begins and ends with voiced components of very high pitch. In the middle of each cry the voice breaks down into a very irregular noise. In this example the components are far enough apart so that they are easily resolved with the wide filter. However, the narrow filter permits the exact frequencies of the components to be determined. Sections (C) and (D) analyze the sound of snoring. The wide filter shows that the inspiration phase consists of a series of sharp, regularly spaced clicks, with the frequency distribution modified by resonances in two portions of the frequency range. The expiration phase is practically random noise but also shows reenforcement by resonance in definite frequency regions. The narrow filter reveals that the resonances are unexpectedly sharp considering the nature of the oral cavities.

Figure 25 illustrates some bird songs analyzed with the wide and narrow filters. Sections (A) and (B) show the song of the nightingale. There are two distinct types of song in this illustration. One is a rapidly falling note with a double trill at the end. The other is a rising and falling note with an almost linear trend in both directions. It will be seen that each note is accompanied by some noise components. This is recognized with more assurance with the wide filter than with the narrow filter because the narrow filter tends to produce a fuzzy trailing edge when it scans across a component. Since the wide filter has

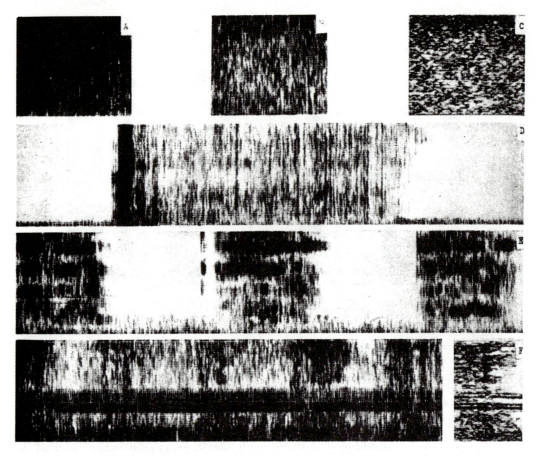

FIG. 23. Some sounds other than speech. Sections (A), (B) random noise at two levels, 300-cycle filter. (C) random noise, 45-cycle filter. (D) sound of striking a match, and the roar of the flame. (E) filing on metal plate. (F) machinery noise.

sharper time resolution, a higher level of signal can be used and thus a wider range of levels can be explored without fuzziness. The noise components in this sample are therefore definitely not a result of the analyzing process.

Sections (C) and (D) represent the song of the wood thrush. Here again a higher level can be used with the wide filter. This song is remarkable for two reasons. The middle portion contains a rapid succession of two distinct notes repeated with great precision. The fainter trace at the top of this section is a second harmonic which was not necessarily generated by the bird but may have been produced in the recording and reproducing processes. The last section of the song however, shows two distinct notes pro-

duced at once, namely an extremely rapid high pitched trill accompanied by a steady note of lower pitch. Since these two notes cannot be multiples or submultiples of each other, they are not harmonically related and must therefore have been produced by the bird with two distinct emitting mechanisms. The rapid trill is almost completely blurred by the narrow filter. Incidentally, these bird songs (and others to be shown later) were taken from phonograph records. They included frequencies above the normal 3500-cycle range of the spectrograph. The phonograph records were therefore played at less than their normal speed so that all frequencies were reduced sufficiently to fall within the range. When this method is used, the actual frequencies can be

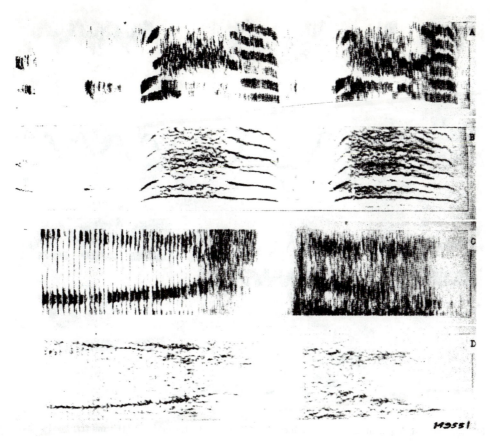

FIG. 24. Comparing the two analyzing filters. Sections (A) and (B) infant crying. (C) and (D) sound of snoring.

computed by dividing the apparent frequencies, as read from the spectrogram, by the speed reduction ratio. The nightingale sample covers about 4500 cycles, and the wood thrush about 6000 cycles.

Figure 26 gives further examples of the behavior of the two filters with signals that vary rapidly in frequency. These are spectrograms of warble tones produced by varying the frequency of a single tone sinusoidally. Sections (A) (narrow filter) and (B) (wide filter) show four different rates of warble from 40 per second to 80 per second. It can be seen that as the frequency of warble is increased, the picture made by the narrow filter tends to exhibit a horizontal structure. In other words, the narrow filter sees this signal as a frequency modulated wave which consists mathematically of side bands around the average frequency. Sections (C) and (D) show higher frequencies of warble and also somewhat greater excursions. The breaking up into discrete components is complete at 100 cycles with the narrow filter and at higher frequencies even the wide filter shows the same effect. Mathematically, both of these representations are correct; the signal may be regarded either as a set of distinct frequency components or as a rapidly varying single component. The spectrograph therefore does not give a false picture. It is simply a matter of choice which interpretation of the signal is more convenient.

Incidentally, all of the illustrations used in this section were made without any form of compression. In exploring an unknown signal it is generally advantageous to make this kind of analysis first because it gives a better picture of

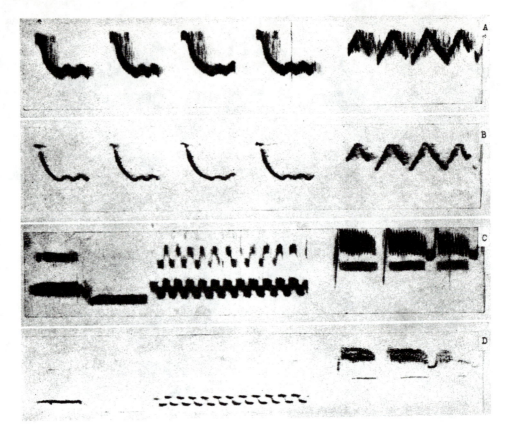

FIG. 25. Two bird songs analyzed with both filters. Sections (A) and (B) nightingale. (C) and (D) wood thrush.

amplitude relations. If the existence of weaker components is suspected, these can be explored with the help of the control circuits if desired.

In Fig. 27 are some spectrograms in which frequency analysis is not the purpose but only the means to an end. Section (A) is the output of an oscillator whose frequency was varied by means of a motor driven condenser. It was desired to determine how the frequency varied with time, and this is immediately apparent from the spectrogram. This type of information could have been obtained by making an oscillogram of the output and determining the frequency *versus* time by counting cycles and making proper interpolations, which would have been an extremely laborious procedure particularly if the determination of slight irregularities were important.

Section (B) portrays the output of a sweep frequency generator showing that the sweep is substantially linear and the return substantially instantaneous. Section *C* illustrates an experiment in which it was desired to determine the manner of acceleration of a phonograph record when released on a moving turntable. The record contained a single frequency tone and a spectrogram of this tone during release proved that the frequency varied linearly from the time the record was released to the time it reached full speed. The duration of the acceleration period can be measured directly on the time scale.

Incidentally, the spectrograms in Fig. 27 cover an 11,000-cycle range instead of the normal 3500 cycles. This was accomplished by recording the signal at the high speed normally used for reproducing. With this arrangement the time covered by the spectrogram is reduced by a factor of three and the frequency scale is multiplied

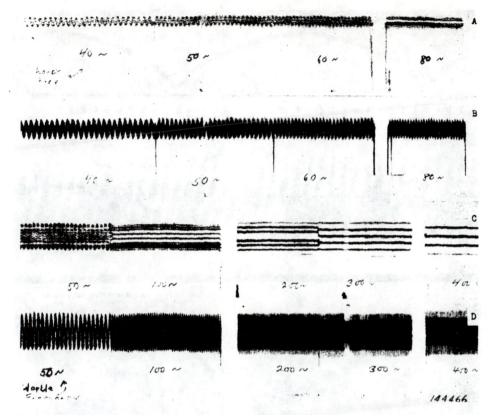

FIG. 26. Tones warbled at various rates. (A) and (C) narrow filter. (B) and (D) wide filter. When the warble rate is comparable to the filter width the warble breaks up into discrete sideband frequencies.

by the same factor. The effective filter width, however, is also multiplied by the same factor, but the apparent width, that is, the width of the trace in the spectrogram, remains the same.

Figure 28 illustrates another application in which the determination of frequency variation rather than analysis was the objective. These spectrograms portray the output of an oscillator whose frequency was governed by a fluctuating d.c. voltage on its grid. The instantaneous frequency can easily be determined at any point with a suitable frequency scale. The fuzziness which is apparent in certain sections results from very rapid amplitude or frequency modulation superposed on the lower frequency modulation. Here the spectrograph takes the place of a string oscillograph, and it avoids the necessity for a d.c. amplifier with sufficiently high output current to drive the low impedance string.

Figure 29 presents another frequency modulation series. In this case a complex wave having both odd and even harmonics was varied in frequency at several rates. The high and low points are marked on the spectrograms. In the uppermost sample the frequency became so low that even the narrow filter resolved the beats. In all these spectrograms "harmonics" will be noted which appear to slope in the opposite direction from the real frequency variation. The effect is due to the fact that the filter, with a rather slow response, is scanning across components at such a rate as to generate a kind of interference pattern. Without attempting to go into the matter thoroughly here, the effect might be compared to the phenomenon of the spokes of a wheel apparently turning backwards in motion pictures. Spurious components like those in Fig. 29 are sometimes visible in analyses

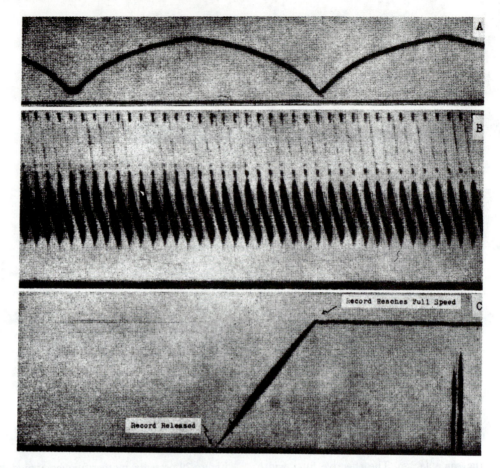

Fig. 27. In these illustrations spectrograms were used to determine *frequency vs.* time rather than energy distribution. Section (A) the output of a motor-driven warbler oscillator. (B) a time base wave. (C) determination of the mode and speed of acceleration of a phonograph disk when released on a moving turntable.

of speech. A good example of this effect can be seen in Fig. 22.

Figure 30 illustrates an interesting application of the spectrograph which should prove very useful. Section (A) shows speech after it has passed through a long loaded line. The line had a cut-off at about 1800 cycles as may be seen by the absence of speech components above that frequency. In addition, however, there is a curious curvature to each syllable. This same curvature can be seen in the small section at the right which represents a click sent over the same line. Ordinarily a click, as mentioned previously, appears as a straight line across the frequency range. The curvature here produced is due to

the fact that different frequencies were delayed by different amounts in transmission over the line. Section (B) shows the same material after a delay correction network had been added to the line. Here the speech and the click are nearly normal. In Section (C) the speech was transmitted through the network alone, resulting in the opposite kind of curvature. This illustrates that the spectrograph may be used to investigate the delay characteristics of filters or other networks which are difficult and sometimes practically impossible to handle mathematically when they include dissipation. These characteristics can be determined by simply measuring the de-

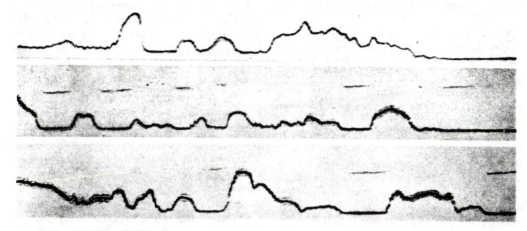

FIG. 28. Another application where spectrograms were used to record frequency *vs.* time. This shows the output of an oscillator whose frequency was governed by a d.c. voltage. The spectrograph here performed the function of a d.c oscillograph.

FIG. 29. Here a complex wave rich in harmonics is varied in frequency at several rates. The maximum and minimum frequencies are marked on the margins. In Section (A) the frequency becomes so low that the narrow filter shows vertical striations due to beats. In all the samples, spurious components may be seen which slope in the opposite direction from the true frequency change.

lay *versus* frequency for clicks sent through the networks.

This section will be concluded by presenting a variety of sounds with a wide variety of patterns. First in Fig. 31 are some additional bird songs. Ornithologists have long been trying to analyze and record the songs of various birds accurately. Even after the songs have been slowed down by recording and reproducing at different speeds, it is still difficult for the ear to follow the rapid changes in frequency. Even if the ear were adequate there still remains the problem of a suitable notation for indicating the complex time and frequency relations. With the spectrograph these analyses can be made objectively, and the results recorded unequivocally.

In Fig. 32 are a few additional voice sounds. They require no particular comment except to note that the song in Section (A) is that of a very high pitched voice which is resolved with the wide filter. The amplitude and pitch variations in the vibrato are clearly shown. Presumably the spectrograph will have application in voice training.

Figure 33 contains a variety of animal sounds and Fig. 34 some miscellaneous familiar sounds. The various kinds of components occurring in these sounds have been pointed out in the previous discussion.

VI. SOME VARIABLES

As already indicated above, the general plan of the spectrograph is capable of very wide variations depending upon the application to which it is to be put. For instance, the time scale can be made extremely short for investigating transient phenomena or the like, or it can be made very long for making long spectrograms or for plotting the course of very slowly varying phenomena. The frequency range is also very flexible. Extremely low frequency sounds could be handled by recording very slowly and using a high speed-up ratio. Extremely high frequencies could be handled by recording at high speeds or by the use of modulating processes to bring the high frequencies down to where they could be handled in the normal way.

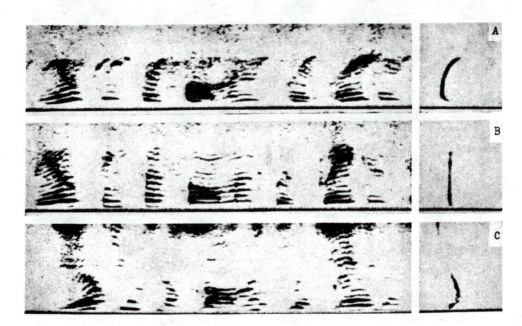

FIG. 30. Illustrating transmission delay in a long loaded line. In Section (A) speech and a click show a cut-off at 1800 cycles, and a curvature which results from the fact that different frequencies were transmitted with different speeds. In Section (B) a delay correction network has been added, restoring the speech and the click to normal. Section (C) shows transmission through the network alone, with the opposite curvature.

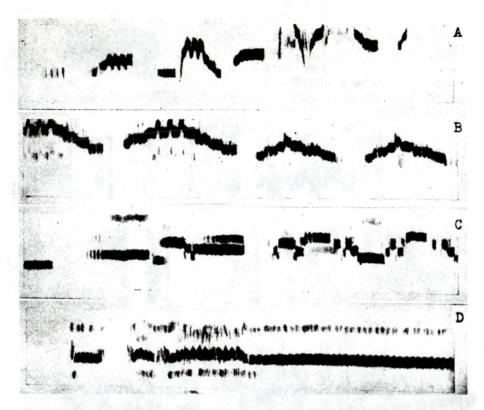

FIG. 31. Some additional bird songs. (A) olive backed thrush. (B) veery. (C) hermit thrush. (D) rooster.

In the present paper all the spectrograms have a linear frequency scale. For some applications, a logarithmic frequency scale would appear to be more logical. In music for instance, the notes are separated by logarithmic intervals. Also, the ear has a natural scale, as shown by differential pitch perception, which is more nearly logarithmic than linear. It might be advantageous to use scales in the spectrograms which approximate those occurring in the ear so that the pictures might be made to look the way they sound. In this connection, the analyzing filters might also be made to simulate more closely the operation of the ear. For instance, a narrow filter might be used in analyzing the low frequencies, with the filter gradually widening towards the high frequencies. The shape of the filter characteristic is also important. In the present spectrograph the narrow filter has extremely steep attenuation characteristics. The wide filter is also

very steep with a relatively flat pass band. Different representations can be obtained with filters having different characteristics.

Figure 35 illustrates a few experiments along this line. Sections (A) and (B) were made with the wide and narrow filter, respectively. The subject matter consists of a series of sharp clicks and at the right a calibration tone consisting of all the odd harmonics of 60 cycles. Section (C) was made with a filter which is just about as wide as the one used in Section (B). However, the sides do not slope quite so steeply. It will be noted that in Section (B), the clicks are fuzzy on both the leading and trailing edges. In Section (C), the leading edge is much sharper. In Section (D), the filter is actually narrower than (B) and still retains a sharper leading edge than (B). In Section (E), the pass band is about the same as (B) but the sides slope much more gradually. Here the total width of the clicks is about the

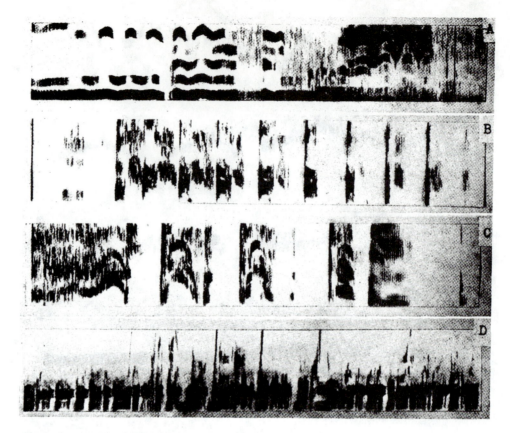

FIG. 32. Some additional voice sounds. (A) trained soprano. (B) laugh. (C) cough. (D) gargling with water.

same as in (B), but the leading edges are about as sharp as with the 300-cycle filter. Obviously, this is a large subject and these illustrations merely indicate the possibilities.

The time requisite for analysis is also subject to wide variation. Time can be saved by reducing the number of lines or by raising the speed-up ratio. If this is carried to sufficiently high frequencies, the patterns might be made substantially instantaneously on a cathode-ray tube.

Various types of signal recording mediums might be used. The magnetic tape seemed desirable because it can be used over and over again. Magnetic recording on wire might be used instead of tape with the advantage that the analyzed samples could be stored. Film recording techniques might be used although this seems

rather slow and expensive. On the whole some of the newer types of magnetic recording look most promising for spectrograph applications.

Similarly, various types of facsimile recording mediums can be used. The particular medium used in the present spectrograph is paper with the trade name Teledeltos. This has the advantage of requiring no processing and is permanent. There are other types of facsimile papers in commercial use, including some which are saturated with a chemical which changes color when current passes through it. These require much less power to mark them and would be adaptable to higher speeds. For a wide range of density, photographic film appears to be best. It has, of course, the disadvantage of requiring processing and is rather expensive.

It might be mentioned that all the variables

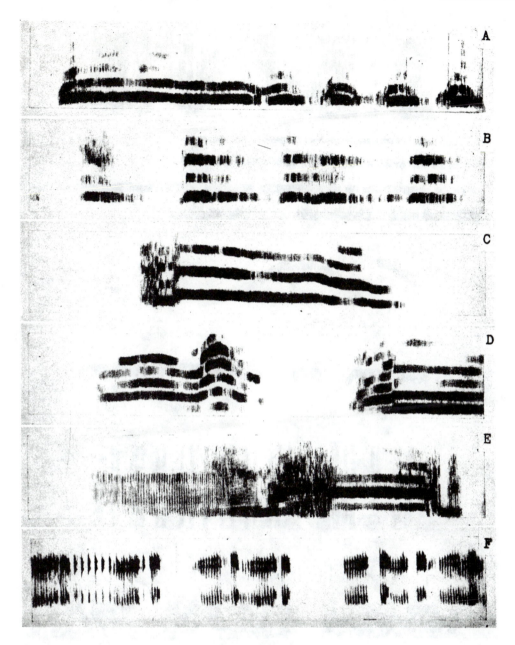

FIG. 33. Some animal sounds. (A) Newfoundland dog. (B) small dog. (C) and (D) wolf. (E) cow. (F) frogs.

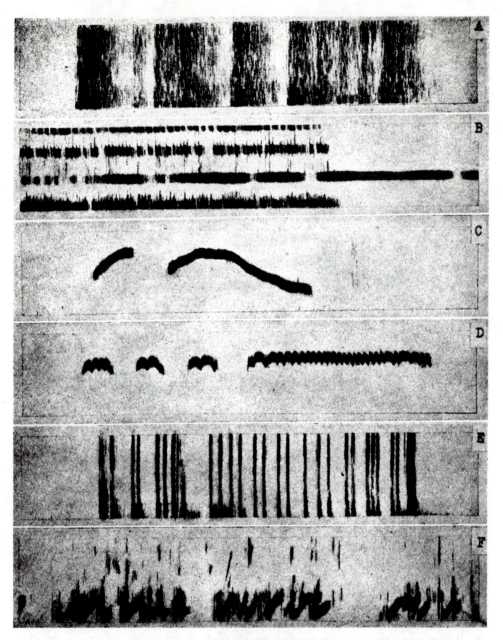

FIG. 34. Some familiar sounds. (A) snare drum. (B) telephone bell. (C) man whistling. (D) police whistle. (E) riffling cards. (F) bubbles blown through water.

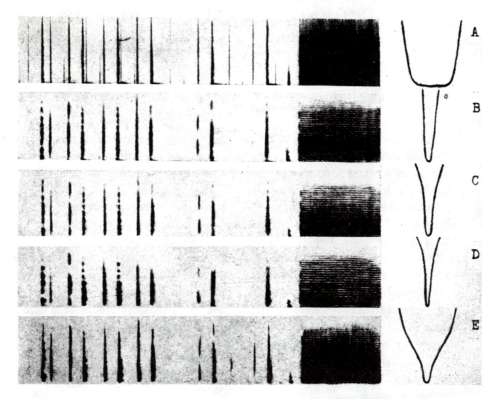

FIG. 35. Illustrating the effect of different filter response characteristics. (A) and (B) the "normal" 300- and 45-cycle filters, respectively. (C), (D), (E) narrow filters with different characteristics. Filters with gradual slopes give sharper pictures of clicks than steep filters.

mentioned in this section have been tried at least in exploratory experiments.

One very important variable should be noted in conclusion. This is the matter of amplitude representation. In the spectrograms presented above, the time and frequency scales are reproducible and subject to precise measurement. The density or amplitude scale, however, is non-linear and not reproducible. The total range of photometric density is not very great, and furthermore there are many variables such as ambient temperature and humidity, stylus pressure, stylus width, the condition of the drum surface, and so forth, which affect the density scale. In some applications, it is necessary to know the amplitudes of the components quantitatively. Various methods have therefore been devised for representing amplitudes in spectrograms in such a way that they can be interpreted quantitatively. It is planned to cover this subject in a subsequent paper.

ACCURACY AND LIMITATIONS OF SONA-GRAPH MEASUREMENTS

BJÖRN LINDBLOM

SUMMARY

In the following we shall briefly review the basic terms involved in the description of speech spectra. We shall point out that the acoustic specification of vowel sounds in terms of formant patterns owes its simplicity to the introduction of the *pole* concept in the description. This is often overlooked.

Among the sources of error in specification by sound spectrography some are inherent in the speech wave itself and others are caused by the analyzing instrument. Fig. I shows a few examples of common sonagraphic displays.

The accuracy in vowel formant measurements from sonagrams was found to be about 40 c/s in an experiment with synthetic vowels.

Is it possible to find a simple formula that automatically transforms spectral data into formant frequency values? Probably not. An alternative procedure is described which uses an inventory of *standard envelopes* or standard formant shapes which are applied to the spectrum under consideration.

THEORY

A fundamental concept in the acoustic description of a speech sound is that of the *spectral envelope*. Its constituent parts are the transfer function of the vocal tract and more or less constant factors such as source characteristics and radiation. Mathematically any envelope is most simply described in terms of *poles* and *zeros* which are points in the complex frequency plane. Poles correspond to resonances within the vocal tract and zeros to anti-resonances. The shape of a pole curve, or a zero curve, is completely specified by data on its frequency and bandwidth (Fig. IIa). The mathematical description of an envelope is equivalent to a decomposition of this envelope into a number of known functions, poles (and zeros), which, if multiplied by each other or summed on a dB scale, would restore the original shape of the envelope (Fig. IIb). Since bandwidths can be predicted from pole or formant frequencies, the measure to take on a zero-free vowel is simply the pole frequencies. More elaborate specifications would in ideal cases be redundant (1, 2).

In a harmonic spectrum (the [ɑ]-sample in Fig. I) the levels and the frequencies

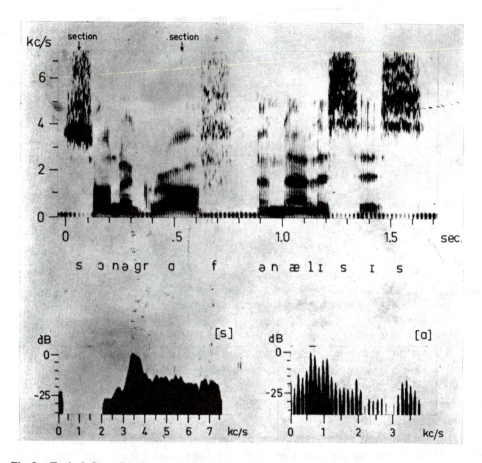

Fig. I. Typical Sona-Graph records. Wide-band spectrogram of the utterance "Sona-Graph analysis". Below wide-band section of the first [s] and narrow-band section of the [ɑ]

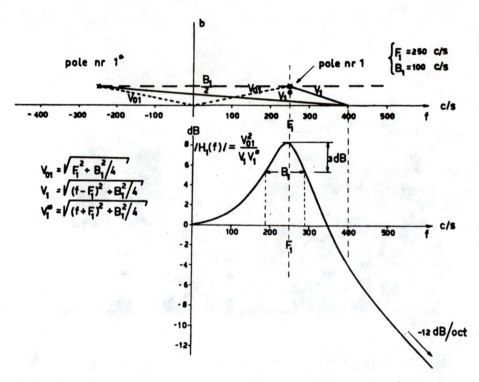

Fig. IIa   Shows how a pole curve can be derived when pole frequency and bandwidth are given. (After Fant).

of the components define the envelope in a number of points; the lower the fundamental frequency the better defined the envelope. The position of the *strongest partial* within a *formant* or *energy maximum* is independent of that of the corresponding *envelope peak*; they may or may not, coincide depending upon the interrelations between pole frequency and fundamental frequency. The *pole* has no direct spectrographic manifestation.

It is thus clear that, when we measure the formant frequencies of a vowel we always aim at estimating the pole frequencies. Unless our measurements stand for poles they have no theoretical justification. On the other hand the difference between the frequency location of an envelope peak and the corresponding pole is negligible except in cases when two poles, or a pole and a zero, come very close together. In reality this implies that, if we succeed in determining the locations of the envelope peaks we shall, in most cases, have obtained a good estimate of the pole frequencies or the *F-pattern*. Given the poles we are able to reconstruct the envelope and thus our description covers all the relevant information that the spectrum may contain.

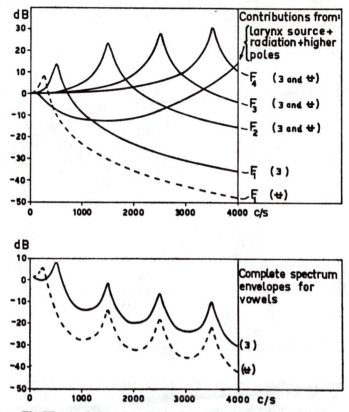

Fig. IIb. Analysis and synthesis of vowel envelopes. (After Fant).

SOURCES OF ERROR INHERENT IN THE SPEECH WAVE

In considering the factors that may jeopardize the precision of formant frequency measurements we find difficulties inherent in the structure of the speech wave itself and limitations imposed by the Sona-Graph. Several investigators (3, 4, 12) have brought attention to the following sources of error in vowel analysis.

(1) The higher the fundamental frequency the less information on the envelope shape. Fig. IIIa exemplifies this difficulty. We see that the partials in this idealized vowel spectrum indicate only one spectral peak whereas the envelope displays two. It is interesting to note that, in spite of the identical envelopes, the ear would probably not equate Fig. IIIa and Fig. IIIb with respect to phonetic quality; Fig. IIIb could be transcribed [ɑ] whereas Fig. IIIa would sound more [ɔ]- like (5).

(2) The more asymmetrical a formant, the more distant the envelope peak may be from the strongest partial within the formant. In Fig. IIIb the envelope is fairly well defined by the relatively dense pattern of partials. There is, however, a certain degree of asymmetry in the second formant. The asymmetry is also obvious in F1 of

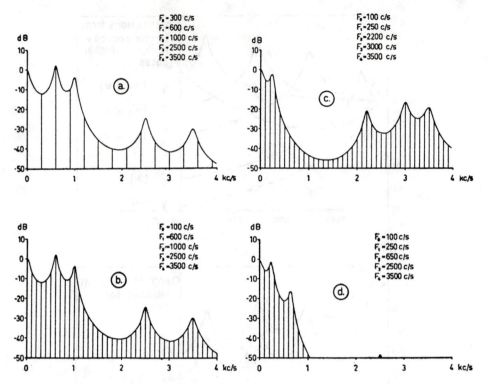

Fig. III illustrates cases where envelopes may be hard to draw on basis of the particular configurations of partials. The difficulty may be caused by too high a fundamental component (a), asymmetry in formants (b, c, d), and by lack of information in the energy distribution in high frequency regions (d). The envelope curves were produced by a computer which was programmed to make a mathematical synthesis of four elementary resonance curves, source function, radiation and higher-pole correction.

Fig. IIIc and F1 and F2 of Fig. IIId. F1 of a close [i]-sound often exhibits negative skewness. The use of a weighting formula for deriving the formant frequency[1] would in these cases fail to give a good result.

(3) In close vowels only one slope may be visible in the first formant.

(4) The first two formants of back vowels are often badly defined since they are usually close together. In these cases it might be worth while to consult the wide-band spectrogram which displays the continuity of the F-pattern.

(5) Close back vowels have only a slight amount of energy in the upper formants. Considerable high-frequency pre-emphasis may be needed to make them appear. This is evident in Fig. IIId.

(6) Zeros, i.e., anti-resonances, appear as spectral minima. They originate from

---

[1] E.g., the one suggested by Potter and Steinberg (6), $F = \dfrac{\Sigma \, \omega_i f_i}{\Sigma \, \omega_i}$ where ω refers to the level and f to the frequency of the ith component within the spectral maximum.

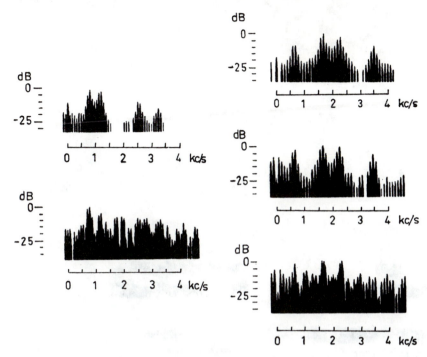

Fig. IV. Samples of steady-state synthetic vowels approaching [a] (left column) and [æ] (right column). The top sections pertain to non-distorted versions. The spectra below exemplify various degrees of distortion.

the source (cf. Flanagan (7)) or a superimposed nasalization. If there is a pole in the vicinity of such a zero the frequency of the corresponding envelope peak may deviate considerably from that of the pole. Moreover, the existence of a zero may give rise to extra formants, i.e., "spurious" formants which do not belong to the F-pattern proper.

(7) In non-stationary intervals the time position of the sample must be chosen more or less arbitrarily. Perceptual experiments may throw some light upon this problem (8).

INSTRUMENTAL SOURCES OF ERROR

There are several instrumental factors to bear in mind when attempting to minimize irrelevant contributions to the speech sample under analysis.

Distortion

Spurious formants may often be artefacts produced by the Sona-Graph. The upper spectra of Fig. IV pertain to relatively pure samples of synthetic [a] and [æ].

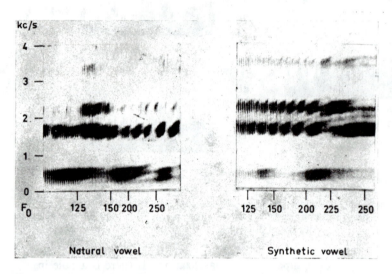

Fig. V. Natural vowel (left) and synthetic vowel (right) on continuously rising fundamental frequency. Subjective estimations of formant frequencies are likely to be influenced by the specific patterns of partials within the formants.

The others display various degrees of distortion. These intermodulation effects could be avoided, however, by keeping the position of the Sona-Graph input control fixed at a high level of amplification and by regulating the level before the Sona-Graph, e.g., on the attached tape-recorder. The critical value on the VU-meter has to be determined by experience.

Time location and sample durations of sections

The time position of a section is apt to vary somewhat owing to the mechanical properties of the microswitch. This uncertainty is about ± 10 msec.

The process of integration involves a weighting of the energy according to a "memory" function. The shape of this function determines the contribution of energy from points along the negative time axis up to the one selected for sectioning (4). The integration time is dependent upon the width of the analyzing filter and the integrating circuitry. The sample durations of narrow-band and wide-band sections are about 30 msec. and 5 msec. respectively.

When sections are made of random noise segment it is important that the time constant of the integrating circuitry is much larger than that of the band-pass filter. In the Kay-Electric Sona-Graph this requirement is not fulfilled and random irregularities appear in wide-band, and still more in narrow-band, spectral sections of e.g., voiceless fricatives. These irregularities may be mistaken for "true" spectral maxima and minima (9).

Among the causes of *spurious formants* we have thus found nasalization and pecularities in the source and instrumental factors such as distortion and limitations in the smoothing filter in the Sona-Graph sectioning device.

Pre-emphasis

A prefiltering of + 6 dB/octave may give rise to certain inaccuracies in formant measurements. As a general rule a bass attenuation means that the lower a formant is in frequency the more its true shape will be mutilated and the further up in the spectrum we will find its peak. Too steep a bass cut will be a serious source of error in the case of analysis with a "600"-c/s filter.[2] This method which requires the use of a magnified frequency scale, produces a spectrographic display which makes accurate measuring very difficult. Experimental results show errors of 150 c/s in judgments of F_1 of synthetic [i]. On the other hand the time resolution of this analysis is accurate and the method lends itself readily to purposes other than precise frequency measurements.

---

[2] A reduction of the speed of the input signal by a factor of two results in halving all the frequencies of the speech. The 300–c/s filter will pass twice as many partials as it would if the signal were played back at normal speed. Its effective width is thus 600 c/s. This type of analysis has been recommended for the study of high-pitched voices.

Calibration

The instability of the instrument makes facilities for individual calibration of spectrograms desirable. Errors introduced in the manual stages of the measuring procedure and by unsatisfactory indication of zero line could to some extent be minimized by the use of harmonic spectra in which frequencies can be measured as fractions of F_0. The fundamental component may be extracted with good accuracy by averaging over e.g., ten partials in a narrow-band spectrogram.

EXPERIMENTAL RESULTS

In order to evaluate the accuracy of formant frequency measurements five experienced investigators were asked to estimate the F-patterns of synthetic vowels on sonagrams. No special instructions were given. The subjects just adhered to "current praxis".

Irrespective of whether the method was wide-band spectrogram, wide-band or narrow-band section, the mean error in a fairly large number of measurements was about 40 c/s for male voices.[3]

The major variable influencing judgments seemed to be fundamental frequency. With increasing fundamental frequency the error tended to become larger than 40 c/s. Only rarely did it exceed $F_0/4$ however. This figure is in many cases larger than the difference limen for vowel formant frequencies, which is roughly of the order of 3% (10, 11).

There is a clear tendency for the investigator to be influenced by the strongest component within a formant. This is readily understood when looking at Fig. V, which shows a synthetic and a natural vowel both on a rising pitch. We see the wavy motion of the strongest partials through the resonances. The extent of the motion is an indicator of the errors which might occur in formant frequency measurements.

PROCEDURE

We may now ask a number of questions. For instance, what method of analysis should we choose in order to obtain a maximally precise estimation of the F-pattern of a vowel? Is it possible to state a procedure by which, in a simple way, reliable formant frequency data could be extracted from a Sona-Graph record or any similar spectrographic representation?

It seems reasonable that, for the study of vowels, harmonic spectra will best serve our purposes. In view of the complex variables that influence the shape of the spectral envelope we must conclude that the prospects of finding a formula that will

---

[3] Standard deviation 40 c/s.

be of general application and automatically give us the frequency of the pole are highly unfavorable.

Unless the formant in question is symmetrical the information contained in a spectrographic configuration of partials within this formant will be insufficient. A correction factor for skewness or asymmetry could perhaps be inserted into our formula but this would entail too great complications.

It appears likely that an investigator would profit more by having an *inventory of standard envelopes* at his disposal from which, on basis of his knowledge and experience, he could select the more probable patterns and apply them to the harmonic spectrum. The procedure suggested is a graphical *spectrum matching* technique.

(1) Estimate approximately the pole (–zero) pattern "by eye" and "by ear", i.e., if our vowel under examination approaches [ɑ] our previous experience of analyzing and synthesizing similar sounds tells us that, if it is a male [ɑ], it is likely to have its first formant F_1 at about 650 c/s, F_2 at 1000 c/s, F_3 at 2600 c/s, and F_4 at 3250 c/s. This is a very rough estimate which may be adjusted by preliminary spectral measurements.

(2) We then select the standard envelope from the inventory whose pole (–zero) pattern corresponds most closely to the one just estimated. The F-pattern of the standard envelopes may of course differ somewhat from that of the sample under consideration as we have made up our inventory of a small number of points strategically chosen in the vowel hyperspace. The important point here though is that, whereas there are an infinite number of combinations of parameter values, formant shapes remain fairly constant for a lot of points in the vowel space. Thus it does not matter if the F-pattern of our standard envelope deviates somewhat from that of the analyzed vowel as the shape of each standard formant will in all probability be fairly congruent with the corresponding formant shape in the spectrum under scrutiny.

(3) Enclose the harmonics of the formant to be measured with the selected standard formant(s) (printed on transparent material). Move the standard formant along the frequency scale till an optimal fit has been obtained and read off the frequency value of its envelope peak.

In the case of two poles, or a pole and zero, close together the frequencies of the peaks and valleys could be adjusted so as to approximate more accurately the actual pole (and zero) frequencies.

The development of an inventory of standard envelopes should involve systematic variation of all the relevant parameters responsible for the shape of spectral envelopes of speech sounds. This means primarily the first four formants, formant bandwidths, source function, and "higher pole correction". This inventory will continually be supplemented and revised as our knowledge of speech spectra grows.

Speech Transmission Laboratory
Royal Institute of Technology
Stockholm

LITERATURE

(1) Fant, G., *Acoustic Theory of Speech Production* (Mouton & Co., 's-Gravenhage, 1960), 323 pp.

(2) Fant, G., "On the Predictability of Formant Levels and Spectrum Envelopes from Formant Frequencies", *For Roman Jakobson* (Mouton & Co., 's-Gravenhage, 1956), 109–120.

(3) Ladefoged, P., *The Perception of Vowel Sounds*, Ph.D. Thesis, University of Edinburgh (Edinburgh, 1959).

(4) Fant, G., "Acoustic Analysis and Synthesis of Speech with Applications to Swedish", *Ericsson Technics*, 15, No. 1 (1959), 3–108.

(5) Miller, R. L., "Auditory Tests with Synthetic Vowels", *J. Acoust. Soc. Am.* 25 (1953), 114–121.

(6) Potter, R. K., and Steinberg, J. C., "Toward the Specification of Speech", *J. Acoust. Soc. Am.*, 22 (1950), 807–820.

(7) Flanagan, J. L., "Some Influences of the Glottal Wave upon Vowel Quality", invited paper presented at the Fourth International Congress of Phonetic Sciences, Helsinki, September 4–9, 1961; published in this volume.

(8) Brady, P. T., "Perception of Sounds Generated by Time-Variant Resonant Circuits", Massachusetts Institute of Technology, Research Laboratory of Electronics, *Quarterly Progress Report* No. 58, July 15, 1960, 218–220; and MIT, RLE, *Quarterly Progress Report* No. 59, October 15, 1960, 134–138.

(9) Speech Transmission Laboratory, Royal Institute of Technology, (Stockholm), *Quarterly Progress and Status Report*, 1/1960, October 15, 1960, 11–13.

(10) Flanagan, J. L., "Difference Limen for Vowel Formant Frequency", *J. Acoust. Soc. Am.*, 27 (1955), 613–617.

(11) Flanagan, J. L., "Estimates of the Maximum Precision Necessary in Quantizing Certain Dimensions of Vowel Sounds", *J. Acoust. Soc. Am.* 29 (1957), 533–534.

(12) Peterson, G. E., "Vowel Formant Measurements", *J. of Speech and Hearing Research* 2 (1959), 173–183.

DISCUSSION

Eli Fischer-Jørgensen:

Mr. Lindblom takes it for granted that what we want to find by formant measurements are the pole frequencies (or resonance peaks of the vocal tract). Most phoneticians in measuring formant frequencies will however probably try to find the peaks of the physical spectrum (e.g. of a section taken on the sonagraph). There will however, according to Gunnar Fant, be some differences between these peaks and the pole frequencies.

(1) The falling slope of the larynx spectrum will have the effect that the peaks of the section will be slightly lower than the poles, and this is especially true of the lower poles,

(2) When two poles are close together, the overlapping of their curves will cause the peaks of the resultant physical pattern to come still closer together. This is also true of a low F1 peak in relation to its negative pole. This means that one should make slight corrections for low F1 peaks and for close formant peaks.

It is evident that these corrections should be made if the aim is to find the relations between formant peaks and the configuration of the vocal tract. It is less evident, if the aim is to look for relations between physical stimulus and auditory reaction. –

But it is of course unpractical to have two different notions of formant frequency, and it is possible that the inaccuracy is less disturbing for the physical-auditory relation than for the physiological-physical relation. Both Gunnar Fant and Gordon Peterson seem to prefer identifying formant frequency with pole frequency. At any rate it is important that we all measure according to the same principles. It would be very useful to get practical directions for the corrections to be made.

In Reply:

It is important, I think, that we remain faithful to the mathematical model developed for the acoustic description of vowel sounds whatever the purpose of our investigations. Thus, in the model, there are not "two different notions of formant frequency". Formant frequency is synonymous only with pole frequency. The frequency of a pole alone, gives us the main shape of the corresponding elementary resonance curve since bandwidths are fairly predictable. Several pole frequencies enable us to reconstruct the spectral envelope. Once the spectral envelope and the fundamental frequency are known the relative amplitudes and the frequencies of the individual harmonics are uniquely specified. In other words, we can substitute the lowest four pole frequencies for the amplitudes and frequencies of a large number of partials. A formant frequency measurement is a pole frequency measurement.

Now, where do we find the pole on our spectrographic record? Our best policy is to make an attempt at estimating the frequency of the corresponding envelope peak. As Eli Fischer-Jørgensen points out there may be differences in frequency between a pole and its peak. Even when such factors as those mentioned by Eli Fischer-Jørgensen are taken into account, e.g., the slope of the source function and the distance between two close resonances, it is likely that we should hardly ever meet with differences that exceed 5–10 c/s. To all intents and purposes the number of c/s that an envelope peak deviates from its pole may be regarded as negligible. In comparison with the accuracy that we can achieve in locating peaks this figure is usually extremely small and the answer to our question is that we find the pole at the envelope peak. It should be noted that the frequency of the envelope peak is not the same as the centre of gravity of the spectral maximum or formant. As was said earlier asymmetry in formants renders this measure inaccurate. Thus the world of phonetics is not divided into those who content themselves with envelope peaks and those who, being more exacting, measure pole frequencies. We all make pole frequency measurements when trying to estimate the location of envelope peaks.

So far our discussion has treated of ideal cases i.e., non-aspirative, non-nasalized vowels without anomalies in the larynx spectrum. To complete the picture it should be added that, whereas a well-defined envelope peak is usually indicative of a pole, the pole is not always manifested as a peak in the transfer function; zeros in the vicinity and a large bandwidth may spoil the peakedness of a resonance. Instead of a peak the envelope just has a plateau. A formant manifests a transfer function pole as a *potential* spectral energy maximum. The success of pole-zero matching techniques shows however, that, in spite of these complications, the model is basically sound.

In discussing physical-auditory relations we should think of our vowel sound as a complex stimulus in which, in ideal cases, the distribution of energy is most simply described by the lowest four poles and the fundamental frequency component. Considering what is known so far about auditory processes it is not justifiable to exchange the pole specification for a description that considers arbitrarily the "formants" in isolation. *Not the formants but the entire spectrum constitutes our stimulus.*

To sum up, the procedure of formant frequency measurements is theoretically a search for pole frequencies. In practice poles and peaks coincide. Thus good accuracy is obtained if we succeed in finding envelope peaks. As a help to finding envelope peaks I suggest the use of standard envelopes mathematically derived as mentioned in my paper.

SOUND SPECTROGRAPHY

GUNNAR FANT

1. ACOUSTIC PHONETICS

The scientific study of speech has developed considerably during the last 24 years since the last international congress of phonetic sciences.

The traditional articulatory or rather physiological phonetics is being supplemented more and more by acoustic phonetics. In part this is due to the increasing interest in speech research from communication engineering quarters (11). Progress in methods of speech transmission and speech data processing presupposes advanced knowledge of human speech on all levels of specification including speech production, acoustic speech structure, and speech perception. The basic notion of speech as signals which are transmitted through successive stages within both the listener and speaker part of the system and transformed into different physical forms by a coding process in each of these stages is a commonly used model (28), which stems from information theory.

Acoustic phonetics centers around the speech wave as defined by the sound pressure fluctuations affecting a microphone in front of the speaker. Our most important means of studying the physical structure of the speech wave is through spectrographic records but there exist many supplementary means of analysis, e.g. through oscillograms and records of speech intensity and voice fundamental frequency, etc.

The acoustic speech wave is more open for insight than any other physical manifestation of a human utterance. This potentiality is of a considerable advantage once the language of Visible Speech is known (32, 33). Beginners will certainly have difficulties – those who are more sophisticated will have to admit that there still remains very much to learn about this language. A maximally complete description can be achieved at the price of an overdetailed representation only.

Spectrographic records may possess undeniable artistic qualities but they are not studied for the sake of their own beauty. Acoustic phonetics aims at relating speech wave data to any other observable aspect of the speech act. Of primary interest is to relate to the speech wave data to linguistically defined signs and categories belonging to the message aspect (15). The success of such a task is much dependent on our insight in the codes whereby the sound patterns may be related to the function of the human speaking organs (3, 10, 41) and to the capacities of the hearing mechanism.

These general constraints of what can be said and what can be heard are of basic importance for the development of specificational schemes. The rules for physiological interpretation of spectrograms provide the key for learning to read Visible Speech.

With access to this code the reading of spectrographic records provides a very interesting and stimulating insight in the speaker's particular oral behavior in producing a specific utterance. In this respect the spectrographic records supplement the auditory transcription of an informant's speech. It is true that the predictability of articulation from speech wave patterns is not as single valued as translating from speech production to speech waves. However, the possibilities of compensatory modes of articulation providing the same speech wave patterns are not very serious if sufficient evidence is taken into account. Here the interests of traditional articulatory phonetics (24) and modern acoustic phonetics (6, 16) meet. The more experienced a phonetician is in articulatory phonetics, the easier it will be for him to learn the elements of Visible Speech.

A knowledge of the general constraints of the auditory system as a sound analyzer and its response to speech-like stimuli is much needed for a proper evaluation of the relative importance of various sound pattern aspects. Synthetic speech has been of considerable value for studying these criteria (12, 17, 18) but there are many other important techniques for speech pattern evaluations of e.g., by means of small differential eliminations or substitutions of the sound within specific time (43, 44) and frequency intervals.

The raw data from a spectrogram is never subjected to an auditory evaluation in all its details. A single harmonic does not have an independent auditory significance. The spectrographic patterns must first be expressed in a simplified form pertaining to the essentials of the energy distribution in frequency and time. The specific constraints on such energy distributions imposed by the properties of the speech generating mechanism, for instance the relations between formant intensities and the pattern of formant frequencies (5, 7, 10) allow for valuable simplifications in the specifications and provide a guide for a natural choice of parameter for a systematic variation of the composition of speech-like stimuli in speech perception experiments.

However, the procedure sketched above is more of a theoretical strategy than an established procedure in speech research. Our knowledge of speech wave structure and of speech production and speech perception is still rather incomplete. Although there has been considerable advance in speech research the last 15 years we are still in a rather early stage of development. It was stated by Joos in 1948 (16) and I expressed the same opinion in Oslo 4 years ago (6) that acoustic phonetics is still in its infancy. In view of the fact that speech spectrography has existed for a long time it is astonishing that so few large scale experimental studies have been accomplished. The reason for this slow development is in part due to instrumental difficulties, in part due to a lack of a rationale for specification and interpretation of experimental results. The investigator too easily drowns in a sea of details of unknown significance if he attempts to make use of all observable data.

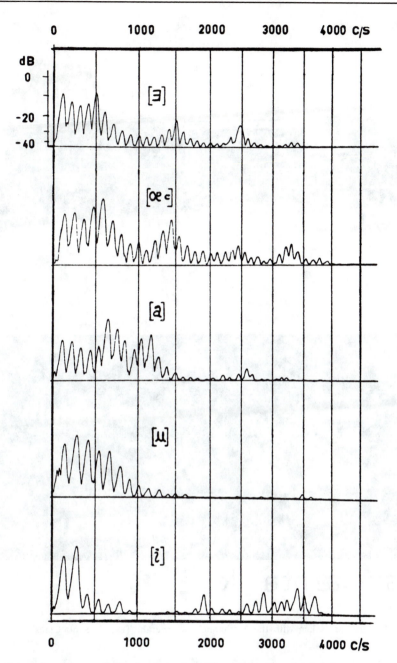

Fig. 1.   Sweep frequency analysis of sustained speech sounds.   The sign [ɘ] denotes a neutral reference vowel produced from OVE I. The 4000 c/s range has been run through in 3 seconds with a 31 c/s-wide filter.   Mingograph recorder.

Fig. 2.   The Sona-Graph spectrograph.

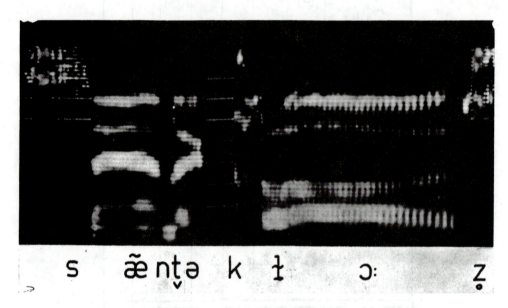

Fig. 3.   Spectrogram taken with the 48-channel spectrograh. Text is "Santa Claus". Compare with Fig. 10.

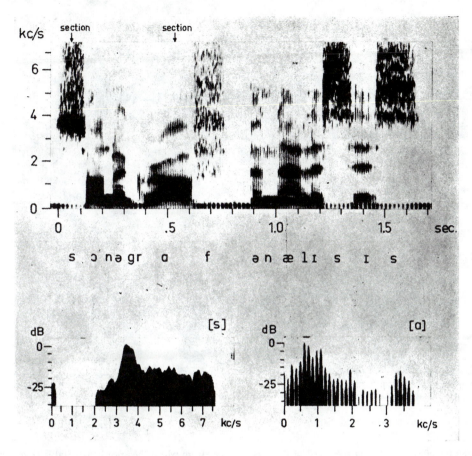

Fig. 4. Broad-filter spectrogram and narrow-filter sections taken with the Sona-Graph.

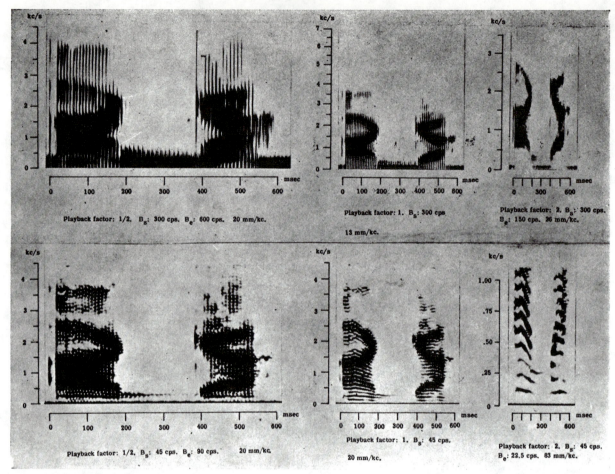

Fig. 5.   Spectrograms illustrating the effects of varying the speed of the tape-recorder from which the speech material is trans-
ferred to the Sona-Graph.   Broad-filter analysis above, narrow-filter analysis below.   Half speed to the left, normal speed in
the middle, and double speed to the right.   The utterance is the VCV syllable "agga".

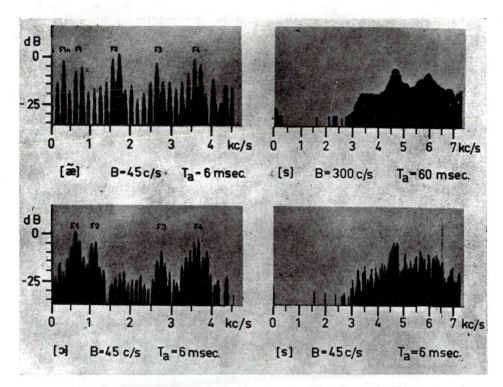

Fig. 6. To the left normal narrow-filter Sona-Graph sections of the vowels [æ̃] and [ɔ:]. Observe the split first formant of the nasalized [æ̃]. – Upper-right section pertains to the fricative [s] analyzed with the broad filter and an extra large integration time constant. Lower-right section pertains to the same [s] sample but analyzed with the narrow filter and the normal integration time constant of the instrument. – The rugged fine structure of the lower section is an instrumental artefact related to the low product of analysis filter bandwith B and integration time constant T_a.

SOUND SPECTROGRAPHY

2. SPECTRUM ANALYSIS TECHNIQUES

The sound spectrograph is perhaps the most important research tool in present-day speech research both in phonetic laboratories and at communication engineering institutions. This statement may not be agreed upon by all those present here. Some may speak up for speech synthesizers, others for high speed digital computers, especially in view of the fact that large, versatile digital computers can be made to simulate both analysis and synthesis processes.

However, the common feature of analysis and synthesis methods lies in the spectral representation of speech waves. It is a well established fact that the speech spectrum provides a much more useful reference than oscillographic displays.

The human ear is an effective sound analyzer that we would like to be able to duplicate instrumentally in all its major functions. The major trouble is the brain part of the system that determines important aspects of the auditory functions that have as yet not been sufficiently investigated in psychoacoustic experiments. The mere fact that the selectivity and discriminability of time events are not constant but appear to be functions of the overall type of stimulus indicates the level of the difficulties we meet with when attempting to predict the auditory functions in response to the rather complicated speech wave structure.

Aside from the difficulties of reaching a complete insight in the black box we label hearing it is appearent that simplified spectrum analysis by hearing has been of considerable importance in the early history of experimental phonetics, e.g. in the works of Helmholtz (14), Paget (26), Stumpf (42). I have the greatest respect for the accurate formant frequency analysis of Danish vowels performed by Smith (37) by hearing alone.

Fourier analysis of oscillographically determined wave forms was one of the earliest methods of objective analysis. I would like to mention the pioneering work of the Finnish phonetician Pipping (31) who derived the complete amplitude and phase spectra of vowels by this method as early as 80 years ago. Fourier analysis of speech wave forms now incidently enjoys a renaissance thanks to high speed computer techniques (23).

Sweep frequency analysis of sustained sounds has been an important technique but has the obvious drawback that its use is limited to prolonged isolated sounds and thus excludes the study of connected speech. The sweep frequency analyzers currently in use 30 years ago required a subject that could maintain a steady sung vowel for a period of one or two minutes. I have in mind the analysis performed by Barczinski and Thienhaus (1) and by Sovijärvi (38). In modern design the time of analysis is brought down to the order of 4 seconds for the analysis of a 4000 c/s frequency range with a 32 c/s-wide filter (6) and the method may supplement standard sound spectrography for detail studies of well reproducible stationary sounds. Amplitude versus frequency spectra recorded by the sweep frequency method are exemplified in Figure 1. Such recordings generally display a clear and well defined harmonic structure.

In the Key Electric Sona-Graph and other modern sound spectrographs the frequency location of the analyzing filter is shifted through the frequency range of interest just as in the sweep frequency method. The essential difference is that the speech to be analyzed is played through the spectrograph a large number of times during the course of analysis. The memory for storage of the speech material is a magnetic recording drum which has a time span of 2.4 seconds. The time needed for the analysis process is of the order of 5 minutes in the Sona-Graph.

The origin of the Sona-Graph is the sound spectrograph developed for the Visible Speech Project at the Bell Telephone Laboratories (32, 33, 29). Several laboratory constructions of spectrographs have been made according to these principles. The most exact and versatile apparatus of this type I have seen is that at Gordon E. Peterson's Laboratory, University of Michigan, Ann Arbor, Michigan.

The common drawback of these spectrographs is the relative long time required for the processing but they have the benefit of a very detailed spectral portrayal and an optimally fine resolution in time allowing a detailed insight in the time varying spectrum of connected speech. The restrictions in the speed of analysis have been overcome in a recent design of Gill (13) employing a circulating memory which the speech continuously enters and leaves after having been rotated round the memory loop many times at a very high speed. This causes a translation of the speech material by a very large factor in frequency at a retained time scale allowing a very large reduction of the time required for analysis. A related method making use of phase coincidence (2) filters has been tried in an American spectrograph, the Simaramic, designed for studies of under-water sounds.

One important class of high speed sound analyzers makes use of a large set of band-pass filters working in parallel the outputs of which are scanned by a rotating switch. Our 48-channel analyzer (6) designed by H. Sund is one of the few analyzers of this type in use for phonetic research. A recent design according to similar principles is that of P. Denes for University College, London. The time-frequency-intensity sound spectrum is recorded on continuous photographic film in these two analyzers and that of Gill (13). The advantage is that very long pieces of speech may be analyzed in a very short time. This is an advantage when one merely intends to use the spectrogram as a reference record for a large speech material. The frequency resolution of these high speed analyzers, with the possible exception of that of Gill is not quite as good as in the Sona-Graph, compare for instance Figure 3 with that of Figure 7. It should be appreciated that these high speed analyzers can in a short time produce a spectrographical material that may keep a phonetician busy for a life time.

The sound spectrograph of the Sona-Graph type and its use in phonetic research has been extensively described in the literature (29, 32, 33). A few practical hints on the use of the Sona-Graph will be given here in addition to those discussed by Lindblom in his paper for this congress (21). The normal type of spectrograms and sections are illustrated by Figure 4. It is possible to expand the time scale and compress simultaneously the frequency scale. This is achieved by a play-back speed reduction of a factor of 2 when playing speech material into the Sona-Graph. This process will increase the effective bandwidth of the analysis filter to twice the normal value which in case of the broad-band filter implies a $2 \times 300 = 600$ c/s effective width. This feature is sometimes of value for avoiding the appearence of a harmonic fine structure in "broad-band analysis" of high pitched female voices. Another apparent advantage is the increased time resolution which emphasizes the periodicity aspect of low pitched male voices. Similarly, a play-back speed increase will compress the time scale and expand the frequency scale which is of some benefit in voice fundamental frequency analysis. The effective reduction of the filter width will provide an increased resolution in the harmonic analysis.

There are several practical precautions which should be made in using the Sona-Graph. One is to prevent overloading by careful check of the input signal level to the instrument (see Lindblom's paper (21)). Spectral sections of fricatives should not be taken with the narrow-band filter since the overlaid statistical fluctuation will be considerable. Instead the broad-band filter should be used and the integration time of the intensity processing part of the analyzer should be increased by a factor of 2–3.

Other suggestions for instrumental improvements would include a reshaping of the pre-emphasis filter HS to provide a smooth 6-dB/octave rise from 200 c/s to 5000 c/s instead of the present fairly constant response at frequencies below 800 c/s followed by a rapid rise in the response. This change will contribute to clean up the F1 and bass-band region of the spectrogram thus avoiding excessive marking in this region. Another suggestion is to replace the present mechanical sampling switch for sectioning by an electronically gated switch. This would improve the accuracy in sampling. Most spectrographs are nowadays supplied with a frequency scale expander, which is very helpful for intonation studies based on narrow-band harmonic analysis.

3. INTERPRETATION OF SPECTROGRAPHIC DATA

It was stated in the first chapter that we cannot make full use of all observable data from a spectrogram, at least not on a quantitative basis. The purpose of analysis is rather to obtain answers to specific questions of a phonetic nature. Quantitative measurements have generally been limited to formant frequencies of vowel-like sounds (7, 30) but this is by no means an inherent restriction of the instrument. Sound spectrographs deserve to be used more than they have been but they need all the engineering care they can get to function satisfactorily.

Some of the general problems encountered in taking formant frequency measures are ventilated in the paper by Lindblom. The accepted general definition of a formant is a maximum in the sound spectrum. Alternative definitions could be adopted for the formant frequency but it is nowadays commonly accepted to refer to the frequency

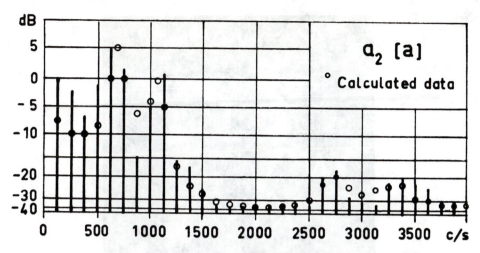

Fig. 7.   Spectrum of a sustained vowel [a]. The calculated points have been derived from a set of preselected formant frequencies. (From *Ericsson Technics*, Vol. 15, No. 1, 1959).

of the corresponding vocal resonance (pole). In a well isolated formant the difference between the peak frequency of the spectrum envelope and the corresponding resonance frequency is of academic interest alone since it is much less than the uncertainty set by the harmonic structure.

The formant frequencies are not merely the basic correlates of vowel quality as judged from several studies. It can be shown that the essential shape features of a vowel spectrum are predictable from a knowledge of the formant frequencies (5), see also the paper by Mártony et al. (22). One of these basic rules interrelating formant frequencies and the intensity level of any part of the spectrum is that a decrease in formant frequency F_1 will cause a shift down in the spectrum level of the entire spectrum above F_1 at a rate of 12 dB per octave shift in F_1. The implications of this rule for phonetic theory, and syllable division in particular, is apparent. Articulatory narrowing is the cause of decrease in F_1 which is automatically followed by the above mentioned intensity reduction. At constant phonatory power, i.e. vocal source strength, the articulatory movements alone thus have the power of determining the time-variable intensity changes from a vowel to a following voiced consonant.

One important aspect of these relations is the converse. The intensity level at one part of the vowel spectrum compared with the levels at other parts of the spectrum carries some information on the frequencies of all formants. The accuracy in formant frequency measurements may thus be improved by taking into account data from the spectrum outside the region of the formant peak. This is practically accomplished by the spectrum matching technique, also known under the name of "analysis-by-synthesis", from the work at M.I.T. (40). The technique is examplified in Figure 7 which shows to what extent the measured harmonic line spectrum of a vowel [a] is predictable from the analytical model based (7) on the formant frequencies. The

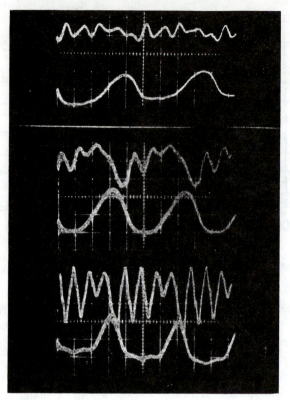

Fig. 8.   Oscillograms of the vowel [æ] and of the regenerated glottal flow function. Low, medium, and high voice efforts are illustrated from the top to the bottom of the figure.

figure exemplifies the first stage of the matching based on the first guess of formant frequencies. The matching proceeds with a systematic variation of formant frequencies until the difference between the synthetic and natural spectrum is minimal.

The pronounced dip at 800 c/s which marks a deviation from the ideal model is a typical property of the vocal source spectrum of the particular speaker.

Spectrum matching according to these principles is outside the technical resources of most phonetic laboratories. The gross relations between spectrum shape and the pattern of formant frequencies should, however, be known by any phonetician attempting to collect data on formant frequencies of the separate vowels of a particular language or dialect. This knowledge constitutes an insurance against errors in the identification of a formant number. I know of several vowel studies which are invalidated by inconsistent formant specifications, e.g. F_3 labeled as F_2 etc. Simple continuity considerations can be relied upon for the practical evaluations.

The time domain correspondence of spectrum matching is the inverse filtering technique whereby each formant is compensated until the oscillographic display of the vowel shows a residue which is merely a pulse train at the rate of the voice fundamental. This method, if carefully planned, provides valuable information on the glottal functions (25, 8), see Figure 8, but the primary aim is generally to measure the formant frequencies. We do not yet have sufficient experience of this speech microscope[1] method to fully evaluate it but one can anticipate trouble in case of nasalized vowels containing two separate first formants, one nasal and one oral as in the [æ̃] of Figures 3 and 10.

The most powerful method in investigating the acoustic correlates of phonetic entities is to construct contrastive sentences differing only in terms of the category to be studied. The importance of the concept of distinctive features in phonemic theory is undeniable; no less is its importance in practical experimental work. Without the elimination of the conditioning effects due to the speaker's individuality and all contextual factors it is often difficult to get a clear view of the information bearing elements of the speech wave. An example of a minimum distinction, that of the continuant /v/ versus the interrupted /b/, is shown in Figure 9. The difference in the degree of articulatory closure accounts for the less attenuated second formant of /v/ as compared with /b/. This acoustic difference is paralleled by the higher frequency of F_1 in /v/ compared with /b/ in comformity with the general relations between articulatory narrowing, F_1, and the level of higher formants discussed above. This is a typical example of how a knowledge of the articulation-speech wave relations and the interrelations of the acoustic variables of specification contributes to the interpretation of spectrographic records.

A systematic study of the general principles of taking spectrographic measures in connected speech is at present being undertaken at our laboratory. The basic problem is how to divide the visible pattern in a succession of natural units. Are there any such units? The answer is positively yes. The sound spectrogram provides an excellent basis for the study of the durations of phonetic units. There are sharp breaks in the pattern associated with the major discontinuities in speech production, such as the onset of a fricative following a vowel or the step to or from complete closure in the vocal tract. Less unambiguous speech segment boundaries may be defined by variations in the formant pattern or by the appearance or disappearance of nasalization cues, i.e. the split versus single first formant.

The present specificational system[2] is based on a primary division of sound features in two basic categories; those determining *segment boundaries* which will be called *segment type features* and those specifying the contents of speech segments beyond the categorization inherent in the type features which we call *segment pattern features*. Segment type features thus concentrate on the discontinuous aspects of speech, in phonetic terminology referred to as manner of production. The segment pattern features, on the other hand, correspond more to the place of articulation.

[1] So called by W. Lawrence who has developed this method.
[2] A more detailed presentation of this tentative system is given in the Royal Institute of Technology, Speech Transmission Laboratory, *Quarterly Progress and Status Report* No. 2/1961, pp. 1–11. The system is related to that of Fant-Jakobson-Halle (15) but has a broader purpose.

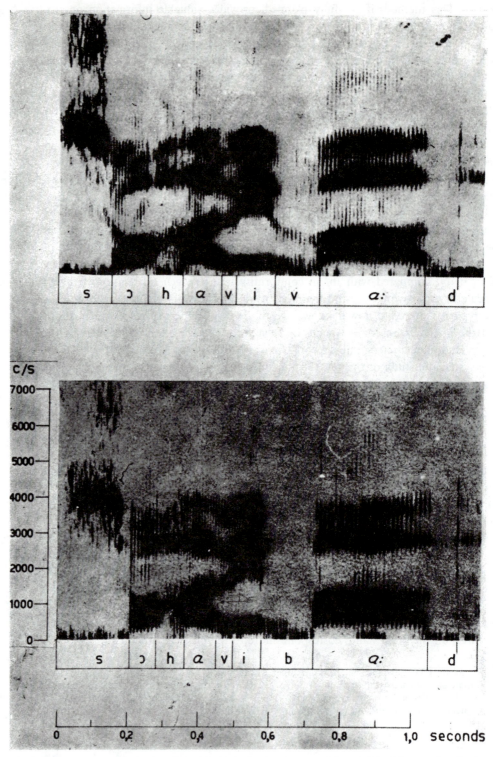

Fig. 9.   Spectrograms illustrating the minimal distinction between [v] and [b].   The speaker is the Norwegian phonetician Ernst Selmer.

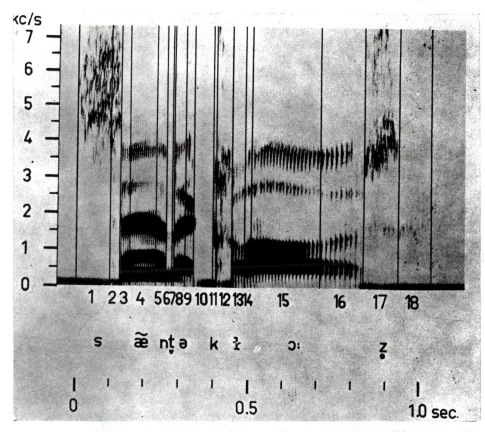

Fig. 10.   Segmentation of a broad-band spectrographic record. Text: "Santa Claus."

SEGMENT TYPE FEATURES

Sources features	1	voice
	2	noise
	3	transient
Resonator features	4	occlusive
	5	fricative
	6	lateral
	7	nasal
	8	vowellike
	9	transitional[3]

The specification of any segment thus starts out with a number of binary decisions as to the presence or absence of each of the type features. The analysis then proceeds with the segment pattern features which are measured in terms of more or less continuous functions the particular choice of which depends upon the segment type classification. These data may finally be interpreted in terms of the most probable place of articulation. In automatic speech recognition the data from a number of successive segments should enable a phonemic or allophonic identification.

Most of the segment pattern features may be quantized in terms of an arbitrary number of standard articulatory positions or in terms of the acoustic parameter values allowing such identifications. A final identification of the phonemes of a piece of speech sometimes requires a few additional acoustic data such as intensity, duration, and voice fundamental frequency within segments supplementing the place of articulation data. In other words, not all of the segment pattern features are related to the place of articulation. The articulatory patterns may be described acoustically on the basis of two basic categories of measures, the *F-pattern* defined by the formant frequencies F_1 F_2 F_3 F_4 and *spectral energy distribution* generally defined by a spectrum envelope (10). In vowellike sounds the essential shape of the spectrum envelope is predictable from the F-pattern[4] and the F-pattern is then a sufficient basis for the specification.

In the case of fricatives and stops, on the other hand, both the F-pattern and the spectral energy distribution aid in signaling the specific place of articulation. The greater the energy content in the consonantal sound segment the greater perceptional importance its spectral energy distribution will have. A typical example is the difference between the relative intense burst of unvoiced stops compared with the relatively low intensity burst of voiced stops. Similarly, the nasal consonants differ more in terms of formant transitions as defined by the F-pattern, than by their inherent spectrum.

---

[3] An intermediate degree of feature 9 labeled glide has been adopted in some of the preliminary studies (Figure 11). Although phonemic motivations exist for this extra distinction it does not seem practical to maintain it in the acoustic analysis.

[4] Specific deviations from this rule define the lateral and nasal type features.

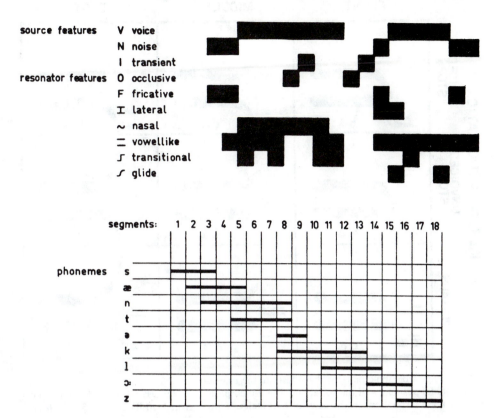

Fig. 11. Classification of the acoustic segments of the utterance Santa Claus, Fig. 10, in terms of segment type features. Estimated phoneme-segment dependency is indicated below.

The view of speech as composed of one sound segment for each phoneme is an oversimplification which is allowable on a phonemic level only. A purely phonetic segmentation according to the principles above of a specific sentence, see e.g. Figure 10, results in a larger number of sound segments than phonemes. Each sound segment generally carries cues for the identification of several successive phonemes and each phoneme is generally associated with several successive sound segments, see Figure 11. Well-known examples of these interrelations are the dual role of vocalic segments in signaling a vowel and an adjacent consonant and the dependency of a stop sound on the burst and a following vocalic element.

There is a wealth of information collected on the perceptional importance of the various cues in speech from the synthesis work at Haskins Laboratories (17, 18). Figure 12 exemplifies the nature of the systematic variations of transitional cues and spectral energy distribution cues.

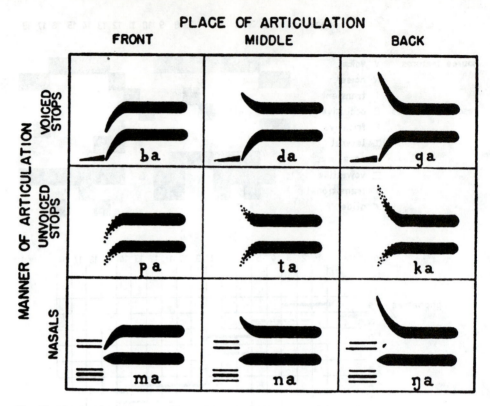

Fig. 12.   Spectrographic patterns that illustrate the transition cues for the stop and nasal consonants in initial position with the vowel /a/. The dotted portions in the second row indicate the presence of noise (aspiration) in the place of harmonics. (After Alvin M. Liberman, 1957, *J. Acoust. Soc. Am.*, 29 (1957, pp. 117–123).

It would be interesting to follow up these classical experiments with synthesizers that retain the natural constraints of the human speaking mechanism. I am considering not only articulatory analogs such as DAVO (36) of M.I.T. but in particular synthesizers of the OVE II type (34, 35, 8, 4) which are coded in terms of acoustic parameters but retain the natural relations between formant frequencies and spectrum shapes, as discussed in connection with Figure 10. But now I am approaching the subject of the next paper for this congress.

Speech Transmission Laboratory
Royal Institute of Technology
Stockholm

REFERENCES

(1) Barczinski, L., Thienhaus, E., "Klangspektren und Lautstärke deutscher Sprachlaute", *Arch. Néerland. Phon. Exp.*, 11 (1935), pp. 47–58.

(2) Bickel, H. J., "Spectrum analysis with delay-line filters", *Ire Wescon Convention Record* (1959), Part 8, pp. 59–67.

(3) Delattre, P., Liberman, A. M., Cooper, F. S., "The physiological interpretation of sound spectrograms", *PMLA*, LXVI (1951), pp. 864–875.

(4) Fant, G., "Speech communication research", *IVA*, 24 (1953), pp. 331–337.

(5) Fant, G., "On the predictability of formant levels and spectrum envelopes from formant frequencies", *For Roman Jakobson* ('s-Gravenhage, 1956), pp. 109–120.

(6) Fant, G., "Modern instruments and methods for acoustic studies of speech", *Acta Polytechnica Scandinavica*, 246/1958, 84 pp., also publ. in *Proc. of VIII Internat. Congress of Linguists, Oslo 1958*, pp. 282–358 (1958).

(7) Fant, G., "Acoustic analysis and synthesis of speech with applications to Swedish", *Ericsson Technics*, 15, No. 1 (1959), pp. 1–106.

(8) Fant, G., "The acoustics of speech", *Proc. of the 3rd Internat. Congress on Acoustics, Stuttgart 1959*, ed. by L. Cremer, Vol. I (Amsterdam, 1961), pp. 188–201.

(9) Fant, G., "Descriptive analysis of the acoustic aspects of speech", paper given at the Wenner-Gren Foundation for Anthropological Research Symposium on Comparative Aspects of Human Communication, Burg Wartenstein, Austria 1960; to be publ. in *LOGOS*, the Bulletin of the National Hospital for Speech Research (1962).

(10) Fant, G., *Acoustic Theory of Speech Production* ('s-Gravenhage, 1960).

(11) Fischer-Jørgensen, E., "What can the new techniques of acoustic phonetics contribute to linguistics?", *Proc. of VIII Internat. Congress of Linguists, Oslo 1958*, pp. 433–478.

(12) Flanagan, J. L., "Difference limen for vowel formant frequency", *J. Acoust. Soc. Am.*, 27 (1955), pp. 613–617.

(13) Gill, J. S., "A versatile method for short-time spectrum analysis in 'real-time'", *Nature*, 189 (1961), pp. 117–119.

(14) Helmholtz, H., *On the Sensations of Tone* (New York, 1954) (Second English Edition).

(15) Jakobson, R., Fant, G., Halle, M., "Preliminaries to speech analysis", Massachusetts Institute of Technology, Acoustics Laboratory, *Techn. Report* No. 13 (1952), 3rd printing.

(16) Joos, M., "Acoustics phonetics", *Language*, 24 (1948), pp. 1–136.

(17) Liberman, A. M., "Some results of research on speech perceptions", *J. Acoust. Soc. Am.*, 29 (1957), pp. 117–123.

(18) Liberman, A. M., Ingemann, F., Lisker, L., Delattre, P., Cooper, F. S., "Minimal rules for synthesizing speech", *J. Acoust. Soc. Am.*, 31 (1955), pp. 1490–1499.

(19) Lindblom, B., et al., "Evaluation of spectrographic data sampling techniques", Speech Transmission Laboratory, R.I.T., Stockholm, *QPSR*, 1/1960, pp. 11–13.

(20) Lindblom, B., "Formant frequency measurement", Speech Transmission Laboratory, R.I.T., Stockholm, *QPSR*, 2/1960, pp. 5–6.

(21) Lindblom, B., "Accuracy and limitations of Sona-Graph measurements", paper presented at the IV Internat. Congress of Phonetic Sciences, Helsinki 1961; see this volume. pp.

(22) Mártony, J., et al., "Zur Analyse und Synthese von Vokalen und Geräuschlauten", paper presented at the IV Internat. Congress of Phonetic Sciences, Helsinki 1961; see this volume, pp.

(23) Mathews, M. V., Miller, J. E., David, E. E., Jr., "Pitch synchronous analysis of voiced sounds", *J. Acoust. Soc. Am.*, 33 (1961), pp. 179–186.

(24) Menzerath, P., de Lacerda, A., *Koartikulation, Steuerung und Lautabgrenzung* (Berlin-Bonn, 1933).

(25) Miller, R. L., "Nature of the vocal cord wave", *J. Acoust. Soc. Am.*, 31 (1959), pp. 667–677.

(26) Paget, R., "The production of artificial vowel sounds", *Proc. Royal Soc.*, A 102 (1923), p. 75, and *Human Speech* (London, 1930).

(27) Peterson, G. E., "The information bearing elements of speech", *J. Acoust. Soc. Am.*, 24 (1952), pp. 629–637.

(28) Peterson, G. E., "Fundamental problems in speech analysis and synthesis", *Proc. of the VIII Internat. Congress of Linguists, Oslo 1958*, pp. 267–281.

(29) Peterson, G. E., "Parameters of vowel quality", *J. of Speech and Hearing Research*, 4 (1961), pp. 10–29.

(30) Peterson, G. E., Barney, H. L., "Control methods used in a study of the vowels", *J. Acoust. Soc. Am.*, 24 (1952), pp. 175–184.

(31) Pipping, H., *Om klangfärgen hos sjungna vokaler* (Helsinki, 1890).

(32) Potter, R. K., et al., "Technical aspects of visible speech", Bell Telephone System, *Monograph* B–1415, 1946; *J. Acoust. Soc. Am.*, 17 (1946), 89 pp.

(33) Potter, R. K., Kopp, A. G., Green, H. C., *Visible Speech* (New York, 1947).

(34) *Quarterly Progress and Status Report*, Speech Transmission Laboratory, R.I.T., Stockholm, STL–QPSR 1/1961 (January–March), April 15, 1961.

(35) *Quarterly Progress and Status Report*, Speech Transmission Laboratory, R.I.T., Stockholm, STL–QPSR 2/1961 (April–June), July 15, 1961.

(36) Rosen, G., "Dynamic analog speech synthesizer", *J. Acoust. Soc. Am.*, 30 (1958), pp. 201–219.

(37) Smith, S., "Analysis of vowel sounds by ear", *Arch. Néerland. Phon. Exp.*, XX (1947), pp. 78–96.

(38) Sovijärvi, A., "Die wechselnden und festen Formanten der Vokale erklärt durch Spektrogramme und Röntgengramme der finnischen Vokale", *Proc. III Internat. Phonet. Conf., Ghent 1938*, pp. 407–420.

(39) Sovijärvi, A., *Die gehaltenen, geflüsterten und gesungenen Vokale und Nasale der finnischen Sprache* (Helsinki, 1938).

(40) Stevens, K. N., "Toward a model for speech recognition", *J. Acoust. Soc. Am.*, 32 (1960), pp. 47–55.

(41) Stevens, K. N., House, A. S., "Studies of formant transitions using a vocal tract analog", *J. Acoust. Soc. Am.*, 28 (1956), pp. 578–585.

(42) Stumpf, C., *Die Sprachlaute* (Berlin, 1926).

(43) Truby, H. M., *Acoustico-cineradiographic analysis considerations with especial reference to certain consonantal complexes.* Thesis work, *Acta Radiologica*, Suppl. 182 (Stockholm, 1959).

(44) Öhman, S., "On the contribution of speech segments to the identification of Swedish consonant phonemes", Speech Transmission Laboratory, R.I.T., Stockholm, *QPSR*, 2/1961, pp. 12–15.

(45) Öhman, S., "Relative importance of sound segments for the identification of Swedish stops in VC and CV syllables", Speech Transmission Laboratory, R.I.T., Stockholm, *QPSR*, 3/1961, pp. 6–14.

Parameter Relationships In The Portrayal Of Signals With Sound Spectrograph Techniques

Gordon E. Peterson

APPLICATIONS of the sound spectrograph (1) have been made in a number of fields. The chief interest in the instrument, however, has come from students of speech and language. The following discussion is intended to present the relationships among a number of factors which are fundamental in the visual display of signals on the sound spectrogram. An understanding of these relationships is often of value in the interpretation of patterns produced with the sound spectrograph and in calibrations or modifications of the instrument. This discussion deals with the conventional pattern in which frequency is presented along one axis, time is presented along the other, and intensity is shown by blackness on the paper.

In the conventional revolving paper drum sound spectrograph, the pattern is constructed by drawing a series of lines in time which are adjacent in frequency; one line is drawn for each repetition of the signal. The signal frequencies are continuously shifted by means of a modulator so that they are slowly passed across the analyzing filter.

If the filter is narrower in frequency than the number of cycles traversed

Gordon E. Peterson (Ph.D., Louisiana State, 1939) is engaged in research at the Bell Telephone Laboratories, Murray Hill, N. J.

per line, then portions of the signal will be omitted in the portrayal. In order to avoid such 'skipping,' it is desirable to have:

A. $$\frac{\text{cps}}{\text{line}} = r \times \text{filter width}$$

where r is a quantity such that $1 > r > 0$.

In the revolving paper drum sound spectrograph:

B. $$\frac{\text{cps}}{\text{line}} = \frac{\text{cps/inch}}{\text{lines/inch}}$$

In the use of Teledeltos paper the lines are burned with a metal stylus. The character of the marking is shown in Figure 1 which shows enlargements of portions of spectrograms with lines drawn by three different stylus widths. These spectrograms were produced by placing a single tone on the spectrograph and allowing it to mark continuously. The automatic gain control in the spectrograph was eliminated, the level at the top of each picture was started well above the overload, and the reproduce gain was reduced 2 db for each 5 lines marked. In the original spectrograms, of which these are enlargements, the lines are at .010 inch spacings; the marking stylus width for (a) is .002 inch, for (b) .012 inch, and for (c) .020 inch. To obtain a usable stylus stiffness both the .002 inch stylus and the .020 inch stylus were

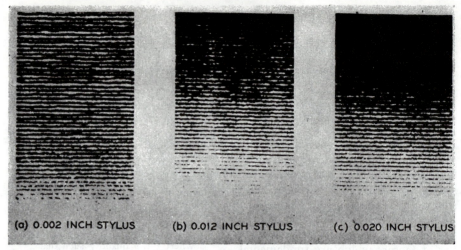

(a) 0.002 INCH STYLUS   (b) 0.012 INCH STYLUS   (c) 0.020 INCH STYLUS

FIGURE 1. Enlargement of portions of spectrograms marked with a continuous tone.

obtained by flattening and grinding the tip of a .012 inch stylus. One was oriented to mark in the narrow direction, and the other was adjusted to mark in the broad dimension.

It is seen in each case that as the level to the stylus is reduced the degree of blackness remains approximately the same, but the line width decreases—and the marking becomes more erratic.

It would appear that if fringe effects from neighboring lines are to be avoided, the lines as marked should not completely fill the space, even at full blackness. Thus, for distinct portrayal a stylus should be chosen such that at maximum marking:

C.

$$\text{width marked (in inches)} = \frac{q}{\text{lines/inch}}$$

where q is a quantity such that
$$1 > q > .75 \quad (\text{approximate}).$$

Resolution and Quantization

As long as r is maintained within the limits indicated in A the degree of frequency resolution is primarily determined by the filter width. We may define the *minimum frequency resolu-* tion as the smallest separation of two tones in frequency which is portrayed as two distinguishable signals on the sound spectrogram. It should be noted that a signal tone which is appreciably narrower than the analyzing filter will be marked on the spectrogram with the full filter width. The value of the minimum frequency resolution thus approaches the analyzing filter width.

The analyzing filter width may be expressed in terms of distance on the spectrogram:

D.

$$\Delta F \text{ (in inches)} = \text{filter width (inches)}$$
$$= \frac{\text{filter width (in cps)}}{\text{cps/inches}}$$

In a similar manner, the degree of time resolution obtained on the sound spectrogram primarily depends upon the transient time of the filter. Since we may write approximately:

F.

$$\frac{1}{\text{filter width (in cps)}} = \frac{\text{filter transient}}{\text{time (in seconds)}}$$

Then we may consider the *minimum time resolution* as approaching the

value of $\dfrac{1}{\text{filter width}}$.

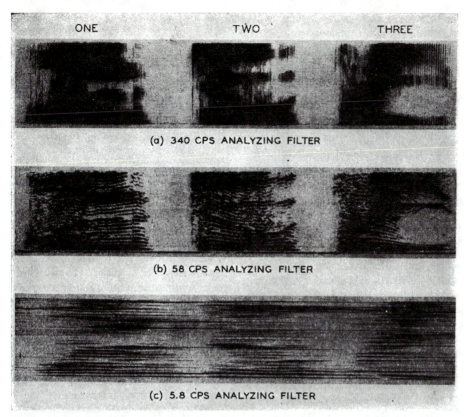

ONE   TWO   THREE

(a) 340 CPS ANALYZING FILTER

(b) 58 CPS ANALYZING FILTER

(c) 5.8 CPS ANALYZING FILTER

FIGURE 2. Spectrograms of the digits 'one, two, three.'

$\triangle F$ (in inches)

$\triangle T$ (in inches)

the product of cps/inch × seconds/inch

This factor we define as aspect product:

M.

aspect product = cps/inch × seconds/inch

It will be noted that aspect ratio has the dimensions of 1/seconds squared and that aspect product has the dimensions of 1/inches squared.

Appendix A

As long as r in equation A is maintained constant there is an advantage to the use of a very narrow analyzing filter under certain conditions. In particular, if the signal tones remain appreciably narrower than the filter, an improvement in signal-to-noise ratio should be realized in the display. This follows from the fact that the noise power through the filter increases with the bandwidth of the filter, whereas the energy passing the filter due to a tone much narrower than the filter will be independent of the bandwidth of the filter. Thus the marking due to noise will be reduced, and that due to steady tones will remain the same when the filter is made narrower. When the filter width is made narrower, appropriate changes in such factors as cps/line must be made, however, in order to achieve satisfactory portrayal.

For example, consider the use of a filter one-tenth that of the present narrow filter in the model D spectrograph, which was the type of instrument employed in making most of the pictures of visible speech (2).

In the instrument employed in marking Figures 1 and 2, in Effective Values:

filter width = 58 cps

cps/inch = 1750

lines/inch = 100

seconds/inch = .2

from B cps/line $= \dfrac{1750}{100} = 17.5$

The distance on the spectrogram occupied by the transient time of the filter is given by the relation:

G. ΔT (in inches) = filter transient (in inches) =

$$\frac{1}{\text{filter width (in cps)}} \times \frac{1}{\text{seconds/inch}}$$

For some purposes it is convenient to consider the spectrogram as composed of a series of elementary areas or quanta, each having the dimensions of $\triangle$F $\times$ $\triangle$T.

Effective Values

The above equations are valid either when the units pertain to the dimensions of the original signal or when the units pertain to the analyzing circuits, so long as the two systems are not confused, of course: The former we shall call 'effective'—E, the latter 'spectrograph'—S.

Signal transformations are normally obtained by changes in speeds of a separate recorder or by linear shifts in frequency by means of modulation. Such transformations are normally obtained with equipment external to the spectrograph, and the resulting signal is then supplied electrically to the sound spectrograph. In either the case of changes in recorder speeds, shifts by means of modulation, or both the relations between E and S for that portion of the signal which falls within the range of the spectrograph will be presented by the following: Let:

R$_r$ = recording speed of the separate recorder

R$_p$ = playback speed of the separate recorder

S$_r$ = spectrograph recording speed

S$_p$ = spectrograph playback speed

H. E cps/inch = S cps/inch $\dfrac{R_r \; S_r}{R_p \; S_p}$

I. E seconds/inch = S seconds/inch $\dfrac{R_p \; S_p}{R_r \; S_r}$

J. E filter width = S filter width $\dfrac{R_r \; S_r}{R_p \; S_p}$

In the case of the revolving paper drum sound spectrograph:

K. analyzing time (in seconds) =

$$\frac{\text{full band width (in cps)}}{\text{cps/line} \times \text{spectrograph play rps}}$$

Spectrogram Aspect

Consider two spectrographs which cover the same range of frequency and time, but which mark pictures which are different in size. The same signal may be supplied to both of these instruments and the spectrogram from one can be enlarged to the same dimensions as the spectrogram from the other instrument.

If these two spectrograms are to appear the same, there are three fundamental factors which must have the same value in both instruments:[1]

  filter width
  cps/line
  the relation of cps/inch to seconds/inch

This latter factor we may define as aspect ratio:

L. aspect ratio = $\dfrac{\text{cps/inch}}{\text{seconds/inch}}$

When signals in which the record or reproduce speeds have been altered are played to the same sound spectrograph, the resulting spectrograms again have three factors in common:[2]

---

[1] In addition to the three factors named, it is obvious that if the cps/line and the frequency range are the same in the two spectrograms, the total number of lines must be the same.

[2] Obviously the lines/inch and the total number of lines will be the same in the spectrograms.

from A
$$r = \frac{17.5}{58} = .302$$

Thus the limits of r specified in A are observed.

minimum frequency resolution $= 58$ cps
minimum time resolution $= .017$ seconds

from D ΔF (in inches) $= \dfrac{58}{1750}$
$$= 3.3 \times 10^{-2} \text{ inches}$$

from G ΔT (in inches) $= \dfrac{1}{58} \times \dfrac{1}{.2}$
$$= .086 \text{ inches}$$

from L aspect ratio $= \dfrac{1750}{.2} = 8.75 \times 10^3$

from M aspect product $= 1750 \times .2 = 350$

from K analyzing time $= \dfrac{3500}{\dfrac{78}{60} \times 17.5}$ sec.
$$= 2.56 \text{ minutes}$$

The Desired Effective Values

If we maintain the same value of r then A becomes:

cps/line $= .302 \times 5.8 = 1.75$

If we maintain cps/inch the same then according to B:

$$\text{lines/inch} = \frac{1750}{1.75} = 1000$$

minimum frequency resolution $= 5.8$ cps

minimum time resolution $= .172$ seconds

from D ΔF (in inches) $= \dfrac{5.8}{1750} = 3.3 \times 10^{-3}$

from G ΔT (in inches) $= \dfrac{1}{5.8} \times \dfrac{1}{.2} = 0.862$

L and M show that the aspect ratio and aspect product remain unchanged. There are two losses, however, which result from the increase in frequency resolution achieved by dividing the filter width by a factor of 10.

a. ΔT has been increased by a factor of 10, so that transient signals will be stretched out in time on the spectrogram. This may be corrected in part by compressing the time dimension on the spectrogram, that is, by employing a smaller paper drum or by employing a larger reproducing disc so that more time may be analyzed.

b. According to K the analyzing time has been increased by a factor of 10.

$$\text{analyzing time} = \frac{3500}{\dfrac{78}{60} \times 1.75} \text{ seconds}$$
$$= 25.6 \text{ minutes}$$

Figure 2 has been made to illustrate the effect of filter width upon the various parameters. The words 'one, two, three' were recorded on the model D spectrograph and were then analyzed with the three filters whose characteristics are shown in Figure 3. Since the reproduce speed in this spectrograph is approximately 3.12 times the recording speed, the effective filter widths are approximately one-third those shown in

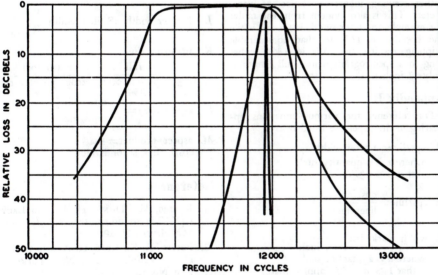

FIGURE 3. The frequency characteristics of the three filters employed in marking Figure 2.

TABLE 1. Effective values of the various parameters of Figure 2.

	(a)	(b)	(c)
filter width (in cycles)	340	58	5.8
cps/inch	1750	1750	1750
seconds/inch	.2	.2	.2
cps/line	17.5	17.5	17.5
stylus width (in inches)	.012	.012	.012
minimum frequency resolution (in cps)	340	58	5.8
minimum time resolution (in seconds)	.0029	.017	.172
Δ F (in inches)	.194	3.3×10^{-2}	3.3×10^{-3}
Δ T (in inches)	.0147	.086	.862
aspect ratio	8.75×10^3	8.75×10^3	8.75×10^3
aspect product	350	350	350

Figure 3. Filter width is expressed here in terms of points 3 db below the maximum.

Figure 2 (a) is for the 340 cps filter, 2 (b) is for the 58 cps filter, and 2 (c) is for an approximation to the 5.8 filter. Full band control was employed in marking 2 (a) and narrow band control, with the same conditions of gain preceding the analyzing filter, was employed in 2 (b) and 2 (c).

To summarize, the effective values of the various parameters of Figure 2 are listed in Table 1.

The spectrogram in Figure 2 (c) is displaced relative to the others due to the slow build-up time of the filter. While traces of the digits can be found in Figure 2 (c) it is evident that this condition represents a rather striking incorrect choice of parameters. This is also evident from the table: for example, the filter width is 5.8 cps whi'e the cps/line is 17.5, so that considerable skipping results; also ΔT is 0.862 inches long in a spectrogram whose full length is only 12 inches.

Appendix B

For reference the various equations appearing in the paper are listed below.

A. cps/line $= r$ filter width

where r is a quantity such that $1 > r > 0$

B. cps/line $= \dfrac{\text{cps/inch}}{\text{lines/inch}}$

C. width marked $= \dfrac{q}{\text{lines/inch}}$

where q is a quantity such that $1 > q > .75$ (approximate)

D. ΔF (in inches) $= \dfrac{\text{filter width (in cps)}}{\text{cycles/inch}}$

F. $\dfrac{1}{\text{filter width (in cps)}} = $ filter transient time (in seconds)

G. ΔT (in inches) $=$
$\dfrac{1}{\text{filter width}} \times \dfrac{1}{\text{seconds/inch}}$

H. E cps/inch $=$ S cps/inch $\dfrac{R_r S_r}{R_p S_p}$

I. E seconds/inch $=$ S seconds/inch $\dfrac{R_p S_p}{R_r S_r}$

J. E filter width $=$ S filter width $\dfrac{R_r S_r}{R_p S_p}$

K. analyzing time $=$
$\dfrac{\text{full band width (in cps)}}{\text{cps/line} \times \text{spectrograph play rps}}$

L. aspect ratio $= \dfrac{\text{cps/inch}}{\text{seconds/inch}}$

M. aspect product $=$
cps/inch $\times$ seconds/inch

References

1. KOENIG, W., DUNN, H. K. AND LACY, L. Y. The sound spectrograph. *J. acoust. Soc. Amer.*, 17, 1946, 19-49.
2. POTTER, R. K., KOPP, G. A. AND GREEN, H. C. *Visible Speech.* New York: D. Van Nostrand, 1947.

PART II
Spectrographic Characteristics of Normal Speech

Spectrography is used to measure important spectral and temporal parameters of speech so that linguistic, developmental, diagnostic, and experimental questions can be answered. For this reason, publications that present clear and useful spectrograms and provide accurate, well-defined sets of spectrographic measures are particularly valuable. These articles serve as a handy reference, a dictionary of measures and spectrograms that illustrates what particular speech samples should look like and how important acoustic properties can be measured.

Spectrographic displays vary widely. The greatest variability is associated with the differing articulatory and acoustic properties of the phonemes within the sound pattern of a language. Further variability is associated with the linguistic and phonetic structure of the utterance, as well as with recording conditions, and the dialect, sex, age, and pathology of the speaker. The speaker's anatomic, physiologic, and behavioral idiosyncracies also contribute. Still, there is enough consistency to allow highly trained specialists to produce accurate phonetic transcriptions and qualitative impressions of the normality of a speaker's output on the basis of visual inspection of a spectrogram.

The articles in this section were selected, therefore, to display not only handsome spectrograms but also clever, well-defined, and rationalized measurements of interesting populations of speakers. Spectrographic cues for natural classes of consonants are represented in the papers of Halle, Hughes, and Radley (1957), Lehiste and Peterson (1960), Lisker and Abrahamson (1964), Klatt (1975), and Dalston (1975). Peterson and Lehiste's (1960) article provides a carefully reasoned, elaborately explained methodology for segmenting the consonant from the vowel based on specific acoustic clues observed in the spectrogram. The rules and procedures they devised have been widely adopted as standards for the interpretation of spectrographic data.

Perhaps the most seminal article in all of acoustic phonetics is the one by Peterson and Barney (1952). It clearly defines the relationship between production and perception of English vowels, tabulates formant frequencies and fundamental frequencies for children, women, and men, and defines the variability inherent in both the measures and the listener's response to vowel sounds. Most importantly, it provides the classic plots of the $F_1 - F_2$ phonetic space for the vowels.

Other articles that we have included in Part II provide model spectrograms (especially Fant, 1969, 1970) and important data that are necessary to the assessment of normality and to drawing inferences concerning articulatory movements on the basis of acoustic patterns. Particularly helpful to the beginner, in this regard, are the chapters taken from Pickett (1980), which provide a simple, concise, and clear presentation of the spectral properties of English speech sounds along with sufficient articulatory mechanics and acoustic theory to define how articulation results in a stream of speech sounds.

Readings

Pickett, J. M. (1980). *The Sounds of Speech Communication* (Chap. 4, pp. 57–78; Chap. 6, pp. 103–120; Chap. 7, pp. 121–132). Baltimore: University Park.

Peterson, G. E., and Barney, H. L. (1952). Control methods used in a study of the vowels. *Journal of the Acoustical Society of America, 24,* 175–184.

Peterson, G. E., and Lehiste, I. (1960). Duration of syllable nuclei in English. *Journal of the Acoustical Society of America, 32,* 693–703.

Fant, G. (1970). *Acoustic Theory of Speech Production* (App. A1). The Hague: Mouton.

Fant, G. (1969). Stops in CV syllables. *Speech Transmission Labs Quarterly Progress Reports, 41.*

Halle, M., Hughes, G. W., and Radley, J. -P. A. (1957). Acoustic properties of stop consonants. *Journal of the Acoustical Society of America, 29* 107–116.

Klatt, D. H. (1975). Voice onset time, frication, and aspiration in word-initial consonant clusters. *Journal of Speech and Hearing Research, 18,* 686–706.

Lisker, L., and Abrahamson, A. S. (1964). A cross-language study of voicing in initial stops. *Word, 20,* 384–422.

Lehiste, I., and Peterson, G. E. (1961). Transitions, glides, and diphthongs. *Journal of the Acoustical Society of America, 33,* 268–277.

Dalston, R. M. (1975). Acoustic characteristics of English /w, r, l/ spoken correctly by young children and adults. *Journal of the Acoustical Society of America, 57,* 462–469.

CHAPTER 4

THE SPECTRA OF VOWELS

CONTENTS

> In...vowels sounded on a succession of different larynx notes...what the ear hears...is the...resonant characteristics of the cavities through which that larynx note has passed...due to the relative volume and areas of orifices produced by the different attitudes of the tongue and lips.
>
> R. A. S. Paget, 1924

Thus far vowel sounds have been described according to vocal tract shape and its effects on the formant locations. A complete description of a vowel sound also includes characteristics arising from the action of the glottis. In this chapter the effects of vowel shape and glottal action are combined. First the glottal action and how it affects the spectrum of the glottal source-sound is described. Then the effects of the vocal tract resonances on the glottal spectrum are presented, using the source-filter theory of vowel production. We also study the effects on the vowel spectrum of low- and high-pitched voice, of vocal effort, and of nasalization. Finally, typical spectrograms are given of English vowels and diphthongs.

THE GLOTTAL SOUND SOURCE

The production of voiced speech sounds begins with the repeated opening and closing of the glottis, in response to the tracheal air pressure; this action forms a train of glottal pulses, which is the basic sound source for vowels and all other voiced sounds. The spectrum of this sound source depends on just how the glottis forms the pulses. For each glottal pulse, the exact form of the airflow through the glottis has an effect on the glottal sound spectrum, so we must first examine how the glottal airflow occurs.

The action of the glottis to produce a sound source is called *phonation*. Phonation depends on how the airflow interacts with the muscular and elastic tensions of the vocal folds; these interactions are now described following the widely accepted *aerodynamic-myoelastic theory of phonation*.

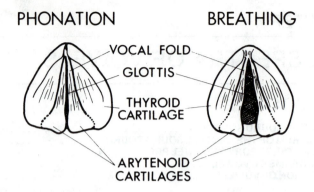

Figure 22. Diagrams of the larynx as seen from above, illustrating the positions of the arytenoid cartilages and vocal folds for breathing and for phonation.

The vocal folds are held in various positions by the arytenoid cartilages, to which the rear portions of the folds are attached (see Figure 22). During breathing the arytenoid cartilages are held outward, keeping the glottis open in a wide-open position. When phonation is about to begin, the arytenoids move inward and bring the vocal folds together; this closes the glottis and blocks the flow of air from the trachea. The chest and lungs press inward, causing the air pressure below the glottis to rise. When this subglottal pressure is sufficiently higher than the air pressure above the glottis, the closing tension on the folds is overcome and they begin to open in a glottal slit between the folds. The sequence of events that then occurs to produce glottal pulsing is as follows: as the glottal slit opens, air begins to flow out through the glottis. The subglottal pressure continues to force the glottis to open wider, and there is an increasing airflow[1] through the glottis, until the natural elastic tension of the folds, which increases dynamically with increased opening, balances the separating force of the air

[1]The term *airflow* is called glottal volume velocity in acoustic research on speech. It is equal to the area of the glottal opening multiplied by the air molecule velocity through the glottis. The air molecule velocity, to a first approximation, is simply proportional to the difference in air pressure above and below the glottis. This transglottal pressure difference is approximately constant throughout a cycle of glottal action, although, of course, it is under the influence of external changes in pressure from the chest action or from a narrow constriction in the vocal tract above the glottis and may be slowly rising or falling due to these influences.

Recent theory of glottal action is discussed in Ishizaka and Flanagan (1972) and Titze (1973, 1974).

pressure. Then the glottal opening and the rate of airflow through the glottis have reached their maximum value. At this point the kinetic energy that the vocal folds received during the opening movement is stored as elastic recoil energy, resulting in a restoring force large enough to overbalance the separating force of the airflow. This stored energy also causes the folds to begin to move inward. The inward movement gathers momentum and continues. When the glottis becomes sufficiently narrow, the high velocity of movement of the air particles within the narrow glottis creates a suction effect, which tends to further pull the vocal folds toward each other. This suction is an example of a physical flow effect called the Bernoulli force.[2] The elastic restoring force and the Bernoulli force together act to close the glottis. The Bernoulli force especially comes into play just before closure; as the glottal slit becomes very narrow there is a further increase in the velocity of the air particles moving through the glottis, thus increasing the suction of the Bernoulli force, and causing the glottis to close very abruptly, completely stopping the airflow. Elastic restoring forces during this collision of the vocal folds, in conjunction with the subglottal pressure, then start a new cycle of action similar to the cycle just described.

To summarize the forces in the cycle of glottal action, the subglottal pressure forces the vocal folds to open and then move outward; the momentum of the movement forces the folds to an extreme of elastic tension where they reverse and then move inward; the momentum of inward movement and, finally, the increased suction of the Bernoulli effect cause the vocal folds to close abruptly; the subglottal pressure and elastic restoring forces during closure cause the cycle to begin again.

As long as the subglottal pressure remains at a sufficiently high level and the arytenoid cartilages hold the vocal folds together, voicing phonation occurs and the glottis will continue to emit a rapid series of air pulses; there is one air pulse emitted during each open-close cycle of glottal action.

---

[2] The Bernoulli pressure is a difference in pressure that must exist to maintain equal energy in a duct with varying cross section. The total flow energy depends on the pressure and air particle velocity. The particle velocity at a constriction is higher than it is at the adjacent larger areas; therefore, because the total flow energy must remain constant, the pressure in the constricted area is lower than the pressure in the adjacent areas.

A Bernoulli force exists wherever there is a difference in fluid pressure between opposite sides of an object. Two other examples of a Bernoulli force in a constricted area of flow are: 1) blowing between parallel sheets of paper held close together (they pull together instead of flying apart because the air velocity is greater, and the pressure is lower, between the sheets than on the outer sides) and 2) the attraction of a hose nozzle toward the bottom of a pail because of the increased velocity of the water when the nozzle is near the bottom (if the nozzle outlet is too close to the bottom, the Bernoulli suction is strong enough to completely shut off the water flow in spite of the water pressure outward through the nozzle).

THE SPECTRUM OF THE GLOTTAL SOUND SOURCE

The exact form of the pulses of air emitted by the glottis is extremely important because this form is the waveform of the glottal sound source and the spectrum of this waveform is the spectrum of the glottal sound source. For this reason the spectrum of the glottal source has been studied by many scientists. However, only recently have we had powerful experimental techniques that promise to lead to a complete description of all the factors that affect the glottal spectrum. The first modern technique, ultra high speed cinematography of the movement of the vocal folds during phonation, was developed at Bell Laboratories (Farnsworth, 1940). The method was to take several thousand pictures per second through a small mirror looking down on the glottis. A series of such pictures is shown in Figure 23. These pictures showed the change in degree of opening between the vocal folds, which can then be converted to an open-area measurement for each picture. This method was used by W. W. Fletcher in 1950 at Northwestern University to determine glottal area waveforms in time, and to study how these waveforms were related to voice intensity. Flanagan (1958) used Fletcher's waveforms, and certain physical flow assumptions about how the area waves would be related to the wave shapes of airflow pulses, to derive the first detailed plots of the spectrum of glottal pulses. Flanagan and his colleagues at Bell Laboratories then proceeded to develop a computer model of the action of the vocal folds (Flanagan and Landgraf, 1968). Computer models produce directly their own wave forms of glottal pulses, and assumptions about the area-flow relationship are not necessary. This is because a computer model can simulate many of the anatomic and physical conditions, the forces on the air in the glottis, and the resulting actions of the vocal folds. In the computer simulation, an input of constant subglottal pressure produces movements of simulated vocal folds and corresponding pulses of air escaping through the simulated glottis between the folds.

The veracity of the glottal pulses produced by computer models has been checked by other methods. One of the best methods is to analyze actual speech waves by filtering to remove the effects of the resonances of the pharyngeal-oral tract, and leave as an output from the filters the original glottal pulses. This method is called inverse filtering; it consists of first determining the resonant frequencies and bandwidths of the main formants of a steady portion of a vowel sound, then setting inverse filters at the same frequencies and bandwidths, and finally passing the vowel sound through this inverse filter set. The output wave has the same wave shape as the pulses of glottal airflow. For examples of the resulting waves of glottal airflow see Rothenberg (1973).

Next consider the spectrum of the glottal sound source, the *glottal source spectrum*. This spectrum is the basis of the spectrum characteristics of all voiced sounds. The spectrum depends on the shape of the glottal wave form.

Figures 24 and 25 illustrate the origin of the source spectrum; Figure 24 shows a wave form of the glottal area for two cycles of vocal fold vibration and the resulting waves of glottal airflow, and Figure 25 shows the spectrum of the glottal airflow waveform. The waves of Figure 24 were generated by an advanced computer model of the vocal folds; the model incorporated typical conditions of the subglottal pressure, of the physical characteristics of the folds, and of the muscle tensions on the folds. This biomechanical model of phonation was developed by Titze and Talkin (1979), who kindly furnished the curves of Figure 24. The pressure and tension conditions were chosen to produce an idealized glottal source spectrum having a slope with the same general pattern as found at Bell Laboratories, and by other investigators in previous studies of the actual glottal spectrum.

There are two characteristics of the glottal spectrum that are especially important: 1) the frequency spacing of the spectral components, i.e., the fundamental and the harmonics, and 2) the amplitude pattern of the components over frequency. The frequency spacing depends on the repetition rate of the pulses in the glottal wave. The amplitude pattern of the spectral components depends on the exact shape of the pulses.

The spacing of the components of the glottal wave of Figure 25 is 100 Hz between components; this spacing corresponds to the repetition rate of the glottal pulses and to the fundamental frequency of the glottal wave. In other words, the glottal pulses repeat at a rate of 100 pulses per second, the corresponding fundamental frequency of the wave of glottal pulses is 100 Hz, and the harmonics in the spectrum of this wave are spaced 100 Hz apart. The fundamental frequency of the spectrum shown in Figure 25 is typical for a low-pitched adult male voice, that is, a fundamental frequency of 100 Hz.

The amplitudes of the components in the glottal spectrum have a pattern that generally decreases from low frequency harmonics to higher ones; that is, the spectrum slopes generally downward. The intensity slopes downward at an average of 12 dB per octave change (doubling) in frequency. The spectrum of the glottal flow wave in Figure 25 therefore has a slope of −12dB/octave.

For actual glottal waves there are variations in the component amplitudes of the glottal spectrum that are related to the degree of rounding of the corners, the duration of the closure, and other fine details of the glottal waveform. These relate physiologically to the style and force of speak-

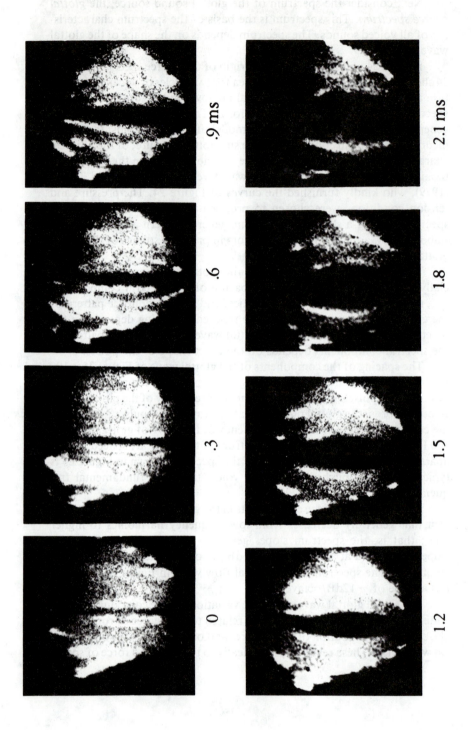

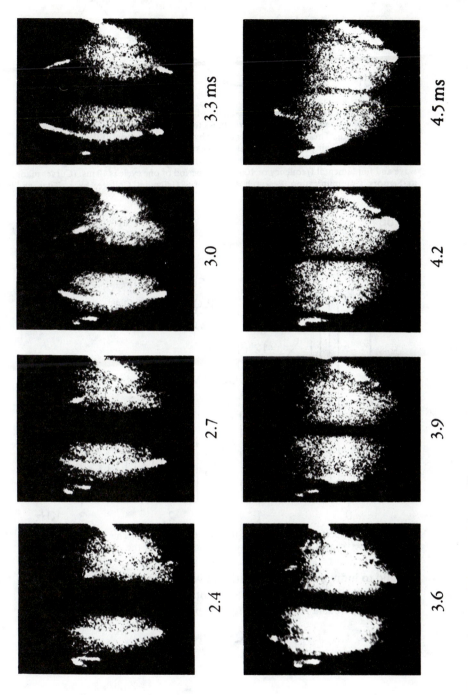

Figure 23.   A series of high speed photographs of one cycle of glottal voicing action. The pictures are taken looking down on the glottis; the arytenoid cartilages are out of view at the bottom of the picture. The speaker was a high-pitched adult male: this one cycle required only 4.5 ms. The pictures were taken at a rate of 10,000 frames per second; only every third frame is shown. (Photos courtesy of W. Wathen-Dunn, H. Soron, and P. Lieberman, taken at the Air Force Cambridge Research Laboratories.)

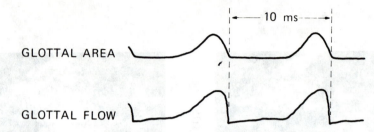

Figure 24.   The upper curve shows an example of how the area of the glottal opening varies in time in phonation and the lower curve shows the corresponding variation of the airflow through the glottis. These curves were generated by a computer model of the vocal folds activated by subglottal air pressure from below. The model was adjusted with typical values of pressure and muscle tension to produce a smoothly sloping spectrum for the glottal flow wave and fundamental frequency of 100 Hz; the period of one cycle is 10 ms. (Curves made at Sensory Communication Research Laboratory, Gallaudet College, by I. Titze and D. Talkin.)

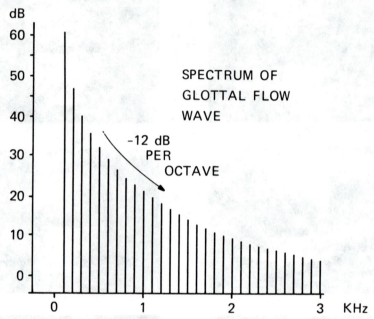

Figure 25.   The spectrum of the glottal flow wave of Figure 24. This is an idealized spectrum, which serves well as a model of the source spectrum for the vowel sounds.

ing, and to individual characteristics of vocal fold behavior. However, an idealized glottal spectrum with a smooth slope of −12 dB/octave is a good, normal basis for describing the spectra of voiced sounds.

The pitch or fundamental frequency of the glottal pulsing depends on the tension on the vocal folds, on the effective mass of the vocal folds, and on the subglottal pressure. The effective mass depends on the size of the vocal folds, which in turn depends on age, sex, and the individual. For example, the vocal folds are progressively larger, as we go from children to women to adult males. This corresponds to a change in voice pitch or fundamental pulse rate going from higher to lower pulsing rates as we go from the smaller vocal folds to the larger ones. Information about the speaker's control of voice pitch by means of tension on the vocal folds is presented in the next chapter.

SOURCE-FILTER THEORY OF VOWEL PRODUCTION

In the formation of vowel sounds the action of the glottis produces the basic source of sound, as was just described; this sound is then propagated, or transmitted, through the pharynx and oral tract to the outside air. We can think of the tract as a filter that emphasizes some of the components of the source sound, namely, those at and near the resonant frequencies of the tract. Therefore we can think of the formation of vowels as the result of a filtering action of the pharyngeal-oral tract on the sound source produced by the glottis. This view of vowel production is called the *source-filter theory of vowel production*. This theory led to the first production of model vowel sounds based on vocal tract shape, as already described in Chapter 3. The source-filter theory helps us explain how the details of vowel spectra arise from the combination of: 1) the spectrum of the glottal sound source and 2) the filtering of this spectrum by its transmission through the vocal tract.

You will recall from our discussion of vowel shaping in Chapter 3 that the vowel resonant peaks depend for their frequency locations on the positions of the tongue and lips. Thus, in order to describe how the spectrum of a vowel is formed, all we need to do is describe the effect on the glottal spectrum of the resonant peaks of the vocal tract. The resonant peaks determine the filtering curve or transmission response of the tract. When we apply this filter curve to the spectrum of the glottal sound source, the resulting spectrum is the vowel sound spectrum.

In other words, it is as if the glottal sound spectrum were passed through a certain filter that determines what the vowel will be. This is illustrated in Figure 26, where diagrams show how the spectrum of the glottal sound source is modified according to filter curves of the oral-pharyngeal tract to form the different vowel sound spectra for several vowels. The fundamental frequency is 100 Hz and thus the harmonics are

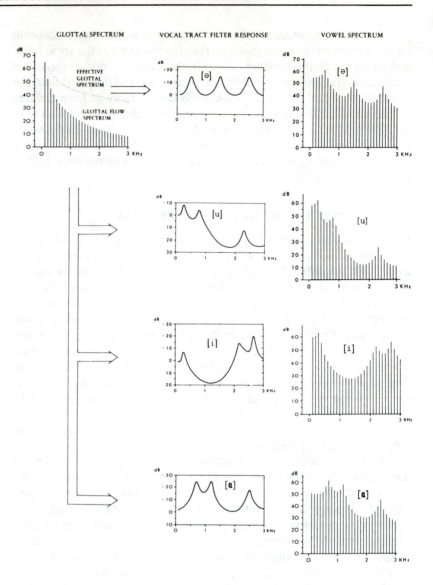

Figure 26.   The production of model vowels according to the source-filter theory. An idealized spectrum sloping −12 dB/octave is assumed as the spectrum of the basic waveform of glottal airflow. However, radiation of the vowel sound from the mouth is more efficient for high than for low frequencies, on a slope of about + 6 dB/octave. This constant factor is added to the glottal flow spectrum to give an effective glottal source spectrum sloping −6 dB/octave for all the vowels. It is modified by the filter responses of the vocal tract, shown for the different vowels, to produce the final vowel spectra on the right. The filter shapes were calculated from combinations of ideal resonators. (Adapted from Fant, 1960; Stevens and House, 1961.)

at all the multiples of 100 Hz. The effective glottal spectrum has a slope of −6 dB/octave instead of the −12 dB/octave of the average glottal spectrum; the slope of the effective glottal spectrum is the sum of the −12 dB/octave glottal source spectrum and a +6 dB/octave constant factor because of radiation characteristics of the mouth-opening in the human head.

The important things to note in Figure 26 are that the spectrum of the glottal sound source is the same for all the different vowels and this sound spectrum is then changed by the filtering of the vocal tract to produce vowel sounds that have different spectral patterns.

First consider the spectrum envelopes of the vowel spectra, ignoring the individual components. Examine the relations between the formant peaks in the spectrum and the overall slope of the spectrum from low to high frequencies.

The general slope of the spectral envelopes of vowels stems both from the spectrum of the glottal sound source and from the degree of proximity of the formant frequencies. The slope is affected by any formants that are very close to each other. In the case of the vowel [u], for example, the first and second formants are close in frequency and at a low location; the two close resonances reinforce each other and thus raise the low frequency part of the spectrum to a higher amplitude than for the neutral vowel and very high in relation to the third formant of [u]. In the case of the vowel [i] the second formant is close to the third formant, and thus they reinforce each other and raise the high frequency end of the vowel spectrum relative to the middle. However, both F2 and F3 are now very far away from F1, which is in a low position for the vowel [i]. Because of the distance between them, the reinforcing effect of the first formant on the second and third formants is much less. The net result on the spectrum of [i] is that the amplitude level of the spectrum in the region of F3 is still low compared with the amplitude level in the low frequencies, but it is much higher than for [u] and substantially higher than for [ə] and [ɑ]. Thus we see that the particular locations of formant peaks, which are determined by the shape of the vocal tract, will affect not only the location in frequency of the vowel spectrum peaks but also the amplitudes of the peaks in relation to each other and the relative strengths of F3 and higher formants. The amplitudes of components in the F1 region are greater than the amplitudes of components lower in frequency.

In addition to the effect of the tract shape on the vowel spectrum envelope the conditions of glottal action have their effects on the resulting vowel spectrum. There are two main glottal factors: one is the fundamental pulsing rate at the voice pitch frequency, and the other is the amount of vocal effort. The factor of voice pitch affects only the frequency positions

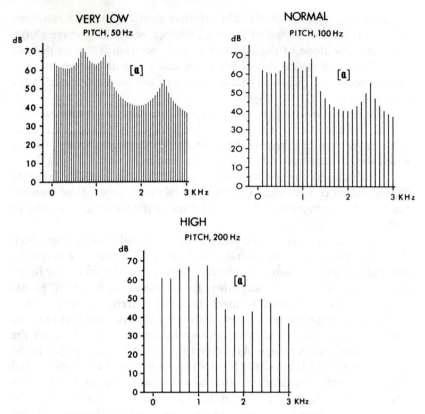

Figure 27.   Effects of voice pitch on a model vowel spectrum. The vowel spectrum envelope is constant but the harmonic spacing changes with fundamental frequency or pitch.

of the individual harmonic components in the spectrum and does not affect the shape of the spectrum. The effects on the spectrum of changes in voice pitch frequency are illustrated in Figure 27. On the left side of Figure 27 is the spectrum for a voice pitch that is lower than the fundamental frequency of 100 Hz that was assumed for the vowels of Figure 26. The low pitch causes the spectrum components to be spaced more closely together, compared with the vowel on the right side of the figure, which has a fundamental frequency of 100 Hz. The low-pitched spectrum on the left is for a fundamental voice frequency of 50 pulses per second. Thus the spectrum components in the vowel are at 50-Hz intervals. A voice pitch as low as 50 Hz occurs for extremely low-pitched voices as sometimes heard in radio announcers. At the bottom of Figure 27 is the spectrum for a high-pitched voice where the voice fundamental frequency is 200 pulses per second. For this vowel the spectral components occur at intervals of 200 Hz and the density of components is thus lower.

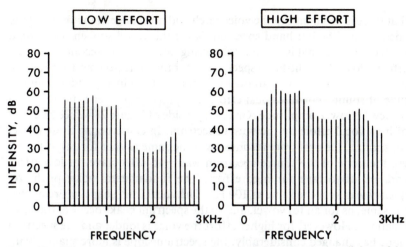

Figure 28. Effects of vocal effort on the vowel spectrum. Note that the overall slope of the vowel spectrum is steep for low effort and more gradual for high effort. The second and higher formants are relatively more intense under high vocal effort. See text for further explanation.

It should be especially noted in Figure 27 that the shape of the spectrum envelope, which is determined by the positions of the formants and their relations to each other, is not changed by changes in the voice pitch. Only the spacing of the component frequencies, that is, the spacing of the harmonics corresponding to the fundamental pulse rate, is changed by changes in voice pitch. How these components are shaped to form the spectrum envelope depends only on the vocal tract shape and not at all on the frequency of the voice pulsing rate.

The glottal wave assumed for Figures 26 and 27 had a smooth spectrum envelope with slope of −12 dB/octave. The spectra of real glottal pulses do not have such a smooth spectrum slope, but the 12-dB slope is a good representation for average speech spoken for specimen or citation purposes. In more relaxed phonation the glottal pulses are more rounded on the corners, causing the glottal spectrum to slope downward more steeply. A typical spectrum slope for this type of phonation is −15 dB/octave; this value would correspond to a relaxed conversational level of vocal effort. If the style of speaking is very forceful, the glottal pulses can have very steep sides and sharper corners, because of higher subglottal pressure on the opening of the vocal folds and higher Bernoulli suction before the closing. With such high effort, the glottal spectrum slope will be more shallow than −12 dB/octave, say about −9 dB/octave (see Fant, 1959; Flanagan, 1958; Mártony, 1965; Rothenberg, 1973).

Figure 28 shows the effect of a change in vocal effort on the vowel spectrum of a model [ɑ] vowel. For the purposes of the figure we assume that there is no change in the voice pitch and no change in the shape of the vocal tract. The left-hand spectrum is for the vowel spoken softly on a pitch of 100 Hz, that is, the glottal pulsing rate is 100 per second and vocal effort is low; the right-hand spectrum is for the same [ɑ] vowel at the same pulse rate but with a high amount of effort and producing a higher amplitude of sound. For low vocal effort the spectrum is steeper in slope and the level is low in amplitude. On the right side of Figure 28 we see an effect of high vocal effort on the vowel spectrum. In constructing these model [ɑ] spectra, the oral tract response was the same as that for [ɑ] in Figure 26; the slope of the source spectrum was −15 dB/octave for low effort and −9 dB/octave for high effort. The fundamental voice pitch frequency was kept the same at 100 Hz. The vocal tract shape has remained the same, as for an [ɑ] vowel, and so the spectrum peaks occur at the same locations. However, for higher effort the voice is louder and the spectrum slope has changed considerably; the spectrum slope is more shallow with higher amplitudes at the high frequencies, and the amplitudes of the formant peaks of the spectrum are higher than for normal effort, but the fundamental component is lower in amplitude. In other words, the increased voice loudness with high effort is due to increases in the amplitudes of the resonant oscillations.

In addition to the effects of glottal pulse shape on the overall slope of the glottal spectrum, the individual spectrum components are affected in amplitude by the general time features of the glottal wave. The time features are the duration of the open portion, the ratio of the open portion to the closed portion, and the degree of symmetry of the opening and closing legs of the pulse. These features cause variations in component amplitudes above and below the average slope of the spectrum. These variations give a scalloped effect to the source spectrum envelope by lowering the amplitude of about every fourth or fifth harmonic. In addition there is often a narrow depression in the source spectrum, somewhere in the region between 600 and 1000 Hz, which is due to absorption of sound by the subglottal spaces. Research on glottal function is currently concerned with relating these aspects of the glottal waveform to various conditions of phonation. Systematic rules about the glottal spectra for various styles and types of phonation should result from this research, but at present we do not have these rules.

Individual anatomic characteristics of the vocal folds and voice training can also affect the spectrum of the glottal pulses. However, at present we do not have enough systematic knowledge to explain how these individual characteristics arise. In general a highly efficient, "strong" speaking voice is attributable to a steep offset of the glottal pulse before the closed portion and not to the vocal tract resonances per se; the resonances are more strongly excited by a more efficient shape of glottal pulse. However, professional singers are able to adjust their pharynx to raise the vowel spectrum in the region F3 to F5 (Sundberg, 1973).

SPECTROGRAMS OF VOWELS

Spectrograms[3] of spoken examples of the vowels [i], [ɑ], and [u] are shown in Figure 29 to illustrate the variables in vowel formation. The vowels were spoken by an adult male in words beginning with [h] and ending with [d]. Next to the spectrogram of each vowel is a spectral section taken at one time point during the vowel. The spectrograms and sections were made on a Kay Sona-graph adjusted to apply an upward tilt to the spectrum above 500 Hz of 3½ dB/octave. The sections show the effects on the spectrum envelope of the vocal tract shape differences between [i], [ɑ], and [u]. The sections also show the effects on the glottal source spectrum for low- and high-pitched voices: the voice pitch is reflected in the frequency spacing of the harmonic components, with wider spacing for high pitch than for low pitch. The effects of high vocal effort appear in the amplitudes of F2 and F3 between 1 and 3 kHz, which are seen to be much more intense relative to the F1 region for high effort vs. low effort.

The pitch of the voice can be seen in a spectrogram as well as in the spectrum sections. In the spectrogram there is a pulse of sound energy for each pulse of the glottis, which forms the source of the vowel sound. On the spectrogram each glottal pulse appears as a dark striation running from low to high frequencies. The striations succeed each other in time exactly in synchrony with the glottal pulses. Since the glottal pulses are more widely spaced in time for a low-pitched voice, the spectrogram pulses are farther apart for vowels spoken on a low voice pitch. For the high-pitched voice the glottal pulses and the striations in the spectrogram are more closely packed together, because for a high-pitched voice the glottal pulses succeed each other more rapidly in time.

Spectrograms of all of the vowels and diphthongs are shown in Figure 30, as spoken by an adult male in syllables beginning with [h] and ending with [d], except for [ə], which was spoken in the phrase *a toy* [ətɔɪ]. The speaker used his native General American dialect except for the vowel [a] where he imitated a native of Massachusetts saying the word *hard*. Going across the top row of spectrograms (A), we go through the series of front vowels starting with [i] and going through [ɪ], [e], [ɛ], [æ], and [a]; you will note that the second formant comes down from high to low frequencies through this series of front vowels, and the first formant rises from a low to a high frequency position, through the series. You will also

---

[3]If you are not already familiar with spectrograms, you should review the operation of the sound spectrograph described in Chapter 2.

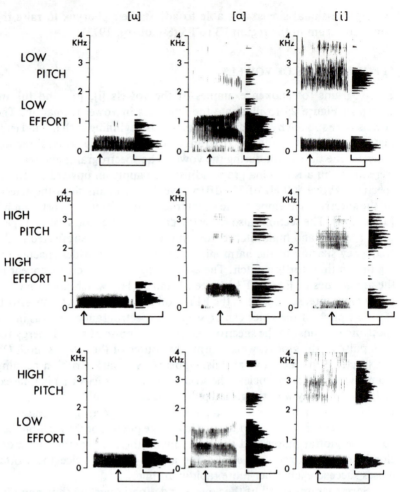

Figure 29.   Spectrograms and spectral sections of natural vowels under different combinations of voice pitch and vocal effort. For the spectral sections each vowel was sampled at the point in time indicated by the arrow. The sections show how the harmonic spacing changes with voice pitch and how the intensity of the components in the higher formant regions increase, relative to the fundamental, with high vocal effort.

note that two of the front vowels, namely, [ɪ] and [ɛ], are shorter in duration than the other vowels. Of course any vowel can be deliberately shortened or prolonged in pronunciation, but, as they occur in naturally spoken English, certain vowels have shorter durations than the other vowels. The average durations of vowels in stressed one-syllable words, spoken by American talkers, was found to be about 230 ms for long vowels and 180 ms for the short vowels (Peterson and Lehiste, 1960). The vowel durations in Figure 30 are similar to these values.

The second row of spectrograms (B) shows the sound patterns of the back vowel series starting with [u] and going through [ʊ], [o], [ɔ], and [ɑ]. You will note in this series that the first and second formant resonances go from low frequency positions to higher frequency positions. In the series of back vowels there is one short vowel, [ʊ].

Figure 30 (C) shows the spectrograms of the three central vowels [ʌ], [ə], and [ɚ]. The short central vowel is [ə]. The diphthongs [ɑɪ], [iu], and [ɔi] and [ɑʊ] are shown in (D); they are longer in duration. Diphthongs are similar to double vowels and they include a glide in articulation from one vowel position to another. In the spectrograms of the diphthongs you can see both the first and second formant frequency positions changing in time as the vocal tract shape changes from one vowel conformation to the other.

NASALIZATION OF VOWELS

Normally the vowel sounds of English are spoken with the velum raised against the walls and back of the pharynx to shut off the nasal passages completely from the pharynx and oral tract. However, speakers of American English often seem to nasalize their vowels slightly by allowing the velum to remain slightly open. Nasalization also occurs in vowels that are adjacent to nasal consonants, especially in the portions of the vowel immediately next to the consonant.

In pathologic speech, such as that of a person who has a cleft palate, which opens the oral tract into the nasal passages, or a person with an undeveloped velum or abnormally sluggish velum action, there may be extreme nasalization of all sounds. Persons who were born deaf sometimes speak with nasalized sounds.

The important acoustic effects of nasalization have been determined through research on vocal tract models (House and Stevens, 1956). Electrical models were built of the cavities of the nasal tract and the oral tract, and the two tracts were connected together through circuits representing greater or lesser amounts of opening between them. It was found that the main effect on a vowel of an opening at the velum is to produce changes in the filter curve of the oral tract. One effect was that the first formant became broader and less peaked than before, because of the damping of the formant resonance by the loss of energy through the opening into the nasal tract.

Another change is to apply negative resonant peaks to the oral tract response. These negative resonances are called *zeroes*. Zeroes are antiresonances; they are exactly the opposite of resonances in their effect on the spectrum. Instead of reinforcing and amplifying the spectrum at and near the resonant frequency, an antiresonance selectively absorbs sound so

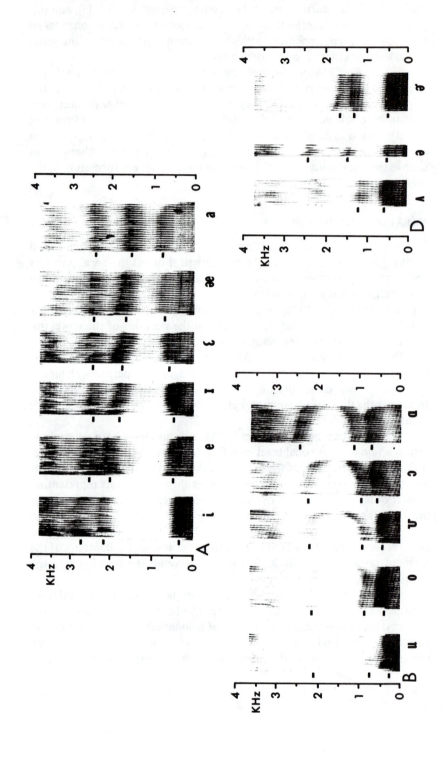

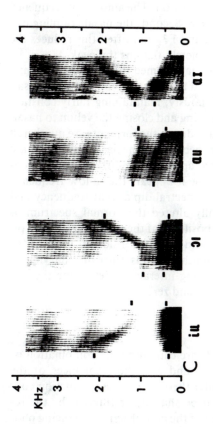

Figure 30. Spectrograms of examples of the vowels and diphthongs of American English. The approximate midvowel locations of formants are indicated by the bars beside each spectrogram.

that it greatly reduces the amplitudes of components at and near the anti-resonant frequency. In addition, for each zero there is an extra formant. The amount of these effects depends on the amount of opening between the pharyngeal-oral tract and the nasal tract. That is, the nasalization effects on the spectrum depend on the *amount of coupling* between the two tracts. The amount of coupling also affects the frequency positions of the zeroes and extra formants. The total effect on the spectrum is complex but there are two general effects. First, the presence of a low frequency zero below F1 tends to make the spectral peak in the region of F1 appear to be higher in frequency than it would normally be. Thus the effects of nasalization on F1 are to reduce the amplitude, and to move the apparent F1 in this region to a higher frequency position. The amount of frequency shift in the apparent F1 is 50 to 100 Hz. Second, the nasal coupling can also cause zeroes in the region of F2 and F3, and often this reduces the peakedness of these formants or completely flattens the peaks.

Some effects of nasalization are diagrammed in Figure 31, showing spectrum envelopes for a natural [ɑ] and for the same vowel heavily nasalized. The talker spoke the [ɑ] continuously, maintaining fairly constant positions of tongue and jaw while opening and closing the velum to nasalize and denasalize the vowel. The peaks due to the formants are numbered 1, 2, and 3 for the normal [ɑ]; for the spectrum of the nasalized [ɑ], z's are drawn to indicate spectral regions that appear to be influenced by zeroes in the vocal tract response. In this case it appears that a low frequency zero at about 600 Hz has produced a spectral dip at that frequency and that two higher zeroes have radically altered the normal spectrum at points near the third resonance. The positions of these zeroes may be typical for heavily nasalized [ɑ] but should not be considered to hold for milder degrees of nasalization, nor for other vowels, since the pharyngeal-oral shape and amount of velar opening interact to determine the frequency positions of the nasal formants and zeroes.

SUMMARY

The spectral characteristics of vowels are caused by the combination of the spectrum of the glottal source sound and the resonances of the pharyngeal-oral tract. The source-filter theory of vowel production considers the glottal source spectrum to be shaped, or filtered, by the response of the vocal tract, independent of the glottal action of voicing phonation. Factors that affect the glottal spectrum operate through changes in the pulse form of the airflow through the glottis in forming each glottal pulse. Vocal fold tension affects the fundamental pulsing rate and the airflow velocity causes a suction force (Bernoulli force) between the folds,

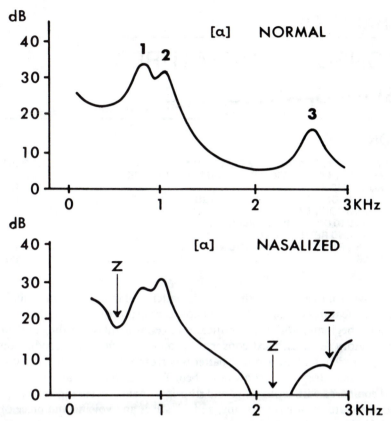

Figure 31.   An example of the effects of vowel nasalization on the vowel spectrum. The spectrum envelopes of a normal [ɑ] and a nasalized [ɑ] are plotted as derived from spectral sections. The first three formants are labeled in the normal vowel; reductions in spectrum level in the nasalized vowel, presumably because of the addition of zeroes to the vocal tract response, are indicated by "z."

which affects the pulse shape. The spacing in frequency of the glottal spectrum components depends on the voice pitch (fundamental pulsing frequency); the slope of the spectrum depends on the pulse shape, which is sensitive to the amount of vocal effort.

The formant resonances of the vowels and diphthongs, and the effects of changes in pitch and vocal effort, are exemplified in spectrograms of natural speech.

Vowel sounds may be nasalized and this causes a reduction in F1 amplitude and the insertion of antiresonances (zeroes) and extra formants in the transmission of the pharyngeal-oral tract, thus altering the normal vowel spectrum.

CHAPTER 6

CONSONANT FEATURES, GLIDES, AND STOPS

CONTENTS

We now turn to a study of the acoustic patterns of consonants. The main acoustic features of consonants and how each feature is produced are described, beginning with the classification of consonants according to their articulatory features. Next consonant production and vowel production are compared, and the acoustic patterns corresponding to each of the different articulatory features are described. The glide features are explained and compared with diphthongs and stop consonants. In subsequent chapters the features of nasals, stops, and fricatives and voicing and place of articulation are described.

ARTICULATORY FEATURES OF CONSONANTS

Phonetic study of the consonants has developed a classification of consonants according to their articulatory features. Certain acoustic features correspond to the articulatory features, and in turn the acoustic features are the basis for the perceptual distinction of one consonant from another by a listener. The relations among articulatory, acoustic, and perceptual features form a theory of distinctive features. A theory of distinctive features constructs category systems for phonemes; the categories are intended to cover all languages. Each feature category is derived by joint consideration of three levels of linguistic analysis: the perceptual level, the acoustic level, and the articulatory level. Thus the purpose of distinctive feature theory is to provide a single consistent framework for specifying the phonology, i.e., the communicative sound structure, of any language (Chomsky and Halle, 1968; Jakobson et al., 1967).

Table 2. Articulatory classification of consonants

| Place of articulation | Manner of articulation | | | | | |
| | | | Stop | | Fricative | |
	Glide	Nasal	Voiced	Unvoiced	Voiced	Unvoiced
Front						
Bilabial	w,ʍ	m	b	p		
Labiodental					v	f
Middle						
Dental					ð	θ
Alveolar	j,l	n	d	t	z	s
Palatal	r				ʒ	ʃ
Back						
Velar	w,ʍ	ŋ	g	k		
Pharyngeal						h
Glottal			ʔ			

Distinctive feature theory has been highly useful in the study of speech communication. However, the purpose here is more limited. We deal only with English, and primarily with physiological and acoustic phonetics. Thus, the description of the acoustic patterns of consonants follows a classification according to articulatory features rather than distinctive features. The articulatory features of consonants are of three types: 1) features of manner of articulation, 2) the voicing feature, and 3) features of place of articulation. The manner and voicing features are types or states of articulation that can occur with any place of articulation; the voicing feature is either voiced or unvoiced; the manner features are glide, stop (plosive), nasal, and fricative. There are three subsidiary types of glide articulation: semi-vowel [w, j], lateral [l], and retroflex [r]. There are three general places of articulation—front, middle, and back— and at each general place there are two or three subsidiary places. The English consonants are shown in Table 2 arranged in rows corresponding to place of articulation and in columns corresponding to voicing and manner of articulation.

You may already be familiar with articulatory classification of consonants from a study of general phonetics. If not, you should memorize the classification because it is so commonly used in discussing consonants and it forms the basis for our study here.

CONSONANT PRODUCTION COMPARED WITH VOWEL PRODUCTION

Consonants differ from vowels in two main ways: 1) in vocal tract shaping and 2) in sound sources. The *sound source* for vowels is always periodic, but a consonant may be produced with a periodic sound source, an aperiodic sound source, or a combination of periodic and aperiodic sources. Aperiodic sources of consonant sound are caused by constrictions in the vocal tract. Consonants often include aperiodic sound because the tract constrictions for many consonants are so narrow that the airflow of the breath stream becomes turbulent. Turbulent airflow generates an aperiodic sound. The periodic sound source for consonants is the airflow fluctuations resulting from the periodic movements of the vocal folds, just as for vowels.

The *vocal tract shaping* of consonants constricts the tract to a larger degree than for vowels. The stop consonants, such as [p, b, t], obstruct the breath stream completely during a portion of the articulatory gesture. The fricative consonants, such as [ʃ, s, z], are formed with a very narrow constriction. Even the glide consonants, [w] and [j], constrict the oral tract more than do the corresponding close vowels, [u] and [i].

The constriction differences cause important general differences in sound pattern between consonants and vowels. The openness of the oral tract during vowels gives them the general characteristic of strong, voice-pulsed sound. In contrast the constrictedness of consonants causes them to have weaker voiced sound, aperiodic sound, or absence of sound. These differences are discussed briefly now, and later in more detail for the various types of consonants.

The stop or plosive consonants [p, t, k, b, d, g] are produced by a movement that completely occludes the vocal tract. During the occlusion there is either complete silence or only weak, low frequency sound. There is a complete silence for an unvoiced stop; during the occlusion of a voiced stop there is only the sound of the very lowest harmonics as long as voicing is maintained during the occlusion. As we shall see later, certain conditions often suppress the voicing.

When the occlusion of a stop consonant is released to form a following vowel, a transient and, for unvoiced stops, a burst of noise-like sound occur during the release. Thus, in contrast to the continuous, strong, voiced sound of vowels, the stop consonants have an interval that is silent, or nearly so, followed by a release burst of sound.

The continuant, nonplosive consonants are the glides [w, j, r, l], the nasals [m, n, ŋ], and the fricatives [s, ʃ, f, θ, z, ʒ, v, ð]. These are produced by movements that form partial constrictions of the vocal tract. Partial constriction causes either a reduced voiced sound during the constriction or, for fricatives, a noise-like, aperiodic sound caused by a turbulent sound source. The voiced sound produced during the constrictions of the glides and nasals is weaker than for vowels, especially in the region of F2 and above. Usually the noise-like sounds of the unvoiced fricatives [s, ʃ, f, θ] have more energy at middle and high frequencies, above 2 kHz, than at lower frequencies; in contrast, voiced sounds always have more energy in the low frequencies, below 1 kHz, than at higher frequencies.

GLIDE CONSONANTS AND DIPHTHONGS

The following description of consonant features concentrates first on the manner features, then on the voicing feature, and finally on the place features. This order is the order of importance of the features in their phonemic function in English (Carterette and Jones, 1974; Denes, 1963). We can begin our study with glide consonants, taking advantage of the fact that glides are similar to the vowels that we have already studied.

The remainder of this chapter concerns the articulatory actions for the glide features and their corresponding acoustic features: first the contrast between glide consonants and diphthongs and voiced stops, and then the differences among the voiced glides [w, j, r, l]. The unvoiced glide [ʍ] is discussed in the chapter on voicing.

The semivowel glide consonants, [w] and [j], when combined with vowels, are similar to diphthongs; the differences are that the glide consonants are produced with a constriction that is greater than the closest vowels and the articulatory movements to and from the glide constriction are faster than the movement between the two vowels of a diphthong.

Let us examine how the glide consonants are produced. The production of a consonant involves four important physiological factors: 1) the constricting effect of the consonant articulation on the oral tract, 2) the subglottal air pressure, 3) the air pressure in the mouth, and 4) the state of the vocal folds. Figure 36A shows the action of each of these factors in the production of the phrase *a Y* [əwɑɪ]. This phrase contains the glide [w] and the diphthong [ɑɪ] for comparison.

Each of the first four numbered rows in Figure 36 represents the movement, state, or pattern of one of the four factors. The last row (5) shows a spectrogram of the sound patterns of the phrase marked with lines to show how the sound patterns are related to the four production factors. The articulatory factors are schematic; the spectrogram was made from the utterance of an adult male speaker.

In row 1 the basic phases of the oral tract movement are traced. These are as follows: open during vowels, transitional closing from vowel to consonant, constricted phase of the consonant, and transitional opening from consonant to vowel. The movements shown are schematic; the forms of movement shown are based partly on inferences from acoustic patterns and partly on high speed motion pictures of lip and tongue movement (Fujimura, 1961; Houde, 1968; Kent and Moll, 1969; Perkell, 1969; Truby, 1959).

In row 1 of Figure 36A, the oral tract is initially in an open position for the neutral vowel [ə]. About 60 ms after the start of the vowel, the lips and tongue begin to move toward constriction for [w]. The transition time from open to narrow constriction is about 75 ms; the constriction lasts about 100 ms; the opening transition is about 75 ms. The total duration of the consonant movement is about 250 ms. During the period of narrowest constriction, the amount of constriction changes only slowly, compared with the rapid transitions to and from the constriction. After the opening transition of [w], the diphthong [ɑɪ] lasts about 350 ms. The oral tract is more constricted during the [ɪ] portion than during the [ɑ] portion. These durations are fairly typical for the utterance in a citation style of a short vowel, glide consonant, and a stressed diphthong.

The open phases of vowels can vary considerably in duration, depending on regional accent, on the identity of the vowel, on the consonants with which it is coarticulated, and on whether it is stressed or unstressed, or receiving special emphasis. For the various consonants, the closed time, or the constricted time, is generally in the range of 75 to 150 ms; longer times can occur on fricative consonants. On the average the duration of the period of constriction per consonant in rapid, fluent speech is about 100 ms.

Keeping in mind the basic open-constricted movement cycle, as sketched in row 1, we can explain how these movements will affect the sound patterns. First there must be speech sound generated by sound sources. Rows 2 and 4 indicate how these sound sources are produced and how they fit in with the open-constricted movement cycle to produce the phrase *a Y.*

The subglottal air pressure and the vocal fold action produce sound that is modified by the open-to-constricted cycle of the oral tract movement. In Figure 36 the articulations are coordinated in time, as shown schematically in rows 1 through 4; the corresponding sound patterns are shown in the spectrogram below. Before phonation of the [ə] begins, the vocal folds are brought close together (row 4) and the subglottal pressure begins to rise (row 2). When this pressure is high enough the vocal folds begin their opening and closing action to produce the basic sound source for the vowel [ə]. This voicing action continues until, at the end of the phrase, the subglottal pressure becomes too low to produce any vocal fold action. The pressure variations generated by the pulses of glottal airflow are seen as the small oscillations in the subglottal pressure. The average subglottal pressure is rather constant through the vowel [ə] and through

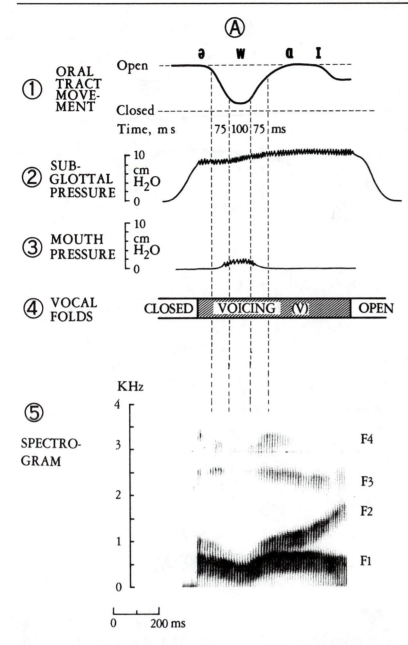

Figure 36. The patterns of articulation, air pressure, and phonation in relation to the spectrographic acoustic patterns for the phrases *a Y* [əwaɪ] and *a buy* [əbaɪ]. A full explanation of

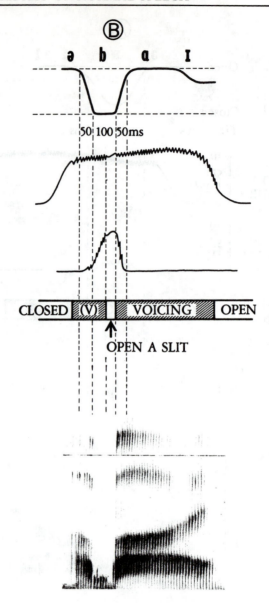

each numbered line, 1 through 5, is given in the text. The acoustic patterns are of actual utterances and the other patterns are drawn schematically to illustrate typical conditions for such utterances. The pressure unit cm H_2O is equal to 9.806×10^2 dyne/cm².

part of the consonant constriction. It then rises to a maximum and falls off again during the [ɑɪ]. This rise is what produces the stress on the second syllable of the phrase.

Row 3 indicates the amount of air pressure in the mouth relative to atmospheric pressure as zero. When the articulation is fairly open, as it is for all vowels, the pressure in the mouth is zero; however, whenever the articulation becomes constricted, there is a rise in the air pressure behind the constriction. The state of pressure during consonant constrictions depends on specific patterns of articulation, and this pressure is extremely important in generating certain sound patterns for the consonants. For the consonant [w] there is a considerable amount of lip constriction, and thus there is a small rise in pressure. The rise is small because the lips do not close completely.

The spectrogram shows how the sound patterns of the phrase are related to the articulation events above. When the voicing excitation of the oral tract begins, F1 is located at about 500 Hz, F2 at 1000 Hz, and F3 at 2500 Hz. The low F2 position may be due to a slight back constriction by the tongue. The formants drift downward from these positions for about 60 ms until the lips and tongue begin to move rapidly toward the [w] constriction. Then both F1 and F2 turn down in frequency because of the increasing constriction at the lips and the more back-constricted tongue; these changes in F1 and F2 frequencies are what we would expect according to the F1 and F2 constriction rules of Chapter 3. As the transition continues and the constriction becomes greater, the frequency positions of F1 and F2 become lower and lower. These changes in the formant locations are the formant transitions for [w]. As indicated by the dashed vertical lines, the formant transitions are correlated in time with the changes in constriction in row 1, which cause the formants to move to lower and lower frequencies with more and more constriction during the onset of the [w] consonant and to rise again as the lips open and the tongue moves toward the [ɑ] position. The lip constriction also causes F3 and F4 to go down in frequency and to be greatly reduced in intensity; F1 and F2 are also lower in intensity during the narrowest part of the constriction. During and after the opening transition from the constriction, the tongue articulation moves to [ɑ] then to [ɪ], causing F2 to rise farther and F1 to fall again for the [ɪ].

The timing of the formant transitions is an important aspect of the glide consonant sound. The basic transition, caused by the movement into and away from the constriction, takes about 75 ms. This is seen most directly in the F1 transition, because the frequency of F1 is more closely related to the amount of constriction. If the vowel formants are located far from the glide consonant formants, then the F2 transitions may require more than 75 ms while the F1 transition lasts only about 75 ms.

The glide [w] differs in three ways from the vowel [u]. First, the lips constrict more for [w] than for [u]. This causes lowered intensity of F1 and F2, and great reduction of the intensity of F3 and the higher formants. Second, [w] may be formed in front of any tongue position; the tongue position is affected by the adjacent vowels. A slight back constriction of the tongue may accompany the [w] constriction at the lips. The vowel [u], on the other hand, requires a narrow back tongue constriction in addition to lip constriction. Third, the speed of oral tract movement is faster in producing [w] than in movements between two vowels; this is seen by comparing the speeds of F1 transition in Figure 36. The F1 transition on the opening of [w] into [ɑ] is much faster than the F1 transition from [ɑ] to [ɪ]. These differences are typical of the differences between glide consonants and diphthongs.

GLIDE AND VOICED STOP

Now that we have seen how the glide consonant [w] is produced, and how it is different from vowels and diphthongs, we need to compare it with other consonants. First, we compare [w] with [b]. The consonant [b] is a voiced stop produced at the same place of articulation as [w], i.e., by a constriction of the lips. Figure 36B is a schema of the production of [b], in the phrase *a buy,* for comparison with the production of [w].

We see that the vocal folds are again closed at first and that the subglottal pressure rises in time. When the subglottal pressure is high enough, vocal fold voicing action begins, thus producing the source sound for the vowel [ə]. This pulsing continues throughout the vowel and through the transitional phase from open to constricted. So far all is similar to [w]. The similarity ends, however, at the point where the constriction of the lips to form the [b] reaches an amount of constriction sufficient to impede and then block the breath stream. Then the air pressure in the mouth immediately begins to rise, as shown in row 3. After the lips close completely, the mouth pressure continues to rise; it approaches the level of the subglottal pressure. During part of the rise in mouth pressure there is still enough pressure drop across the glottis to maintain vocal fold voicing, although at a decreasing pulse rate (because of the decreasing pressure drop across the glottis). Finally the pressure drop is not large enough to cause vocal fold movement and there is a period of complete silence. The silence lasts about 25 ms until the lips begin to open in the transition from the completely closed state toward the following vowel.

As soon as the lips are even slightly open the dammed-up air in the mouth begins to flow very rapidly through the lips, and soon the mouth pressure goes back down to zero, the atmospheric base line; the release of this pressure takes only 10 to 20 ms. This release of the pressured air in the mouth produces two sounds: an abrupt transient of increased sound pressure followed by a very brief burst of turbulent sound. The turbulent sound occurs when there is sufficient air velocity, through the barely parted lips, from the brief airflow outward in response to the higher than atmospheric air pressure inside the mouth.

During all this time the vocal folds are still held together in a position ready for voicing, probably forming a slit; as soon as the air pressure in the mouth has dropped far enough, there is a sufficient difference between the mouth pressure and the subglottal pressure for voicing action to resume. In other words, as the mouth pressure goes down because of airflow through the opening lips, and the pressure drop across the glottis becomes large enough, the vocal fold voicing begins again for the following vowel. Voicing then continues throughout the rest of the transition to the vowel and during the vowel phase.

As the vowel continues, the subglottal pressure curve reaches a maximum, giving the stress to the [ɑɪ], and then begins to decline especially toward the end of the vowel.

Now examine the sound patterns of the phrase *a buy* in row 5 of Figure 36B. Note that the formant transitions are very similar to the transitions for [w] except that they seem to be cut short by the closure of the lips. Theoretically, F1 reaches zero frequency at the moment of complete lip closure, and thus the F1 transition of [b] can reach a lower frequency than that of [w]; this is sometimes seen when a voicing pulse happens to occur during the final 10 ms or so of the closing movement of the lips.

While the lips are completely closed there is no sound present except weak sound in the very low frequencies, at the fundamental frequency, and perhaps at the second harmonic; these frequencies are low enough to be transmitted at low intensity through the closed lips and the cheeks. The sound in the region of F2 and above is completely suppressed by the closure of the oral tract; indeed F2 and the higher formants are partially suppressed and lowered in frequency during the last phase of the transitional part of the consonant movement because of the progressively smaller lip opening.

At the end of the closed phase when the lips part and the mouth pressure releases through the lips, the release transient and a very brief, 10-ms burst of turbulent sound are seen in the spectrogram. Just before this pressure release, during the latter part of the closed phase, the vocal fold voicing has stopped and there is complete silence. After the release burst has dissipated enough of the mouth pressure, voicing begins again and there are corresponding vertical striations in the spectrogram, one for each airflow pulse emitted by the glottis. The lips continue to open and the tongue has already moved toward the [ɑ] position. As the lips continue to open F1 rises, producing a transition to a level of about 650 Hz for the [ɑ], and the F2 frequency also rises to about 1150 Hz. The reappearance and upward transitions of F3 and F4 are also seen. After the transition interval is over, the formant frequencies remain at rather steady locations until the formants begin moving toward the [ɪ] part of the diphthong.

Now compare the two consonants [w] and [b]. We see that their sound patterns differ mainly in that sound is very weak or absent during the complete closure of the [b] and there is a release-burst of sound upon opening, whereas for [w] there is strong low frequency sound present throughout and no transient burst with the opening movement. These differences arise in the oral tract movement: the [b] movement closes the tract rapidly and completely but the [w] movement goes only as far as a narrow constriction and then begins to open again. Because the [b] closes completely, three acoustic features of a voiced stop are produced: 1) weak or absent low frequency sound, 2) a brief burst of air pressure release just before voicing begins again for a following vowel, and 3) a rapid F1 transition. The transition is typically 50 msec for a stop vs. 75 msec for a glide.

The formant transitions associated with [w] and [b] are very similar in direction. This is because the transitions are produced by constricting the oral tract at the lips.

GLIDE AND STOP AT MIDDLE PLACE

We now examine the production of the glide [j]. This glide is produced by a movement of the tongue to form a constriction at the front of the palate.

In Figure 37 we have schematized the factors in production of the glide [j] in contrast to the voiced stop [d], using two phrases, *a yacht* in Figure 37A and *a dot* in Figure 37B. The constrictive movements for [j] and [d] are similar to those of [w] and [b] in Figure 36; in other words, the tongue makes a glide-consonant movement toward and away from the palate for [j] that is very similar to the movement of the lips in forming [w]; and for [d] the tongue makes a stop-consonant movement to and away from the alveolar ridge that is very similar to the movement of the lips for [b].

Also the same patterns of manipulation of the subglottal pressure, mouth pressure, and vocal fold action occur for [j] and [d] as for [w] and [b].

Therefore, the sound patterns seen in the spectrograms of [j] and [d] are similar to those seen in the spectrograms of [w] and [b] except for a difference caused by the difference in the place of constriction. This difference is seen largely in the transitions of F2. According to the formant constriction rules for F2, constriction at an alveolar or front palatal posi-

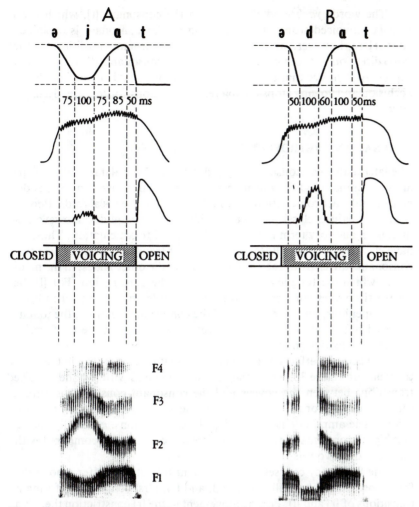

Figure 37.   Schematic relations of factors in the production of alveolar glide and stop consonants, exemplified in the spoken phrases *a yacht* [əjɑt] and *a dot* [ədɑt]. A full explanation of each line, 1 through 5, is given in the text for Figure 36 and this figure. The pressure unit cm H_2O is equal to 9.806×10^2 dyne/cm^2.

tion causes F2 to rise in frequency, but constriction of the lips causes F2 to decrease in frequency. For F1 the constriction has the same effect at both locations: a lowering of the F1 frequency during the transition from vowel to consonant and a rise in F1 frequency during the transition from consonant to vowel. The F2 transitions in *a yacht* and *a dot* show a rapid rise in frequency during the onset of the consonant constrictions and a rapid fall in frequency at the offset into the stressed vowel [ɑ].

The words *yacht* and *dot* end with the consonant [t], which is an alveolar unvoiced stop. The production of this consonant is explained later. Here, however, we can see that [t] has formant transitions in the same direction as those of the other alveolar consonant [d], as we might expect. Also notice that the mouth pressure rises suddenly during the [t] occlusion and voicing stops completely; the reasons for this are discussed later.

LATERAL AND RETROFLEX GLIDES

The lateral alveolar consonant [l] and the retroflex palatal consonant [r] are very similar to glide consonants in the speed of movement, in the degree of oral tract constriction, and in the action of the vocal folds. Phoneticians sometimes classify [l, r] as liquids rather than glides. However, liquid is an auditory term not necessarily related to articulation. Thus, we have classified [l, r] as glides, based on their transition speed. These two consonants differ from each other, and from the other glides, in the manner in which the tongue is shaped to form the constriction. For [l] the tongue tip makes contact with the alveolar ridge but is shaped to leave lateral openings, one on each side of the contact area. For [r], the tongue is flexed back and curved upward (retroflexed) so that the tip forms a moderate constriction at the palate.

The acoustic effects of [l] and [r] articulation can be seen in the spectrograms of Figure 38, where they can be compared with [w] and [j]. The transitions between the vowels and the consonant constrictions have a similar duration for all four consonants, as seen especially in the F1 transitions. The amplitude is low during the constrictions, especially for F2 and higher formants, because of the greater constriction compared with the more open vowels.

The frequency courses of the formant transitions differ among the four consonants, especially in F2, F3, and F4. First compare the formant transitions of [r] and [l]. For the movement to the [r] constriction there is a large F3 transition downward to about 1300 Hz, because of the increasing constriction of the oral tract at the middle of the palate by the retroflexed tongue tip; there is also a slight downward transition in F2 and F4. For the movement to the [l] constriction there is a slight downward transition in F2 but little or no transition in F3 or F4. These aspects of [r] and [l] contrast with [j]. For [j] there are upward transitions of F2, F3, and F4 going from [ə] to the constriction and downward again for the [ɑ]. For [w] F2 makes a large downward transition to the constriction, but F3 is not affected in frequency; F4 makes a smaller downward transition than F2.

The F1 transitions are similar for all the glides, and the transition duration is about 75 to 100 ms. The [l] has two discontinuities in the spec-

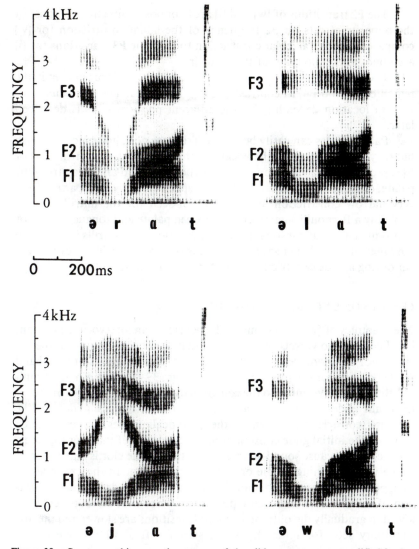

Figure 38.   Spectrographic acoustic patterns of the glide consonants exemplified in the phrases *a rot* [ərɑt], *a lot* [əlɑt], *a yacht* [əjɑt], and *a watt* [əwɑt]. See text for description of the important acoustic differences and similarities between these consonants.

trum and amplitude, which are seen especially in the F1 and F2 regions; this is because the tongue tip makes, holds, and then releases its contact with the alveolar ridge. The other glides [r, w, j] are not articulated with a tongue-tip contact and therefore their formant transitions change smoothly in time without discontinuities.

The F2 transitions of [w] and [j] are in opposite directions because of the opposite effects on F2 frequency of the labial constriction for [w] compared with the alveolar constriction for [j]. The F3 transitions for [j] are opposite the direction of those for [r].

The formant pattern of [l] during the constriction is prominent in the region of F3 and F4, in contrast to the other glides. The formants of [l] vary in location depending on the adjacent phonemes, as is described later.

Palatal glides can easily be trilled. Trills are not phonemic in English but they are often part of the vocal repertoire of children. A trilled [r] or [l] is produced by a vibration of the tongue tip toward and away from the palate, causing a rapid alternation in the spectrum between a pattern for a very narrow constriction and the pattern seen for the untrilled glide. Probably a Bernoulli suction effect between palate and tongue is a factor in producing trilled consonants. The alternation rate of trills is usually in the range of 20 to 30 per second, and thus two to three trill cycles may occur during a glide constriction of 100 ms (1/10 second).

EFFECTS OF UTTERANCE POSITION

The examples of [w, j, l, r] thus far have been in an intervocalic position, i.e., between two vowels. A consonant may also occur initially at the beginning of an utterance or finally, at the end. Spectrograms of initial and final glide-like consonants are shown in Figure 39. The patterns of the initial glides are very similar to the constricted and releasing phases of the intervocalic glides in Figure 38; also the patterns of the final glides are like the onset-constriction patterns of the intervocalic glides. The constricted phase of the initial glide consonant may be more brief than for the intervocalic glide because sound-source production by the glottis may not start at the very beginning of the oral tract constriction. In the examples of final position, [r] and [l] are more diphthong-like and drawn out in duration of the constriction because phonation is not shut off but merely allowed to gradually die out; the formant transitions are slower and the discontinuity seen for initial [l] is not seen for final [l] for one of the speakers.

The position of a glide consonant is often adjacent to another consonant, forming a compound consonant or consonant cluster. Then the glide consonant articulation strongly affects the adjacent vowel.

SUMMARY

For acoustic phonetic study the consonants are classified according to their articulatory features rather than according to distinctive feature

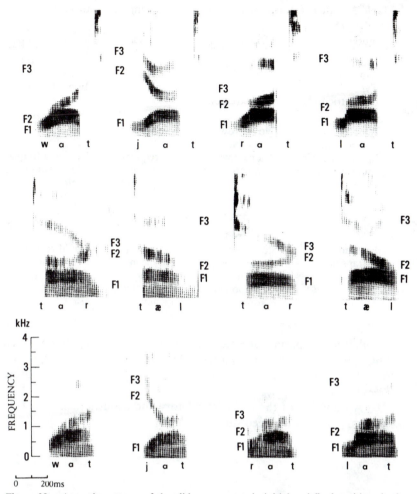

Figure 39. Acoustic patterns of the glide consonants in initial and final positions in the words *watt* [wɑt], *yacht* [jɑt], *tar* [tɑr], and *tal* [tæl]. The important points to note are described in the text. Two different male speakers spoke each word; the speaker for the top row of spectrograms has very even, regular glottal pulses and highly resonant formants, compared with the speaker in the bottom row, who was the author.

theory. The articulatory features of consonants are of three types: features of manner of articulation, voicing, and place of articulation.

Features of the articulation of glide consonants are: 1) a speed of articulation that is faster than that for diphthongs but slower than that for stops, 2) a degree of constriction that is greater than that for vowels, and 3) occurrence of lateral and retroflex forms of tongue articulation. The acoustic patterns of glides show formant transitions of intermediate

Table 3. Main features of glide consonants compared with voiced stops and diphthongs

Features	Diphthongs	Glides	Voiced stops
Timing			
Oral articulation	Slow	Medium-fast	Fast
Type of constriction	(No narrow constriction)	Brief constriction	Brief closure
Spectral			
Intensity during constriction	(No narrow constriction)	Strong	Weak
Spectrum during constriction	(No narrow constriction)	Low frequencies strong up to about 600 Hz; midfrequency energy weaker than in diphthongs	Very low frequencies; fundamental alone, lowered in pitch; no energy in F2, F3 and higher regions
Formant transitions	Slow formant transitions between the two component vowels	Medium-fast transitions appropriate to place, lateral opening, or retroflexion	Rapid formant transitions

speed, weak amplitude of F2 and higher formants during the constriction phase, and characteristic F patterns depending on lateral (F2), retroflex (low F3), labial (low F2), or alveolar (high F2) constriction characteristics.

A summary of the main articulatory and acoustic features of diphthongs, glides, and voiced stops is given in Table 3.

CHAPTER 7

CONSONANTS: NASAL, STOP, AND FRICATIVE MANNERS OF ARTICULATION

CONTENTS

This chapter contains a description of the articulation and acoustic features for three more manners of articulation that produce phonemic distinctions among the consonants of English: nasal, stop (or plosive), and fricative. These three manner-features are extremely important. Together they account for about 80% of all the consonantal distinctions (Denes, 1963).

The nasal consonants have some acoustic similarities to glides, so the nasal manner of articulation is described before discussing how nasals differ from glides. The nasals are also compared with voiced stops. Fricative consonants are then described, especially as compared with stops.

NASAL CONSONANTS

The nasal consonants [m,n,ŋ] are articulated by a combination of two movements: 1) movement of the tongue or lips to completely occlude the oral tract and 2) lowering of the velum. Velar lowering introduces an opening from the pharynx into the nasal passages; this opening is called the velopharyngeal port or simply the *velar port*. The oral occluding movements for the nasals are similar to those for the corresponding voiced stops [b,d,g] in that the constricting movement of the tongue or lips is rapid and a complete oral occlusion is formed. Because of this similarity some linguists classify the nasals as stops having the feature of nasalization.

During the oral occlusion of a nasal consonant the sound produced by the glottal action of phonation is propagated through the velar port

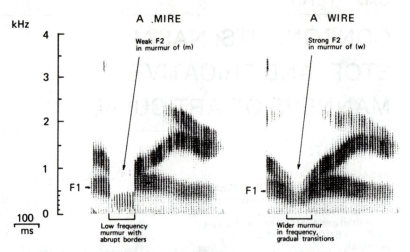

Figure 40. Spectrograms of *a wire* [əwaɪr] and *a mire* [əmaɪr] to compare the transitions and constriction murmurs between glide and nasal consonants. The transitions are more abrupt for the nasal. The strongest part of the murmur ranges up to about 800 Hz for the glide but only to about 300 Hz for the nasal.

and the nasal passages, and out through the nose. This sound from the nose is called a nasal murmur; its spectrum is dominated by low frequency sound determined mostly by the main resonance of the large volume of the nasal passages constricted by the small nose openings. The nasal passages of a speaker remain constant in shape and size for the different nasal consonants. For this reason the murmur spectrum does not differ greatly among [m,n,ŋ].

NASAL-GLIDE-STOP DIFFERENCES

Figure 40 compares the nasal and glide consonants showing spectrograms of the phrases *a wire* [əwaɪr] and *a mire* [əmaɪr]. The spectrograms show differences between nasal and glide consonants in the transitions to and from the consonant constrictions and also during the murmurs of the constriction intervals. The strong low frequency portion of the nasal murmur is similar to that in the glide constriction intervals except that in the nasal murmur it is limited to the region below about 300 Hz, whereas the strong low frequency energy in the constriction of glides ranges up to about 800 Hz. The nasal murmur has abrupt borders compared to the more gradual transitions of the glide constriction from vowel to constriction and back to vowel. The abruptness of onset and offset of the nasal murmur results from two circumstances: 1) the oral occlusion is sudden in onset and offset and 2) the nasal port is already wide open at the onset of the occlusion and remains so throughout.

There are important differences between nasals and glides in the spectrum of the murmur sound above the low frequency part. The nasal murmurs are much less intense above 800 Hz than are the murmurs of the glides, and the pattern of formant frequencies in this upper region is not consistently definitive among the nasals [m,n,ŋ] as it is among glides.

We next compare the nasal and voiced stop consonants. The nasal vs. stop acoustic differences are somewhat complicated but they can be easily understood if the production factors are kept in mind. There are three main acoustic differences between voiced stops and nasals: 1) the stops have release bursts but the nasals do not; 2) the nasals have stronger intensity of the constriction murmur; and 3) the vowels adjacent to nasals are nasalized, but not for stops. The movement of the oral tract for nasals is similar to that of stops, with rapid transitions, abrupt onset and offset of occlusion, and an occlusion interval of about 100 ms. However, during the occlusion interval of nasals there is present the relatively strong, low frequency sound of the murmur compared with weak or absent sound during stop occlusions. The murmur and nasalization patterns can be compared in Figure 41. Let us now see how all these acoustic differences are produced.

Release Bursts and Murmur Intensity

During the closed period of voiced stops, the vocal folds continue to open and close, emitting pulses of subglottal air into the closed oral cavity. As this continues, the air pressure in the mouth increases until it is high enough to stop phonation or until the release of the oral closure. At the moment of release the oral pressure is higher than the atmospheric pressure. Thus, upon release, there is a burst consisting of a transient (momentary), step-like increase in the pressure of the air in front of the lips and following formant resonances; then phonation starts for the following vowel sound. In contrast, the release of a nasal consonant is not accompanied by a burst because, due to the open state of the velar port, there has been no build-up of air pressure in the oral-pharyngeal cavity during the oral occlusion.

The first event in the burst is the step-like, instantaneous increase in sound pressure; this is followed by damped oscillations at resonant frequencies (formants) determined by the location in the vocal tract of the sound source (the step change) and the vocal tract shape at that moment. The voiced stop release bursts are brief, lasting only 10 to 20 ms. The release burst of the [b] in Figure 41 was visible on the original spectrogram but cannot be seen in the reproduced figure.

The nasal murmur during the oral occlusion of the nasals is more intense than the constriction murmurs that are seen during voiced stops; the reason is that much more sound can radiate through the nostrils during

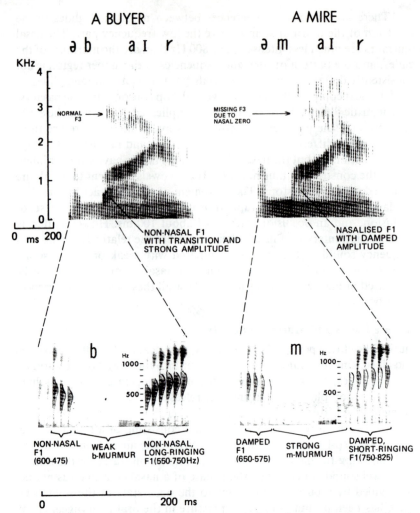

Figure 41.   Spectrograms of *a buyer* [əbaɪr] and *a mire* [əmaɪr] to compare the acoustic patterns of nasal vs. voiced stop consonants. In the upper spectrogram, the stop has a very weak murmur during the occlusion interval and a release transient and the nasal has a strong murmur and no release transient. Nasalization adjacent to the nasal causes differences in the vowel spectrum compared with that adjacent to the stop. In the bottom spectrograms, the murmurs and transitions in the vowels are presented on an expanded time scale. The expansion makes visible the individual formant-ringing intervals of the vowel. These ringing intervals have been outlined on the spectrogram and look like "lozenges," which are straight on the left leading edge and round on the right trailing edge. Because nasalization damps the ringing of F1, the lozenges are thinner (shorter ringing time) near the nasal than the stop. The time expansion was accomplished on a Kay Sona-graph (late 1950s model) by making the original recording on "reproduce" speed, which gives a 3:1 time expansion and 3:1 frequency compression relative to the normal procedure. The frequency scale was then re-expanded on reproduction using an accessory, the Kay Scale Magnifier Sr., Model S.

the nasal consonant than can radiate through the walls of the closed vocal tract during the voiced stops.

Thus there are two main differences distinguishing nasals and voiced stops that stem from the articulatory conditions during the oral occlusion, the absence or presence of a release burst and the intensity of the murmur.

On the release (or opening) of the oral occlusion of nasals the oral opening movement is a little slower compared with releases of stops. This difference is due to the air pressure in the mouth during stop closures compared with the lack of this pressure on nasals because of the open velar port and nose. The pressure of air behind the stop closure causes a slightly faster opening movement just after the release than is seen for the nasals (Fujimura, 1961).

Nasalization of Vowels Adjacent to Nasal Consonants

The movement downward of the velum for a nasal consonant begins well before the beginning of oral tract movement toward occlusion, and thus the opening of the velar port is already accomplished by the time the oral tract becomes closed; also the velar port remains open during the release and opening of the oral occlusion. The lead and lag of velar opening and closing, preceding and following the oral tract occlusion, are typically about 100 ms. This causes nasalization of portions of vowels for about 100 ms preceding and following nasal consonants.

The effects of the leading and lagging nasalization are seen in Figure 41 by comparing the vowels adjacent to the stop in *a buyer* with the vowels adjacent to the nasal in *a mire*. Nasalization of vowels introduces extra resonances and antiresonances into the response of the oral tract because of the tuning effects of the velar opening and connected nasal cavities. It should be emphasized that these nasalization effects are mainly caused by changes in the response of the oral tract, not by added sound coming out of the nose, a sound that is negligible because of its low amplitude in the frequencies above about 500 Hz, relative to the vowel sound. In mathematical descriptions of the response of the vocal tract, the resonances (or formants) are called *poles* and the antiresonances are called *zeroes;* these terms are used in describing the effects of nasalization on the vowel spectrum.

Nasalization introduces a pole at a very low frequency, which intensifies the fundamental, and a zero at a frequency just above the pole, which reduces the energy in the spectrum above the fundamental, in the F1 region. If the normal oral tract F1 is low in frequency the zero can cancel the F1 resonance, leaving a flat spectrum. If F1 is normally high, the zero reduces the spectral energy in an area between the fundamental and F1. The zeroes often show in the spectrogram as light patches or light areas in the

F1 region, and these can be seen in Figures 41 and 42. Nasalization also introduces zeroes in the regions of F2 and F3.

In areas of the spectrum where zeroes are present the spectrogram has missing or depressed harmonics, and there is an overall broadening in frequency bandwidth and reduction in intensity of the oral formants relative to those seen near the stop consonant closures where there is no nasalization. These effects are clearly visible, especially in the expanded sections of the spectrograms in the lower half of Figure 41. The F1 intensity is weaker adjacent to the [m] than the [b], the F1 transitions are less extensive (starting and ending frequencies of the F1 transitions are given in parentheses on the spectrogram), and the resonant ringing of F1 is damped out more rapidly. In the expanded spectrograms the ringing period of the formant forms a lozenge-shaped pattern, which has been hand-outlined on the spectrogram for each formant pulse; it will be seen that the formant-ringing lozenges are thinner near the [m] than near the [b].

The frequency locations of the poles and zeroes due to nasalization depend greatly on the amount of opening of the velar port. The velar port changes in size, from small to larger before the oral occlusion and from large to smaller during the opening of the occlusion. These changes in amount of velar opening cause changes in the frequency locations of the poles and zeroes, making the spectral effects of nasalization extremely variable, depending on the time course of velar movement and the particular combination of vowel and consonant.

The F1 formant transitions of nasal consonant articulation are often somewhat overridden by the changing pole-zero pattern from nasalization. This is seen in Figure 41, comparing the F1 transitions adjacent to the closures of [b] vs. [m]. The F2 transitions in Figure 41 are not so much affected by nasalization as are the F1 transitions.

Figure 41 also shows a case of suppression of F3 by a zero, where after the [b] the F3 of the following vowel starts immediately upon release of the [b] occlusion; on release of the [m] occlusion, however, F3 is apparently suppressed because it is seen only after a delay of about 50 ms.

Initial and Final Nasals and Stops

Initial and final nasal consonants are similar to the intervocalic nasals in timing and spectral pattern. Examples are shown in the spectrograms of Figure 42. When a syllable begins and ends with a nasal consonant the lag and lead of nasalization cause the entire vowel to be nasalized. Compare *mom* and *bob* in vowel pattern; note that the formants are weaker throughout the nasalized [ɑ̃] of *mom* compared with the [ɑ] of *bob*. A weak or blank area below F1 indicates the presence of a zero in the oral

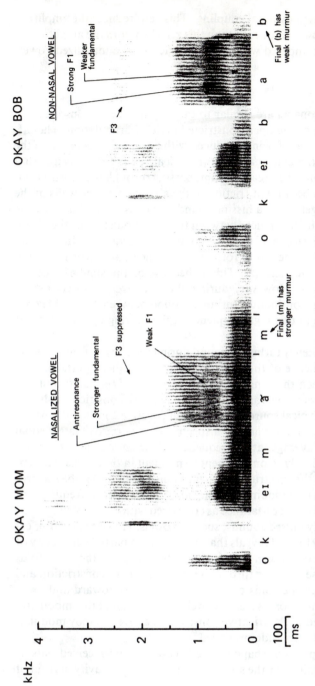

Figure 42. Spectrograms of *Okay Bob* and *Okay Mom* to compare initial and final voiced stop and nasal consonants. The lag and lead of the velar opening for the nasal consonant causes complete nasalization of the [ɑ] in *Mom* in contrast to the "normal" [ɑ] in *Bob*. The important effects of the nasalization are noted in the spectrograms and discussed in the text.

tract response caused by nasal coupling. This zero reduces the amplitude of F1. A pole of lower frequency than this zero increases the amplitude of the fundamental compared with its amplitude in the unnasalized vowel.

FRICATIVE CONSONANTS

The fricative consonants are similar to the stop and nasal consonants in the general timing of the open-constricted cycle of articulation. The difference is that, instead of being produced with a complete occlusion of the oral tract during the consonant gesture, fricatives are produced with a narrow constriction. The breath stream, passing through the constriction, becomes turbulent because of friction of the airstream on the walls of the constriction; this generates a hissing sound, which is the hallmark of the fricatives. The main differences between the sound patterns of the alveolar voiced fricative, stop, and glide are compared in Figure 43. In the spectrograms we see that the vowel formant frequencies and their transition are similar for the [d] and [z]. This is because of the similarity of the tongue articulations. However, during the fricative constrictions for [z] there is a strong, continuous, turbulent sound between 4 and 5 kHz but a complete silence in this high frequency region during the occlusion of the [d].

The high frequency turbulent sound during the constriction of the [z] is caused by turbulence of the airstream as it passes through the narrow constriction between the tongue and the alveolar ridge. Air turbulence produced in this way, by various kinds of narrow constrictions in the vocal tract, is the typical source sound for all fricative consonants. At the source it is a random noise having a spectrum with approximately equal amplitude, on the average, at all frequencies. The amplitude at each frequency varies randomly, from moment to moment in time. This randomness can be seen in the spectrum of the [z] sound in Figure 43; the spectrogram of a sound with randomly varying amplitudes at each frequency of the sound has a mottled appearance as compared with the striated appearance of periodically pulsed sounds, such as vowels. However, a closer examination of the [z] sound reveals that there is also a partial periodicity of amplitude. This is often seen in voiced fricatives because the vocal folds are held fairly close together throughout the consonant constriction and the airflow through the folds causes them to vibrate toward and away from each other, more or less as in vowel phonation, and this modulates the airflow supplied to the fricative constriction above, thereby modulating the turbulence amplitude produced.

The overall spectrum shape of the fricative sound received outside the mouth is determined by the size and shape of the oral cavity in front of

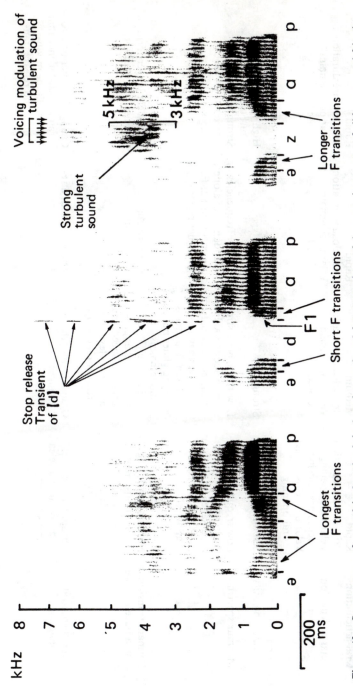

Figure 43. Spectrograms of *a yap* [əjap], *a dap* [ədap], and *a zap* [əzap] for comparison of the acoustic patterns of glide, stop, and fricative. Acoustic features are noted on the spectrogram and further discussed in the text.

Table 4.   Summary of main features of nasals, glides, voiced stops, and voiced fricatives

Features	Nasals	Glides	Voiced stops	Voiced fricatives
Timing				
Oral articulation	Rapid	Medium	Rapid	Rapid
Velar articulation	Brief closure duration Velar port opening leads oral closing Velar port closing lags oral opening	Brief closure duration Velar port remains closed	Brief closure duration Velar port remains closed	Brief closure duration Velar port remains closed
Spectral				
Murmur intensity	Strong	Strong	Weak	High frequency turbulence Strong in high frequencies (above 2.5 kHz)
Murmur spectrum	Low frequency resonance of nasal passages up to about 300 Hz; very weak above this	Low frequencies strong up to about 800 Hz; midfrequency pattern stronger than nasals; different F patterns among glides but not among nasals	Very low frequencies (fundamental alone); no energy in F2, F3 or higher regions	
Formant transitions in adjacent vowel	Nasalization during the transitions, may obscure expected transitions; F1 of adjacent vowels is weakened	Long formant transitions appropriate to speed, place, and retroflexion (r articulation only)	Short formant transitions	Somewhat longer formant transitions than for stops
Overall spectral changes	Abrupt onset and offset, without a release transient	Gradual, smooth changes	Abrupt and with a release transient	Change from periodic to random turbulence that is amplitude modulated; no release transient

the constriction. The spectrum of fricatives is usually much more intense in the frequencies above about 2.5 kHz than at lower frequencies. The spectra of fricatives are discussed in more detail under the topic of the shape and place features of consonants (Chapter 9).

The formant transitions in F1 and F2 during the closing and opening movements should be compared between [z] and [d]. It will be seen that the transitions are slightly longer and slower for [z] than for [d]. Perhaps this difference is because the tongue must form a certain shaped narrow passage against the palate in order to produce the fricative turbulence of [z], and this adjustment requires a controlled slowing down of the constricting movement compared with the movement for [d], which can attain occlusion simply by collision with the palate; there is some evidence from an x-ray study that this may be the case (Perkell, 1969).

Note in the figure that the release of [d] has a sharp transient containing energy up to 7.5 kHz followed by brief formant ringing at F1, F2, F3, and F4, and a silent gap of about 15 ms before the first vocal fold pulse of the vowel and its very strong F1; this delay in voicing may have occurred because the last half of the occlusion period was de-voiced, indicating a high mouth pressure that had to be dissipated before vowel voicing could begin. A similar release gap in voicing does not appear after the [z].

Figure 43 also includes a spectrogram of the phrase *a yap* so that the alveolar glide [j] can be compared in rate and extent of formant transitions with [d] and [z]. The transitions have been marked on the spectrograms. It will be seen that the transitions of [j] are more extended than those for [d] and [z].

There is an additional manner of fricative articulation, called affricate, which includes the consonant sounds [tʃ], as in *church,* and [dʒ], as in *judge;* sometimes affricates are considered to be unitary phonemes, the sounds of which are symbolized by [č] and [ǰ]. The affricates are produced like fricatives that are preceded by an occlusion instead of a more open articulation. The occlusion is formed at the same place as the ensuing constriction for the friction part, which is usually of shorter duration than in a fricative.

SUMMARY

Table 4 summarizes the articulatory and acoustic features of all four manner distinctions among consonants: nasality, glide, stop (plosive), and fricative.

Control Methods Used in a Study of the Vowels

Gordon E. Peterson and Harold L. Barney

Bell Telephone Laboratories, Inc., Murray Hill, New Jersey

(Received December 3, 1951)

Relationships between a listener's identification of a spoken vowel and its properties as revealed from acoustic measurement of its sound wave have been a subject of study by many investigators. Both the utterance and the identification of a vowel depend upon the language and dialectal backgrounds and the vocal and auditory characteristics of the individuals concerned. The purpose of this paper is to discuss some of the control methods that have been used in the evaluation of these effects in a vowel study program at Bell Telephone Laboratories. The plan of the study, calibration of recording and measuring equipment, and methods for checking the performance of both speakers and listeners are described. The methods are illustrated from results of tests involving some 76 speakers and 70 listeners.

INTRODUCTION

CONSIDERABLE variation is to be found in the processes of speech production because of their complexity and because they depend upon the past experience of the individual. As in much of human behavior there is a self-correcting, or servomechanism type of feedback involved as the speaker hears his own voice and adjusts his articulatory mechanisms.[1]

In the elementary case of a word containing a consonant-vowel-consonant phoneme[2,3] structure, a speaker's pronunciation of the vowel within the word will be influenced by his particular dialectal background; and his pronunciation of the vowel may differ both in phonetic quality and in measurable characteristics from that produced in the word by speakers with other backgrounds. A listener, likewise, is influenced in his identification of a sound by his past experience.

Variations are observed when a given individual makes repeated utterances of the same phoneme. A very significant property of these variations is that they are not random in a statistical sense, but show trends and sudden breaks or shifts in level, and other types of nonrandom fluctuations.[4] Variations likewise appear in the successive identifications by a listener of the same utterance. It is probable that the identification of repeated sounds is also nonrandom but there is little direct evidence in this work to support such a conclusion.

A study of sustained vowels was undertaken to investigate in a general way the relation between the vowel phoneme intended by a speaker and that identified by a listener, and to relate these in turn to acoustical measurements of the formant or energy concentration positions in the speech waves.

In the plan of the study certain methods and techniques were employed which aided greatly in the collection of significant data. These methods included randomization of test material and repetitions to obtain sequences of observations for the purpose of checking the measurement procedures and the speaker and listener consistency. The acoustic measurements were made with the sound spectrograph; to minimize measurement errors, a method was used for rapid calibration of the recording and analyzing apparatus by means of a complex test tone. Statistical techniques were applied to the results of measurements, both of the calibrating signals and of the vowel sounds.

These methods of measurement and analysis have been found to be precise enough to resolve the effects of different dialectal backgrounds and of the nonrandom trends in speakers' utterances. Some aspects of the vowel study will be presented in the following paragraphs to illustrate the usefulness of the methods employed.

EXPERIMENTAL PROCEDURES

The plan of the study is illustrated in Fig. 1. A list of words (List 1) was presented to the speaker and his utterances of the words were recorded with a magnetic tape recorder. The list contained ten monosyllabic words each beginning with [h] and ending with [d] and differing only in the vowel. The words used were *heed, hid, head, had, hod, hawed, hood, who'd, hud,* and *heard.* The order of the words was randomized in each list, and each speaker was asked to pronounce two different lists. The purpose of randomizing the words in the list was to avoid practice effects which would be associated with an unvarying order.

If a given List 1, recorded by a speaker, were played back to a listener and the listener were asked to write down what he heard on a second list (List 2), a comparison of List 1 and List 2 would reveal occasional

[1] Bernard S. Lee, J. Acoust. Soc. Am. **22**, 824 (1950).
[2] B. Bloch, Language **24**, 3 (1948).
[3] B. Bloch, Language **26**, 88 (1950).
[4] R. K. Potter and J. C. Steinberg, J. Acoust. Soc. Am. **26**, 807 (1950).

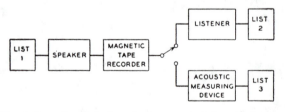

Fig. 1. Recording and measuring arrangements for vowel study.

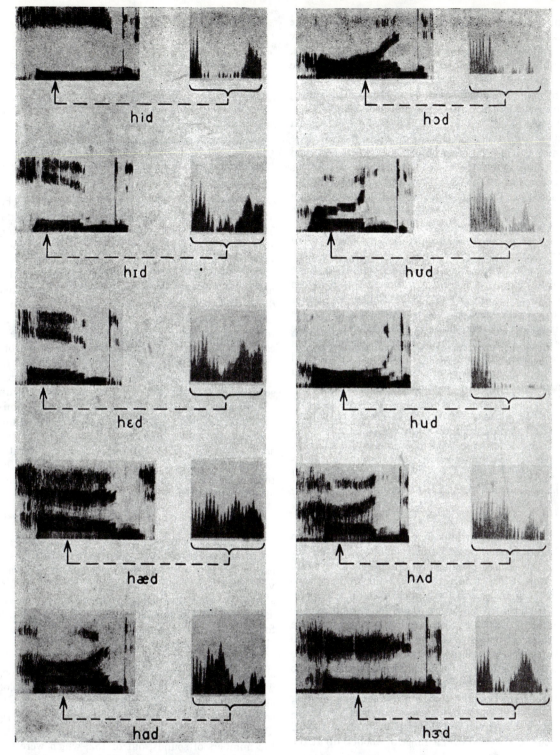

FIG. 2. Broad band spectrograms and amplitude sections of the word list by a female speaker.

differences, or disagreements, between speaker and listener. Instead of being played back to a listener, List 1 might be played into an acoustic measuring device and the outputs classified according to the measured properties of the sounds into a List 3. The three lists will differ in some words depending upon the characteristics of the speaker, the listener, and the measuring device.

A total of 76 speakers, including 33 men, 28 women and 15 children, each recorded two lists of 10 words, making a total of 1520 recorded words. Two of the speakers were born outside the United States and a few others spoke a foreign language before learning English. Most of the women and children grew up in the Middle Atlantic speech area.[5] The male speakers represented a much broader regional sampling of the United States; the majority of them spoke General American.[5]

The words were randomized and were presented to a group of 70 listeners in a series of eight sessions. The listening group contained only men and women, and represented much the same dialectal distribution as did the group of speakers, with the exception that a few observers were included who had spoken a foreign language throughout their youth. Thirty-two of the 76 speakers were also among the 70 observers.

The 1520 words were also analyzed by means of the sound spectrograph.[6,7]

Representative spectrograms and sections of these words by a male speaker are shown in Fig. 3 of the paper by R. K. Potter and J. C. Steinberg;[4] a similar list by a female speaker is shown here as Fig. 2.[8] In the spectrograms, we see the initial [h] followed by the vowel, and then by the final [d]. There is generally a part of the vowel following the influence of the [h] and preceding the influence of the [d] during which a practically steady state is reached. In this interval, a section is made, as shown to the right of the spectrograms. The sections, portraying frequency on a horizontal scale, and amplitude of the voiced harmonics on the vertical side, have been measured with calibrated Plexiglass templates to provide data about the fundamental and formant frequencies and relative formant amplitudes of each of the 1520 recorded sounds.

LISTENING TESTS

The 1520 recorded words were presented to the group of 70 adult observers over a high quality loud speaker system in Arnold Auditorium at the Murray Hill Laboratories. The general purpose of these tests was to obtain an aural classification of each vowel to supplement the speaker's classification. In presenting the words to the observers, the procedure was to reproduce at each of seven sessions, 200 words recorded by 10 speakers. At the eighth session, there remained five men's and one child's recordings to be presented; to these were added three women's and one child's recordings which had been given in previous sessions, making again a total of 200 words. The sound level at the observers' positions was approximately 70 db re 0.0002 dyne/cm², and varied over a range of about 3 db at the different positions.

In selecting the speakers for each of the first seven

[5] C. K. Thomas, *Phonetics of American English*, The Ronald Press Company (New York, 1947).
[6] Koenig, Dunn, and Lacy, J. Acoust. Soc. Am. **17**, 19 (1946).
[7] L. G. Kersta, J. Acoust. Soc. Am. **20**, 796 (1948).
[8] Key words for the vowel symbols are as follows: [i] heed, [ɪ] hid, [ɛ] head, [æ] had, [ɑ] father, [ɔ] ball, [ʊ] hood, [u] who'd, [ʌ] hud, [ɜ] heard.

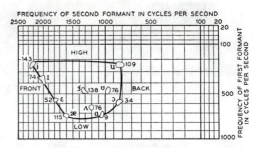

FIG. 3. Vowel loop with numbers of sounds unanimously classified by listeners; each sound was presented 152 times.

sessions, 4 men, 4 women, and 2 children were chosen at random from the respective groups of 33, 28, and 15. The order of occurrence of the 200 words spoken by the 10 speakers for each session was randomized for presentation to the observers.

Each observer was given a pad containing 200 lines having the 10 words on each line. He was asked to draw a line through the one word in each line that he heard. The observers' seating positions in the auditorium were chosen by a randomizing procedure, and each observer took the same position for each of the eight sessions, which were given on eight different days.

The randomizing of the speakers in the listening sessions was designed to facilitate checks of learning effects from one session to another. The randomizing of words in each group of 200 was designed to minimize successful guessing and the learning of a particular speaker's dialect. The seating positions of the listeners were randomized so that it would be possible to determine whether position in the auditorium had an effect on the identification of the sounds.

DISCUSSION OF LISTENING TEST RESULTS

The total of 1520 sounds heard by the observers consisted of the 10 vowels, each presented 152 times. The ease with which the observers classified the various vowels varied greatly. Of the 152 [i] sounds, for instance, 143 were unanimously classified by all observers as [i]. Of the 152 sounds which the speakers intended for [ɑ], on the other hand, only 9 were unanimously classified as [ɑ] by the whole jury.

These data are summarized in Fig. 3. This figure shows the positions of the 10 vowels in a vowel loop in which the frequency of the first formant is plotted against the frequency of the second formant[9] on mel scales;[10] in this plot the origin is at the upper right. The numbers beside each of the phonetic symbols are the numbers of sounds, out of 152, which were unanimously classified as that particular vowel by the jury. It is of interest in passing that in no case did the jury agree unanimously that a sound was something other than what the speaker intended. Figure 3 shows that

[9] R. K. Potter and G. E. Peterson, J. Acoust. Soc. Am. **20**, 528 (1948).
[10] S. S. Stevens and J. Volkman, Am. J. Psychol. 329 (July, 1940).

[i], [ɜ], [æ], and [u] are generally quite well understood.

To obtain the locations of the small areas shown in Fig. 3, the vowels were repeated by a single speaker on twelve different days. A line enclosing all twelve points was drawn for each vowel; the differences in the shapes of these areas probably have little significance.

When the vowels are plotted in the manner shown in Fig. 3, they appear in essentially the same positions as those shown in the tongue hump position diagrams which phoneticians have employed for many years.[11] The terms "high, front, low back" refer to the tongue positions in the mouth. The [i], for instance, is made with the tongue hump high and forward, the [u] with the hump high and back, and the [ɑ] and [æ] with the tongue hump low.

It is of interest that when observers disagreed with speakers on the classification of a vowel, the two classifications were nearly always in adjacent positions of the vowel loop of Fig. 3. This is illustrated by the data shown on Table I. This table shows how the observers classified the vowels, as compared with the vowels intended by the speakers. For instance, on all the 152 sounds intended as [i] by the speakers, there were 10,267 total votes by all observers that they were [i], 4 votes for [ɪ], 6 votes for [ɛ], and 3 votes for [ɔ]. Of the 152 [ɑ] sounds, there was a large fraction of the sounds on which some of the observers voted for [ɔ]. [ɪ] was taken for [ɛ] a sizable percentage of the time, and [ɛ] was called either [ɪ] or [æ] (adjacent sounds on the vowel loop shown in the preceding Fig. 3) quite a large number of times. [ɑ] and [ɔ], and [ʌ] and [ɑ] were also confused to a certain extent. Here again, as in Fig. 2, the [i], [ɜ], [æ], and [u] show high intelligibility scores.

It is of considerable interest that the substitutions shown conform to present dialectal trends in American speech rather well,[12] and in part, to the prevailing vowel shifts observable over long periods of time in most languages.[13] The common tendency is continually to shift toward higher vowels in speech, which correspond to smaller mouth openings.

The listener, on the other hand, would tend to make the opposite substitution. This effect is most simply described in terms of the front vowels. If a speaker produces [ɪ] for [ɛ], for example [mɪn] for [mɛn] as currently heard in some American dialects; then such an individual when serving as a listener will be inclined to write *men* when he hears [mɪn]. Thus it is that in the substitutions shown in Table I, [ɪ] most frequently became [ɛ], and [ɛ] most frequently became [æ]. The explanation of the high intelligibility of [æ] is probably based on this same pattern. It will be noted along the

vowel loop that a wide gap appears between [æ] and [ɑ]. The [a] of the Romance languages appears in this region. Since that vowel was present in neither the lists nor the dialects of most of the speakers and observers the [æ] was usually correctly identified.

The [i] and the [u] are the terminal or end positions in the mouth and on the vowel loop toward which the vowels are normally directed in the prevailing process of pronunciation change. In the formation of [i] the tongue is humped higher and farther forward than for any other vowel; in [u] the tongue hump takes the highest posterior position in the mouth and the lips are more rounded than for any other vowel. The vowels [u] and [i] are thus much more difficult to displace, and a greater stability in the organic formation of these sounds would probably be expected, which in turn should mean that these sounds are recognized more consistently by a listener.

The high intelligibility of [ɜ] probably results from the retroflexion which is present to a marked degree only in the formation of this vowel; that is, in addition to the regular humping of the tongue, the edges of the tongue are turned up against the gum ridge or the hard palate. In the acoustical pattern the third formant is markedly lower than for any other vowel. Thus in both physiological and acoustical phonetics the [ɜ] occupies a singular position among the American vowels.

The very low scores on [ɑ] and [ɔ] in Fig. 3 undoubtedly result primarily from the fact that some members of the speaking group and many members of the listening group speak one of the forms of American dialects in which [ɑ] and [ɔ] are not differentiated.

When the individuals' votes on the sounds are analyzed, marked differences are seen in the way they classified the sounds. Not only did the total numbers of agreements with the speakers vary, but the proportions of agreements for the various vowels was significantly different. Figure 4 will be used to illustrate this point. If we plot total numbers of disagreements for all tests, rather than agreements, the result is shown by the upper chart. This shows that [ɪ], [ɛ], [ɑ], [ɔ], and [ʌ] had the most disagreements. An "average" observer would be expected to have a distribution of disagreements similar in proportions to this graph. The middle graph illustrates the distribution of disagreements given by observer number 06. His chief difficulty was in distinguishing between [ɑ] and [ɔ]. This type of distribution is characteristic of several observers. Observer 013, whose distribution of disagreements is plotted on the bottom graph, shows a tendency to confuse [ɪ] and [ɛ] more than the average.

The distributions of disagreements of all 70 observers differ from each other, depending on their language experience, but the differences are generally less extreme than the two examples shown on Fig. 4. Thirty-two of the 70 observers were also speakers. In cases where an observer such as 06 was also a speaker, the remainder of the jury generally had more disagreements

[11] D. Jones, *An Outline of English Phonetics* (W. Heffer and Sons, Ltd., Cambridge, England, 1947).

[12] G. W. Gray and C. M. Wise, *The Bases of Speech* (Harper Brothers, New York, 1946), pp. 217–302.

[13] L. Bloomfield, *Language* (Henry Holt and Company, New York, 1933), pp. 369–391.

with his [ɑ] and [ɔ] sounds than with the other sounds he spoke. Thus it appears that if a speaker does not differentiate clearly between a pair of sounds in speaking them, he is unlikely to classify them properly when he hears others speak them. His language experience, as would be expected, influences both his speaking and his hearing of sounds.

Since the listening group was not given a series of training sessions for these tests, learning would be expected in the results of the tests.[14] Several pieces of evidence indicate a certain amount of practice effect, but the data are not such as to provide anything more than a very approximate measure of its magnitude.

For one check on practice effect, a ninth test was given the jury, in which all the words having more than 10 disagreements in any of the preceding eight tests were repeated. There was a total of about 175 such words; to these were added 25 words which had no disagreements, picked at random from the first eight tests. On the ninth test, 67 words had more disagreements, 109 had less disagreements, and 24 had the same number of disagreements as in the preceding tests. The probability of getting this result had there been no practice or other effect, but only a random variation of observers' votes, would be about 0.01. When these data are broken down into three groups for the men, women and children speakers, the largest differences in numbers of disagreements for the original and repeated tests was on the childrens' words, indicating a larger practice or learning effect on their sounds. The indicated learning effect on men's and women's speech was nearly the same. When the data are classified according to the vowel sound, the learning effect indicated by the repetitions was least on [i], [ɝ], and [u], and greatest on [ɑ] and [ɔ].

Another indication that there was a practice effect lies in the sequence of total numbers of disagreements by tests. From the second to the seventh test, the total number of disagreements by all observers diminished consistently from test to test, and the first test had considerably more disagreements than the eighth, thus strongly indicating a downward trend. With the speakers randomized in their order of appearance in the eight tests, each test would be expected to have approximately the same number of disagreements. The probability of getting the sequence of numbers of total disagreements which was obtained would be somewhat less than 0.05 if there were no learning trend or other non-random effect.

It was also found that the listening position had an effect upon the scores obtained. The observers were arranged in 9 rows in the auditorium, and the listeners in the back 4 rows had a significantly greater number of disagreements with the speakers than did the listeners in the first 5 rows. The effect of a listener's position

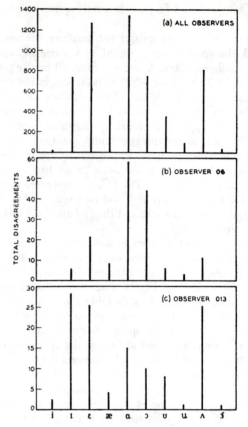

FIG. 4. Observer disagreements in listening tests.

within an auditorium upon intelligibility has been observed previously and is reported in the literature.[15]

ACOUSTIC MEASUREMENTS

Calibrations of Equipment

A rapid calibrating technique was developed for checking the over-all performance of the recording and analyzing systems. This depended on the use of a test tone which had an envelope spectrum that was essentially flat with frequency over the voice band. The circuit used to generate this test tone is shown schematically in Fig. 5. It consists essentially of an overloading amplifier and pulse sharpening circuit. The wave shapes which may be observed at several different points in the test tone generator are indicated in Fig. 5.

The test tone generator may be driven by an input sine wave signal of any frequency between 50 and 2000 cycles. Figure 6(a) shows a section of the test tone with a 100 cycle repetition frequency, which had been recorded on magnetic tape in place of the word lists by the speaker, and then played back into the sound spectrograph. The departure from uniform frequency response of the over-all systems is indicated by the shape of the envelope enclosing the peaks of the 100

14 H. Fletcher and R. H. Galt, J. Acoust. Soc. Am. 22, 93 (1950).

15 V. O. Knudsen and C. M. Harris, *Acoustical Designing in Architecture* (John Wiley and Sons, New York, 1950), pp. 180–181.

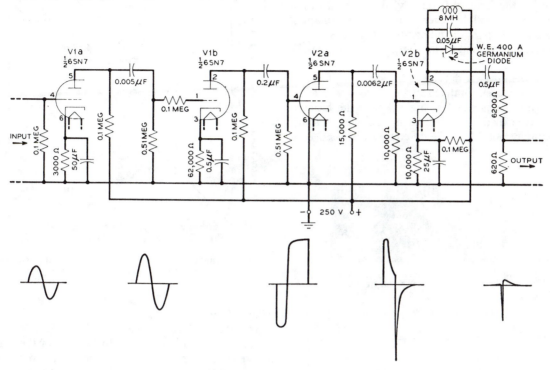

FIG. 5. Schematic of calibrating tone generator.

cycle harmonics. With the 100 cycles from the Laboratories standard frequency oscillator as the drive signal, the frequency calibration of the systems may be checked very readily by comparison of the harmonic spacing on the section with the template scale. The amplitude scale in 6(a) is obtained by inserting a pure tone at the spectrograph in 5 db increments. The frequency scale for spectrograms may also be calibrated as shown in Fig. 6(b). The horizontal lines here are representations of the harmonics of the test tone when the test tone generator is driven by a 500 cycle standard frequency. These lines further afford a means of checking the amount of speed irregularity or wow in the over-all mechanical system. A calibration of the time scale may be obtained by using the test tone generator with 100 cycle drive and making a broad band spectrogram as shown in Fig. 6(c). The spacings between vertical striations in this case correspond to one-hundredth of a second intervals.

In the process of recording some of the word lists, it was arranged to substitute the calibrating test tone circuit for the microphone circuit, and record a few seconds of test tone between the lists of words. When the word lists were analyzed with the spectrograph, the accompanying test tone sections provided a means of checking the over-all frequency response of the recorder and analyzer, and the frequency scale of the sectioner.

The effect of speed variations in either the recorder or the sound spectrograph is to change the frequency scale. A series of measurements with the 100 cycle test tone showed that the tape recorder ran approximately one percent slower when playing back than it did on recording.

The speed variations on the sound spectrograph were measured with the test tone applied directly, and the maximum short time variations were found to be ±0.3 percent. Such direct calibrations of the frequency scale of the spectrograph, during a period of four weeks when most of the spectrographic analysis was done, showed maximum deviations of ±30 cycles at the 31st harmonic of the 100 cycle test tone. During that period a control chart[16] of the measurements of the 3100 cycle component of the test tone showed a downward trend of about 10 cycles, which was attributed to changes in the electonic circuit components of the spectrograph. As a result of these calibration tests, it was concluded that the frequency scale of the sound spectrograph could be relied upon as being accurate within ±1 percent.

Formant Measurements

Measurements of both the frequency and the amplitude of the formants were made for the 20 words recorded by each of the 76 speakers. The frequency position of each formant was obtained by estimating a weighted average of the frequencies of the principal components in the formant. (See reference 4 for a discussion of this procedure.) When the principal components in the formant were symmetrically distributed about a dominant component, such as the second formant of [ʌ] *hud* in Fig. 2, there is little ambiguity

[16] "A.S.T.M. manual on presentation of data," Am. Soc. Testing Materials (Philadelphia, 1945), Appendix B.

in choosing the formant frequency. When the distribution is asymmetrical, however, as in the first formant of [ɜ] *heard* in Fig. 2, the difference between estimated formant frequency and that assigned by the ear may be appreciable.

One of the greatest difficulties in estimating formant frequencies was encountered in those cases where the fundamental frequency was high so that the formant was poorly defined. These factors may account for some, but certainly not all, of the differences discussed later

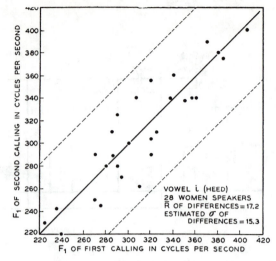

FIG. 7. Accuracy-precision chart of first formant frequencies of [i] as spoken by 28 women.

between vowel classification by ear and by measured values of formant frequencies.

Amplitudes were obtained by assigning a value in decibels to the formant peak. In the case of the amplitude measurements it was then necessary to apply a correction for the over-all frequency response of the system.

The procedure of making duplicate recordings and analyses of the ten words for each of the speakers provided the basis for essential checks on the reliability of the data.

One method by which the duplicate measured values were used is illustrated by Fig. 7. This is a plot of the values for the first formant frequency F_1 of [i] as in *heed*, as spoken by the 28 female subjects. Each point represents, for a single speaker, the value of F_1 measured for the *heed* in the first list, *versus* the value of F_1 for the *heed* in the second list. If the F_1 for the second list or calling was greater than that for the first calling, the point lies above a 45-degree line; if it is less, the point lies below the 45-degree line. The average difference $\bar{R}$ between the paired values of F_1 for first and second callings, was 17.2 cycles. The estimated standard deviation σ derived from the differences between pairs of F_1 values was 15.3 cycles. The dotted lines in Fig. 7 are spaced $\pm 3\ \sigma$ cycles from the 45-degree line through the origin. In case a point falls outside the dotted lines, it is generally because of an erroneous measurement.

Each of the three formant frequencies for each of the 10 vowels was plotted in this way. There were 760 such points for each formant, or a total of 2280 points plotted on 90 accuracy-precision charts like Fig. 7. Of these 2280 points, 118 fell outside the $\pm 3\ \sigma$ limits. On checking back over the measurements, it was found that 88 of the points were incorrect because of gross measurement errors, typographical errors in transcribing the data, or because the section had been made during the influence period of the consonants instead of in the

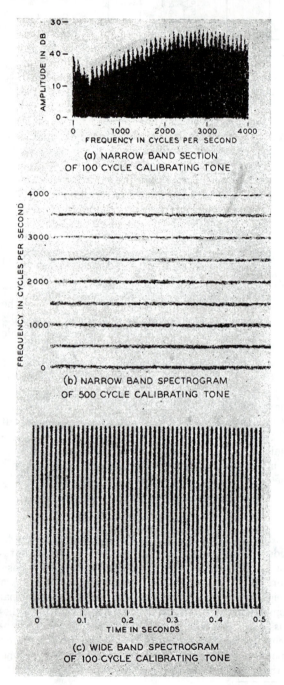

(a) NARROW BAND SECTION OF 100 CYCLE CALIBRATING TONE

(b) NARROW BAND SPECTROGRAM OF 500 CYCLE CALIBRATING TONE

(c) WIDE BAND SPECTROGRAM OF 100 CYCLE CALIBRATING TONE

FIG. 6. Spectrograms and section of calibrating tone.

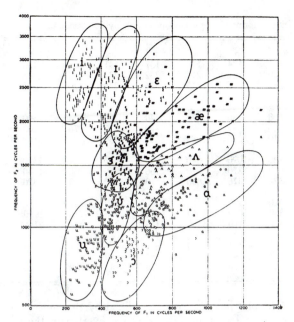

FIG. 8. Frequency of second formant *versus* frequency of first formant for ten vowels by 76 speakers.

steady state period of the vowel. When corrected, these 88 points were within the $\pm 3\,\sigma$ limits. Of the remaining 30 points which were still outside the limits, 20 were the result of the individuals' having produced pairs of sounds which were unlike phonetically, as shown by the results of the listening tests.

The duplicate measurements may also be used to show that the difference between successive utterances of the same sound by the same individual is much less significant statistically than the difference between utterances of the same sound by different individuals. An analysis of variance of the data in Fig. 7 shows that the differences between callings of pairs are not significant. However, the value for the variance ratio when comparing speakers is much larger than that corresponding to a 0.1 percent probability. In other words, if the measurements shown in Fig. 7 for all callings by all speakers were assumed to constitute a body of statistically random data, the probability of having a variance ratio as high as that found when comparing speakers would be less than one in a thousand. There-

fore it is assumed that the data are not statistically random, but that there are statistically significant differences between speakers. Since the measurements for pairs of callings were so nearly alike, as contrasted with the measurements on the same sound for different speakers, this indicated that the precision of measurements with the sound spectrograph was sufficient to resolve satisfactorily the differences between the various individuals' pronunciations of the same sounds.

RESULTS OF ACOUSTIC MEASUREMENTS

In Fig. 3, as discussed previously, are plotted areas in the plane of the second formant F_2 *versus* the first formant F_1. These areas enclose points for several repetitions of the sustained vowels by one of the writers. It is clear that here the vowels may be separated readily, simply by plotting F_2 against F_1; that is, on the $F_2 - F_1$ plane, points for each vowel lie in isolated areas, with no overlapping of adjacent areas, even though there exists the variation of the measured values which we have discussed above.

The variation of the measured data for a group of speakers is much larger than the variation encountered in repetitions with the same speaker, however, as may be shown by the data for F_1 and F_2 for the 76 speakers. In Fig. 8 are plotted the points for the second calling by each speaker, with the points identified according to the speaker's word list. The closed loops for each vowel have been drawn arbitrarily to enclose most of the points; the more extreme and isolated points were disregarded so that in general these loops include about 90 percent of the values. The frequency scales on this and Fig. 9 are spaced according to the approximation to an aural scale described by Koenig, which is linear to 1000 cps and logarithmic above.[17]

Considerable overlapping of areas is indicated, particularly between [ɜ] and [ɛ], [ɜ] and [ʊ], [ʊ] and [u], and [ɑ] and [ɔ]. In the case of the [ɜ] sound, it may be easily distinguished from all the others if the third formant frequency is used, as the position of the third formant is very close in frequency to that of the second.

The data of Fig. 8 show that the distribution of points in the $F_1 - F_2$ plane is continuous in going from sound to sound; these distributions doubtless represent

TABLE I. Classifications of vowels by speakers and by listeners. Vowels as classified by listeners.

		i	I	ɛ	æ	ɑ	ɔ	ʊ	u	ʌ	ɜ
	i	10267	4	6	...	...	3	...	...	...	...
	I	6	9549	694	2	1	1	...	...	...	26
	ɛ	...	257	9014	949	1	3	...	...	2	51
	æ	...	1	300	9919	2	2	...	...	15	39
Vowels intended by speakers	ɑ	...	1	...	19	8936	1013	69	...	228	7
	ɔ	...	...	1	2	590	9534	71	5	62	14
	u	...	...	1	1	16	51	9924	96	171	19
	u	...	...	1	...	2	...	78	10196	...	2
	ʌ	...	1	1	8	540	127	103	...	9476	21
	ɜ	...	...	23	6	2	3	...	...	2	10243

[17] W. Koenig, Bell Labs. Record **27**, (August, 1949), pp. 299–301.

TABLE II. Averages of fundamental and formant frequencies and formant amplitudes of vowels by 76 speakers.

		i	ɪ	ɛ	æ	ɑ	ɔ	ʊ	u	ʌ	ɝ
Fundamental frequencies (cps)	M	136	135	130	127	124	129	137	141	130	133
	W	235	232	223	210	212	216	232	231	221	218
	Ch	272	269	260	251	256	263	276	274	261	261
Formant frequencies (cps)											
F_1	M	270	390	530	660	730	570	440	300	640	490
	W	310	430	610	860	850	590	470	370	760	500
	Ch	370	530	690	1010	1030	680	560	430	850	560
F_2	M	2290	1990	1840	1720	1090	840	1020	870	1190	1350
	W	2790	2480	2330	2050	1220	920	1160	950	1400	1640
	Ch	3200	2730	2610	2320	1370	1060	1410	1170	1590	1820
F_3	M	3010	2550	2480	2410	2440	2410	2240'	2240	2390	1690
	W	3310	3070	2990	2850	2810	2710	2680	2670	2780	1960
	Ch	3730	3600	3570	3320	3170	3180	3310	3260	3360	2160
Formant amplitudes (db)	L_1	−4	−3	−2	−1	−1	0	−1	−3	−1	−5
	L_2	−24	−23	−17	−12	−5	−7	−12	−19	−10	−15
	L_3	−28	−27	−24	−22	−28	−34	−34	−43	−27	−20

large differences in the way individuals speak the sounds. The values for F_3 and the relative amplitudes of the formants also have correspondingly large variations between individuals. Part of the variations are because of the differences between classes of speakers, that is, men, women and children. In general, the children's formants are highest in frequency, the women's intermediate, and the men's formants are lowest in frequency.

These differences may be observed in the averaged formant frequencies given on Table II. The first formants for the children are seen to be about half an octave higher than those of the men, and the second and third formants are also appreciably higher. The measurements of amplitudes of the formants did not show decided differences between classes of speakers, and so have been averaged all together. The formant amplitudes are all referred to the amplitude of the first formant in [ɔ], when the total phonetic powers of the vowels are corrected so as to be related to each other by the ratios of powers given by Fletcher.[18]

Various methods of correlating the results of the listening tests with the formant measurements have been studied. In terms of the first two formants the nature of the relationship is illustrated in Fig. 9. In this figure measurements for all vowels of both callings are plotted in which all members of the listening group agreed with the speaker. Since the values for the men and the children generally lie at the two ends of the distributions for each vowel, the confusion between vowels is well illustrated by their data; thus the measurements for the women speakers have been omitted.

The lines on Fig. 9 are the same as the boundaries drawn in Fig. 8. As indicated previously, some vowels received 100 percent agreement much more frequently than others.

The plot has also been simplified by the omission of [ɝ]. The [ɝ] produces extensive overlap in the [ʊ] region in a graph involving only the first two formants. As explained previously, however, the [ɝ] may be isolated from the other vowels readily by means of the third formant.

When only vowels which received 100 percent recognition are plotted, the scatter and overlap are somewhat reduced over that for all callings. The scatter is greater, however, than might be expected.

If the first and second formant parameters measured from these words well defined their phonetic values; and if the listening tests were an exact means of classifying the words, then the points for each vowel of

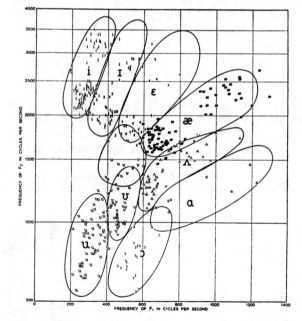

FIG. 9. Frequency of second formant *versus* frequency of first formant for vowels spoken by men and children, which were classified unanimously by all listeners.

[18] H. Fletcher, *Speech and Hearing* (D. Van Nostrand Company, Inc., New York, 1929), p. 74.

Fig. 9 should be well separated. Words judged intermediate in phonetic position should fall at intermediate positions in such a plot. In other words, the distributions of measured formant values in these plots do not correspond closely to the distributions of phonetic values.

It is the present belief that the complex acoustical patterns represented by the words are not adequately represented by a single section, but require a more complex portrayal. The initial and final influences often shown in the bar movements of the spectrograms are of importance here.[19] The evaluation of these changing bar patterns of normal conversational speech is, of course, a problem of major importance in the study of the fundamental information bearing elements of speech.

A further study of the vowel formants is now nearing completion. This study employs sustained vowels, without influences, obtained and measured under controlled conditions. The general objectives are to determine further the most fundamental means of evaluating the formants, and to obtain the relations among the various formants for each of the vowels as produced by difference speakers. When this information has been obtained it is anticipated that it will serve as a basis for determining methods of evaluating and relating the changing formants within words as produced by various speakers.

SUMMARY

The results of our work to date on the development of methods for making acoustic and aural measurements on vowel sounds may be summarized as follows.

1. Calibration and measurement techniques have been developed with the sound spectrograph which make possible its use in a detailed study of the variations that appear in a broad sample of speech.
2. Repeated utterances, repeated measurements at various stages in the vowel study, and randomization in test procedures have made possible the application of powerful statistical methods in the analysis of the data.
3. The data, when so analyzed, reveal that both the production and the identification of vowel sounds by an individual depend on his previous language experience.
4. It is also found that the production of vowel sounds by an individual is not a random process, i.e., the values of the acoustic measurements of the sounds are not distributed in random order. This is probably true of many other processes involving individuals' subjective responses.
5. Finally, the data show that certain of the vowels are generally better understood than others, possibly because they represent "limit" positions of the articulatory mechanisms.

ACKNOWLEDGMENTS

The work which we have discussed has involved the contributions of a number of people. We should like to acknowledge the guidance of Mr. R. K. Potter and Mr. J. C. Steinberg in the plan of the experiment, and the contribution of Dr. W. A. Shewhart who has assisted in the design and interpretation of the study with respect to the application of statistical methods. We are indebted to Miss M. C. Packer for assistance in statistical analyses of the data. We wish to acknowledge also the assistance given by Mr. Anthony Prestigiacomo, Mr. George Blake, and Miss E. T. Leddy in the recording and analysis of the sounds and in the preparation of the data.

[19] Potter, Kopp, and Green, *Visible Speech* (D. Van Nostrand Company, Inc., New York, 1947).

Duration of Syllable Nuclei in English*

Gordon E. Peterson and Ilse Lehiste

Speech Research Laboratory, University of Michigan, Ann Arbor, Michigan

(Received February 26, 1960)

This study deals with the influence of preceding and following consonants on the duration of stressed vowels and diphthongs in American English. A set of 1263 CNC words, pronounced in an identical frame by the same speaker, was analyzed spectrographically, and the influences of various classes of consonants on the duration of the nucleus were determined. The residual durational differences are analyzed as intrinsic durational characteristics, associated with each syllable nucleus. The theory is tested with a set of 30 minimal pairs of CNC words, uttered by five different speakers.

INTRODUCTION

IN the investigation of the relation of basic speech parameters to their linguistic interpretation, there appear to be two general approaches which may be taken. In one approach speech synthesis is employed, and the parameters under study can be controlled individually and accurately. The limitation of speech synthesis is that it may be necessary to employ incomplete sets of parameters or parameters which do not correspond closely in their properties to those generated in human speech. In the second approach, actual speech is recorded for analysis, and thus the parameters may be procured in their natural form. The limitation of this method is that it is sometimes difficult to measure the parameters accurately, and it is even more difficult to obtain their precise control. It appears that in the present stage of speech technology, useful information can be derived from both techniques of investigation.

The present study involves the latter method, in which samples of actual speech are recorded and analyzed. This paper reports some of the results of a study of stressed syllable nuclei in English, and deals with certain aspects of duration.

Duration may have different linguistic functions in different languages. In certain languages, a meaningful difference may be associated with a change in the duration of a consonant or vowel. In some languages, however, changes in the duration of a sound may be determined by the linguistic environment and may be associated with preceding or following segmental sounds, initial or final position in an utterance, or type and degree of stress. Such durational changes in turn may become cues for the identification of the associated phonemes. In a recent study of acoustical cues to word boundaries,[1] it was found that allophonic variations of sounds at juncture points included significant changes in duration. In order to identify changes in duration which are cues to juncture, it is necessary to isolate such changes from durational features that form an integral part of the distinctive properties characterizing the various English phonemes.

It has been observed before that the duration of the vocalic part of a monosyllabic word may be conditioned to some extent by the class of consonants which follow the syllable nucleus. House and Fairbanks,[2] and more recently Denes,[3] have shown this to be the case for English; Zimmerman and Sapon[4] have examined the problem cross-linguistically and have suggested that such observed variations are a part of the phonetic system of English rather than a general principle applicable to all languages induced by physiological factors.

This paper represents a further examination of some of the characteristics of duration in English. If the factors that condition the duration of syllable nuclei can be isolated and described, and if their influence on the syllable nucleus can be determined, the remaining durational differences, if any, might be defined as intrinsic durational differences associated with each vowel pattern. If such intrinsic durational differences exist, it would be of interest to determine their relation to various types of syllable nuclei, as monophthongs, glides, and diphthongs. Thus durational aspects might contribute to the arrangement of the phonetic data of syllable nuclei into a phonemic pattern.

MATERIALS AND PROCEDURES

Connected speech was used for the experiments. The material studied consisted of two sets of data. The first set involved 1263 words, selected on the basis of frequency of occurrence, and recorded by one speaker in an identical sentence frame, with determined stress and pitch patterns. The words all have the same structure, consisting of one of fifteen common syllable nuclei of English, preceded and followed by a consonant phoneme. The list is described in more detail in a previous publication.[5] The second set involved 70 minimally

* This research was supported (under contract) by the Information Systems Branch of the Office of Naval Research.

[1] I. Lehiste, "An acoustic-phonetic study of internal open juncture," Rept. No. 2, Speech Research Laboratory, University of Michigan, Ann Arbor, Michigan (August, 1959).

[2] A. S. House and G. Fairbanks, J. Acoust. Soc. Am. 25, 105–113 (1953).

[3] P. Denes, J. Acoust. Soc. Am. 27, 761–764 (1955).

[4] S. A. Zimmerman and S. M. Sapon, J. Acoust. Soc. Am. 30, 152–153 (1958).

[5] I. Lehiste and G. E. Peterson, J. Acoust. Soc. Am. 31, 280–286 (1959).

different words, including 60 CNC words forming 30 minimal pairs, and 10 disyllabic words constituting five additional minimal pairs; the 70 words were uttered by five different speakers of the same general dialect. These five speakers used the same frame sentence and pitch and stress pattern as the speaker for the larger set of material. The 1263-word CNC list and the 350 items recorded by five speakers were analyzed acoustically by various techniques. Broadband and narrow-band spectrograms were made of the total set. Analyses were also made of the total set with the Mingograph at the Royal Institute of Technology in Stockholm. These analyses included two intensity curves with high-frequency and low-frequency pre-emphasis, a Grützmacher pitch curve, and a duplex oscillogram. The smaller set of 350 items was also processed through the 48-channel spectrograph available at Stockholm.[6] The data measured from the spectrograms form the primary basis for the observations presented in this paper.

SEGMENTATION

An essential problem in the measurement of the duration of syllable nuclei is that of segmentation. Segmentation has long been and continues to be a major problem in speech analysis. Basic difficulties in the concept of segmentation have been discussed previously by one of the present authors.[7] Since vowel and consonant lengths contrast in some languages there can be no question but that duration may be linguistically distinctive. The specification of those cues which are perceptually significant in linguistic judgments of duration is a subject which should receive further study.

Successive speech sounds not only involve physiological targets and controlled movements, but they often involve changes from one sound type to another. These changes often occur at distances far removed from the targets and, for the purposes of this study, were considered the segment boundaries. Such changes obviously represent major points of transition in the activities of the vocal mechanism. If speech perception is closely correlated with these activities, it seems probable that the transitional regions may be of considerable linguistic significance. The perceptual and linguistic significance of such boundaries merit much further investigation. For purposes of automatic speech recognition, it is obviously necessary to employ some procedure for segmentation or quantization.

There are many instances in which the cues signalling the beginning and the end of a syllable nucleus are relatively unambiguous, but there are many other instances where it is very difficult to specify the point of segmentation. An attempt will be made to describe the major cues that were used in the segmentation basic to the measurements of the present study. It should be emphasized that the procedures employed in this study sometimes involved a great deal of human judgment. In several instances, segmental cues of a type not anticipated were observed. We are in no position to consider the universality of these cues, but it appears profitable to investigate some of them further.

In the present study, instrumental accuracy is in general considerably greater than the accuracy with which the segmental boundaries can be determined. It was usually possible to determine segmental boundaries within one or two centiseconds. In some instances, however, the transitions between consonants and vowels involve an overlapping of cues, and in such instances it does not appear meaningful to attempt to determine exact time boundaries.

1. Initial and Final Plosives

The release of a voiceless initial plosive appears as a spike on the spectrogram. The duration of the explosion depends on the bandwidth of the major resonance and is followed by a period of frication and a period of aspiration.[8] Two separate measurements were made for syllable nuclei following aspirated plosives, one from the center of the releasing spike and the other from the onset of voicing immediately after the aspiration. There was usually a measurable concentration of fricative energy in the regions of higher formants throughout the aspiration period, and it was difficult to decide whether at a given moment the pattern in these formants represented breathy phonation or modulated fricative energy. The onset of voicing could be determined relatively accurately, however, by observing the first formant. There was often a weak energy concentration at the frequency of the first formant during the period of aspiration, and the onset of voicing was clearly distinguishable. Thus it was usually possible to determine the frequency of the first formant, both immediately after the release of the plosive and at the onset of voicing after the aspiration. In vowels involving high first formants (particularly /a/, /æ/, and /ɔ/), the energy concentration in the region of the first formant during aspiration was often comparable to that at other formant frequencies, but the onset of voicing was usually clearly distinguishable as the moment in time at which periodic striations started in the first formant frequency.

After voiced initial plosives, the period of aspiration was absent, but the period of frication following the

---

[6] The Mingograph, a recording oscillograph with a relatively high-frequency response, and the 48-channel spectrograph are described by C. G. M. Fant, "Modern instruments and methods for acoustic studies of speech," *Proceedings of the VIII. International Congress of Linguists* (Oslo University Press, Oslo, 1958).

[7] G. E. Peterson, Language **31**, 414–427 (1955).

[8] The distinction between explosion and frication is a matter of source. Explosion is considered to be the sound produced by the shock excitation of the vocal cavities due to the pressure release, and frication is the sound which originates from turbulence produced by the flow of air through the narrow passage which is formed immediately after the release. Cf. Fant, footnote reference 6, pp. 307–308.

spike was usually more prominent than in the case of voiceless plosives. The measurements were again made from the center of the spike, so that the frication period was included in the duration of the vowel. The duration of the frication varied between about 0.5 and 2.5 csec.

The beginning of final voiceless plosives was determined by the abrupt cessation of all formants. The final voiced plosives were often pronounced with full voicing and a voiced release; under the conditions of recording, a considerable amount of energy was present in the voiced plosives, and up to fifteen harmonics appeared in some of the narrow-band spectrograms. Thus the cessation of voicing was not a proper cue for the termination of the syllable nucleus. Instead, the beginning of final voiced plosives was determined by comparing narrow-band and broad-band spectrograms, from which the moment in time when the energy in the higher harmonics was suddenly greatly diminished could be ascertained. In general, it was possible to specify the boundary with an accuracy of about one vocal-fold period.

Examples of initial and final plosives may be seen on Figs. 1–4. Figures 3 and 4 illustrate initial voiced and voiceless plosives; Figs. 1 and 2 contain examples

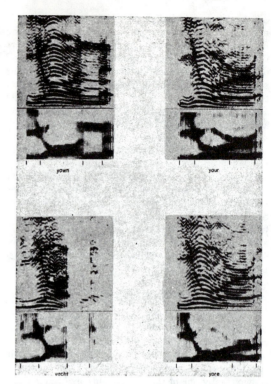

Fig. 2. Broad-band and narrow-band spectrograms of four CNC words spoken by informant GEP. Approximate segmentation points for identifying the boundaries of initial and final consonants have been provided.

of final voiceless plosives, and Fig. 4 contains examples of both voiced and voiceless final plosives.

2. Initial and Final Nasals

In the measurement of syllable nuclei durations, initial nasals offered no difficulty. It was usually possible to identify the vocal-fold period which followed the velar closure by observing the abrupt change from steady formant pattern to rapid onglide movement. Final nasals share the characteristic of steady resonances with initials. In the case of two speakers from the smaller set of data, however, the vowels were nasalized considerably. This had no significant effect upon the identification of the initial boundary of the syllable nucleus, but for these two speakers the nasalization of the vowels obscured the transition from the syllable nucleus to the final nasal consonant on the broad-band spectrograms. The control set of 70 words contained 14 final nasals, but only 3 initial nasals; the relative ease of identifying the boundaries of initial nasals may be due to the very limited data. In the narrow-band spectrograms for these speakers, it was possible to locate the approximate boundaries as the position at which there was a sudden change in the relative marking of the various harmonics. Those

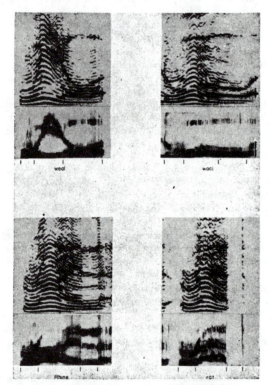

Fig. 1. Broad-band and narrow-band spectrograms of four CNC words spoken by informant GEP. Approximate segmentation points for identifying the boundaries of initial and final consonants have been provided.

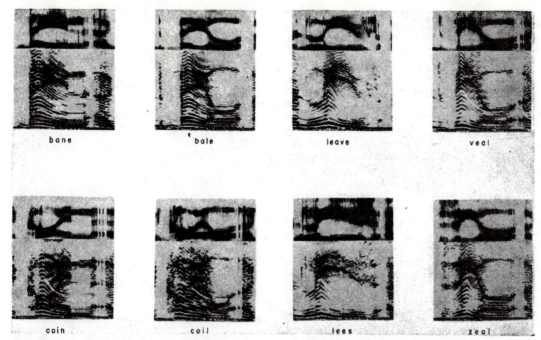

FIG. 3. Broad-band and narrow-band spectrograms of eight CNC words uttered by informant GEP. The tenth harmonic has been traced in white paint on the narrow-band spectrograms; the fifth harmonic has been traced with a dotted white line on some of the spectrograms.

harmonics that were not within the frequency region of either the oral or nasal resonances were marked much more lightly following the vocalic period, and thus a boundary point could be established. Information on relative changes in energy level among the vowel and nasal formants and the minima (or valleys) between is not yet available. Thus the extent to which the marking changes are due to energy-level changes cannot be specified at present. The pattern changes result in part, of course, from the automatic adjustments of the

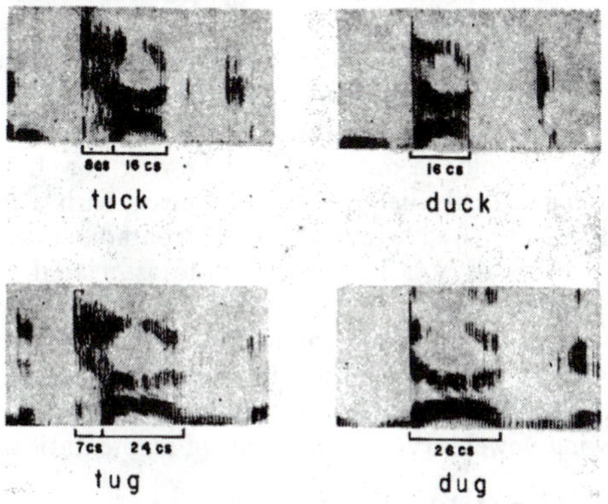

narrow-band marking control to the decrease in over-all output energy during the formation of nasals.

Some examples of final nasals may be found on Figs. 1, 2, and 3. The narrow-band patterns in Figs. 1 and 2 are particularly good illustrations of the changes in marking of the harmonics outside the resonances.

3. Initial and Final Fricatives

The beginning of a vowel after an initial voiceless fricative was determined by the onset of voicing in the region of the first formant. This cue was also employed in determining the beginning of the syllable nucleus after an initial /h/, as formant movements were not adequate indications of the points of transition. In such cases, the intensity curves provided a valuable additional reference. There was a period of "breathy" quality for initial /h/ on broad-band spectrograms after the onset of voicing (noise pattern superimposed upon a rather clear formant pattern), but the intensity curves provided a relatively unambiguous cue. Some of the initial voiceless fricatives registered considerable energy on both Mingograph traces and the oscillogram, but there was a cessation of fricative energy before the onset of phonation, and a sharp minimum in the intensity curves provided an appropriate boundary point.

The terminal boundaries of initial voiced fricatives were, in general, rather easily recognized on broad-band spectrograms. The superimposed noise usually ended

FIG. 4. Broad-band spectrograms of four CNC words spoken by informant GEP. The duration of the aspiration following a voiceless initial plosive has been presented separately from the duration of the voiced part of the syllable nucleus.

abruptly. Final voiceless fricatives were recognized by the onset of random noise: The vowel was considered terminated at the point where the noise pattern began, even though voicing in a few low harmonics continued for a few centiseconds in most cases. Final voiced fricatives were more troublesome. In broad-band and narrow-band spectrograms, the transition between vowel and consonant appeared rather gradual, but the onset of high-frequency energy in the case of /z/ and /ʒ/ provided a clear boundary on the intensity curves. The boundaries preceding final /v/ and /ð/ were recognized chiefly by the rapid decrease of energy that could usually be detected on the intensity curves.

Figure 5 presents 4-channel Mingograph tracings of two of the frame utterances spoken by informant Br. Curves a and b display the sound intensity; low-frequency pre-emphasis was employed in constructing curve a and high-frequency pre-emphasis was employed for curve b; c is a fundamental frequency contour, and d a duplex oscillogram.[6] The top utterance represents the sentence "Say the word 'voice' again," and may be compared with "Say the word 'noise' again," presented in the lower half of the illustration. The sharp boundary between initial /s/ and the following vowel in *say* can be observed in both utterances. The boundaries of the voiceless sibilant /s/ in *voice* are more clearly demarcated than the initial boundary of the /z/ in *noise*; curve b, which emphasizes energy in the higher frequencies, provides the best clue for isolating final /z/. The initial voiced fricative /v/ in *voice* can be best isolated on curve a, with low-frequency pre-emphasis. Initial and final voiced fricatives may also be observed on Fig. 3, which is a good illustration of the difficulty of finding a clear-cut boundary line for final voiced fricatives if only broad-band and narrow-band spectrograms are used for the analysis.

4. Initial /w/ and /y/

Both of these initial consonants involved a steady-state period. Since they were fully voiced and had only a minimal amount of friction, the formant movements from the consonant to the syllable nucleus were uninterrupted. Nevertheless, certain cues appeared with a fair amount of regularity, and together provided reasonably usable criteria for segmentation. For initial /w/ the region in which the slope of the second formant acquired a positive value was considered the boundary. This directional change was often accompanied by a sharp increase in energy, and the energy change was accompanied on the narrow-band spectrogram by a darker marking of the harmonics not in the frequency regions of resonance. Such energy cues were particularly useful in sequences where /w/ was followed by a vowel with a low second formant. Figure 1 contains initial /w/ followed by a front and a back vowel. A steady state for /w/ is followed by a rather sharp upward inflection of the second formant in the sequence /wi/;

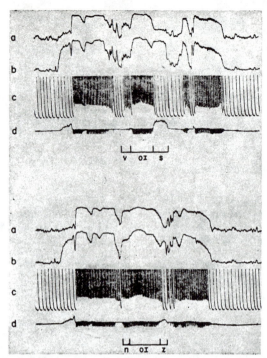

FIG. 5. Four-channel Mingograph tracings of two utterances by informant Br: "Say the word 'voice' again," and "Say the word 'noise' again." Curve a is an intensity curve with low-frequency pre-emphasis; curve b is an intensity curve with high-frequency pre-emphasis; curve c is a pitch curve (modified Grützmacher method); and curve d is a duplex oscillogram. The analysis was performed at the Royal Institute of Technology in Stockholm.

there is a noticeable change in the marking of the formants and also in the harmonics not within the resonance regions in the case of the sequence /wʊ/.

In these data, initial /y/ had a steady state, in which the frequency of the third formant was much greater than that for any simple vowel nucleus. The point, however, at which the transition to the following vowel began was at a considerably lower position in frequency. Thus the third formant of /y/ performs a rapid dip in frequency before rising back to the third-formant position of the vowel. The position in time of the frequency minimum of the third formant was thus considered the point of onset of the following vowel. This cue is most easily determined for vowels with a high third-formant frequency. Figure 2 contains illustrations of initial /y/. The steady state associated with the initial /y/ is characterized by a high third formant and a relatively weak intensity of the harmonics between the resonances; the minimum in the movement of the third formant from the steady state of /y/ to the following vowel serves as the point of segmentation.

5. Initial and Final /l/ and /r/

Both initial /l/ and /r/ had periods of steady resonances. The onset of a vowel after /l/ was usually unambiguously defined on the narrow-band spectrograms by the sudden change in marking of the harmonics between the various resonances at the change from steady formants to onglide. Initial /r/ often had a slight fricative quality. In addition, the frequency movements of the third formants usually provided a clue for the segmentation.

Final /l/ and /r/ presented particularly difficult problems. Very often the formant movements were quite smooth, and the establishment of a boundary on the basis of broad-band spectrograms was questionable. Intensity curves were helpful in instances where the vowel had an intrinsic energy considerably different from that of /l/ or /r/. In the transition from the vowel nucleus to /l/ a frequency minimum or a relatively rapid rise in the frequency of the third formant was sometimes present and was used as the basis of the segmentation. In the total set of data, the third formant of /l/ had an average frequency value of 2635 cps, and the change from the usually lower third-formant position of the vowel to that of /l/ sometimes involved a well-defined change point. But in a rather large number of instances, the formant movements appeared smooth, there was no significant change in the intensity, and the determination of a boundary had to be accomplished by some other criterion.

It was observed that the fundamental voice-frequency curve employed in each utterance had certain characteristic distributional features. The initial consonant of the word in the frame appeared to determine the occurrence of the peak of the fundamental curve. When the initial consonant was voiced, the peak occurred in the middle of the nucleus of the target word, with a rather smooth glide of the fundamental (usually upward but often down on voiced plosives) during the initial voiced consonant. If the consonant was voiceless, and particularly when the consonant was a voiceless fricative, the peak occurred immediately at the onset of voicing, and the fundamental on the syllable nucleus thereafter decreased. The total drop in pitch normally took place during the vocalic part of the syllable. When the final consonant was voiceless, this might have been expected. But when the final consonant was voiced, the fundamental pitch reached its minimum value by the beginning of the consonant and remained almost completely level for the duration of the consonant. This pattern was observed with very great regularity, and we concluded that in this type of utterance the region where the fundamental has become essentially level may be considered the consonant part.

Figure 3 illustrates the parallelism between such words as *coin* and *coil*, where the fundamental voice frequency was used to determine the boundary between the syllable nucleus and final /l/. The tenth harmonic has been traced in white, and provides a visual representation of the fundamental movement associated with this intonation. Some examples of initial /l/ are also included in Fig. 3 to illustrate that in initial position,

the rise in pitch takes place during the pronunciation of the voiced resonant; level fundamental frequency is not a characteristic of all /l/ sounds.

Examples of final /r/ may be found on Fig. 2, where the segmentation has been based on two clues: the steady fundamental frequency associated with final position, and the change in the third-formant frequency. Initial /r/ sounds are represented in Fig. 1. Approximate segmentation may be achieved by comparing the relative markings of the harmonics in the narrow-band spectrogram and by identifying the position at which the third formant begins to rise rapidly in frequency in the broad-band spectrogram.

PROBLEM OF TEMPO

In order to observe the intrinsic duration of syllable nuclei and the influence of preceding and following segmental sounds upon the duration of syllable nuclei, variability in duration due to the suprasegmental features of pitch, stress, and tempo should be eliminated. Since the recorded utterances involved a uniform stress and intonation pattern, it seems reasonable to assume that stress and pitch affected each test word in essentially the same manner. The chief remaining variable to be considered is speaker rate.

There are several different ways in which speaker rate might be defined for such a set of material. For example, speaker rate might be considered constant if the durations of the sentence frames remained constant. In order to study the durations of the sentence frames, the duration of each test word was subtracted from the duration of the entire utterance. It was found that in both sets of data a glottal stop was often inserted following the test word, and the duration of this stop was included in the measurement of the duration of the test frame. The average durations in centiseconds of the frames for the 70 utterances by each of the five speakers were: 122, 130, 144, 150, and 177. Ten samples of 50 sequential frame sentences each were also extracted from the 1263 words of the larger set of data. The average duration of the frame was 174 csec, with a standard deviation of 6.9 csec. The mean for the five speakers was 144, which differs from the average for the speaker of the large set of data by 30 csec. The average durations of the syllable nuclei contained in the test words in the smaller set of data were: 24, 25, 26, 30, and 31 csec, with an average of 27 csec. The average of the nuclei in the same words for GEP was 28 csec. Thus there was much greater relative variation in the average duration of the frame than in the average duration of the stressed syllable nuclei contained in the test words.

The foregoing data imply that differences in tempo may affect stressed and unstressed words in different ways. It has been suggested previously[9] that in English

[9] A. Classe, *The Rhythm of English Prose* (Basil Blackwell, Oxford, 1939).

there is a tendency for stress groups to assume approximately the same duration. Such a principle would require that the length of syllables vary, particularly in the case of stress groups containing different numbers of syllables. Thus we might consider whether the speakers spaced the main stresses at regular intervals. If so, the differences in the durations of stressed test words might be compensated by varying the durations of unstressed syllables.

The durations of the intervals between successive test words were measured for the same set of utterances that was used for computing the average duration of the frames. The selection of a time mark, either within the frame or within the test word, is somewhat arbitrary. If the rate of uttering the unstressed syllables of the frame varied according to the duration of the stressed test words, then a recurrent point in the test frames would not provide a satisfactory measure. On the other hand, since the test words all differ, it is obviously difficult to specify a common point within the test words. The selection of the point of maximum stress within the syllable nucleus might seem most appropriate, but it is undoubtedly influenced by both fundamental voice frequency and intensity in a way which is not yet understood, and the peaks for the two are not necessarily concurrent within the stressed syllable. Since the point of release of the initial consonant of the stressed syllable may be physiologically significant, and since it is a point which can be specified fairly accurately, it was chosen as the time mark for the measurements. The duration of the intervals between successive test words was measured accordingly for the same set of utterances that was used for computing the average durations of the frames.

Figure 6 presents a sequence chart for the durations of the time intervals between successive initial consonant releases of the test words (i.e., the total intervals), the durations of the test words, and the durations of the syllable nuclei. In the graph, relatively long pauses for inhalations, irregular breathing patterns, and relatively uniform rate accelerations and decelerations are all evident.

Figure 7(A) shows the duration of the test word versus the total time interval duration, and (B) shows the duration of the syllable nucleus vs the total time interval duration for 100 utterances by GEP. None of these graphs implies a strong relation between the interval duration measure which we chose and the duration of the test word or the syllable nucleus.

In general, the test word represents only a small fraction of the total duration of the interval. Also, the variation in the interval was small relative to the total interval duration, of the order of 3–5%, or approximately 5 to 15 csec. These facts suggest that variations in rate of utterance by any given speaker had little effect upon the duration of the stressed syllables under study.

A further brief experiment was devised to explore

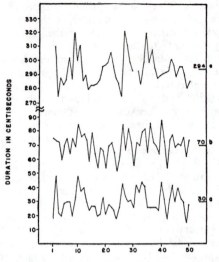

FIG. 6. Utterances 1–50 by informant He. Curve *a* presents the durations of the syllable nuclei, curve *b* the durations of the test words (occurring in random order), and curve *c* the duration of the time intervals between successive initial consonant releases of the test words. The break in curve *c* between items 30 and 31 represents the turning of the page from which the randomized test words were read.

whether stressed and unstressed syllables are similarly affected by a controlled change in tempo. A selected set of test utterances was recorded by three of the speakers. In one instance the spacing in time between the stressed syllables was controlled to be 2 seconds by asking the subjects to speak in synchronism with a periodic pulse produced over an earphone; in a second similar set of recordings, the spacing between stressed syllables was 1 second. The pulse and the speech were recorded on an SPL recorder and on magnetic tape. The durations of the words spoken at both rates of speech were measured, and the speedup factors were computed. In this experiment, the duration of the syllables with main stress changed less than the duration of the unstressed syllables: When the rate of utterance was increased by a factor of two, the stressed words decreased in duration by a factor of approximately 1.5. Under these conditions the actual durations for the stressed words were very similar for the three speakers.

Further investigations of the relations of tempo and stress to duration appear necessary before this variable can be specified adequately. For the present study, however, it seems reasonable to assume that the duration measurements of the test words were not greatly influenced by variations in tempo during the recording by any given speaker.

INFLUENCE OF PRECEDING AND FOLLOWING CONSONANTS

If the influence of suprasegmental factors is eliminated, the remaining durational differences may be

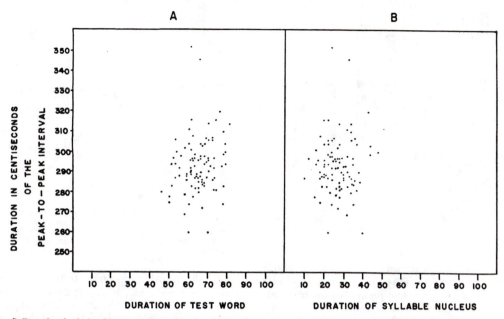

Fig. 7. Durational relationships between test word, syllable nucleus, and total time interval for 100 utterances by GEP. (A) shows the total time interval duration vs the duration of the test word, and (B) shows the total time interval duration vs the duration of the syllable nucleus.

due either to the influence of preceding and/or following consonants, or to intrinsic durational differences. The influence of consonants was considered next. Some of the syllable nuclei are represented by a larger number of words in the CNC list than others. Since we assumed that vowels may have different intrinsic durations, all occurrences of a particular consonant could not be included, as the results would then be weighted according to the predominance of intrinsically short or long syllable nuclei associated with the consonant. Therefore, several smaller subsets, consisting of minimal pairs present in the list, were analyzed. For example, in determining the influence of a following voiced or voiceless consonant on the duration of the preceding syllable nucleus, the durations of the syllable nuclei in such pairs as *beat-bead, sight-side*, etc., were compared. There were 118 minimal pairs in the larger set of data, differing in the voicing of the final consonant. The average duration of the syllable nucleus before the voiceless member of the consonant pair was 19.7 csec, and before the voiced member was 29.7 csec. The comparable values for the control group of five speakers were 19.3 csec and 29.1 csec. Thus, for this set of data, the ratio of vowel before voiceless consonant to vowel before voiced consonant is approximately 2:3.

The homorganic nasals influence the preceding vowel in much the same manner as the voiced stops. In 46 instances of triple contrasts, such as *back-bag-bang*, the average values of the syllable nuclei before the voiced stop and nasal were 29.8 csec for the voiced stop and 30.2 for the nasal in the larger set of recordings, and

28.9 csec and 30.0 csec for the stop and nasal, respectively, for the five speakers.

The voiced fricatives appear to have a further lengthening effect. Of the 21 minimal pairs in the set in which the effect of a final voiced plosive could be compared with the effect of the final homorganic voiced fricative, the duration of the syllable nucleus before the voiced plosive was 30.0 csec, whereas the comparable duration before the voiced fricative was 37.9 csec. There were nine sets where four contrasts were represented—sets of such words as *rice-rise-ride-right*. The average durations of the syllable nuclei, in ascending order, were: 18.4 csec before the voiceless plosive, 22.8 csec before the voiceless fricative, 28.0 csec before the voiced plosive, and 37.6 csec before the voiced fricative.

Initial voiced-voiceless contrasts presented no easily discernible pattern. There were 68 minimal pairs in the larger set of data which differed in the voicing of the initial consonant. Figure 8 presents graphically the results of the measurements on these minimal pairs. It appears that there is practically no durational difference associated with an initial /f/—/v/ contrast; in the case of /s/—/z/ and /č/[tʃ]—/j/[dʒ], the effect of voicing appears contradictory, the voiceless member of the pair being followed by a longer syllable nucleus in the case of the /s/—/z/ contrast, but by a shorter syllable nucleus in the case of an initial /č/—/ǰ/ contrast. Initial plosives present a special problem. If aspiration is considered part of the syllable nucleus, then voiceless plosives are regularly associated with longer syllable nuclei than voiced plosives; if, however,

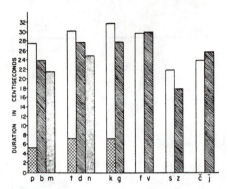

FIG. 8. The duration of syllable nuclei, measured from 68 minimal pairs differing in the voicing of the initial consonant, presented as a function of the initial consonant. The cross-hatched area associated with the columns representing the duration of syllable nuclei following voiceless plosives indicates the duration of aspiration.

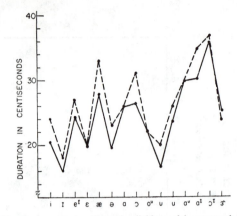

FIG. 9. Average durations of syllable nuclei, measured from minimal pairs differing in the voicing of the final consonant. The solid curve is for a large set of CNC words spoken by GEP; the dotted curve represents the values for 30 minimal pairs uttered by five speakers.

the duration of the aspiration is discounted, the syllable nucleus following a voiceless plosive is usually shorter than that following a voiced plosive. In the phonemic analysis of English, voiceless aspirated plosives are commonly analyzed as single phonemes, although they consist of a sequence of acoustical segments.

The aspiration has also been considered as part of the following vowel.[10] According to this opinion, the voiceless part represents the influence of the voiceless consonant as partial progressive assimilation which extends over a certain portion of the duration of the vowel.

The average duration of the aspiration after an initial |p| was 5.8 csec (for 81 different items); after an initial |t| the aspiration lasted 6.9 csec (in 73 instances), and for initial |k| the duration of the aspiration lasted 7.5 csec (for 83 items). These data suggest that aspiration may become progressively longer as the point of articulation shifts farther back in the mouth, but this observation was not supported by a separate analysis of the two main allophones of /k/, [c] and [k]. The average for the front allophone, [c], followed by front vowels (39 instances), was 7.8 csec, whereas the average for the velar allophone [k], followed by back vowels (44 instances), was 7.2 csec. Nevertheless, the /t/ aspirations were consistently shorter than the aspirations associated with either of the allophones of /k/.

If differences in the duration of the aspiration are conditioned and, therefore, nonsignificant, the question could be raised as to whether the duration of the aspiration is irrelevant to the duration of the syllable nucleus. If it is, then the aspiration may be considered as part of the consonant rather than the vowel. In some instances, this actually seemed to be the case.

---

[10] E. Fischer-Jørgensen, *Misc. Phonetica* 2, 42–59 (1954).

Figure 4 shows such an instance. In the spectrogram for *duck*, the vowel seems as long as the vowel in *tuck*; if the duration of the aspiration is included in the duration of the syllable nucleus, the total duration is more like the duration of the vowel in *dug*.

If we exclude aspiration, the average duration of the syllable nucleus after a voiceless consonant was 25.1 csec; when aspiration is included, it was 30.8 csec; the average duration after voiced consonants was 27.4 csec. These figures represent the average values for all 68 minimal pairs. Perhaps the most obvious conclusion is that, in our data, the influence of an initial consonant on the duration of the syllable nucleus followed no simple regular pattern.

INTRINSIC DURATIONS OF SYLLABLE NUCLEI IN ENGLISH

If the duration of a syllable nucleus is conditioned by the presence or absence of voicing in the following consonant, the intrinsic duration of the syllable nucleus might be defined as the average duration of the respective minimally contrastive pairs. Such average durations were computed for both the large and the small sets of data. In Fig. 9, the solid curve represents the averages for one speaker, and the dashed curve the averages for five speakers. Table I presents the actual values upon which the graph in Fig. 9 is based. The third row adds, for purposes of comparison, the average durations of the syllable nuclei in all instances in which the syllable nucleus occurred in the CNC list before those final consonants that were involved in the respective minimal pairs. In most instances, there is good agreement between the values computed from minimal pairs and the values averaged from a larger number of occurrences. There is also a considerable similarity between the two curves in Fig. 9.

TABLE I. Intrinsic durations of syllable nuclei
in American English.

TABLE I. Intrinsic durations of syllable nuclei
in American English.

Syllable nucleus	Average for five speakers (in csec)	Average for GEP in minimal pairs	Average for all occurrences in CNC list
i	24	20.6	20.7
ɪ	18	16.0	16.1
eɪ	27	24.3	20.0
ɛ	20	20.3	20.4
æ	33	28.0	28.4
ə	23	19.3	18.1
ɑ	26	26.1	26.5
ɔ	31	26.5	25.0
oʊ	22	22.0	22.2
ʊ	20	16.3	16.3
u	26	23.8	23.5
ɑʊ	30	30.2	30.2
ɑɪ	35	30.3	31.0
ɔɪ	37	36.0	36.0
r	24	25.3	25.6

It appears rather clear that the vocalic syllable nuclei may be subdivided into classes according to their durations. As a first approximation, the syllable nuclei may be considered as consisting of four short nuclei, [ɪ], [ɛ], [ʊ], and [ə], and nine long syllable nuclei.

The average duration of the nuclei preceding each consonant was next computed, and Fig. 10 presents these durations as a function of the final consonant phoneme. Only minimal pairs were included in constructing the two curves of Fig. 10 and in the accompanying Table II. The top curve is for all long syllable nuclei, and the bottom curve is for the four intrinsically short syllable nuclei. The voiceless-voiced contrasting influence on syllable nucleus duration is clearly evident in the variations of both curves. It is interesting that

TABLE II. Duration of syllable nuclei as a function
of the following consonant.

Following consonant	Duration of short syllable nucleus (in csec)	Duration of long syllable nucleus (in csec)
p	13.8	18.8
b	20.3	30.7
t	14.7	21.0
d	20.6	31.8
k	14.5	20.0
g	24.3	31.4
m	22.0	31.3
n	21.6	32.2
ŋ	21.8	35.0
f	19.2	26.1
v	23.1	37.4
θ	20.8	26.5
ð	26.0	38.1
s	19.9	26.9
z	26.2	39.0
ʃ	21.2	27.8
ʒ	. . .	41.0
r	22.6	29.6
l	21.8	29.3
č	14.5	19.8
ǰ	19.1	30.0

there is durational overlap between the durations of long nucleus plus voiceless consonant and short nucleus plus voiced consonant, for example in such sets as *bead-beat-bit-bid*. A further interesting fact is that the affricates [tʃ] and [dʒ] affect the preceding vowel durations in the same manner as the plosives. There is a possible historical basis for this similarity. Other characteristics of the two durational classes of syllable nuclei will be discussed in a subsequent issue.

CONCLUSION

It appears from the data analyzed during the present study that the durations of all syllable nuclei in English are significantly affected by the nature of the consonants that follow the syllable nuclei; the influence of the initial consonants upon the durations of the syllable nuclei appears to be negligible. In general, the

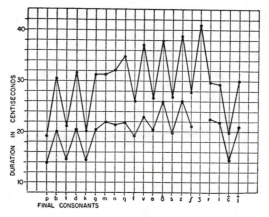

FIG. 10. Duration of syllable nuclei as a function of the final consonant phoneme, computed from minimal pairs of CNC words spoken by GEP. The top curve presents the average durations for all long-syllable nuclei and the bottom curve the averages for four short-syllable nuclei.

syllable nucleus is shorter when followed by a voiceless consonant, and longer when followed by a voiced consonant. In a large number of minimal pairs of CNC words differing in the voicing of the final consonant, the ratio of the durations of the vowels was approximately 2:3, the syllable nucleus before the voiced consonant being longer in every case. As a class, plosives are preceded by the shortest syllable nuclei; nasals had approximately the same influence as voiced plosives. Syllable nuclei were longest before voiced fricatives. Assuming that a voiced consonant has a lengthening influence on a syllable nucleus that is comparable to the shortening influence of a voiceless consonant, the intrinsic duration of syllable nuclei may be defined as the average duration of the syllable nucleus measured from minimal pairs differing in the voicing of the final consonant. Such intrinsic durations were computed for all stressed syllable nuclei in English. Two groups may be established according to this procedure: intrinsically short syllable nuclei, comprising the four vowels [ɪ, ɛ, ə, ʊ], and intrinsically long syllable nuclei, consisting of [i, eᴵ, æ, ɑ, ɔ, oᵁ, u, r, ɑᵁ, ɑᴵ, ɔᴵ].

ACKNOWLEDGMENT

The authors wish to express their appreciation to Dr. C. Gunnar M. Fant of the Royal Institute of Technology in Stockholm for his courtesy in providing mingograph tracings and continuous spectrograms of the data described here.

A.1 SPEECH WAVE ANALYSIS

A.11 *Intensity Measurements*

All measurements of the speech wave, of an oscillographic as well as of a spectro-graphic nature, involve the specification of amplitude or intensity measures. The term amplitude refers to the instantaneous or time average value of sound pressure, volume velocity, or particle velocity at a particular point in the sound field, or to the corresponding voltages or currents as delivered by a microphone. Any particular numerical value of the amplified, filtered, and by other means processed version of this electrical copy of the acoustic wave is also referred to by the term amplitude.

Sound intensity is the energy per unit time transmitted through a unit area. In the *cgs* system, which is the most common reference system in the acoustic literature and adopted in this work, the unit of intensity is erg per second per square centimeter. One such unit is 10^{-7} *watts/cm²*. In a plane or spherical free-progressive sound wave the intensity in the direction of the propagation is

$$W = P^2/\varrho c \; erg\text{-}sec^{-1}/cm^2, \tag{A.1-1}$$

where P is the *r.m.s.* sound pressure in *dynes/cm²*, ϱ is the density of the medium in *g/cm³*, and c the velocity of propagation in *cm/sec*. The product ϱc is the specific acoustical resistance of the medium which is *41.4 dynes sec/cm³* at *20 ⁰C* and *40.0* at *35 °C*, the latter value appropriate for the wave propagation within the vocal cavities.

Speech intensity is almost never measured directly. Pressure-sensitive microphones are utilized and the intensity, if of any interest, is calculated by means of *Eq. A.1-1*. Amplitude and intensity have become synonymous in a general sense because of this one-to-one correspondence. Sound pressure or intensity data are generally specified on a logarithmic scale with the unit decibel (*dB*) relative to a fixed reference. The standardized sound pressure reference is $P_0 = 0.0002 \; dynes/cm^2$ which corresponds closely to a reference intensity of $W_0 = 10^{-16} \; watt \; /cm^2$.

The sound intensity level is defined as

$$L = 10 \log_{10}(W/W_0) \; dB, \qquad\qquad (A.1\text{-}2)$$

which is identical with the sound pressure level

$$L = 20 \log_{10}(P/P_0) \; dB, \qquad\qquad (A.1\text{-}3)$$

provided P_0 is related to W_0 by means of *Eq. A.1-1.* A sound pressure reference of $P_0 = 1 \; dyne/cm^2$ is sometimes utilized in acoustics, especially in connection with microphone calibrations. The average sound pressure level at *30 cm* distance from a speaker is of this order of magnitude.

When evaluating the performance of an intensity meter it is necessary to consider:

(a) The prefiltering if any;

(b) The type of rectification;

   1. Half-wave or full-wave;

   2. Linear, square, or intermediate rectifier characteristics;

(c) The integration time and the shape of the temporal weighting function;

(d) The amplitude calibration, whether linear or logarithmic or of an intermediate degree of amplitude compression in the final presentation.

Auditory criteria can be applied to all of these design stages, but it should be remembered that the relations between the physical constants of complex time variable sounds and the loudness sensations they evoke, are too complicated to be successfully materialized in the physical design of a reliable loudness meter. In addition, the psycho-acoustic basis is not sufficiently well established with regard to speech-like stimuli. Technical comments on the standardization of sound level meters are given by Hardy and others (1957).

A prefiltering stage is often incorporated in an intensity meter. The function of this filter is to perform a weighting of the relative contributions from spectral components of different frequencies so that components of the intermediate frequency range *1000-4000 c/s* are emphasized. The standard sound level meter for noise measurements, see e.g., Beranek (1949), has three weighting networks, so-called frequency correction or emphasis networks.[1]

Human speech covers an intensity range of about *30 dB*. Vowels carrying a main stress have a sound pressure level of approximately *65 dB* at one meter's conversational distance (Dunn and White, 1940), and the unvoiced consonants are on the average *20 dB* weaker (Fant, 1949). These data could motivate the use of an *A-curve* pre-emphasis for measuring unvoiced consonants and the *B-curve* for collecting data on vowels. However, as an alternative to the loudness criteria it might be desired to

---

[1] These are labeled *A, B,* and *C.* The *A*-curve is recommended for use in the sound level range of *20-55 dB.* This filter has maximum transmission at *2500 c/s* and a low frequency attenuation that reaches *25 dB* at *100 c/s.* The small high-frequency suppression specified for the *A*-filter can be neglected for phonetical applications. The *B*-filter is recommended for use in the sound level range of $L = 55\text{-}85 \; dB.$ Its frequency characteristics are intermediate between those of the *A*-curve and the purely flat *C*-curve, but closer to the latter. Thus the low frequency suppression is only *6 dB* relative to the level at *1000 c/s.*

obtain intensity measurements that are less influenced by the particular phonetic quality of a vowel, as specified by the F-pattern, and more directly related to the speaker's voice effort. In this respect, the use of the *C-curve* is more advisable since the first formant will then determine the major part of the intensity. A more effective method is the use of an integration, i.e., a low frequency boost, and the ideal procedure would be to remove the formants entirely in order to regenerate the voice source. This possibility is being investigated.

The rectifier characteristics are less important. Full wave rectification is recommended since otherwise one-half of the speech wave, that above or below zero pressure amplitude, will be ignored. The difference is noticeable in the case of deep pitched male voices, especially at the boundaries between speech sounds and if the rectifier characteristics are non-linear. The difference between linear mean value and square-law rectifiers can be expressed in terms of the summation of spectral components, the latter providing the ideal summation of the squares of the amplitudes of the frequency components. A linear and a square-law instrument may be calibrated to give the same scale reading for a sine wave. When they are used for speech measurements the linear device shows on the average *0-3 dB* too low values, the larger deviation applicable for sounds composed of several partials of not too different amplitudes. One simple test of the summation is to superimpose two sine waves of the same amplitude on the measuring device. The square-law instrument will show a *3 dB* higher level than for one sine wave only, but the corresponding figure is only *2 dB* for the linear instrument. The difference of *1 dB* in the indications of the two instruments is also found in measurements on random noise (Beranek, 1949, p. 453); see also the comments of Snow (1957).

Unless combined with a root extracting device, the square-law rectification provides an intensity proportional measure. Square-law rectification probably has a greater auditory significance than linear-law rectification, but the difference is not very great and can generally be taken into account in the calibration procedure.[2] It should also be observed that the linearly operating device is phase dependent (Haase and Vilbig, 1956). Linear rectifier characteristics are preferable for most practical applications because of the simpler design and the lesser degree of compression needed in the final stage.

If the output from the rectification stage of an intensity meter is fed into an oscillograph directly and not via an integrating stage, there results merely an oscillogram of the instantaneous intensity. This has the form of an ordinary oscillogram in which all negative excursions of the curve have been folded up to the positive side. There is also an expansion of the amplitude scale provided the rectifiers have square-law characteristics. Obviously such a curve is not very practical to use because of the unnecessary detail structure that is retained.

The integrating or smoothing process inherent in the function of a low-pass filter

---

[2] The square-law system is not an established ideal from a perceptional point of view and peak measurements may be of the same significance as loudness correlates of wide-band complex sounds.

is analogous to calculating the area under the unsmoothed intensity curve at a definite interval, for instance, a voice fundamental period. A graphic-mathematical procedure of this type operates according to a rectangular weighting function; that is, the same importance is laid on the contributions from all parts within the predetermined interval. Auditory perception is not, however, so highly time selective and neither is any physical filter. A continuous weighting of the contributions from the past according to a specific memory function occurs in both instances. In addition, however, the memory function presumably varies with the type of stimulus and with the context.

Any particular point on a recorded intensity curve represents the accumulated intensity value from a smoothly bounded interval of the speech wave. The effective duration of this interval, called the *integration time* or *averaging time*, is the area under the memory curve divided by the ordinate value at its center of gravity (Laurent, 1953). In a large class of *LC*-low-pass filters this point on the memory function is close to the maximum value. The location of this effective center of the memory function relative to the instant of observation is called the *delay time* which is another characteristic time constant of the integrating device. In one class of smoothing filters, the simple *RC*-low-pass filter specified by a simple exponential memory function

$$h(t) = h_0 \cdot e^{-t/RC}, \tag{A.1-4}$$

the peak of the memory, h_{max}, occurs at the instant of observation, but the delay time according to the precise definition of Laurent (1953) will be equal to $T_d = RC$, and the averaging time will be $T_a = e \cdot RC$.

In general, the averaging time is of the order of

$$T_a = 1/2B, \tag{A.1-5}$$

where B is the cutoff frequency of the low-pass filter. The delay time is of no concern in the evaluation of speech records except when several differently processed derivates of the speech wave have been recorded on a multichannel oscillograph and a synchronous sampling of the data is desired. If, instead of the oscillographic display, the intensity values are presented as needle deflections on a meter, it is the mechanical inertia of the system which performs the integration.

The combination of a rectifier and a low-pass filter of *RC*-type with a large time constant can be designed to perform a peak detection. The instrument reading reaches a maximum value very quickly within a time of the order of a voice fundamental period and discharges slowly. The instrument does not respond to a peak amplitude unless this exceeds the value remaining from the previous charge. In a piece of connected speech of about *3* seconds' length, the highest instantaneous peak is of the order of *20 dB* above the long time average value, the latter defined from the energy of the sample divided by its duration (Dunn and White, 1940).

The auditory inertia, called *smear* by Joos (1948), cannot very exactly be described by time constants of the type defined above, but it appears that both the delay and the averaging times are of the order of *20-200 msec*. Experiments on the perception of simple sine waves presented in pulses of different duration have shown that an increase of pulse duration beyond the order of *0.18-0.25 sec* causes no increase in the loudness sensation. Longer pulses are merely sensed as a prolongation and shorter pulses are evaluated on the basis of both intensity and duration; see e.g., von Békésy (1929). The relative contribution from each of these parameters varies with the level at which the stimuli are presented (Munson, 1947) and with the individual subject of the test (Garner, 1949). Short bursts of random noise are perceived with an averaging time of the order of *50 msec* (G. A. Miller, 1948).

Much is still unknown about auditory time constants. It appears that different aspects of the speech wave are perceived with different amounts of auditory inertia and that no single time constant is sufficient. Some information reaches the higher centers very quickly via short and direct nervous transmission paths and other data, processed more intricately, are delayed and smoothed out to a greater extent. Sound pulses of large amplitude travel faster than those of a lower amplitude.

A direct reading intensity meter of the standardized *VU*-type has an averaging time of the order of *250 msec*, which is somewhat longer than the voiced part of an average syllable, the latter providing a meter deflection of *2 dB* above the long time average (Boeryd, 1957). Because of the non-uniqueness of a single auditory time constant, it is not advisable to design an intensity meter with too large an integration time. If this time constant is chosen small enough, it is possible, by means of graphical integration, to simulate the effect of any particular smear.

On the other hand it should be observed that if the integration time is chosen smaller than the reciprocal value of the speaker's voice fundamental frequency F_0, a ripple of this frequency will be found superimposed on the intensity curve. This ripple is harmless as long as it is small compared with the mean intensity, and it may be made use of for measuring F_0. An integration time of *10 msec*, according to *Eq. A.1-5*, corresponding to a low-pass smoothing filter of cutoff frequency *50 c/s*, has been found to be satisfactory and conforms with the concept of *mean speech power*, as recommended by Fletcher (1929). A *20 msec* integration time will effectively remove all voice frequency ripple even from very low-pitched segments but causes too large a smear for the study of the decay and onset characteristics of the burst interval of a stop sound.

The shape of the memory function should also be taken into account. If a passive *RC*-network is utilized for the smoothing, the memory function will have a considerably faster onset than decay. If a very short impulse from the speech wave, for instance, a very short stop burst, enters such a filter and the impulse duration is shorter than the averaging time, the resulting curve will merely reflect the memory function of the filter.[3]

---

[3] The present practice developed at the Speech Transmission Laboratory is to use phase-compensated *LRC*-filters with *18 dB/octave* attenuation above the cutoff frequency. The memory curve of our standard filters is fairly symmetrical and has a negligible overshoot. Design data will be given elsewhere (Fant, 1959).

The final amplitude calibration of the intensity record should be expressed by a table or curve relating the amplitude of the intensity curve in millimeters to the sound pressure level of the speech in *dB* relative to the reference pressure. The *dB* calibration is natural if the final stage contains a logarithmic transformation of the output from the integrating stage but can also be adopted in a purely linear display. A compromise between linear and logarithmic presentation can be obtained with a very simple compressing device which performs a logarithmic translation of large and medium size amplitudes but a linear translation of small amplitudes. The resulting amplitude scale, referred to as compressed, could be more representative of hearing than the purely logarithmic display inasfar as the minimum perceptible intensity difference in *dB* is larger at the threshold of hearing than at higher sensation levels. These *DL*-values range from *0.5 to 5 dB*. The *DL* for vowel intensity is close to *1 dB*, as reported by Flanagan (1957a). According to S. S. Stevens (1956), an increase in stimulus level of *10 dB* causes a doubling of the loudness sensation. These data enable an estimate of the accuracy needed in collecting intensity data.

As a physical correlate to stress it has been proposed to measure, from a linear amplitude recording, the area under the syllabic peaks, thus combining intensity and duration in a single measure (Fant, 1949, 1957).[4] This is motivated by the dependency of loudness on duration and the experience from speech analysis and synthesis that a shortening alone can have the effect of changing a listener's stress response. This area measure, tentatively called *impulse index*, has the dimension of energy only if the rectifier characteristics are quadratic. The area measure obtained from linear rectification has a conceptual similarity to energy but is strictly of the dimension of sound pressure multiplied by time. It is practical to express the impulse index on a *dB* scale, with reference to area ratios. Assuming quadratic rectifiers, a *3 dB* intensity increase of a syllable, i.e., a doubling of its amplitude, will accordingly be considered equivalent to a doubling of its duration. A linear rectification and recording will give less weight to the intensity, since a doubling of the amplitude of the intensity curve means a *6 dB* increase. There is not yet enough experience accumulated for a decisive recommendation of any particular scale and form of presentation. Linear rectification seems to be the more practical solution, and a linear recording should be utilized.

A.12 *Spectrum and Waveform Measurements*

Present techniques of spectrographic and oscillographic speech analysis provide the following data:

1. Instantaneous amplitude;
2. Intensity averaged over a short time of the order of *10-20 msec*;
3. Spectral composition in terms of one of the alternative forms:
   A. Fourier series containing amplitude and phase of the fundamental and harmonics;

---

[4] Other stress correlates are the increase of voice fundamental frequency F_0 and the increased vowel/consonant contrast in stressed syllables; see further Fant (1957).

B. Amplitude and phase of the outputs of a set of band-pass filters of sufficient
   number to cover the frequency range of interest.

The phase concept referred to here is that of instantaneous phase $\varphi_m(t)$ of the output
$v_m(t)$ of a band-pass channel *No. m* of center frequency $F_m = \omega_m/2\pi$.

$$v_m(t) = V_m(t) \cos [\omega_m t + \varphi_m(t)], \qquad (A.1\text{-}6)$$

where $V_m(t)$ represents the amplitude information. Both $V_m(t)$ and $\varphi_m(t)$ are
considered to vary only by small amounts within the period time $2\pi/\omega_m$. The
oscillation of center frequency F_m is introduced as a carrier of the amplitude and
phase information. After rectification and smoothing, only the amplitude information
$V_m(t)$ remains. Any observed value $V_m(t)$ represents a sample of the effective
duration $1/B_m$, where B_m is the bandwidth of the analyzing filter. This is due to the
integrating function of the filter. Observe the similarity with the integrating function
of a low-pass filter *Eq. A.1-5* and the difference with regard to a factor of *2*.

Phase information is of very little importance for the perception of speech and can
generally not be recorded by our present analyzers. Phase information is generally
predictable from the amplitude information. The reverse relation holds partially so
that phase-frequency analysis can, to some extent, be substituted for amplitude-
frequency analysis (Huggins, 1952). Phase is thus of a more theoretical interest. A
large frequency-dependent phase shift in a transmission system or in a recording
system results in a delay in the time of arrival of spectral components. If the phase
shift is not linearly related to the frequency, there will be separate time delays for
separate frequency intervals of the spectrum.

The intensity-versus-frequency distribution of very short clicks is the same as in
white noise, i.e., uniform. In other words, the spectrum level per unit bandwidth is
the same in every part of the spectrum. In the click, all frequency components are
in phase. In random white noise, on the other hand, the phase is distributed at
random throughout the spectrum. From this example it might appear important to
measure phase. In view of the foregoing discussion, however, it is quite sufficient to
restrict the specification to amplitude and time of arrival of separate spectral components of bandwidth *B* and duration $1/B$ distributed within the frequency-time plane
of spectrographic representation. The response of the filter to an impulse of infinitely
short duration is identical with its memory weighting function, the effective duration
of which is $1/B$. Only if the duration of the noise is shorter than $1/B$ will the spectrograph fail to distinguish the click from the short burst of noise.

Graphical Fourier analysis, the so-called harmonic analysis, is nowadays seldom
carried out, since it is so much easier to utilize a filtering method. Harmonic analysis
has, however, been of great importance in an earlier period of experimental phonetics
(Crandall, 1925; Steinberg, 1934; Lewis, 1936; Sovijärvi, 1938a; Tarnóczy, 1948).
One unnatural aspect of the classical Fourier frequency analysis is that it is equivalent
to the use of an analyzing filter of infinitely narrow bandwidth. The representation
in terms of elementary frequency-time limited spectral components applied above

not only provides a useful theory for describing the function of a spectrograph, it also serves as a better signal representation than Fourier series and Fourier integrals when discussing auditory phenomena (Gabor, 1946, 1953). There is, however, need for more accurate data on the effective bandwidths and time constants for the perception of different spectral aspects as well as of the shape of the memory function; compare the discussion in *Section A.11.*

Joos's preference for narrow bandwidth in spectrographic analysis was motivated by the *50 msec* smear time he suggested as representative of auditory integration. However, the *smear* effect in spectrographic analysis depends in part on the band-pass filters, in part on the integrating circuitry following the filters, and these may be designed to perform the essential part of the integration. It seems more probable that the auditory organs function like a broad-band analyzer, the multiple channel outputs of which are rectified and smoothed and intercorrelated in the nervous system (Licklider, 1952) with an integration time which is large as compared with the reciprocal of the bandwidth of the peripheral filters and of the order of *20-200 msec*. There are also indications that the multipathway connections for transmission of spectral information are associated with different time constants (Gabor, 1946). The frequency analysis discussed so far is concerned with the *quality* or *timbre* aspects of speech sounds. The perception of the fundamental pitch and thus of intonation appears to be related, at least in part, to a separate auditory process. To make the analogy to broad-band spectrography complete, this might be thought of as a process of counting the number of energy maxima per unit time within any or all of the band-pass channels, i.e., a detection of the time function envelope periodicity. It must be stressed that this analogy is not intended to explain the auditory mechanism, but to discuss some aspects of its function.

In one class of spectrographs the amplitude information from a number of separate frequency bands is displayed almost simultaneously by a rapid scanning process, e.g., in the *48*-channel spectrograph at the R.I.T. (Sund, 1957). In other analyzers requiring repeated playback for the analysis, e.g., the Kay Electric Sonagraph originating from the Bell Telephone Laboratories (1946) sound spectrograph, the mid-frequency of a single filter is shifted by a small amount for each completed loop of the playback.

The Sonagraph provides time-frequency-intensity records, so-called spectrograms, of a maximum length of *2.4 seconds*. The time scale is horizontal, the frequency scale vertical, and the intensity of spectral components is represented by a continuous black-grey-white marking scale. Amplitude, or more precisely intensity level versus frequency sections, can be taken at various desired positions along the time scale. Both spectrograms and sections may alternatively be produced with a narrow analyzing filter, $B = 45\ c/s$, or with a broad-band filter $B = 300\ c/s$. A section constitutes a sample of a definite center position in time with an extent in time equal to the averaging time of the integrating circuitry, the inertia of the band-pass filter included. The latter is decisive for the sample duration of a narrow-band section which is of the order of *30 msec*. In broad-band analysis the integrating circuitry following the filter determines a sample duration of the order of *5 msec*.

Sonagraph analysis is exemplified in *Fig. A.1-1*. In narrow-band analysis, see *A* and *C*, in this figure the individual harmonics are resolved. They constitute a fine structure of fairly horizontal lines running through the formants of the frequency-intensity-time spectrograms. They appear as individual peaks within the sections. The width of one of these harmonic lines is equal to the bandwidth of the filter.

Formant frequency, formant bandwidth, and formant level can be defined from the envelope which can be drawn to enclose smoothly the harmonics within the spectral maximum (Fant, 1956). The frequency of a formant is generally measured as the frequency position of the envelope maximum, but this point cannot be utilized for an unambiguous definition. Difficulties are encountered in case of highly asymmetric formants and when the voice fundamental frequency F_0 is high. A center of gravity definition as proposed by Potter and Steinberg (1950) could have some bearing on perception but does not solve the problem. It is preferable to attempt an estimate of the corresponding resonance frequency of the vocal tract filter function for the benefit of the F-pattern specification; see *Sections 1.22* and *1.32*. The formant level is generally defined as the envelope level, i.e., the sound pressure level in *dB* of the envelope peak.[5] It is also possible to define the formant level from the sum of the intensities of the individual harmonics within the formant. If the voice pitch F_0 is greater than the formant bandwidth, there is less than *1 dB* difference between the intensity level and the envelope peak level. These relations will be discussed in more detail in a separate publication. Formant bandwidth is measured by drawing a line parallel to the frequency axis *3 dB* below the envelope peak. The bandwidth is the distance between the two points where the envelope is intersected.

Provided the fundamental pitch is not too high, the broad-band spectrograms will fail to show the individual harmonics. This is because more than one harmonic at a time will be passed through the filter. A large bandwidth *B* means a small integration time $1/B$. Thus the intensity variations within a voice fundamental period will be detected. The vertical striations typical for a spectrogram of a low pitch male voice are indications of each vocal cord period. Each pulse of air from the glottis injected into the vocal cavities will give rise to a damped oscillation.

A formant in the frequency domain is mathematically identical with a damped oscillation in the time domain. If this had been quite clear *50* years ago, the classical Helmholtz theory and the Hermann-Willis theory of speech production would never have been opposed to each other as being different. This was pointed out already by Lord Raleigh (1896); see further Chiba and Kajiyama (1941); Trendelenburg (1950).

The apparent width of the formant bands in a broad-band spectrogram is the sum of the true formant bandwidth and the bandwidth of the analyzer, of which the latter is by far the larger—at least when dealing with the first three formants. If a speaker's average F_0 is high and of the same order of magnitude as the width of the broad

---

[5] Peterson and Barney (1952) use the term *amplitude* for the *dB*-value of the formant peak. As long as the unit and procedure for measurements are defined, it does not matter what term is used.

analyzing filter, the spectrographic display will show the individual harmonics during sound intervals of high F_0, i.e., at intonation peaks, but the formant structure may appear properly or in mixture with the harmonic fine structure at sound intervals of low F_0. This may be rather confusing, and it is recommended to make supplementary spectrograms with the tape played back at half speed, thus reducing both F_0 and the formant frequencies by a factor of 2. The formant structure will then appear but at the expense of a reduced selectivity. Close-lying formants may not be sufficiently well separated.

Recent developments of instruments for collecting spectrum data of speech have been reported in an earlier publication (1957). One very accurate but rather time-consuming method of deriving amplitude-versus-frequency sections is to make amplitude-versus-time oscillograms of the speech wave from the outputs of a number of band-pass filters covering the appropriate part of the frequency scale or from a single band-pass filter that is shifted in mid-frequency after each completed cycle of the entire recording. This was the technique adopted for deriving the sections shown in the *Appendix* and utilized here for comparisons with calculated data. It has been utilized earlier for the analysis of stop sounds (Fant, 1949).

One of the early instrumental methods for spectral analysis of speech was the sweep-frequency analysis, *Suchtonanalyse*, performed with a wave analyzer of continuously variable carrier frequency. This method provides constant bandwidth, but continuously gliding center frequency of the effective filter function of the instrument. The instrumentation utilized by, for instance Sovijärvi (1938a,b) and Barczinski and Thienhaus (1935), required a time of analysis of the order of two minutes. Trained singers were required to sustain a stationary sound of that length. The present techniques of this method (Meyer-Eppler, 1950; Fant, 1957) have been improved so that the sounds to be analyzed need not be sustained more than the theoretical minimum, which is the extent of the frequency scale to be covered divided by the square of the filter bandwidth utilized in the analysis. Sweep frequency analysis covering a frequency range of *8000 c/s* thus requires a time of analysis of *2 sec* when a *63 c/s* bandwidth is utilized, and only *0.5 sec* for a *125 c/s* filter. It does not pay to reduce the time of analysis below *0.5 sec*, since the temporal fine structure from successive voice periods will then be too disturbing. The vowel analysis exemplified in *Fig. A.1-2* shows the high quality spectral tracings[6] obtained by connecting the

---

[6] The curves of *Fig. A.1-2* were obtained without any high frequency pre-emphasis. It has been found that a simple high-pass *RC*-network specified by a zero at *200 c/s* and a pole at *5000 c/s*, both on the negative real axis, provides a generally useful degree of correction for the low frequency emphasis typical of the spectra of most speech sound, thus permitting weaker high frequency formants to be seen better. This correction curve has the desirable property of being simple and symmetric around *1000 c/s* and represents a compromise between the demands of a compensation for the long time average speech spectrum and the frequency dependent perception of loudness. The network approximates a *40 phone* equal loudness curve for frequencies below *3000 c/s*. In our experience it appears to provide better spectral balance than the Sonagraph high frequency pre-emphasis. For routine presentation of spectrum curves it would also be desirable to utilize a frequency scale such as the mel scale (Stevens and Volkman, 1940) so that the visual impression of the

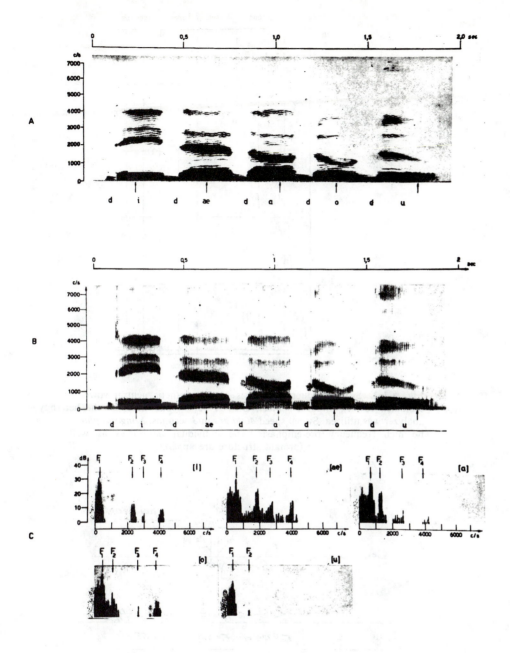

Fig. A.1-1. Spectograms: A. narrow band, B. broad band, and C. sections, obtained with a *Sonagraph*. Speech material [didædadodu], American subject, H.T. The time locations of the sections are indicated by arrows under the spectrograms.

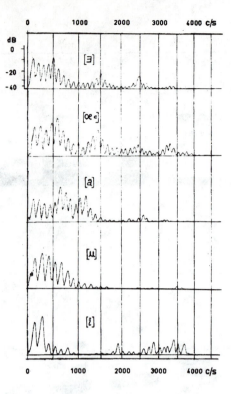

Fig. A.1-2. Sweep frequency analysis of the synthetic neutral vowel and some sustained vowels, Swedish subject, G.F. A *31 c/s* bandwidth of the heterodyne analyzer was utilized. Sweep speed *4000 c/s* in *3* seconds. *Mingographic* recording, no high frequency ·pre-emphasis. The individual harmonics as well as the formant structure are apparent.

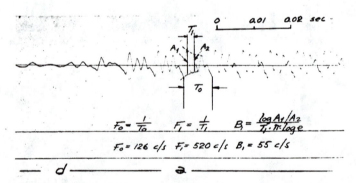

Fig. A.1-3. Waveform analysis of the fundamental pitch F_0 and of the frequency F_1 and bandwidth B_1 of the first formant in the fourth period of the vowel [ə] in [də] *Mingograph* high-speed oscillogram with half-speed tape-recorder playback.

analyzer output to a direct-writing oscillograph recorder of high frequency response. This method is especially suited for voice quality studies.

From an engineering point of view it seems rational to measure and to define the formant from the time function. Given a high-speed oscillogram of the speech wave, with a prefiltering arranged to isolate the formant of interest, the formant frequency can be measured from the time of a full period of the oscillation. The initial amplitude of the oscillation may then be adopted as an alternative measure of formant intensity. The bandwidth is defined as $B = \sigma/\pi$ where $1/\sigma$ is the time it takes for the oscillation to decay *8.6 dB*, i.e., a factor e; see *Fig. A.1-3*. This method has the advantage of providing formant frequency data in conformity with the F-pattern definition.

Frequency and intensity measures taken from the time function generally agree quite well with data from spectral sections. Formant bandwidths obtained from frequency domain measurements are constantly greater than the measure obtained from the time domain as described above. The latter are physically more correct. There is always some bandwidth broadening owing to the time-averaging effects in filters or in Fourier series expansions.

The voice fundamental frequency, see *Eq. 1.1-2*, is defined as $1/T_0$ where T_0 is the duration of a fundamental period measured from an oscillogram or from the vertical striations in a broad-band spectrogram. Any observable harmonic of known number can be utilized for direct measurements of fundamental frequency from narrow-band spectrograms or cross-sections. Automatic pitch extracting instruments can also be used, instead of the spectrographic or oscillographic methods. Present devices originate more or less from the Grützmacher and Lottermoser (1937) pitch extractor. It provides a continuous curve of the voice fundamental frequency within voiced sections of the speech wave. Such devices, however, are not always reliable.

The following symbols will be used:

F_n = frequency of formant number n in *c/s*;

B_n = bandwidth of formant number n in *c/s*;

L_n = level of formant number n in *dB*;

F_n = formant number n without specific reference to its dimensions. The first formant is thus denoted by $F1$ and its frequency by F_1 and so on;

F_0 = frequency of the voice fundamental in *c/s*;

$F0$ = the voice fundamental without specific reference to its dimensions.

---

spectral distribution should conform to the auditory importance of various frequency regions. A common linear scale gives too much prominence to higher frequencies and a logarithmic scale will overemphasize the low frequency end. The Koenig (1949) scale is a first order approximation specified as linear below *1000 c/s* and logarithmic above *1000 c/s*. A better approximation would be to relate the abscissa distance x *cm* to the frequency f by the formula $x = k \log(1 + f/1000)$, (Fant, 1949). It has the advantage that the interval discontinuity at *1000 c/s* is removed. Since most spectrum recording devices are designed for either logarithmic or linear frequency scale and since it is laborious to replot spectral curves, it is generally customary to retain the frequency scale of the original recording.

The natural range of variation of the voice fundamental frequency and of formant frequencies for non-nasal voiced sounds uttered by average male subjects is as follows:

$$F_0 \quad 60\text{-}240 \quad c/s$$
$$F_1 \quad 150\text{-}850 \quad c/s$$
$$F_2 \quad 500\text{-}2500 \quad c/s$$
$$F_3 \quad 1500\text{-}3500 \quad c/s$$
$$F_4 \quad 2500\text{-}4500 \quad c/s$$

Females have on the average one octave higher fundamental pitch but only *17* per cent higher formant frequencies; see Peterson and Barney (1952); Fant (1953b). Children about *10* years of age have still higher formants, on the average *25* per cent higher than adult males, and their fundamental pitch averages *300 c/s*. The individual spread is large.

At an average voice level, the level of the first formant measured at a distance of *1 m* is *60-65 dB* re *0.0002 dynes/cm²* (Dunn and White, 1940; Fant, 1949). Higher formants have decreasing levels and they vary according to the particular formant frequencies, as will be discussed later.

The first two formants have bandwidths of the order of *30-100 c/s*. Higher formants have increasing bandwidths, B_3 and B_4, ranging from *40-200 c/s*. These data were obtained from oscillographic measurements. They are considerably smaller than the bandwidth data reported by Bogert (1953). The systematic differences are due to the measuring technique as discussed earlier. Recent data provided by House and Stevens (1957) and Stevens (1958) as well as the data of van den Berg (1953) conform closely to the order of magnitudes stated above.

A.13 *Spectrographic Illustrations of the Speech Material Utilized for the Control of the Consonant Calculations*

The following illustrations labeled *A.13-1* to *A.13-19* contain speech wave characteristics of monosyllabic test words of the type consonant plus [a] spoken by the subject used for the X-ray photography. The original recording was made in an anechoic chamber and included the syllables

Fig.			Fig.			Fig.		
A. 13-1	[ma]	[m,a]	A. 13-6	[fa]	[f,a]	A. 13-13	[ča]	[ca]
A. 13-2	[na]	[n,a]	A. 13-7	[va]	[v,a]	A. 13-14	[pa]	[p,a]
A. 13-3	[la]	[l,a]	A. 13-8	[sa]	[s,a]	A. 13-15	[ba]	[b,a]
A. 13-4	[ra]	[r,a]	A. 13-9	[za]	[z,a]	A. 13-16	[ta]	[t,a]
A. 13-5	[ja]		A. 13-10	[xa]		A. 13-17	[da]	[d,a]
			A. 13-11	[ša]	[šča]	A. 13-18	[ka]	[k,a]
			A. 13-12	[ža]		A. 13-19	[ga]	

spoken in succession and at the rate of approximately two syllables per second.

The analysis comprises spectrograms (*Sonagraph*), intensity curves with various types of pre-filtering, and section samples at places of interest within the consonants to be studied. The amplitude-versus-frequency sections were compiled from a number of *Mingograph* recordings of the output of a wave analyzer with a bandwidth of *150 c/s* and variable center frequency.[7] These sections are more time-consuming to prepare than those obtainable from the Sonagraph, but they provide a better intensity resolution. Thus, *F*2 and *F*3 of a voiced occlusion may generally be detected. They have been utilized as control material for estimating the practical potentialities of the techniques for predicting speech spectra from X-ray data.

The time location of each section is specified by reference to a specific point on the time scale of the spectrogram. For analysis of unvoiced stops, sections have been taken at three different sampling points or intervals within the burst labeled *I*, *II*, and *III*. These correspond to explosion, frication (fricative interval), and aspiration respectively; see for instance [t,] and [k,]. Generally the first two or the last two of these events are more or less mixed.

The following synchronous time functions were recorded:

(1) Oscillogram with *B-curve* (see *Section A.11*) suppression of low frequencies. The upper frequency limit is that of the *Mingograph* or approximately *800 c/s*;

All intensity-versus-time characteristics (2)-(8) were recorded with an effective integration time of *10 msec*, corresponding to the *50 c/s* low-pass cutoff frequency of the smoothing filter. Full-wave linear rectification was utilized. The amplitude scale is logarithmic for (2) and (3) and linear for (4), (5), and (6) but is calibrated in *dB* in all instances. The following pre-filtering was utilized for the separate time functions.

(2) Sound level meter *A-curve* pre-emphasis. This is essentially a low frequency suppression; see *Section 1.11*;

(3) High-pass filtering, cutoff frequency *1500 c/s*;

(4) Band-pass filtering, *1400-1800 c/s*;

(5) Band-pass filtering, *2800-3600 c/s*;

(6) High-pass filtering, cutoff frequency *4000 c/s*.

Several observations of general interest may be made from these illustrations,[8] e.g., the difference in temporal intensity envelope comparing stops, affricates, and fricatives. The stops display a relatively short burst interval or at least a short fricative interval within the burst. The duration of the affricate is longer than for the stops but shorter than for continuants. The stop burst has a much shorter onset interval than decay interval. These are of about the same length for the affricate and in the case of continuants in initial position the rising interval occupies a major part of the sound owing to the increasing over-pressure associated with the onset of a breath pulse; compare *Fig. A.2-2*. These onset, duration, and decay characteristics have been summarized quantitatively by Halle (1954).

[7] Halle and Hughes participated in the initial stage of this work.
[8] The very weak third formant of the vowel as seen in several of the spectrograms is merely a personal characteristic of the speaker. As shown in *Section 2.42*, there is a theoretical possibility that a critically small degree of nasal coupling can produce this effect, the third formant gaining in intensity at larger or no nasal coupling; compare [la] with [na] and [za], *Fig. A. 13-3, A. 13-2,* and *A. 13-9.*

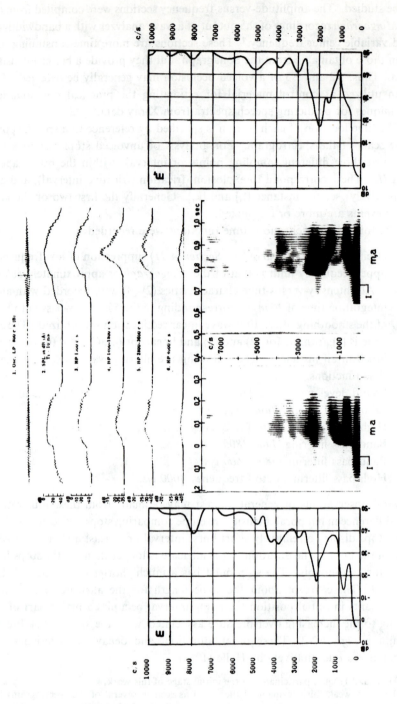

Fig. A.13-1. [ma], [m,a].

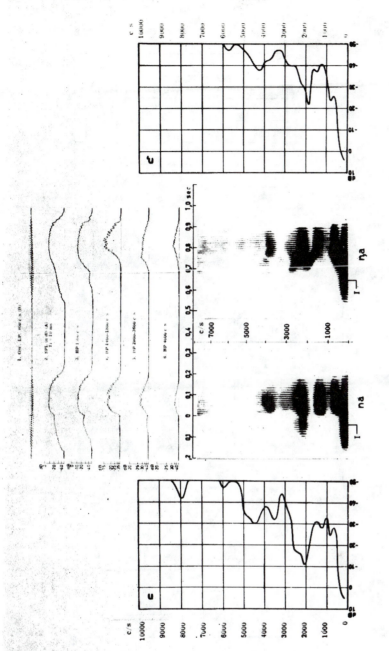

Fig. A.13-2. [naɪ], [n,a].

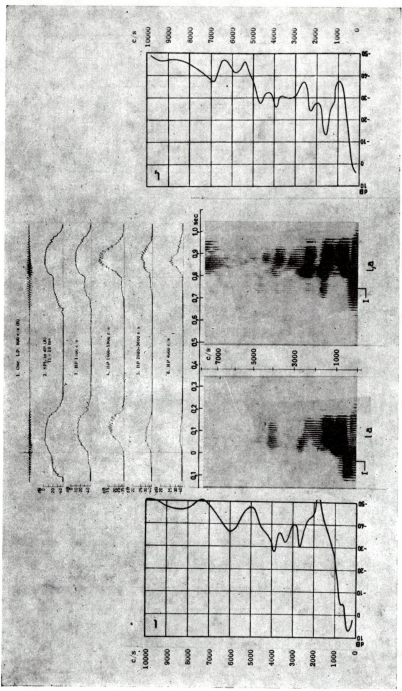

Fig. A.13-3. [Ia], [I,a].

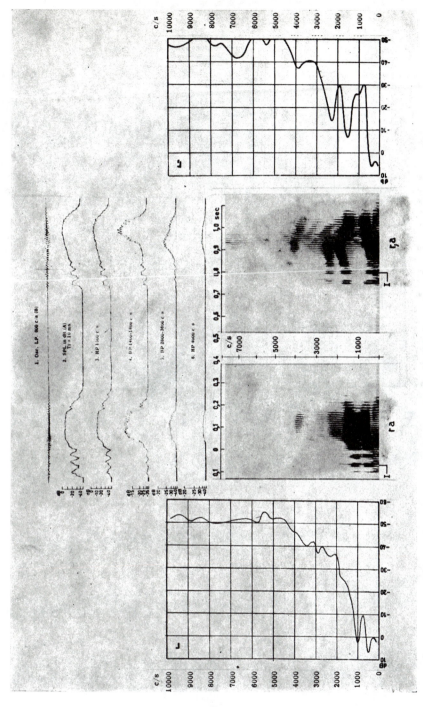

Fig. A.13-4. [ra], [r,a].

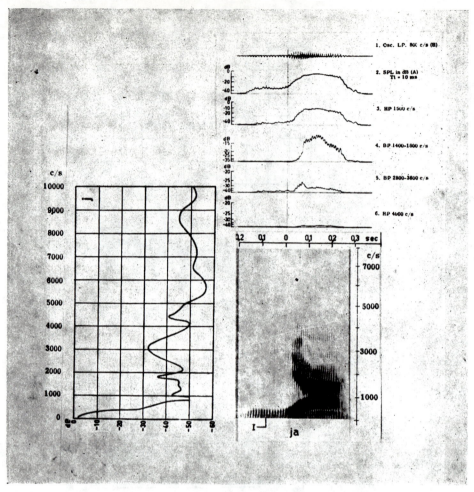

Fig. A.13-5. [ja].

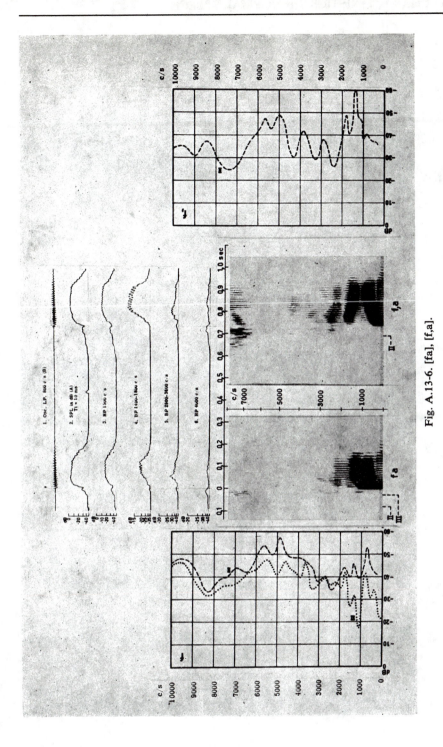

Fig. A.13-6. [fa], [f,a].

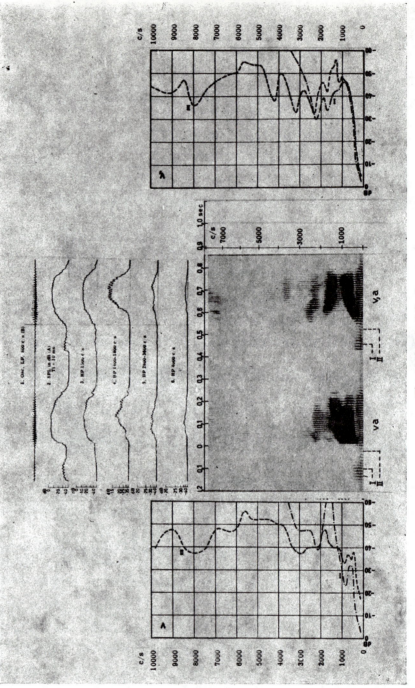

Fig. A.13-7. [va], [v,a].

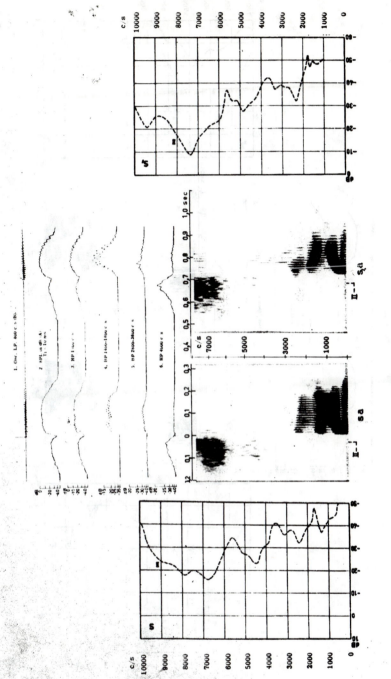

Fig. A.13-8. [sa], [s,a].

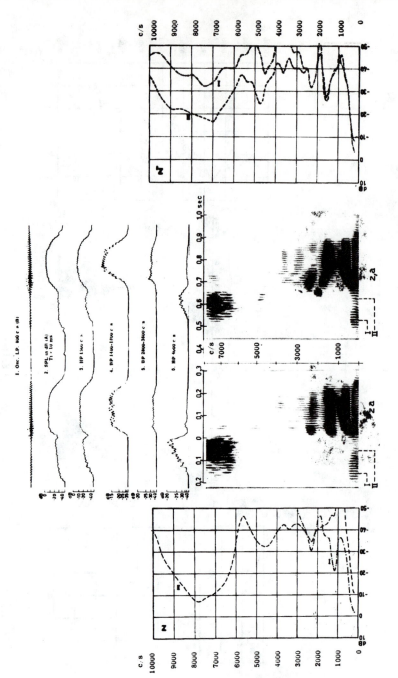

Fig. A.13-9. [za], [z,a].

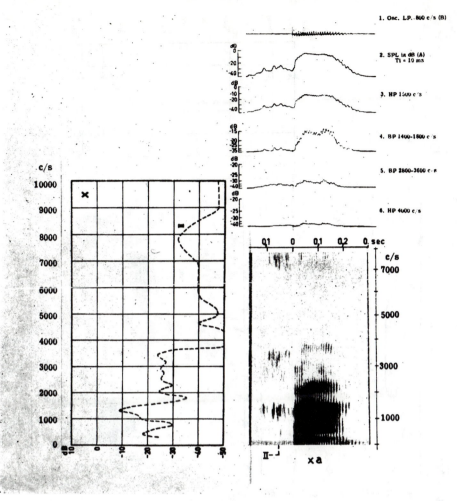

1. Osc. LP. 800 c/s (B)

2. SPL in dB (A)
   Ti = 10 mS

3. HP 1500 c/s

4. BP 1400-1800 c/s

5. BP 2800-3600 c/s

6. HP 4000 c/s

Fig. A.13-10. [xa].

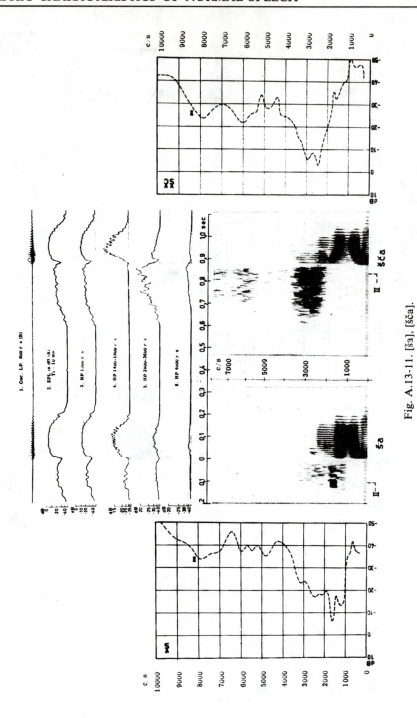

Fig. A.13-11. [ša], [šča].

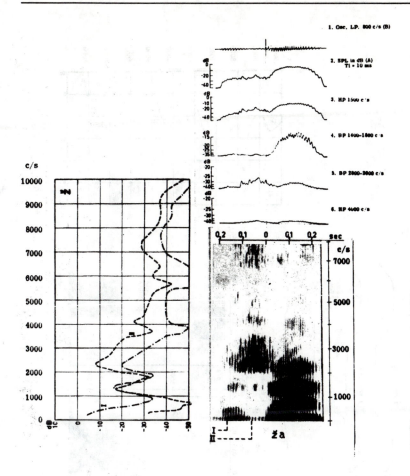

Fig. A.13-12. [ža].

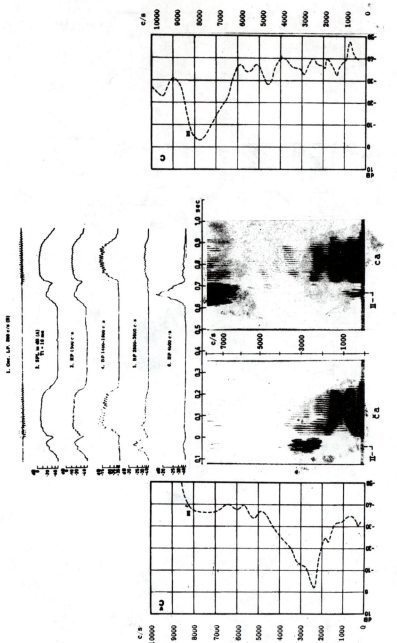

Fig. A.13-13. [ča], [ca].

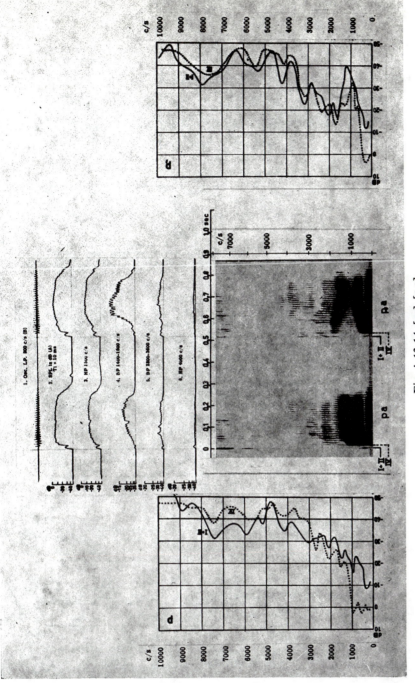

Fig. A.13-14. [pa], [p,a].

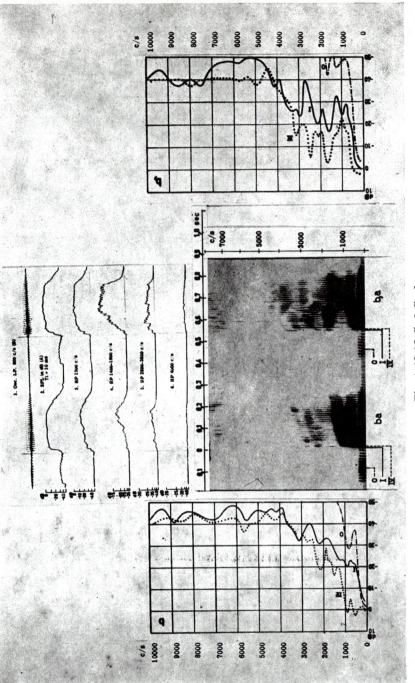

Fig. A.13-15. [ba], [b,a].

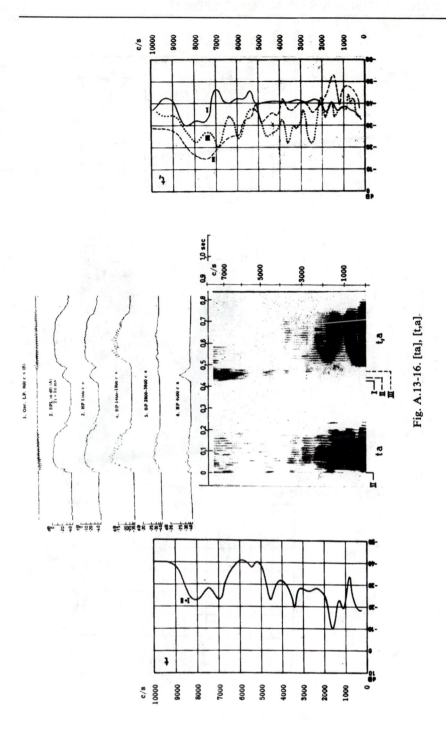

Fig. A.13-16. [ta], [t,a].

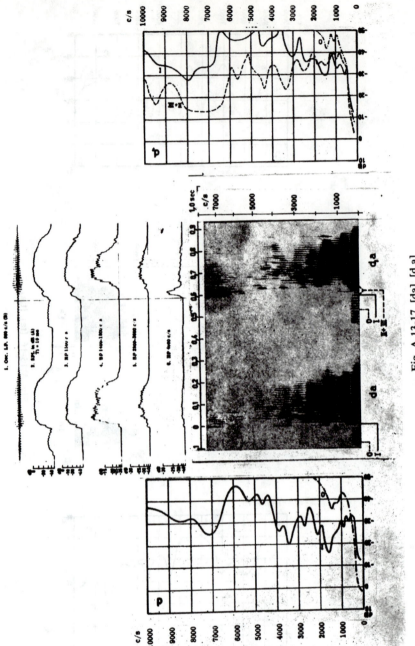

Fig. A.13-17. [da], [d.a].

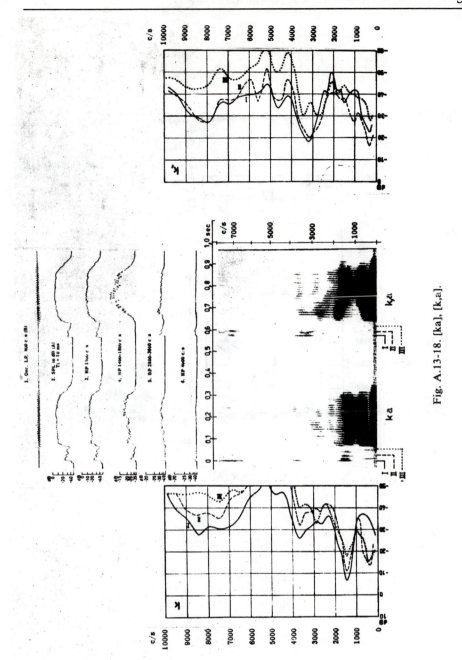

Fig. A.13-18. [ka], [k,a].

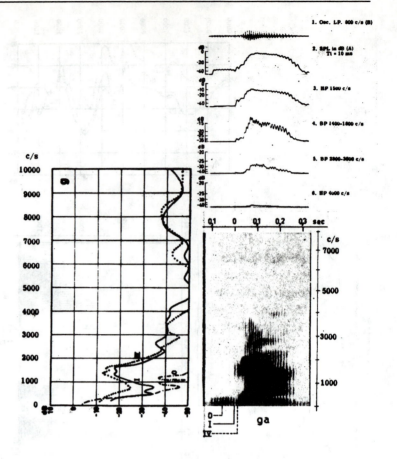

Fig. A.13-19. [ga].

I. SPEECH ANALYSIS

A. STOPS IN CV-SYLLABLES
G. Fant

Introduction

The following study is an attempt to analyze a spectrographic material on stops in CV-syllables in terms of measurable pattern characteristics that can be given a phonetic interpretation. Several aspects are treated:

(1) Segment durations.

(2) Spectral patterns.

(3) Coarticulation and syllable organization.

(4) Discussion of data with respect to production theory.

(5) Discussion of data with respect to perception and feature correlates.

Since the material is limited to one speaker this is a pilot study which exemplifies what problems can be treated and how they can be attacked. The results are discussed in relation to established theory and should have some significance for synthesis strategies as well as for general phonetic theory.

Material

The six Swedish stops [k][p][t][b][d][g] in syllable initial position were combined with each of the nine long vowels [u:][o:][a:][ɛ:][e:][i:] [y:][ʉ:][ø:]. These CV-syllables were spoken in isolation by Björn Lind-blom at regular intervals of about 2 seconds. The complete set of spectrograms was published by Fant, Lindblom, and Mártony (1963). Part of the spectrographic material has appeared in other publications, Fant (1957/68) and Fant (1968). The voiced and unvoiced stops before the vowels [a:] [i:][ø:] and [u:] are illustrated here in Figs. I-A-1 - I-A-4.

Some theory, data, and discussion on segment durations

A fully developed unvoiced stop in stressed, initial position can be decomposed in five successive segments, Fant (1968). These are:

(1) Occlusion, voiced or silent.

(2) Transient. This is the response of the vocal tract to the pressure release, exclusive of any turbulence effects. The duration of the transient phase is that of the time constants of vocal resonances. It is of the order of 2-30 ms and generally less than 10 ms. The formant structure of the transient phase is often obscured by highly time-varying effects and by the same zero function as fricative segments.

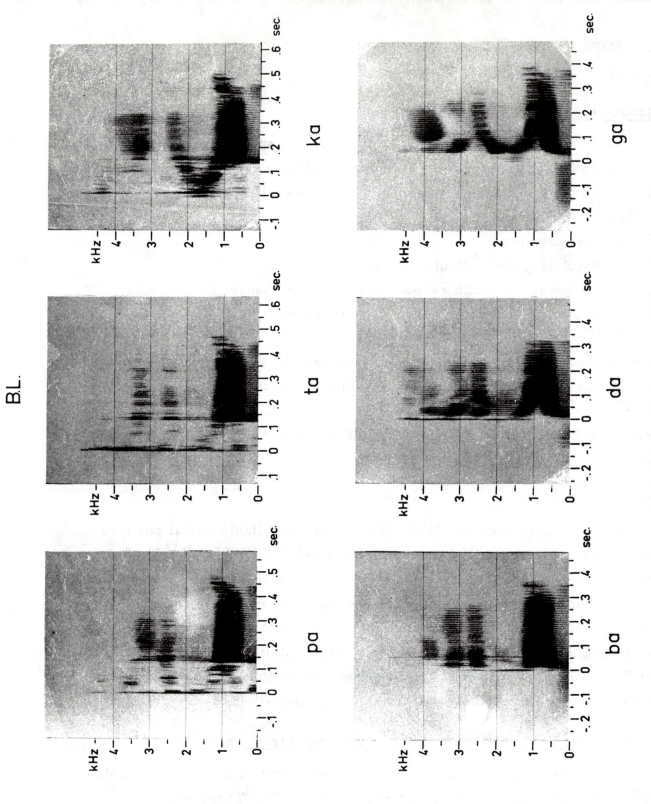

Fig. I-A-1.   Spectrograms of [p][t][k][b][d][g] before the vowel [a:].   Subject B.L.

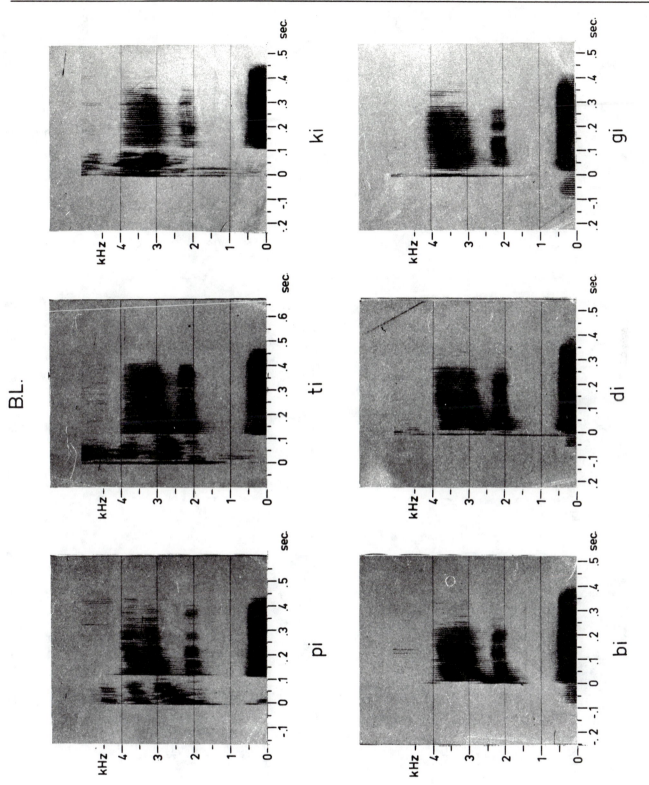

Fig. I-A-2.   Spectrograms of [p][t][k][b][d][g] before the vowel [i:].   Subject B.L.

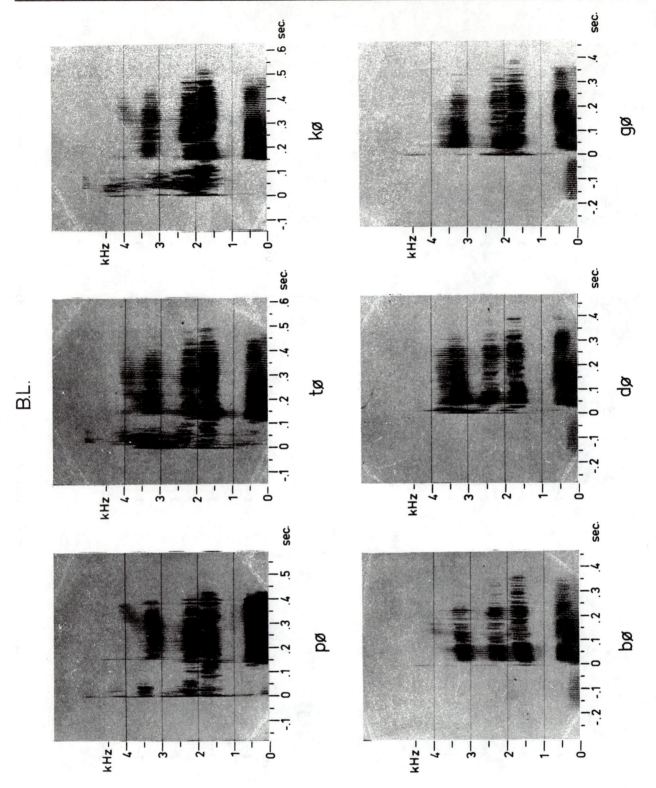

Fig. I-A-3.   Spectrograms of [p][t][k][b][d][g] before the vowel [ǿ:].   Subject B.L.

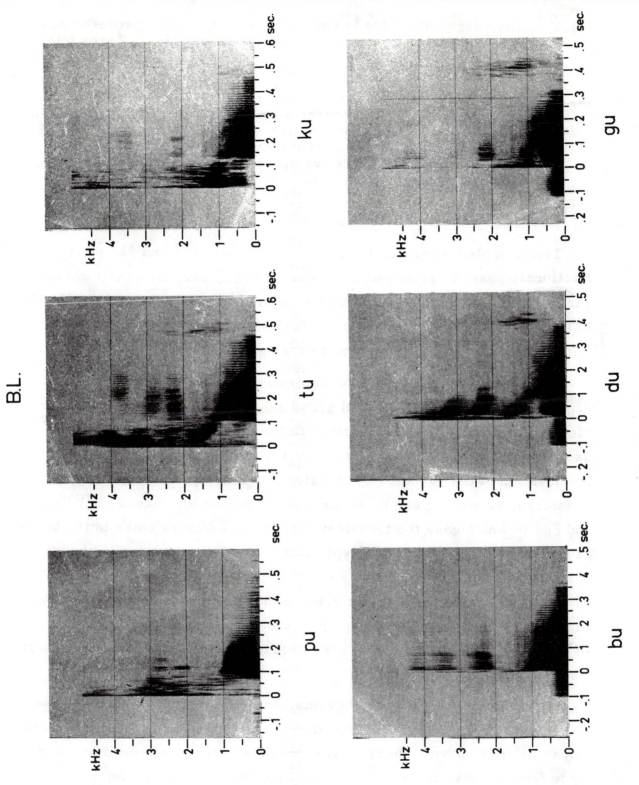

Fig. A-4.   Spectrograms of [p][t][k][b][d][g] before the vowel [u:].   Subject B.L.

(3) Fricative segment. This is characterized by a noise produced at the consonantal constriction as in a homorganic fricative. Zeros interact so as to cancel "back cavity" formants, while "front cavity" formants prevail.

(4) Aspirative segment. This is characterized by an "h-like" noise originating from a random source at the glottis or from a supraglottal source at a relative wide constriction exciting all formants. F2, F3, and F4 are the most typical constituents. The aspirative segment can in part cooccur with the fricative segment but takes over as the degree of articulatory opening proceeds.

(5) The initial part of a following voiced sound to the extent that it is influenced by coarticulation with the stop.

This complete sequence is typical of aspirated [t] and [k] whereas the frictional phase is rather weak or absent in [p] because of the low noise generating efficiency of the bilabial structure and the rapid delabialization. In the terminology of the classical Haskins' synthesis the transient plus friction plus aspiration is treated as a single segment called the "burst".

Voiced Swedish stops lack the aspiration phase. A short frictional segment can be seen in [d] and [g]. The [g] has the most apparent transient segment which can be ascribed to the high Q of the front cavity resonance and lacking dispersion effects of the main formant. Accordingly, the duration of the [g] and [k] transients is longer than in any other stops. Uninterrupted voicing can be superimposed during all phases of [b][d] and [g] in which case the transient appears as an extra spike in the background of voicing. It is more typical, however, that voicing is absent or very weak, some 50 ms before and 10-30 ms after the transient. The period of weak voicing after the release thus corresponds to the aspirative segment (4) in unvoiced stops and may coincide with a fricative segment in [d] and [g]. We shall return to the production theory in the later feature discussion.

A first inspection of spectrograms, see Figs. I-A-1 - I-A-4, reveals some apparent aspects of the voiced-voiceless distinction. The unvoiced stops [k][p][t] have a "burst", i.e. unvoiced segment defined by the distance from release transient to the full voicing onset in the following vowel which is of the order of 125 ms compared with 10-25 ms for the corresponding segment in [b][d][g].

However, the duration of the voiced part of the vowel is approximately the same after all stops, voiced as well as unvoiced. Thus the temporal organization is not simply a matter of delay in voicing in [k][p][t] compared with [b][d][g] at the expense of the vowel length.

Table I-A-1.A provides quantitative data on these segmental aspects.
The observed differences between vowel lengths in voiced and unvoiced
contexts and with respect to the labial dental or velar place of stop articulation are rather small and need to be checked by studies on larger materials
involving several speakers. Our data indicate that open vowels are somewhat shorter than close vowels in this context, contrary to established
rules of vowel length increasing with degree of opening, Elert (1964) and
Lindblom (1968).

TABLE I-A-1.A

Vowel durations in CV (C = stop) syllables

		ms
Mean values all contexts	[i]	350
	[e]	345
	[ε]	335
	[ʉ]	370
	[y]	360
	[ø]	325
	[u]	340
	[o]	330
	[a]	320
average		345
After voiced stop		350
After unvoiced stop		340
After labial stops		340
After dental stops		350
After velar and palatal stops		

One factor that seems to add to the observed durations of close Swedish vowels is that they tend to be diphthongized with a homorganic fricative. Since my criterion for the termination of the vowel segment was the disappearance of F1 in the spectrogram the vowel accordingly incorporates any frictional termination which is voiced. As shown in Table I-A-1.B the duration of the burst is somewhat shorter before [u] and [i] than before other vowels thus tending to reduce differences in the overall duration of syllables comprising various vowels after unvoiced stops.

The main finding above that the duration of the voiced part of a vowel is not substantially influenced by the nature of the preceding consonant conforms with the observations of Peterson and Lehiste (1960), as illustrated by their fig. 4 exemplifying spectrograms of "tug" and "dug", "tuck" and "duck". However, their average findings indicate that the vowel after a voiced stop exceeds the length of the voiced part of a vowel after an unvoiced stop by approximately one-half of the burst duration or 30 ms. Their vowel lengths are about 20 per cent shorter than those reported here whilst the absolute value of their burst durations were of the order of 60 per cent of ours indicating a heavier aspiration of the Swedish stops.

TABLE I-A-1.B

Voicing onset delay in ms after release in CV syllables

	i	e	ε	ʉ	y	ø	u	o	a	mean
p	100	130	120	100	95	130	100	130	125	115
t	120	125	125	125	120	105	100	125	120	120
k	120	130	150	125	130	150	115	130	140	130
mean	115	130	130	115	115	130	105	130	130	120
db	<10	<10	<10	<10	10	15	0	0	15	<10
gd	10	15	30	40	25	40	10	10	15	20
g	25	25	20	15	35	15	15	20	35	25

These differences are probably related more to the complexity of the test words, CVC versus CV, than to language specific pronunciation as judged by other speech material at our disposal. Tempo and level of stress should also be considered. These conditional factors as well as the effect of location within a complex string of syllables need to be investigated further. As seen in Fig. I-A-5 aspiration is not lost in sentence initial unstressed syllables.

In these CVCV:CV words spoken by the same subject, B.L., the duration of the burst is of the order of 50-90 ms in stressed positions and 50-70 ms in unstressed sentence initial position.

Interesting material for comparison is offered by Öhman (1965). He used test words of the type CVCen (with C=g and k, V=long [ɑ:] and short [ɑ] with accent 2 word intonation) inserted in a carrier sentence (säga ... igen). The durations of his [k]-bursts were more or less constant 80 ms. When two utterances differing by the voiced/voiceless distinction of the first C were compared and synchronized with respect to overall intonation pattern he found that the instant of stop release had to come 40 ms earlier in [k] than in [g].

Öhman also claims that the same relative timing pattern occurs if the articulation of the following vowel and not the intonation is taken as a basis of comparison. This rule also appears to hold in the present CV material as shown by Fig. I-A-6 exemplifying the overlaying of traced formant patterns of [tɑ:] and [dɑ:], [kɑ:] and [gɑ:]. Here the release of the [t] is located 30 ms ahead of the release of [d] and the same holds for [k] compared with [g]. This means that the articulatory gesture after release is different in the voiced and unvoiced plosives. This difference can have two dimensions. One is that the articulatory pattern is different at the instant of release and eventually reaches the same dynamical pattern although at different times for the two stops or that the initial articulatory pattern is more or less the same, except for the larger glottal opening at the release of the unvoiced stop, whilst the offset gesture proceeds at a slower rate in the first 40 ms after release of the unvoiced stop*. The latter appears to be the case with palatal stops and possibly also for most dental stops. The terminal F-patterns are not so different comparing

---

* Articulatory data on English stop+vowel dynamics published by Houde (1967) are of some interest in this connection.

SPEAKER: B.L.

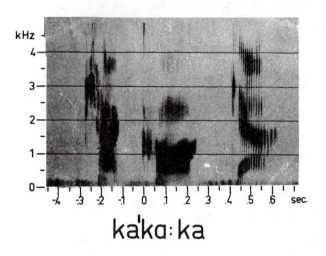

ka'ka:ka

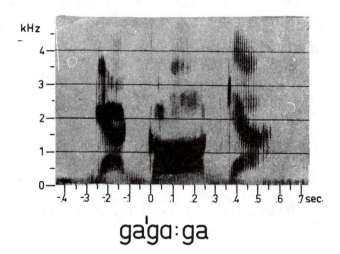

ga'ga:ga

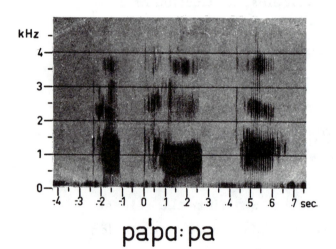

pa'pa:pa

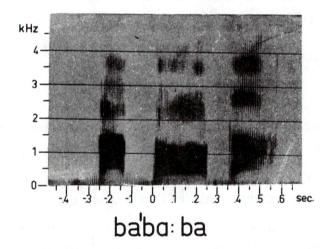

ba'ba:ba

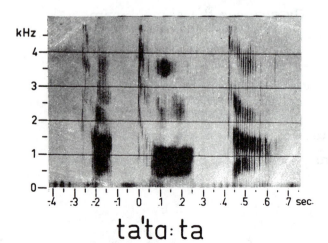

ta'ta:ta

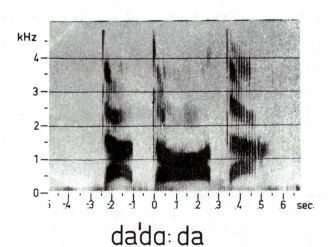

da'da:da

Fig. I-A-5.   Ca'Ca:Ca with C = [k][g][p][b][t][d].   Same subject as in Figs. I-A-1 - I-A-4.

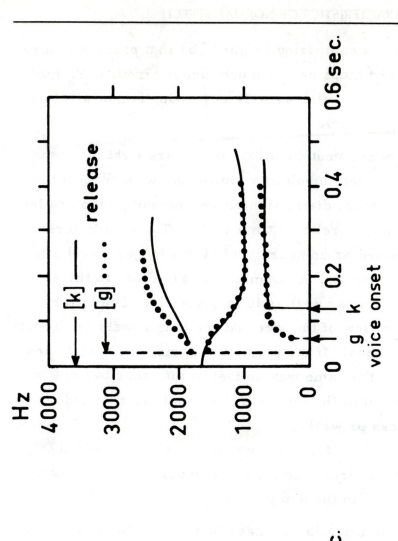

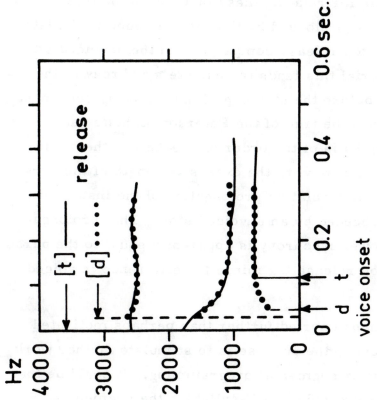

Fig. I-A-6.   F-patterns of voiced and unvoiced stops matched for articulatory synchrony.

[g] and [k] or [d] and [t] as comparing [p] and [b] in a position before a back vowel where unvoiced stops have a much higher terminal F_2 than voiced stops. This holds for Swedish as well as for English as will be shown in a later part of this article.

Returning to matters of segment durations it appears first of all that available data on the differences in voiced vowel length with respect to the influence of the voiced/voiceless distinction of the preceding stop are less variant on an absolute than on a relative time scale. Thus the Peterson-Lehiste data can be expressed as an average of 30 ms longer vowel after voiced than after unvoiced stop and the Öhman data are close to the 40 ms difference which holds in short as well as in long vowels. The latter observation is remarkable in view of the fact that the long vowels are about 60 % longer than the short ones. If the present material of CV syllables is to be analyzed in exactly the same way as that of the other two studies mentioned above we must add to the length of the vowel after voiced stop the duration of the voiceless or weakly voiced interval between release transient and visible onset of the following vowel. In all we would then have a 20 ms vowel length difference in the g-k comparison, a 25 ms in the d-t contexts, and a 25 ms in the b-p contexts.

A simple numerical rule for relating these facts would be that the vowels after voiced stops are prolonged by the same amount as the latency of the instant of voiced stop release compared with the unvoiced stop release. In Öhman's material this leads to absolute synchrony of the instant of vowel termination before the stop gap of the following consonants. Approximately the same could be true of the Peterson-Lehiste data since the difference in vowel lengths is of the order of one-half of the burst length. In our CV-material, however, the excessive length of the burst, average 125 ms, accounts for a relative prolongation of the instant of voice offset of the vowel preceded by an unvoiced stop. This prolongation assuming maximum vowel synchrony is apparently equal to the burst length minus the voiced stop release lag minus the difference in voiced vowel length.

This discussion is perhaps carried further than perhaps motivated by our meager data. However, the purpose is to stimulate further work on the formulation of rules for segmental programming. It could be that in the specific mode of reading isolated CV-syllables the segmental programming is governed mainly by a rhythmical demand of producing equally spaced, equally loud vowel nuclei. Tests on the timing of syllable production in synchrony with a periodically repeated auditory signal performed by Lindblom and Sundberg* indicate that the instant of major intensity increase in the syllable, a special case of which is the instant of switching from voiceless to voiced segment, governs the timing. These data support the syllabic timing rules proposed by Kozhevnikov and Chistovich (1965).

One typical example of the role of voicing boundary as a determinant of segmental organization can be studied in the [CaCà:Ca] (C=k, p, t, g, b, d) spectrograms of Fig. I-A-5. The time interval between onset of voicing in the first and the second vowel and between the second and final vowel is shown below together with data on the duration of the three vowels.

TABLE I-A-2

CaCà:Ca segmental analysis, time in ms						
C=	k	g	p	b	t	d
Onset V_2 - onset V_1	260	250	270	250	270	240
Onset V_3 - onset V_2	370	360	365	360	370	350
Duration V_1	85	125	75	110	85	120
Duration V_2	180	240	180	240	190	250
Duration V_3	170	180	170	160	170	170

The stability of these temporal reference points of vowel onsets holds for variations in place of articulation within 10 ms and within 30 ms for the voicing distinction. The increase in consonant length with unvoicing is somewhat larger than for reduction of the vowel length. Thus the V+C intervals of Table I-A-2 are about 15 ms longer when C is unvoiced than when C is voiced. The initial vowel is close to 40 ms longer when the consonant is voiced in agreement with previous findings. The second and fully stressed vowel is 60 ms longer in a voiced context whereas the final vowel which is unstressed does not vary much in length depending on the voicing of the consonant. The latter observation conforms with the far going reduction of the acoustical distinction between voiced and unvoiced

* unpublished data.

stops in non-initial unstressed position. The relative large effects on the second vowel could be ascribed to the added influence from both previous and following consonants. A further discussion of the k/g, p/b, and t/d distinctions follows in a later part of this article.

Before leaving the topic of segmental structure some words should be said about the terminal boundary of a vowel followed by a stop. If voicing is continued straight through the occlusion the boundary is set by the articulatory closure as seen by the termination of the F_1 transition towards base-line position. Vowels followed by unvoiced stops are terminated by an active devoicing gesture of the vocal cords which is synchronized to turn off voicing at or just before the articulatory closure. The articulatory closing gesture may well contribute to the final interruption of the voice source but this is not a necessary requirement. In heavily stressed positions the voicing has died out well before the articulatory closure.   Vowel duration is influenced more by the following consonant than by a preceding consonant, see Peterson and Lehiste (1960), Elert (1964), and a forthcoming report*.

Transitional patterns

The purpose of the following section is to discuss the material on formant patterns and transitions in the CV-material in relation to earlier studies, notably those of Lehiste and Peterson (1961), Öhman (1966), and Fant (1959).

By formant transitions is understood the dynamic variation of the F-pattern, i.e. $F_1 F_2 F_3 F_4$ as a function of time. The extent to which the F-pattern dynamics signals the place of articulation is one problem of general interest. Another is the possibility of inferring coarticulation features from F-pattern analysis. We shall attempt to compare voiceless and voiced stops in Swedish and English accordingly. As a control on some of the measurements using a vocal tract model we shall simulate transitions that are difficult to follow in spectrograms. Finally we shall discuss data, vocal tract theory, and proposed models of perception in relation to feature theory of stop sounds.

---

* A thesis study by Inger Karlsson and L. Nord support this view.

First a few words about transitions and sampling techniques. The main object of our measurements has been to sample the F-pattern extrapolated to the instant of the beginning of the transient release of the stop closure. This is not an unambiguous process. The first part of the transition after release may be very rapid and difficult to follow. A fact which often is overlooked is that a CV-transition is often complex, comprising a first rapidly progressing part related to the release of the consonantal obstruction plus an overlayed transition of longer time constant related to the main tongue body movement. This is typically the case with labials but also with alveolars and dentals.

It may be difficult to follow a formant transition in unvoiced segments but the reverse can also be true. An intense aspiration may provide more favorable conditions for F-pattern tracking than a very low pitched voiced segment. It was considered of interest to sample the F-pattern of unvoiced stops not only at release but also at the initiation of voicing after aspiration.

The collected F-pattern data on F_2, F_3, and F_4 are documented in Tables I-A-3 and I-A-4. No F_1 data are included. The limiting value of F_1 in the occlusion is of the order of magnitude of 200 Hz for all voiced stops. On the other hand F_1 at onset of voicing after unvoiced stop is generally close to the target value of F_1 except in occasional instances of unvoiced stop plus $[a{:}]$. Other aspects of articulatory movements such as tongue body place shifts, or a labial or palatal closing gesture may continue during the vowel. Obviously, a simple time constant one for each formant independent of consonant and its vocalic context is not sufficient for CV-synthesis.

The first object of the analysis was to explore how much the initial F_2 and F_3 values of a stop vary with respect to the associated vowel. It can be seen from Table I-A-3 that the extreme low $F_{2i}=1400$ Hz of $[p]$ occurs with the vowel $[o{:}]$ and the maximally high $F_{2i}=1800$ Hz with the vowels $[i{:}]$, $[e{:}]$, and $[y{:}]$. The voiced cognate $[b]$ has the same maximum F_{2i} value and a minimum $F_{2i}=900$ Hz. Such data on extreme ranges of second and third formant terminal frequencies are summarized in Fig. I-A-7.

Fig. I-A-8 shows a set of corresponding data extracted from an article by Lehiste and Peterson (1961). A first glance at the two figures reveals basic similarities; the small range of variation for dentals,

TABLE I-A-3

$F_2F_3F_4$ at instant of release

	i	e	ε	ʉ	y	ø	u	o	a	for-mant	range min-max
p	1800	1800	1700	1750	1800	1700	1600	1100	1750	F_2	1400-1800
	2250	2200	2200	2300	2200	2100	2100	?	2250	F_3	2100-2300
	3200	?	?	3200	3300	3300	?	?	3400	F_4	3200-3400
b	1700	1800	1600	1600	1600	1400	900	900	1000	F_2	900-1800
	2300	2300	2250	2300	2150	2150	2200	2200	2400	F_3	2150-2400
	3200	3300	3200	3200	3200	3050	3200	3400	3050	F_4	3050-3300
t	1800	1850	1800	1800	1850	1850	1700	1600	1700	F_2	1600-1850
	2600	2700	2700	2650	2600	2700	2400	2700	2700	F_3	2400-2700
	3600	?	?	3300	3250	3300	3200	3500	3500	F_4	3200-3600
d	1850	1850	1650	1700	1750	1800	1600	1400	1400	F_2	1400-1850
	2600	2500	2600	2500	2500	2650	2400	2400	2600	F_3	2400-2650
	3400	3300	3300	3400	3200	3200	3200	3200	3300	F_4	3200-3400
k	2100	2200	2200	1900	2000	1900	1200	1200	1600	F_2	1200-2200
	3100	3200	2950	2400	2600	2200	2000	2000?	1900	F_3	1900-3200
	3500	3800?	3600	3400	3300	3000	?	?	?	F_4	3000-3800?
g	2000	2100	2000	1800	2000	1700	1100	1000	1600	F_2	1000-2100
	3100	3000	2900	2300	2600	2100	2300	2000	1900	F_3	1900-3100
	3600	3500	3350	3400	3400	3300	?	2800	3100	F_4	2800-3600

TABLE I-A-4

F_2, F_3, F_4 at instant of voice onset after unvoiced stops

	i	e	ε	ʉ	y	ø	u	o	a
p	1900	1950	1950	1750	1750	1600	800	700	1000
	2750	2650	2500	2200	2200	2100	2200	2400	2500
	3500	3200		3200	3250	3200			3250
t	2000	2100	1900	1750	1950	1650	1000	900	1050
	2750	2700	2600	2350	2500	2250	2200	2500	2500
	3550	3600	3550	3350	3400	3300	2900	3200	3300
k	2100	2200	2000	2000	2000	1750	850	750	1100
	3050	3050	2800	2250	2500	2200	2100	2200	2150
	3600	3600	3500	3400	3400	3300			3250

the large range for velars, and palatals as a single group with the overlap of F_{2i} and F_{3i} ranges. The greater range for voiced than for unvoiced labials, already mentioned above, is found in the Swedish as well in the English data. A detail analysis reveals that the extended initial F-pattern range of voiced labial stops can be ascribed to a closer coarticulation with back vowels [u:][o:] and [ɑ:] whereas unvoiced labial stops start from a more neutral tongue position at the instant of release. A similar trend appears with Swedish dentals. The lower bound of the F_{2i} domain for Swedish [g] is also somewhat lower than that of [k]. Following the co-articulation model developed by Öhman (1967) these effects could at least in part be ascribable to the relative timing of articulatory programming. As discussed previously in connection with Fig. I-A-6 the voiced stop tongue movement is equal to that of the unvoiced one released 30 ms earlier. If we hypothesize the same semi-neutral tongue body target of voiced as well as unvoiced stops the mere translation of the vowel influence curve to the "right" in time for the unvoiced stop would reduce the effect of vowel coarticulation on the terminal values of formant frequencies.

The range of terminal F-pattern variations would be even greater if we inserted different vowels before the consonants, i.e. if both the following and the previous vowels were varied independently as in the study of Öhman (1966). Our study above can be regarded as a special case where the consonant is preceded by a neutral vowel. Öhman has shown that in V_1CV_2 syllables with C=voiced stop [g][b] or [d] and V_1 and V_2 equally stressed vowels [u:][ɑ:][ø:] or [i:] varied independently the transitional pattern in any part of the test words is influenced by both vowels and the consonant. Thus the initial F-pattern after release as well as the following transition of the CV_2 part depend on the particular V_1 and conversely the V_1C offglide transition is influenced by V_2.

One pattern aspect studied by Öhman was the consonant "locus" in the specific Haskins Laboratories' sense. Their "locus" is defined as a common point on the frequency scale about 50 ms ahead of the release which is regarded as the virtual starting point of F_2 transitions from one and the same consonant to all possible vowels that can follow. Delattre, Liberman, and Cooper (1955) claimed from synthesis experiments that [d] has a locus of 1800 Hz, [b] a locus of 720 Hz, and [g] if produced with non-back vowels 3000 Hz. The articulatory significance of the loci are claimed to be invariant vocal tract configurations. This is an over-simplification and the significance of the "locus" is primarily limited to two-formant synthesis rules. Öhman states that given a specific V_1 and C the four possible V_2 of this test provide transitions that can be extrapolated back to a common "locus" providing C is either [d] or [b] and

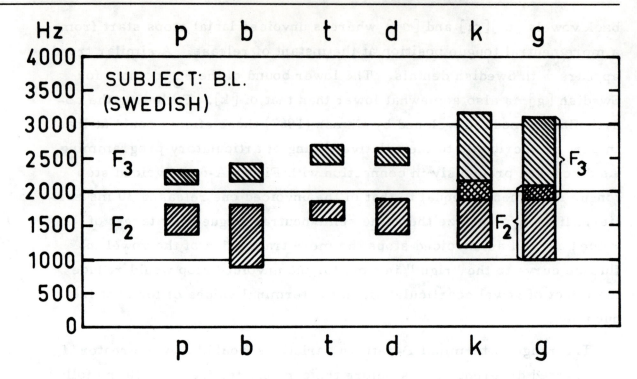

Fig. I-A-7.   Range of initial F_2 and F_3 of Swedish stops in combinations with all possible long vowels.

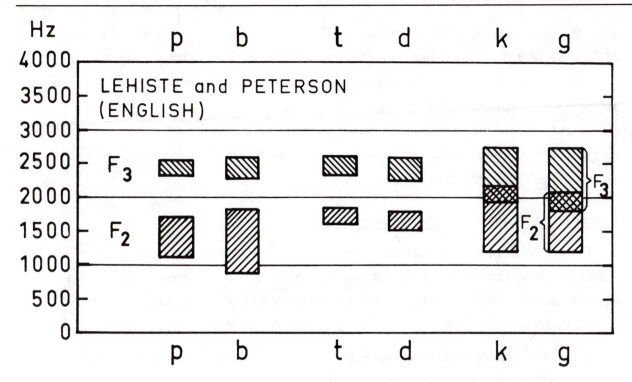

Fig. I-A-8.   Lehiste-Peterson data on range of initial F_2 and F_3 of stops.

with the locus being a function of the F_2 of V_1. However, a closer view
of Öhman's data shows that the invariance of [b] loci with respect to V_2
is not very good. A brief study of the spectrograms of our CV material
supports the notion that [b] does not have a unique locus. That [g] has
a variable locus was evident already in the early Haskins Laboratories'
work although they choose to speak of two [g] loci, one for front vowels
and one for back vowels.

Transitions studied by analog simulation

Before entering a discussion on the relative importance of various
acoustic cues for stop consonant identifications it is worth-while to consult production theory in the support of some of the more uncertain
measurements and to provide some general basis for feature analysis.

The transitions of labial stops to a following vowel are not always
easy to follow in the spectrogram. The major part of the labial opening
phase is often completed in less than 20 msec. Production theory,
Fant (1960), states that an increase in lipsection area, everything else
being equal, cannot result in a downward shift of any formant located at
a frequency lower than $c/4\ell_o$, where ℓ_o is the length of the lip passage
which in practice applies to all observable formants of the F-pattern.
However, the extent of the upward shift of formant frequencies varies
with the particular formant and the vocal tract configuration. As earlier pointed out a superimposed tongue body movement may produce a
transition of opposite sign to that induced by the lip passage opening and
it generally extends over a longer period of time. A relative prominent
falling transition may result, see [pɑ:] in Fig. I-A-1 and [pu:] in Fig.
I-A-4. The same feature if found in Danish [p^ho], Fischer-Jørgensen(1954).

An obscure detail in the [bɑ:] spectrum is the vertical spectral line
from 1000-2000 Hz in the released transient. It was observed already
in my spectrographic work at the Ericsson Telephone Co. in 1946-1949,
see Fant (1959), Fig. 42. One object of the analog calculations would
be to find out if it had anything to do with F_2 and F_3 transitions. Another
object was the study of formant transitions from [b] to a front vowel [i].
For this purpose I adopted for a simulation study with our line analog
LEA the   lipopening cross-sectional area as a function of time, see
Fig. I-A-9, experimentally determined by Fujimura (1961). The area

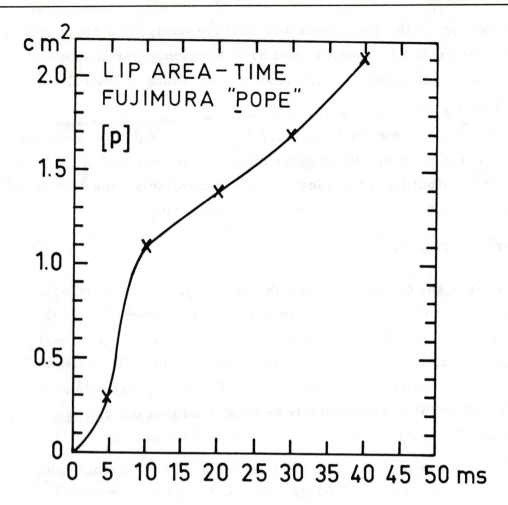

Fig. I-A-9.   Fujimura (1961) data on lip opening as a
function of time for the test word "pope".

function of the rest of the vocal tract was kept constant. One set of measurements* were made with a vocal tract area function, appropriate for the Russian vowel [a:], one for [i:], and one pertaining to the palatized [p,], see Fant (1960).

At the interval of complete lip closure F_1 should not drop to zero but to a limiting value of about 150 Hz determined by the enclosed air volume and the mass distribution at the vocal walls. Accordingly, see Fant (1960), all F_1 values were corrected by a root square summation

$$F_{1e} = (F_1^2 + 150^2)^{\frac{1}{2}}$$

The results of the calculations are shown in Fig. I-A-10 and Table I-A-5. According to Fig. I-A-9 the lipopening has reached 50 % of the final value at 10 ms and then proceeds at a slower rate. A major part of the F_1 and F_2 transitions are also completed at 10 ms after release. All transitions are positive as expected. The F_2 and F_3 transitions of [ba:] are small and it can accordingly be concluded that the release transient above F_2 should be disregarded in transition studies.

In [bi:] F_{2i} jumps up 500 Hz on the first 5 ms. The terminal value 1200 Hz is lower than the F_{2i}=1700 Hz measured from spectrograms. This difference could be explained by limited means of following such a rapid transition in the spectrogram. Another source of deviation of the model from the spoken data could be that the tongue body configuration at the instant of release in [bi:] is not that of a pure [i:] but is perturbed in the direction of a neutral position as in the palatalized [b,] of Fig. I-A-10 where the terminal value of F_{2i} is closer to 1500 Hz and the extent of the F_2 transition is smaller. In view of the wide range of coarticulation induced by a previous vowel in CVC-contexts and possible fluctuations in initial tongue configuration in production of CV-syllables it is, anyhow, apparent that variations in F_{2i} of [bi:] can be expected.

On the whole, however, disregarding the lack of information on the first 5 ms the calculated dynamical F-pattern of [bi:] in Fig. I-A-10 agrees well with measured data. One pattern aspect wellknown from spectrograms is that the F_3 transition goes on for a longer time than the F_2 transition and, with disregard to the first 5 ms, covers a greater frequency span than F_2.

---

* I am indebted to Doc. J. Sundberg for carrying out this work.

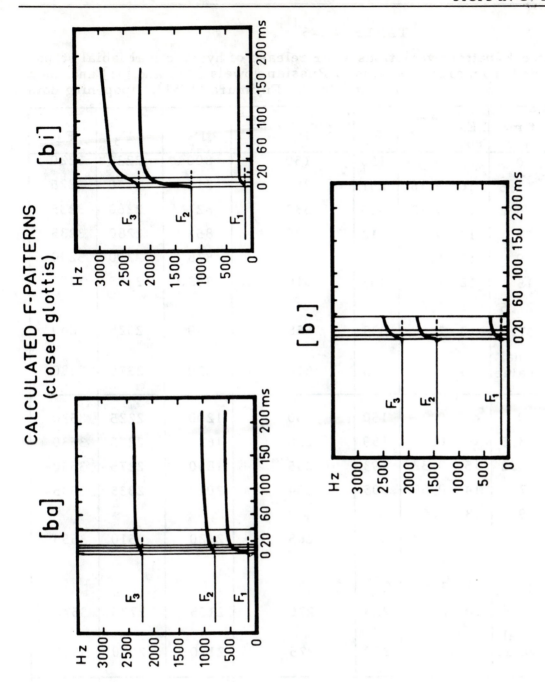

Fig. I-A-10.   Calculated dynamic F-patterns of voiced labial stops.

TABLE I-A-5

Calculated F-pattern variations after release of hypothetical labial stops constructed from area functions of Russian vowels [a:] and [i:] and the soft labial stop [p,], from Fant (1960). Fujimura (1961), lipopening data.

	time ms	LEA no.	Area cm^2	F_1	$(F_1^2+150^2)^{\frac{1}{2}}=F_1^1$ / F_1	F_2	F_3	F_4
[pa:]	0	∞	0	150	150	800	2230	3220
	3.5	16	0.16	251	293	813	2250	3225
	5.2	15	0.32	325	380	827	2260	3235
	7	14	0.65	412	439	853	2280	3235
	9	13	1.0	464	486	876	2290	3240
	15	12	1.3	495	516	898	2305	3250
	27.5	11	1.6					
	37.5	10	2.0	538	558	939	2325	3260
	final value	6		595	614	1039	2375	3280
[pi:]	0	∞	0	150	150	1200	2225	3520
	3.5	16	0.16	169	226	1625	2245	3530
	5.2	15	0.32	193	245	1860	2275	3530
	7	14	0.65	205	254	2010	2335	3535
	9	13	1.0					
	13			218	265	2120	2510	3555
	15	12	1.3					
	27.5	11	1.6					
	37.5	10	2.0	225	270	2155	2725	3570
	final value			230	275	2170	2930	3595
[p,]	0	∞		150	150	1440	2106	3420
	4.4	16/15		206	255	1600	2200	3436
	5.2	15		230	275	1640	2240	3440
	7	14		263	303	1710	2320	3450
	9	13		277	317	1740	2465	3460
	15	12		288	326	1760	2410	3470
	27.5	11		298	334	1780	2450	3470
	37.5	10		307	342	1790	2490	3470

F_1 = uncorrected, F_1^1 = corrected with respect to cavity wall vibration

As seen in Fig. I-A-2 the transitional pattern of the [pi:] aspiration is not less apparent than that of [bi:]. The main part of the F_3 transition is completed in 40 ms according to the simulation in Fig. I-A-10. In this time F_3 has moved from the 2200 Hz terminal value to 2750 Hz. This compares very well with measurements from the spectrogram in Fig. I-A-2. The F_3 transition in the following and later part of the spectrogram reaches a higher target value than in the simulated syllable which can be ascribed to the tongue body movement up to a higher degree of closure typical for the diphthongization of Swedish [i:]. However, apart from this added F_3 movement the longer duration of the F_3 transition compared with the F_2 transition is related to a higher, differential influence of the lip parameter on F_3 than on F_2 at relative large degrees of lipopening. In terms of resonator theory this is explained by the fact that F2 is a standing wave resonance of the pharynx and once the lipopening has reached a value high enough so as to not compete with the palatal stricture the F_2 influence will be minimal. Also, since F_3 of [i:] is a mouth cavity resonance it will be highly susceptible to variation in the lip area.

Experimental check of occlusion F-pattern

Vocal tract simulation is an indirect means of studying the F-pattern in articulatory closed parts of the utterance. It would be handy if a continuous tracking of the F-pattern were possible in all parts of real speech. If we limit our object to voiced stops there exist some limited possibilities of studying F_1F_2 and F_3 during occlusion providing a high frequency emphasis and extra gain is utilized in the spectrographic analysis. A small pilot study* has provided us with data that support the findings above concerning [bɑ:] and [bi:]. It was thus found that F_{2i} of [bɑ:] was 1000 Hz and of [bi:] 1700 Hz as measured from a separate recording of the same subject. During [bi:] and [gɑ:] there were prominent transitions within the occlusion.

One technical difficulty in the analysis was the need for high input levels to the spectrograph and thereby the risk of overloading with intermodulation formants appearing. Another difficulty is the low level of the voice source immediately before release.

---

* This pilot study was carried out by S. Pauli utilizing both the Voiceprint Spectrograph and the 51-channel analyzer. A separate report on these studies is planned.

Identification of spectral components

Ambiguity often arises as what is the true release transient of palatal and velar stops. As pointed out already by Fischer-Jørgensen (1954) there often occur double or triple spikes indicating a sequence of interrupted air injections through the articulatory stricture, see Fig. I-A-1*. These multiple spikes could reflect a suction reaction at the articulatory stricture by the Bernoulli pressure just as in the normal voice source. In voiced velar stops they may occur superimposed on the regular voice source operating in a breathy mode so as to damp out F1. This reduction occurs both before and after the release and is thus not in itself indicative of the instant of release. The double spikes of the [k] burst could also originate from a reaction on the glottis at the release resulting in a momentary flow reduction. Further investigations are needed to reach a better understanding of these phenomena. Another problem of interest is the F_1 locus of unvoiced stops. The subglottal impedance shunting the supraglottal impedance in a circuit theory model would account for a substantial increase in F_1 and could also introduce traces of subglottal resonances. Because of the low energy level of F1 in the aspiration it is hard to get reliable measures of an initial F_1 just before release. Just after release one observes values of the order of 300-600 Hz depending on the particular vowel, see Figs. I-A-1 - I-A-4. However, F1 of the aspiration is not very important for either perception or for synthesis and recognition work.

Acoustic characteristics and synthesis rules

When discussing the stops as a specific ensemble we need not worry about distinctive features in a general sense. We can proceed to discuss the relation of the subset [k][p][t] to that of [g][b][d] and further on investigate the triangular place relations within each subset, e.g. what pattern aspects or cues are typical for each of the members within the subset in relation to each of the other members. We do, of course, find the expected similarities k/g = p/d = t/d etc. underlying the four natural categories which are traditionally referred to as 1) unvoiced/voiced, 2) velars and palatals, 3) labials, and 4) dentals. In this limited material of stressed and isolated CV-syllables the distinction between voiced and unvoiced stops is very clear, as has been discussed in the previous sections.

---

* See also illustrations of several speakers' [ka] and [ga] in Fant (1957/68).

A synthesis of CV-stop plus long vowel syllables of the type studied here could proceed as follows:

(1) Determine first, if needed with respect to the phrase prosody, a point on the time scale where the vowel shall start. If preceded by a voiced stop this is the instant of the stop release transient. If preceded by an unvoiced stop this is the instant of voicing onset after aspiration.

(2) Choose the vowel length after more or less detailed rules starting from a mean value of 250-350 ms for long vowels according to tempo and degree of emphasis required. Add 30 ms to the vowel if preceded by a voiced stop. The instant of release transient of an unvoiced stop is placed 80-120 ms ahead of the voicing onset.

(3) An appropriate F-pattern for the whole voiced stop plus vowel sequence is generated. This can be used as an approximation also for the corresponding unvoiced stop if synchronized to have its release transient coincide with a point 30 ms after the release of the unvoiced stop. The F-pattern for the initial 30 ms of the burst is traced by rules for linear extrapolation back in time. Labials before back vowels require separate F-patterns for voiced and unvoiced stops. These can, however, probably be derived from coarticulation rules. A minor correction for the effect of glottal opening on the F-pattern should be added. An open glottis increases F_2 and F_3 by about 50-100 Hz.

(4) Make the F_0 contour synchronous with respect to the F-pattern. For unvoiced stops add an F_0 increment in the first 50 ms after voicing onset.

(5) Choose an appropriate dynamic pattern of intensity and spectral distribution of the voice source. Our speaker consistently shifted his voiced source spectral balance to a more high-frequency de-emphasized shape in the later half or third of the vowel. An aspirative final termination of voicing is frequent in the vowel [a:]. Although some of these characteristics vary with speaker the trend of decreasing vocal effort with time is typical of the sentence final position.

(6) Apply rules for spectrum and time shaping of release transients and fricative segments. These rules have yet to be worked out on the basis of production theory, Fant (1960), and more quantitatively aimed pattern matchings, as will be discussed later. In general, see Fant and Mártony (1962), the release transient should be synthesized with a DC-stop source and a friction segment with an appropriately shaped noise source. The release transient and the friction are both synthesized with the "K-filter", whereas the following aspiration is shaped with the "F-filter".

The initial F-pattern as a place correlate

We shall now return to a study of the data on F-patterns and transitions in order to evaluate how distinctive they are in identifying "place" of articulation of the consonant and what additional cues should be taken into consideration.

It is well known and rather obvious that the transitional patterns in the voiced part of a vowel after a heavily aspirated stop pertain to instances in time where the articulators have moved so far away from the consonant that their movements do not retain much distinctiveness. In Table I-A-6 [p][t] and [k] are compared in terms of F_2 and F_3 at the voicing boundary. The reduction is especially apparent comparing [t] and [p] before the vowel [a:] and unrounded front vowels. The loss of transitional information within the stop burst is specified by Table I-A-7. The amount by which voiced and unvoiced stops differ in F_2 and F_3 at the instant of the release transient is shown in Table I-A-7. The earlier discussed differences in articulation of voiced and unvoiced labials before back vowels are apparent. In other combinations the differences are not larger than 300 Hz and generally smaller than 200 Hz.

TABLE I-A-6

F_2 and F_3 differences at instant of voice onset
as place correlates within unvoiced stops

	i	e	ε	ʉ	y	ø	u	o	a
$F_{2t}-F_{2p}$	100	150	-50	0	200	50	200	200	50
$F_{3t}-F_{3p}$	0	50	100	150	300	150	0	100	0
$F_{2k}-F_{2t}$	100	100	100	250	50	100	-150	-150	50
$F_{3k}-F_{3t}$	300	350	200	-100	0	-50	-100	-300	-350

TABLE I-A-7

Extent of F_2 and F_3 transitions within unvoiced
segments (from release to voice onset)

	i	e	ε	ʉ	y	ø	u	o	a
ΔF_{2p}	-100	-150	-250	0	50	100	800	700	750
ΔF_{3p}	-500	-450	-300	100	0	0	-110	?	-250
ΔF_{2t}	-200	-250	-100	100	-100	200	700	700	650
ΔF_{3t}	-150	0	100	300	100	450	200	200	200
ΔF_{2k}	0	0	200	-100	0	150	350	450	500
ΔF_{3k}	50	150	150	150	100	0	-100?	-200?	-250

The discriminative power of the second and third formant frequencies F_{2i} and F_{3i} is illustrated in Fig. I-A-11 and Fig. I-A-12. The following general conclusions can be drawn. The main characteristic of dentals compared with labials is the 350-500 Hz. higher F_{3i}. Dentals may have higher F_{2i} than labials if compared in context with the same vowel. The palatal [k] and [g] before the unrounded front vowels [ɨ][e] and [ɛ:] comprise a peripherally located subset of higher F_{3i} and also somewhat higher F_{2i} than any dental. The [k] and [g] before rounded front vowels [y:] [ʉ:] and [ø:] differ from labials and dentals by a somewhat higher F_{2i} only. The velar [k] and [g] before the back vowel [a:] has a lower F_{3i} than any labial plus vowel.

It is interesting to note that the initial F_2F_3 pattern differentiates unvoiced stops somewhat better than voiced stops which is fully in line with the previously inferred finding that at the instance of release the unvoiced stops appear to be less coarticulated with the following vowel than is corresponding voiced stops. This is also apparent by the smaller spread of the unvoiced data with respect to vowel context as already pointed out in connection with Fig. I-A-7. The detail data on the unvoiced-voiced differences in F_{2i} and F_{3i} are given in Table I-A-8. The negative values of $F_{3p}-F_{3b}$ are ascribable to the difference in coarticulation as is typically $F_{2p}-F_{2b}$ of [u:][o:] and [a:]. It should be kept in mind that the glottal shunt contributes to the trend of positive signs of the data with an average amount of the order of +100 Hz.

Thus with the exception of the infiltration of [gu:] and [gʉ:] in the labial area in Fig. I-A-10 all dentals are confined to one area of the place and all labials are confined to a separate area and the velar-palatals to a large range of peripheral locations outside these areas. For the corresponding unvoiced stops, Fig. I-A-11, there is no overlapping. The vowel targets are included in Fig. I-A-10 so as to allow a derivation of the direction of CV-transitions.

Spectral energy cues. General feature discussion

An effective approach for testing the relevance of these transitional cues is to look up pairs of consonants in the same vowel context where the F-pattern data are the same or almost the same and then see what other cues there are to note. This technique was used by Öhman (1966) in his V_1CV_2 studies. He found that the CV_2 part of [ybo] was the same

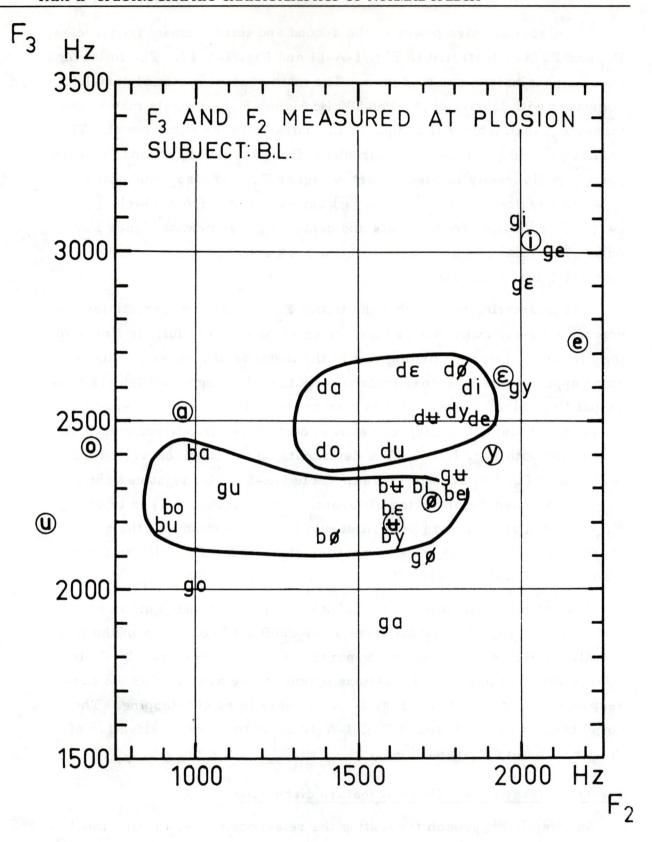

Fig. I-A-11.   Initial F_2 and F_3 of voiced Swedish stops, subject B.L.
The vowel targets are indicated in the figure.

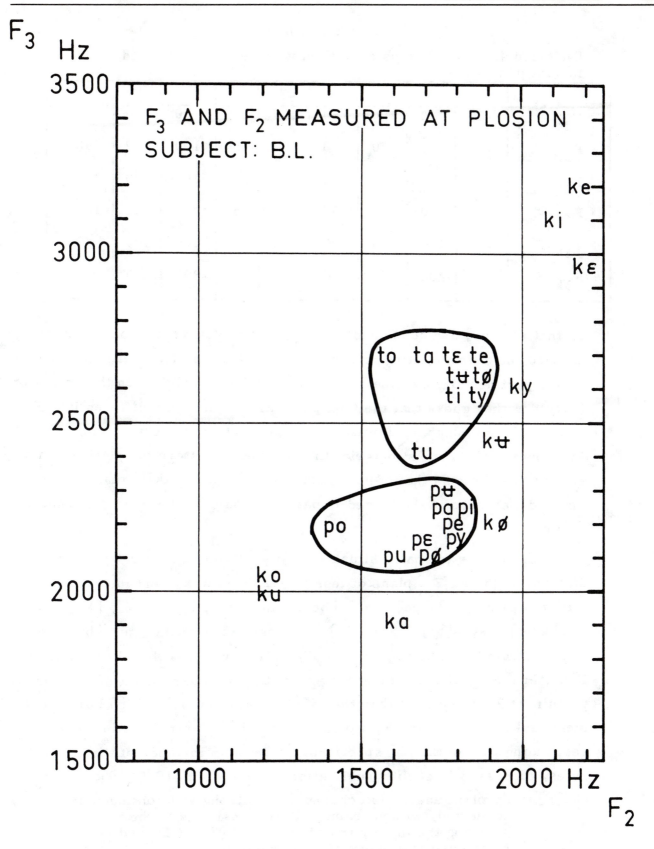

Fig. I-A-12.   Initial F_2 and F_3 of unvoiced Swedish stops, subject B. L.
The vowel targets are indicated in the figure.

TABLE I-A-8

Unvoiced and voiced stops compared with respect to F_2 and F_3 at instant of release

	i	e	ε	ʉ	y	∅	u	o	ɑ
$F_{2p}-F_{2b}$	100	0	100	150	200	300	700	500	750
$F_{3p}-F_{3b}$	-50	-100	-50	0	50	-50	-100	?	-150
$F_{2t}-F_{2d}$	-50	-50	150	0	50	0	100	200	300
$F_{3t}-F_{3d}$	0	200	100	150	100	50	0	300	100
$F_{2k}-F_{2g}$	100	100	200	100	0	200	100	200	0
$F_{3k}-F_{3g}$	0	200	50	100	0	100	-300?	0?	0

as that of [ygo] and concluded that V_1 and the V_1C transitional pattern carried the differentiating information. It would be interesting to check this experimentally by time segmentation of V_1C and CV_2 in the occlusion. I would rather guess that the CV_2 part carries the main differentiating information although not immediately apparent from the spectrogram. Moreover, in Öhman's material the stylized F-pattern of [∅go] is almost exactly the same as that of [∅bo]. It does not seem likely that some small differences in the traced F-patterns could be the main differentiating cue.

There exists an analog situation in my CV-material. A vectorial distance in the $F_{2i}F_{3i}$ plane of less than 250 Hz was found in the following minimal pairs [ko]-[po], [go]-[bo], [kʉ]-[pʉ], [gʉ]-[bʉ], [kʉ]-[tʉ], [gu]-[bu], [ky]-[ty], [gy]-[dy]. A closer view of the [gu]-[bu] distinction from the spectrograms of Fig. I-A-4 verifies that the dynamical F-pattern is about the same. However, the [g] burst has a much more prominent F2 component than that of [b]. Moreover, the [g] burst segment lacks energy in the F_1 range whereas F1 is prominent in the corresponding part of the [b] spectrum. This is an instance of the general rules, discussed in earlier publications, Fant (1958)(1960)(1968).

[k][g]   Spectral energy is concentrated, strong and continuously connected, without rapid initial transitions to the formant carrying the main pitch of the vowel (F_2 or F_3 and even F_4 in case of a prepalatal articulation).

[p][b]   Spectral energy is weak, more spread than in [k][g], and with an emphasis on lower frequency than [t][d]. Initial transitions are rapid and rising.

[t][d]   Spectral energy is spread, generally strong, with emphasis on higher frequencies than in [p] and [b] and extending higher than the main [k][g] formant.

An extension of the range of analysis to higher frequencies than 4000 Hz adds to the distinctiveness of these visually defined cues, mainly by displaying the high frequency components of the [t] and [d] bursts.

The statements above concerning "spectral energy" refer to the first 10-30 ms after the release which appears to carry the main information on the place of articulation. Transient burst and the first part of a vowel when appearing within this segment should be regarded as a single stimulus rather than as a set of independent cues, Fant (1960, p.217), Stevens (1967). When relating data from real speech to experiments with synthetic speech one should keep this in mind. As stated already by E. Fischer-Jørgensen (1954): "The listener does not compare explosion with explosion and transition with transition but compares artificial syllables comprising either explosion or transition with natural syllables that always contain both".

When discussing transitions it seems wise to distinguish two categories: 1) those related to the overall tongue body movement within the whole of a previous or a following vowel and 2) those related to the break of a consonantal obstruction or the movement towards closure. Those belonging to category 1) mainly reflect vowel coarticulation and are less distinctive than those of category 2). A typical example is the falling transition from labial stop to back vowel, see Fig. I-A-4, which reflects the tongue body movements whereas the labiality cues may be confined to the first 10 ms only and may not be visible in the spectrogram.

Production theory, Fant (1960), provides a basis for explanation of the origin of the general characteristic discussed above and is the starting point for derivation of synthesis strategies. Thus the main formant of the [k][g] sounds derives from the cavity in front of the tongue constriction and is represented by a free pole. The diffuse spectrum of [p] and [b] release originates from the lack of any front cavity. At release the dispersion effect is pronounced, pole frequencies rapidly moving in positive direction away from associated zeros which neutralize the poles before release.

The [k][g], on the other hand, have a free pole before release. In the critical segment after release this pole cannot display very rapid movements. The [t] and [d] have a small and narrow front channel behind the source which is associated with a high-pass sound filtering.

TABLE I-A-9

Burst formant areas of [k] and [g]

	i	e	ε	ʉ	y	ø	u	o	α
[k]	3200	3200	3100	2500	2600	2000	1300	1200	1750
[g]	3400	3500	3000	2200	2600	1950	1050	1000	1650
	F_3F_4	F_3F_4	F3	F3	F3	F_2F_3	F2	F2	F2

TABLE I-A-10

Target values of subject's formant frequencies towards the end of the vowel

	i	e	ε	ʉ	y	ø	u	o	α
F_1	225	300	370	250	200	375	250	350	650
F_2	2100	2200	2000	1600	1900	1700	550	600	950
F_3	3050	2700	2600	2100	2850	2300	2200	2500	2500
F_4	3600	3500	3500	3050	3200	3200	3000	2850	3050

The mean frequency of the [k] and [g] bursts and their F-pattern
associations in different vowel contexts have been measured and the data
are presented in Table I-A-9.   The data vary over a 2500 Hz range from
1000 Hz to 3500 Hz.   The observed differences with respect to voicing
are not very significant in view of the limited data.

Secondary correlates to the place of articulation for [k] and [g] are
the approximately 30 ms delay from release transient to the appearance
of the formant structure in the following vowel.   The F_1 transitions after
[b][d] and [g] are not much different except that the F_1 rise tends to be
somewhat slower after [g].   The differences in vowel targets conditioned
by the particular place of articulation of the consonant could be measured
but appear to be too small to be of any appreciable perceptual significance.
The F_0 cues also contribute.   Approximate vowel targets for the subject
B.L. are shown in Table I-A-10.   They pertain to the final part of the
vowel, in case of close vowels (lowest level F_1) to the diphthongal termination.   In [u:] and [ʉ:] this is a lip closure which accounts for the
falling F_2 and F_3.   For [i:] and [y:] the diphthongal element is made

with the tongue pressing harder against the palate. This accounts for the rise in F_3 at constant lipopening in [y:] and [i:]. A more detailed discussion of Swedish vowels was given by Fant (1969).

Intensity-frequency sections of the transient and burst spectra of Swedish stops have earlier been published by Fant (1959) and corresponding data on Russian stops by Fant (1960). These data support the conclusions above and support the feature frame of Jakobson, Fant, and Halle (1952/67) as [k][g] being compact, [p][b] diffuse and grave, [t][d] diffuse and acute (nongrave).

Although Chomsky and Halle (1968) improved the feature system by introducing tongue body features separate from the place of articulation features they have not been equally successful in defining "place" features that irrespective of cooccurrence with other features retain some perceptual invariance or at least similarity. Furthermore, they are highly disputable even on the level of production control, Fant (1969). Although the feature "anterior" takes over the function of "diffuse" and thus could inherit the same correlates there is a real trouble with the "coronal" feature, which loses its physiological basis when separating dentals from labials. The class of labial consonants is accordingly selected by reference to the negative of a feature referring to activities in muscles which have nothing to do with the lips.

From the perceptual point of view the feature [+coronal] separating dentals from labials when combined with the feature [+anterior] implies a high versus low frequency emphasis. When the coronal feature is used to differentiate [-anterior] fricatives, e.g. Swedish [ʂ] and [ç], with respect to the tip of the tongue being up [+coronal] or down [-coronal] the acoustic effect appears to be the opposite, the [+coronal] (retroflexion) accounting for a lowering of the mean frequency of the spectrum. I cannot find any other spectral characteristics of the "coronal" feature that would be retained in combination with both + and - anterior. The "coronal" feature would not display this acoustical ambiguity if restricted to the class of [-anterior] consonants.

Stevens' (1967) theory of perceptual invariance conforms with the general statement on stop features above and has elements in common with that of Fant (1960, p. 217) and Jakobson, Fant, and Halle (1952/67). Thus, his treatment of velar sounds is almost the same as my earlier. His

floating reference of spectral energy with respect to the following vowel
being low in labials is valid for the short (=10 ms) delabialization segment only and requires that the aspiration is identified with the vowel.
I have a feeling that the reference to the vowel is not needed for discriminating [p] and [t]. Stevens' treatment of [g] as acoustically of
lower pitch than a retroflex [ɖ] is valid for velar [g] only. In my view
it is more natural to oppose velar [g] to palatal [g] pitch wise whereas
the relation of [ɖ] to [g] is basically a matter of spread versus concentrated energy. The [ɖ] should rightly be opposed to [d], the [ɖ] being
more "flat" and also less spread than [d]. The role of the feature "distributed" in this connection is not clear.

References

CHOMSKY, N. and HALLE, M. (1968): Sound Pattern of English (New York).

DELATTRE, P., LIBERMAN, A.M., and COOPER, F.S. (1955):
"Acoustic Loci and Transitional Cues for Consonants", J.
Acoust. Soc. Am. 27, pp. 769-773.

ELERT, C-C. (1964): Phonological Studies of Quantity in Swedish
(thesis, Uppsala).

FANT, G. (1957/68): "Den akustiska fonetikens grunder", Report No. 7,
KTH, Speech Transmission Laboratory (Stockholm), new edition.

FANT, G. (1959): "Acoustic Analysis and Synthesis of Speech with Applications to Swedish", Ericsson Technics No. 1, pp. 3-108.

FANT, G. (1960): Acoustic Theory of Speech Production ('s-Gravenhage).

FANT, G. (1968): "Analysis and Synthesis of Speech Processes" in
Manual of Phonetics ed. by B. Malmberg, pp. 173-277
(Amsterdam).

FANT, G. (1969): "Distinctive Features and Phonetic Dimensions",
pp. 1-18, STL-QPSR 2-3/1969.

FANT, G. and MÁRTONY, J. (1962): "Speech Synthesis", pp. 18-24,
STL-QPSR 2/1962.

FANT, G., LINDBLOM, B., and MÁRTONY, J. (1963): "Spectrograms
of Swedish Stops", p. 1, STL-QPSR 3/1963.

FISCHER-JØRGENSEN, E. (1954): "Acoustic Analysis of Stop Consonants",
Miscel. Phonetica 2, pp. 42-59.

FUJIMURA, O. (1961): "Bilabial Stop and Nasal Consonants: A Motion
Picture Study and its Acoustical Implications", J. of Speech and
Hearing Research 4, pp. 233-247.

HOUDE, R.A. (1967): "A Study of Tongue Body Motion During Selected
Speech Sounds", (thesis, Univ. of Michigan, Ann Arbor).

JAKOBSON, R., FANT, G., and HALLE, M. (1952/67): "Preliminaries
to Speech Analysis: The Distinctive Features and Their Correlates", MIT, Acoust. Lab., Techn. Rep. No. 13 (1952);
7th edition publ. by MIT Press (Cambridge, Mass.).

ref. cont.

KOZHEVNIKOV, V.A. and CHISTOVICH, L.A. (1965): Speech: Articulation and Perception (transl. from Russian), US Dept. of Commerce, JPRS:30, 543 (Washington).

LEHISTE, I. and PETERSON, G.E. (1961): "Transitions, Glides, and Diphthongs", J.Acoust.Soc.Am. 33, pp. 268-277.

LINDBLOM, B. (1968): "On the Production and Recognition of Vowels" (thesis, Stockholm).

PETERSON, G.E. and LEHISTE, I. (1960): "Duration of Syllable Nuclei in English", J.Acoust.Soc.Am. 32, pp. 693-703.

STEVENS, K.N. (1967): "Acoustic Correlates of Certain Consonantal Features", paper C6 presented at the 1967 Conf. on Speech Communication and Processing, Nov. 6-8, Cambridge, Mass., pp. 177-185.

ÖHMAN, S.E.G. (1965): "On the Coordination of Articulatory and Phonatory Activity in the Production of Swedish Tonal Accents", pp. 14-19, STL-QPSR 2/1965.

ÖHMAN, S.E.G. (1966): "Coarticulation in VCV Utterances: Spectrographic Measurements", J.Acoust.Soc.Am. 39, pp. 151-168.

ÖHMAN, S.E.G. (1967): "Numerical Model of Coarticulation", J.Acoust.Soc.Am. 31, pp. 310-320.

Acoustic Properties of Stop Consonants*

M. Halle,† G. W. Hughes,‡ and J.-P. A. Radley§

Research Laboratory of Electronics, Massachusetts Institute of Technology, Cambridge, Massachusetts

(Received September 6, 1956)

The two major cues for stop consonants, the burst of the stop release and the formant transitions in the adjacent vowel, were investigated. Detailed energy density spectra of the bursts were prepared. The transitions were studied by means of sonagrams. Possible criteria for identification were developed and tested. In order to assess the efficacy of the two types of cue, perceptual tests were conducted with isolated segments that contained either stop bursts or vowel transitions alone. Common acoustical properties of bursts and formant transitions are noted; differences as well as similarities are discussed in the light of different varieties of pitch judgments.

THE stop sounds, /p/ /t/ /k/ /b/ /g/, are produced by a complex of movements in the vocal tract. With the nasal cavity closed, a rapid closure and/or opening is effected at some point in the oral cavity. Behind the point of closure a pressure is built up which is suddenly released when the closure is released.

During the period of closure the vocal cords may or may not vibrate; if they do, we have a voiced stop; if they do not, we have a voiceless stop. Although in many instances the presence or absence of voicing serves to distinguish /b/ /d/ /g/ from /p/ /t/ /k/, in English voicing is not crucial to this distinction. The essential difference between these two classes of stops lies in the fact that in the production of the latter more pressure is built up behind the closure than in the production of the former. This difference in pressure results in higher intensity bursts and accounts for the well-known fact that /p/ /t/ /k/ bursts are often followed by an aspiration, which is not present in the case of /b/ /d/ /g/. Differences in the spectra of the bursts of these two classes of stops and in the duration of the preceding vowel can also be observed (see below). Since the role of the vocal-cord vibrations is thus relatively less important, the traditional terms "voiced" and "voiceless" seem somewhat inappropriate and will not be used here. Instead we shall refer to /p/ /t/ /k/ as "tense" and to /b/ /d/ /g/ as "lax" stops.[1]

The acoustic correlates of the complex of movements involved in the production of stops are rapid changes in the short-time energy spectrum preceded or followed by a fairly long period (of the order of at least several centiseconds) during which there is no energy in all bands above the voicing component (above 300 cps).

This "silence" is a necessary cue for the perception of a stop sound: if the "silence" is filled by any other type of sound except voicing, a stop is not perceived.

When the stop is adjacent to a vowel, the movement in the oral cavity to and/or from the closure results in rapid changes in the formant frequencies. These rapid changes in the vowel formants adjacent to a silence are known as *transitions* and they are important cues for the perception of the different classes of stops.[2]

The rapid opening of the oral cavity is commonly accompanied by a short burst of noise. The spectral properties of the burst constitute another set of cues for the perception of the different classes of stops.

When a stop sound is adjacent to a vowel, we usually have all three cues: silence, burst and transition, or transition, silence and burst, as in "tack" in Fig. 1. Of these three, however, only the silence is a necessary cue—the silence with either transition or burst is a sufficient cue for identifying a stop. Thus, for example, in words like "task" (see Fig. 1) the identification of the final stop must evidently be attributed to the spectral properties of the stop burst; since the stop is not adjacent to any vowel, there can be no transition cue. On the other hand, in the ordinary pronunciation of words like "tact" (see Fig. 1), there is only a single silence followed by a single burst, although two stops /k/ and /t/ are perceived. The cue for the stop /k/ must, therefore, be contained in the transitions of the vowel formants preceding the silence.

* This work was supported in part by the U. S. Army (Signal Corps), the U. S. Air Force (Office of Scientific Research, Air Research and Development Command), and the U. S. Navy (Office of Naval Research); and the National Science Foundation.

† Also Department of Modern Languages, Massachusetts Institute of Technology.

‡ Also Department of Electrical Engineering, Massachusetts Institute of Technology.

§ Now at Air Force Cambridge Research Center, Hanscom Field, Bedford, Massachusetts.

[1] Jakobson, Fant, and Halle, Preliminaries to Speech Analysis, Technical Report 13, Acoustics Laboratory, Massachusetts Institute of Technology, May, 1952, pp. 36–39. The phonetic symbols used in this article are those of the International Phonetics Association (IPA).

[2] Ever since it became clear that vowels are products of the resonances of different configurations of the vocal tract, it has also been obvious that these resonances had to change as the geometrical configuration of the vocal tract changed. Not until the development of the sonagraph was it possible to follow these changes easily, although single investigators with unusually acute ears, like the Russian phonetician, A. Thomson, drew attention to these changes more than half a century ago. Thomson wrote: "Depending on the pitch of the proper tone of the mouth cavity ('pitch' refers to the second formant—M. H.) in its articulation of the preceding consonant, the vowel often begins considerably higher or lower, and then continuously and rapidly moves to its characteristic pitch on which it is held for a relatively long time. Towards the end, as it approaches the following consonant, the vowel again rapidly rises or drops, depending on the shape of the resonator characteristic of that consonant . . . even in the central part of the vowel there is no complete constancy in pitch. The same movement from the characteristic pitch of the preceding consonant to that of the following consonant continues here too." A. I. Thomson, Russ. Filol. Vestnik 54, 231 (1905).

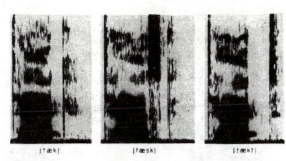

FIG. 1. Sonagrams of the words "tack" "task" "tact" (male speaker *G*) illustrating the role that transitions and bursts play in the perception of stops. In the /k/ of "tack" both transition and burst are present; in that of "task" only the burst is present; while in that of "tact" the transition alone is present.

The objective of the research reported below was to study the burst and transition separately in order to establish ways in which they could be used in a mechanical identification procedure.

SPECTRAL PROPERTIES OF STOP BURSTS

For this phase of the study our corpus consisted of monosyllabic words spoken in isolation by two males and one female. The list of words contained the six stops of English in position before and after the vowels /i/ /ɪ/ /ʌ/ /ɑ/ /u/. In addition, the list contained the voiceless stops in nonvocalic contexts, e.g., in the word "whisk," as well as words ending in the vowels /i/ /u/ /ɑ/.

Since we propose to study the bursts in isolation, the question might well be raised: Is a listener able to identify stop bursts isolated from their context as /p/ /t/ or /k/? We tried to answer this question by performing the following experiment. Words ending in stops produced with a burst and without vocal-cord vibration ("leap," for example) were selected from the corpus. The first 20 msec of each stop burst was gated out and rerecorded. Care was taken not to introduce any perceptible gating transients. The gated stop bursts were presented to listeners with instructions to judge them as /p/ /t/ or /k/. In the initial experiment, we experienced great difficulty in obtaining a reasonable response from our subjects, but with a certain amount of training it was possible to elicit fairly consistent responses. Our five best subjects gave the following percentages of correct responses: 65, 70, 75, 80, and 96. The last three subjects had had a considerable amount of experience with bursts in isolation; the first two subjects had received only a few minutes of instruction before the test. Since the percentages of correct responses of these five subjects were at least twice the percentages that might be obtained by guessing, we concluded that the bursts in isolation are identifiable as particular stops by listeners.

We hypothesized that the clues that make possible the identification of the bursts as different stops, reside in the spectrum. Consequently, we prepared detailed spectra of the stop bursts of all the words in our corpus. The first 20 msec of each stop burst, or the interval from the onset of the burst to the onset of the vowel—whichever was shorter—was fed into a filter of fixed band width whose center frequency was continuously variable over the range from 250 cps to 10 000 cps. For our filter we used a Hewlett Packard 300 A wave analyzer modified so that its band width was approximately 150 cps. The output of the wave analyzer was amplified, full-wave rectified, and integrated, and the resultant dc voltage was fed to a holding circuit and meter.[3] Samples of spectra are shown in Figs. 2, 3, and 4.

In examining the spectra, we note that the three classes of stops associated with different points of articulation differ from each other as follows:

/p/ and /b/, the labial stops, have a primary concentration of energy in the low frequencies (500–1500 cps).

/t/ and /d/, the postdental stops, have either a flat spectrum or one in which the higher frequencies (above 4000 cps) predominate, aside from an energy concentration in the region of 500 cps.

/k/ and /g/, the palatal and velar stops, show strong concentrations of energy in intermediate frequency regions (1500–4000 cps).

The differences among the various speakers were not very regular or marked. Much greater were the differences in the spectra of tense and lax stops. Since most of our lax stops were pronounced with vocal-cord vibration their spectra contained a strong low-frequency component. This component does not appear in the examples in Figs. 2, 3, and 4, because we passed all lax stops through a 300 cps high-pass filter before measuring them. The lax stops also show a significant drop in level in the high frequencies. This high-frequency loss is a consequence of the lower pressure associated with the production of lax stops and is therefore a crucial cue for this class of stops.

The most striking differences, however, were found in spectra of /k/ and /g/ in position before different vowels. Before front vowels (i.e., vowels having a second formant above 1200–1500 cps) the spectral peak of the bursts was in the region between 2000 and 4000 cps; before back vowels (second formant below 1200 cps) the spectral peaks were at much lower frequencies. These differences are not surprising, since it is well known that in English the phonemes /k/ and /g/ have two distinct contextual variants; one, before front vowels, produced with a closure nearer the front of the vocal cavity, and the other, before back vowels, produced with a closure more to the rear of the oral cavity. In position after vowels these contextual

---

[3] G. W. Hughes and M. Halle, J. Acoust. Soc. Am. **28**, 303–305 (1956), gives a detailed description of measuring procedure and equipment characteristics.

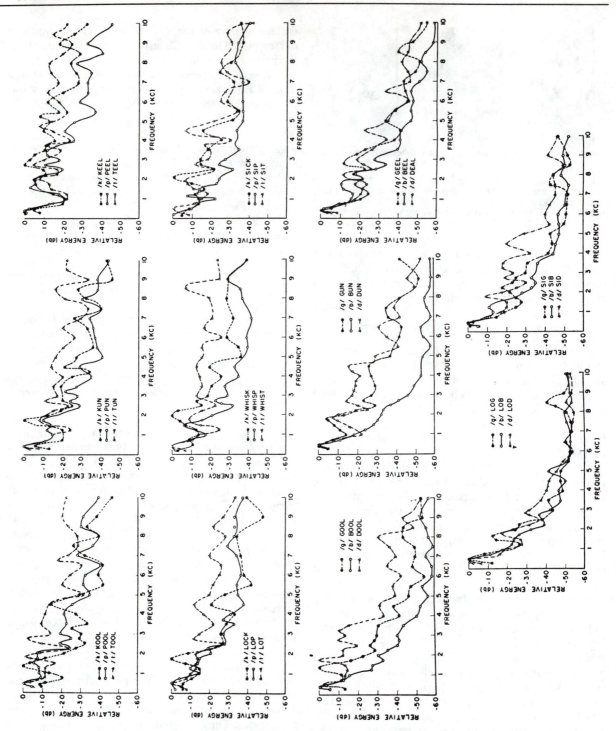

Fig. 2. Energy density spectra of stop bursts as spoken by speaker *G* (male).

differences were much less marked, which is to be expected since the "silence" between the end of the vowel and the burst was of the order of 100 msec.

A number of spectra deviated from the norms described above. Two particularly striking examples are given in Fig. 5; others can be found in Figs. 2, 3, and 4.

In spite of these divergences, the spectra possessed enough uniformity to make possible a statement of criteria that separate the spectra into three classes which are associated with the different points of articulation: First, the intensity in the 700–10 000 cps and 2700–10 000 cps bands was measured for all bursts. When the burst possessed significant energy in

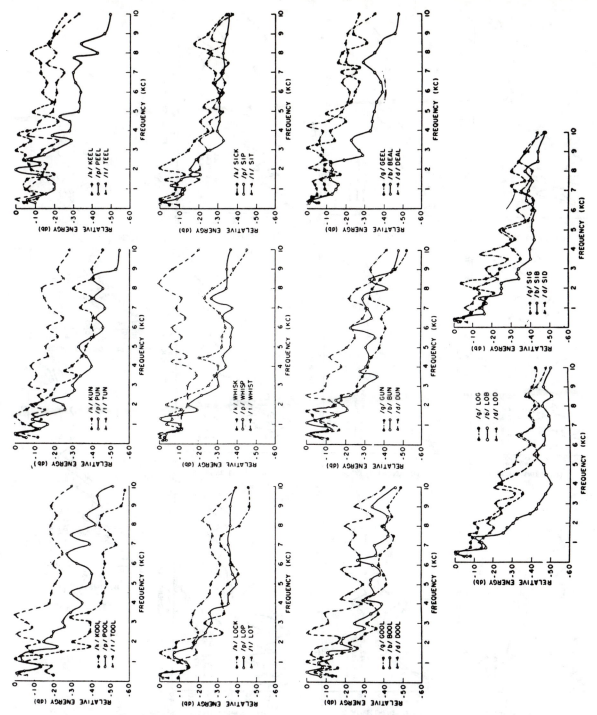

FIG. 3. Energy density spectra of stop bursts as spoken by speaker *A* (male).

the upper frequencies, these two values differed little (5 db for tense stops, 8 db for lax stops). When there was no significant energy in the higher frequencies, the two measurements differed greatly. As we have remarked, significant energy in the high frequencies is a characteristic of /t/ and /d/ and of the front variants of /k/ and /g/, while /p/ and /b/ and the back variants of /k/ and /g/ are characteristically weak in the high frequencies. We subjected our entire catalog of sounds to these two measurements and obtained correct classifications in 95% of the cases.

This step classified all the sounds into two classes; one, which we shall call the *acute* class, contained /t/ /d/ and the front variants of /k/ and /g/; the

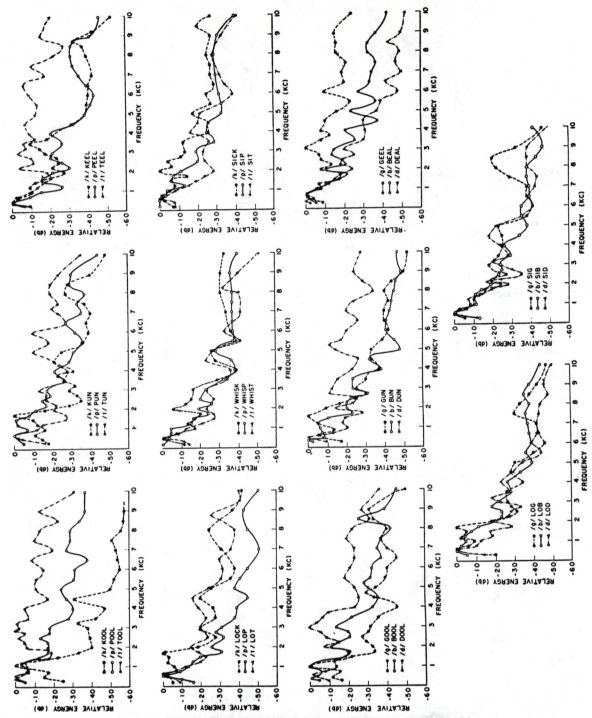

FIG. 4. Energy density spectra of stop bursts as spoken by speaker *R* (female).

other, which we shall call the *grave* class, contained /p/ and /b/ and the back variant of /k/ and /g/.[4] Acute /k/ and /g/ variants were rare in final position due to the "silence" that separates the burst from the preceding vowel. The next task involves subdividing

these two classes again into two; thus obtaining the correct identification of the stops. In order to do this we found it necessary to apply a different procedure for the grave consonants than for the acute.

For the grave consonants, we noted the difference in levels between the two most intense spectral maxima and plotted it as a function of the frequency position

[4] See R. Jakobson *et al.*, reference 1, pp. 26–36, for an explanation of the terms "grave" and "acute."

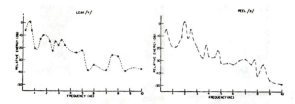

FIG. 5. Deviant spectra of stop bursts /k/ in "leak" (male speaker G) and /p/ in "peal" (male speaker A).

of the maximum of highest frequency. Such a plot is shown in Fig. 6. By the simple expedient of drawing straight lines across these graphs (the higher line for tense than for lax stops can easily be justified on the grounds of correcting the effects of the high-frequency drop that is characteristic of lax stops), we obtained correct separation of 85% of the tense bursts and approximately 78% of the lax bursts. The only really bad cases are the four low /g/ in final position. No special significance is to be attached to the shape or the position of the line other than that it separates what we know to be different.

We separated the acute stops into /t/ /d/ and /k/ /g/ by measuring graphically the average level of the spectrum between 300 cps and 10 000 cps and comparing it with the average level of the spectrum between 2 kc and 4 kc. Since /k/ and /g/ had an energy concentration in the central frequencies, the spectrum level in these frequencies considerably exceeded (5 db for tense stops, 8 db for lax stops) the average level of the entire spectrum. These values yielded the correct classification in approximately 85% of the cases. This procedure was very efficient in the case of the tense stops; for the lax stops it was not quite as reliable.[5]

TRANSITIONS

The other major class of cue that is important in the identification of the stop consonants is the transitions in the formants of the adjacent vowel. In recent years, a great deal of valuable information concerning this class of cue has been gathered by the researchers at the Haskins Laboratories in their work on the perception of synthetic speech stimuli in which certain features were systematically varied.[6] The problem, as we saw it, was to determine to what extent the uniformities observed with synthetic stimuli were applicable to natural speech.

We approached this problem from two directions: (1) by studying a large number of spectrograms and attempting to correlate the observed formant transitions with the stop that was uttered by the speaker;

and (2) by conducting perceptual tests that were similar to those carried out by the Haskins group except that natural speech was used in place of synthetic stimuli.

Spectrographic Studies[7]

For examining the transitions, the principal tool was a Kay Electric sonagraph. The sonagraph has certain limitations for a study of this kind, the most serious of which are the restricted range of automatic gain control and the fixed band widths of its analyzing filter which make it impossible to obtain clearly defined formants for certain speakers. Nevertheless, in the majority of our samples the presentation was quite satisfactory.

The corpus in this study consisted of words, primarily monosyllables, in which the English vowels /i/ /ɪ/ /e/ /ɛ/ /æ/ /ɑ/ /ʌ/ /ɔ/ /o/ /u/ and /ʊ/ were combined with the six stops in initial and final position. The list was read twice by three males and one female whose dialects varied somewhat.

Our first problem, how to define a transition, illustrates well the difficulties that are encountered in the study of natural speech, but can easily be avoided when one has control over the stimulus.[8] In the sonagrams, shown in Fig. 7, there are a number of stop transitions that differ greatly in duration, rate of change, and their terminal (beginning and end) points. In Fig. 7(a), the final transition is considerably longer than 50 msec. The stop transition cannot be distinguished here from the change in the position of the vowel formants arising from the diphthongal pronounciation of the vowel. In Fig. 7(b), the vowel lasts only 100 msec and it is difficult to find any steady-state

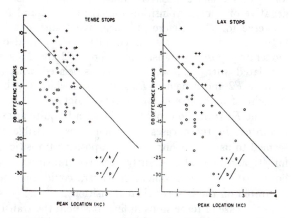

FIG. 6. Plots of the intensity differences of the two most intense spectral maxima as a function of the frequency position of the maximum of highest frequency. The straight lines in each plot divide /k/ and /g/ bursts from /p/ and /b/ bursts.

[5] Attention is drawn to a similar scheme proposed for the identification of Russian stop sounds in a forthcoming book: M. Halle and L. G. Jones, *The Russian Consonants* (Mouton and Company, 'S-Gravenhage, Netherlands, to be published).

[6] Liberman, Delattre, Cooper, and Gerstman, "The role of consonant-vowel transitions in the perception of stop and nasal consonants," Psychological Monographs No. 379, 1954; see also publications cited therein.

[7] For the material (including more than 500 sonagrams) on which the following discussion is based, see J.-P. A. Radley, "The role of transitions in the identification of English stops," S.M. thesis, Department of Electrical Engineering, Massachusetts Institute of Technology, 1955.

[8] Delattre, Liberman, and Cooper, J. Acoust. Soc. Am. **27**, 769–773 (1955).

portion or to decide where the transition begins. In Fig. 7(c), the final transitions of the different formants start at different times. Note that here the final $F2$ transition lasts only 20 msec. The initial $F2$ and $F3$ transition can only be discerned with the greatest difficulty even if the aspiration is included with the vowel transition.

All of these difficulties show that it is not easy to decide what segment on a given sonagram constitutes a transition. Specifically, it is often impossible to identify a transition by examining on a single sonagram a fixed time interval before or after a silence or by looking for certain rates of change in the formant center frequency or the formant band width.

We find, however, that by looking at sets of sonagrams of minimally different words, e.g., "seep," "seat," "seek," differences in the formant transitions, if they exist, can be easily pointed out. The transition, like so many other linguistic concepts, must be defined with respect to a set of entities that are otherwise identical.

The regularities that we observed were considerably more complex than the elegant "locus" rules that summarize the results of the Haskins experiments. We found dependencies not only on the steady-state position of the adjacent vowel, but also on the position of the stop with respect to the vowel (preceding or following), and of the feature tense-lax in both the consonant and the vowel.[9]

The least satisfactory group was that of the tense stops in initial position. For these stops, generalizations are only possible about transitions in the lax vowels /ɪ/, /ʌ/, and /ʊ/ and in the tense vowel /u/. Before /ʌ/, $F2$ and $F3$ have neutral or negative transitions for /p/; $F2$ has a positive transition and $F3$ has a negative or neutral transition for /t/; and $F2$ and $F3$ converge for /k/. Before /ɪ/, negative transitions in both $F2$ and $F3$ are associated with /p/, neutral or moderately positive transitions in both $F2$ and $F3$ are correlated with /t/, while /k/ is associated with a positive $F2$ and a neutral $F3$ transition, which can be thought of as a case of convergence. Before /ʊ/ and /u/, the $F3$ transition could not be seen in quite a few instances; in those cases in which it was visible it seemed to us to be neutral. $F2$ had positive transitions for /t/ and neutral or slightly negative transitions for both /p/ and /k/, which, however, could not be separated on the basis of their transitions.

In the case of tense stops in final position, the transitions are considerably more uniform. A partial explanation for this may be that imploded stops are quite common in final position. In these cases, the transition

[9] See K. N. Stevens and A. S. House, J. Acoust. Soc. Am. **28**, 578–585 (1956). Following common usage, we call a transition "negative" if its terminal (beginning or end) point is of lower frequency than the steady-state or average position of the formant in the vowel; "positive" if it is of higher frequency; and "neutral," if it is of the same frequency.

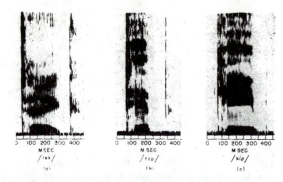

FIG. 7. Sonagrams illustrating the great variety of transitions encountered in actual speech. (a)—"take" (male speaker *R*); (b)—"tip" (male speaker *B*); (c)—"keep" (male speaker *H*).

cue is not supplemented by a burst cue, as it is in initial position. The transitional cues fall into two classes: after /i/ /ɪ/ /ɛ/ /e/ /æ/ /ɑ/ /ɔ/ /ʌ/ and after the rounded back vowels /u/ /ʊ/ /o/. In the former class /p/ induces a markedly negative transition in $F2$, which is absent for /t/ and /k/. The latter two can be distinguished by noting that /k/ has a convergence of $F2$ and $F3$. In the case /u/ /ʊ/ /o/ the cue for /t/ is a markedly positive $F2$ transition, which sometimes meets a descending $F3$, while the absence of such an $F2$ transition is the cue for /p/ and /k/, which do not differ significantly from each other.

For lax stops in initial position, /b/ has a more negative or less positive $F2$ and $F3$ transition than /d/ for every vowel except /i/, where the transitions may be similar. As we move along the vowel triangle from /i/ to /u/, /d/ gives progressively more positive $F2$ transitions, in conformity with the results obtained in the Haskins perceptual tests; but it was not possible to specify a "locus" frequency. Before the front vowels, /i/ /ɪ/ /e/ /ɛ/ /æ/, /g/ has a more positive $F2$ transition than the other two stops, while before the back vowels, /g/ has a less positive transition than /d/. Convergence of $F2$ and $F3$ is common, though not universal, for /g/ transitions, particularly before back vowels.

In the case of the lax stops in final position, the rules are fairly similar to those stated for tense stops in final position. As with /p/, there is the very marked negative transition before /b/ in all vowels except those with the lowest $F2$: /u/ /o/. Again we find something like a "locus" phenomenon in the behavior of /d/ transitions, which are slightly negative or neutral with vowels having a high second formant and become progressively more positive as $F2$ of the vowels is lower. After front vowels, /g/ has a more positive transition than /d/, and is further distinguished from /d/ by a negative $F3$, thus giving convergence. For the back vowels, however, the $F2$ transition is considerably more positive for /d/ than for /g/. In these instances, /g/ transitions cannot be differentiated consistently from /b/ transitions.

TABLE I. Responses of the listeners to syllables from which the final stop bursts were gated out. Each box contains the results of tests with syllables beginning with the consonant plus vowel sequence indicated. The vertical columns show the number of different consonant judgments made with respect to a single stimulus.

		Final stop in stimulus syllable /la-/							
		/p/	/t/	/k/	/#/	/b/	/d/	/g/	Total
Number	/p/	5	0	1	0	3	0	0	9
of listener	/t/	9	25	21	0	0	0	0	45
judgments	/k/	5	1	2	0	0	0	0	8
	/#/	9	1	6	25	3	1	0	45
	/b/	2	0	0	4	22	0	3	31
	/d/	0	2	0	0	2	29	20	53
	/g/	0	0	0	1	0	0	7	8
	Total	30	29	30	30	30	30	30	

		Final stop in stimulus syllable /li-/							
		/p/	/t/	/k/	/#/	/b/	/d/	/g/	Total
Number	/p/	26	14	20	0	3	0	0	63
of listener	/t/	3	12	9	0	0	1	1	26
judgments	/k/	0	1	1	0	0	0	5	7
	/#/	0	3	0	20	8	13	19	63
	/b/	0	0	0	6	15	1	5	27
	/d/	1	0	0	3	4	24	4	36
	/g/	0	0	0	1	0	1	1	3
	Total	30	30	30	30	30	40	35	

		Final stop in stimulus syllable /lu-/							
		/p/	/t/	/k/	/#/	/b/	/d/	/g/	Total
Number	/p/	18	2	11	0	2	0	0	33
of listener	/t/	5	24	4	0	0	0	0	33
judgments	/k/	1	1	4	0	0	0	0	6
	/#/	6	1	9	27	30	4	17	94
	/b/	0	2	2	2	7	0	12	25
	/d/	0	0	0	1	1	26	0	28
	/g/	0	0	0	0	0	0	1	1
	Total	30	30	30	30	40	30	30	

		Final stop in stimulus syllable /sʌ-/						
		/p/	/t/	/k/	/b/	/d/	/g/	Total
Number	/p/	21	0	2	9	0	0	32
of listener	/t/	7	27	16	0	0	10	50
judgments	/k/	1	1	11	0	0	0	13
	/b/	1	0	0	11	0	4	16
	/d/	0	2	0	7	19	7	35
	/g/	0	0	1	3	1	19	24
	Total	30	30	30	30	20	40	

		Final stop in stimulus syllable /sɪ-/						
		/p/	/t/	/k/	/b/	/d/	/g/	Total
Number	/p/	23	5	0	5	0	0	33
of listener	/t/	6	23	1	1	7	1	39
judgments	/k/	0	0	27	0	0	2	29
	/b/	1	0	0	24	1	2	28
	/d/	0	2	0	0	22	1	25
	/g/	0	0	2	0	0	23	25
	Total	30	30	30	30	30	29	

Perceptual Tests

It was, unfortunately, impossible to carry out large-scale perceptual tests. The data reported below are, therefore, to be taken as preliminary results.

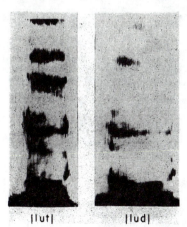

FIG. 8. Sonagrams of the words "lute" "lewd" (male speaker G) illustrating the differences in duration between the vowels preceding tense and lax stops.

In the tests, listeners were presented with monosyllables recorded by one female and two male speakers. The syllables contained the vowels /i/ /ɑ/ /u/ /ɪ/ /ʌ/ followed by each of the six stops. The first three vowels were also contained in open syllables. Thus, a representative paradigm contained the following stimuli: /lip/ /lit/ /lik/ /lib/ /lid/ /lig/ /li/. By means of an electronic gate each syllable including the open one (i.e., the one ending in a vowel) was terminated immediately after the vowel so that no stop burst appeared in the test. The subjects were asked to identify the end of the syllable as one of the six stops or as "nothing" (#). After the lax vowels, where in English an open syllable is impossible, the judgment "nothing" was omitted. The results of the tests are given in Table I.

Because of the very marked difference in duration of vowels before tense and before lax stops (see Fig. 8), the subjects had little difficulty in distinguishing tense from lax stops. Subjects never confused an open syllable with a syllable ending in a tense stop, but occasionally an open syllable was thought to end in a lax consonant. On the other hand, closed syllables, particularly those ending in lax stops, were rather frequently judged to be open. The "mistakes" are correlated with the position of first formant of the preceding vowel. They seem to indicate that negative transitions of the first formant played a particularly significant role in the identification of stops as class. Where $F1$ was high and, consequently, free to move downward, closed syllables were relatively rarely thought to be open; where $F1$ was low and its downward movement restricted, closed syllables were frequently judged to be open.

Somewhat unexpectedly, in the light of previous studies, but not quite so surprisingly, in view of the transition data reviewed in the preceding section, the greatest differences in response were correlated with the differences between tense and lax vowels. After lax vowels, the transitions seemed, in general, easier to judge correctly than after tense vowels. Especially great difficulties were experienced with stimuli ending in /k/ and /g/ preceded by tense vowels. Here /k/ and /g/ judgments were avoided to such an extent that they constituted only 5% of the responses, although syllables ending in /k/ and /g/ accounted for 28.5% of the stimuli. This compares with 25.5% /k/ and /g/ responses vs 36% of the stimuli for the transitions in the lax vowels.

As for individual vowels, we must note the extreme reliability of the judgments for the vowel /ɪ/, which is explained by the very clear transitions of this vowel; see Fig. 9. The other lax vowel in our corpus /ʌ/ was also judged with fair reliability, although not nearly as reliably as /ɪ/. It is significant that /k/ and /g/ judgments are again the least reliable. After /u/ there was a very marked tendency to consider syllables ending in a lax stop as open, which is explained by the total absence of transitions (see Fig. 10). In view of the restricted size of the sample, the tendencies in the /i/ and /a/ transition judgments are not sufficiently marked to warrant specific conclusions.

CONCLUDING REMARKS

The data just reviewed, though fragmentary and in need of further elaboration, give support to the common view that, in the perception of stop sounds, information from the burst as well as from the transition is normally required. This view, however, presents us with the paradoxical situation that what appear to be the two most disparate acoustical phenomena, formant movements and bursts of sound, are perceptually equated. We shall try to account for this by considering some acoustical properties of bursts and transitions and their relation to the perception of speech.

Physically speaking, a formant[10] reflects organization

---

[10] We distinguish between "resonance" and "formant." The former refers to a maximum in the frequency response of a resonator that is computed by taking into consideration only the geometrical properties of the resonator and by specifically neglect-

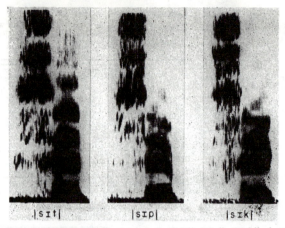

FIG. 9. Sonagrams of the words "sit" "sip" "sick" (male speaker *G*) illustrating the exceptionally unambiguous transitions in the end of the vowel /ɪ/. Note that in "sit" $F2$ and $F3$ transitions are neutral; in "sip" both transitions are negative; while in "sick" $F2$ has a positive transition and $F3$, a negative transition, and the two formants converge.

of the acoustic energy in the frequency domain and no organization in the time domain; while a burst represents organization of acoustic energy in the time domain and no organization in the frequency domain. In the case of an ideal formant, there is no energy outside the infinitely narrow resonance frequency, but the sound lasts forever. An ideal burst (impulse), on the other hand, has an infinitely short duration; i.e., the energy is present only at a given instant, but its band width is infinite.

When a resonance is changing in frequency, the formant band width increases. The more rapid the movement, the broader the band width. In the limiting case of instantaneous movement, the band width is infinite; i.e., we have a phenomenon of strictly limited duration and infinite band width. But these are exactly the terms in which we previously described the burst. The burst can, therefore, be considered as an extreme

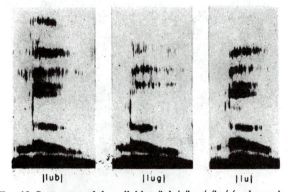

FIG. 10. Sonagrams of the syllables /lub/ /lug/ /lu/ (male speaker *A*) showing almost no differences in the transitions.

---

ing the special effects that are produced when the resonator is excited in a particular manner and its output measured by a particular device and procedure. The term "formant" takes all these factors into consideration; thus it refers to a frequency region of maximal intensity in an actually measured spectrum.

case of transition in which the changes in the short-time energy-density spectrum are very rapid and the organization of the energy in the frequency domain is replaced by organization in the time domain.

It is usually assumed that moving formants are perceived in a manner similar to that of stationary formants. This view seems to be an oversimplification, for no reasons have been advanced that would justify ignoring the fact that when a resonance is changing in frequency the problem of measuring this frequency is complicated by increases in the formant band width. It is obvious that in the case of instantaneous change of resonance frequency, it is meaningless to specify a formant frequency, or formant movement. In intermediate cases, the rate of change (or the formant band width) at which it becomes meaningless to specify a formant frequency depends upon the properties of the measuring apparatus,[11] which, in the case of interest here, are those of the human auditory system.

In experiments with damped sine waves, K. N. Stevens[12] has shown that, as the resonance band width is increased by increasing the damping, it becomes increasingly difficult to match the pitch of such a resonance to that of a pure tone. Although Stevens' experiments were not carried out with enough values of damping to provide conclusive evidence on this point, they indicate that, at some critical band width, which we estimate to be 300 cps, the train of damped sine waves can no longer be matched in pitch to a pure tone. This does not mean that all pitch judgments become impossible; for example, different trains of damped sine

waves can still be ordered from high to low with some consistency.

It is interesting that we observe similar facts in judging the pitch of vowels and consonants. On the one hand, the vowels can be matched in pitch to pure tones without much difficulty; such matches have been performed with amazing accuracy ever since the seventeenth century, when Samuel Reyherr, in his book *Mathesis mosaica* (Cologne, 1679), gave in musical notation the "characteristic pitches" (second formant) of German and French vowels.[13] On the other hand, consonants cannot be matched easily in pitch to pure tones; and all "pitch" determinations of consonants are completely unconvincing and usually refer to the terminal stage of the second formant in the adjacent vowel.[14]

One might, therefore, suggest as an hypothesis that the distinction between vowels and consonants, which is the fundamental dichotomy of phonetics, is based on the organism's ability to perform much more elaborate pitch judgments with respect to certain classes of physical stimuli (vowels and undamped or moderately damped sine waves) than with respect to other classes (consonants, tonal masses, noises, and highly damped sine waves). Formant transitions would then be intermediate structures whose assignment to the vowels or to the consonants is a function of their band width, which in turn is dependent on their rate of change.

---

[11] L. L. Beranek, *Acoustic Measurements* (John Wiley and Sons, Inc., New York, 1949), pp. 538–542.

[12] K. N. Stevens, "The perception of sounds shaped by resonance circuits," Sc.D. thesis, Department of Electrical Engineering, Massachusetts Institute of Technology, 1952.

[13] Compare C. Stumpf, *Die Sprachlaute* (Berlin, 1926), p. 148.

[14] Compare the following remark of a nineteenth century English phonetician who attempted to determine the "pitch" of consonants: "When freed from connection with any vowel, the resonance of *f* can be carried a long way both up and down in pitch without at all spoiling the *f* itself. . . . It becomes clear that the essential quality of *f* is but vaguely linked with the actual pitch of its resonance." R. J. Lloyd, Proc. Roy. Soc. (Edinburgh) **22**, 224 (1898).

VOICE ONSET TIME, FRICATION, AND ASPIRATION IN WORD-INITIAL CONSONANT CLUSTERS

DENNIS H. KLATT

Massachusetts Institute of Technology, Cambridge

The voice onset time (VOT) and the duration of the burst of frication noise at the release of a plosive consonant were measured from spectrograms of word-initial consonant clusters. Mean data from three speakers reading English words in a sentence frame indicated that the VOT changed as a function of the place of articulation of the plosive and as a function of the identity of the following vowel or sonorant consonant. Burst durations varied in a similar way such that the remaining interval of aspiration in /p, t, k/ was nearly the same duration in comparable phonetic environments. The VOT was longer before sonorants and high vowels than before mid- and low vowels. Aspiration was also seen in an /s/-sonorant cluster. To explain these regularities, production strategies and perceptual cues to a voicing decision for English plosives are considered. Variations in VOT are explained in terms of articulatory mechanisms, perceptual constraints, and phonological rules. Some VOT data obtained from a connected discourse were also analyzed and organized into a set of rules for predicting voice onset time in any sentence context.

The timing of voice onset relative to plosive release (VOT) and other acoustic cues to the voiced/voiceless distinction for plosives have been studied previously in a number of phonetic environments in English (Lisker and Abramson, 1964; 1967; Halle, Hughes, and Radley, 1957) and other languages. Measurements have been made of VOT in English plosives followed by vowels in word-initial, medial, and word-final positions in both stressed and unstressed syllables. However, the detailed acoustic characteristics of plosive consonants have not been systematically investigated in consonant cluster environments.

The acoustic events that take place at the release of a plosive consonant in various consonant cluster environments can be analyzed to see if there is any recoding of articulatory events or changes required in strategies for the coordination of laryngeal and supralaryngeal gestures. The problem in interpreting the acoustic evidence is to determine whether the changes occur at a phonological level, or whether they are automatic consequences of low-level articulatory or perceptual constraints. Several tentative articulatory and perceptual constraints are suggested by the data to be described.

METHOD

A list of monosyllabic words was constructed to include five examples for each of 25 different word-initial clusters. Words beginning with a single plosive consonant were also recorded. The five examples included four monosyllabic words involving the syllabic nuclei /i, ε, ay, u/ and a bisyllabic word that was generated by adding a second syllable to one of the four monosyllabic words. For example, the /str/ words were *street, stress, strike, strewn,* and *stressful.* In some cases a related vowel had to be used to make a legitimate English word.

The word list was randomized and recorded at a moderate speaking rate in an anechoic chamber by three adult male speakers. All words were spoken in the frame sentence "Say _____ instead" to produce speaking rates more nearly in line with conversational speech, and to minimize the effects of prepausal lengthening in utterance-final position.

Broad-band spectrograms were made of the phrases (Presti, 1966). Vertical lines were drawn on the spectrograms at the release of a plosive consonant and at voice onset time following plosive release. Plosive release can usually be determined in a spectrogram by the onset of a burst of frication noise following the closure interval. The VOT is indicated by the sudden onset of vertical striations in the second and higher formants. Spectrograms of three words containing alveolar plosives are shown in Figure 1 to illustrate the measurement procedure.

If a voiced stop is preceded by a phonetic segment that is also voiced, as

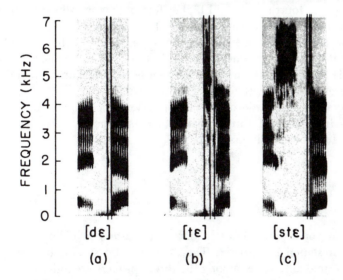

FIGURE 1. Broad-band spectrograms of word-initial plosives that have been excised from the frame sentence "Say _____ instead." Vertical lines have been drawn on the spectrograms at plosive release, at the end of visible frication noise, and at voicing onset.

KLATT: *Voice Onset Time, Frication, and Aspiration*

in the frame sentence, voicing normally continues during closure. Voicing energy can be observed at low frequencies during the early part of the closure interval for the /d/ shown in Figure 1. Indications of weak voicing may extend throughout closure and continue during the frication burst, or the vocal folds may discontinue vibration as the oral pressure increases. Since the presence or absence of prevoicing is not phonemic in English (Lisker and Abramson, 1964) and is frequently difficult to establish spectrographically because of the limited dynamic range of the spectrogram paper, any prevoicing will be ignored in this investigation. Instead, voice onset is defined to follow the frication burst in a voiced stop, coinciding with the onset of normal voicing where a number of formants are excited and visibly manifested on the spectrogram as voicing striations.

When possible, the VOT interval in voiceless plosives has been divided into two phases: (1) the initial phase, during which frication noise is generated at the expanding vocal tract (oral) constriction, and (2) the terminal phase during which the sound output is primarily aspiration noise generated at the glottis. Frication and aspiration can be generated simultaneously if the oral and glottal constrictions are about the same size, so that a visual boundary determination must be interpreted with caution.

The spectral characteristics of frication generated during the production of /t/ and /k/ are sufficiently different from aspiration spectra to determine the approximate location of the transition between frication and aspiration in most cases, as illustrated in Figure 1. Aspiration noise is weaker in intensity and tends to excite all but the first formant (Stevens and Klatt, 1974). Strong excitation of the fourth, fifth, and higher formants is usually seen in the burst of frication noise at the release of a /t/. The /k/ burst is distinguished by a strong concentration of noise energy that is continuous with the third formant before front vowels, or continuous with the second formant before back vowels. The frication burst in /p/ is frequently too weak and spectrally diffuse to be differentiated from the aspiration interval.

Spectrograms were made of 15 samples of each consonant cluster, that is, five words from each of three speakers. Measurements were made of VOT and burst duration, as discussed above.

RESULTS

Voice Onset Time

The mean voice onset times in different clusters involving plosive consonants are presented in Table 1. The data are also summarized in Figure 2. Voice onset time differences among the three speakers are indicated in Table 1. Speaker differences were generally small except that one of the speakers, DK, typically used shorter voice onset times (and a faster speaking rate) than the others.

Variability within and across speakers was of the same order of magnitude

TABLE 1. Voice onset time (in msec) for selected consonant clusters for speakers KS, RK, and DK. Each entry represents an average value obtained from five different words. The average across speakers is presented in the right-most column.

Cluster	KS	RK	DK	Average
Voiced				
/b/	12	14	6	11
/d/	23	17	11	17
/g/	36	25	19	27
/br/	16	18	9	14
/dr/	30	25	20	25
/gr/	36	32	38	35
/bl/	18	11	9	13
/gl/	34	24	21	26
Voiceless				
/p/	50	48	42	47
/t/	77	64	53	65
/k/	68	74	66	70
/pr/	64	64	48	59
/tr/	94	107	79	93
/kr/	87	89	77	84
/pl/	66	59	59	61
/kl/	81	80	69	77
/tw/	113	106	86	102
/kw/	92	97	93	94
/s/ clusters				
/sp/	14	13	8	12
/st/	28	22	20	23
/sk/	39	25	27	30
/spr/	19	19	15	18
/str/	44	39	29	37
/skr/	42	26	37	35
/spl/	18	12	17	16
/skw/	48	32	36	39

as in data reported by Lisker and Abramson (1964; 1967) and by Cooper and Nager (1975). Standard deviations of VOT measurements were computed for each consonant cluster for each individual. The standard deviation of a VOT measurement was on the order of 5 msec for the voiced plosives /b, d, g/ and about 11 msec in clusters containing the voiceless aspirated plosives /p, t, k/. Some of this variability is due to measurement errors, some to speaker variability, and some to the influence of different following vowels.

Averaging across place of articulation, the mean VOT for voiced plosives is 18 msec before a vowel and 23 msec before a sonorant consonant. The corresponding means for voiceless plosives (not preceded by /s/) are 61 msec before a vowel and 81 msec before sonorant consonants. The values before vowels are somewhat smaller than have been reported for stressed mono-syllabic words spoken in isolation (Lisker and Abramson, 1964), and they are somewhat larger than have been reported for comparable words excised from spoken sentences (Lisker and Abramson, 1967).

KLATT: *Voice Onset Time, Frication, and Aspiration*

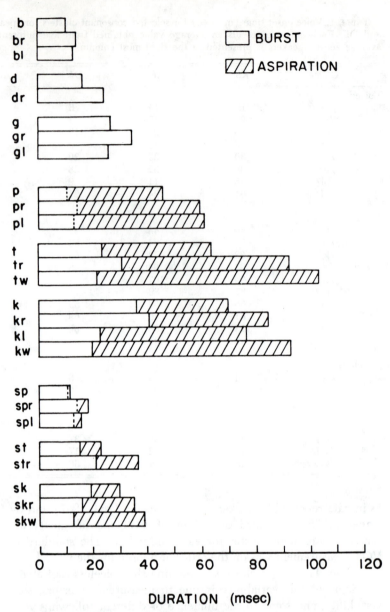

FIGURE 2. Unfilled bars indicate the duration of a burst of frication noise at plosive release. Crosshatched bars indicate the duration of an interval of aspiration. The voice onset time is the sum of the burst duration and the aspiration duration. Dashed lines separate burst and aspiration for /p/ because the burst duration was not measurable. The burst duration obtained from /b/ is used in the figure.

When a voiceless plosive is preceded by the consonant /s/ in the same word, the VOT is considerably reduced. The average VOT following /s/ is 22 msec before vowels and 29 msec before sonorant consonants. These values are similar to the data for voiced plosives. However, a brief interval of aspiration was frequently seen in these consonants, whereas no such interval was seen in the voiced-plosive data.

The data in Table 1 indicate that the VOT is approximately 10 msec less than average for labial plosives and approximately 10 msec greater than average for velar plosives. Lisker and Abramson (1964) have found a similar relationship across several languages.

The VOT for voiceless plosives was not greatly changed in two-syllable words. The VOT for /p, t, k/ in two-syllable words was on the average, 8% shorter than in the corresponding one-syllable word. The duration of the plosive closure interval was on the average, 4% shorter, and the duration of the syllable nucleus was on the average, 36% shorter in a two-syllable word.

The VOT in voiceless plosives followed by a vowel was found to be greater if the syllable nucleus was a high vowel. The difference in VOT for /p, t, k/ as a function of the following vowel is presented in Table 2. The VOT is 15%

TABLE 2. Voice onset time (in msec) as a function of the following vowel. Each entry is the average of 30 tokens of voiceless plosives not preceded by /s/. The average durations of the consonant and following vowel are also given in msec.

Vowel	VOT (msec)	Consonant Duration (msec)	Vowel Duration (msec)
/i/	78	98	157
/ɛ/	71	96	137
/ay/	73	92	192
/u/	90	97	171

longer before the high vowels /i, u/ than before /ay, ɛ/. This difference is significant at the 0.01 level. Vowel duration does not explain the effect; the average vowel durations shown in Table 2 indicate that the shortest vowels are /i, ɛ/. Lisker and Abramson (1967) reported no vowel-conditioned effects in a similar study, but their data sample may have been insufficient to evaluate this question (Lisker[1]). The VOT for /p, t, k/ is also greater by about 10 to 40 msec before sonorant consonants, suggesting that the VOT increases in general if the first formant is low in frequency for the following segment.

Burst Duration

The average duration of the burst of frication noise is presented in the list on page 692 and Figure 2 (in msec) for each cluster involving a plosive consonant. Each entry in the list is the average of five tokens from each of three

---

[1] L. Lisker, personal communication.

KLATT: *Voice Onset Time, Frication, and Aspiration*

speakers. Frication burst and aspiration could not be differentiated in clusters involving /p/. By definition the burst duration is equal to the VOT in voiced-stop environments. Data for /p/ are estimates based on the VOT observed in /b/.

The burst durations for /b, d, g/ average to be approximately 13, 21, and 29 msec, respectively. The same ordering of burst durations was seen by Halle et al. (1957). Burst durations are five to 10 msec longer for voiceless aspirated plosives than for voiced plosives. Frication bursts also appeared to be somewhat more intense in voiceless plosives, but this additional acoustic cue to the voicing distinction could not be accurately quantified from the spectrographic representation.

Cluster	Burst Duration	Cluster	Burst Duration
Voiceless:		Voiced:	
/p/	–	/b/	11
/t/	24	/d/	17
/k/	37	/g/	27
/pr/	–	/br/	14
/tr/	31	/dr/	25
/kr/	41	/gr/	35
/pl/	–	/bl/	13
/kl/	23	/gl/	26
/tw/	22		
/kw/	20		
/s/-clusters:			
/sp/	–		
/st/	15		
/sk/	19		
/spr/	–		
/str/	21		
/skr/	16		
/spl/	–		
/skw/	13		

Comparison of burst durations and voice onset times in Figure 2 for each of the voiceless plosives, shows that both measurements increase from /p/ to /t/ to /k/. The difference between voice onset time and burst duration is the length of the aspiration interval. The data indicate that the aspiration duration is approximately the same for labial, dental, and velar plosives having identical phonetic environments.

Burst durations in the clusters /kw, kl, tw, skw/ appear to be shorter than in the environment where the plosive is followed by a vowel. It may be, however, that the frication burst is simply less intense and not as visible in these clusters because of the low first- and second-formant frequencies in /w, l/ and the presence of a secondary constriction in front of the frication source location.

Aspiration in /s/-Sonorant Custers

An aspiration interval appears following the cessation of visible frication energy in an /s/. The interval of aspiration is as much as 30 to 50 msec if the /s/ is followed by a sonorant consonant. Average data (in msec) are presented below for consonant clusters involving /s/ followed by a sonorant consonant. Each entry is the average of 15 tokens. A spectrographic example of aspiration following an /s/ is shown in Figure 3.

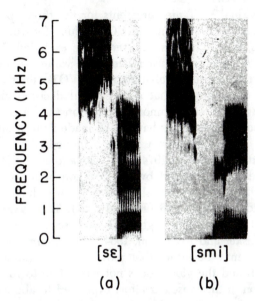

FIGURE 3. Broad-band spectrograms are shown of portions of the words *set* and *smear*. An interval of aspiration can be seen following the termination of high-frequency frication noise for the /s/ in *smear*.

Cluster	Aspiration Duration
/s/	12
/sw/	49
/sm/	38
/sn/	32
/sl/	29

The 12-msec average aspiration interval, when /s/ is followed by a vowel, may not be an accurate indication of aspiration; it may simply reflect the fact that the /s/ frication noise intensity became less than the marking threshold of the spectrogram paper. Nevertheless, it is clear from changes in the spectral composition of the noise that a prolonged interval of true aspiration is present in the /s/-sonorant transitions.

DISCUSSION

There is a wide variation in the average voice onset time for plosives in different consonant cluster environments. The average VOT for voiced plosives ranges from 11 msec for /b/ to 35 msec for /gr/. The average VOT for voiceless unaspirated plosives ranges from 12 msec for /sp/ to 39 msec for /skw/, and the average VOT for voiceless aspirated plosives ranges from 47 msec for /p/ to 102 msec for /tw/.

When the individual VOT measurements for the three speakers were compared, some overlap was seen in the VOT values for voiced and voiceless aspirated plosives, even when /s/ clusters were excluded. Eleven words involving /g/ or a /g/-sonorant cluster had VOT values greater than or equal to 40 msec, while eight words involving /p/ had VOT values less than or equal to 40 msec. The data suggest that a perceptual decision about the voicing feature for an English plosive cannot be made on the basis of VOT alone. A place-of-articulation decision may have to be made first, or acoustic cues such as the presence of low-frequency energy immediately following release (Stevens and Klatt, 1974; Lisker, 1974) may play a role.

The VOT is nearly unchanged by the addition of a second syllable to a word. However, the added syllable shortens the vowel duration in the original syllable by a factor of about 0.66 (Klatt, 1973b). Thus VOT is not a simple function of vowel duration, although VOT does seem to vary with speaking rate and stress (Lisker and Abramson, 1964, 1967; Summerfield and Haggard, 1972). The reason may be either that plosive closure duration is shorter in more rapid speech and the glottis does not have time to fully open, or there may be a reduction in the muscular effort expended to abduct the vocal folds in rapid speech and in unstressed environments.

The longer VOT for /p, t, k/ preceding a high vowel is consistent with a phonological rule of Japanese in which high vowels become voiceless if surrounded by voiceless obstruents (McCawley, 1968). In some way, high vowels seem to influence the behavior of the larynx such that the laryngeal fundamental frequency is higher (House and Fairbanks, 1953) and voicing is less easy to initiate or sustain than in other vowels.

The increased voice onset time in /p, t, k/-plus-sonorant clusters and the aspiration interval following /s/ in /s/-plus-sonorant clusters has been described previously in the phonetics literature (see, for example, Jones, 1969; Heffner, 1950). The sonorant is said to be voiceless in these environments. The present VOT data have been compared with the durational characteristics of sonorants in these environments (Klatt, 1973a). Comparisons indicate that the perceptual impression is not entirely correct; the sonorant is aspirated for only about half of its duration. Of particular interest is the fact that sonorant consonants are longer in duration following /p, t, k/ than following /b, d, g/. It is as if the sonorant is lengthened after /p, t, k/ by a phonological rule so that the major portion of the subsequent sonorant-vowel formant transitions are voiced.

The inherent differences in burst durations for labials, dentals, and velars may be explained by observing the time course of the pressure developed across the oral closure following release. A labial release is quite rapid and the generated burst spectrum is weak in intensity because there is no resonator in front of the lips (Fant, 1960). Both factors contribute to the acoustic appearance of a short burst.

A velar release involves the entire tongue body. The constriction increases in area more slowly, due in part to the mass involved, and in part to the fact that the release vector of the tongue motion is usually not perpendicular to the long dimension of the acoustic tube formed by the vocal tract (Houde, 1967). The release vector of the tongue tip for /t, d/ is more nearly perpendicular, except perhaps before /r/, where burst durations are observed to be somewhat longer.

The VOT differences between /p, t, k/ cannot be explained by a similar argument. It is true that the burst durations differ, but voicing onset occurs considerably later, that is, at a time when the oral pressure is zero. Possible explanations for the observed VOT differences among /p, t, k/ are discussed in a later section.

Several aspects of our voice onset time data are in agreement with data recently published by Davidsen-Nielsen (1974). In a study of word-medial /s/-plosive clusters, using British and American speakers, he included a few words involving other clusters. These limited data are in agreement with our observations that the VOT increases from /p/ to /t/ to /k/, that the VOT increases when the plosive is followed by a sonorant consonant, and that the VOT for /s/-plosive clusters is similar to VOT values for the corresponding voiced plosive.

Perceptual (Acoustic) Cues to the Voiced/Voiceless Distinction for English Plosives

The acoustic differences between voiced and voiceless plosives of English in various phonetic environments can be separated into about six distinct types of cues that are described below and illustrated in Figure 4. While voice onset time and low-frequency energy cues are perhaps of greatest perceptual importance, there are situations where the other cues (burst loudness, fundamental frequency, segmental duration, and prevoicing) have a potentially greater influence on the voicing decision for a plosive.

Voice Onset Time. If voicing onset is delayed by more than about 20 to 25 msec relative to plosive release, burst and voicing onset are perceived as two separate events and a voiceless plosive is likely to be heard (Stevens and Klatt, 1974). If the VOT is less than about 20 msec, the burst and voicing onset are perceived as occurring simultaneously, as in a voiced plosive. The time of

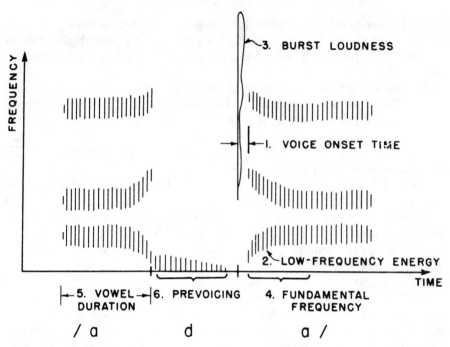

FIGURE 4. Six perceptual cues to the voiced-voiceless distinction in English as proposed and discussed in the text.

voicing onset can be detected as a separate event in an aspirated /p, t, k/ because voicing differs from aspiration and frication in spectral composition. The spectral level of the noise is at least 15 to 25 dB less intense in the frequency region of the first formant due to differences in the source spectra (Stevens, 1971; Stevens and Klatt, 1972) and to an increase in the bandwidth of F1 when the vocal folds are abducted (Fant, 1960).

A subsidiary cue to VOT is the presence or absence of aspiration noise. The perceptual importance of the aspiration noise is suggested by an experiment reported by Winitz, LaRiviere, and Herriman (1975). They replaced the 40 msec following the frication burst in, for example, a /da/ syllable by silence and found that subjects heard /da/, not /ta/.

Low-Frequency Energy/Rapid Spectrum Change. The presence of low-frequency energy due to the voiced excitation of a low first-formant frequency immediately following plosive release suggests a voiced plosive. In a voiceless plosive, the formant transitions that indicate release of an oral occlusion (first formant) and place of articulation (second and third formants) are nearly completed before voicing onset and the low-frequency energy cue is absent (at least for a following vowel with a high first formant). Experiments by Stevens and Klatt (1974) have shown that there is a perceptual trading relationship between VOT and the presence or absence of a significant first-formant transition following voicing onset. The phoneme boundary, as measured in terms of voicing onset, may be delayed by as much as 15 msec if there is a significant rise in the first formant frequency starting at voicing onset.

Stevens and Klatt (1974) propose that the relevant acoustic cue is the presence or absence of a rapid spectrum change following voicing onset. Summerfield (1974) has shown that, if this is the case, then only motions of the first formant are effective. New data and arguments presented by Lisker (1974) suggest that it is primarily the presence of low-frequency energy at the beginning of a rapid spectrum change that is perceptually effective in signaling a voiced plosive. The argument is as follows. According to Stevens and Klatt (1974), the presence of a rapid spectrum change following plosive release in, for example, /da/ indicates a voiced plosive. However, little or no first-formant change is seen in the syllable /di/ because /i/ has a low first formant. Therefore one should begin to hear /ti/ sooner as the VOT is increased in a synthetic /ti/-/di/ continuum. The opposite result has been observed. Cooper (1974) and Summerfield (1974) obtained shifts in the perceptual phoneme boundary of plus 6 msec when switching from a /ta/-/da/ continuum to a /ti/-/di/ continuum. Our production data are in agreement with the boundary shift; there is generally a longer VOT before the vowel /i/ than before /a/.

The relevant cue must be the presence or absence of energy in the frequency region below 300 Hz following voicing onset. The conclusion is reinforced by the perceptual data of Summerfield (1974) who found that increasing the rate of change of all formant transitions in a set of synthetic stops differing by VOT modified the /ka/-/ga/ perceptual boundary, but had little effect on the /ki/-/gi/ boundary.

The low-frequency energy cue is presumably much more important for clusters involving /g/ where the VOT usually exceeds the simultaneity threshold. Assuming that one need not determine place of articulation before making a voicing decision, the presence of low-frequency energy following voice onset for /g/ could explain the voiced quality that is heard.

Burst Loudness. The peak intensity and the duration of the burst of frication noise are greater at the release of a voiceless plosive. The reason is that the pressure drop across the oral occlusion is 1–2 cm H_2O higher at release (Lubker and Parris, 1970; Lisker, 1970)—and more importantly, the pressure drop across the expanding oral constriction remains high longer when the vocal folds are abducted. One need not postulate a greater pressure for voiceless plosives (Chomsky and Halle, 1968) to explain these effects. In fact, the subglottal pressure may be 1–2 cm H_2O lower for aspirated plosives due to the pressure drop in the lower airways that occurs at very high airflows.

The physical intensity of the frication noise is proportional to the three-halves power of the pressure drop across the constriction, all else being equal (Stevens, 1971). The perceptual loudness of the burst is proportional to both its intensity and and its duration because the burst is short in duration relative to the averaging time constant for loudness judgments (Miller, 1948). While burst intensity differences were not quantified in this study, differences in duration are sufficient to make the burst perceived at least four dB louder in a voiceless plosive. An additional 3 to 6 dB greater intensity for voiceless plosives could be expected on the basis of observed differences in oral pressure. No data concerning the contribution of this cue to the voiced/voiceless distinction in perception are known to the author.

Fundamental Frequency. The fundamental frequency averaged over the duration of a vowel placed between voiceless plosives is about 5% higher than in a vowel placed between voiced plosives (House and Fairbanks, 1953). The difference is greatest, about 15%, immediately following voicing onset (Lehiste and Peterson, 1961a; Lea, 1973). A much smaller difference is found in the vowel preceding the stop. Theoretical considerations suggest that the difference in onset fundamental frequency is due in part to the greater transglottal pressure and greater vocal fold stiffness at voicing onset for a voiceless plosive (Halle and Stevens, 1971). However, the hypothesized vocal fold stiffening gesture must take place during oral occlusion to account for the delay in the fundamental frequency rise. Fujimura (1971) and Haggard, Ambler, and Callow (1970) have shown that a rapid rise or fall in fundamental frequency following voice onset is perceived as a change in voicing of the plosive if all other cues have been neutralized.

Segmental Duration. Potential durational cues include the duration of the previous segment and the duration of the plosive itself. In English, a vowel or sonorant followed by a voiceless plosive is significantly shorter in duration than it would be before a voiced plosive (House and Fairbanks, 1953; Peterson and Lehiste, 1960). The durational difference in the segment preceding the plosive is as much as 34% in phrase-final syllables, but the contrast is not as great in other positions (Klatt, 1973b; 1975). The perceptual relevance of vowel duration as a cue to the voicing feature of a following consonant has been demonstrated by Denes (1955).

The vowel duration contrast before a plosive, while small, is present in many other languages (Chen, 1970; Fischer-Jorgensen, 1954). One possible explanation for the seemingly universal tendency to encroach on the duration of the vowel if a voiceless segment follows, concerns the relative timing of the oral closing gesture and the glottal opening gesture. A slightly delayed glottal opening gesture is likely to produce a few cycles of vibration during closure, which is an undesirable cue for voicing. Since perfect synchrony of glottal and supraglottal activity is difficult, the vocal folds are normally abducted somewhat early to avoid generation of a false voicing cue. Consistent with this hypothesis is the observation that formant transitions are slightly truncated before final voiceless plosives (Lehiste and Peterson, 1961b; Broad and Fertig, 1970). Of course English has expanded on this universal tendency for vowel duration to be shorter before /p, t, k/; English speakers have adopted a phonological rule making the durational difference large enough to be perceptually relevant, that is, phonemic.

The duration of the plosive closure interval may also function to distinguish between voiced and voiceless plosives under some circumstances. In prestressed position, voiced and voiceless plosives have about the same duration (Lisker,

1969; Klatt, 1973a). However in poststressed intervocalic phonetic environments, such as in the minimal pair *rapid-rabid,* the closure duration for the voiced consonant is shorter (Lisker, 1957). Closure duration has been shown to be a perceptually adequate cue to distinguish between such word pairs, but the distinction is not always maintained; the consonants /t, d/ are frequently flapped in this phonetic environment.

Prevoicing. A plosive will be prevoiced whenever the vocal folds are positioned for voicing before the oral occlusion is achieved, that is, when a transglottal pressure drop is present at the onset of the closure interval. Utterance-initial voiced plosives usually are not prevoiced in English (Lisker and Abramson, 1964) indicating that English speakers habitually effect an oral closure before glottal closure when beginning an utterance with a plosive. On the other hand, voiced plosives preceded by a vowel or a voiced consonant are frequently prevoiced in English. Prevoicing is seen on a spectrogram as low-frequency vertical striations.

The spectrum of prevoicing contains only low-frequency harmonics because the first formant is low (about 200 Hz during closure) and sound radiation through the tissues attenuates higher frequencies. If the closure duration is long, the amplitude of prevoicing is likely to decrease, or prevoicing may cease entirely as oral pressure builds up. It is not known whether the presence of prevoicing will change the voiced/voiceless perception of an otherwise ambiguous intervocalic plosive in English, but the cue is probably perceptually relevant.

The prevoicing cue may be related to the second cue described above, low-frequency energy. Both involve the presence or absence of low-frequency energy, but this energy must be present before plosive release in one case and after release in the other. If the temporal order of events were not important in plosive perception, the two physical cues could be playing the same perceptual role.

Articulatory Differences between Voiced and Voiceless Plosives in English

As can be seen, a good deal is known about the acoustic cues that determine whether an English plosive is heard as voiced or voiceless. This evidence has been used to argue for a model of speech perception in which the outputs of a number of special purpose feature detectors are weighted and combined, leading to a voicing decision for each segment in the speech stream. These simple models have some appeal as characterizations of the peripheral processing that must take place, but they tend to underemphasize the influence of such factors as speaking rate (Summerfield and Haggard, 1972) and phonetic, prosodic, syntactic, and semantic expectations on segmental feature-identification decisions.

The acoustic data can be used to deduce certain articulatory differences between voiced and voiceless plosives in singleton and cluster environments. For a voiceless aspirated plosive, the vocal folds must be abducted and

KLATT: *Voice Onset Time, Frication, and Aspiration*

stiffened to prevent vibrations and permit aspiration generation when the oral occlusion is released (Halle and Stevens, 1971). For a voiced plosive, the vocal folds must be abducted and slackened to facilitate voicing at release when a significant transglottal pressure is developed.

The actual instructions to control the larynx must be somewhat more complicated than these simple goal-directed statements indicate because the muscle commands will depend on the glottal state for the preceding segment, plosive duration and other requirements such as the desired fundamental frequency and voice quality in the next vowel or sonorant segment. The following rules, while tentative, summarize certain aspects of the organization of motor commands to the laryngeal musculature during the production of voiced and voiceless plosives. The rules describe acoustic events, but it seems clear that the laryngeal control system has learned to preplan motor commands to the larynx and vocal tract articulators without the need for closed-loop acoustic feedback. Examples of the timing relationships specified in each rule are presented in schematic form in Figure 5.

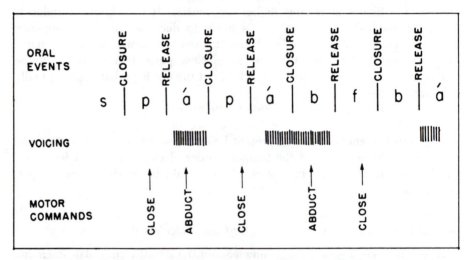

FIGURE 5. Expected timing relationships between laryngeal and oral events for English /p/ and /b/ are illustrated in different phonetic environments. The example is not a possible phonetic sequence in English, but it serves to illustrate all possible combinations of voiced-voiceless transitions. Also shown are approximate times of initiation of motor commands to the primary laryngeal abductor muscles (posterior cricoarytenoids) and adductor muscles (interarytenoids and lateral cricoarytenoids).

1. If /p, t, k/ are preceded by a voiced segment, execute a command to abduct and stiffen the vocal folds such that vibrations normally cease a few milliseconds before plosive closure. Initiate the glottal closing gesture at a time such that the vocal folds begin to vibrate at a fixed time after the end of the burst of frication noise.

2. If /p, t, k/ are preceded by a voiceless segment, keep the vocal folds

abducted and stiff during oral closure. The adducing rule is the same as above.

3. If /b, d, g/ are preceded by a voiced segment, keep vocal folds approximated and slack throughout closure.

4. If /b, d, g/ are preceded by a voiceless segment, set the timing of a vocal folds adduction command so as to ensure that the vocal folds are approximated before plosive release.

5. If /p, t, k/ are preceded by an /s/ in the same word, begin the vocal fold closure gesture earlier so that voicing onset occurs a few msec after the frication burst is over.

The implications of this set of instructions include the prediction that formant transitions into a voiceless plosive will be somewhat truncated relative to transitions into a voiced plosive. Also, voice onset times should be positively correlated with burst durations. The rules suggest that it is possible to have a small amount of aspiration in an /sp/, /st/, or /sk/ cluster, but not in a voiced plosive between voiced segments. All predictions are consistent with the present data.

This control strategy might result in VOT's for aspirated /p, t, k/ being a function of closure duration. If the VOT depends on the amount of time available to open the glottis, then the VOT will get shorter as closure duration shortens, because the glottis cannot be fully opened before the closing command is issued. This prediction is born out by the data of Coker and Umeda (in press) and our own sentence data to be described below. However, the prediction is not in agreement with a correlation analysis performed by Cooper and Nager (1975) which showed no correlation between closure duration and VOT for repetitions of the nonsense utterance /rə ′pi/. Perhaps the observed shortening of VOT with shorter closure durations in different sentence contexts is preprogrammed rather than being an automatic consequence of a limited velocity of glottal adjustments.

The commands to the laryngeal musculature must precede the events of glottal opening and closure because it is known that it takes about 50 to 80 msec between the first EMG activity is observed in the posterior cricoarytenoid or interarytenoid before actual opening or closure is achieved (Hirose and Gay, 1972). Thus it is necessary to begin closing the vocal folds in an aspirated plosive before oral release and the concomitant decrease in oral pressure.

We had argued previously that the decrease in oral pressure could trigger the laryngeal adduction gesture reflexively, at least during the language-acquisition stage when VOT values for /p, t, k/ may be very large (Port and Preston, 1972). In this way, the VOT differences between /p/, /t/, and /k/ are explained by a physiological constraint, the duration of the plosive burst (Klatt, 1973c). It now appears that a more plausible reason for the difference is to be found in the perceptual domain. A longer VOT is needed in a voiceless plosive with slower formant transitions, such as /k/, to prevent listeners from hearing the low-frequency energy cue that would indicate a /g/. There is probably a rule of English phonology that delays glottal closure in /k/ relative to /p, t/, which share the same laryngeal feature assignment. We seem to have the unexpected state of affairs that the VOT differences among /b, d, g/ are due on physiological constraints, while the VOT differences among /p, t, k/ are implemented by a phonological rule whose existence is due to a perceptual factor.

Prediction of Voice Onset Times in Sentences

The acoustic characteristics of plosive consonants in cluster environments are not the same in all sentence contexts. Voice onset time and burst characteristics depend on the sentence stress pattern, the position of the cluster within a word, and phonetic features of the segment appearing before the cluster. A connected discourse containing about 1500 segments was read by one of the speakers used in the present study (DK) to compare voice onset time data in the two situations and devise a set of rules for predicting voice onset times in all sentence contexts. These rules are summarized in the Appendix.

Plosives in Prestressed Positions

Agreement is good between values obtained in the discourse and in the controlled cluster study. The median VOT of 10 tokens of prestressed /t 'V/ was 60 msec in the connected discourse. This compares with a value of 53 msec for DK in the systematic consonant cluster sudy. Averaging across all examples of /p, t, k/ in prestressed clusters in the discourse, the VOT was found to be 4 msec longer than the corresponding values obtained in the carrier sentence. The VOTs for prestressed /b, d, g/ were also found to be in good agreement between the two studies.

There is more variability in the discourse, but the VOT of a prestressed plosive does not appear to depend on whether the cluster is word-initial or word-medial; nor does it seem to matter whether the preceding segment is voiced or voiceless. The VOTs may be somewhat shorter in syllables assigned secondary lexical stress, but there were insufficient tokens to quantify the degree of change.

The VOT is about 10-15 msec shorter if the segment before /p, t, k/ is a nasal. The reason is probably because the prestressed plosive is shorter in duration and the vocal folds do not have time to fully abduct.

Plosives in Postvocalic and Preunstressed Positions

The VOTs for /b, d, g/ are about the same whether prestressed or not. Voiced plosives have a slightly longer duration burst, and thus by definition a longer VOT, if preceded by a voiceless consonant.

The VOTs for /p, t, k/ are generally much shorter in postvocalic and pre-unstressed positions. Similar observations have been made by Lisker and Abramson (1967). In intervocalic positions, /p, t, k/ and /p, t, k/-sonorant clusters had VOTs that averaged about 15 msec shorter in word-initial position (the previous word ended in a vowel), and about 35 msec shorter in other intervocalic positions within or at the end of a word. It appears that word-initial unstressed /p, t, k/ are produced with a somewhat greater glottal opening gesture than other unstressed examples of /p, t, k/.

The same tendency appears in nonintervocalic positions as well, leading to the conclusion that word boundary locations can influence the acoustic characteristics of phonetic segments not normally distinguished in their segmental or suprasegmental feature representation. To describe this regularity, a phonological description of English would have to preserve word boundary information as a part of the low-level phonetic description, or a phonological rule will have to be devised to assign some special feature value to a word-initial plosive. (The special nature of preunstressed word-initial positions is not accounted for by the restricted occurrence of alveolar flapping; all examples of flap /t/ were excluded from the calculations.)

There exists a number of phonological rules that modify the expected characteristics of unstressed plosives, including alveolar flapping, replacement by glottal stop, and shortening of plosives in homorganic nasal plosive clusters. Tentative formulations for some of these rules are included in the Appendix.

Unstressed clusters beginning with a plosive had a longer VOT if the preceding segment was voiceless. This tendency is in agreement with the observation that the VOT is shorter in intervocalic unstressed positions because less effort is made to open the glottis (Sawashima et al., 1970). The less-effort hypothesis also accounts for the frequently observed devoicing of an unstressed vowel between a plosive and a voiceless consonant (for example, the second vowel in *multiply* and the first vowel in *to select*). An insufficient gesture is made to close the glottis between two voiceless segments because unstressed syllables can be produced with less articulatory effort.

There were seven examples of the word *to* in the corpus and only in one instance was the /t/ flapped. Unstressed word-initial /t/ is usually flapped if the preceding segment is a sonorant, but the only flap occurred in the verbal auxiliary phrase *continue to be*. In the remaining examples, the word functioned as a preposition, thus beginning a new phrase. It appears that the presence of the phrase boundary may block application of the phonological rule involving alveolar flapping, at least for this speaker. We have other indications that phrase boundary locations are phonetically distinctive in normally spoken sentences. The syllable preceding a phrase boundary is longer in duration than it would normally be (Klatt, 1975), and there is a strong likelihood that a glottal stop will be inserted if the next phrase begins with a vowel or sonorant consonant.

In word-medial positions before a stressed vowel, /s/-plosive clusters usually behave as a cluster, with a weakly aspirated plosive. However, the

KLATT: *Voice Onset Time, Frication, and Aspiration*

plosive may be aspirated if there is an obvious morpheme boundary and the stem forms a word and this word is fairly infrequent (Davidsen-Nielsen, 1974).

ACKNOWLEDGMENT

This research was supported in part by National Institutes of Health Grant 5 R01 NSO 4332-12. Requests for reprints should be directed to Dennis H. Klatt, Room 36-523, Massachusetts Institute of Technology, Cambridge, Massachusetts 02139.

REFERENCES

BROAD, D. J., and FERTIG, R. H., Formant frequency trajectories in selected CVC-syllable nuclei. *J. acoust. Soc. Am.,* **47,** 1572-1582 (1970).

CHOMSKY, N., and HALLE, M., *Sound Pattern of English.* New York: Harper and Row (1968).

CHEN, M., Vowel length variation as a function of the voicing of the constant environment. *Phonetica,* **22,** 129-159 (1970).

COKER, C. H., and UMEDA, N., Subphonemic variations in American English. In L. Chisitovich and G. Fant (Eds.), *Proceedings of the Symposium on Speech Analysis and Perception.* Leningrad, August 1973 (in press).

COOPER, W. E., Contingent feature analysis in speech perception. *Percept. Psychophys.,* **16,** 201-204 (1974).

COOPER, W. E., and NAGER, R. M., Perceptuo-motor adaptation to speech: An analysis of bisyllabic utterances and a neural model. *J. acoust. Soc. Am.,* **58,** 256-265 (1975).

DAVIDSEN-NIELSEN, N., Syllabification in English words with medial sp, st and sk. *J. Phonetics,* **2,** 15-45 (1974).

DENES, P., Effect of duration on the perception of voicing. *J. acoust. Soc. Am.,* **27,** 761-764 (1955).

FANT, G., *Acoustic Theory of Speech Production.* The Hague, Netherlands: Mouton (1960).

FISCHER-JORGENSEN, E., Acoustic analysis of stop consonants. *Misc. Phonetica,* **2,** 42-59 (1954).

FUJIMURA, O., Remarks on stop consonants: Synthesis experiments and acoustic cues. In L. L. Hammerich, R. Jakobson, and E. Zwirner (Eds.) *Form and Substance: Phonetic and Linguistic Papers Presented to Eli Fischer-Jorgensen.* Denmark: Akademisk Foilag, 221-232 (1971).

HAGGARD, M. S., AMBLER, S., and CALLOW, M., Pitch as a voicing cue. *J. acoust. Soc. Am.,* **47,** 613-617 (1970).

HALLE, M., HUGHES, G. W., and RADLEY, J. P. A., Acoustic properties of stop consonants. *J. acoust. Soc. Am.,* **29,** 107-116 (1957).

HALLE, M., and STEVENS, K. N., A note on laryngeal features. *Research Laboratory of Electronics Quart. Progr. Rep. No. 101.* Cambridge, Mass.: MIT, 198-213 (1971).

HEFFNER, R-M. S., *General Phonetics.* Madison, Wis.: Univ. of Wisconsin Press (1950).

HIROSE, H., and GAY, T., The activity of the intrinsic laryngeal muscles in voicing control: An electromyographic study. *Phonetica,* **25,** 140-164 (1972).

HOUDE, R. A., A study of tongue body motion during selected speech sounds. Doctoral dissertation, Univ. of Michigan (1967).

HOUSE, A. S., and FAIRBANKS, G., The influence of consonantal environment upon the secondary acoustical characteristics of vowels. *J. acoust. Soc. Am.,* **25,** 105-113 (1953).

JONES, D., *An Outline of English Phonetics.* (19th ed.) Cambridge, Eng.: Heffer (1969).

KLATT, D. H., Durational characteristics of prestressed word-initial consonant clusters in English. *Research Laboratory of Electronics Quart. Progr. Rep. No. 108.* Cambridge, Mass.: MIT, 253-260 (1973a).

KLATT, D. H., Interaction between two factors that influence vowel duration. *J. acoust. Soc. Am.,* **43,** 1102-1104 (1973b).

KLATT, D. H., Voice onset time, frication and aspiration in word-initial consonant clusters.

Research Laboratory of Electronics Quart. Progr. Rep. No. 109. Cambridge, Mass.: MIT, 124-136 (1973c).

KLATT, D. H., Vowel lengthening is syntactically determined in a connected discourse. *J. Phonetics*, 3, 161-172 (1975).

LEA, W. A., Influences of phonetic sequences and stress on fundamental frequency contours of isolated words. *J. acoust. Soc. Am.*, 53, 346 (abstract) (1973).

LEHISTE, I., and PETERSON, G. E., Some basic considerations in the analysis of intonation. *J. acoust. Soc. Am.*, 33, 419-425 (1961a).

LEHISTE, I., and PETERSON, G. E., Transitions, glides and diphthongs. *J. acoust. Soc. Am.*, 33, 268-277 (1961b).

LISKER, L., Closure duration and the intervocalic voiced-voiceless distinction in English. *Language*, 33, 43-49 (1957).

LISKER, L., Stop duration and voicing in English. *Haskins Lab. Status Rep. SR 19/20.* 27-35 (1969).

LISKER, L., Supraglottal air pressure in the production of English stops. *Lang. Speech*, 13, 215-230 (1970).

LISKER, L., Is it "VOT" or a first-formant transition feature detector? Paper presented at the annual meeting of the American Association of Phonetic Sciences, St. Louis, Missouri (1974).

LISKER, L., and ABRAMSON, A. S., A cross-language study of voicing in initial stops: Acoustical measurements. *Word*, 20, 384-422 (1964).

LISKER, L., and ABRAMSON, A. S., Some effects of context on voice onset time in English stops. *Lang. Speech*, 10, 1-28 (1967).

LUBKER, J. F., and PARRIS, P. J., Simultaneous measurements of intraoral pressure, force of labial contact and labial electromyorgraphic activity during the production of the stop cognates /p/ and /b/. *J. acoust. Soc. Am.*, 47, 625-633 (1970).

McCAWLEY, J. D., *The Phonological Component of a Grammar of Japanese.* The Hague, Netherlands: Mouton (1968).

MILLER, G. A., The perception of short bursts of noise. *J. acoust. Soc. Am.*, 20, 160-170 (1948).

PETERSON, G. E., and LEHISTE, I., Duration of syllablic nuclei in English. *J. acoust. Soc. Am.*, 32, 693-703 (1960).

PORT, D. K., and PRESTON, M. S., Early apical stop production: A voice onset time analysis. *Haskins Lab. Status Rep. SR 29/30,* 125-149 (1972).

PRESTI, A. J., High-speed sound spectrograph. *J. acoust. Soc. Am.*, 40, 628-634 (1966).

SAWASHIMA, M., ABRAMSON, A. S., COOPER, F. S., and LISKER, L., Observing laryngeal adjustments during running speech by use of a fiberoptics system. *Phonetica*, 22, 193-201 (1970).

STEVENS, K. N., Airflow and turbulence noise for fricative and stop consonants: Static considerations. *J. acoust. Soc. Am.*, 50, 1180-1192 (1971).

STEVENS, K. N., and KLATT, D. H., Current models of sound sources for speech. In B. D. Wyke (Ed.), *Ventilatory and Phonatory Control Systems: An International Symposium.* London: Oxford Univ. Press (1972).

STEVENS, K. N., and KLATT, D. H., The role of formant transitions in the voiced-voiceless distinction for stops. *J. acoust. Soc. Am.*, 55, 653-659 (1974).

SUMMERFIELD, Q. A., Processing of cues and contexts in the perception of voicing contrasts. *Proceedings of the 1974 Stockholm Speech Communication Seminar.* August 1-3, 1974, Uppsala: Almquist and Wiksell (In press).

SUMMERFIELD, Q. A., and HAGGARD, M. P., Speech rate effects in the perception of voicing. *Speech Synthesis and Perception No. 6.* Cambridge, Eng.: Psychological Laboratory Univ. of Cambridge (1972).

WINITZ, H., LaRIVIERE, C., and HERRIMAN, E., Variations in VOT for English initial stops. *J. Phonetics*, 3, 41-52 (1975).

Received March 4, 1975.
Accepted June 15, 1975.

APPENDIX

Expected voice onset times in sentence contexts. These rules express general tendencies. Individual VOT values may differ from the predictions due to unaccounted for variability, especially in unstressed environments.

Voiced plosives /b, d, g/:
- —use the average voice onset time values given in Table 1
- —if the plosive is preceded by a voiceless consonant, multiply these values by 1.3
- —if the plosive is preceded by a nasal, multiply these values by 0.8

Voiceless plosives /p, t, k/ in prestressed clusters:
- —use the average voice onset time values given in Table 1

Voiceless plosives /p, t, k/, not prestressed:
Word-initial
- —if the plosive is preceded by a voiceless consonant or silence, multiply Table 1 values by 0.9
- —otherwise multiply Table 1 values by 0.7

Word-medial and word-final
- —if the plosive is preceded by a voiceless consonant, multiply Table 1 value by 0.7
- —otherwise multiply Table 1 value by 0.4
- —if the plosive is preceded by a homorganic nasal consonant, set the VOT to zero
- —/t/ becomes a glottal stop (VOT = 0) if followed by syllabic /n/ or if preceded by /n/ and followed by /m, n, l/
- —/t/ becomes a flap intervocalically (no burst and a VOT = 0)
- —there is a burst, but essentially no aspiration if the plosive is followed by a fricative

LEIGH LISKER
and *ARTHUR S. ABRAMSON*——————————————

A Cross-Language Study of
Voicing in Initial Stops:
Acoustical Measurements*

I. INTRODUCTION

Theoretical background. In diagnosing the phonetic basis for our ability to distinguish between phonemic categories, linguists often invoke the dimension of voicing to call some categories "voiced" and others "voiceless". In the case of stop consonants it is usual to label as voiced, categories characterized by the presence of glottal buzz during the interval of articulatory closure, while absence of buzz during this interval is a mark of voiceless stops. Acoustically the two kinds of stops are in most cases easily distinguished by reference to their spectrographic patterns; for voiced stops the formantless segment corresponding to the closure interval is traversed by a small number of low-frequency harmonic components, while in the case of voiceless stops the closure interval is essentially blank. But while this difference is an adequate basis for the physical separation of stop categories in many languages, there are some, like English, for which it works only in part. Although in medial position English /b d g/ are voiced and /p t k/ voiceless, in initial position both sets are commonly produced with silent closure intervals and should therefore be classed as voiceless according to the definitions cited. While phoneticians rarely call initial /b d g/ out-and-out voiceless stops, they regularly cite at least one other phonetic attribute, that of aspiration, which reliably distinguishes /p t k/ from /b d g/ both in initial position and medially before a stressed syllabic.

*A preliminary report, "Voicing Lag and English Initial Stops," was read before the Sixth Annual Conference on Linguistics of the Linguistic Circle of New York, held on May 6, 1961. Earlier versions of the present cross-language study were presented at the Sixty-Sixth Meeting of the Acoustical Society of America, Ann Arbor, Michigan, November 6–9, 1963 and the Thirty-Eighth Annual Meeting of the Linguistic Society of America, Chicago, Illinois, December 28–30, 1963. This work was supported in part by the National Science Foundation under Grant G-23633.

In many non-final positions,[1] then, /b d g/ are voiced and /p t k/ voiceless, while in some, /p t k/ are released with an audible explosion and an interlude of noise and /b d g/ are not. Thus, differences of voicing and aspiration, either singly or in conjunction, are said to separate the two sets of English stop phonemes, although neither is alone sufficient to distinguish them over the entire range of contexts in which both are found.

In addition to voicing and aspiration a third phonetic dimension, one of articulatory force, is widely cited as still another basis for separating the stop categories of English and many other languages. Although the assessment of articulatory force appears ultimately to be a matter of proprioceptive judgment, this judgment is said to depend directly on the audible features of closure duration and the loudness of the stop explosion.[2] Thus it is said that English /p t k/ are in general more forcefully articulated than /b d g/. In fact it is often asserted that this fortis/lenis difference is the primary mark of the /p t k/:/b d g/ set of contrasts, on the ground that it alone is operative in every position in which these contrasts are observed. In the current terminology, the fortis/lenis difference is the distinctive feature separating the two categories, while any concomitant differences of voicing and aspiration are systemically redundant, quite aside from whatever importance they might have as cues for perception.

In seeking to determine experimentally the acoustic cues by which listeners distinguish between English /b d g/ and /p t k/, we have of course been interested in discovering some single best measure by which to separate the two phoneme categories. In trying to use accepted phonetic descriptions of English as a guide to our research, we have been hampered by certain ambiguities in the treatment of articulatory force. Many phonetic statements imply that the three dimensions of voicing, aspiration and force of articulation are taken to be mutually independent coordinate dimensions of description; and yet there are reasons for wondering whether this is so. No one of the physical measures, whether physiological or acoustic, that have been proposed as correlates of the fortis/lenis

[1] As for final position, our impression of the literature on English phonemics is that three *observable* phonetic features, voicing, release and vocalic length, are attested for the contrast between /b d g/ and /p t k/. The occlusion of /b d g/, it is said, may be partially voiced or not voiced at all. If the final stops are audibly released, as they sometimes are, /p t k/ will have a stronger, more aspirated release. The single differentiating feature that all descriptions agree is regularly present is the greater length of vowels followed by /b d g/, but this is usually treated as a matter of vowel allophonics. (See, for example, the references cited in footnote 22.)

[2] See K. L. Pike, *Phonetics* (Ann Arbor, 1951), pp. 128–129; R-M. S. Heffner, *General Phonetics* (Madison, 1949), p. 120; R. Jakobson, C. G. M. Fant and M. Halle, *Preliminaries to Speech Analysis* (M.I.T. Technical Report No. 13, 1952), p. 36.

dimension, has been shown *not* to be significantly connected with voicing or aspiration. And in fact an examination of the phonetic literature generally fails to turn up any language which is said to possess stop categories that differ only in force of articulation.[3] For languages in which the fortis/lenis difference is invoked, it is too often the case to be accidental that voiceless and aspirated stops are discovered to be fortis, while voiced and un-aspirated ones are at the same time lenis. In languages whose stop categories are said to differ on all three dimensions, the total number of such categories seems never to exceed four. The ambiguous status of the terms "fortis" and "lenis" (or "tense" and "lax") is also reflected in statements by several writers[4] to the effect that a number of phonetic features, *among them voicing and aspiration*, may be taken as manifestations of an underlying division of stops on the basis of a fortis/lenis opposition. So far as we are aware, only one recent study, Gunnar Fant's *Acoustic Theory of Speech Production*,[5] suggests that the ensemble of acoustic features that are used as evidence for a dimension of articulatory force may be plausibly grouped together without any need for positing an independent fortis/lenis difference; in fact Fant associates all these features instead with differences in the position and activity of the glottis during the various phases of stop production, and our own work convinces us that Fant's views are entirely correct.

The acoustic features that we may suppose to be useful physical correlates of the manner contrasts between stop categories are in part readily visible in spectrograms,[6] although in general there is all too little solid evidence for asserting that any given feature is to be connected exclusively with some one of the phonetic dimensions of voicing, aspiration and articulatory force. At the same time it is reasonable to claim as a salient acoustic correlate of voicing the periodic character of a speech signal, which shows up in narrow-band spectrograms as a set of one or more harmonic traces and in wide-band spectrograms as a series of regularly spaced vertical striations. Aspiration too is spectrographically unambiguous; it registers as noise (i.e., random stippling), mostly at the frequencies of the second and third formants of contiguous pattern segments. In the case of the fortis/lenis relation, as has been said, the dimension of articulatory force seems

[3] In the occasional instance that appears in the literature, the description never clearly excludes the involvement of aspiration, presumably because any distinguishing aspiration present is taken to be a sign of fortisness.

[4] See, e.g., R. Jakobson and M. Halle, "Tenseness and Laxness," in *Roman Jakobson: Selected Writings*, I. *Phonological Studies* (The Hague, 1962), pp. 554–555.

[5] The Hague, 1960, pp. 224–225.

[6] These are listed, for example, in L. Lisker, "Closure Duration and the Intervocalic Voiced-Voiceless Distinction in English," *Language* XXXIII (1957), pp. 43, 45.

to us to be of doubtful status; certainly none of the acoustic features which have been suggested as correlates of a fortis/lenis dimension[7] is demonstrably independent of voicing.

The two features correlated with voicing and aspiration—periodic pulsing at the frequency of the voice pitch and noise in the frequency range of the higher formants—have an interesting relation to one another, at least in the case of the stops in English; each feature tends to be prominent in spectrograms only where the other is absent. Thus if a portion of a spectrographic pattern indicates the presence of voicing, then the noise feature is absent or much obscured, while if noise is strongly marked then periodic pulsing is usually not discernible. Now if we locate a pattern segment with reference to the instant of release of the stop closure,—and this event is marked by an abrupt increase in the amplitude and frequency spread of the signal—then we may define the amount or degree of voicing of a stop as the duration of the time interval by which the onset of periodic pulsing either precedes or follows release. In thus giving up the absolute definition of the term "voiced stop" with which we began, we are free to say that a difference of voicing not only separates voiced from voiceless stops,[8] but that it equally well distinguishes aspirated from unaspirated stops, where the latter are both commonly called voiceless. The noise feature of aspiration, instead of being considered coordinate with voicing, is then regarded simply as the automatic concomitant of a large delay in voice onset. In English, at least, this seems reasonable: /b d g/ and /p t k/ probably differ everywhere in the time of voice onset relative to release, but in certain positions the presence of aspiration noise tells us something about the absolute magnitude of delay in the onset time following /p t k/ releases.

On the basis of the considerations just presented it seems reasonable to begin a study aimed at finding the acoustic features which serve as cues for the manner differentiation of stops by fixing attention on the timing relation between voice onset and the release of occlusion. This measure is both easy to make and at the same time most promising as providing the single best basis for the physical discrimination of stop manner categories. Moreover, while this timing relation is to be connected immediately to the phonetic dimension of voicing, the underlying glottal mechanism which controls it is also responsible, presumably, for generating some of the features that have been taken to be acoustic manifestations of aspiration

---

[7] See especially Jakobson, Fant and Halle, 1952, pp. 36, 38. Additional references and discussion are to be found in L. Lisker, "On Hultzén's 'Voiceless Lenis Stops in Prevocalic Clusters'," *Word* XIX (1963), 376–387.

[8] As defined absolutely.

and articulatory force.[9] Finally, in choosing this feature, we took into account the fact that any findings based on spectrographic analysis would ultimately have to be corroborated, by experiments involving the use of speech synthesis. The synthesizers available at the Haskins Laboratories permit us to manipulate most precisely and conveniently the relative timing of the acoustic features marking release and the onset of voicing.

It may be objected that much of the foregoing discussion applies only to English, where the features of voicing and aspiration are distributed within the stop categories according to a particular pattern. The present study was undertaken to gather the data needed in order to determine, with some degree of precision, just how important our measure of the relative timing of voice onset is for the physical specification of stop categories in languages generally.

Purpose of the study. The purpose of the present study is to see how well a single dimension, voice onset time, serves to separate the stop categories of a number of languages in which both the number and phonetic characteristics of such categories are said to differ. Attention will be limited to word-initial position before vowels. For each of the languages chosen the phonetic features for which differentiating functions are usually claimed were such that we could expect to find initial stop categories marked by differences in voice onset time. For two of the languages, however, Hindi and Marathi, we did not expect this feature to mark off the so-called voiced aspirates. The eleven languages that were examined fall into three groups according to the number of stop categories: (1) two-category languages: American English, Cantonese, Dutch, Hungarian, Puerto Rican Spanish, and Tamil; (2) three-category languages: Korean, Eastern Armenian, and Thai; (3) four-category languages: Hindi and Marathi.

Procedure. The general procedure involved the spectrographic analysis of high-quality tape recordings made in an acoustically treated room. Each of our informants, seventeen in all,[10] produced a set of words chosen to include a sampling of all the initial prevocalic stops[11] found in his language.

[9] See G. Fant, *Acoustic Theory of Speech Production* (The Hague, 1960), p. 279.

[10] The number of informants used for each language depended upon availability. They were all educated speakers of standard varieties of their languages. For Tamil some further specification of dialect is given.

[11] The linguist may wish to include affricates among the "stops" or "plosives" in his phonemic analysis of a language. We have excluded affricates from the present study, e.g. in Hungarian and Cantonese, limiting ourselves to plain prevocalic stops, namely occlusives that have an abrupt rather than a fricative release.

For each word the informant was then told to make up two sentences to show its use in initial and non-initial positions. He was urged to utter these sentences with the fluency and naturalness of normal conversation. The informant recorded each word and each sentence twice. Departures from this elicitation procedure are noted for English and Thai sentences in Part III.

Wide-band spectrograms[12] of the recordings were made, and from these, voice onset times were measured by marking off the interval between the release of the stop and the onset of glottal vibration, that is, voicing. The point of voicing onset was determined by locating the first of the regularly spaced vertical striations which indicate glottal pulsing, while the instant of release was found by fixing the point where the pattern shows an abrupt change in overall spectrum. Oral closure is marked spectrographically by the total or almost total absence of acoustic energy in the formant frequency range; oral release is marked by the abrupt onset of energy in the formant frequency range.[13] In Figure 1, which shows wide-band spectrograms with displays of relative amplitude, we have three stop+vowel syllables illustrating three common conditions of voice onset time. In the first, voicing begins before the release of the stop; in the second, just after the release; in the third, voice onset lags considerably behind the release. According to their usual phonetic descriptions, the first stop is voiced and unaspirated, the second is voiceless and unaspirated, and the third is voiceless and aspirated. We have adopted the convention of assigning zero-time to our reference point, the instant of release; thus, measurements of voice onset time before the release are stated as negative numbers and called voicing lead, while measurements of voice onset time after the release are stated as positive numbers and called voicing lag. Each measurement was rounded to the nearest five milliseconds as a reasonable estimate of attainable precision.

In some few cases where word-initial stops were medial in sentences, it was not possible to equate the presence of vertical striations with audible glottal vibration. In such cases the striations[14] were very faint and confined

[12] The sound spectrograph used was the Sona-Graph of the Kay Electric Company, Pine Brook, New Jersey. The wide-band setting rather than the narrow one was used for its better time resolution; this effect was enhanced by substituting a large drum for the standard one to provide an expanded time scale on the paper of 7.5 in./sec. as against 5 in./sec.

[13] This acoustic energy may be concentrated just at the formant frequencies, or it may take the form of a "burst" or very brief interval of noise having a somewhat broader frequency spread.

[14] These inaudible pulses are undoubtedly the result of glottal activity, for they occur at the same frequencies as the audible variety. For further discussion of this phenomenon, see **Inferences as to glottal mechanisms** in IV.

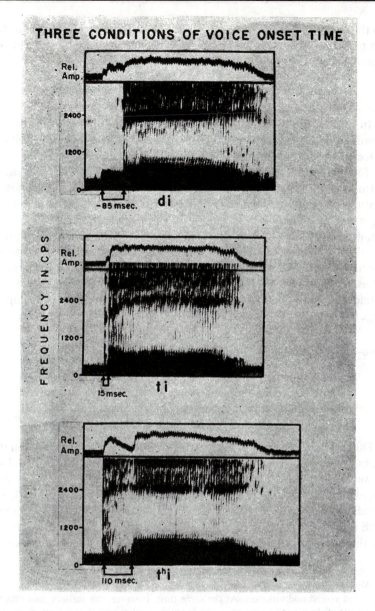

FIGURE 1. Wide-band spectrograms showing three conditions of voice onset time: voicing lead, short voicing lag, and long voicing lag. (Examples from Thai.)

to the bottom of the pattern. Moreover, careful listening tests showed that no pulses could be detected by ear. In carrying out our measurements, we ignored these striations.

II. Stops in Isolated Words

In this section we present our findings for the initial stops of isolated words in each of the eleven languages studied. These languages fall into three groups, depending on whether they have a maximum of two, three, or four categories of stops at each place of articulation. Each language is introduced by a chart of its stop phonemes with a statement of the phonetic features commonly recognized as distinctive for the stops. This is followed by a table of averages and ranges of voice onset time for all the stop phonemes of the language. The frequency distributions underlying these numbers are then shown graphically in Figures 2–4 for the two-category languages and Figures 5–7 for the three- and four-category languages. Thus, for example, the bilabial stops of the first language, Dutch, are to be found in Figure 2, the dental stops in Figure 3, and the velar stops in Figure 4.

Two-category languages.

1. Dutch

LABIAL	b	p
DENTAL	d	t
VELAR		k

Dutch is said to have a contrast of voiced and voiceless unaspirated stops,[15] except in the velar position where only /k/ is found. Moulton, however, simply calls them lenis and fortis.[16] In Table 1 we show data based on measurements of initial stops uttered by a single native speaker of standard Dutch. The first line gives average values of voice onset time for each category; the second line shows the ranges of values observed; and the third line records the number of tokens of each stop phoneme measured.

[15] See A. Cohen, C. L. Ebeling, K. Fokkema and A. G. F. van Holk, *Fonologie van het Nederlands en het Fries* (s'-Gravenhage, 1961), pp. 33–34, in which the two stop series are called voiced and voiceless. At the same time, however, the authors note that "in most parts of the world voicing goes together with another articulatory feature, one that is referred to by the term *lenis* or *soft*. The voiceless sounds are characterized as *fortis* or *sharp*." (Our translation.)

[16] William G. Moulton, "The Vowels of Dutch: Phonetic and Distributional Classes," *Lingua* XI (1962), p. 308.

4—w.

TABLE 1. Voice Onset Time in Msec: Dutch
(1 speaker)

	/b/	/p/	/d/	/t/	/k/
Av.	−85	10	−80	15	25
R.	−145: −50	0:30	−115: −45	5:35	10:35
N.	22	46	32	56	60

2. Puerto Rican Spanish

LABIAL	b	p
DENTAL	d	t
VELAR	g	k

Puerto Rican Spanish is said to have a contrast of voiced and voiceless unaspirated stops.[17] The allophonic complexity of these stops will be discussed in Table 13, where it is relevant.

TABLE 2. Voice Onset Time in Msec: Spanish
(2 speakers)

	/b/	/p/	/d/	/t/	/g/	/k/
Av.	−138	4	−110	9	−108	29
R.	−235: −60	0:15	−170: −75	0:15	−165: −45	15:55
N.	17	20	16	16	14	20

3. Hungarian

LABIAL	b	p
DENTAL	d	t
VELAR	g	k

The two sets of Hungarian stops are described as voiced and voiceless unaspirated respectively.[18] A palatal set /ɟ c/, which is often classed with the stops, will not be included here. (See footnote 11).

[17] In this respect it is like other dialects of Latin American Spanish as well as Iberian Spanish. See Tomás Navarro, *El Español en Puerto Rico* (Río Piedras, P. R., 1948), p. 58. But the two sets of Spanish stops are said to be distinguished by the tense/lax feature in Sol Saporta and Heles Contreras, *A Phonological Grammar of Spanish* (Seattle, 1962), p. 39.

[18] R. A. Hall, Jr., *An Analytical Grammar of the Hungarian Language* (Baltimore, 1938), pp. 16–17; J. Lotz, *Das ungarische Sprachsystem* (Stockholm, 1939), p. 27; József Tompa, ed., *A mai magyar nyelv rendszere. Leíró nyelvtan.* I. (Budapest, 1961), p. 81.

TABLE 3. Voice Onset Time in Msec: Hungarian
(2 speakers)

	/b/	/p/	/d/	/t/	/g/	/k/
Av.	−90	2	−87	16	−58	29
R.	−125: −65	0:10	−130: −65	10:25	−70: −35	20:35
N.	8	12	7	12	6	7

4. Tamil

LABIAL	b	p
DENTAL	d	t
VELAR	g	k

Our data for the Tamil initial stops are taken from the speech of an educated Brahman of South Arcot District in Madras State; they may be considered fairly representative of the speech of well educated Tamilians in the area that includes Madras City and the country to the east and south. Of the more recently published statements on the phonology of the language of this region some[19] describe the initial stops as voiced and voiceless, but at least one study[20] states categorically that "in stop consonants paired by similarity of articulatory position, tenseness is the significant feature in opposition to laxness, rather than voicelessness in opposition to voice." In addition "tense stops, unless affricated, are aspirated" (p. 361).

TABLE 4. Voice Onset Time in Msec: Tamil
(1 speaker)

	/b/	/p/	/d/	/t/	/g/	/k/
Av.	−74	12	−78	8	−62	24
R.	−100: −55	0:45	−105: −35	0:30	−110: −35	15:35
N.	8	42	16	8	13	13

5. Cantonese

LABIAL	p	p^h
DENTAL	t	t^h
VELAR	k	k^h

The two sets of stops are described[21] as being voiceless unaspirated and

[19] L. Lisker, "The Tamil Occlusives: Short vs. Long or Voiced vs. Voiceless?" *Indian Linguistics*, Turner Jubilee Vol., I (1958), 294–301.

[20] Murray Fowler, "The Segmental Phonemes of Sanskritized Tamil," *Language* XXX (1954), 360–367.

[21] Yuen Ren Chao, *Cantonese Primer* (Cambridge, Mass., 1947), p. 20; Diana Kao, *The Structure of the Cantonese Syllable* (Ph.D. dissertation in preparation, Columbia University, 1964), chap. 2.

voiceless aspirated respectively. In addition to the three places of articulation given in our chart an alveolar series is often included among the stops; these are phonetically affricates, however, and are therefore excluded from consideration (see footnote 11). Sometimes a fourth series of labialized velars is posited, but these too will not be treated here.

TABLE 5. Voice Onset Time in Msec: Cantonese
(1 speaker)

	/p/	/pʰ/	/t/	/tʰ/	/k/	/kʰ/
Av.	9	77	14	75	34	87
R.	0:20	35:110	5:25	45:95	25:55	70:115
N.	15	15	12	15	15	15

6. English

LABIAL	b	p
ALVEOLAR	d	t
VELAR	g	k

Recent descriptions of English are in general agreement that initial /p t k/ are aspirated and /b d g/ are not, but there is considerable diversity as to the relative emphasis put on differences in voicing and differences in force of articulation. For certain writers[22] the two series differ primarily in voicing, but the voiced set may be additionally characterized as produced with weaker articulatory force than the voiceless set. Other writers, however, prefer to place primary stress on the difference in articulatory force, while the voicing difference is said to be secondary, on occasion even absent.[23]

TABLE 6. Voice Onset Time in Msec: English
(4 speakers)

	/b/	/p/	/d/	/t/	/g/	/k/
Av.	1/−101	58	5/−102	70	21/−88	80
R.	0:5/−130:−20	20:120	0:25/−155:−40	30:105	0:35/−150:−60	50:135
N.	51/17	102	63/13	116	53/13	84

[22] J. S. Kenyon, *American Pronunciation*, 10th ed. (Ann Arbor, 1951), pp. 41, 45, 121–131; C. F. Hockett, *A Manual of Phonology* (Baltimore, 1955), pp. 115–116; A. A. Hill, *Introduction to Linguistic Structures* (New York, 1958), p. 32; A. J. Bronstein, *The Pronunciation of American English: an Introduction to Phonetics* (New York, 1960), pp. 59–60; H. A. Gleason, *An Introduction to Descriptive Linguistics*, 2nd ed. (New York, 1961), pp. 22, 24, 247–248; M. W. Bloomfield and L. Newmark, *A Linguistic Introduction to the History of English* (New York, 1963), p. 67.

[23] G. L. Trager and H. L. Smith, Jr., *An Outline of English Structure* (Norman, Okla., 1951), p. 29; A. C. Gimson, *An Introduction to the Pronunciation of English* (London, 1962), pp. 146–147.

It should be noted that we give two sets of values for /b d g/. To have given a single set of values would have meant lumping positive and negative values of voice onset time as items of a single population, and it appeared rather that these are distributed within two discontinuous ranges. In such a situation it would be misleading to determine single average values of onset time for the members of the /b d g/ set. Moreover, it is relevant that instances of positive and negative values do not occur randomly in our material. In the following table we see how the two kinds of /b d g/ were distributed for each of our four speakers of American English.

TABLE 6a. Number of Occurrences of Lag and Lead

Speaker	/b/	/d/	/g/
AA	+ 6	+30	+18
	− 0	− 0	− 0
LL	+22	+16	+18
	− 0	− 0	− 0
CC	+22	+17	+17
	− 0	− 1	− 1
TR	+ 1	+ 0	+ 0
	−17	−12	−12

A single speaker TR was responsible for 95% of all the stops produced with voicing lead, while one other speaker, CC, produced the remainder of such stops. Conversely, speaker TR produced 41 of his 42 /b d g/ tokens with voicing lead; CC, for his part, had positive values (lag) in 56 of the 58 /b d g/ stops he produced. Thus it appears that our speakers do not randomly produce such stops with positive and negative values of relative onset time; rather, each speaker, in isolated words at least, always or nearly always produces a single kind of /b d g/.

Three-category languages.

1. Eastern Armenian

LABIAL	b	p	pʰ
DENTAL	d	t	tʰ
VELAR	g	k	kʰ

The three series are called mediae, tenues and aspiratae by the author of one recently published textbook;[24] these terms are presumably equivalent to voiced, voiceless unaspirated and voiceless aspirated. Another source[25] characterizes these stops as voiced, voiceless glottalized

[24] P. L. Movsessian, *Armenische Grammatik* (Vienna, 1959), p. 17.

[25] G. H. Fairbanks and E. W. Stevick, *Spoken East Armenian* (New York, 1958), pp. xv–xviii.

unaspirated and voiceless aspirated. The very much earlier description by Rousselot[26] referred to them as lenis, fortis and aspirated.

TABLE 7. Voice Onset Time in Msec: Eastern Armenian
(1 speaker)

	/b/	/p/	/pʰ/	/d/	/t/	/tʰ/	/g/	/k/	/kʰ/
Av.	−96	3	78	−102	15	59	−115	30	98
R.	−195:−35	0:15	60:105	−195:−90	10:20	35:80	−190:−150	15:50	60:135
N.	23	12	10	13	14	8	14	14	16

2. Thai

LABIAL	b	p	pʰ
DENTAL	d	t	tʰ
VELAR		k	kʰ

The stops of Thai are most often described as voiced, voiceless unaspirated and voiceless aspirated.[27] Hockett adds the comment that the voiceless unaspirated stops "do not tend to be non-distinctively glottalized."[28]

TABLE 8. Voice Onset Time in Msec: Thai
(3 speakers)

	/b/	/p/	/pʰ/	/d/	/t/	/tʰ/	/k/	/kʰ/
Av.	−97	6	64	−78	9	65	25	100
R.	−165:−40	0:20	25:100	−165:−40	0:25	25:125	0:40	50:155
N.	31	32	33	33	33	33	32	38

3. Korean

LABIAL	p	pᶜ	pʰ
DENTAL	t	tᶜ	tʰ
VELAR	k	kᶜ	kʰ

Our choice of symbols for representing the stops of Korean is not based on the practices of linguists specializing in the language; it represents rather a simple broad transcription based on our own phonetic judgments of the productions of several speakers of the Seoul dialect. Published phonetic descriptions of the stops show considerable variation.[29] The first

[26] P.-J. Rousselot, *Principes de phonétique expérimentale*, Vol. I (Paris, 1924; 1st pub., 1901–1908), pp. 596–599.

[27] M. R. Haas, G. V. Grekoff, R. C. Mendiones, W. Buddhari, J. R. Cooke and S. C. Egerod, *Thai-English Student's Dictionary* (Stanford, 1964), p. xi. This analysis has been presented by M. R. Haas in numerous earlier publications. See also A. S. Abramson, *The Vowels and Tones of Standard Thai: Acoustical Measurements and Experiments* (Bloomington, 1962), p. 4.

[28] Hockett, *Manual*, p. 115.

[29] S. E. Martin, "Korean Phonemics," *Language* XXVII (1951), 519–533; F. Lukoff, *A Grammar of Korean* (Ph.D. dissertation, University of Pennsylvania, 1951), pp. 5–8; Mieko S. Han, *Acoustic Phonetics of Korean*, Technical Report No. 1 (University of California, 1963), pp. 20–21.

series, /p t k/, have been called voiceless, tense, long, and glottalized, though not all these terms have been used by everyone. The series /pᶜ tᶜ kᶜ/ are said to be, in initial position, voiceless, lax, and slightly aspirated. /pʰ tʰ kʰ/ are described as voiceless and heavily aspirated, but lax. Although for our present purpose it is efficient to regard the stops of each series as unit phonemes, two well known analyses establish only the second type as unit phonemes, while those of the first and third types are represented as sequences of two phonemes each; the first type is taken either as a case of gemination or as a sequence of the simple stop phoneme and a phoneme of "glottal tension," while the third type is a sequence of the simple stop followed by a phoneme /h/. For our purpose the choice of one of these analyses over the others is a matter of no consequence.

TABLE 9. Voice Onset Time in Msec: Korean
(1 speaker)

	/p/	/pᶜ/	/pʰ/	/t/	/tᶜ/	/tʰ/	/k/	/kᶜ/	/kʰ/
Av.	7	18	91	11	25	94	19	47	126
R.	0:15	10:35	65:115	0:25	15:40	75:105	0:35	30:65	85:200
N.	15	30	21	16	24	12	16	34	12

Four-category languages.

1. Hindi

LABIAL	b	bʰ	p	pʰ
DENTAL	d	dʰ	t	tʰ
DOMAL	ḍ	ḍʰ	ṭ	ṭʰ
VELAR	g	gʰ	k	kʰ

The Hindi stops may be arranged, with respect to the place and manner dimensions of phonetic description, in a 4 × 4 array. The manner dimension itself is, in turn, analyzed into the two independent components of voicing and aspiration, so that the sixteen categories may also be located in a 2 × 2 manner array:

	voiced	voiceless
unaspirated	b d ḍ g	p ṭ ṭ k
aspirated	bʰ dʰ ḍʰ gʰ	pʰ tʰ ṭʰ kʰ

It is of course possible to argue that the aspirated categories are better analyzed into phoneme sequences consisting of either voiced or voiceless stop and a phoneme /h/.[30] For our purpose, however, it makes no difference whether the aspiration is taken as a phonetic component of half the stop categories or as the manifestation of a phoneme /h/.

[30] See John J. Gumperz, "Phonological Differences in Three Hindi Dialects," *Language* XXXIV (1958), 212–224; also C. F. Hockett, *Manual*, esp. p. 107.

TABLE 10. Voice Onset Time in Msec: Hindi
(1 speaker)

	/b/	/bh/[31]	/p/	/ph/	/d/	/dh/	/t/	/th/
Av.	−85	−61	13	70	−87	−87	15	67
R.	−120: −40	−105:0	0:25	60:80	−140: −60	−150: −60	5:25	35:100
N.	16	15	18	18	18	18	16	16

	/ḍ/	/ḍh/[31]	/ṭ/	/ṭh/	/g/	/gh/	/k/	/kh/
Av.	−76	−77	9	60	−63	−75	18	92
R.	−115: −30	−110:0	0:20	45:80	−95: −30	−160: −40	10:35	75:100
N.	18	15	18	18	17	16	16	18

2. Marathi

LABIAL	b	bh	p	ph
DENTAL	d	dh	t	th
DOMAL	ḍ	ḍh	ṭ	ṭh
VELAR	g	gh	k	kh

In general the Marathi stops are phonetically similar to the Hindi; distributionally they differ in that Marathi /ḍ/ and /ḍh/ do not occur in word-initial position (and thus are not represented in the body of data given below). The four categories differ phonetically with respect to the two intersecting dimensions of voicing and aspiration, although at least one recent statement[32] characterizes the voiceless stops as also fortis, the voiced as lenis, and the aspirated voiced stops as "rather fortis."

TABLE 11. Voice Onset Time in Msec: Marathi
(1 speaker)

	/b/	/bh/	/p/	/ph/	/d/	/dh/	/t/	/th/
Av.	−117	−95	11	76	−111	−87	10	65
R.	−160: −80	−160: −65	0:25	40:110	−175: −65	−110: −40	0:20	40:85
N.	14	16	11	14	20	19	17	14

	/ṭ/	/ṭh/	/g/	/gh/	/k/	/kh/
Av.	0	63	−116	−89	24	87
R.	0:10	35:75	−160: −75	−120: −45	10:40	60:105
N.	10	14	18	18	14	14

Overall relations. From a comparison of the mean values and ranges given in the tables just presented it is quite clear that, on the whole, differences in

[31] In each of the categories /bh/ and /ḍh/ there was a single aberrant production with voicing lag: +20 for one word said to begin with /bh/ and +25 for one of the words recorded for /ḍh/. Both were excluded from our table, since careful listening led us to believe that they might well be regarded by the speaker as faulty productions, although it seemed very unlikely that they would be identified as any stops other than /bh/ and /ḍh/.

[32] A. R. Kelkar, *The Phonology and Morphology of Marathi* (Ph.D. dissertation, Cornell University, 1958), pp. 4, 16.

voice onset time may serve as a basis for separating the various manner categories in each of the languages examined. At the same time, however, there is some indication that the measure of voice onset time is also, to a certain extent, sensitive to the *place* of stop closure, for the velars seem to have consistently higher values than the other stops. Because this may well have the effect of producing apparently overlapping distributions if stops of the same manner but different places of articulation are taken together, we shall keep separate the data for the three general positions of stop closure. An example of this effect is the relation between English /b d g/ and /p t k/; the two classes of stops overlap in the +20 to +30 range, but this is in fact almost entirely a matter of overlap between /g/ and /p/, for our data show no range of values common to /b/ and /p/ or to /d/ and /t/ or to /g/ and /k/. With our present data we can not rule out the possibility that some of the remaining overlap is a function of the uncontrolled variable of vocalic environment.

In order to see in detail just how the measure of voice onset time serves as a device for separating stop categories it is perhaps easier to display our data in the form of graphs of frequency distribution. These graphs enable us to see at a glance whether the values determined for items belonging to any particular category tend to cluster near some favored or "modal" value. In Figs. 2–7 each category is represented by a family of vertical lines, where the height of any one line indicates the percentage of items belonging to the category whose values of voice onset time fall within a ten milli-second interval at the value shown by the location of the line along the horizontal axis of the graph. It is assumed that as the number of measured items is increased the family of lines representing them will tend more and more to conform to one or another type of "smooth" distribution, that is, that the line connecting the ends of those lines will increasingly approximate a smooth curve. A number of categories represented in our figures show frequency distributions that are far from smooth, but in general our data provide a reasonably good indication of the range of values that a larger sample of stops in the various languages might occupy.

If we begin by looking at the frequency distributions for the two-category languages (Figs. 2, 3, 4) we see, first of all, that four of the languages (Dutch, Spanish, Hungarian, Tamil) are grossly similar in having one set of stops with negative values and the other with zero or small positive values of voice onset time. Cantonese is similar to these in having a category whose values lie in the region at and just above zero, but its second category shows considerably higher positive values. English resembles Cantonese, except for the lone speaker (of the four who served as informants) who produced /b d g/'s with negative values of voice onset

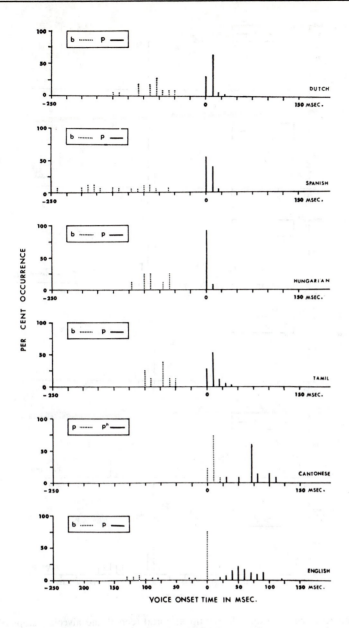

FIGURE 2. Voice onset-time distributions: labial stops of two-category languages.

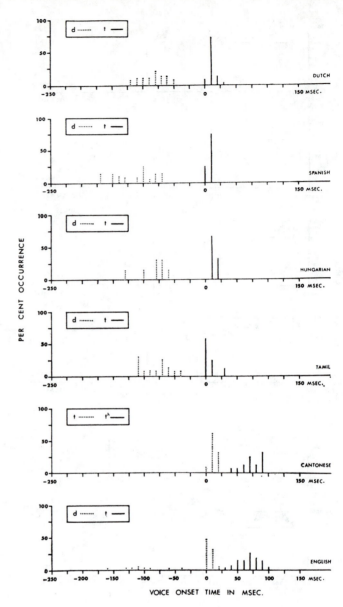

FIGURE 3. Voice onset-time distributions: apical (dental and alveolar) stops of two-category languages.

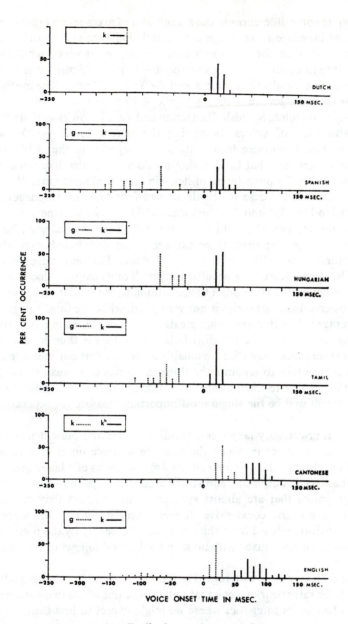

FIGURE 4. Voice onset-time distributions: velar stops of two-category languages.

time. Despite some differences in the magnitudes of averages and ranges of values from language to language the overall similarity among these six languages is striking, for it appears that the stop categories overall fall generally into three ranges—one from about -125 to -75 msec, one from zero to $+25$ msec, and a third from about $+60$ to $+100$ msec. The median values for these ranges are -100, $+10$ and $+75$ msec respectively. Thus we may say that Dutch, Spanish, Hungarian and Tamil show essentially the same distribution of values, occupying the ranges about -100 and $+10$ msec, that Cantonese locates its stop categories in the $+10$ and $+75$ msec ranges, and that English shows values distributed like those of Cantonese, except for a scattering of items in the -100 msec range.[33]

The situation in the case of the three- and four-category languages is represented in Figs. 5, 6 and 7. Values measured for Eastern Armenian and Thai line up very precisely with the ranges which the two-category languages occupy jointly; their three categories are distributed over the ranges centering at -100, $+10$ and $+75$ msec. The remaining three-category language, Korean, is peculiar in that all of its stops are located in the positive half of the voice onset time continuum; the resolution between the two lower-valued categories is not very good, while the third category shows average values that are rather greater than those found in any of the other languages. But while the distribution of values is thus somewhat anomalous, we cannot say with reasonable assurance that our measure of voice onset time fails to separate the three categories of Korean stops; it will certainly suffice to distinguish the aspirated set from the other two and it may still well be the single most important measure for separating the latter.

The two four-category languages, Hindi and Marathi, present us with our only clearcut cases in which the measure of voice onset time is insufficient for distinguishing among all the stop categories of a language. To be sure, the voiced unaspirated and voiced aspirated stops show differences in average values that are almost systematic; nevertheless they occupy ranges that are nearly coextensive. It seems very likely that the voiced aspirates are distinguished from the other voiced category by the presence of low amplitude buzz mixed with noise in the interval following release of the stop.

Two final observations with regard to the data of Figs. 2–7 can be made. The first is the rather curious one that not a single one of the two-category languages locates its categories where we might expect to find them, that

[33] Very recently Lawrence Raphael of Queens College of the City University of New York examined initial stops in isolated Persian words and found them to be much like English stops in the way they lie along the dimension.

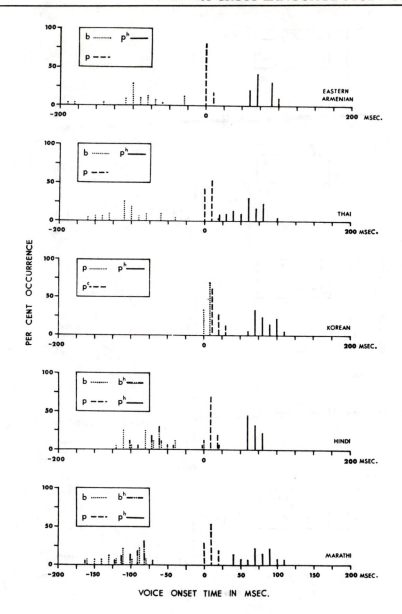

FIGURE 5. Voice onset-time distributions: labial stops of three- and four-category languages.

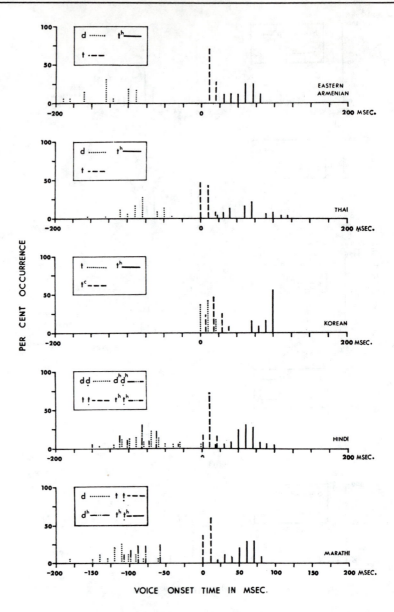

FIGURE 6. Voice onset-time distributions: apical (dental and domal) stops of three- and four-category languages.

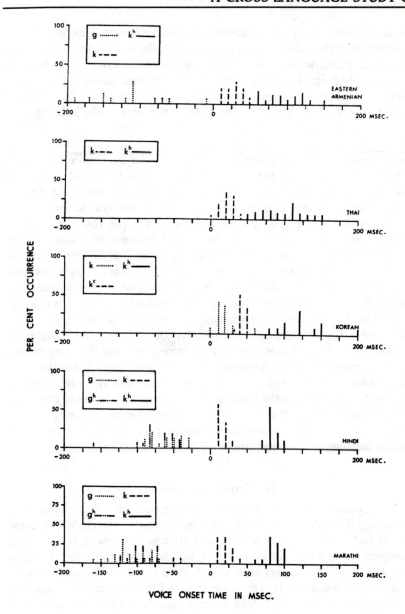

FIGURE 7. Voice onset-time distributions: velar stops of three- and four-category languages.

is, at opposite ends of the continuum of voice onset time. This fact, if it is a reflection of the situation in languages generally, is evidence for the view that in the phonetic "realization" of phonemic contrasts human beings fall considerably short of utilizing all the phonetic space available to them. The second observation concerns the relation between frequency distribution and the existence of "holes" in the phonemic inventory of a language. In both Dutch and Thai the velar series of stops is deficient as compared with the labial and apical sets, and we might plausibly expect to find that the velars found in those languages have rather broader distributions than the other stops. This is not the case, however; instead the distributions for Dutch /k/ and Thai /k/ and /kʰ/ are exactly what they would be if their velar series conformed in number of phonemes to the other series.

Finally, it is of interest to see how values for the voice onset time measure are distributed for all eleven of our languages taken together. In Figure 8 the overall frequency distributions for each of our three general places of articulation are given after normalizing so that all stop categories in each language are in effect represented by the same number of measurements. From this figure it appears that the distribution of values is essentially tri-modal, corresponding generally to the ranges centering at -100, $+10$ and $+75$ msec. The three modes differ considerably in their degree of peakedness and in the sharpness of their separation from the other modes of the distribution. It is furthermore apparent from Figure 8 that the positive modes for the velar place of articulation have somewhat higher values than either the labial or the apical stops. It should also be noted that each of the three frequency distributions shows a "hole" in the region just below zero, although at the moment there is no evidence to support speculation on the meaning of the observation.

III. Stops in Sentences

The ultimate usefulness of measuring voice onset time depends on how effectively it enables us to identify the stops in running speech. We have not as yet had a really serious look at long stretches of speech, but we have compared values for words spoken in isolation with those for the same words embedded in longer sentences, both in initial and non-initial positions (see **Procedure** in I). The sentence data for our eleven languages are presented in Tables 12–22. The average value and range of voice onset time in milliseconds, as well as the number of items measured for each phoneme, are given in the same format as in Tables 1–11, except that a separate set of items for non-initial position appears in each table.

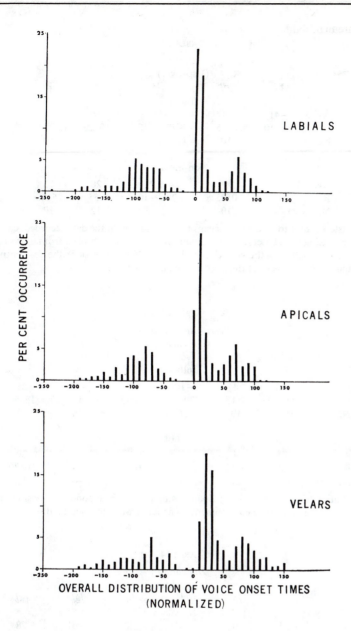

FIGURE 8. Overall frequency distributions of voice onset-time values, normalized so that all stop categories are equally represented.

Measurement data.

TABLE 12

Dutch
(1 speaker)

	/b/	/p/	/d/[34]	/t/	/k/
			Initial		
Av.	−41	11	−51	16	34
R.	−65:0	0:25	−70: −40	10:20	25:60
N.	10	10	11	9	10
			Non-initial		
Av.	*	9	−40*	20	33
R.	—	0:25	−70: −10	0:55	25:40
N.	—	10	2	12	10

* An asterisk next to an average means that in addition to the data recorded, cases of unbroken voicing were observed, i.e., voicing that proceeds unbroken from a preceding voiced environment into the stop-closure interval. If an asterisk is the sole entry, it means that all occurrences of the stop showed unbroken voicing.

TABLE 13

Puerto Rican Spanish
(2 speakers)

	/b/	/p	/d/	/t/	/g/	/k/
			Initial			
Av.	−110	4	−109	7	−92	25
R.	−175: −35	0:15	−170: −55	0:15	−145: −50	15:55
N.	15	19	16	14	16	19
			Non-initial			
Av.	−90*	4	*	8	*	20
R.	−90	0:15	—	0:15	—	10:30
N.	1	21	—	16	—	18

*In addition to unbroken voicing, Spanish stop phonemes in non-initial position have fricative allophones in some environments. The latter were not measured.

TABLE 14

Hungarian
(1 speaker)

	/b/	/p/	/d/	/t/	/g/	/k/
			Initial			
Av.	−55	0	−70	20	−61	28
R.	−70: −35	0	−90: −35	10:35	−95: −40	20:45
N.	6	6	6	6	6	6

[34] One occurrence of initial /d/ showed a voicing lag, not lead, of 10 msec.

Non-initial

Av.	*	4	*	24	*	34
R.	—	0:15	—	20:30	—	10:45
N.	—	6	—	6	—	6

TABLE 15
Tamil
(1 speaker)

	/b/	/p/	/d/	/t/	/g/[35]	/k/
			Initial			
Av.	−61	12	−64	10	−56	27
R.	−75:−40	0:45	−100:−45	0:25	−80:10	15:40
N.	10	37	13	8	13	11

[35] Two occurrences of initial /g/ showed voicing lag. One was 10 msec and the other, 5 msec.

Non-initial

Av.	*	6	*	6	*	10
R.	—	0:20	—	0:15	—	10:30
N.	—	43	—	8	—	10

TABLE 16
Cantonese
(1 speaker)

	/p/	/pʰ/	/t/	/tʰ/	/k/	/kʰ/
			Initial			
Av.	11	58	15	62	34	68
R.	10:15	50:75	10:25	45:85	25:50	55:80
N.	6	6	4	5	6	6
			Non-initial			
Av.	9	39	15	66	23	67
R.	0:15	20:55	10:25	45:110	10:45	60:75
N.	5	5	6	6	5	6

TABLE 17[36]
English
(4 speakers)

	/b/	/p/	/d/	/t/	/g/	/k/
			Initial			
Av.	7/−65	28	9/−56	39	17/−45	43
R.	0:15/−65	10:45	0:25/−90:−20	15:70	0:13/−45	30:85
N.	24/2	24	45/5	26	24/1	25

[36] The investigation of voice onset time in English was conducted before the format for the present study had been set, and the method of obtaining stops embedded in

Non-initial

Av.	4/−63*	34	7*	37	16*	49
R.	0:20/−90: −50	15:70	0:20	15:95	0:40	15:90
N.	47/4	86	34	99	53	138

TABLE 18

Eastern Armenian
(1 speaker)

	/b/	/p/	/pʰ/	/d/	/t/	/tʰ/	/g/	/k/	/kʰ/
				Initial					
Av.	−72	5	51	−107	13	35	−66	23	83
R.	−140: −55	0:10	35:65	−150: −70	10:15	30:40	−130:0	15:30	55:100
N.	14	6	6	3	2	2	7	7	8
				Non-initial					
Av.	−47*	7	53	*	10	47	−21*	27	76
R.	−55: −30	0:10	35:65	—	10	45:50	−35:0	15:55	45:95
N.	3	6	6	—	2	2	4	8	8

TABLE 19[37]

Thai
(1 speaker)[38]

	/b/	/p/	/pʰ/	/d/	/t/	/tʰ/	/k/	/kʰ/
				Initial				
Av.	−35	8	37	−53	15	63	15	69
R.	−50: −20	0:15	25:45	−60: −45	15	55:70	15	55:90
N.	2	4	3	2	2	2	2	4
				Non-initial				
Av.	−66*	11	50	−38*	8	43	16	74
R.	−90: −20	0:20	25:80	−60: −20	0:20	20:95	0:25	30:135
N.	8	5	12	10	6	18	6	29

sentences was different. We simply composed several lists of sentences containing not only the words of Part II but also many other words with initial stops. The informants were told to read them as naturally as they could. For the double entries under /b d g/, see the discussion accompanying Tables 6 and 6a.

[37] As in the case of English, voice onset time in Thai was investigated before the format for this study had been set. To obtain stops embedded in sentences we listened to high-quality tape recordings of about half an hour's worth of unrehearsed conversational and narrative material and picked out passages containing prevocalic stops. The only phones accepted as utterance-initial stops were those that appeared after juncture, which was taken to be any break in discourse such that what followed was impressionistically equivalent to the initiation of speech. This procedure yielded somewhat fewer initial stops than non-initial ones.

[38] This speaker is one of the three entered in Table 8.

TABLE 20
Korean
(1 speaker)

	/p/	/pᶜ/	/pʰ/	/t/	/tᶜ/	/tʰ/	/k/	/kᶜ/	/kʰ/
					Initial				
Av.	7	22	89	11	30	100	20	48	125
R.	0:15	15:40	55:115	0:20	15:40	75:130	0:30	35:75	80:175
N.	14	28	24	15	21	12	14	35	10
					Non-initial				
Av.	5	13*	75	12	22*	78	21	44*	93
R.	0:10	10:20	40:130	0:25	10:45	50:120	10:35	30:65	55:175
N.	14	10	23	16	12	10	14	11	10

* The noteworthy thing about unbroken voicing (see Table 12) in Korean is that it occurs in the middle category rather than the leftmost one. The matter will be brought up again in the general discussion of the sentence data.

TABLE 21
Hindi
(1 speaker)
Initial

	/b/	/bʰ/	/p/	/pʰ/	/d/	/dʰ/	/t/	/tʰ/
Av.	−89	−65	12	63	−88	−78	11	63
R.	−115:−75	−105:0	5:20	50:75	−120:−50	−105:−65	5:20	35:80
N.	8	8	8	8	8	8	8	8

	/ḍ/	/ḍʰ/	/ṭ/	/ṭʰ/	/g/	/gʰ/	/k/	/kʰ/
Av.	−74	−74	11	57	−47	−59	16	84
R.	−140:−30	−90:−35	5:15	50:65	−70:−35	−85:−30	10:25	65:105
N.	8	8	8	8	8	8	8	8

Non-initial

	/b/	/bʰ/	/p/	/pʰ/	/d/	/dʰ/	/t/	/tʰ/
Av.	*	*	9	46	0*	*	14	45
R.	—	—	0:20	35:55	0	—	10:20	30:70
N.	—	—	8	8	1	—	8	8

	/ḍ/	/ḍʰ/	/ṭ/	/ṭʰ/	/g/	/gʰ/	/k/	/kʰ/
Av.	0*	*	8	48	10*	*	21	63
R.	0	—	0:15	15:60	10	—	0:35	50:80
N.	1	—	8	8	1	—	8	8

TABLE 22
Marathi
(1 speaker)
Initial

	/b/	/bʰ/	/p/	/pʰ/	/d/	/dʰ/	/t/	/tʰ/
Av.	−106	−73	0	35	−93	−71	11	54
R.	−145: −85	−90: −60	0	25:55	−110: −75	−85: −60	10:15	35:80
N.	4	4	4	4	8	8	4	4

	/t/	/tʰ/	/g/	/gʰ/	/k/	/kʰ/
Av.	11	35	−81	−67	21	73
R.	10:15	30:40	−90: −70	−85: −40	20:25	60:80
N.	4	4	6	6	4	4

Non-initial

	/b/	/bʰ/	/p/	/pʰ/	/d/	/dʰ/	/t/	/tʰ/
Av.	*	*	0	45	*	0*	15	60
R.	—	—	0	40:50	—	0	15	50:70
N.	—	—	4	2	—	1	3	4

	/t/	/tʰ/	/g/	/gʰ/	/k/	/kʰ/
Av.	3	53	*	*	13	66
R.	0:10	40:65	—	—	0:20	60:75
N.	4	4	—	—	4	4

Comparison with words. Tables 12 to 22 reveal that by and large the sentence data are congruent with the word data. Although the voice onset time dimension effectively separates stop categories in sentences, there is, nevertheless, some effect of embedding the stops in running speech. First of all, for categories with voicing lead, we find that in non-initial position voicing usually proceeds unbroken from a preceding voiced environment into the closure interval; any interruption of glottal buzz depends on what sounds occur before the stop. This effect is also observed in categories with short voicing lag in two languages, English /b d g/ (Table 17) and the Korean middle category /pᶜ tᶜ kᶜ/ (Table 20).[39] It is difficult to see, off-hand, why it should be the Korean middle category and not the lowest one that

[39] It must be understood that while the negative as well as positive marking of the categories named affects the absolute magnitude of voice onset time, it does not cause a weakening of the power of the dimension; indeed, it enhances it. Where Korean and English stops have unbroken voicing (i.e., voicing that has started earlier in the utterance and not stopped at the time of the stop closure), they are better separated from the categories with interrupted voicing and lag than they are in other environments.

takes on unbroken voicing;[40] however, it should be noted that in all the other languages but English, categories with zero onset time or very short lag are like Korean /p t k/ in not showing unbroken voicing. Another effect of embedding stops in sentences is that voice onset time values, both lead and lag, tend to be a bit compressed in comparison with the values measured in the citation forms of words. If this tendency, admittedly not a strong one, persists in a larger sampling of utterances, it suggests that not only vowel duration but also voice onset time is likely to be affected by temporal compression in rapid speech. In the several cases where this compression occurs, there is, of course, a reduction of the gap separating those categories from each other along the voice onset time dimension. There is no question, however, of a reduction to the point of serious over-lap between otherwise distinct categories.

Several uncontrolled variables in the sentence data have to be mentioned. In our desire to get normal connected speech, we made no attempt to control the rate of utterance, but simply told the informants to say the sentences naturally. Stress variation was considerable, especially in English where we did not hesitate to examine stops that occurred in initial position in words other than the key words. (See footnote 36.) No control over vocalic environments was exercised. When feasible, we had the informant, or some other speaker of the language, check his recordings, but we are quite sure that occasional losses of contrast have remained in our data because of informants' slips. Aside from accidental losses of contrast, there is also the question of unstable contrasts. If, in a given language system, two phonemes tend to alternate with some freedom, e.g. English /ð/ and /θ/, one might wonder whether that contrast is not in a state of flux. The phonemic descriptions available to us indicated nothing as to the relative stability of the stop contrasts, yet we suspect that this may be a factor in some of our data, for example, the Korean. In spite of these variables, which may in part be uncontrollable, the resolving power of the voice onset time dimension is good.

IV. Discussion and Plans

Inferences as to glottal mechanisms. In phonetic investigations one would like to show what physiological mechanisms underlie acoustic features that differentiate phonemes. We believe that certain inferences about glottal behavior will explain the findings of this study, as well as other studies, of

---

[40] See, however, S. Martin (1951) for the positing of a glottal component for the lowest-valued category in Korean. Glottalization has been attributed to the stops of other languages too. All such assertions, based on auditory evaluation, clearly require physiological confirmation.

the voicing distinction in stops. It is to be understood that this is not merely the obvious question of whether or not there is laryngeal vibration. Instead, it seems evident that a fairly complicated acoustic output is dependent upon the relatively simple matter of varying the area of the glottis. If the speaker closes the glottis down enough for phonation, he does not directly "command" the vocal folds to vibrate;[41] rather, he makes the necessary muscular adjustments that set the conditions for vibration when sufficient airflow is supplied.[42]

At this point it may be useful to go through a brief review of the salient features of voice production.[43] The myoelastic-aerodynamic theory, involving a counterbalancing of aerodynamic forces and muscular tensions, is the most widely accepted explanation of phonation. When air pressure beneath the closed glottis is sufficiently high, the vocal folds are blown apart and a puff of air is released into the supralaryngeal cavities. With the resulting drop in subglottal air pressure, the folds snap together again[44] under the impact of two restoring forces: (1) tension of the intrinsic muscles of the larynx, and (2) a drop in air pressure along the margins of the folds caused by air rushing through the glottis (the Bernoulli effect). Voice onset can occur either with the folds completely adducted or somewhat abducted. The laryngeal repetition rate (fundamental frequency) is regulated by the length, mass and tension of the vocal folds in conjunction with varying amounts of air pressure from the lungs.[45] The puffs of air thus repeatedly released by

[41] Unless one accepts Husson's generally discredited theory of direct neural triggering of laryngeal pulses. See R. Husson, "Etude des phénomènes physiologiques et acoustiques fondamentaux de la voix chantée," Thèse. *Revue Scientifique* (Paris, 1950). For criticism, see the works cited below in footnotes 43 and 45.

[42] A theory of the perceptual relevance of motor commands is presented in A. M. Liberman, F. S. Cooper, K. S. Harris and P. F. MacNeilage, "A Motor Theory of Speech Perception," *Proceedings of the Speech Communication Seminar*, Vol. II, Royal Institute of Technology (Stockholm, 1962).

[43] For good anatomical drawings of various views of the larynx, see, e.g., Raymond C. Truex and Carl E. Kellner, *Detailed Atlas of the Head and Neck* (New York, 1948), Figures 66–74.

[44] This is a commonly observed mode of vibration. The description does not take into account the way the mode varies with different voice registers. For example, the system can be kept in oscillation with little or no contact between the folds at the end of each cycle.

[45] For a good exposition in greater detail, see, e.g., Giles W. Gray and Claude M. Wise, *The Bases of Speech*, 3rd ed. (New York, 1959), pp. 163–171. For a critical survey of work on phonation, see Janwillem van den Berg, "Myoelastic–Aerodynamic Theory of Voice Production," *Journal of Speech and Hearing Research*, I (1958), 227–244. For work on subglottal air pressure, see Peter Ladefoged, "Sub-Glottal Activity during Speech" in *Proceedings of the Fourth International Congress of Phonetic Sciences*, ed., A Sovijärvi and P. Aalto (The Hague, 1962), pp. 73–91.

the glottis excite the resonant frequencies of the vocal tract, producing voice.

The glottis can vary considerably in size and shape. This is effected principally by movements of the arytenoid cartilages under the control of the intrinsic muscles of the larynx. The vocal folds extend from the thyroid cartilage in front to the vocal processes (anterior angles) of the arytenoid cartilages in back. These pyramidal cartilages, set on the upper back edge of the cricoid cartilage of the trachea, can tilt backwards, stretching and possibly tensing the folds, and forward, relaxing them. They can glide toward and away from each other, and rotate to bring the vocal processes together or apart;[46] thus the front three-fifths of the laryngeal opening, the membranous glottis, can be closed while the cartilaginous glottis in back is open, or the whole glottis can be open or shut. Consequently, wide variations in the area and shape of opening are possible.[47]

By and large, the concept of voice onset time offers no physiological difficulty. Phonation simply starts at some point in time relative to the release of the stop closure. (During a voicing lag, aspiration will be heard if the vocal tract resonates to turbulent air passing through the open glottis.) It must be acknowledged that in making this physical measure one may be misled into including a short span of pulsation, perhaps just one cycle, that is too weak to be audible. We are certain that occasional errors of this sort can make no significant difference in the way the stop categories have been shown to lie along the dimension.

The question of audibility of glottal pulses is a crucial one. There is no point, it would seem, in speaking of the distinctive relevance of a phonetic feature that is not perceptible. In the **Procedure** we stated that from time to time, in an environment of preceding voicing, non-initial stops with apparent voicing lag showed faint vertical striations at glottal rates near the baseline of the spectrogram below the clearly aperiodic high-frequency noise of aspiration. It seems that some investigators[48] have observed such cases and seized upon them to cast doubt on the primacy of the voiced/ voiceless distinction. This may reflect a failure to discriminate between acoustic features and their preceptual correlates; that is, there is a danger of giving primary emphasis to an instrumentally detectable acoustic disturbance that, in the situation, can have no auditory consequences. Despite the almost negligible number of our recorded utterances that showed this

---

[46] Harold M. Kaplan, *Anatomy and Physiology of Speech* (New York, 1960), p. 120.

[47] Kaplan, pp. 128–129.

[48] For example, Fred W. Householder in his review of Ernst Pulgram, *Introduction to the Spectrography of Speech, International Journal of American Linguistics* XXVII (1961), p. 178.

phenomenon, we feel we must discuss the matter, if only to satisfy the observers who have made so much of it. Donning our phoneticians' caps, we listened carefully and repeatedly to the utterances in question without detecting voicing in the hold or release of the stops. In addition, in passing the tapes over the playback head of the tape recorder at extremely slow speeds and very high amplification, a procedure which yields a distinct impression of periodic pulsing in the case of normal voicing, we heard nothing but the noise of release and aspiration. We believe that inferences can be made from the available knowledge of glottal mechanisms to account for these anomalous cases.

To date it has not been possible to look directly at the action of the vocal folds in running speech; therefore we can only make inferences from other kinds of evidence. Spectrograms suggest that the laryngeal oscillations of a preceding voiced environment may simply continue for a while even after the glottis has begun to open for a voiceless stop; these vibrations are so low in intensity that any auditory effect they might have by themselves seems to be masked out by the stop burst and the noise of turbulent air rushing through the glottis. We propose the term "edge vibrations" for this hypothesized behavior.[49] That edge vibrations occur at all in speech is evident in the high-speed motion pictures of the larynx now available. These films are limited so far to speech with the mouth wide open. In her film "Vocal Cord Action in Speech: a High-Speed Study,"[50] Elizabeth Uldall shows vowel productions with laryngeal vibrations occurring before the glottis has closed at the beginning of the vowel and after the glottis has opened at the end of the vowel. Vibration occurs with an even wider glottal aperture for an initial [h].

A way of directly photographing edge vibrations, or indeed any laryngeal vibrations, during consonant articulations has not yet been worked out. The method of photo-electric glottography, recently developed by B. Sonesson,[51] affords an indirect way of recording the area of the glottis as it varies in time. The procedure used by us was designed independently by Franklin S. Cooper, who followed suggestions made by Paul Moore of the University of Florida. The system uses a powerful light source, a light guide, and a photoelectric cell. The light guide is a light-conducting rod

---

[49] The spectrum of the edge vibrations seems to consist only of one or two weak harmonics at the low-frequency end. This can be seen better in narrow-band spectrograms.

[50] University of Edinburgh and Swiss Federal Institute of Technology, 1957.

[51] B. Sonesson, *On the Anatomy and Vibratory Pattern of the Human Vocal Folds* (Lund, 1960).

shaped to fit the contour of the roof of the subject's mouth[52] and shower an intense beam of light down onto the larynx. In a darkened room, light passing through the open glottis can be seen coming through the skin of the neck below. The photocell is held against the neck at this point. The amount of light entering the cell varies in proportion to the changing area of the glottis. An oscillographic record of the photocell output reveals whether the glottis is open or closed and whether the folds are vibrating or not.[53]

Through transillumination of the larynx we obtained a number of glottal traces for English voiceless stops in medial position after voiced phones and before both stressed and unstressed vowels. In every instance the glottis opened abruptly, but the vocal folds did not always stop vibrating at the same moment. They sometimes continued to vibrate until the glottis began closing to reach normal phonatory position again. In one production, before the stressed vowel of *depict*, the folds vibrated through the whole open phase, with some weakening of the pulses after the glottis reached its peak opening. These findings are supported by high-speed oscillograms of such utterances recorded simultaneously by means of an air microphone, which picks up the signal as it arrives at the ear, and a throat microphone, which is more directly responsive to laryngeal vibrations. The throat trace will sometimes show very weak glottal modulation (edge vibration) on the wave form of the aspiration noise of English /p t k/, while the air trace shows only noise. Of course, if the edge vibrations are a bit higher in amplitude, although still inaudible, they will appear in the air trace too, just as they do in spectrograms. Further work with improved instrumentation is needed, but the findings of this little side study clearly lend credence to our thoughts on edge vibrations.

Another anomaly that requires explanation is the failure of the dimension of voice onset time to separate the voiced aspirate stops from the voiced inaspirates of Hindi and Marathi. Voicing lead of much the same duration is found in both categories, and indeed it distinguishes the pair from the other stop categories. Auditory impressions suggest that the

[52] The two subjects to try it so far find that they can tolerate the light guide only for short periods of time, but while it is in place, they can articulate pretty well. F. S. Cooper is now designing a modification of the system with a light guide made of a flexible fiber optics bundle that can be passed through the nose to interfere even less with speech. The next step will be to try to supplement transillumination with direct photography by bringing up an image through a separate light bundle to a motion picture camera.

[53] Another indirect method of obtaining the glottal waveform is that of inverse filtering, in which the effects of the resonances of the vocal tract are removed from the speech wave. So far, this method can best be used for sustained sounds and not in running speech.

voiced aspirates are released with breathy voice or murmur.[54] These impressions are supported by spectrograms in which, upon release of the stop, the voicing is seen to take on a special character. There is a period of glottal periodicity, sometimes intermittent, mingled with random noise in the formant regions, all at relatively low amplitude. This voiced aspiration sounds about as long as voiceless aspiration, but it is difficult or even impossible to make physical measurements of its duration, because it merges more or less imperceptibly with the following normal voicing.

Instead of the time of onset of voicing it is the kind of voicing that distinguishes the voiced aspirates; thus, here too we should be able to find a laryngeal mechanism to account for the feature. It is physiologically reasonable to infer that the murmur is characterized by glottal vibration of a sort that allows a steady leakage of turbulent air either through the incompletely closing folds or between the open arytenoid cartilages.[55] In his film "Voice Production: the Vibrating Larynx,"[56] Jw. van den Berg uses a specimen larynx to demonstrate breathy voice. Under contraction of the lateral cricoarytenoid muscles air escapes between the arytenoid cartilages while the membranous glottis is vibrating.[57] We hope to test these inferences by transilluminating the larynx of a native speaker of Hindi or Marathi. It is also possible that there will turn out to be differences in subglottal activity associated with the production of aspirated and unaspirated voiced stops.

Coming back to the more general cases, those in which voice onset time does distinguish stop categories, we often find other features in association with distinctions along the dimension. They are: delay in the onset of the first formant (Fl cutback),[58] differences in buccal air pressure and burst intensity, and the maintenance of contrasts in whispered speech. We believe that these too are susceptible of explanation in terms of glottal mechanisms, but it will be more convenient to discuss these matters in a sequel to this article.[59]

---

[54] In the occasional instance of /bʰ dʰ gʰ/ without voicing lead, the murmured release is nevertheless present.

[55] Eli Fischer-Jørgensen, *Almen Fonetik*, 3rd ed. (Copenhagen, 1960), p. 63.

[56] University of Groningen, the Netherlands, 1960.

[57] Murmur, voiced [ɦ], etc., are discussed in J. Lazicius, *Lehrbuch der Phonetik* (Berlin, 1961), pp. 45, 60–62.

[58] A. M. Liberman, P. C. Delattre, and F. S. Cooper, "Some Cues for the Distinction between Voiced and Voiceless Stops in Initial Position," *Language and Speech* I (1958), 153–166.

[59] "A Cross-Language Study of Voicing in Initial Stops: Experiments in Perception," (in preparation).

The fortis/lenis feature in English. Let us return briefly to a topic presented in the Introduction, the positing of a fortis/lenis distinction for English stop consonants. English /b d g/ used to be regularly labelled "voiced" and /p t k/, "voiceless". At some point however, certain linguists decided that a definition of the terms "voiced" and "voiceless" in strictly phonetic terms made them not completely accurate as descriptors, for we can read, in some accounts at least (see footnotes 22 and 23) that initial allophones of /b d g/ may be more or less voiceless. Such linguists have pretty well adopted the practice of labelling the two sets of stop phonemes "lenis" and "fortis," asserting that the two sets are more generally distinguished on the basis of differences in force of articulation than in voicing. Now, if all these terms are assumed to have phonetic meanings, we must ask whether this change nets us any gain in precision of description, for we have exchanged a phonetic dimension, voicing, which has a clear articulatory and acoustic meaning, for one which is considerably less well defined both articulatorily and acoustically; furthermore, attempts at a purely physiological definition of fortisness in stops have thus far yielded nothing reliable.[60] It seems to us that the greater generality claimed for the fortis/lenis dimension of description depends upon the vagueness of its phonetic reference, a vagueness which makes it difficult to decide whether the new terms really refer to a physical difference which serves to separate the /p t k/ and /b d g/ sets or whether they are merely phoneme-class labels masquerading as phonetic categories. A closer look at the fortis/lenis feature will be taken in the sequel to this article.

Experiments in perception. Although our data generally support the view that the dimension of voice onset time is a sufficient acoustic differentiator of stop categories across a wide variety of languages, it remains to be demonstrated that this feature is perceptually relevant and sufficient.[61] We are preparing series of synthetic-speech syllables of the form stop+vowel in which the voice onset time varies in small steps along a continuum that matches the ranges observed in the present study. That is, each series will encompass the ranges of all eleven languages, as well as many others, although for a given language there will no doubt be variants that are in-

[60] Gloria Lysaught, Robert J. Rosov, and Katherine S. Harris, "Electromyography as a Speech Research Technique with an Application to Labial Stops," *Journal of the Acoustical Society of America* XXXIII (1961), 842 (Abstract); K. S. Harris, G. Lysaught, and M. H. Schvey, "Experimental Studies of the Production of Oral and Nasal Labial Stops," (in preparation).

[61] This has in fact been demonstrated for English (Liberman *et al.*, 1958) but not for the other languages.

appropriate in the sense of both lead and lag. A series will be prepared for each of the three major places of articulation.

Randomized sequences of stimuli of each syllable-type will be presented for phoneme labelling to speakers of several of the languages under consideration. We intend these experiments to test three hypotheses: (1) Perceptual boundaries between phoneme categories will fall along the voice onset time dimension; (2) the phoneme boundaries will vary from language to language in general accord with the measurements obtained from real speech; (3) best synthesis will require that voicing onset be represented acoustically by the simultaneous starting of both periodic pulsation (buzz) and the first formant.[62] Preliminary experimental data, obtained from trials of one such test series, support these hypotheses. Where category boundaries along the dimension are not very sharp, one must look for possible perceptual instability of the phonemic distinction in question. The contrast between the two Korean lower-valued categories seems a likely prospect. A necessary precaution, then, will be to run tests of the intelligibility of the distinction in real speech before turning to the experiments with synthetic speech.

Experiments will also be conducted to determine acuity of perceptual discrimination of stop variants across phoneme boundaries in comparison with discrimination of variants within phoneme categories. The cross-language situation promises to be of much interest in relation to earlier findings of the Haskins group,[63] as well as in connection with more recent thought and work on a possible link between perception and articulation.[64] This line of inquiry is made all the more interesting because the categorical kind of production suggested by the three cross-language modes of Figure 8; attempts at mimicry of the synthetic variants should throw further light on this.

Work on the various experiments in perception is now in progress, and it is hoped that an article presenting the results together with the implications of both studies will soon be ready for publication.

Summary. Linguists often find it useful to divide the phonemes of a language into "voiced" and "voiceless" categories. For stops, some languages are said to utilize aspiration in conjunction with voicing to yield two, three or

---

[62] The third hypothesis is based on the work of Liberman, Delattre and Cooper (1958), p. 64.

[63] A. M. Liberman, K. S. Harris, H. S. Hoffman, and B. C. Griffith, "The Discrimination of Speech Sounds within and across Phoneme Boundaries," *Journal of Experimental Psychology* LIV (1957), 358–368.

[64] A. M. Liberman *et al.* (1962).

four categories, while in other languages categories are said to be distinguished solely by differences in aspiration. Some linguists, moreover, speak of fortis and lenis categories. Despite the fact that these features of voicing, aspiration and force of articulation are usually treated as independent dimensions of phonetic description, there are some grounds for considering them to be plausible consequences of a single underlying variable. In the search for acoustic features which serve as cues for the perception of stop consonants in initial position we have focused our attention on spectrographic measurements of the time interval between the burst that marks release and the onset of periodicity that reflects laryngeal vibration. This measure of voice onset time has been applied to word-initial stops in eleven languages and has been found to be highly effective as a means of separating phonemic categories, although these languages differ both in the number of those categories and in the phonetic features usually ascribed to them. The boundaries between contrasting categories along the continuum of voice onset time vary from language to language, but this variation is so far from random in nature that we may speak of three general phonetic types from which the categories of a particular language are selected. It would seem that such features as voicing, aspiration and force of articulation are predictable consequences of differences in the relative timing of events at the glottis and at the place of oral occlusion.

Department of Linguistics   *Haskins Laboratories*
University of Pennsylvania   *305 East 43rd Street*
Philadelphia, Pa. 19104   *New York, N.Y. 10017*

Transitions, Glides, and Diphthongs*

Ilse Lehiste and Gordon E. Peterson

Communication Sciences Laboratory, The University of Michigan, Ann Arbor, Michigan

The study deals with the formant movements associated with transitions, glides, and diphthongs in spoken American English. The transitional characteristics associated with all initial and final consonant phonemes were studied in a large sample of utterances. The rate of change of the transition from a consonant hub to the steady state vowel formant position and conversely was investigated for vowels which are commonly considered monophthongs. It is assumed that such changes are cues for the perception of the consonants rather than linguistically significant components of the vocalic nucleus. The rate of change associated with syllable nuclei commonly perceived as diphthongs, [ɑɪ], [ɔɪ], [ɑʊ] was investigated and compared with the changes due to consonant transitions in monophthongs. Criteria are suggested by which the formant movements due to transitions may be distinguished from movements that have linguistic signalling value within the syllable nucleus.

INTRODUCTION

THE purpose of the present study is to investigate the distinction between formant movements which serve as cues for consonant identification and formant movements which signal the presence of a complex syllable nucleus, such as a glide or a diphthong. The set of material that was analyzed has been described in a previous publication.[1] Briefly, the materials include 1263 monosyllabic CNC words (consonant phoneme—syllable nucleus—consonant phoneme) recorded by one speaker, and a control set of 70 words, uttered by five speakers of the same general dialect. All words were recorded in random order in an identical sentence frame, with determined stress and pitch patterns. The total set was analyzed acoustically by various techniques.

For this present study, the following measurements were made: the frequencies of the first three formants at the beginning of the onglide, measured from the release of the consonant; the duration of the onglide from the consonant release to the steady state of the syllable nucleus; the formant positions at the steady state; the duration of the steady state; the frequencies of the first three formants at the end of the offglide; and the duration of the offglide.[2] We thus have information about the transitional formant movements associated with each initial and final consonant phoneme, information about the formant frequencies associated with the syllable nuclei, and data for calculating the rates of change associated with each formant movement.

If the rate and direction of formant movements are predictable from the combination of the formant positions of the vowel and the consonant loci, it seems that the movements would serve as cues for the identity of the consonant. The influence which such movements have upon the perception of vowel quality in monophthongs is also an interesting question for future study. If two vowel targets appear between the initial and final consonants of the CNC words, the syllable nucleus is a diphthong. It is possible that if only one target is present, the rate of change associated with either the onglide or the offglide may produce a linguistic contrast. The so-called glide phonemes that occur in some languages may fall in this category.

CONSONANT TRANSITIONS

Previous research about the interaction between vowels and consonants has resulted in the "hub"[3] and "locus"[4] theories. The "hub" theory associates with each consonant a relatively fixed frequency position for the second formant transitions; the "locus" theory adds the requirement that the direction of the movement be taken into consideration and extends the concept to all formants. Both theories appear to assume that the steady state position of the vowel formants remains

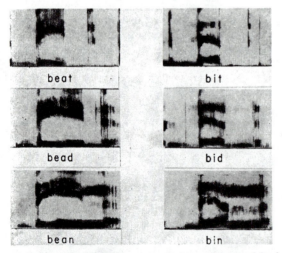

FIG. 1. Broad band spectrograms of six words uttered by informant GEP, illustrating formant transitions associated with the vowels /i/ and /ɪ/ followed by dental-alveolar consonants.

* This research was supported under contract by the Information Systems Branch of the Office of Naval Research of the U. S. Navy.

[1] G. E. Peterson and I. Lehiste, J. Acoust. Soc. Am. 32, 693 (1960).

[2] For the purposes of this study, we have defined onglide as the initial transition from the consonant to the vowel target, and offglide as the final transition from the vowel target to the consonant.

[3] R. K. Potter, G. A. Kopp, and H. C. Green, *Visible Speech* (D. Van Nostrand Company, Inc., Princeton, New Jersey, 1947).

[4] P. C. Delattre, A. M. Liberman, and F. S. Cooper, J. Acoust. Soc. Am. 27, 769 (1955).

essentially the same regardless of the preceding and following consonants. The frequency of the beginning of the onglide and the end of the offglide is commonly assumed to remain relatively constant for the different sets of consonants produced at the same point of articulation. In the literature dealing with the loci of different consonants, it appears furthermore that the frequencies of the initial and final terminations of the transitions are considered to be identical. While the "hub" theory may be considered a generalization from observations made from the speech of several informants (two main informants, one male, one female), the "locus" values are essentially based on one idiolect, that of the pattern playback. The "hub" and "locus" concepts are both valuable as attempts to extract a pattern from the great diversity of actually occurring speech events. It should be kept in mind, however, that this diversity exists. A detailed analysis of additional idiolects may yield values that differ considerably from currently accepted "hub" or "locus" values.

Some of our data show considerable divergence from previously published locus positions; we have also observed directional patterns which differ from those used for establishing the loci of consonants. In our materials, the transitions also differ considerably depending upon the position of the consonant relative to the vowel. Some general illustrations of this fact are presented in Figs. 1–3. A more detailed consideration of second formant transitions is given in the discussion of some of the later tables.

Figure 1 illustrates the formant transitions associated with the vowels [i] and [ɪ] followed by [t], [d], and [n]. The second formant of the vowel [i] in the words *beat*, *bead*, and *bean* moves toward a frequency of approximately 2000 cps; the second formant of [ɪ] in *bit*, *bid*, and *bin* ends in the frequency range of 1400 cps. Both transitions are negative. The expected second formant locus position for the alveolar consonants is approximately 1800 cps; while this value could be obtained by extending the slope of the second formant in

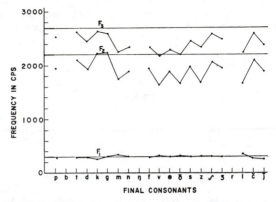

FIG. 2. Positions of the first three formants of the vowel /i/ at the end of the offglide toward all final consonants, based on 105 CNC words uttered by informant GEP.

beat and *bead*, an extension of the falling formant in *bit* and *bid* would yield an even greater difference between the expected value and the measured value.

Given the general direction of the movement, the transition associated with the offglide depends further on whether the following consonant is voiced or voiceless. In the case of voiced final consonants, the preceding syllable nucleus is relatively longer, and the transition proceeds to a frequency value that is greater in a positive transition, or smaller in a negative transition, than the corresponding value before a voiceless consonant. Figure 2 illustrates the formant positions (F_1, F_2, F_3) for the vowel [i] at the end of the offglide toward all final consonants. The values are averaged from the 105 words containing [i] as the syllable nucleus in the larger corpus. Each point represents the average for all occurrences of the [i]+C sequence. The average [i] target positions of the formants are also indicated by the thin horizontal lines, so that the direction of the movement may be inferred. Except for the pair /k/–/g/, the transitions proceed to a lower frequency value when a voiced consonant follows the [i]; the second formant transitions toward both /k/ and /g/ are positive, and

TABLE I. Average formant positions measured at the target.

Syllable nucleus	Averages for 1263 CNC words spoken by GEP			Averages for 350 CNC words spoken by 5 speakers		
	F_1	F_2	F_3	F_1	F_2	F_3
i	315	2200	2700	320	2205	2800
ɪ	415	1750	2470	410	1755	2415
eᴵ	360	2015	2510	335	2105	2630
ɛ	570	1610	2465	540	1705	2415
æ	640	1570	2460	625	1740	2415
ə	610	1185	2565	585	1155	2255
ɑ	645	1110	2540	665	1145	2520
ɔ	505	880	2525	590	985	2365
oᵁ	495	960	2495	435	905	2435
ʊ	450	980	2360	400	1015	2090
u	355	895	2240	350	845	2105
ɑᵁ	655–510	1255–910	2520–2415	655–415	1235–870	2215–2225
ɑɪ	665–485	1200–1790	2540–2450	700–375	1315–1975	2360–2585
ɔɪ	510–505	900–1610	2510–2425	550–370	950–1830	2255–2485
ɝ	475	1245	1680	430	1255	1575

TABLE II. Frequency ranges of second formant transitions.

F_2 "hub"	Labial			Dental-alveolar			Velar			Palatal	
	Initial	Final		Initial	Final		Initial	Final		Initial	Final
p	1725 ɪ 1335 1075 ʊ	1960 i 1225 720 u	t	1825 i 1695 1600 ɔɪ	2105 i, eɪ 1485 1065 u	k	1360 oʊ 1285 1200 ʊ	1045 ʊ 890 680 oʊ	c	2200 i 1880 1495 ɑ	2245 i 1785 1195 ɑ
b	1780 i 1205 900 ɔ	1300 ɑɪ 1010 750 oʊ, u	d	1785 i 1575 1535 ɑ	1960 i 1465 1250 ɑʊ	g	1325 u 1290 1225 ɔ	1055 ɔ 945 830 oʊ	ɟ	2110 eɪ 1875 1465 ɝ	2250 i 1770 1100 ɑ
m	1780 i 1185 825 oʊ	1755 i 1160 705 oʊ	n	1740 i 1450 1290 ɔ	1900 i 1430 1180 oʊ	ŋ		950 ɔ	ɲ		2110 ɪ 1770 1130 ə
Average	1240	1130		1575	1460		1285	930		1875	1775
f	1825 i 1210 800 ɔɪ	1960 i 1355 800 oʊ, u	θ	1625 i 1385 1190 ɔ	1935 i 1375 1100 oʊ				ʃ	1955 i 1650 1390 ɔ	2100 i 1700 965 ʊ
v	1650 i 1270 960 ɔɪ	1650 i 1205 815 oʊ	ð	1575 i 1400 1250 oʊ	1665 i 1395 1200 oʊ				č	1995 i 1610 1325 ɔ	2140 i 1455 1050 u
			s	1685 i 1430 1290 ɔ, ɝ	2000 i 1560 1400 ʊ				ǰ	1865 ɪ 1740 1600 ɔɪ	1925 i 1490 1175 ɑʊ
			z	1625 i 1400 1200 oʊ	1700 i 1480 1300 ɑʊ						
Average	1240	1280		1405	1455					1665	1550
Combined average	1240	1190		1475	1455		1285	930		1750	1665

the second formant proceeds, on the average, toward a higher frequency for the voiced member of the pair. The over-all curve has a certain resemblance to the duration curve presented in the previously indicated paper.[1]

The average value for [i] was taken from Table I which also contains the average target positions for all syllable nuclei included in the study. The smaller corpus of 350 words does not contain a sufficient number of occurrences of each initial and final consonant to offer a reliable comparison with the 1263-word CNC list;

the target values of the syllable nuclei, however, have been included in Table I.[5]

Figure 2 should be compared with Fig. 3, representing formant positions at the onset of the vowel [i] after all consonants.[6] In Fig. 2 it could be seen that voicing of the final consonant influenced the termination of the off-glide, but voicing or voicelessness appears to have no clearly discernible influence on the beginning of the onglide. It should be noted that for corresponding consonants the initiations of the onglides for formants 2 and 3 are, in general, appreciably different from the terminations of the offglides for these formants. Compare, for example, the points for /t/ in Figs. 2 and 3.

A study of specific transitions associated with each consonant-vowel combination is not the primary purpose of this paper; therefore, only the initial and final transitions of the second formant will be given more detailed consideration. Table II contains a summary of the data for the second formant.

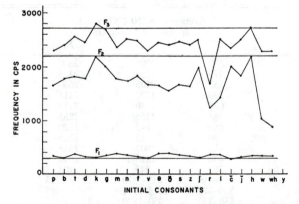

FIG. 3. Positions of the first three formants of the vowel /i/ at the onset of the vowel after all initial consonants, based on 105 CNC words uttered by informant GEP.

[5] The accuracy of formant measurements was within ±25 cps; repeated measurements differed by no more than that amount. The values included in the tables represent averages of these measurements, rounded to the nearest 5 cycles.
[6] The number of actual occurrences of each C+[i] and [i]+C sequence in the CNC list may be seen from Tables II and III of the paper by the present authors on "Transitions, glides, and diphthongs," Studies of Syllable Nuclei, Part II, SRL Rept. No. 4, Ann Arbor (1960). The report contains several additional tables.

The four columns show the average initial and final transitions associated with the labial, dental-alveolar, velar, and palatal consonants. Transitions to and from all vowels were combined in computing the table. Initial transitions will be considered first. It has been suggested that the second formant locus for labials is located at approximately 700 cps, the second formant locus for dental-alveolar consonants at 1800 cps, and that there are two loci for velar consonants, one at a low frequency value, and the other at approximately 3000 cps. If these values are to represent generally applicable locus positions for American English consonants, then in analyzing the speech of various native speakers of standard American English, we should expect to find similar loci with a fairly small range of variation for the combination of each consonant with different vowels. The Table contains both the average beginnings of transitions and the range of average values observed in the corpus. As may be seen from Table II, the average initial transitions for labials began considerably higher than 700 cps for this speaker. The beginning of the onglide from /p/ to a following vowel ranged from 1725 for /pɪ/ to 1075 cps for /pʊ/; similar large variations were observed for all labials. The dental-alveolar series appears to be associated with an initial transition beginning at approximately 1475 cps rather than 1800 cps, as postulated by the locus theory. In this case, the range of fluctuation is somewhat smaller than in the case of labials, but there is a complete overlap of the ranges for the two sets: the highest average initial transition value, associated with /fi/, was 1825 cps, which is identical with the average transition value associated with /ti/, and the lower extreme of the initial hubs associated with the dentals falls within the lower range of the labials. It is difficult to generalize that the palatals and velars are associated with two hubs, considering the very gradual changes in vowel onset frequency associated with the various allophones of the /k/ and /g/ phonemes. The values for velars in Table II were computed for the five syllable nuclei, [ɔ oᵁ ʊ u ɔɪ]; the values for palatals are averaged over the ten remaining syllable nuclei, but the range from 2200 cps for [ci] to 1495 cps for [kɑ] is quite extensive. It might be added that there is a similar gradual scale of onset frequencies associated with /ʃ/ and /č/, phonetically realized as [tʃ]; it appears that if two allophones are assumed for /k/ ([k] and [c]), the allophones of /ʃ/ and /č/ should be described in an analogous way.

Even greater fluctuations are found in final position than were observed in connection with initial transitions. The range of final hubs for labials is from an average of 1960 cps for the sequence /ip/ to 705 cps for the sequence /oᵁm/; the average value of 1190 cps becomes rather meaningless under such circumstances. The final dental-alveolar consonants have an average hub position at 1455 cps, with a range of from approximately 2100 cps for the sequences /it/ and /eɪt/ to about 1065 cps characterizing the average final hub that occurred in the sequence /ut/.

The various final allophones of /k/ present a somewhat different picture from the initial allophones. While the initial /k/ followed by /ə/ and /ɑ/ appeared to pattern with the allophones followed by front vowels (i.e., had relatively high hubs), allophones of /k/ appearing in final position after /ə/ and /ɑ/ belong clearly in the group characterized by a low hub position. The range for the velars and palatals together (i.e., the range associated with all allophones of the /k/ phoneme) extends from 2245 cps for /ik/ to 680 cps for /oᵁk/, which is quite comparable to the range observed for the labials.

Other consonants exhibit similar fluctuations. It appears from our data, furthermore, that the vowel allophones associated with the different consonants show considerable modifications due to the influence of the consonant. (This part of the data will be discussed in a separate publication.) There seems to be no evidence that in the interaction between two sounds in sequence one will remain constant; however, the locus values seem to have been obtained by keeping the vowels constant and varying the consonant transitions. From a linguistic point of view, an allophone is a variant of a phoneme, whose phonetic shape is determined by its environment. Of two sounds in sequence, each constitutes part of the environment of the other; thus a mutual interaction between them might be expected. It may well be that for purposes of automatic speech recognition, it is necessary to specify the beginning of the onglide and the end of the offglide for each consonant and vowel combination separately. If rules for predicting the extent of the influence of consonants upon vowel formants and conversely can be established, such rules should be incorporated in the instructions.

Detailed tabulations of the frequency positions of the beginning of the onglide and the end of the offglide for the first three formants for each of the syllable nuclei, and for the initial and final consonants for the 1263 CNC words, uttered by one speaker, are presented in Tables V–X of the report referred to in footnote 6.

The values listed in Table II are based on measurements made at the point of transition between vowel and consonant; the locus theory also requires a consideration of the slope of the formant at the point of transition. As mentioned above in connection with Fig. 1, we have observed that in a considerable number of instances, even when the syllable nucleus is a monophthong and the initial and final consonants are the same phoneme (in such words as bib, did, cease), both the terminal transition values and the slopes are different for the onglides and offglides. A further complication is that in many instances, particularly in the case of certain final transitions (for example, /k/ and /g/ after front vowels), the second formant has a positive transition, while the third formant has a negative transition. If lines are drawn through the centers of the

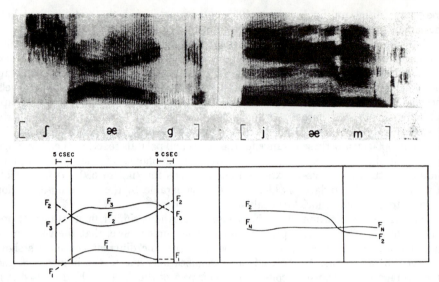

FIG. 4. Broad band spectrograms of the word *shag* uttered by GEP, and the word *yam* uttered by a dysarthric patient. The graphs below the spectrograms represent tracings of the formant positions from the spectrograms.

formants and are continued with their original slopes, they intersect at a value between the two offglide terminal positions. This case is illustrated by the tracing of the spectrogram for [ʃæg] in Fig. 4. For some consonants, previous work with synthesized speech[4] has suggested locus positions for F_2 that are considerably higher than the intersection of the lines drawn as continuations of the two formants. If formants are numbered in ascending order, it appears inconsistent that F_2 should have a locus that is higher than the locus of F_3. The intersection of the lines drawn to represent the continuation of F_2 and F_3 represents a point at which $F_2 = F_3$, and beyond that point the lower in frequency of the two could be called F_2, although the lower line represents a continuation of F_3. If it were possible to assign a single formant to a single cavity resonance, it would seem entirely plausible that the resonance frequencies could overlap. The apparent crossing of formants in the second spectrogram of Fig. 4 indicates that this may occasionally be possible. The spectrogram is for the word *yam* pronounced by a dysarthric patient. A steady nasal resonance may be observed throughout the vowel, and appears to continue into the nasal consonant. The second oral formant of the vowel [æ] apparently crosses this nasal formant during the transition period from the target position of [æ] to [m]. If loci could be defined in terms of specific cavity resonances, perhaps a higher locus for F_2 than for F_3 could be given a satisfactory explanation. From our data it appears that loci established for second formants without considering the directions of the transitions of the third formants are open to question.

DURATION OF TRANSITIONS AND RATE OF CHANGE

In order to compare the relative durations of the onglide, target, and offglide, it appeared necessary to establish a working rule as to what constitutes a target.

The time interval within the syllable nucleus where the formants are parallel to the time axis has been considered the extent of a vowel target. The minimum duration of such a time interval was arbitrarily chosen as 2 csec. There were some instances where no fixed target appeared, but usually somewhere within the syllable nucleus there was a noticeable change in the slope of the moving formant which suggested a target. In addition, the intonation pattern was often helpful in determining the position of the target, since the peak of the intonation contour associated with the CNC word usually coincided with the target of the syllable nucleus. Some uncertainty in determining the actual durations could not be avoided; however, the uncertainty did not appear sufficiently great to affect significantly the general pattern of values which was obtained.

There appear to be many factors which influence the duration of the transition from the release of the initial consonant to the target position of the vowel. To determine whether these durations are used as distinctive characteristics of the vowels, the average durations of initial transitions for all consonant-vowel combinations were computed for the 1263 utterances; these appear in Table III.

This Table shows considerable variation in the durations associated with the different initial consonants and also in the durations associated with the same consonant followed by different vowels. Some generalizations may be made from the variations. It appears that labials usually have shorter initial transitions than lingual consonants. A possible explanation lies in the fact that the tongue does not participate essentially in the articulation of an initial labial consonant but remains free to move toward the articulatory position of the following vowel during the consonant formation. Thus in many instances the transition from a labial consonant to a vowel is shorter than a transition from a lingually articulated consonant to the same vowel. For example,

TABLE III. Average duration of initial transition in centiseconds for 1263 CNC words.

	i	ɪ	eᴵ	ɛ	æ	ə	ɑ	ɔ	oᵁ	ʊ	u	ɑᵁ	ɑɪ	ɔɪ	ɝ	Average
p	8.9	4.4	17.5	5.7	8.4	4.4	5.2	8.0	3.2	4.2	4.7	4.3	5.2	10.0	5.7	6.7
b	6.6	4.3	15.8	4.8	4.9	3.7	3.8	3.3	2.2	2.0	3.3	3.0	4.0	4.0	4.0	5.1
t	11.2	2.6	14.0	3.5	8.0	7.3	6.0	8.2	9.3	7.0	9.0	7.0	8.1	10.0	10.0	7.9
d	8.2	4.0	16.2	4.8	6.2	6.2	5.8	6.4	6.7	...	7.5	6.0	5.7	...	7.0	6.8
k	10.0	6.6	18.2	9.0	9.8	8.5	6.6	6.6	6.3	6.7	7.0	6.0	6.0	7.0	9.1	8.8
g	8.0	3.4	14.9	6.0	7.4	7.0	7.0	6.7	6.8	7.0	6.0	8.0	7.0	...	5.3	7.8
m	4.8	3.3	12.7	5.2	4.0	3.2	2.7	3.6	2.3	...	2.2	2.0	2.8	...	5.0	4.5
n	7.3	3.0	13.5	2.8	4.3	4.0	3.7	4.5	4.8	4.0	2.6	4.0	4.2	6.0	9.0	4.9
f	6.0	3.6	15.7	3.8	5.8	3.3	4.0	3.2	2.3	2.0	3.0	4.0	1.8	2.0	2.0	5.3
v	7.0	4.0	15.5	...	8.0	...	...	...	3.5	...	...	4.5	3.4	2.3	6.0	6.4
θ	8.3	2.0	17.0	...	4.0	4.0	...	3.3	...	...	...	...	3.0	...	6.0	5.3
ð	8.0	6.0	14.9	6.3	4.0	...	...	...	3.0	...	...	...	4.0	...	...	5.2
s	6.8	3.1	13.7	4.2	4.5	4.1	5.2	4.0	4.5	4.0	3.6	4.3	3.8	4.0	5.3	5.5
z	6.0	...	...	...	...	...	6.0	...	7.0	...	4.0	...	...	...	...	5.7
ʃ	5.0	2.3	14.0	4.5	6.0	6.8	5.0	7.5	6.0	4.7	5.0	7.0	5.5	...	4.0	6.3
r	5.6	6.3	14.3	7.0	7.1	3.9	5.0	5.0	4.2	2.0	4.1	4.0	3.9	4.0	...	6.2
l	6.3	4.5	12.9	6.6	7.5	2.2	3.0	2.0	2.0	2.0	3.2	3.3	2.9	2.0	4.7	4.9
č	4.2	2.2	12.8	4.3	5.5	5.0	4.5	6.0	5.0	...	3.0	...	6.0	4.0	4.3	5.2
ǰ	6.0	2.3	17.7	6.8	7.5	8.7	7.2	8.0	7.0	...	5.3	8.0	6.0	6.0	7.0	7.0
h	3.4	2.4	12.0	1.6	2.6	3.1	3.0	3.3	3.2	2.5	6.2	3.0	2.4	...	3.8	3.4
w	4.7	6.7	12.5	8.2	10.0	2.0	7.3	3.6	4.0	2.0	2.0	...	4.3	...	5.6	6.4
wh	7.0	7.6	12.0	10.3	8.0	...	6.0	...	...	...	...	...	2.7	...	4.0	7.2
y	...	4.0	8.0	5.3	5.5	8.0	4.5	7.0	6.0	6.0	5.3	...	...	...	8.0	5.8
aver.	6.6	4.2	14.7	5.4	6.2	4.9	5.2	4.9	4.5	4.0	4.4	5.1	4.3	5.0	5.8	

the average duration of the transition in the sequence /pu/ is 4.7 csec, compared to 9.0 csec for the sequence /tu/. It appears also that there is much more variability in the durations associated with the different vowels following the same lingually articulated consonant than there is in the case where the different vowels follow a labial consonant. For example, the duration of the transition in the sequence /tɪ/ is, on the average, 2.6 csec, and for the sequence /tu/ 9.0 csec; /pɪ/ and /pu/ have average transitions of 4.4 and 4.7 csec. The tongue movement for /tu/ is clearly much more extensive than for /tɪ/. Apparently the tongue anticipates the articulatory position to a considerable extent in /pɪ/ and /pu/.

A study of Table III also reveals other facts about the transitions for this particular speaker. For example, there is very little difference in the duration of the transition from /k/ to front and back vowels. The reason may be found in the fact that the point of articulation for /k/ shifts with the vowel. This change is reflected in the continuous range of transition frequencies associated with the various allophones of /k/. Shorter transitions are, in general, more closely associated with voiced initial consonants than with voiceless initial consonants. It may also be noted that in some instances /h/ appears to have a definite articulatory position of its own; in sequences such as /hu/ and /hɝ/, the liprounding and the retroflection seem to occur during the pronunciation of the vowel.

It appears that the duration of the initial transition is essentially physiologically conditioned. Except for the syllable nucleus /eᴵ/, to be discussed later, the differences in rate of change due to differences in the duration of the initial transition are probably not significant in determining the linguistic interpretation of the vowel. The exact relationships between the rate of articulatory change and the corresponding changes in the resonances can probably best be determined by correlating x-ray studies of articulation with acoustic analysis of the produced sequences.[7]

The rate of change of a vowel formant may be specified as the frequency range in cycles per second through which the formant moves in a given time interval. The interpretation of the rate is complicated, however, by the fact that the initial transitions appear conditioned physiologically. The interpretation is also complicated by the fact that the following consonant in the case of a final transition not only conditions the frequency at which the transition terminates, but also the duration of the preceding syllable nucleus. In such pairs as *bit-bid*, there are differences in both duration of the syllable nucleus and the frequency position of the termination of the offglide which influence the rate of formant transition. Such differences, however, do not cause either of these syllable nuclei to be perceived as glides or diphthongs.

The rate of formant change has been investigated extensively with synthetic speech,[8,9] and the contrast

[7] H. M. Truby, *Acta Radiologica, Supplementum* 182 (Stockholm, 1959).

[8] A. M. Liberman, P. C. Delattre, L. J. Gerstman, and F. S. Cooper, J. Exptl. Psychol. **52**, 127 (1956).

[9] J. D. O'Connor, L. J. Gerstman, A. M. Liberman, P. C. Delattre, and F. S. Cooper, Word **13**, 24 (1957).

between such combinations as [u]+[i] and [w]+[i] can be described in terms of rate of change. According to our data, however, such a contrast is not utilized within the linguistic signalling system of the English speech we analyzed. This type of change may be illustrated with examples from Finnish. In that language, a sequence of vowel plus vowel may contrast with a sequence of semivowel plus vowel in such word pairs as *iäinen* "eternal" vs *jäinen* "icy." In the analysis of a number of contrasts of this type the formant frequencies associated with the targets remained constant, but the change in the rate of formant movement produced a meaningful difference. As another illustration, the diphthongs [ui] and [iu] in Estonian may be compared with the semivowel+vowel sequences /wi/ and /yu/ in English. Again, the slopes of the transitions and the durations of the target positions were the only differences, since the formant positions were identical for the same speaker.

It appears that if the target position remains constant, the slope of the transition is a criterion for defining the difference between diphthongs and glides. The movement in frequency of any one formant, however, is not sufficient to describe the characteristic properties of the syllable nuclei. The changes in the total formant pattern reflect changes in the total articulatory configuration. In the next section it is considered that the time taken to produce this total change, relative to the total duration of the syllable nucleus, may be a criterion for defining characteristic differences among syllable nuclei.

CLASSIFICATION OF SYLLABLE NUCLEI

In the preceding paper[1] the data confirmed previous suggestions that, as a first approximation, syllable nuclei

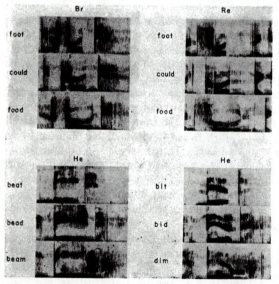

FIG. 5. Broad band spectrograms for nine words uttered by three informants. The words illustrate the difference in the relative durations of the targets and offglides for the tense vowels /u/ and /i/, as compared with the lax vowels /ʊ/ and /ɪ/.

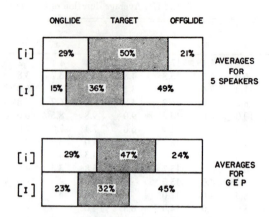

FIG. 6. Relative durations of the onglide, target, and offglide for /i/ and /ɪ/ in CNC words. Averages for the large corpus spoken by GEP are compared with the averages for five speakers of the control set.

may be divided into short and long. The short vowels, [ɪ ɛ ə ʊ], all appear to be monophthongs. An examination of the changes in the formant patterns associated with these vowels shows that they have an additional feature in common. They contrast with the long vowels [i æ ɑ ɔ u] in the relative durations of the two stages we have called target and offglide. The four short vowels have a relatively long offglide and a correspondingly shorter target; the long vowels have a relatively longer target and a shorter offglide.

Figure 5 illustrates the difference in the relative durations of the targets and offglides for two contrasts, /u/—/ʊ/ and /i/—/ɪ/. The contrasts for /u/ and /ʊ/ were uttered by two different speakers, Br and Re; those for /i/—/ɪ/ were spoken by He. The significant difference for the two sets of contrasting vowels is the duration of the offglide relative to the duration of the total syllable nucleus, and not the absolute duration of the transition or the rate of formant change.

Figure 6 compares the relative durations of the three stages for all occurrences of the vowels /i/ and /ɪ/ in both sets of data. The durations are expressed in percentage of total duration to allow for the differences in intrinsic duration. Table IV presents the relative durations in percent of the three formant stages for all syllable nuclei in both sets of data.

Thus it appears that the characteristic difference between the long and short monophthongs may be described as a difference in the articulatory rate of change associated with the movement from target position to the following consonant. The traditional terminology "lax" and "tense" seems appropriate to label this difference. "Lax" vowels, then, are those vowels whose production involves a short target position and a slow relaxation of the hold; for "tense" vowels the target position is maintained for a longer time, and the (articulatory) movement away from the target position is relatively rapid. The relationships of the three stages to the total duration remain approximately constant,

TABLE IV. Relative duration in percent of targets and transitions.

Syllable nucleus	Averages for 1263 CNC words spoken by GEP			Averages for 350 CNC words uttered by five speakers		
	Onglide	Target	Offglide	Onglide	Target	Offglide
i	29	47	24	28	50	22
ɪ	23	32	45	15	36	49
eᴵ	50	30	20	46	39	15
ɛ	23	34	43	17	40	43
æ	20	53	27	22	40	38
ə	24	41	35	31	39	30
ɑ	18	60	22	14	65	21
ɔ	16	59	25	15	56	29
oᵁ	15	25	60	12	42	46
ᴜ	19	40	41	28	29	43
u	17	63	20	20	56	24

	Onglide	Target 1	Glide	Target 2	Offglide	Onglide	Target 1	Glide	Target 2	Offglide
aᵁ	16	26	27	16	15	19	26	27	12	16
aɪ	12	26	31	17	14	21	30	28	15	6
ɔɪ	13	25	30	17	15	15	20	33	18	14
ɝ	22	31			47	10	40			50

regardless of the fluctuation in duration produced by the following consonant. The tense-lax opposition becomes particularly significant when the difference in intrinsic duration is neutralized, as for example in such pairs as *beat-bid* shown in Fig. 5.

The remaining syllable nuclei may be classified again into two groups. The first group, /eᴵ/, /oᵁ/, and /ɝ/, have only one steady state each, and therefore should not properly be classed as diphthongs. Phonetically, these single-target complex nuclei are difficult to segment into a sequence of two sounds. There is no steady state for the first element of /eᴵ/, but a slow glide appears toward the target position, the glide being longer than the target. Often the first part of /eᴵ/ has been called the "full vowel" and the second element the glide or semivowel. In the dialect under study, it is actually the second element that has a steady state and the first element that is phonetically a glide—longer than any other onglide. If the second formant onset position for /eᴵ/ is lower than approximately 1800 cps, the movement of the formant is normally smooth. However, if the preceding consonant is characterized by a higher second formant onset frequency, as in the case of /k/, /g/, /ʃ/, /č/, /ǰ/, the second formant performs a movement toward a frequency of approximately 1800 cps and glides from there toward the second formant target position of approximately 2000 cps. The formant movement is continuous, however, in such instances, and no target according to our definition can be located. The duration of the onglide from the consonant toward this minimum is approximately 30% of the total, and the glide from this minimum toward the steady state portion of the syllable nucleus lasts approximately 20% of the total duration.

Unlike /eᴵ/ which has a long glide as the first element, /oᵁ/ involves a short steady state target as the first element, and a long glide as the second element. The second formant of /oᵁ/ may have a minimum at a frequency of approximately 780 cps, after which the formant bends rapidly toward the point in frequency associated with the end of the offglide for the following consonant. When the second formant transition value associated with the final consonant is lower than the frequency of this approximate minimum, the glide is quite smooth, and it is impossible to detect a steady state for the second element. In the case of a higher transition value for F_2, the total duration of the glide (60% of the syllable nucleus) is divided into a glide toward 800 cps and an offglide from that point, with durations of 38 and 22% of the total, respectively.

The /ɝ/ consists of a relatively short steady state followed by a rather long glide. This glide is unique in

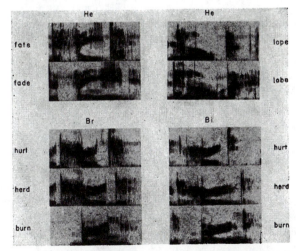

FIG. 7. Broad band spectrograms of seven words, spoken by three informants. The words represent occurrences of single-target complex nuclei.

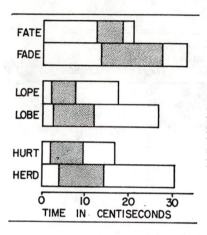

FIG. 8. Average values of the onglide, target, and offglide durations in six words spoken by five informants. The words illustrate single-target complex nuclei.

TABLE V. Average values of rate of change in cps/csec for the glides for five speakers.

	Onglide			Offglide		
	F_1	F_2	F_3	F_1	F_2	F_3
Fate	−8	+52	+31	−8	−62	−54
Fade	−7	+38	+22	−3	−34	−22
Lope	+10	0	−100	−7	−28	0
Lobe	+33	−13	−63	−9	−13	−10
Hurt	0	+19	−63	−8	+29	+29
Herd	0	−3	−26	−3	+15	+13

that it involves parallel movements of the second and third formants. The direction of the movement appears to be determined to a considerable extent by the following consonant. The slow, controlled change in articulatory position appears as the main characteristic of the three sounds, /eᴵ/, /oᵁ/, and /ɝ/.

Figure 7 illustrates some occurrences of single-target complex nuclei; the items were recorded by three speakers, He, Br, Bi. Figure 8 presents the average values for the same words for the five speakers; the durations of the targets are shown by the dotted areas, preceded by the onglide durations and followed by those of the offglides. Table V expresses the glides of the single-target complex nuclei in terms of average values of rate of change in cps/csec. Since all our duration measurements are in centiseconds, the rate of change is expressed in cps per centisecond in Table V; the signs indicate the direction of the rate of change. It is seen from Table V that the rate of change of the movement of any single formant is unsatisfactory for the definition of a specific glide.

The second group, /aɪ/, /aᴜ/, and /ɔɪ/, is characterized by two target positions. In our data the first target is usually longer than the second, but the transitions between targets are longer than either target

position. Neither of the elements comprising the diphthong is ordinarily phonetically identifiable with any stressed English monophthong; for example, in /aɪ/ the first element is neither /ɑ/ nor /æ/, and the second element is neither /i/ nor /ɪ/. The symbols /aɪ/, /aᴜ/, and /ɔɪ/ are adopted tentatively as labels for these syllable nuclei; neither a phonetic nor a phonemic commitment is implied at this moment.

Figure 9 illustrates some of the double-target syllable nuclei. The recordings were made by the three speakers, Br, Re, and He. The significant feature is the appearance of a definite steady state for both elements, but the transitions between the target positions are also quite prominent.

CONCLUSION

It appears that within the rather homogeneous dialect analyzed, and under the restricted conditions of the experiment, the syllabic sounds of American English can be described in terms of fifteen syllable nuclei, subdivided into short and long. The long nuclei are further subdivided into simple and complex nuclei. The four short nuclei are lax monophthongs. The five simple long nuclei are tense monophthongs; the complex long nuclei consist of three single-target nuclei and three double-target nuclei. The single-target nuclei are glides. Only the double-target nuclei are diphthongs. The total inventory of stressed syllable nuclei might then be listed

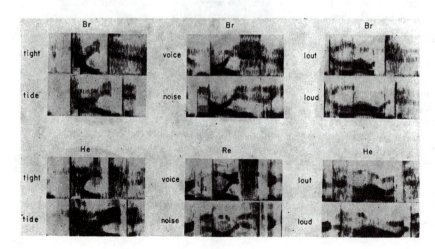

FIG. 9. Broad band spectrograms of six words illustrating double-target complex nuclei, uttered by three informants.

as follows:

Short nuclei: [ɪ] [ɛ] [ə] [ʊ]

Long nuclei:

    (1) Simple: [i] [æ] [ɑ] [ɔ] [u]

    (2) Complex:

        (a) Single target: [eᴵ] [oᵁ] [ɝ]

        (b) Double target: [ɑɪ] [ɑʊ] [ɔɪ].

The following phonetic definitions are suggested:

A *formant transition* is a formant movement in frequency from the initiation of the vowel of a consonant-vowel combination to the target position of the vowel; or a movement of a formant from one target position to the next target position; or a movement from the target position of a vowel to the point at which the vowel terminates for a particular vowel-consonant combination.

A *glide* is a vocalic syllable nucleus consisting of one target position, with associated formant transitions to the target, and formant transitions from the target. The duration of either the onglide or the offglide must be comparable to that of the target. Glides are specified only when both the target position and the duration of the significant part of the transitional movement (onglide or offglide) are described.

A *diphthong* is a vocalic syllable nucleus containing two target positions.

Acoustic characteristics of English /w,r,l/ spoken correctly by young children and adults

Rodger M. Dalston

Northwestern University, Evanston, Illinois 60201
(Received 11 March 1974; revised 11 November 1974)

This report presents the results of a spectrographic analysis of word-initial allophones of /w/, /r/, and /l/ produced by three- to four-year-old children and adults. Information was obtained concerning formant frequencies, steady-state durations, transition durations, and transition rates of each of the first three formants of these sonorants. The results demonstrate that the phonemes investigated are distinguishable on the basis of their temporal, as well as their spectral, acoustic characteristics.

Subject Classification: 70.20, 70.40, 70.70.

INTRODUCTION

It is not at all clear why the sounds /r/ and /l/ appear so late in the speech development of English-speaking children, nor why they are confused so frequently with /w/ when they occur in the initial position in words. It is possible that this confusion arises because children fail to recognize one or more of the acoustic characteristics which adults utilize to distinguish among these sounds. On the other hand, children may preceive the critical differences among /w, r, l/ but be unable to execute the motor patterns necessary to replicate them.

A basic assumption underlying the present investigation was that the development of speech is determined by the perceptual capabilities of the child. That is, it is assumed that the young child manifests the physiologic capability to produce all the sounds of the language but that sounds are not utilized linguistically until the child incorporates into his language system the perceptual basis underlying their identification. Given this assumption, any attempt to determine the basis for sonorant misarticulation in children must begin with a delineation of the acoustic characteristics of these phonemes in the speech of normal adults. Such a delineation is of considerable importance since it can be presumed that the speech of adults serves as a model with which the child compares his own productions.

Some information concerning the acoustic characteristics of adult sonorant productions has been provided by previous spectrographic analyses (Delattre,[1] Fant,[2] Joos,[3] Lehiste,[4] Potter *et al.*,[5] and Tarnoczy[6]). However, these studies have concentrated on specifying the spectral acoustic characteristics of these sounds while ignoring their temporal characteristics.

The importance of temporal acoustic characteristics to the identification of various speech sounds has been demonstrated by numerous investigators. It is well known that English-speaking adults utilize temporal acoustic characteristics to differentiate among different classes of speech sounds (Bastian *et al.*,[7] Denes,[8] Gay,[9] Liberman,[10] and Liberman *et al.*[11-13]) In addition, there is some evidence to suggest that adults use timing information to differentiate among sounds within a given class (Bennett,[14] Powel and Tosi,[15] Stevens,[16] and Tiffany.[17]) Of particular interest here is the fact that data obtained from the synthetic speech studies reported by

O'Connor *et al.*[18] and Ainsworth[19] seem to indicate that temporal information could be of importance to adults in distinguishing among certain English sonorants. These findings take on special significance when it is realized that young children apparently do not discriminate minimally paired words differing by a single temporal acoustic cue as well as do adults (Koenigsknecht[20]). It may be that the difficulty children frequently encounter in learning to produce acceptable /r/ and /l/ phones is related to the temporal acoustic characteristics of these sounds.

An investigation was undertaken to determine the spectral and temporal acoustic characteristics of correct and incorrect /w/, /r/, and /l/ phonemes produced in the word-initial position by young children and adults. The present communication will consider that portion of the investigation concerned with the acoustic characteristics of the adults' and children's correct productions.

I. METHOD

A. Subjects

The subjects for this study were ten children and five young adults. All 15 subjects met criteria of normalcy for medical and psychological history, speech and language development and usage, and hearing sensitivity. The children used in the study were obtained from nursery schools in Evanston, Illinois. They all came from homes in which General American was the only dialect regularly spoken. The six male subjects ranged in age from 3 years, 3 months to 4 years, 3 months, with a mean age of 4 years, 0 months. The four female subjects ranged in age from 3 years, 5 months to 4 years, 3 months, with a mean age of 3 years, 11 months. Thus the children employed in this investigation were comparable in age to the youngest group studied by Koenigsknecht.[20]

All but one of the adult subjects were freshman students enrolled at Northwestern University. The three male subjects ranged in age from 19 years, 9 months to 27 years, 8 months, with a mean age of 25 years, 4 months. The two female subjects ranged in age from 18 years, 6 months to 18 years, 9 months with a mean age of 18 years, 8 months. A General American dialect was required of all subjects. Persons who had received speech therapy or training in phonetics were not included in the study.

B. Speech samples

Each child named a set of 29 stimulus pictures at least six times, while each adult subject read a list of 29 words corresponding to the pictured stimuli utilized with the children. Four of the ten children were particularly cooperative in performing the task and it was possible to record their responses a seventh time. The adults read the word list six times. The nine test words were arranged so that each successive test word was separated by two nontest words. This was done to ensure that the speakers would not become aware of the fact that only certain sounds (/w, r, l/) were being tested. The nine test words enabled the sampling of word-initial /r/, /l/, and /w/ in each of the following contexts: /i/, /ɑ/, and /u/.

All recordings were made at the Northwestern University Speech Science Laboratory in a sound-treated room (IAC, Model 1201.) Recordings were made employing an Ampex Model 350-2 tape recorder, Western Electric 640AA microphone, Western Electric type E preamplifier and Western Electric Condenser Microphone Complement. In order to provide recordings free from distortion, the gain setting of the tape recorder was adjusted during each recording session so that the VU meter peaked in the range −3 to 0. This adjustment was made during the first production of the word list by each speaker. This first set of words was not employed in subsequent analyses, leaving five productions of each test word by every adult and either five or six productions by each child. All productions were subsequently analyzed on a Kay Spectrograph, model 6061A.

C. Data analysis

Two 80–8000-Hz full-range spectrograms were made for each test word produced by each of the adult subjects. The first included a wide-band frequency-by-time record and an amplitude display. The second spectrogram contained narrow-band frequency-by-intensity sections of the calibration tone, the midportion of the sonorant steady state and the midportion of the vowel steady state.

The vowel and sonorant steady states were defined as the place in time during which the formants were undergoing the least frequency shift between contextual phonemes. The following measurements were obtained from the spectrograms of each word:

(a) frequency of each of the first three sonorant formants;

(b) frequency of each of the first three vowel formants;

(c) duration of the steady state of each of the first three sonorant formants, defined as the distance in milliseconds between the visible onset of each formant and the point at which that formant demonstrated a noticeable change in slope;

(d) duration of the transition of each of the first three sonorant formants, defined as the distance in milliseconds during which each formant was undergoing a relatively rapid frequency shift between the sonorant and vowel steady states;

(e) rate of the transition of each of the first three sonorant formants, determined by dividing the duration of the transition (in milliseconds) into the extent of frequency change (in hertz) between the sonorant steady state and the steady state of the succeeding vowel.

The high fundamental frequency of a child's voice results in the resonances of the vocal tract being excited by only a few harmonics. This fact increased the possibility of obtaining spurious peak frequency measurements on spectrograms of the children's productions, even when the broad-band (300-Hz) filter was employed. In an attempt to overcome this problem, the children's productions were analyzed with the input tape recorder set at half speed and the scale magnifier of the spectrograph set at 80–4000-Hz full range. This process effectively doubled the bandwidth of the analysis filter and provided the additional advantage of increasing resolution in the time domain (Fant[21]).

A second spectrogram made of the children's productions contained a number of narrow-band frequency-by-intensity sections of each word recorded at half speed and analyzed with 80–4000-Hz range scale magnification. The points at which these intensity sections were made corresponded to the points analyzed in the adult speech samples. All the measurements made on the adult productions were also made on each of the children's productions. In an attempt to assess the accuracy of each of these words, the children's productions were submitted to a listener judgment analysis.

D. Listener judgment task

A panel of 25 adult listeners was employed to assess the correctness of each child's sonorant productions. Five of these listeners were the adult subjects in this study. For these persons a period of nine months separated the speaking and listening tasks. The other 20 listeners were young adults between 16 and 17 years of age. All listeners spoke with a General American dialect, manifested no hearing loss, and had never received speech therapy or extensive training in phonetics.

The recorded responses of each child were dubbed in random order onto two listening tapes to avoid the possibility that continuous listening to a single child's responses might cause a listener to predict certain patterns of articulation. In order to obtain an indication of intrajudge reliability, 50 randomly selected items were recorded at the end of the second listening tape. The two tapes, containing 536 items, were presented to the 25 listeners in a sound field by means of two Ampex 620 amplifier–speakers connected to an Ampex 354 tape recorder. The listeners were instructed to mark on a record sheet whether each item on the tape began with an *r*, *w*, or *l*. In order for a sound to be classified as a *w* (or *r* or *l*) for the purposes of this study, it had to be judged a *w* by 60% or more of the listeners. Any sound receiving less than 60% agreement among the listeners was not included for consideration here.

TABLE I. The number of correct, incorrect, and unclassified sonorants spoken by each of the children.

Subject	Number of correct productions			Number of incorrect productions			Number of productions with < 60% agreement			Total number of test words
	/w/	/r/	/l/	/w/	/r/	/l/	/w/	/r/	/l/	
1	18	16	8	•••	1	7	•••	1	3	54
2	15	14	5	•••	1	8	•••	•••	2	45
3	15	15	6	•••	•••	7	•••	•••	2	45
4	18	15	18	•••	3	•••	•••	•••	•••	54
5	15	14	15	•••	1	•••	•••	•••	•••	45
6	18	9	7	•••	7	8	•••	2	3	54
7	15	9	1	•••	4	12	•••	2	2	45
8	15	1	12	•••	14	3	•••	•••	•••	45
9	16	2	15	•••	16	•••	2	•••	3	54
10	15	8	15	•••	5	•••	•••	2	•••	45
										486
							Reliability test items			+50
							Total			536

Those repetitions of *r* and *l* words that were judged by 60% or more of the adult listeners to have begun with the sound /w/ were grouped together and considered to be examples of incorrect sonorant productions. Table I shows the number of correct, incorrect and "unclassified" sonorant productions of each child. Spectrographic analyses of the incorrect productions are the subject of an article in preparation. Intrajudge reliability for each of the 25 listeners was determined by calculating the percentage of test–retest agreement. This agreement ranged from 72% to 92%, with a mean of 83%. A panel of judges was not employed to assess the adequacy of the adult sonorant productions. However, it was the considered judgment of the author that none of these productions was incorrect.

II. RESULTS

A. Spectral characteristics

The means and standard deviations for the formant frequencies of the correct productions of /w/, /r/, and

TABLE II. Mean frequency values (hertz) and standard deviations associated with three sonorants produced correctly in three vocalic contexts by children and adults.

	Adult males		Adult females		Children	
	M	SD	M	SD	M	SD
First formant						
/r/	348	45.9	350	38.3	431	49.8
/w/	336	39.2	337	30.4	402	59.7
/l/	344	55.2	365	11.6	412	38.4
Second formant						
/r/	1061	92.5	1165	85.4	1503	191.8
/w/	732	87.6	799	87.8	1020	148.8
/l/	1179	141.2	1340	96.8	1384	175.3
Third formant						
/r/	1546	94.8	2078	346.1	2491	369.8
/w/	2290	335.8	2768	141.7	3547	223.7
/l/	2523	197.8	2935	174.4	3541	283.0

/l/ by the adults and children employed in this study are reported in Table II. All correct productions of each test word by a single speaker were lumped and entered for analysis as a single value. For this reason, the standard deviations reported in this table are a representation of the variability that occurred across individuals and across vowel contexts.

Information obtained from spectrographic analyses of adult real speech (Delattre,[1] Fant,[2] Joos,[3] Lehiste,[4] Potter *et al.*,[5] and Tarnoczy[6]) and studies of synthesized adult speech (Ainsworth,[19] Cooper *et al.*,[22] Delattre,[23] Haggard,[24] and[25] Liberman *et al.*,[26] Lisker,[27] Mattingly,[28] and O'Connor *et al.*[18]) has demonstrated that: (a) the first formants of all sonorants have a characteristically low frequency value which does not serve to differentiate among the sounds within this class; (b) the second formant serves to reliably distinguish /w/ from both /l/ and /r/, and (c) the third formant frequency of /r/ is very low and distinguishes this sound from both /w/ and /l/. The results of the present investigation corroborate these observations and further demonstrate not unexpectedly, that the same distinctions obtain among children's correct productions of these sounds.

It has been suggested by Peterson[29] that, to a first approximation, equivalent vowels produced by different speakers tend to lie along lines of constant frequency ratio. Because of this observation, and in an attempt to facilitate the comparison of the adult productions and the productions of the children employed in this study, the first three formant frequencies of each sonorant utterance were divided by the frequency value of $F1$. This resulted in an $F3 : F2 : F1$ ratio in which $F1$ equaled 1.00. Expressing the frequency values of $F2$ and $F3$ in relation to $F1$ enabled a graphic representation of all three formants to be made on a two dimensional plane, as shown in Figs. 1–3. Despite its simplicity and apparent utility, a review of the literature revealed that analyses of the acoustic characteristics of vowel and vowel-like speech sounds have not involved this type of

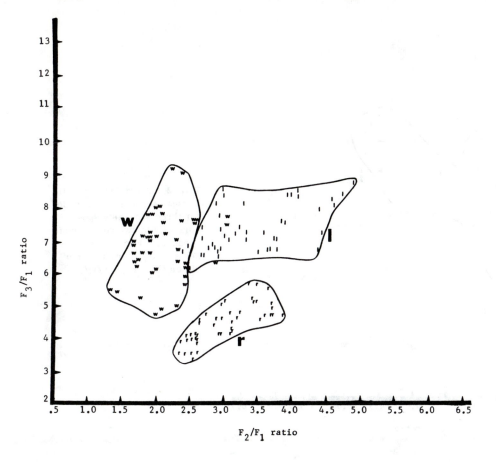

FIG. 1. Third-formant ratio versus second-formant ratio for three sonorants spoken correctly by three adult male speakers. Each point represents a single production of either /l/, /r/, or /w/.

graphic display.

The closed loops appearing in Figs. 1–3 were drawn arbitrarily to include a majority of the points while excluding the more extreme and isolated items. A concerted effort was made to draw these loops in such a way as to minimize overlap among them while still including approximately 90% of the points. Inspection reveals that the loops enclosing the children's productions of each phoneme (Fig. 3) are noticeably larger and manifest more overlap than is the case for the adult productions (Figs. 1 and 2). A cursory inspection of the original data revealed that this overlap would be reduced, but by no means eliminated, by graphing the productions of each child separately. Separate plotting of the productions of the two adult females revealed that overlap persisted in the case of one of these subjects.

B. Temporal characteristics

Tables III and IV summarize the analysis of the temporal characteristics of /w/, /r/, and /l/ spoken correctly by the children and adults. An overall test of significance of sex differences among the variables studied revealed no significant difference between the adult males and females. For this reason, the adult speakers were treated as a homogeneous group.

The significant steady-state duration differences among the sonorants for both the children and adults were further analyzed with a series of multiple comparisons using the Newman–Keuls procedure (Winer[30]). From these tests it was evident that the reliable differences in $F1$ and $F2$ steady-state duration were due to the

fact that the first- and second-formant steady states of /l/ were longer than those associated with /w/ and /r/. This observation may be related to the fact that /l/ is the only one of the three sonorants which requires that contact be made between the tongue and another articulator. The fact that the articulation of /l/ entails such contact suggests that this sound is produced rather ballistically. If this is so, the tongue would be expected to manifest a delay in moving away from the contact, or steady-state position, because it must first overcome the inertial force that was generated as the tongue moved to that contact.

No discernible third-formant shift between the sonorant and the succeeding vowel occurred in 21% of the adults's and 73% of the children's productions of /l/. Similarly, no $F3$ shift was visible in 49% of the adult's and 75% of the children's productions of /w/. In such cases, the $F3$ steady-state duration was recorded as being zero (0). Therefore, the average steady-state duration values for the third formants of these two sounds are understandably low. This also explains the low transition duration and transition rate values for the third formants of these two sonorants (Tables III and IV).

The differences among the sonorants in terms of $F1$ transition duration and $F1$ transition rate are related to the fact that /l/ was characterized by a short $F1$ transition duration and a rapid $F1$ transition rate (Tables III and IV). From his studies of adult real speech, Joos[3] reported that /l/ is always marked either at the beginning or end, or both, by a relatively abrupt shift of for-

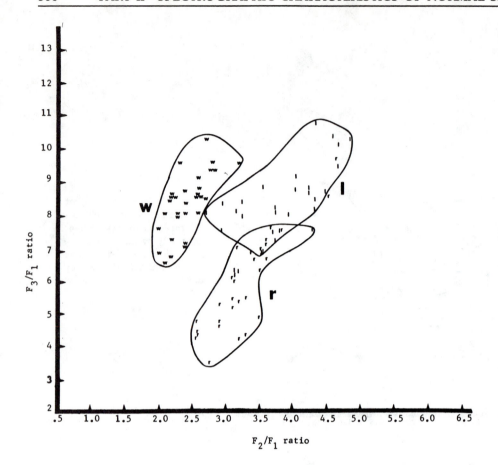

FIG. 2. Third-formant ratio versus second-formant ratio for three sonorants spoken correctly by two adult female speakers. Each point represents a single production of either /l/, /r/, or /w/.

mant structure. Fant[2] appears to be in agreement with this observation, stating that "the identification [of /l/] relies on the sudden shift up of $F1$ from the lateral to the adjacent vowel" (p. 167). The data presented here corroborate these observations. The brief, abrupt $F1$ shift characterizing /l/ apparently reflects the rapid movement of the tongue tip away from the roof of the mouth to the target position of the succeeding vowel.

The rapid shift of the first-formant frequency of /l/ was frequently accompanied by a transient click in the acoustic spectrum of this sound (Fig. 4). This was particularly true in the high-vowel contexts /i/ and /u/, where a click was present in 86% of the adult productions and 70% of the children's productions of /l/. Such transients were never observed in the spectrograms of /w/ and /r/ utterances. Preliminary findings obtained from listener judgments of synthetic speech patterns suggest that a noise transient in the acoustic spectrum of /l/ may be an important acoustic cue underlying the identification of this sound in at least certain vowel contexts. The absence of such a transient source may help to explain the fact that the percentage correct identification of the /l/ patterns generated by O'Connor et al.[18] was rather low (about 70%) even when a first-formant transition duration of 10 msec was employed.

TABLE III. Comparison of the temporal acoustic characteristics of /r/, /w/, and /l/ spoken by the adult subjects. The duration values reported are in milliseconds and the rate values are in hertz/msec.

	/r/		/w/		/l/		
	M	SD	M	SD	M	SD	F ratio[a]
$F1$ steady-state duration	39.2	23.2	39.6	16.1	67.0	19.0	11.63[c]
$F2$ steady-state duration	35.5	14.8	44.4	20.2	57.0	19.9	5.73[b]
$F3$ steady-state duration	30.9	18.7	18.4	20.6	45.4	23.7	7.27[b]
$F1$ transition duration	33.7	20.4	32.7	18.7	21.3	15.7	6.84[b]
$F2$ transition duration	50.4	17.3	58.3	26.8	41.3	26.7	5.57[b]
$F3$ transition duration	71.4	19.7	22.5	19.7	31.1	18.9	39.46[c]
$F1$ transition rate	3.9	2.2	3.5	3.5	8.5	6.6	5.38[b]
$F2$ transition rate	10.5	6.6	11.8	6.9	11.4	4.5	0.54
$F3$ transition rate	12.8	1.5	3.1	3.8	1.5	5.0	65.49[c]

[a]Degrees of freedom = 2, 36.   [c]$p < 0.001$.
[b]$p < 0.01$.

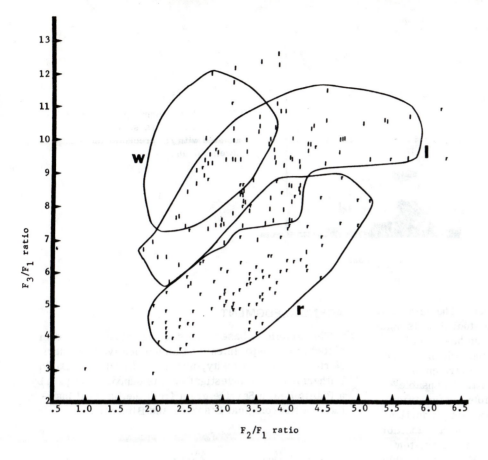

FIG. 3. Third-formant ratio versus second-formant ratio for three sonorants spoken correctly by ten three to four-year-old children. Each point represents a single production of either /l/ or /r/. A closed loop was drawn to encircle 90% of the /w/ points. The /w/ points were deleted to ensure legibility.

Among the productions of both the children and the adults, the second-formant transition duration of /l/ tended to be shorter than that associated with /w/ and /r/. However, the overall difference in this variable among the three sonorants reached significance only for the adult production of these sounds (Table III). The second-formant transition rate clearly did not differentiate among /w, r, l/ as produced by the adults. However, this variable did differentiate among the sonorant productions of the children. Specifically, it was found that the $F2$ transition rate of /r/ was slower than that of either /w/ or /l/. This finding is particulary interesting in light of an observation made by O'Connor et al.[18] with regard to the perception of synthetic speech patterns:

"At 150 msec... an otherwise satisfactory /w/ pattern, before the vowels /i, e, ɛ/, was heard as /wr/; this effect is undoubtedly due to the large rising transition of the second formant coupled with a *comparatively slow rate of frequency change*" (italics added) (p. 36).

III. DISCUSSION

One approach that may be taken in the investigation of the relationship between the various physical parameters of a speech sound wave and its linguistic interpreta-

TABLE IV. Comparison of the temporal acoustic characteristics of /r/, /w/, and /l/ spoken by the children. The duration values reported are in milliseconds and the rate values are in hertz/msec.

	/r/		/w/		/l/		F ratio[a]
	M	SD	M	SD	M	SD	
$F1$ steady-state duration	40.3	15.3	39.0	23.1	56.7	14.6	5.55[d]
$F2$ steady-state duration	41.2	15.0	39.5	21.9	55.4	15.9	5.99[d]
$F3$ steady-state duration	38.9	19.5	13.5	18.0	15.0	16.6	14.69[e]
$F1$ transition duration	32.7	19.2	36.9	18.2	21.8	14.1	3.00[b]
$F2$ transition duration	52.3	21.5	55.0	24.7	41.1	28.1	2.80
$F3$ transition duration	61.0	20.1	10.2	13.0	8.6	9.4	74.82[e]
$F1$ transition rate	8.0	7.7	7.7	7.5	11.2	9.5	3.77[c]
$F2$ transition rate	11.7	6.9	17.4	9.5	19.0	7.0	11.22[e]
$F3$ transition rate	14.3	3.7	1.2	2.1	1.1	4.4	108.33[e]

[a]Degrees of freedom = 2, 51.
[b]$p < 0.059$.
[c]$p < 0.05$.
[d]$p < 0.01$.
[e]$p < 0.001$.

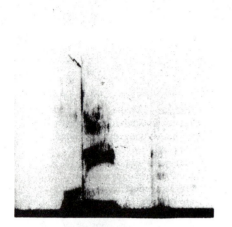

Leap

Loop

FIG. 4.   Broad-band spectrograms demonstrating a transient source associated with /l/ preceding the high vowels /i/ and /u/.

tion entails the analysis of real speech. The advantage here is that the speech signal can be studied in its natural form. However, "if a spectrogram has a fault, ... it is in the abundance of its revelations, which lead an investigator to wonder what, in a given stretch of speech, is linguistically basic and what dispensable" (O'Connor,[18] pp. 25–26). For example, in the present study it was found that among the sonorant productions of the children and adults, the third-formant transition duration and third-formant transition rate consistently differentiated /r/ from /w/ and /l/. It is not possible by means of spectrographic analysis to determine if these characteristics are important to the identification of /r/, if they merely add to the apparent naturalness of this speech sound, or if they are purely the coincidental, perceptually unimportant, result of differences in third-formant frequency. A study employing synthetic speech patterns might be employed to determine the answers to such questions since the use of synthetic speech enables the investigator to isolate, alter, and test by ear any feature present in the spectrographic pattern that is presumed to be of perceptual significance. No such investigation has been undertaken to date.

To the extent that the perceptual importance of temporal acoustic characteristics can be surmised from spectrographic analysis, it would appear from the results reported here that the phonemes investigated are distinguishable on the basis of their temporal, as well as their spectral, acoustic characteristics. It has been suggested that adults are better able to discriminate minimally paired words differing by a single temporal acoustic cue than are young children (Koenigsknecht[20]). One might hypothesize, on the basis of that information, that speech sound perception in young children is dependent primarily upon spectral cues present in the acoustic waveform of speech, while adults make considerable use of both spectral and temporal cue information. The fact that the sonorants studied in this investigation could be differentiated on the basis of acoustic cues to which young children apparently are not attentive lends support to the contention that the late emergence of these sounds may be related to their perceptual, rather than their articulatory, complexity.

ACKNOWLEDGMENT

This article is based on a doctoral dissertation completed in the Department of Communicative Disorders, Northwestern University, under the direction of David Rutherford. The investigation was supported in part by a Public Health Service grant from the National Institutes of Neurological Diseases and Blindness.

[1]P. Delattre, "Acoustic or articulatory invariance," Glossa 1, 3–25 (1967).

[2]G. Fant, *Acoustical Theory of Speech Production* (Mouton, 's-Gravenhage, 1960).

[3]M. Joos, "Acoustic phonetics," Lang. Suppl. 24, 1–136 (1948).

[4]I. Lehiste, "Acoustical characteristics of selected English consonants," Int. J. Am. Ling. 30, 1–197 (1964).

[5]R. K. Potter, G. A. Kopp, and H. G. Kopp, *Visible Speech* (Dover, New York, 1966).

[6]T. Tarnoczy, "Resonance data concerning nasals, laterals and trills," Word 4, 71–77 (1948).

[7]J. Bastian, P. Delattre, and A. M. Liberman, "Silent interval as a cue for the distinction between stops and semivowels in medial position," J. Acoust. Soc. Am. 31, 1568(A) (1959).

[8]P. Denes, "Effect of duration on the perception of voicing," J. Acoust. Soc. Am. 27, 761–764 (1955).

[9]T. Gay, "A perceptual study of English diphthongs," Status Rep. Speech Res.: Haskins Labs. 1–80 (June 1967).

[10]A. M. Liberman, "Some results of research on speech perception," J. Acoust. Soc. Am. 29, 117–123 (1957).

[11]A. M. Liberman, P. Delattre, and F. S. Cooper, "The role of selected stimulus variables in the perception of the unvoiced stop consonants," Am. J. Psychol. 65, 497–516 (1952).

[12]A. M. Liberman, P. C. Delattre, L. J. Gerstman, and F. S. Cooper, "Tempo of frequency change as a cue for distinguishing classes of speech sounds," J. Exp. Psychol. 52, 127–137 (1956).

[13]A. M. Liberman, K. S. Harris, H. S. Hoffman, and B. C. Griffith, "The discrimination of speech sounds within and across phoneme boundaries," J. Exp. Psychol. 54, 358–368 (1957).

[14]D. C. Bennett, "Spectral form and duration as cues in the recognition of English and German vowels," Lang. Speech 11, 65–85 (1968).

[15]R. L. Powel and O. Tosi, "Vowel recognition threshold as a function of temporal segmentations," J. Speech Hear. Res. 13, 715–724 (1970).

[16]K. Stevens, "Effect of duration upon vowel identification," J. Acoust. Soc. Am. **31**, 109(A) (1959).

[17]W. R. Tiffany, "Vowel recognition as a function of duration, frequency, modulation and phonetic context," J. Speech Hear. Res. **18**, 289–301 (1953).

[18]J. D. O'Connor, L. J. Gerstman, A. M. Liberman, P. G. Delattre, and F. S. Cooper "Acoustic cues for the perception of initial /w, j, r, l/ in English," Word **13**, 24–43 (1957).

[19]W. A. Ainsworth, "First formant transitions and the perception of synthetic semi-vewels," J. Acoust. Soc. Am. **44**, 689–694 (1968).

[20]R. A. Koenigsknecht, "An investigation of the discrimination of certain spectral and temporal acoustics cues for speech sounds in three-year-old children, six-year-old children and adults," Ph. D. dissertation, Northwestern U. (1968).

[21]G. Fant, "Sound Spectrography," in *Proceedings of the Fourth International Congress on Phonetic Science* (Mouton, 's-Gravenhage, 1962).

[22]F. S. Cooper, P. C. Delattre, A. M. Liberman, J. M. Borst, and L. J. Gerstman, "Some experiments on the perception of synthetic speech sounds," J. Acoust. Soc. Am. **24**, 597–606 (1952).

[23]P. Delattre, "From acoustic cues to distinctive features," Phonetica **18**, 198–230 (1968).

[24]M. Haggard, "Perceptual study of English /l/ allophones," J. Acoust. Soc. Am. **41**, 1581(A) (1967).

[25]M. Haggard, "Perception of semi-vowels and laterals," Status Reps. Speech Res. Haskins Labs. 143–155 (June 1969).

[26]A. M. Liberman, F. Ingemann, L. Lisker, P. Delattre, and F. S. Cooper, "Minimal rules for synthesizing speech," J. Acoust. Soc. Am. **31**, 1490–1499 (1959).

[27]L. Lisker, "Minimal cues for separating /w, j, r, l/ in intervocalic position," Word **13**, 256–267 (1957).

[28]I. Mattingly, "Synthesis by rule of General American English," Ph. D. dissertation, Yale U. (1968).

[29]G. E. Peterson, "Parameters of vowel quality," J. Speech Hear. Res. **4**, 10–29 (1961).

[30]R. J. Winer, *Statistical Principles in Experimental Design* (McGraw-Hill, New York, 1962).

PART III

Speech Sound Development

The emergence of the normal repertoire of speech sounds reflects maturation of the child's neuromuscular control system and developmental changes in vocal tract anatomy. The evolution of speech motor competence is complex and, of course, is not directly observable. But the consequences of speech system maturation are apparent in the acoustics and timing characteristics of the speech signal, a great deal of which can be seen in routine Sonagrams. From the spectrographic data, it is possible to draw inferences about what is happening in the vocal tract during speech. Knowing what is going on during the various stages of normal development provides a firm foundation for evaluating aberrant or inadequate speech development.

The articles included in this section demonstrate several profitable ways of exploring the acoustic features of speech sound development. At the same time, they illustrate the nature of the inferential process and provide a great deal of useful information about what can be expected at various developmental stages. Of particular interest is the research report of Eguchi and Hirsh (1969), which explores the speed and stability of speech motor control as it matures during childhood. The tutorial article by Kent (1976), provides an excellent over-

view and integrates a great deal of complex information about the acoustic manifestations of speech maturation. Kent and Forner (1979) and Kent and Murray (1982) clearly analyze developmental changes in vowel formants in infancy and childhood, while Bennett (1981) examines them for preadolescents.

Readings

Eguchi, S., and Hirsh, I. J. (1969). Development of speech sounds in children. *Acta Otolaryngologica* (Suppl. 257), 5–48.

Kent, R. D. (1976). Anatomical and neuromuscular maturation of the speech mechanism: Evidence from acoustic studies. *Journal of Speech and Hearing Research, 19,* 421–447.

Bennett, S. (1981). Vowel formant frequency characteristics of preadolescent males and females. *Journal of the Acoustical Society of America, 69,* 231–238.

Kent, R. D., and Forner, L. (1979). Developmental study of vowel formant frequencies in an imitation task. *Journal of the Acoustical Society of America, 65,* 208–217.

Kent, R. D., and Murray, A. (1982). Acoustic features of infant vocal utterances at 3, 6, and 9 months. *Journal of the Acoustical Society of America, 72,* 353–365.

ACTA OTO-LARYNGOLOGICA

SUPPLEMENTUM 257

Central Institute for the Deaf, St. Louis, Missouri

DEVELOPMENT OF SPEECH SOUNDS
IN CHILDREN[1]

S. EGUCHI[2] and I. J. HIRSH

UPPSALA 1969

[1] This research was supported in full by a U.S. Public Health Service, Department of Health, Education and Welfare research grant (NB-03856) from the National Institute of Neurological Diseases and Blindness.
[2] Visiting Research Associate at C.I.D., on leave from Dept. of Otolaryngology, University of Nagasaki.

PRINTED IN SWEDEN BY

Almqvist & Wiksells

BOKTRYCKERI AKTIEBOLAG

UPPSALA 1969

CONTENTS

I. INTRODUCTION

Reviews of the literature concerned with development of speech in children have provided much information on grammatical, contextual and syntactic aspects (Miller and Smith, 1966), but somewhat less on phonetic aspects (Irwin, 1943, 1945, 1948; Morley, 1965; Simon, 1957) of speech development. Phonetic studies, particularly since the introduction of the Sound Spectrograph in 1946, have clarified certain acoustical chracteristics of speech sounds (Potter, Kopp and Green, 1947; Joos, 1948; Peterson and Barney, 1952; Potter and Steinberg, 1950; Peterson, 1959), and these characteristics have been confirmed subsequently by acoustical resonance theory (Dunn, 1950; Stevens and House, 1955, 1961; Fant, 1960; Cooper *et al.*, 1952). Potter and Steinberg (1950) and Peterson and Barney (1952) reported that the vowel formant frequencies of children were about 25% higher than those of the adult male and 20% higher than those of the adult female. The rapid anatomical, physiological and psychological development in childhood would, of course, predict that these acoustical features of the speech sounds or phonemes of children could not remain stable over any long period of time. However, there is a scarcity of acoustical studies concerned with the development of speech sounds or phonemes in children (Okamura, 1966).

The present investigation was designed to clarify the way in which speech sounds or phonemes develop in normal children after the initial stages of language acquisition. Measurement of the formant frequencies that characterize certain vowels in a sentence spoken by children at different ages would provide information on the formant shifts that occur with age. Furthermore, calculation of the variability of such formants in samples of repetitions of the sentences would provide information on the accuracy with which children uttered such vowels. Measurement of the vocal fundamental frequency would provide information on changes with age and another kind of measurement, namely of certain interphonemic time intervals, would provide both mean and variability for at least one aspect of consonant development. Finally, to ascertain what relation might exist between variability of vowel formants and the intelligibility of vowels, certain listening tests were carried out.

II. GENERAL PROCEDURE

Subjects

Eighty-four subjects, ranging in age from 3 to 13 years, and also adults, served as talkers. Subjects older than 10 years were divided into two groups according to sex. Each age or age-sex group contained five or six subjects. All subjects were from the Greater St. Louis area.

Test material

Two sentences, "He has a blue pen", and "I am tall", which are easy to pronounce and available in the daily conversation of children, were selected as the test sentences.

Six vowels, representative of a variety of tongue positions in vowel articulation, were selected for spectrographic analysis, in order from the sentences above: [i], [æ], [u], [ɛ], [a], [ɔ]. (The sound of [a], not normally found in most American dialects, was taken from the first portion of the diphthong [ai] in the word "I".) In addition, the words "blue", "pen" and "tall" were used for the measurement of certain temporal features in the words.

Recording procedures

Tape recordings of the test sentences were made in a room where the signal-to-ambient-noise ratio was 32 dB or better. Each sentence was spoken by each subject on five different occasions, separated by only a few minutes. Children over 7 years of age read the sentences from a card, while younger subjects repeated them after a native American speaker (IJH) who speaks with a general Eastern dialect. Speech samples at approximately 70 dB SPL (re 0.0002 dyne/cm²) were picked up by a condenser microphone at a distance of about 0.5 meter and were recorded on tape by an Ampex (Model 300) tape recorder. Background and internal noise was further reduced by a 300-Hz high-pass filter whose low-frequency response fell at 12 dB per octave.

III. VOWEL FORMANT FREQUENCIES

Method

A Sound-Spectrum Analyzer (Kay, Sona-Graph Model 6061A) was used for the acoustical analysis of reproduced speech sounds. Steady-state portions of the vowels were identified from both wide-band and narrow-band spectrograms. The first and second formant frequencies for each vowel on each repetition of each subject were estimated from the spectrum envelopes drawn on expanded narrow-band sections (0–4000 Hz) (Fig. 1).

In each age group, the mean formant frequencies and between-subject standard deviations were calculated from the mean values of each subject, while intra-subject standard deviations were calculated as the square root of the mean value of the individual variance within each age group.

These intra-subject standard deviations of the distribution of five repetitions within each age group were used as a measure of variability, or the inverse of precision, of articulation and were calculated either in absolute terms or in terms of ratios to the individual means.

Since the present study focuses on measures of variability associated with talker repetitions, age and different vowels, some information about error of measurement of formant frequencies through visual inspection of spectrogram sections is required. Several previous reports have addressed themselves to this problem. With age as a principal variable, Potter and Steinberg (1950) reported no correlation between the fundamental frequency and formant frequency for their three groups of adult males, adult females, and children. More directly related to the present report was their further finding that repeated utterances by a number of talkers showed a standard deviation of 20–40 Hz for the first formant, and 40–70 Hz for the second formant. Corresponding measurements for children (8 years) yielded values about twice as large. Distributions of single utterances from a large number of talkers had standard deviations two or three times as large. Peterson and Barney (1952) reported that the standard deviation for the first formant of a repeated vowel ([i]) by adult females was 15.3 Hz. They did not attribute this value to a specific source but suggested that it represented intra-subject variability, that is, over several trials by the same talker, and they stated further that this value was not easily interpretable in comparing one talker with another. Finally, and more specifically concerned with error of spectrographic measurement, Lindblom (1962) studied the accuracy with which formant frequencies could be estimated from spectrograms of synthesized vowels. He compared the values read by five experienced investigators and obtained a between-reader standard deviation of 40 Hz for adult male voice pitch, that is, a value about one-fourth the fundamental frequency.

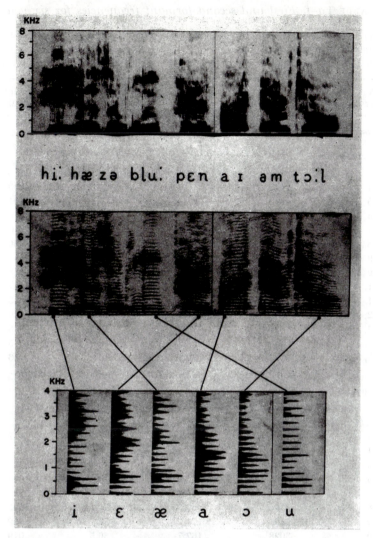

Fig. 1. Spectrogram of a child's rendition of "He has a blue pen. I am tall." Wide-band spectrogram is shown at the top, and narrow-band in the center. At the bottom are seen the sections at the indicated points in time which show the spectral distribution of the vowels up to 4 kHz.

We cannot find any study on intra-reader variability, that is, the reliability with which a single investigator will draw his spectrum envelopes and interpolate the peak values on successive readings of the same recorded sample. Accordingly, one of us (S. E.) estimated from sections the first and second formants of six different vowels spoken by a 6-year-old child and by an adult male. Five sets of narrow-band sections (0–4 kHz) were recorded from the spectrogram and he then made his estimates on different occasions and in haphazard order. The typical standard deviation within any set of five was about 10 Hz, a value considerably lower than any that will

TABLE 1 *a–f. First and second formant frequencies for six vowels.*

In each age or sex-age sub-group, $N = 5$. Each table section concerns one vowel, and within each section the columns represent, in order, the Mean frequency, the Between-subject standard deviation, the Within-subject standard deviation, and the Ratio of the Within-s.d. to the Mean.

Age (yrs.)	Mean	Between-S s.d.	Intra-S s.d.	Ratio of Intra-S s.d. to Mean
a. /i/				
First formant				
3	484	81.2	53.1	.110
4	444	49.5	41.5	.093
5	408	63.3	37.0	.091
6	397	15.2	30.3	.076
7	411	19.5	28.6	.070
8	397	38.1	23.8	.060
9	403	58.9	21.4	.053
10	403	36.9	19.4	.048
11, M	397	17.0	18.5	.047
11, F	423	81.3	18.1	.043
12, M	359	62.1	17.6	.049
12, F	358	35.5	17.3	.048
13, M	355	54.8	16.0	.045
13, F	377	30.2	16.2	.043
Adult, M	288	34.3	15.2	.053
Adult, F	338	21.1	14.9	.044
Second formant				
3	3318	267.1	130.8	.039
4	3050	453.1	104.0	.034
5	3235	346.3	95.8	.030
6	3108	210.3	89.6	.029
7	3204	187.1	76.9	.024
8	3104	67.9	71.1	.023
9	3106	171.5	58.7	.019
10	3028	167.7	56.5	.019
11, M	2778	98.7	46.5	.017
11, F	3134	179.2	46.1	.015
12, M	2877	49.0	39.5	.014
12, F	2940	183.7	40.3	.014
13, M	2727	279.7	34.9	.013
13, F	2907	296.3	41.0	.014
Adult, M	2217	194.4	33.5	.015
Adult, F	2810	72.5	39.4	.014
b. /ɛ/				
First formant				
3	673	77.1	97.8	.145
4	566	68.0	78.7	.139
5	642	61.4	66.4	.103
6	512	61.1	55.3	.108

Table 1 (*continued*)

Age (yrs.)	Mean	Between-S S.D.	Intra-S S.D.	Ratio of Intra-S S.D. to Mean
7	664	134.5	50.2	.076
8	585	77.1	45.5	.078
9	608	119.2	40.3	.066
10	645	106.9	33.2	.051
11, M	671	15.2	27.7	.041
11, F	628	171.2	30.0	.048
12, M	618	82.3	25.3	.041
12, F	687	54.5	24.8	.036
13, M	668	62.5	21.2	.032
13, F	590	141.8	22.1	.037
Adult, M	555	91.7	21.0	.038
Adult, F	589	106.5	21.6	.037

Second formant

3	2683	180.6	144.7	.054
4	2397	205.0	119.6	.050
5	2418	157.8	96.5	.040
6	2281	198.3	92.9	.041
7	2280	104.5	73.1	.032
8	2195	142.2	69.8	.032
9	2296	158.1	69.5	.030
10	2193	163.3	59.5	.027
11, M	2109	73.1	51.4	.024
11, F	2359	187.6	51.5	.022
12, M	2059	123.9	48.2	.023
12, F	2169	104.3	44.5	.021
13, M	1974	196.1	41.8	.021
13, F	2205	226.3	46.0	.021
Adult, M	1726	70.5	38.5	.022
Adult, F	2111	101.5	45.2	.021

c. /æ/

First formant

3	786	107.9	102.2	.130
4	657	121.3	86.5	.132
5	643	90.4	68.8	.107
6	611	98.5	58.8	.096
7	736	113.1	56.1	.076
8	685	77.3	51.1	.075
9	647	53.7	47.0	.073
10	735	47.5	37.3	.051
11, M	620	88.9	34.4	.055
11, F	736	141.4	34.6	.047
12, M	658	48.5	33.9	.052
12, F	700	39.8	33.5	.048
13, M	658	70.1	29.5	.045
13, F	672	86.5	29.4	.044
Adult, M	616	68.6	25.4	.041
Adult, F	761	75.7	30.3	.040

Table 1 (*continued*)

Age (yrs.)	Mean	Between-S S.D.	Intra-S S.D.	Ratio of Intra-S S.D. to Mean
Second formant				
3	2599	205.4	134.6	.052
4	2281	213.4	112.3	.049
5	2423	201.9	101.1	.042
6	2238	144.1	93.9	.042
7	2299	137.2	86.2	.037
8	2222	101.3	85.9	.039
9	2295	102.3	76.3	.033
10	2255	110.6	70.5	.031
11, M	2063	123.3	68.1	.033
11, F	2266	100.1	64.2	.028
12, M	2012	101.5	63.3	.031
12, F	2136	113.2	60.3	.028
13, M	1885	225.7	56.9	.030
13, F	2161	214.9	57.1	.026
Adult, M	1723	63.3	59.5	.036
Adult, F	2054	85.5	61.5	.030

d. /a/

Age (yrs.)	Mean	Between-S S.D.	Intra-S S.D.	Ratio of Intra-S S.D. to Mean
First formant				
3	986	105.9	168.9	.171
4	879	148.7	121.5	.138
5	1037	237.9	110.3	.106
6	809	109.1	87.2	.108
7	950	61.4	74.0	.078
8	921	99.8	69.3	.075
9	1053	109.4	63.5	.060
10	997	131.9	54.8	.055
11, M	884	37.5	39.5	.045
11, F	1005	149.7	47.1	.047
12, M	915	110.5	38.7	.042
12, F	895	58.5	37.5	.042
13, M	900	121.1	34.3	.039
13, F	950	51.0	36.0	.038
Adult, M	813	100.7	34.8	.043
Adult, F	922	95.9	37.4	.041
Second formant				
3	1982	180.8	156.3	.079
4	1858	211.0	137.5	.074
5	1784	116.2	119.6	.067
6	1655	63.3	98.5	.060
7	1652	119.6	83.2	.050
8	1729	153.7	77.1	.045
9	1785	87.2	73.7	.041
10	1709	127.9	66.9	.039
11, M	1538	136.8	53.9	.035
11, F	1752	52.9	55.8	.032

Table 1 (*continued*)

Age (yrs.)	Mean	Between-S S.D.	Intra-S S.D.	Ratio of Intra-S S.D. to Mean
12, M	1573	104.4	50.1	.032
12, F	1734	176.7	50.3	.029
13, M	1526	96.2	46.1	.030
13, F	1719	138.9	43.8	.025
Adult, M	1301	60.3	44.8	.034
Adult, F	1503	110.1	44.2	.029

e. /ɔ/

First formant

3	802	110.3	109.6	.137
4	762	144.6	83.3	.109
5	901	197.0	79.6	.088
6	689	87.2	62.5	.091
7	817	78.8	53.1	.065
8	743	69.7	48.1	.065
9	836	68.7	45.2	.054
10	814	89.6	39.2	.048
11, M	724	67.6	34.5	.048
11, F	799	114.1	31.8	.040
12, M	705	100.5	31.2	.044
12, F	830	89.5	28.1	.034
13, M	744	85.7	24.5	.033
13, F	806	126.1	24.8	.031
Adult, M	653	39.5	23.3	.036
Adult, F	666	38.9	24.1	.036

Second formant

3	1485	70.8	122.1	.082
4	1390	172.7	93.4	.067
5	1513	109.6	80.3	.053
6	1308	117.3	68.1	.052
7	1398	94.9	64.8	.046
8	1359	78.3	63.2	.047
9	1352	116.2	54.7	.040
10	1336	48.9	52.0	.039
11, M	1284	87.5	47.5	.037
11, F	1325	104.9	44.2	.033
12, M	1175	139.3	40.9	.035
12, F	1382	82.5	40.1	.029
13, M	1120	82.8	41.0	.037
13, F	1802	155.9	42.4	.035
Adult, M	1048	67.4	40.6	.039
Adult, F	1135	95.4	41.9	.037

f. /u/

First formant

3	578	74.2	55.7	.096
4	472	21.7	42.0	.089

Table 1 (*continued*)

Age (yrs.)	Mean	Between-S s.d.	Intra-S s.d.	Ratio of Intra-S s.d. to Mean
5	452	41.4	39.2	.087
6	431	28.6	34.2	.079
7	481	49.0	30.8	.064
8	450	65.3	24.9	.055
9	469	63.5	23.1	.049
10	469	35.1	19.3	.041
11, M	448	38.5	15.9	.035
11, F	478	77.1	18.7	.039
12, M	404	47.0	16.0	.040
12, F	422	31.2	16.8	.040
13, M	428	18.6	15.4	.036
13, F	399	31.9	15.9	.040
Adult, M	344	45.9	16.2	.047
Adult, F	356	35.0	14.5	.041
Second formant				
3	1664	309.7	120.6	.072
4	1528	149.4	97.6	.064
5	1477	112.3	86.3	.058
6	1385	117.9	78.2	.056
7	1525	67.8	67.3	.044
8	1437	51.7	64.0	.046
9	1392	115.6	61.7	.044
10	1351	92.8	56.9	.042
11, M	1388	144.6	52.5	0.38
11, F	1474	91.2	49.5	.036
12, M	1253	120.4	46.7	.037
12, F	1436	64.9	47.8	.033
13, M	1347	103.9	45.1	.033
13, F	1420	203.2	46.8	.033
Adult, M	1256	80.5	43.6	.035
Adult, F	1460	72.7	46.1	.029

be described presently. Since this crude measure of reader error was the same for both ages or for all vowels, we conclude that the measures of variability to be described in the following sections are in fact descriptive of the speech productions.

Results

Means for each age group and standard deviation between and within subjects for first-formant and second-formant frequencies are given in Table 1.

Mean values of first-formant and second-formant frequencies. The second-formant frequency (first column, lower half) tended to drop more than did

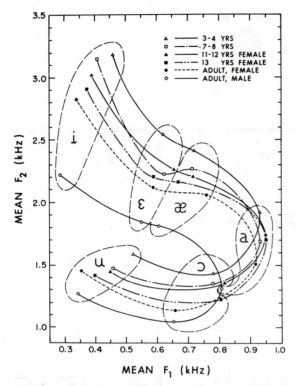

Fig. 2. Mean formant frequencies for combined age groups as shown in the key. Each point represents the combination of Formant 1 and Formant 2 for each of the six vowels, The different symbols together with the lines that join them represent the different ages. The broken circles are drawn around all points for a given vowel.

the first-formant frequency (first column, upper half), with the exception of the first-formant frequency for the vowel [a]. This was especially clear during the period from 3 to 5 years. Formant frequencies of 13-year-old girls were close to those of adult females, while 13-year-old boys had higher formant frequencies than did adult males. Formant frequencies of adults showed almost the same values as those found in the literature (Peterson and Barney, 1952; Fairbanks and Grubb, 1961; Potter and Steinberg, 1950).

In order to assess the dependence of formant frequencies on age, values were averaged for the following age groups: 3 and 4 years; 7 and 8 years; 11 and 12 year-old girls; 13 year-old girls, and male and female adults. The results are shown in Fig. 2 as the familiar F_1–F_2 plot with the vowels of each age group connected to form a "vowel triangle".

Here, the gradual but marked decrease in second formant frequencies, as contrasted with the more stable first-formant frequencies, is shown. Another feature that stands out is that the first-formant frequency for [a] appears to be independent of age.

Between-subject standard deviations. Standard deviations of the distribution of individual subject means (second column) within each age group

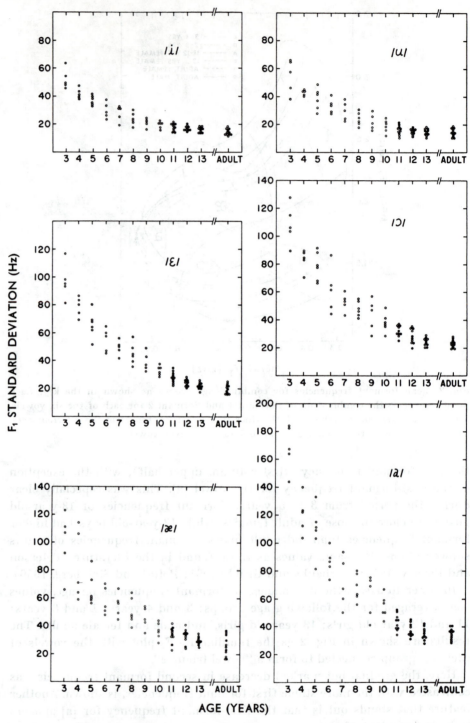

Fig. 3. Intra-subject variability in first formant for six vowels as a function of age. Each point represents the standard deviation in Hz for each subject used in the experiment. Above the age of 10, females are indicated by filled circles, while males are indicated by open circles.

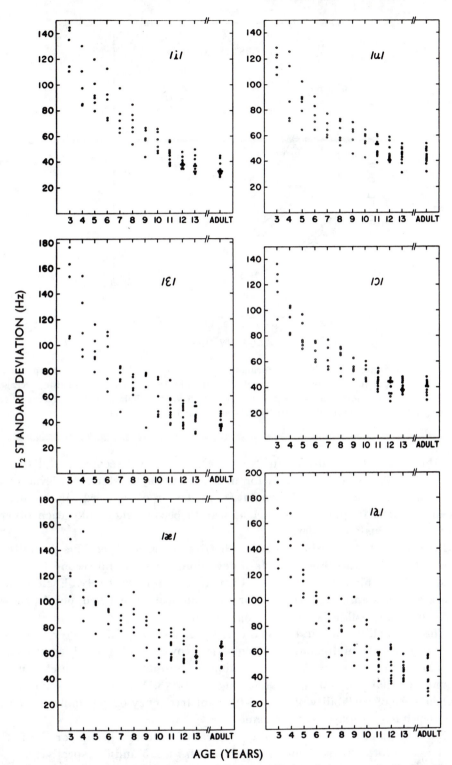

Fig. 4. Intra-subject variability for second formant. Each point represents the standard deviation in Hz for each subject used in the experiment. Above the age of 10, females are indicated by filled circles, while males are indicated by open circles.

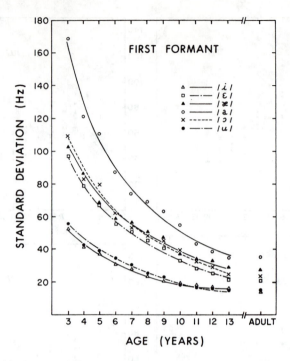

Fig. 5. Intra-subject variability in Formant 1 typical of the different age groups as a function of age. In this figure each point represents the square root of the average variance for the children in each age group. The different symbols and the different lines connecting them for each of the six vowels are identified in the key.

for the first and second-formant frequencies varied between 40 and 450 Hz. Age does not appear to be a factor in between-subject standard deviations for either the first or second-formant frequency. In other words, individual's mean formant frequencies do not appear to become more like each other as the individuals get older.

Intra-subject standard deviations. The five sentence repetitions permitted calculation of intra-subject standard deviations for first and second-formant frequencies, which are shown in Figs. 3 and 4 respectively. Each point represents a standard deviation for each subject. The filled points show data for female subjects above the age of ten.

The variability of first-formant frequencies was higher for middle vowels than for high-front and high-back vowels, but for all vowels the variability decreases with age, reaching a minimum value, which corresponds to that for adults, at about age 11 to 13. While there is no clear dependence of variability of second-formant frequency on particular vowels, the dependence on age was the same.

Summaries of average variability, typical of each age group for the first and second formant frequencies are shown in Figs. 5 and 6 respectively.

The differences in variability of first-formant frequencies among the

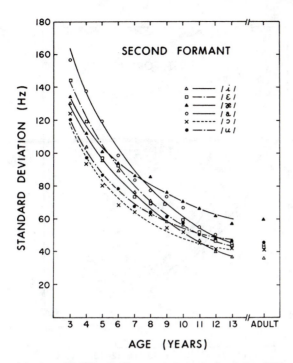

Fig. 6. Intra-subject variability in Formant 2 typical of the different age groups as a function of age. In this figure each point represents the square root of the average variance for the children in each age group. The different symbols and the different lines connecting them for each of the six vowels are identified in the key.

vowels are clear here. Variability of [a] is the highest of all vowels while the variabilities of [i] and [u] are the lowest. The variability of first-formant frequencies is 170 Hz for [a], 55 Hz for [i] and [u], and 100 Hz for [ε], [æ], and [ɔ], at the age of 3. At 13 years, however, it is 35 Hz for [a], 15 Hz for [i] and [u], and 21–29 Hz in [ε], [æ], and [ɔ], the same values as those of an adult. The variability of second-formant frequencies is approximately the same for all vowels. The variability of second-formant frequencies ranged from 120 to 150 Hz at three years and 35 to 57 Hz at thirteen years, reaching adult values.

Ratio of intra-subject standard deviation to mean value. It is obvious from Fig. 5 that the intra-subject variability of first formant for [a] is higher than that for either [i] or [u], but then so is the mean formant frequency. Perhaps variability should be reckoned not as an absolute value, but as a fraction of the mean around which the values vary. Accordingly, we show the same data in Fig. 7, but the ordinate describing variability, is the ratio of the standard deviation in Hz to the *child's own mean* first-formant frequency. Indeed, the differences among the vowels are less distinct. The decrease with age remains as before.

Fig. 6 showed a fair homogeneity of the 'absolute' variability of the

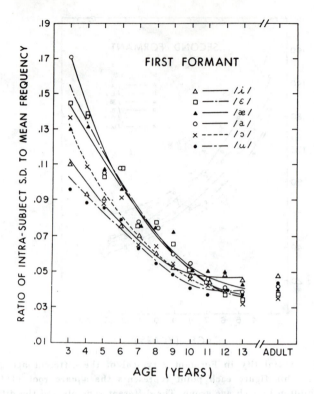

Fig. 7. Re-plotting of first-formant data shown in Fig. 5, but with the variability expressed on the ordinate as the ratio of the standard deviation to the mean formant frequency.

second formants for different vowels in absolute terms, but Fig. 8 shows how the relative variabilities separate according to the mean second-formant frequencies.

The relative variabilities for the first formant for the 3-year-olds are still highest for [a] (0.171) and lowest for [i] and [u] (0.096, 0.11). By the age of five or six, however, the ratios are similar for all vowels (0.09 or 0.1) and they remain the same as they descend to the adult value of 0.03 to 0.05. For the second formant, the s.d./mean ratio is lowest for [i] and higher for [a], [ɔ], and [u], and this finding is independent of age.

Discussion

Acoustical phonetics characterizes phonemes or speech sounds in articulatory terms by places or gestures of the tongue, and in acoustic terms by formants and transitions. In the past, studies on vowel formant frequencies have been reported to clarify some acoustical features of speech sounds. It has been recognized that the vowel formants represent the acoustical resonant properties of vocal tract as shaped in articulation by the tongue (Potter, Kopp and Green, 1947; Joos, 1948; Peterson and Barney, 1952;

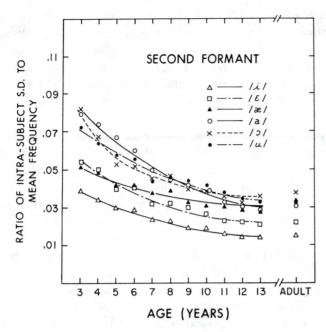

Fig. 8. Re-plotting of second-formant data shown in Fig. 6, but with the variability expressed on the ordinate as the ratio of the standard deviation to the mean formant frequency.

Peterson, 1951, 1959; Potter and Steinberg, 1950; Stevens and House, 1961). Identification of the vowel is chiefly dependent on the first and the second formants.

One simple notion from the past was that the first formant corresponds to the back cavity and the second formant corresponds to the front cavity of the mouth (Joos, 1948). However, it has also been reported that the formants generated by different talkers speaking the same vowel have different frequencies; and that formants generated in producing different vowels may hav the same frequency. A theory based on absolute values for vowel formant frequency has great difficulty (Stevens and House, 1963). Various investigators have considered as a basis for this confusion size of vocal tract, dialect and many other factors.

Recent studies of synthesized speech and measurement of the size of vocal tract on X-ray pictures reveals that the first and second formants are not simply acoustic features of front cavity and back cavity in the vocal tract (Fant, 1960). For example:

"*The first formant.* The frequency of the first formant F_1 is generally dependent more on the back cavity volume than on the volume of other cavities. An exception is the vowel [ɑ], where F_1 is affected equally on a percentage basis by a change in the front cavity volume, and by a change of the back cavity volume. Since the back cavity of [ɑ] is much shorter than the front cavity, the percentage increase of F_1 due to the removal of a small unit length section of the back cavity is larger than the shift caused by a removal of a section of the same length in the middle of the front cavity.

"F_1 of the vowels [e], [i], and [ɨ] is almost completely determined by the back cavity volume and the narrowest section of the mouth cavity. In the vowels [u], [o], and [ɑ] is somewhat more dependent on the front cavity constriction section. The contribution to F_1 of [u] from the back cavity volume is somewhat larger than that from the front cavity.

"*The second formant.* Only in the case of the vowel [ɨ] was the mouth cavity with associated orifices found to be the essential determinant of F_2. F_2 of [i] is clearly a half-wavelength resonance of the back cavity. There is a similar but not at all so apparent tendency of F_2 of [e] to be influenced more by the back than by the front cavity. The second formant of the back vowels [u], [o], and [ɑ] is somewhat more dependent on the front cavity than on the back cavity. Providing the cavity volume changes are introduced on a constant percentage basis, this tendency is apparent, but if the volume changes are performed by means of a constant length reduction, there is found an equal dependency of F_2 on the two cavities for [u] and also for [ɑ]. In the case of [u], F_2 is dependent much more on the relative dimensions of the tongue pass than on the lip section. These two parts of the compound resonator system have about the same effect on F_2 of both [ɑ] and [o]. The lip section is of practically no importance for F_2 of [i] and does not have a very marked influence of [e] either" (Fant, 1960, p. 121).

There are only a few studies of vowel formant frequency of children (Potter and Steinberg, 1950; Peterson and Barney, 1952), especially on the development of formant frequencies (Potter and Peterson, 1948; Okamura, 1966). What is known is that formant frequencies of eight-year old children are about 25% higher than that of adult males and 20% higher than that of adult females.

Okamura (1966) reported, in his study on formant constructions and differentiation of vowel areas in two-formant space, that Japanese vowel formant frequencies can be differentiated from each other by the age of nine.

Needless to say, the vocal tract of a child is smaller in size than that of an adult. But we cannot easily assume that the formants have higher frequencies in proportion to the size of the vocal tract with age as a whole, because different parts of the vocal tract presumably change at different rates.

In a study on the anatomical development of voice and speech organs in children, Negus (1949) pointed out that the larynx develops most rapidly between the ages of 3 and 5 years, and then development of the larynx becomes more gradual with age until puberty is reached.

Our results on formant frequencies can be summarized as follows:

(*a*) There is a clear decrease of first and second formant frequencies between ages 3 and 5 years.

(*b*) Generally, the decrease of the second-formant frequency is greater than that of the first-formant frequency.

(*c*) The first-formant frequency of [a] is independent of age.

(*d*) Between-subject standard deviations of formant frequencies are unrelated to age and sex.

From these results and the work of others (e.g., Negus, and Fant) the following conclusions may be drawn:

(*e*) These acoustical results are in accordance with the rapid anatomical development of the vocal tract between the ages of 3 and 5 years.

(*f*) The development of the front cavity will have a greater influence on changes in formant frequencies than the development of the back cavity.

(*g*) First formant frequencies of [a] are not so clearly influenced by development of vocal tract, but indirectly or mutually influenced by development of front and back cavities, and also other factors (i.e. fundamental frequency, etc.).

(*h*) Variability of formant frequencies for given vowels between subjects is independent of age and sex.

Anatomical factors may not be the only source of these variations, since the development of speech sounds in children is influenced also by psychophysiological development. Further, the perception of vowels is dependent not only on formant frequency, but also on many other information-bearing elements of speech (Peterson, 1952). We should not expect, therefore, to understand the development of vowel formant frequency in children on the basis of the anatomical development of vocal tract alone.

IV. FUNDAMENTAL FREQUENCY

Method

Fundamental frequencies of vowels were estimated from the number of harmonics (up to 4000 Hz) that showed in the narrow-band spectrum at the vowel formant sectioning points (Fant, p. 241). Earlier attempts were made to use a greatly expanded frequency scale to read the fundamental frequency directly from the spectrogram. That procedure involves an expanded harmonic line, whose thickness offsets any increase in accuracy over the harmonic count.

Results

Data for the fundamental frequencies averaged over all vowels are given in Table 2. The means are based on the 5 repetitions, the 6 vowels, and 5 subjects in each age group, in short, an averaged fundamental typical of vowels throughout the sentence. The between-subject S.D. concerns the variation in each age group among the averages of repetitions and vowels. The intra-subject S.D. is the variation among the 5 repetitions, averaged (variance) over all subjects and all vowels. Mean values of fundamental frequencies are shown with between-subject and intra-subject standard deviations in Fig. 9.

Mean values. Fundamental frequency, starting from about 300 Hz at 3 years, decreases slightly with age. However, the largest decrease of fundamental frequency seems to occur between the ages of 3 and 6 years. Thirteen-year-old boys had an average fundamental frequency of 221.1 Hz, still an octave higher than that of adult males (124.2 Hz). Thirteen-year-old girls, on the other hand, had an average fundamental frequency of 239.8 Hz, not very different from that of adult females (220.9 Hz).

Between-subject standard deviation. Between-subject standard deviation was not dependent on age. It ranged from 20 to 45 Hz. Interestingly, 13-year-old boys showed a standard deviation of 66.4 Hz, which is a higher value than that found for all other age groups.

Intra-subject standard deviation and its relation to mean value. Three-year-old children showed about a 40 Hz S.D., yielding a ratio of standard deviation to mean of 0.132. There was a gradual decreasing with age, reaching a minimum value (12 Hz, 0.047) at age ten or twelve; and after that age, there was not further decrease in intra-subject standard deviation of fundamental frequency (0.04 to 0.05). This decrease in relative variability is shown in Fig. 10.

TABLE 2. *Fundamental frequency averaged across all vowels, for the different age groups.*

The columns represent the Mean frequency, the Between-Subject Standard Deviation, the Intra-Subject Standard Deviation, and the Ratio of the Intra-s.d. to the Mean.

Age (yrs.)	Mean	Between-S s.d.	Intra-S s.d.	Ratio of Intra-S s.d. to Mean
3	297.8	30.8	39.2	.132
4	285.6	20.9	26.0	.091
5	288.7	46.3	22.8	.079
6	271.2	27.9	18.4	.068
7	262.5	38.5	17.7	.067
8	261.0	31.1	14.0	.054
9	262.5	35.9	13.7	.052
10	261.9	32.9	12.3	.047
11, M	244.2	24.4	10.5	.043
11, F	252.5	42.5	12.9	.051
12, M	243.2	26.8	10.8	.044
12, F	248.6	19.2	10.9	.044
13, M	221.1	66.4	9.4	.042
13, F	239.8	19.6	9.9	.041
Adult, M	124.2	20.7	5.6	.045
Adult, F	220.9	19.3	10.1	.045

Discussion

It is well known that the fundamental frequencies of children and adult females are higher than those of the adult male. The fundamental frequencies of the vowels of an adult female are about one octave higher than that of the adult male. Children have a fundamental frequency of about 300 Hz even up to the age of 8 and 10 years. There is no significant difference of fundamental frequency of speech between 7 and 8 years, or between boys and girls of those ages (Fairbanks, Herbert and Hammond, 1949; Fairbanks, Wiley and Lassman, 1949; Potter and Steinberg, 1950; Peterson and Barney, 1952).

It is also well known that regulation of fundamental frequency in voice is dependent on many factors, including the length of vocal cord, and the regulation of movement of peripheral voice and speech musculature by central nervous system (Pressman, 1942; Kirikae, 1943). In his anatomical study, Negus (1949) reported that the length of vocal cord is 3 mm at birth, 5.5 mm at 1 year, 7.5 mm at 5 years, 8 mm at age $6\,^1/_2$ years, 9.5 mm at 15 years, 12.5 to 17 mm in the adult female and 17 to 23 mm in the adult male. Vocal cords, generally, lengthen rapidly up to 6 years and gradually after 6 years.

A study of fundamental frequency and the size of larynx of boys from 12 to 15 years reported that rapid development of larynx, as related to change of voice, began at around 13 years and finished at approximately 15 years (Naider, 1965).

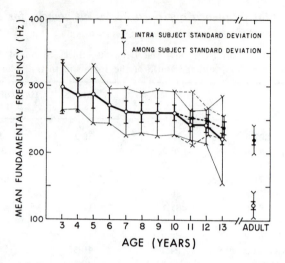

Fig. 9. Fundamental frequencies. The open circles are means averaged across repetitions, vowels, and subjects in each age group. The vertical bars enclosed within horizontal markers show the variation (s.d.) across repetitions, while those between arrowheads show the variation across subjects. The broken line joins means for girls only above the age of 10 years.

The present study shows that fundamental frequency was about 300 Hz at age 3, then there is a remarkable decrease of about 30 Hz between 3 and 6 years, then a gradual decrease after 6 years to 220 Hz in 13-year-old boys. Thirteen-year-old girls have an average of 240 Hz, which is not significantly different from that of adult females (220 Hz).

There is a strong correspondence between the fundamental frequency reported here and the changes in the length of vocal cords reported by Negus (1949). Furthermore, the fact that between-subject standard deviation

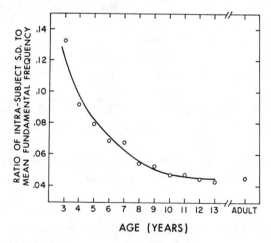

Fig. 10. Variability in average fundamental frequency over repetitions, expressed as ratio of s.d. to mean frequency.

of thirteen-year-old boys was higher than that of other age groups, showed that there are important changes and a rapid decrease of fundamental frequency after about 13 years in boys. This evidence agrees with the results reported by Naider (1965).

In summary, fundamental frequency decreases markedly between the ages of 3 and 6 years, after which the decrease is gradual. At 13 years, girls have almost the same value of fundamental frequency as adult females, while that of boys still decreases after 13 years rapidly reaching the value of the adult male, and corresponding to development of the larynx.

V. TEMPORAL FEATURES

Method

Wide-band spectrograms were used for the measurement of one type of temporal feature in the words. We measured the interval between plosive releases and the subsequent voiced sounds. These time intervals were the gaps between [b] and the release from [l] in the word "blue", between [p] and [ɛ] in the word "pen", and between [t] and [ɔ] in the word "tall" respectively.

Results

Data for temporal features are summarized in Table 3 and Fig. 12.

Mean values. The time interval between [p] and [ɛ] in the word "pen" varied from 49 to 68 msec; and between [t] and [ɔ] in the word "tall" from 60 to 84 msec. No statistically significant difference for the means was found between age groups and therefore we conclude that these time intervals, on the average, are independent of age.

Between-subject standard deviation. Between-subject standard deviation of time intervals between [b] and [l] in the word "blue" showed 7.9 to 21.2 msec; that of [p] and [ɛ] in the word "pen", 8.5–27.7 msec; and that of [t] and [ɔ] in the word "tall", 10.4–22.5 msec. In this case, too, the variability among individuals for this time interval between phonemes is independent of age.

Intra-subject variability. Three-year-old children showed about 27 msec of intra-subject standard deviation and then there was a rapid decrease in variability as a function of age. Variability reached a minimum value (9–10 msec) at age 7 or 8 years, this value corresponding to that of adults. Here, as for the formant frequencies, there is a systematic decrease of individual variability, or an increase in the precision of timing, with age. The variability reaches its minimum or adult value at a somewhat earlier age than for the vowel formants.

Discussion

There are several studies on voice-onset time and formant-transition time as examples of temporal features of consonants (Lisker and Abramson, 1964, 1965; Liberman *et al.*, 1957; Preston, Yem'-Komshian and Stark, 1967; Ohman, 1966). These studies, which have been done on the voice-onset time of adult speech, reported wide variability among subjects. Lisker and Abramson (1965) showed that the mean voice-onset time of [p] was 58 msec with a range of 20 to 120 msec. The mean for [t] was 70 msec, with a range

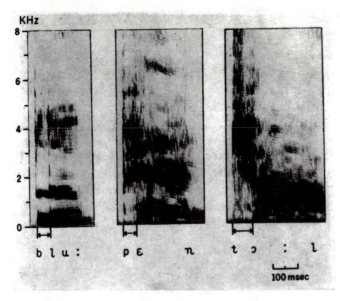

Fig. 11. Portions of spectrograms of the words "blue", "pen", and "tall" illustrating measurement of time interval between plosion and the voiced continuant that follows.

of 30 to 105 msec. Prestin, Yem'-Komshian and Stark (1967) reported that the distribution of the values of voice-onset time for children approximated the adult models.

The present study shows, with the results summarized above, the mean time intervals measured here do not change systematically with age and also that there is wide variation among individuals pronouncing the

TABLE 3. *Time intervals (msec) between plosive sounds and voiced sounds that follow in three different words for all age groups.*

Age (yrs.)	b~l			p~ε			t~c		
	Mean	Between-S s.d.	Intra-S s.d.	Mean	Between-S s.d.	Intra-S s.d.	Mean	Between-S s.d.	Intra-S s.d.
3	73	11.7	27.0	69	12.9	26.1	73	22.5	27.8
4	65	13.9	23.5	66	27.7	19.8	70	18.7	24.2
5	69	21.2	22.2	68	22.8	17.4	84	21.2	22.2
6	85	16.5	15.2	65	8.5	17.1	72	10.4	18.7
7	67	8.5	13.1	49	16.8	11.8	60	14.1	11.3
8	78	11.7	10.8	61	8.8	11.2	70	15.2	10.5
9	67	14.5	10.4	52	10.5	10.8	67	12.1	11.4
10	72	15.6	9.2	61	9.6	10.6	77	15.4	9.9
11	68	17.9	9.3	55	18.1	10.4	65	17.0	9.8
12	68	13.3	9.5	60	12.0	9.9	79	17.2	11.0
13	62	7.9	10.0	56	14.7	10.0	68	14.0	10.6
Adult	70	10.7	9.3	62	18.9	10.3	77	20.4	9.9

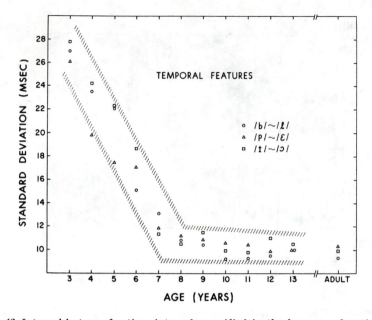

Fig. 12. Intrasubject s.d. for time intervals specified in the key, as a function of age.

same phonetic sequences. These two observations are in accord with those discussed above from other investigators with respect to voice-onset time. The new contribution is the systematic decrease in a subject's own variability as age increases. The apparent fact that this temporal feature of speech production reaches an adult-like minimum value at 7 or 8 years while a spectral feature like vowel-formant frequency continues to increase in individual precision to age about 12 years, suggests that the temporal aspect of speech defines phonemic categories earlier and more easily than does a frequency aspect. Perhaps this dichotomy strengthens the findings concerning discrimination at category boundaries, clearer for consonants (Liberman *et al.*, 1957) than for vowels (Stevens *et al.*, 1964).

VI. IDENTIFICATION OF VOWELS BY
ADULT LISTENERS

Method

A long tape containing 1500 randomly distributed vowel samples was used for a listening task. These samples were taken from the original recordings and contained vowels produced by the subjects: five from age groups 3, 5, 7 and 9 years and ten from age groups 11, 13 and adult. Half of each of the three older groups was male, and half female.

Small segments of tape were cut from the sentence recordings, which segments corresponded to steady, unchanging portions of the target vowel according to a listening criterion of the experimenter. Not all vowel samples remained steady for the same duration and thus the durations were in fact different, ranging from about 100 to 300 msec. According to Joos' (1948) criterion for a minimum of 50 msec required for vowel identification, all of these samples should have been adequately long. A two-way classification analysis of variance of these durations for three widely separated ages showed that the sample durations, averaged over all vowels, were not significantly different for the different ages, but different vowels had different durations, that for [ɔ] being the longest in all cases. There was also a significant interaction between vowel and age.

Fortunately, for present purposes, the longest durations did not yield the highest intelligibility scores (*vide infra*). For example, [ɔ], even though longest in all cases, was not as intelligible as several other vowels. We conclude, therefore, that in spite of variations in the duration of vowel samples used in the listening tests, such variations did not affect the intelligibility scores. The reason probably is that all durations were longer than the minimum necessary.

Each sample was followed by a 5-sec segment of blank tape, before the next sample was joined. Also, during the listening sessions, each block of 80 items was followed by a 2-minute rest period.

Twenty normally hearing adults, 12 men and 8 women, chosen from among the training students at Central Institute for the Deaf, served as listeners. Ten of twenty listeners had to select an identification response from among six simulus alternatives: [i], [ɛ], [æ], [a], [ɔ], and [u]. Another ten listeners made identifications among twelve alternatives: [i], [ɪ], [e], [ɛ], [æ], [a], [ɑ], [ʌ], [ɔ], [o], [ʊ], [u].

Four loudspeakers were hung about 1.5 meters above the heads of listeners seated in two rows. The signal level at the listener's head was approximately 70 dB re 0.0002 dyne/cm² at the peak of the speech sound.

TABLE 4. *Display-cards used by listeners with 6 or 12 alternative responses.*

i beet 1	i beet 1
ɛ bet 2	ɪ bit 2
æ bat 3	e bait 3
a bath 4	ɛ bet 4
ɔ bought 5	æ bat 5
u boot 6	a bath 6
	ɑ bomb 7
	ʌ buck 8
	ɔ bought 9
	o boat 10
	ʊ book 11
	u boot 12

In order to facilitate the identification of the vowel sample, cards on which each vowel was numbered, listed and represented in a key word were distributed to each listener (Table 4). The listener was then to write the number of the identified vowel on an answer sheet. Pretest practice was carried out on 80 items.

Results

A confusion matrix for each age group and listener group was made, and the amount of information transmitted by each age group was calculated.

Six messages–six responses. The results of forced-choice listening with six alternative choices are displayed in the confusion matrix of Table 5. The maximum number in any one cell is the product of 5 children times 5 repetitions times 10 listeners. Inspection of the column totals reveals that, while all six stimuli were presented equally often, the six responses were not given equally often. Three columns deserve particular notice. The choice of [æ] and [ɛ] as distinct vowels was not a happy one for the dialect of St. Louis. Fig. 2 showed that the mean formant frequencies for these two vowels are not very far apart. Speakers in this region do not distinguish clearly the vowels in "pen" and "has". Furthermore, the listeners, including a greater variety of dialects, did not distinguish the two, giving as many as three times the response [ɛ] as [æ]. In addition the low response frequency for [a] probably comes about because in a non-Eastern dialect this vowel never exists except as the first part of the diphthong [aɪ]. On the response card the [a] was exemplified by the word "bath" and the experimenter explained that the word was an example of the sound only in some Eastern dialects where the vowels of "bat, bath and Bob" are all different. Nonetheless, the vowel as illustrated on the card does not represent a much used phonemic category in the speech of most of our listeners.

The diagonal cells shows the number of correct identifications out of 250. Expressed as percentages these measures of intelligibility of the six vowels are given in Table 6 and Fig. 13 for the several ages.

TABLE 5. *Confusion matrices (6 stimuli and 6 response alternatives) for vowels spoken by subjects at different ages.*

Age (yrs.)	Spoken vowel	Identified vowel					
		i	ε	æ	a	ɔ	u
3	i	177	32	5		1	35
	ε	57	151	22	4	13	3
	æ	7	171	49	8	6	9
	a	1	57	86	85	15	6
	ɔ		1	6	96	139	8
	u	4	14	4	11	13	204
	Total	246	426	172	204	187	265
5	i	183	34	8	1		24
	ε	1	194	52			3
	æ	13	185	28	2	1	21
	a	1	26	81	116	8	18
	ɔ	1	2	8	153	70	16
	u	12	20	2	5	4	207
	Total	211	461	179	277	83	289
7	i	237	7				6
	ε		190	53	4	2	1
	æ	11	202	29			8
	a		8	64	158	19	1
	ɔ			3	95	150	2
	u	8	7		1		234
	Total	256	414	149	258	171	252
9	i	223	18	1	1		7
	ε	3	212	28	4	2	1
	æ	12	205	9	2	2	20
	a		14	91	132	13	
	ɔ		1	4	92	152	1
	u	2	2			1	245
	Total	240	452	133	231	170	274
11, M	i	168	39				43
	ε		194	38	5	6	7
	æ	15	164	19	6	5	41
	a		8	53	148	40	1
	ɔ		2	1	41	204	2
	u	8	1		2	3	236
	Total	191	408	111	202	258	330
11, F	i	243	4				3
	ε	3	217	20	3		7
	æ	6	230	8	1	1	4
	a		10	69	144	23	4
	ɔ		2	4	79	164	1
	u	8	1			1	240
	Total	260	464	101	227	189	259

Age (yrs.)	Spoken vowel	Identified vowel					
		i	ɛ	æ	a	ɔ	u
13, M	i	231	12			1	6
	ɛ		223	20	3	3	1
	æ	8	210	10	3	1	18
	a		11	75	139	24	1
	ɔ		18	9	51	172	
	u	21	5			1	223
	Total	260	479	114	196	202	249
13, F	i	224	17				9
	ɛ	9	167	57	4	2	11
	æ	16	194	20	3		16
	a		11	78	143	17	1
	ɔ		1	6	86	157	
	u	24	7	1		1	217
	Total	273	397	162	236	177	254
Adult, M	i	236	8				6
	ɛ		193	14	24	9	10
	æ	2	207	18	3	3	17
	a	2	3	29	173	43	
	ɔ	1	1	2	17	229	
	u		1				249
	Total	241	405	63	217	284	276
Adult, F	i	233	16				1
	ɛ	1	201	41	5	1	1
	æ		197	41	7	4	1
	a		2	36	181	31	
	ɔ		1	1	62	184	2
	u	15	2			2	231
	Total	249	419	119	255	222	236

It is clear that intelligibility of all vowels increases with the age of the talker and we assume that this effect is due to the change in variability that characterizes the consistency of repetition of such vowels, as discussed above in the measurement of formant frequencies.

From these values it is also clear that the several vowels are not equally intelligible, [i] and [u] being the highest. On the other hand, these measures of relative intelligibility are contaminated by the response biases discussed above and illustrated by the column totals of Table 5.

Four types of analyses were made on the data of the confusion matrices, shown in Table 5. These were, (a) conventional calculation of values of intelligibility indices for each vowel as spoken by each age group (Table 6), (b) determination of the amount of information transmitted within each confusion matrix, (c) estimation of the pairwise discriminability among

TABLE 6. *Intelligibility of six vowels spoken by subjects of different ages.*

Uncorrected scores equal to number of correct responses divided by number of correct responses divided by number of vowels spoken for the six-alternative response. The last three rows give averaged results of both sexes in the groups 11 and 13 years, and adult.

Age	i	ɛ	æ	a	ɔ	u	Overall
3	70.8	60.4	19.6	34.0	55.6	81.6	53.6
5	73.2	77.6	11.2	46.4	28.0	82.8	53.2
7	94.8	76.0	11.6	63.2	60.0	93.6	66.5
9	89.2	84.8	3.6	52.8	60.8	98.0	64.9
11, M	67.2	77.6	7.6	59.2	81.6	94.4	64.6
11, F	97.2	86.8	3.2	57.6	65.6	96.0	67.7
13, M	92.4	89.2	4.0	55.6	68.8	89.2	66.5
13, F	89.6	66.8	8.0	57.2	62.8	86.8	61.9
Adult, M	94.4	77.2	7.2	69.2	91.6	99.6	73.2
Adult, F	93.2	80.4	16.4	72.4	73.6	92.4	71.4
11, M + F	82.2	82.1	5.4	58.4	73.6	95.2	66.2
13, M + F	91.0	72.0	6.0	56.4	65.8	88.0	64.2
Adult, M + F	93.8	78.8	11.8	70.8	82.6	96.0	72.3

the vowels by use of the Constant Ratio Rule, for vowels spoken by all but the two youngest groups, and (d) estimation of the probability of a correct identification of each of the vowels as spoken by each age group, after applying a correction for response biases.

The intelligibility indices for each vowel were calculated by dividing the number of times that vowel was correctly identified by the number of presentations of that vowel. These are the measures shown in Table 6 and Fig. 13. They demonstrate a general improvement of performance on the identification task as a function of the age of the speakers, for all vowels with the exception of [æ], which apparently was something of a mystery to

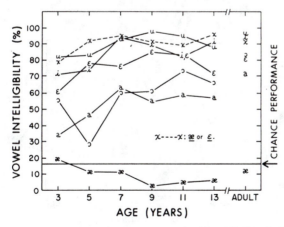

Fig. 13. Intelligibility (percentage of items correctly identified) of the different vowels for seven of the age groups.

TABLE 7. *Average information transmitted per vowel over all vowels spoken by talkers at different ages.*

Age	It	Age	It
3	1.020	11, F	1.699
5	1.169	13, M	1.571
7	1.582	13, F	1.374
9	1.593	Adult, M	1.644
11, M	1.245	Adult, F	1.645

the listeners. (The broken line in this figure is discussed in a later section.)

The amount of information transmitted within each confusion matrix yields a measure of identification performance averaged across the six vowels. This index may thus give a clearer picture of the general improvement in the discriminability of vowels as the speaker's age increaes. Information transmitted (I_t) was calculated as suggested by Garner and Hake, by finding the difference between response information (I_r) and response equivocation (E_r), where

$$I_r = - \sum_{k=1}^{m} [p(a_k) \cdot \log_2 p(a_k)],$$

and

$$E_r = - \sum_{i=1}^{m} p(A_i) \cdot \sum_{k=1}^{m} [p(a_k | A_i) \cdot \log_2 p(a_k | A_i)],$$

for a matrix of m rows (i) and columns (k). Information transmitted as a function of age of the speaker (shown in Table 7, Fig. 14), reaches close to its maximum value by 7 years.

Consideration of the original confusion matrices demonstrates some problems not treated in the two preceding forms of analysis. As noted earlier, the responses were not used equally often, and both information transmitted

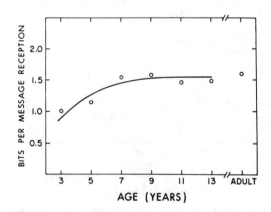

Fig. 14. Information transmitted in a vowel spoken by different age groups.

and intelligibility (simple per cent correct) may be degraded artificially by such response biases. That is, even though ability to identify each of the vowels be equal, differences in response probability might yield the illusion of real variance in their identifiability. That this is not a trivial issue may be seen by examining the relative proportions of the responses [æ] and [ɛ] in Table 5. Also it is fairly clear in the original matrices that these same two vowels are never very discriminable, one from the other, although they do appear to bear information in the sense that either on tends to lead to *one* of the two appropriate responses.

One method for handling these problems is through application of the "Constant Ratio Rule", proposed by Clarke (1957). Clarke's rule simply provides that, "... the ratio between any two entries in a row of a submatrix is equal to the ratio between the corresponding two entries in the master matrix". In the present case this means that the pairwise discriminability of any two vowels can be estimated from the four entries associated with these vowels in the original six-vowel matrix. For example, the vowels [a] and [ɔ] were correctly identified 1060 and 1262 times, when pronounced by speakers from ages nine through adults. (In this analysis we have deleted data for the three younger groups, speakers from which were clearly less precise in their pronunciation than the older speakers.) The vowel [a] was identified as [ɔ] 191 times and [ɔ] as [a] 428 times. The constant ratio rule thus predicts that the results of an experiment on the discriminability of these two vowels would yield a matrix of conditional probabilities of the form,

		Response	
		/a/	/ɔ/
Stimulus	/a/	.847	.153
	/ɔ/	.253	.747

It can be seen from this matrix that the response [a] is expected on fifty-five per cent of the presentations of a vowel sound, while [ɔ] is only expected to be used on forty-five per cent (more serious imbalances may be found in the original confusion matrices). A now-familiar index of discriminability which is relatively independent of such a response bias in the statistic introduced in signal detection theory, d'. It is sufficient for this discussion to identify d' as the separation, in normal deviates, between a pair of overlapping, equal-variance, normal distributions which could give rise to this discrimination matrix. (This statistic, and its application to confusion matrices has been discussed in detail by Egan (1957).) Another way of expressing the discriminability between two such vowels is in terms of the maximum possible per cent of correct identifications ($P_{max}(C)$), if they were presented equally often. This measure is somewhat similar to an intelligibility index that has been corrected for "guessing", but it relies on well-demonstrated relations between response probability and the probability

TABLE 8. *Discriminability (d') within all possible pairs of the 6 vowels spoken (a). Part (b) shows the maximum pairwise discrimination possible in terms of percent correct.*

	d'					
	i	ε	æ	a	ɔ	u
a. *Pairwise discriminability (ages 9-Adult)*						
i	(0)	3.80	3.50	5.00	6.00	3.30
ε		(0)	−0.28	3.52	4.10	4.20
æ			(0)	1.50	3.28	3.50
a				(0)	1.71	5.00
ɔ					(0)	4.50
u						(0)
b. *Maximum possible pairwise discrimination in terms of 90 Correct* *(50 = chance performance)*						
i	(50)	97	99	99	99	95
ε		(50)	44	96	98	98
æ			(50)	77	95	98
a				(50)	80	99
ɔ					(50)	99
u						(50)

that the responses are correct (as opposed to older techniques which assumed that listeners make pure guesses, i.e. that when wrong they are responding totally independently of the immediate sensory stimulus). The value of P_{max} (C) is obtained by determining the particular criterion along a decision axis which maximizes the number of correct responses. In the case of equally-probably stimuli it is the point where the probability that a given stimulus configuration is a sample from one distribution is the same as the probability that it is from the other. Table 8 *a* gives the pairwise discriminability between the vowels, as estimated by the constant-ratio rule, in terms of the statistic *d'*, for the vowels pronounced by talkers of age nine through adults. Table 8 *b* presents the same information, but in terms of P_{max} (C). It can be seen from these tables that discriminability among most of the vowels was quite good, nearly perfect in many cases. However, one of the combinations, [æ] versus [ε], actually produced negative values of *d'*. Also the discriminations of [ɔ] from [a] and of [a] from [æ] are considerably poorer than the other twelve pairs which yielded positive values of *d'*.

In a further analysis we used a method similar to that described above to estimate the entries in the discrimination matrices, had they been made without response biases. Each of the six-by-six matrices was reduced to six different two-by-two matrices by the following technique. For each vowel (*x*) a matrix was constructed consisting of two rows, the stimulus vowels $\bar{x}$ and "not-*x*" ($\bar{x}$) and of two columns, the identifications of *x* and $\bar{x}$, where $\bar{x}$ represents all vowels other than *x*. Values of *d'* and of P_{max} (C) were

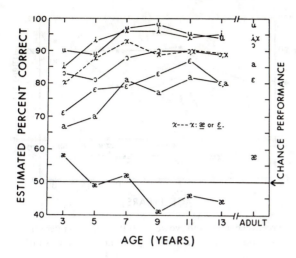

Fig. 15. Corrected estimate of intelligibility that takes into account chance performance and the unequal probabilities of response for the different vowels.

determined for each such matrix. P_{max} (C) here represents performance estimated under the assumption that x and $\bar{x}$ are presented equally often, rather than with the ratio 1 : 5 as was actually the case. This assumption means only that 50% correct can be regarded as chance performance, and it has no effect on the inter-relation of the measures for the various vowels.) Fig. 15 shows the estimated values of P_{max} (C) for each vowel as a function of age of the speakers. The trend discovered in the original intelligibility measures can be seen slightly more clearly here. It is reassuring to see that the major effects are not artifacts associated with response biases.

In the analysis using the constant-ratio rule to determine the pairwise discriminability of the vowels, for the older speakers, it was noted that the vowel [ɛ] was not discriminated from [æ] at better than a chance level. On further examination it was found that these two were likewise indiscriminable when spoken by the younger groups. Therefore the two vowels were treated as a single one, to which either response was considered correct. Values of d' and P_{max} (C) were estimated for each age of speaker, from the matrices of the form

	/ɛ/ or /æ/	$\overline{/ɛ/ \text{ or } /æ/}$
/ɛ/ or /æ/		
$\overline{/ɛ/ \text{ or } /æ/}$		

and the latter values are shown by the x's which are connected by the dashed line in Fig. 15. It can be seen that identification of the pair, [ɛ] *or* [æ], is quite accurate at all ages. A similar pairing of these two vowels was also made when calculating the initial intelligibility indices, and the results are shown by the dashed line and x's of Fig. 13. That the intelligibility

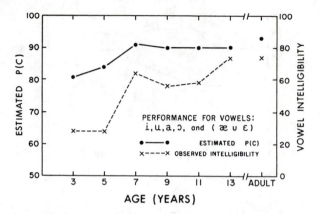

Fig. 16. Estimated percent correct and vowel intelligibility (uncorrected) averaged over five vowels ([æ] and [ε] combined) as a function of the age of the talker.

measures for this pair seem to show it to be more accurately identifiable than any single vowel is an example of the misleading effects of response bias.

The values of P_{max} (C) for the combined vowel [æ] *or* [ε], and for the five single vowels were averaged for each age group and are shown in Fig. 16, along with the corresponding averages of the intelligibility scores. These two curves demonstrate fairly clearly that the major improvement of identification performance as a function of the age of the speakers has been completed by age seven and also that the 'corrected' scores yield a considerably more stable function than the raw intelligibility measures. (The P_{max} (C) values here are related to the left-hand ordinate and the intelligibility scores to the right, for reasons indicated earlier.)

Six stimuli, twelve responses

In view of the variability among the speech-sound repetitions, particularly of the younger children, we wished to determine whether certain produced vowels sounded to adults like vowels not included in the original set of six. Half of the adult listeners were, therefore, given 12 alternatives from which to choose—a set that almost exhausts the repertory of American English. The results are shown in the confusion matrices of Table 9. The overall intelligibility (ratio of diagonal cells to 250) of the six intended vowels is shown in Table 10. The intelligibility of [i] rises from 42% at age 3 to values around 70%, while that for [u] starts at 53%. The other values are lower except for [ε] whose apparently high intelligibility is confounded by high response frequency for that vowel. The response frequencies for each group can be seen in the column totals in Table 9. Note that now many of the [i] stimuli are called [ɪ], probably because of short durations. Note also that many responses to [a] and [ɔ] are distributed under [ɑ] and [ʌ], choices not

TABLE 9. *Confusion matrices (6 stimuli and 12 possible responses) for vowels spoken by talkers at different ages.*

In this case the talkers had only 6 alternatives to produce, while the listeners could choose from among 12 alternatives, the 12 containing the talker's 6 and 6 others.

Age (yrs.)	Spoken vowel	Identified vowel											
		i	ɪ	e	ɛ	æ	a	ɑ	ʌ	ɔ	o	ʊ	u
3	i	106	53	38	15		1		1	1	1	12	22
	ɛ	31	48	20	105	12	4	1	19	4	4	2	
	æ		34	10	133	45	5	3	2	3	8	3	5
	a	2	6	5	34	55	15	69	41	9	4	7	3
	ɔ					1	5	90	34	85	25	4	2
	u	1	5		10	3			12		42	44	133
	Total	140	146	73	297	116	30	163	109	105	84	72	165
5	i	107	85	8	17	8	1		1		2	9	12
	ɛ		21	5	174	37	3		4			3	3
	æ	1	67	6	130	14	7	1	6		2	5	11
	a		5		18	69	20	68	38	5	1	12	14
	ɔ				1	3	6	159	22	38	2	9	10
	u	8	16		3	1			8		9	58	147
	Total	116	194	19	343	132	37	228	79	43	16	96	197
7	i	208	30	2	1	5						3	6
	ɛ		14	7	184	35	7		2	2		1	
	æ	1	85	4	121	22	3		2		3	3	6
	a			1	7	55	11	96	52	22	6		
	ɔ			1	5	3	5	74	51	91	16	4	
	u	7	6	1	1				1		9	71	154
	Total	216	135	16	319	120	26	170	108	115	34	82	166
9	i	181	52	3	4				1	1		4	4
	ɛ		23	3	187	23	4	1	6	1	1		1
	æ	1	79	4	130	6	3	1	2		5	11	8
	a				7	66	31	82	46	17	1		
	ɔ				1	2	4	86	38	111	5	3	
	u	3	1		1	1					4	65	175
	Total	185	155	10	330	98	42	170	93	130	16	83	188
11, M	i	121	105	8	4		2	1	1			4	4
	ɛ		19	1	177	30	6	1	11		3	1	1
	æ		75	6	96	4	2	1	8	1	15	19	22
	a		2		10	25	21	87	71	30	2	2	
	ɔ				1	2	4	39	42	149	11	1	1
	u	2	2		1				2	1	13	60	169
	Total	123	203	15	289	61	35	129	135	181	44	87	197
11, F	i	195	46	6	2								1
	ɛ	1	40	4	165	21	4	2	6			2	5
	æ	2	89	1	136	6		2	7		2	1	4

Table 9 (*continued*)

Age (yrs.)	Spoken vowel	i	ɪ	e	ɛ	æ	a	ɑ	ʌ	ɔ	o	ʊ	u
	a	1	3	4	6	57	21	74	56	23	1	2	2
	ɔ					4	6	64	52	106	17		1
	u	7	2	1							3	45	192
	Total	206	180	16	309	88	31	142	121	129	23	50	205
13, M	i	171	56	5	2				3		2	2	9
	e		5	3	224	10			6		1	1	
	æ	1	115		97	6			5	1	3	12	10
	a		3	2	6	60	22	87	59	11			
	ɔ			3	20	6	6	23	65	113	11	3	
	u	5	8	1	2						6	49	178
	Total	177	187	14	351	82	28	110	138	125	23	67	197
13, M	i	156	81		3				2			2	6
	ɛ		71	5	102	49	7	1	3	1	1	4	6
	æ	1	122	4	94	12	5		1			8	3
	a	1	1	3	15	55	30	90	43	10	1		1
	ɔ		1		1	2	7	86	12	137	3		
	u	7	15	3	1	1		1			5	38	179
	Total	165	291	15	216	119	49	178	59	150	10	52	195
Adult, M	i	198	38	1	2								11
	ɛ		35	4	156	15	9	3	17	4	2	3	1
	æ		34	7	184	6	1	3	3		8	1	3
	a			2	1	13	14	129	48	39	2	2	
	ɔ						1	18	11	174	31		
	u	1			1						1	16	231
	Total	199	107	14	344	34	25	153	79	217	44	22	246
Adult, F	i	184	53	9	1	1							2
	ɛ		16	5	174	39	8		5	1		1	
	æ		7	5	191	17	7	2	6	2	12		1
	a				1	22	23	152	34	17	1		
	ɔ				2		6	62	12	139	29		
	u	1	6						4			35	204
	Total	185	82	19	369	79	44	216	61	159	42	36	207

available to listeners under six alternatives. Finally, and again probably reflecting the influence of short durations, many responses to [u] are now [ʊ].

The difficulties in any further analysis of a rectangular instead of a square matrix force us to provide this brief description only. In general the "high" vowels are sometimes identified as their neighboring [ɪ] or [ʊ], and the middle vowels, already less intelligible under six alternatives, show a still more complicated pattern of response.

TABLE 10. *Intelligibility of 6 vowels spoken by subjects at different ages when the listeners did not know which were 6 alternatives of the talkers, but only that they might have been any of 12.*

Age (yrs.)	i	ɛ	æ	a	ɔ	u	Overall
3	42.4	42.0	18.0	6.0	34.0	52.8	32.5
5	42.8	69.6	5.6	8.0	15.2	58.8	33.3
7	83.2	73.6	8.8	4.3	36.4	61.5	44.7
9	72.4	74.8	2.4	12.4	44.4	70.0	46.1
11 (♂)	48.3	70.8	1.6	8.4	59.5	67.5	42.7
11 (♀)	78.0	66.0	2.4	8.4	42.4	76.7	45.6
13 (♂)	68.4	89.6	2.4	8.7	45.1	71.2	47.6
13 (♀)	62.4	40.8	4.8	12.0	54.8	71.6	48.3
Adult (♂)	79.2	62.4	2.4	5.6	69.6	92.3	51.9
Adult (♀)	73.6	69.6	6.8	9.2	55.6	81.6	49.4

Discussion

The present results on vowel intelligibility agree in several respects with those of previous studies (Peterson and Barney, 1952; Miller and Nicely, 1955; and Fairbanks and Grubb, 1961). Previous intelligibility scores over all vowels are about 75%, ranging from 53 to 92%. The vowels [i] and [u] appear always to be more intelligible than the middle vowels. The present results for adults show an average intelligibility of 72%, with scores of 94 to 96% for [i] and [u] and 70% for [a]. The higher scores are associated with only six alternatives while previous studies have mostly used a vocabulary of from 10 to 12 vowels. The use of 12 alternative responses in the present study does not facilitate the comparison, since those responses were to be associated with only six stimulus alternatives.

The main effect, of course, is that the identification of vowels increases with the age of the talker, no matter whether vowel identification is measured by raw intelligibility scores, by amount of information transmitted, or by an estimate of maximum percent correct that is free of listeners' response biases. Our interpretation is that, particularly in these cases of listening where the listener has no opportunity to "tune up" to the speech of any talker, the intelligibility of vowels depends in part on the consistency with which a given talker utters them. This consistency is the inverse of the intra-subject variability discussed above. The two effects are not completely parallel, however, since vowel-formant variability continues to diminish as age increases to about 12 years, while the listening results reach maximum values for talker ages of only 7 years.

Variability among vowel formant frequencies is not a new phenomenon. Peterson and Barney (1952) displayed graphically the magnitude of variability among talkers by showing areas of overlap on a Formant-1-Formant-2 plot, where exactly the same combination of frequencies represented two different intended vowels. Our results on vowel intelligibility agree with their further report that if the entries were restricted to those that are identified correctly, then the areas of overlap are considerably reduced. Furthermore, if now one plots only vowels identified as correct by the talkers themselves, still less overlap is observed (Fairbanks and Grubb, 1961).

With the present results, we assume that a different kind of variability, namely variability within subjects that occurs over repetitions, yields less confusion or less overlap as the age of the talker increases. A similar notion is advanced by Okamura (1966) who demonstrated a striking reduction in these areas of overlap as the age of the children increased. What is different is that he showed this reduction and consequent improvement in vowel identification in two-dimensional plot of derivations of F_2 and F_3, given by $10 \log F_2/(F_1F_2F_3)^{-3}$ and $10 \log F_3/(F_1F_2F_3)^{-3}$ respectively.

VII. GENERAL CONCLUSIONS AND DISCUSSION

The results from acoustical measurements of sentences spoken by 84 subjects show that the mean fundamental frequency and the mean first and second formant frequencies change systematically with the age of the talker, roughly in accordance with predictions based on anatomical and physiological considerations. Changes in these means are most rapid in those early ages from 3 to 6 years when anatomical change has been noted as most rapid by others.

Of greater interest for present purposes was the change in precision or reproducibility of certain aspects of the speech sounds, namely the first and second formants of the vowels and one temporal aspect of the transition from a plosive consonant to the following vowel or semi-vowel. Both formants show a clear decrease in variability on the successive repetitions of sentences for all vowels, though there are differences among the individual vowels in absolute values. The implication is clear that 3-year-old children do not move their tongues to exactly the same position for a particular vowel as it occurs in repetitions of the same sentence, at least not so exactly the same as older children and adults. The varability decreases until about age 11.

Similarly, the time interval between the explosion of a stop consonant and the following voiced sound is not exactly repeated time after time, but rather shows a certain variability. This variability decreases from a maximum value at 3 years (the youngest age tested) to a minimum value at about age 8, somewhat earlier than was the case for minimum variability in the vowel formants.

The impetus for the present study came from observations of both authors on the intelligibility of speech of children in the countries where the authors' second languages were spoken, observations quite closely related to the concept of "phonemic category", as required in a motor theory of speech perception. Foreigners appear to have more difficulty understanding the speech of native children than do native speakers. If this difficulty is related to inaccuracy or sloppiness in the reproduction of the sounds of language, then it would appear that at least children's speech cannot be well described by relatively fixed sound categories. The present results on the decrease of this variability with age imply that a motor theory of speech perception must somehow be restricted to adults and older children where speech sounds can be regarded as relatively distinct habits.

Concepts of motor behavior controlled in part by sensory feedback are as old as the distinction between sensory and motor systems made around

1811 by Bell and Magendie. Early theories concerned voluntary movement and the idea was extended to nonvoluntary systems especially under the name of homeostasis.

Control of a motor system from sensory information arising in the motor system itself has been likened to the servo-system developed in several aspects of engineering theory (MacColl, 1945; Wiener, 1948; Shannon and Weaver, 1949; Davis, 1951; Peterson, 1953; Fairbanks, 1954; Brown and Campbell, 1948; Mysak, 1959, 1966).

The sensory information that is utilized for control of speech production arises in several sensory modalities. While there is much current interest in the forms of feedback from the musculature and articulating surfaces of the speech mechanism, we assume that the principal modality is auditory. We believe that our results illustrate the rather large error signals that arise in the early years of speech production, but also that the subsequent formation of rather fixed articulatory habits of position and of gesture involves smaller error signals and perhaps even less dependence on sensory feedback. That the feedback never goes to zero in normal talkers is shown by the deterioration of speech that follows the onset of moderate to severe losses of hearing.

In order for the auditory system to provide information about error to the speech-production system, the deviations in the speech output must, of course, be discriminated in hearing. With respect to the adult values for variability of formant frequencies, shown in Figs. 3–8, one might ask why does there remain an average global standard deviation of about 25 Hz for the first formant, and about 40 Hz for the second formant? Surely, listeners can detect changes in the frequency of a pure tone that are smaller. On the other hand, changes in the peak region or formant of a complex tone are somewhat more difficult to discriminate, as was shown by Flanagan (1955). Using the MIT POVO speech synthesizer, he created artificial vowels in which one formant at a time could be varied in frequency. By presenting pairs of vowels in which either F_1 or F_2 was different, he obtained difference limens or just-noticeable differences of the order of 25 Hz for the first formant and about 40–80 Hz for the second formant, the latter depending more on the value of the comparison F_2. In short the present variability measures on speech production are about as low as they could be, if discriminable differences to the ear were the controlling or limiting factor.

It is not at all clear how perceptual discrimination develops. In the child's younger years, when his formant frequencies are so much more variable than those of the adult would his formant discrimination be similarly poor? Though formant discrimination has not been tested in young children, some recent observations on temporal features may provide a clue.

Variability in the time interval between the explosion in a plosive consonant and the voicing that follows, as illustrated in Fig. 12, reaches a minimum value (standard deviation) for the adult of approximately 10 msec. This rather precise performance, in a language that contains only two classes of plosive consonants, is necessary for some of the sharp distinctions involved in separating voiced from voiceless consonants. Such discrimination, however, appears already in the listening behavior of 3-year-old children, according to Winterkorn *et al.* (1967), who showed that such children accepted as "da" only those synthetic syllables with voice-onset time of 20 msec or less, and as "ta" those stimuli with 45 msec or more. But this is at an age when the present results show very great variability (Fig. 12), with standard deviations as large as 26–28 msec.

While this line of evidence is neither abundant nor simple, it appears that the variability under investigation in the present work is descriptive more of the motor control process than of perceptual capability at different ages.

SUMMARY

Sound spectrograms were made of recordings of standard sentences spoken by each of 84 subjects—children ranging in age from 3 to 13 years, and adults. Sentences were repeated by each subject five times. Acoustical measures and statistical calculations concerned fundamental frequency and the first and second formant of vowels, and interphonemic temporal features of words. Adult listeners identified vowel segments taken from the recordings of several age groups.

Intra-subject variability, that is, the acoustical repeatability of certain sounds in the sentences, for the vowel formant frequencies decreases as the age of the talker increases to 11 or 13 years. At least one interphonemic temporal feature also shows a decrease in variability with age, but it reaches its minimum at an earlier age, 7 or 8 years. Intelligibility of the vowels for adult listeners also increases with the age of the talker, reaching maximum values for talkers of ages 8 or 9 years. Other results show changes in the mean fundamental frequency and the mean formant frequencies with age.

Relations between these results and anatomical-physiological development are discussed, as are also relations to language learning and phonemic categories.

SOMMAIRE

On a enregistré (magnetophone) des phrases parlées par chacun des 84 sujets, de l'âge 3 ans jusqu'à l'âge de 13 ans, et adultes. Chaque sujet a répété les phrases 5 fois. Les mesures acoustique, tirées des spectrogrammes, et les calculs statistiques ont concerné la fréquence fondamentale, les formants des voyelles, et certaines intervalles interphonémiques. De plus, des auditeurs adultes ont identifié les voyelles.

La variabilité intra-sujet pour les formants — c'est-à-dire l'inverse de la précision de la répétition des sons dans les phrases — décroît avec l'augmentation de l'âge du locuteur, jusqu'à l'âge de 11 ou 13 ans, dès que la valeur est égale à la valeur adulte. La variabilité des intervalles temporales entre les consonnes plosives et les voyelles suivantes décroît aussi avec l'âge, mais le minimum apparaît à l'âge de 7 ou 8 ans.

L'intelligibilité des voyelles pour les auditeurs adultes s'augmente avec l'âge des locuteurs, mais celle-la achève le maximum dès l'âge de 8 ou 9 ans. Des autres resultats concernent la changement avec l'âge des moyens des fréquences fondamentales et des fréquences formantes.

Des rapports entre ces resultats et le développement anatomique et physiologique, ainsi que le développement du language et les catégories phonémiques, compriment la base de la discussion.

ZUSAMMENFASSUNG

Sprachspektrogramme von Sätzenaufnahmen gesprochen von 84 Versuchspersonen im Alter von 3 bis 13 Jahren waren gemacht. Jede Versuchsperson wiederholte die Sätze fünfmal. Akustische Messungen und statistische Berechnungen der Grundfrequenz der Stimme, der ersten und zweiten Formantfrequenzen der Vokale und der interphonemischer Zeitcharakteristiken waren durchgeführt. Vokalsegmente, die aus den originalen Aufnahmen von verschiedenen Altersgruppen genommen waren, waren mit erwachsenen Zuhörern identifiziert.

Die Intraversuchspersonvariabilität, das heisst, der Mangel der akustischen Wiederholungsfähigkeit einiger Laute in Sätzen, für die Formantfrequenzen der Vokale vermindert sich, als das Alter zu 11. oder 13. Jahre steigt. Es vermindert sich mit dem Alter die Variabilität auch wenigstens einer interphonemischen Zeitcharakteristike, diese reicht aber Minimum im Alter von 7 bis 8 Jahren. Auch die Verständlichkeit der Vokale, die mit erwachsenen Zuhörern geprüft war, steigt mit dem Alter des Sprechers, und reicht maximale Werte bei 8 bis 9-jährigen Sprechern. Es waren dargestellt andere Ergebnisse, die die Veränderung der mittleren Grundfrequenz der Stimme und der mittleren Formantfrequenzen zeigen.

Die Verhältnisse zwischen diesen Ergebnissen und der anatomisch-physiologischen Entwicklung so wie auch das Verhältnis zum Lernen der Sprache und zu phonemischen Kategorien sind gezeigt.

REFERENCES

Bell, C. and Magendie, F., 1811: cited in *Physiology of the nervous system* (by Fulton, J. F.). Oxford Univ. Press, 1943.

Brown, G. S. and Campbell, D. P., 1948: *Principles of servo mechanisms.* Wiley and Sons Inc., New York.

Chase, R. A. *et al.,* 1961: A developmental study of change in behavior and delayed auditory feedback. *J. Genet. Psychol., 99,* 101.

Clarke, F. R., 1957: Constant-ratio rule for confusion matrices in speech communication. *J. Acous. Soc. Amer., 31,* 759.

Cooper, F. S. *et al.,* 1952: Some experiments on the perception of systhetic speech sounds. *J. Acous. Soc. Amer., 24,* 597.

Davis, H., 1951: Auditory communication. *J. Speech Hearing Dis., 16,* 3.

Dunn, H. K., 1950: The calculation of vowel resonances and an electrical vocal tract. *J. Acous. Soc. Amer., 22,* 740.

Egan, J. P., 1957: Message reception, operating characteristics, and confusion matricies in speech communication. Technical Report, Indiana Univ. Hearing and Communication Lab.

Fairbanks, G. and Grubb, P. A., 1961: A psychophysical investigation of vowel formant. *J. Speech Hearing Res., 4,* 203.

Fairbanks, G., Herbert, E. L., and Hammond, J. M., 1949: An acoustical study of vocal pitch in seven-and eight-year-old boys. *Child development, 20,* 63.

Fairbanks, G., Wiley, J. H., and Lassman, F. M., 1949: An acoustical study of vocal pitch in seven- and eight-year-old girls. *Child development, 20,* 71.

Fairbanks, G., 1954: Systematic research in experimental phonetics: 1. A theory of the speech mechanism as a servosystem. *J. Speech Hearing Dis., 19,* 133.

Fant, G., 1960: *Acoustic theory of speech production.* Mouton & Co., 's-Gravenhage.

Flanagan, J. L., 1955: A difference limen for vowel formant frequency. *J. Acous. Soc. Amer., 27,* 613.

— 1958: Pitch discrimination for synthetic vowels. *J. Acous. Soc. Amer., 30,* 435.

Garner, W. R. and Hake, H. W., 1951: The amount of information in absolute judgments. *Psychol. Rev., 58,* 446.

Irwin, O. C., 1943: Speech sound elements during the first year of life: A review of literature. *J. Speech Hearing Dis., 8,* 109.

— 1945: Reliability of infant speech sound data. *J. Speech Hearing Dis., 10,* 229.

— 1948: Infant speech: Development of vowel sounds. *J. Speech Hearing Dis., 13,* 31.

Joos, M., 1948: Acoustic phonetic, Language monograph No. 23. *Jour. of the Linguistic Soc. of Amer., 24,* No. 2., Suppl.

Kirikae, I., 1943: Über den Bewegungsvorgang an den Stimmlippen und die Öffnungs- und Verschlusszeit der Stimmritze während der Phonation. *Jap. Z. Oto-Rhino-Laryng., 46,* 236.

Kirikae, I. *et al.,* 1965: An experimental study on perturbations in vocal pitch. *Jap. Jour. Otol. Tokyo., 68,* 364.

Lenneberg, E. H., 1966: Speech development: its anatomical and physiological concomitants. In: Carterette, E. D. (Ed.) *Brain function,* Vol. III. Speech, Language and Communication. Univ. of Calif. Press.

Liberman, A. M. *et al.*, 1957: The discrimination of speech sounds within and across phoneme boundaries. *J. Exp. Psych.*, *54*, 358.

Lindblom, B., 1962: Accuracy and limitation of Sona-Graph measurements. In: *Proceedings of the fourth international congress of phonetic sciences, Helsinki, 1961.* Mouton & Co., 's-Gravenhage.

Lisker, L. and Abramson, A. S., 1964: A cross language study of voicing in initial stop: Acoustical measurement. *Word, 20*, 384.

— 1965: Voice onset time in the production and perception of English stops. Speech Research, Haskins Laboratories, SR-1.

MacColl, L. A., 1945: *Fundamental theory of servosystems.* D. van Nostrand, New York.

Miller, G. A. and Nicely, P. E., 1955: An analysis of perceptual confusions among some English consonant. *J. Acous. Soc. Amer., 27*, 338.

Morley, M. E., 1965: *The development and disorders of speech in childhood.* Williams & Wilkins Co., Baltimore.

Mysak, E. D., 1959: A servo model for speech therapy. *J. Speech Hearing Dis., 24*, 144.

— 1966: *Speech pathology and feedback theory.* Thomas, Ill.

Naider, von J., 1965: Die pubertalen Veränderungen der Stimme bei Jungen im Verlauf von 5 Jahren. *Folia Phomat., 17*, 1.

Negus, V. E., 1949: *Comparative anatomy and physiology of the larynx.* Grune & Stratton, New York.

Okamura, M., 1966: Acoustical studies on the Japanese vowels in children. The formant construction and the developmental process. *Jap. Jour. Otol. Tokyo., 69*, 1198.

Öhman, S. E. G., 1966: Coarticulation in VCV utterances, Spectrographic measurement. *J. Acoust. Soc. Amer., 39*, 151.

— 1966: Perception of segments of VCCV utterances. *J. Acous. Soc. Amer., 40*, 979.

Peterson, G. E., 1951: The phonetic value of words. *Language, 27*, 541.

— 1952: The information bearing elements of speech. *J. Acous. Soc. Amer., 24*, 629.

— 1953: Basic physical system for communication between two individuals. *J. Speech Hearing Dis., 18*, 116.

— 1959: Vowel formant measurement. *J. Speech Hearing Res., 2*, 173.

Peterson, G. E. and Barney, H. L., 1952: Control method used in a study of the wovels. *J. Acous. Soc. Amer., 24*, 175.

Potter, R. K., Kopp, G. A., and Green, H. C., 1947: *Visible speech.* D. van Nostrand Co., New York.

Potter, R. K. and Steiberg, J. L., 1950: Toward the specification of speech. *J. Acous. Soc. Amer., 22*, 807.

Potter, R. K. and Peterson, G. E., 1948: The representation of vowels and their movements. *J. Acous. Soc. Amer., 20*, 528.

Pressman, J. J., 1942: Physiology of the vocal cords in phonation and respiration. *Arch. Otolaryngol., 35*, 355.

Preston, M. S., Yeni-Komshima, Grace, and Stark, R. E., 1967: Voicing in initial stop consonants produced by children in the prelinguistic period from different language communities. Annual Report, Neurocommunication Lab., The Johns Hopkins Univ., School of Medicine.

Shannon, C. E. and Weaver, W., 1949: *The mathematical theory of communication.* Univ. of Ill. Press, Urbana.

Simon, C. T., 1957: The development of speech. In: Travis, L. E. (Ed.), *Handbook of speech pathology.* Appleton-Century-Crofts, Inc., New York.

Smith, F. and Miller, G. A., 1966: *The genesis of language. A psycholinguistic approach.* MIT Press.

Stevens, K. N. and House, A. S., 1955: Development of a quantitative description of vowel articulation. *J. Acous. Soc. Amer., 27*, 484.

— 1961: An acoustical theory of vowel production and some of its implications. *J. Speech. Hearing Res., 4*, 303.

— 1963: Perturbation of vowel articulations by consonantal context: Acoustical theory. *J. Speech Hearing Res.*, 6, 111.

Stevens, K. N. *et al.*, 1964: Crosslinguistic study of vowel discrimination. *J. Acous. Soc. Amer.*, *36*, 1989 (A).

Wiener, N., 1948: *Cybernetics*. Wiley & Sons Inc., New York.

Winterkorn, J. M. S. *et al.*, 1967: Perception of voiced and voiceless stops in three-year-old children. Haskins Laboratories Status Report No. 11, p. 41–44.

ANATOMICAL AND NEUROMUSCULAR MATURATION OF THE SPEECH MECHANISM: EVIDENCE FROM ACOUSTIC STUDIES

R. D. KENT

University of Wisconsin, Madison

Editor's Note: This is the second in JSHR's new series of invited tutorial articles intended to be of use to the readership and to potential contributors to JSHR. During recent years a strong swing has occurred toward research on many aspects of speech, hearing, and language development. Much of the relevant information on these topics is scattered in a wide range of journals of different disciplines. In this article, Raymond Kent has taken on the task of surveying and interpreting acoustic studies of speech development and considering the available data with respect to anatomical and neuromuscular maturation of the speech mechanism. Kent is a frequent contributor to JSHR and won its Editor's Award for articles he contributed in 1972 and 1974.

This paper surveys acoustic studies of speech development and discusses the data with respect to the anatomical and neuromuscular maturation of the speech mechanism. The acoustic data on various aspects of speech production indicate that the accuracy of motor control improves with age until adult-like performance is achieved at about 11 or 12 years, somewhat after the age at which speech sound acquisition usually is judged to be complete. Other topics of discussion are (1) problems in the spectrographic analysis of children's speech, (2) formant scale factors that relate children's and adults' data, and (3) identification and diagnosis of developmental disorders through acoustic analyses of speech sounds.

The past two decades have been witness to an increasing application of acoustic analysis to the study of speech development in children. Acoustic data have been collected in three major areas: (1) vocal fundamental frequency (f_o), (2) static formant patterns of vocalic sounds, and (3) temporal properties such as voice onset time, rates of formant movement, and segment duration. In contrast, very little work has been done on the analysis of frication or burst noise, nasalization, and formant transitions associated with stop consonants. Consequently, the research background can be organized with respect to the first three areas outlined above. In terms of general implications for the development of structure and function, these three areas speak to, respectively, (1) the adjustment of the phonatory apparatus, (2) the shaping of the vocal tract, and (3) the timing and coordination of articulation. Although the physiologic and phonetic interpretation of acoustic data are sometimes uncertain, acoustic analyses are appropriate to test certain hypotheses about developmental changes in anatomy, motor control, and phonological function. This paper is concerned primarily with the normal developmental process, but reference also will be made to the application of acoustic analysis to the identification and diagnosis of developmental disorders.

LIMITATIONS OF ACOUSTIC ANALYSES OF CHILDREN'S SPEECH

Compared with other experimental methods such as aerodynamic recordings, electromyography, and X ray, acoustic analysis of children's speech is safe and convenient. However, the feasibility of acoustic investigation often is hampered by peculiarities of a child's speech production or by limitations of analysis techniques that have been perfected largely on adult speech. An example of the former obstacle is a tendency of some children to use inappropriate nasalization, which complicates the interpretive task through the introduction of unexpected resonances and antiresonances. Another example along this line is the occurrence of hoarseness or breathiness, which contribute noise components that may obscure other acoustic details. An example of an obstacle that arises from limitations of the analysis technique is the likelihood of formant-harmonic interaction occasioned by the unsuitability of conventional analyzing bandwidths to voices with a high f_0. The crux of the problem is that the harmonics of the laryngeal spectrum are so widely spaced that an analyzing bandwidth of 300 Hz resolves them individually, to produce a spectrogram in which formant structure is obscured by harmonic detail. This interference occurs infrequently with adult male voices because the filter bandwidth usually is wide enough to contain more than one harmonic.

The problem of formant-harmonic interaction can be solved in part by increasing the analyzing bandwidth. The increase can be accomplished either by modification of the original equipment (installing a filter with a 400- or 500-Hz bandwidth) or by reducing the playback speed of the recorded speech signal as it is fed to the spectrograph. The latter practice really compresses the spectrum of the signal but the effect is like that of using a wider analyzing bandwidth. For further discussion of this subject and an illustration of formant-harmonic interaction, see Fant (1968).

The high f_0 of children's voices also contributes to an inherently large error in the estimation of formant frequencies. As f_0 increases, the probability decreases that a harmonic component will lie proximal to the center frequency of a formant. The problem that results is essentially one of increased sampling error: the widely spaced harmonics associated with a high f_0 give a poor resolution of the resonance characteristics. The investigator might mistakenly judge a strong harmonic to be the peak, or center frequency, of a formant. This issue has been discussed at length by Lindblom (1962, 1972), who determined that the hypothetical error of formant estimation related to f_0 is equal to $f_0/4$. Hence, if a child has a f_0 of 400 Hz, the error in estimating the formant frequencies will be about 100 Hz. The magnitude of the error declines with the child's age because f_0 decreases as the child matures. The most accurate estimates of formant frequencies can be made for adult males, for whom the mean f_0 is about 125 Hz and the hypothetical error is therefore 30 Hz or so.

VOCAL FUNDAMENTAL FREQUENCY

Developmental Changes in Mean Fundamental Frequency

The graph in Figure 1 summarizes the developmental course of the mean f_0 from the first few days of life to adulthood. This graph consolidates the data from a number of investigations, which are compiled in Appendixes A and B according to the age of the subjects. The f_0 values are distinguished by sex only after the age of 11 years, although small sex differences might occur before that age. The f_0 drops slightly during the first three weeks or so, but then increases until about the fourth month of life, after which it stabilizes for a period of approximately five months. Beginning with the first year, f_0 decreases sharply until about three years of age, when it makes a more gradual decline reaching to the onset of puberty at 11 or 12 years of age. A sex difference is apparent by the age of 13 years, which marks the beginning of a substantial drop for male voices, the well-known adolescent voice change. in the case of females, the decrement in f_0 from infancy to adulthood is some-

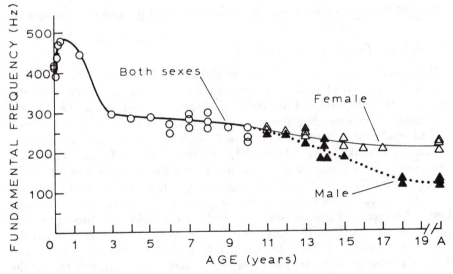

FIGURE 1. Mean fundamental frequency (f_0) plotted as a function of age of subject. The data for males and females are combined until the age of 11 years. The graph consolidates data from the studies compiled in Appendixes A and B. A = adult.

what in excess of an octave, whereas males exhibit an overall decrease approaching two octaves. The ages of most rapid change in mean f_o are the first four months, the period of one-three years, and the period of 13-17 years. Little change in the mean f_o occurs during the period of three-five years, which Negus (1962) identified as an interval of rapid laryngeal growth. The developmental variation in f_o is in better agreement with Kaplan's (1960) summary of structural changes in the developing larynx. He noted that laryngeal growth occurs primarily during the first three years and during puberty.

Because the f_o curve in Figure 1 is based on limited data for many of the ages represented, the pattern shown may not be representative of the actual developmental course. Moreover, it is by no means certain that the mean f_o values for different ages can be validly compared. Possibly, the age-related differences in mean f_o are caused as much by variations in the vocalization activities as by anatomical and physiological maturation. The data for infants often were derived from cry vocalizations, which may be quite different physiologically from the speaking vocalizations of older children and adults. For that matter, a number of variables must be considered even in the comparison of f_o values for children of the same age. Actual f_o values obtained for infants depend upon the means of stimulation and the condition of the infant (Prescott, 1975). In addition, f_o ranges of up to two-three octaves have been observed for young children (van Oordt and Drost, 1963; Ostwald and Peltzman, 1974), and f_o values for some infants may be distributed bimodally (Fairbanks, 1942). Given these factors, the determination of central tendency for f_o is a problem to be approached cautiously. Hence, the developmental course pictured in Figure 1 may at best be a tentative view of the age-related changes in mean f_o. The first three years of life are in especial need of further investigation, and new data may revise this portion of the graph markedly.

Variability of Fundamental Frequency

Relatively little is known about developmental changes in the range or variability of f_o. Most of the literature on the newborn infant's cry indicates that f_o falls in the range of 400-600 Hz, although the infant appears to have the capability of extending this range appreciably in either direction. Ringel and Kluppel (1964) reported a range of 290-508 Hz for 10 infants aged four to 40 hours. Fairbanks (1942) observed a range of 153-888 Hz for an infant in the first month of life and a range of 63-2631 Hz for the first nine months of life. McGlone's (1966) investigation of children aged between one and two years revealed a total range of 16.2 tones, or about two octaves. Van Oordt and Drost (1963, p. 297) concluded from a study of 126 children in two age groups (zero-five years and six-16 years) that ". . . even in very young children the physiological range of the voice has a broad, almost 'adult' range . . ." and that, "The change in the frequency of the speaking voice parallels that of the lowest reachable physiological tone. . . ." Their data indicate that even young children have a f_o range of two-and-one-half to three octaves. If a conclusion is forced from these rather limited data, it would be that the range of vocal frequency does not change appreciably during maturation.

As far as the variability of f_0 is concerned, the most extensive study is that of Eguchi and Hirsh (1969), who collected data for 84 subjects representing adulthood and the age levels of three-13 years at one-year intervals. Spectrographic analyses were made of five recitations each of the two sentences *He has a blue pen* and *I am tall*. The measurements included f_0 and the first two formant frequencies (F1 and F2) of the vowels /i/, /æ/, /u/, /ɛ/, /a/, and /ɔ/, as produced in the sentence contexts. Various aspects of this investigation will be discussed throughout this paper, but for the moment, one conclusion is pertinent: intrasubject standard deviations for the f_0 measurements progressively decreased with age until a minimum was reached at about 10-12 years. If the standard deviations are taken as an index of the accuracy of the laryngeal adjustments during vowel production, then the accuracy of control improves continuously over a period of at least seven to nine years. This conclusion is supported by either the absolute magnitudes of the standard deviations or by relative values defined by the ratio of the standard deviations to the corresponding mean f_0 values.

The discovery that f_0 variability diminishes with age has important implications for the quantitative investigation of speech development. It is not known at what age this apparent refinement of control begins to occur. In a study of two infants during the first 141 days of life, Sheppard and Lane (1968) reported a rather small and constant variability in f_0 values. However, Prescott (1975) discovered small developmental increases in the within-utterance f_0 variability within the first nine months of life. Possibly, at the same time that a child gains control over the accuracy of his laryngeal adjustments, he begins to vary f_0 to achieve intonationlike effects. Of course, to some degree, accuracy of adjustment is requisite to controlled variation. Concerning this subject, studies of infant intonation have revealed evidence that definite patterns are established during the first year of life. Tonkova-Yampol 'skaya (1968) reported that development of intonational forms during the first year adheres to the following sequence: discontent, placid sound, laughter, happiness, exclamatory delight, request, and question. Thus, by the time a child has reached his first birthday, he is capable of producing at least seven distinct intonational forms. Rather limited data are available on the intonational patterns of American infants (for a review of studies in this area, see Crystal, 1973).

Applications to the Identification and Diagnosis of Developmental Disorders

Within the past decade especially, acoustic analyses of infant cries have been directed toward the identification and diagnosis of developmental disorders, upon the assumption that many of these disorders are signaled by deviations in an infant's sound production. This work was motivated largely by reports that certain characteristics of an infant, such as age, identity, and condition, could be appreciated by listening to its cry (Karelitz, Karelitz, and Rosenfeld, 1960; Formby, 1967). Given the apparent validity of the perceptual inferences, investigators hypothesized that acoustic properties such as f_0 could provide a basis for the identification and diagnosis of pathological conditions. For reviews of work in this area, see Vuorenkoski et al. (1966), Wasz-Hockert et al. (1968), Ostwald (1971), Ostwald and Peltzman (1974), Michelsson (1971), Crystal (1973), and Tenold et al. (1974). Most studies of f_0 have determined statistical properties such as the mean, range, standard deviation, or histogram, but others have examined the individual intonation pattern (temporal variation of f_0) in infant cries. To date, relatively few attempts have been made to measure perturbations in fundamental frequency (that is, cycle-to-cycle variations in the fundamental period), although such a measure may have value in describing the stability of laryngeal control (see Lieberman, 1963). This issue is of interest because Bosma, Truby, and Lind (1965) proposed that an infant's neurological maturity might be evaluated from such factors as the stability of laryngeal coordinations and the mobility of vocal tract components during crying.

General conclusions about the diagnostic value of f_0 measurements are difficult to make because such measurements are helpful in certain pathological conditions but not in others. According to Vuorenkoski et al. (1971), an abnormally high f_0 may be expected for infants with asphyxia, brain damage, and hyperbilirubinemia, whereas a low f_0 may be expected for infants with Down's syndrome. An abnormally high f_0 also has been reported for newborn infants with drug-addicted mothers (Blenick, Tavolga, and Antopol, 1971). These reports raise interesting possibilities for neonatal examination, especially because neurological disorders currently may not be detected during the first few weeks of life (Ostwald and Peltzman, 1974).

FORMANT PATTERNS OF VOCALIC SOUNDS
Development of the Vocal Tract and Formant Scale Factors

One of the first spectrographic investigations of the formant patterns of children's speech was the classic study of Peterson and Barney (1952), who pioneered in the spectrographic measurement of the acoustic speech signal. Although this paper is primarily of historical interest here, it set forth one basic conclusion about formant patterns that has not been completely resolved in the acoustic theory of speech production. This conclusion is that the formant frequencies of children's vowels are higher than the values obtained for adult females and higher yet than the values obtained for adult males. On the one hand, this result is to be expected given the differences in the length of the vocal tract between children and women and between children and men. On the other hand, mathematical prediction of the observed differences has been the subject of several papers, right up to the present. If growth of the vocal tract were uniform, then prediction would be simple enough. However, Fant (1966) argued that there are differences other than size between the vocal tract anatomies of men and women, and that children apparently are more like women in the configuration of their vocal tracts. Hence, as a boy grows into manhood, the changes that occur in the formant structure of his vowels cannot be likened exactly to the changes in resonant frequencies that are observed as a uniform acoustic tube is lengthened. The problem of the scaling of formant patterns is important for speech perception, because of the implications it holds for the recognition of phonemes and speakers. This issue has been discussed in several papers (Broadbent, Ladefoged, and Lawrence, 1956; Gerstman, 1968; Fujisaki and Kawashima, 1968).

But the principle of uniform growth of the vocal tract is not without proponents. Mol (1963) replotted the data of Peterson and Barney (1952) to reveal an apparently linear change in formant structure among children, women, and men. He ascribed this linear change to the "principle of uniform axial growth." A graph similar to that used by Mol is shown in Figure 2. The mean formant frequency values that Peterson and Barney recorded for the vowel productions of children, women, and men are plotted in a linear F1-F2 plane, and the three mean data points for each vowel are fitted with a straight line that intersects the origin. Generally, the linear fit with rotation about the origin is good, such that the formant values for each vowel fall along fairly distinct vectors in the plane.

Because Mol tested his hypothesis of uniform axial growth only against the limited data of Peterson and Barney, it is of interest to determine if his hypothesis predicts other data equally well. After Mol introduced this hypothesis, an extensive developmental study of formant frequencies was reported by Eguchi and Hirsh (1969). Some details of this study were reviewed in the preceding discussion of f_o. Given the relative wealth of information in the Eguchi and Hirsh investigation, their data on formant frequencies of children, women, and men have been plotted in Figure 3 according to the method that Mol used to evaluate the principle of uniform axial growth. If this principle was valid, then for each vowel, the data points that Eguchi and Hirsh obtained for subjects of different ages should fall roughly along straight lines intersecting the origin. The graph shows that the linear fit is really quite poor, with a linear tendency appearing only for the vowel /i/. For the sake of comparison, the straight lines constructed in Figure 2 from the data of Peterson and Barney are included in the figure. The agreement between the data in the two investigations is fair for the vowels /i/ and /ɛ/ but rather poor for the other vowels. Generally, the data of Eguchi and Hirsh give little support to Mol's principle of uniform axial growth.

Linear relationships in the formant data of men, women, and children also were described by Nordstrom and Lindblom (1975). They suggested that departures from linearity in the Peterson and Barney data may be explained by articulatory differences among the speakers, especially because not all of the speakers in the investigation were native Americans.

Fant (1966) compared the formant frequencies of adult male and adult female vowels by means of scale factors based on ratios as follows.

(1) First-formant scale factor

$$k_1 = \left[\dfrac{\text{F1 of female}}{\text{F1 of male}} - 1\right] \times 100$$

(2) Second-formant scale factor

$$k_2 = \left[\dfrac{\text{F2 of female}}{\text{F2 of male}} - 1\right] \times 100$$

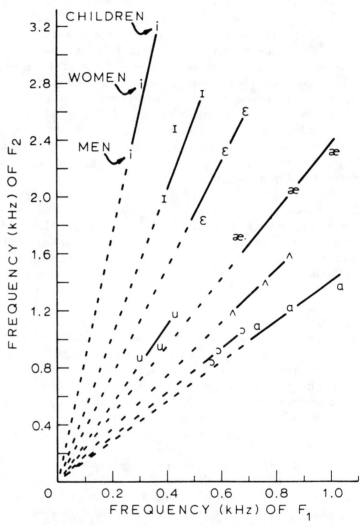

FIGURE 2. Plot of second-formant (F2) frequency versus first-formant (F1) frequency for the vowel data of Peterson and Barney (1952). The data are plotted according to Mol's (1963) method of linear scaling to reveal the nearly linear relationships among the data for the three subject groups, men, women, and children.

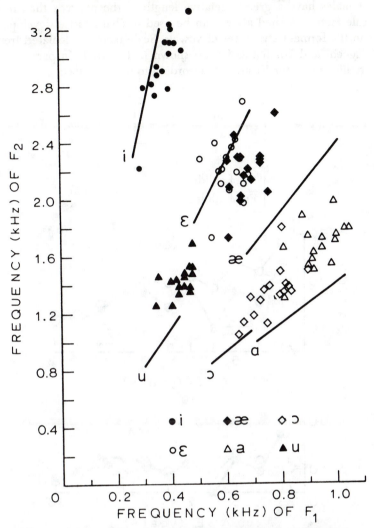

FIGURE 3. Plot of second-formant (F2) frequency versus first-formant (F1) frequency for the vowel data of Eguchi and Hirsh (1969). The data are plotted according to Mol's (1963) method of linear scaling, as in the case of Figure 2. The straight lines are the lines of best linear fit established for Peterson and Barney's (1952) data in Figure 2.

Fant concluded from his calculations that the scale factors relating male and female data vary with the class of the vowels, with the average scale factor about 18%. In addition, he determined that the scale factors for both F1 and F2 were low for rounded back vowels, that the scale factor for F1 was low for any close or highly rounded vowel, and that the scale factor for F1 was high for very open front or back vowels. Fant pointed out that these differences are consistent with differences in vocal tract anatomy between males and females, insofar as males have a greater relative length of the pharynx than females.

The scale factors defined above can be used to characterize developmental changes in the formant structures of vowels. Scale factors calculated from the data of Eguchi and Hirsh (1969) are shown in Figure 4. In part (a), scale factors are illustrated for F1 and F2 according to the formulas:

$$(3) \qquad k_1 = \left[\frac{\text{F1 of children}}{\text{F1 of adult male}} - 1 \right] \times 100$$

$$(4) \qquad k_2 = \left[\frac{\text{F2 of children}}{\text{F2 of adult male}} - 1 \right] \times 100$$

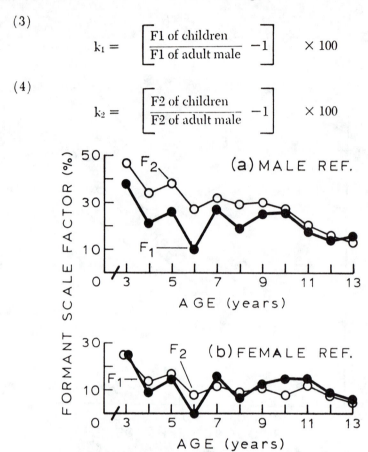

FIGURE 4. Formant scale factors calculated from the data reported by Eguchi and Hirsh (1969) for the vowels of children aged three-13 years. Adult male data were used as the reference in (a) and adult female data were used as the reference in (b).

In part (b), the scale factors are based on the same formulas, except that adult female values are used as the reference (denominator). In both (a) and (b) of Figure 4, the data for male and female children are combined until the age of 11 years, after which only the data for children of the same sex as the adult referent are used. (Eguchi and Hirsh did not distinguish their data by sex until 11 years.)

A developmental trend in formant frequency values appears more strongly in part (a) than in part (b) of Figure 4. That is, when adult male data are used as the referent in computing scale factors k_1 and k_2, both factors tend to decline with age, although several irregularities are seen for k_1. A developmental trend appears only weakly in part (b), and the curve for k_1 indicates that the children in the Eguchi and Hirsh study often had average F1 values approaching those for the adult female subjects. For example, the children aged six years had average F1 values equal to those for the women subjects. In fact, for some vowels, the children actually had lower F1 values than those for adult females. In view of this unusual result, the formant frequency values reported by Eguchi and Hirsh should be treated cautiously. Considering the data for F2, which are more systematic than those for F1, the scale factor in part (a) decreases at an average rate of about 3.4% per year and the scale factor in part (b) decreases at an average rate of about 1.5-2% per year. That is, during the developmental period of three-13 years, k_2 changes at the annual rates of 3.4% for an adult male referent and about 2% for an adult female referent.

The formant scale factors graphed in Figure 4 represent the averaged data for six vowels and therefore obscure the fact that the magnitudes of the scale factors vary from vowel to vowel. The variations in the magnitude of the scale factors are shown for four vowels in Figure 5 (scale factor k_1) and

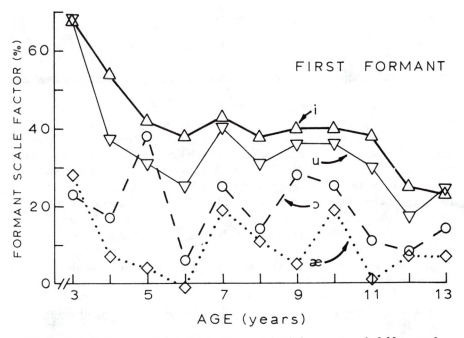

FIGURE 5. Scale factors relating the first-formant (F1) frequencies of children to those of adult males for four vowels. The scale factors were calculated from the data of Eguchi and Hirsh (1969).

Figure 6 (scale factor k_2). The factors in these figures were derived from formulas (3) and (4), in which the formant frequencies of children are compared to the formant frequencies of adult males. The largest values of k_1 (Figure 5) occur for the high vowels /i/ and /u/, and the smallest values

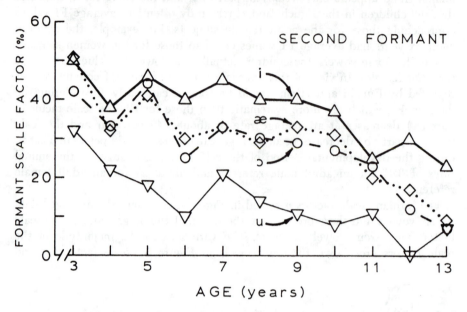

FIGURE 6. Scale factors relating the second-formant (F2) frequencies of children to those of adult males for four vowels. The scale factors were calculated from the data of Eguchi and Hirsh (1969).

generally occur for the low-front vowel /æ/. The largest values of k_2 (Figure 6) occur for the vowel /i/, the smallest values occur for vowel /u/, and intermediate values are seen for /æ/ and /ɔ/. The relationships in Figures 5 and 6 do not always follow the principles that Fant (1966) laid down for the comparison of male and female formant patterns. For example, Fant concluded that k_1, the scale factor for F1, was large for open vowels but small for close vowels. The opposite relationship holds for the comparisons of children's vowels with men's vowels in Figure 5. The results in Figure 6 are in better agreement with Fant's principles, insofar as k_2, the scale factor for F2, is small for rounded back vowels.

The following tentative conclusions about child-adult scale factors may be drawn from Figures 5 and 6:

1. The scale factor for F1 is large for the high vowels but small for the low vowels.
2. The scale factor for F2 is large for the front vowels but small for the close back vowels.

Variability in Children's Formant Patterns for Vowels

Apparently the only substantial source of data in this area is the investigation of Eguchi and Hirsh (1969), which was cited earlier in a similar discussion dealing with the variability of f_0 in children. Eguchi and Hirsh calculated intrasubject standard deviations of both F1 and F2 for five vowel segments in five recitations each of the sentences *He has a blue pen* and *I am tall*. For both F1 and F2, the standard deviations revealed a fairly uniform decrease in variability as subject age increased from three to 11 years. This reduction in variability was apparent for both the absolute values of the standard deviations and for relative values expressed as the ratio of each standard deviation to its corresponding mean. The relative values are plotted in Figure 7 for F1,

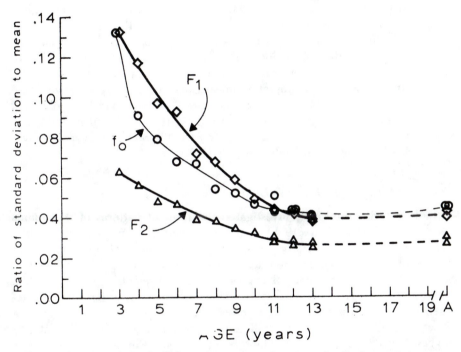

FIGURE 7. Ratios of standard deviation to mean frequency for fundamental frequency (f_0), first-formant frequency (F1), and second-formant frequency (F2), plotted as a function of age of subject. The values used are the means calculated from the data of Eguchi and Hirsh (1969). A = adult.

F2, and f_0. The three curves reach an asymptote at about age 11 or 12, at which age the variability of the children's data is about the same as the variability of the adult data. Eguchi and Hirsh (1969) viewed their data on F1 and F2 as evidence that the young children were more inaccurate in articulatory positioning than the older subjects. They remarked as follows (p. 44):

The implication is clear that three-year-old children do not move their tongues to exactly the same position for a particular vowel as it occurs in repetitions of the same sentence, at least not so exactly the same as older children and adults. The variability decreases until about age 11.

Unfortunately, the validity of the conclusion that Eguchi and Hirsh reached on this matter is somewhat in doubt. Lindblom (1972) objected to the investigation on the grounds that it is hazardous to infer from the spectrographic data that adultlike precision in articulation is not achieved until the age of 11-12 years. Lindblom questioned Eguchi and Hirsh's assumption that the variability of F1 and F2 is descriptive of instability in articulatory positioning. The question arises because, as mentioned earlier in this paper, the accuracy with which formant frequencies can be estimated from spectrograms is limited by the fundamental frequency of the speaker's voice: the higher the f_o, the greater is the variability (error) in estimating the formant frequency value. Lindblom showed that a hypothetical curve relating the error of formant frequency estimation to the fundamental frequency is similar in form to the age-dependent standard deviation curve presented by Eguchi and Hirsh. In other words, measurement error might be a significant factor in the variability data derived from the spectrographic measurements. The problem would be easier to evaluate if estimates of the measurement error had been obtained separately for each age group used in the study. However, Eguchi and Hirsh reported measurement errors based only "on six different vowels spoken by a 6-year-old child and by an adult male" (p. 18).

Formant Structure of Children's Consonants

Studies in this area have investigated the formant patterns of the liquids /w/, /r/, and /l/. Klein (1971) compared spectrographic data on syllable-initial /r/ for two subject groups: (1) the six most intelligible subjects in his sample of 24 preschool children and (2) the six least intelligible subjects in the sample. Klein determined that good and poor attempts at /r/ production could be distinguished reliably by two spectrographic measurements, the frequency of the F2 origin and the frequency difference between the origins of F2 and F3. On the basis of the differences between adult and child data, he suggested that ". . . children may be trying to match the appropriate distinctive features in adult speech rather than absolute values" (Klein, 1971, p. 543). This comment apparently was made in response to the fact that children had higher formant frequencies than adults. The stability of the children's productions cannot be determined from Klein's study because he recorded only two samples of /r/ from each child, using the syllables /rit/ and /rut/.

Dalston (1975) performed spectrographic analyses of /w/, /r/, and /l/ produced by adults and children three to four years of age. Formant frequency patterns, plotted as the F3/F1 ratio as a function of the F2/F1 ratio, revealed that the distributions of data points for the three sonorants were larger and more overlapping for the children than for the adults. Even for sounds that were judged to have been produced correctly, the children exhibited a greater group variance than the adults. Dalston also reported that the children's productions of /w/, /r/, and /l/ could be distinguished on the basis of temporal characteristics such as durations of formant steady states and rates of formant transitions. Thus, children produced these three sounds with distinctive differences in formant frequency origins, durations of steady state portions, and rates of formant movement.

Applications to the Identification and Diagnosis of Developmental Disorders

To a limited extent, analyses of formant patterns have been made of infant cries. A recent example is the investigation of Tenold et al. (1974), who used cepstral and stationarity analyses to compare the cries of full-term and premature neonates. The cepstrum is the Fourier transform of the logarithm of the amplitude spectrum of a signal. Thus, the cepstrum is a transform of a transform and derives its name from a transposition of the letters in the word *spectrum*. The independent variable in a cepstrum is reciprocal frequency (time) and, again by transposition, is known as *quefrency*. The effect of taking the logarithm of the amplitude spectrum is to separate the source and system characteristics as additive components, assuming, as Fant (1970) does, that the source and system characteristics are spectrally multiplicative. That is, in Fant's notation, the sound spectrum of speech, $|P(f)|$, is the product of the source spectrum, $|S(f)|$, and the filter function, $|T(f)|$, or, $|P(f)| = |S(f)| \cdot |T(f)|$. The fundamental frequency, f_o, is a property of the source spectrum $|S(f)|$, and the formant structure is a property of the filter function $|T(f)|$. To obtain a cepstrum, the logarithm is taken of both sides of the equation above to yield $\ln|P(f)| = \ln|S(f)| + \ln|T(f)|$. Then, Fourier transforms (properly, inverse Fourier transforms) are taken to obtain $F\ln|P(f)| = F\ln|S(f)| + F\ln|T(f)|$.

Fundamental frequency can be determined by the cepstral technique because $F\ln|S(f)|$ has a strong component at the quefrency T_o, the fundamental period of laryngeal vibration. The formant maxima are found in $F\ln|T(f)|$ and occur at relatively low quefrency values (because of the reciprocal relationship between frequency and time).

Tenold et al. used the reciprocal of the quefrency at the highest cepstral peak to estimate f_o and reported that their analyses did not reveal differences in the variability of f_o between full-term and premature infants. Variability of formant frequencies was tested indirectly by a stationarity test based on fast Fourier transforms of blocks of cry data. The stationarity analyses revealed that the cry spectra were more variable for the premature infants. The authors interpreted this greater variability to mean that the premature infants had less postural stabilization than the full-term infants. The work of Tenold et al. demonstrates that analysis techniques based on the source-filter theory of vowel production (Fant, 1970) can provide information on both the control of laryngeal vibration and the control of the resonating vocal tract. Actually, spectrograms also are suitable for such purposes, especially if narrow-band spectrograms are used to estimate fundamental frequency and broad-band spectrograms are used to evaluate changes in the supraglottal resonating system.

Beyond the question of postural stability, formant patterns, either relative or absolute, might have some value in the identification and diagnosis of deviant development. However, many conditions that are sufficiently severe so as to affect formant structure are readily signaled by gross changes in physical appearance, such as congenital malformations of the head and neck. Perhaps, though, formant patterns can be used as one index of normal anatomical development, especially during the first two years of life, when the distance between the larynx and the oral cavity gradually increases to form a pharyngeal tube (Negus, 1962; Lieberman et al., 1972; Lieberman, 1973). Abnormalities that affect the development of the pharyngeal cavity conceivably could be detected by appropriate measurements of formant structure.

DEVELOPMENTAL STUDIES OF TEMPORAL FEATURES

Studies of Voice Onset Time

One of the most frequent objects of systematic, quantitative research on speech development is voice onset time (VOT) for stop cognates in syllable-initial position. VOT is defined as the time interval between release of the stop (identified by a noise burst on a spectrogram) and the onset of voicing for a following vocalic element (identified by the appearance of fine vertical striations on a wide-band spectrogram). Measurements of VOT in children's speech have been reported by Preston and Yeni-Komshian (1967), Preston, Yeni-Komshian, and Stark (1967), Preston and Port (1968), Preston and Port (1969), Eguchi and Hirsh (1969), Port and Preston (1972), and Zlatin (1972). The account of VOT changes given below is based upon the data in these reports.

Changes in the VOT distributions that occur during the first six years of life appear to be fairly systematic. The VOT distribution of a child's first words is unimodal, with most of the productions falling in the short lag range of the VOT continuum. That is, the majority of the stops in these early words are characterized by the occurrence of a short delay between articulatory release and the onset of vocal fold vibration. Shortly thereafter, and typically before the age of three years, the VOT distributions of children begin to assume a bimodal form, similar to that for adult speakers of American English, who exhibit two, nonoverlapping ranges of VOT values for the voiced and voiceless stops. However, many children at this age rely on a primary mode falling in the voiced range of the continuum. As a consequence of this preference, VOT values for voiced stops occupy a small portion of the continuum, whereas the values for voiceless stops occupy a much larger portion, with a fairly uniform saturation. By the age of six, VOT distributions generally are bimodal, but the ranges of values for voiced and voiceless stops overlap to a greater degree than for adults. Eventually, values of VOT produce a distinctly bimodal distribution, characterized by little or no overlap of the values for voiced and voiceless stops. Voicing lead (negative values of VOT, for which voicing precedes articulatory release) becomes more common with maturation, especially for bilabials. In addition, the variability of VOT decreases so that adultlike stability of production is noted at about eight years of age. Developmental changes in VOT distributions are illustrated with hypothetical histograms in Figure 8. As a child matures from about two to six years of age, his VOT distributions change from unimodal to bimodal (top to bottom in the figure).

Research on the developmental changes in VOT distributions is an archetype

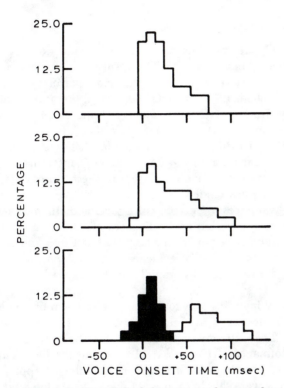

FIGURE 8. Hypothetical histograms showing the expected changes in voice onset time (VOT) as a child matures from two to six years of age. The expected percentage of responses is plotted as a function of VOT. The top histogram applies to a child of about two years of age, and the bottom histogram, to a child of about six years of age. In the bottom histogram, the portion shown in black pertains to voiced stops and the portion shown in white pertains to voiceless stops.

of attempts to quantify the process of speech development. These studies are based on a measurement that is reliable and interpretable. Despite the relatively large number of studies on this problem (large, that is, compared to other aspects of speech development), many interesting features of VOT have yet to be studied developmentally. Recent studies of adult speakers have revealed that VOT for a given stop depends upon several features of phonetic context (Summerfield, in press; Klatt, 1975). Hence, the variability of VOT values in speech would seem to be partly attributable to contextual dependencies that are regular and lawful. It is of interest to know at what ages these regularities appear, because they provide a further opportunity to use a single acoustic dimension in the description of speech development. Moreover, contextual dependencies may help to explain part of the variability that has been observed in developmental studies of VOT.

Studies of Other Temporal Features

Other than VOT, temporal aspects of speech production have received scant attention in developmental studies. This neglect is unfortunate because timing may be the most critical factor in skilled motor performance (Lashley, 1951; Martin, 1972; Michon, 1974). The developmental literature contains very little information even about such gross aspects of speech timing as the durations of vowels and consonants. Acoustic studies along this line recently were reported by DiSimoni (1974a, b, c), who made oscillographic measurements of vowel and consonant durations in CVC and VCV utterances of children aged three, six, and nine years. One conclusion in these studies was that the variability of the durations tended to decrease with age, a result which parallels the age-related variances in the study of Eguchi and Hirsh (1969). In addition, the durational data revealed that influences of context and utterance length on segment durations began to appear between three and six years of age. DiSimoni interpreted his data as evidence of a developmental pattern in which the control of duration changes rapidly in the period between three and six years.

One of the few investigations to address the problem of timing in phrase- or sentence-length utterances in children's speech was reported by Tingley and Allen (1975). They attempted to account for the variance associated with children's performance of two tasks: (1) reciting the lines *Twinkle, twinkle, little star; how I wonder what you are* and (2) finger tapping with a steady rhythm. Subjects were 20 children aged five, seven, nine, and 11 years (five subjects at each age). Among the significant conclusions of this research were the following:

1. The results gave evidence of a definite developmental pattern, with all of the 11-year-old children performing within adult limits of relative variance.
2. The data yielded no evidence of peripheral feedback as a means of speech timing control, even for the five year olds.

3. A linear statistical model (Allen, 1973) accounted for 83-98% of the experimental variance.

The study of Tingley and Allen (1975) has important implications for the development of timing control for speech. First, their results indicated that relative variance falls within adult limits by the age of 11 years, a result which conforms with the data of Eguchi and Hirsh (1969) on various spectral properties of speech. Second, they interpreted their data to mean that motor patterns for speech are largely preplanned rather than feedback controlled even at the age of five years. Thus, it appears that five-year-old children have learned strategies for the preprogramming of motor control, even though the precision of motor control continuously improves for a period of at least four more years (until the age of nine or 11). It is a logical hypothesis that the acquisition of motor programs for speech is conditioned by the learning of phonological regularities. Some support for this hypothesis is provided by a comparison of the results of Tingley and Allen (1975) with those of DiSimoni (1974a, b, c). That is, Tingley and Allen's data indicated that five year olds were not dependent on feedback, and DiSimoni's results showed that certain phonological regularities were present in the speech of six year olds. Thus, there is at least weak evidence for a temporal correspondence between preplanned motor behavior and the appearance of phonological regularities. This correspondence may be evidence of a parallel development of motor strategies and phonological patterns.

Applications to the Identification and Diagnosis of Developmental Disorder

Slight use has been made of temporal properties of speech production in the evaluation of developmental abnormalities. Because of the importance of timing variables in any motor skill, this area may prove to be especially valuable. Investigations of adult speech have revealed that the timing of speech movements is under fine control, such that successive movements in the production of a phonetic sequence may be separated by as little as 10 msec. Kent and Moll (1975) reported that in the consonantal cluster /spl/, the lingua-alveolar constriction for the /s/ is released about 10-20 msec after formation of the bilabial closure for the /p/. Similarly, the lingua-alveolar contact for /l/ precedes the release of the bilabial closure for /p/ by about 20 msec. Thus the seriation of articulatory movements in adult speech routinely involves temporal intervals of very short duration. It is not known at what age children acquire this precision of motor control, but if research on VOT for stop consonants is any indication, then it may be as late as 10 years before children exhibit reliable control over the coordination of articulatory movements. It is likely that timing variables could provide a sensitive metric for the evaluation of the neuromuscular maturation of the speech mechanism. As Tingley and Allen (1975) noted, studies of timing in various motor tasks have revealed a progressive refinement of control ". . . from the earliest age tested through puberty" (p. 186). Thus, motor timing for both speech and nonspeech activities may develop along a continuum that spans at least 12 years of life.

DISCUSSION

A general conclusion that may be drawn from acoustic studies of speech development is that, beginning by at least three years of age, the variability of speech motor control progressively diminishes until the age of eight-12 years, when adultlike stability is achieved. The exact age at which minimum variability is attained probably depends upon several factors, but of certain importance are (1) the child's individual pattern of motor development and (2) the particular type of speech behavior that is under examination.

The spectrographic measurements of Eguchi and Hirsh (1969) focused on three general properties of speech production: (1) positioning of the articulators for vowels (measurements of formant frequencies), (2) laryngeal adjustments for vowels (measurements of f_0), and (3) articulatory-laryngeal coordination (measurements of VOT for stops). In the case of formant frequencies, intrasubject standard deviations progressively decreased in magnitude as the age of the subjects increased from three to 11. Similarly, the intrasubject standard deviations for f_0 progressively decreased with age until a minimum was reached at about 10-12 years. Finally, the temporal feature of VOT showed diminishing intrasubject variability over the period of three to eight years. Thus, the declining variabilities for the three types of measurements appear to reflect an increasing precision of motor control over a five- to eight-year interval. The studies of DiSimoni (1974a, b, c) and Tingley and Allen (1975) indicate that various temporal aspects of speech production also come under increasingly precise control as a child grows older. Interestingly, the 11-year-old children in the Tingley and Allen investigation had a relative variance of timing like that for adults, whereas younger children had greater relative variances. Thus, both the study of Tingley and Allen and the study of Eguchi and Hirsh indicate that an adultlike precision of motor control is acquired only by about 11 years of age. That is, the maturation of the motor skills in speech is not completed until the child enters puberty.

If the age of two or three years is assumed as the beginning of a child's extensive speech usage on a daily basis, then between eight and nine years pass before the precision of his motor control compares with that of an adult. Given that 90% of children possess the consonant sounds of American English by the age of about eight years (Sander, 1972), it appears that the motor skills of speech continue to be perfected even after the child's phonetic repertoire is judged to be complete. Perhaps phonetic judgments give only a gross indication of motor development for speech and are rather insensitive to developmental continua involving motoric variables such as coordination, timing, and placement. Figure 9 allows a comparison of Sander's profile of consonant mastery with the ages at which adultlike precision is observed for formant frequencies and VOT.

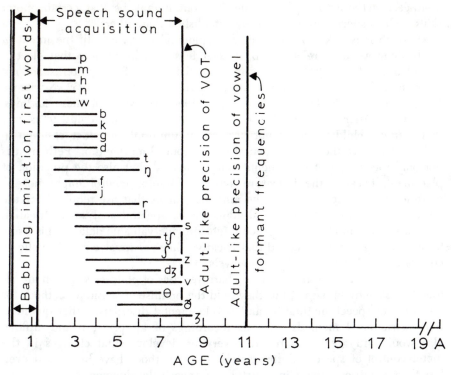

FIGURE 9. Chronological profile of various aspects of speech maturation. The ages of acquisition of various consonant sounds are indicated by the horizontal lines, which begin at the median age of customary articulation for the sound in question and terminate at the age at which 90% of children possess that sound (Sander, 1972). The vertical lines in the center of the illustration indicate the ages at which children achieve an adultlike accuracy in the control of voice onset time (VOT) for stops and the control of formant frequencies for vowels (based on the data of Eguchi and Hirsh, 1969). A = adult.

It is intriguing to consider a maturational endpoint for speech of 11-12 years in the light of Lenneberg's (1967) suggestion that beyond a critical period, which normally ends at puberty, it is impossible for a person to learn a language as a native speaker does. Lenneberg's conclusion was based on evidence from aphasic, deaf, and retarded subjects, but it seems that data on normal speech development also point to a culminative stage around puberty. One hypothesis that might be entertained here is that motor control for speech becomes highly ingrained at about 11 years, after which time new phonetic systems can be acquired only with considerable difficulty. Of course, new syntactic and lexical systems also may be difficult to acquire beyond this age. The rigidity of the motor control that is acquired for a particular phonetic system is indicated by the tenacity of accents (see von Bonin, 1962). It is quite rare that an adult can learn to produce a second language without telltale residuals of his native motor-phonetic background. Whether the motor organization of speech is more resistant to change than the motor organization of nonspeech activities is open to question, but it may be that certain motor skills such as speech are more firmly established than others.

Although it is risky to compare developmental patterns with the intent of establishing a causal relationship, it is at least worthy of note that electro-encephalographic (EEG) studies indicate that adult EEG patterns are not found in children until sometime around puberty (Lindsley, 1952; Novikova, 1961; Tanner, 1962; Dustman and Beck, 1966). In view of these findings, Tingley and Allen (1975, p. 187) remarked, "It thus appears logical to assume that younger children might not perform as uniformly as older children in tasks that involve the use of a neural timing-control mechanism." Perhaps it is not only the timing of movements that is affected, but also the precision of placement, because the immature system of motor control might not be capable of accurately gauging the muscular forces that are required for the performance of delicate structural adjustments. Spectral analyses of frication and burst noise in children's speech might provide valuable data on this issue, because it is generally believed that fricatives like /s/ involve a more delicate control of the articulators than do vowels.

The existing data on the acoustic characteristics of children's speech are all too often sketchy in nature, but they hold the promise of sensitive methods for the study of speech maturation and developmental disorders. Other quantitative instrumental methods, such as recordings of air pressure and airflow, also would aid greatly in the discovery of developmental changes in the motor control of speech. Unfortunately, these methods have been used even less than acoustic analyses in the study of speech development.

By way of summary, some of the major acoustic changes that occur during the process of speech development are listed in Appendix C. Most of the observations reported in this table are rather gross, but they serve to identify at least a few of the transitional periods in the maturation of the speech mechanism.

ACKNOWLEDGMENT

This work was supported by Public Health Service Research Grant NS-12281 from the National Institute of Neurological and Communicative Disorders and Stroke. Requests for reprints should be addressed to the author at the Waisman Center on Mental Retardation and Human Development, 2605 Marsh Lane, University of Wisconsin, Madison, Wisconsin 53706.

REFERENCES

ALLEN, G. D., Segmental timing control in speech production. *J. Phonetics,* 1, 207-225 (1973).

BLENICK, G., TAVOLGA, W., and ANTOPOL, W., Variations in the birth cries of newborn infants from narcotic addicted and normal mothers. *J. Obstet. Gynaec.,* 110, 948-958 (1971).

BOE, L.-J., and RAKOTOFIRINGA, H., A statistical analysis of laryngeal frequency: Its relationship to intensity level and duration. *Lang. Speech,* 18, 1-13 (1975).

BONIN, G. VON, Brain and mind. In S. Koch (Ed.), *Psychology: A Study of a Science.* 4, 100-118. New York: McGraw-Hill (1962).

Bosma, J. F., Truby, H. M., and Lind, J., Cry motions of the newborn infant. *Acta Paediat., Scand., Suppl. 163*, 61-92 (1965).

Broadbent, D. E., Ladefoged, P., and Lawrence, W., Vowel sounds and perceptual constancy. *Nature* (Lond.), **178**, 815-816 (1956).

Crystal, D., Non-segmental phonology in language acquisition: A review of the issues. *Lingua*, **32**, 1-45 (1973).

Curry, T., The pitch characteristics of the adolescent male voice. *Speech Monogr.*, **7**, 48-62 (1940).

Dalston, R. M., Acoustic characteristics of English /w, r, l/ spoken correctly by young children and adults. *J. acoust. Soc. Am.*, **57**, 462-469 (1975).

DiSimoni, F. G., Influence of vowel environment on the duration of consonants in the speech of three-, six-, and nine-year-old children. *J. acoust. Soc. Am.*, **55**, 360-361 (1974a).

DiSimoni, F. G., Influence of consonant environment on duration of vowels in the speech of three-, six-, and nine-year-old children. *J. acoust. Soc. Am.*, **55**, 362-363 (1974b).

DiSimoni, F. G., Influence of utterance length upon bilabial closure for /p/ in three-, six-, and nine-year-old children. *J. acoust. Soc. Am.*, **55**, 1353-1354 (1974c).

Duffy, R., The vocal pitch characteristics of eleven, thirteen and fifteen year-old female speakers. Doctoral dissertation, State Univ. of Iowa (1958).

Dustman, R. E., and Beck, E. C., Visually evoked potentials: Amplitude changes with age. *Science*, **151**, 1013-1014 (1966).

Eguchi, S., and Hirsh, I. J., Development of speech sounds in children. *Acta otolaryng. Suppl. 257* (1969).

Fairbanks, G., An acoustical study of the pitch of infant wails. *Child Dev.*, **13**, 227-232 (1942).

Fairbanks, G., Herbert, E., and Hammond, J., An acoustical study of vocal pitch in seven and eight year-old girls. *Child Dev.*, **20**, 71-80 (1949).

Fairbanks, G., Wiley, J. H., and Lassman, F., An acoustical study of vocal pitch in seven and eight year-old boys. *Child Dev.*, **20**, 63-69 (1949).

Fant, G., A note on vocal tract size factors and non-uniform F-pattern scalings. *Quart. Prog. Stat. Rept., Speech Trans. Lab.*, Royal Inst. Tech., Stockholm, No. 4, 22-30 (1966).

Fant, G., Analysis and synthesis of speech processes. In B. Malmberg (Ed.), *Manual of Phonetics*, Amsterdam: North-Holland, 173-227 (1968).

Fant, G., *Acoustic Theory of Speech Production.* The Hague: Mouton (1970).

Flatau, T. S., and Gutzman, H., Die stimme des sauglings. *Arch. laryng. Rhino.*, **18**, 139-151 (1906).

Formby, D., Maternal recognition of infant's cry. *Develpm. Med. child Neurol.*, **9**, 293-298 1967).

Fujisaki, H., and Kawashima, T., The roles of pitch and higher formants in the perception of vowels. *IEEE Trans. Audio-Electro-acoustics*, **AV-16**, 73-77 (1968).

Gerstman, L. J., Classification of self-normalized vowels. *IEEE Trans. Audio-Electro-acoustics*, **AV-16**, 78-80 (1968).

Hollien, H., and Malcik, E., Adolescent voice changes in Southern Negro males. *Speech Monogr.*, **29**, 53-58 (1962).

Hollien, H., and Malcik, E., Evaluation of cross-sectional status of adolescent voice change in males. *Speech Monogr.*, **34**, 80-84 (1967).

Hollien, H., Malcik, E., and Hollien, B., Adolescent voice change in Southern white males. *Speech Monogr.*, **22**, 87-90 (1965).

Hollien, H., and Paul, P., A second evaluation of the speaking fundamental frequency characteristics of post-adolescent girls. *Lang. Speech*, **12**, 119-124 (1969).

Kaplan, H. M., *Anatomy and Physiology of Speech.* New York: McGraw-Hill (1960).

Karelitz, S., Karelitz, R., and Rosenfeld, L. S., Infants' vocalizations and their significance. In P. W. Bowman and H. V. Mautner (Eds.), *Mental Retardation. Proceedings of the First International Medical Conference, Portland, Maine, 1959.* New York: Grune and Stratton, 439-446 (1960).

Kent, R. D., and Moll, K. L., Articulatory timing in selected consonant sequences. *Brain Lang.*, **2**, 304-323 (1975).

Klatt, D. H., Voice onset time, frication, and aspiration in word-initial consonant clusters. *J. Speech Hearing Res.*, **18**, 686-706 (1975).

KLEIN, R. P., Acoustic analysis of the acquisition of acceptable *r* in American English. *Child Dev.*, **42**, 543-550 (1971).

LASHLEY, K., The problem of serial order in behavior. In L. A. Jeffress (Ed.), *Cerebral Mechanisms in Behavior*. New York: Wiley and Sons, 112-136 (1951).

LENNEBERG, E. H., *Biological Foundations of Language*. New York: Wiley (1967).

LIEBERMAN, P., Some acoustic measures of the periodicity of normal and pathologic larynges. *J. acoust. Soc. Am.*, **35**, 344-353 (1963).

LIEBERMAN, P., HARRIS, K. S., WOLFF, P., and RUSSELL, L. H., Newborn infant cry and nonhuman primate vocalizations. *J. Speech Hearing Res.*, **14**, 718-727 (1972).

LIEBERMAN, P., On the evolution of language. *Cognition*, **2**, 59-94 (1973).

LINDBLOM, B., Accuracy and limitations of sonagraph measurements. *Proceedings of the Fourth International Congress of Phonetic Sciences, Helsinki*. The Hague: Mouton, 188-202 (1962).

LINDBLOM, B., Comments on paper 15 "Development of speech sounds in children," by S. Eguchi and I. J. Hirsh. In G. Fant (Ed.), *International Symposium on Speech Communication Ability and Profound Deafness*. Washington, D.C.: Alexander Graham Bell Association for the Deaf, 159-162 (1972).

LINDSLEY, D. B., Psychological phenomena and the electroencephalogram. *J. Electroenceph. clin. Neurophysiol.*, **4**, 443-456 (1952).

LINKE, E., A study of pitch characteristics of female voices and their relationship to vocal effectiveness. Doctoral dissertation, Iowa State Univ. (1953).

MARTIN, J. G., Rhythmic (hierarchical) versus serial structure in speech and other behavior. *Psychol. Rev.*, **79**, 487-509 (1972).

McGLONE, R., Vocal pitch characteristics of children aged one and two years. *Speech Monogr.*, **33**, 178-181 (1966).

McGLONE, R., and McGLONE, J., Speaking fundamental frequency of eight-year-old girls. *Folia phoniat.*, **24**, 313-317 (1972).

MICHEL, J. F., HOLLIEN, H., and MOORE, P., Speaking fundamental frequency characteristics of fifteen, sixteen, and seventeen-year-old girls. *Lang. Speech*, **9**, 46-51 (1966).

MICHELSSON, K., Cry analyses of symptomless low-birth-weight neonates and of asphyxiated newborn infants. *Acta Paediat., Scand., Suppl. 216*, 1-45 (1971).

MICHON, J. A., Programs and "programs" for sequential patterns in motor behavior. *Brain Res.*, **71**, 413-424 (1974).

MOL, H., *Fundamentals of Phonetics. Janua Linguarum, No. 26*. The Hague: Mouton (1963).

NAIDR, J. VON, ZBORIL, M., and SEVCIK, K., Die pubertalen veranderungen der stimme bei jungen im verlauf von 5 jahren. *Folia phoniat.*, **17**, 1-18 (1965).

NEGUS, V. E., *The Comparative Anatomy and Physiology of the Larynx*. New York: Hafner (1962).

NORDSTROM, P.-E., and LINDBLOM, B., A normalization procedure for vowel formant data. Paper presented at the Eighth International Congress of Phonetic Sciences, Leeds, England (August 1975).

NOVIKOVA, L. A., Age features in the electrical activity of the brain in children and juveniles. *Pavlov. J. higher nerv. Activ.*, **11**, 61-71 (1961).

OSTWALD, P., The sounds of infancy. *Devel. Med. child Neurol.*, **14**, 350-361 (1971).

OSTWALD, P., and PELTZMAN, P., The cry of the human infant. *Scient. Am.*, **230**, 84-90 (1974).

PETERSON, G. E., and BARNEY, H. L., Control methods in a study of the vowels. *J. acoust. Soc. Am.*, **24**, 175-184 (1952).

PORT, D. K., and PRESTON, M. S., Early apical stop production: A voice onset time analysis. *Haskins Laboratories Status Report on Speech Research, SR-29/30*. New Haven, Conn.: Haskins Laboratories, 125-149 (1972).

PRESCOTT, R., Infant cry sound: Developmental features. *J. acoust. Soc. Am.*, **57**, 1186-1191 (1975).

PRESTON, M. S., and PORT, D. K., A report on a study of voicing in initial stop consonants produced during the second year of life. *Johns Hopkins School of Medicine, Annual Report of Neurocommunications Laboratory*, No. 3, 211-222 (1968).

PRESTON, M. S., and PORT, D. K., Further results of voicing in stop consonants in young children. *Haskins Laboratories Status Report on Speech Research, SR-13/14*. New Haven, Conn.: Haskins Laboratories, 181-184 (1969).

PRESTON, M. S., and YENI-KOMSHIAN, G., Studies on the development of stop consonants in children. *Haskins Laboratories Status Report on Speech Research, SR-11*. New Haven, Conn.: Haskins Laboratories, 49-53 (1967).

PRESTON, M. S., YENI-KOMSHIAN, G., and STARK, R. E., Voicing in initial stop consonants produced by children in the prelinguistic period from different language communities. *Johns Hopkins Univ. School of Medicine, Annual Report of Neurocommunications Laboratory*, No. 2, 305-323 (1967).

RINGEL, R. L., and KLUPPEL, D. D., Neonatal crying: A normative study. *Folia phoniat.*, 16, 1-9 (1964).

SANDER, E., When are speech sounds learned? *J. Speech Hearing Dis.*, 37, 55-63 (1972).

SHEPPARD, W. C., and LANE, H. L., Development of the prosodic features of infant vocalizing. *J. Speech Hearing Res.*, 11, 94-108 (1968).

SNIDECOR, J., The pitch and duration characteristics of superior female speakers during oral reading. *J. Speech Hearing Dis.*, 16, 44-52 (1951).

SUMMERFIELD, Q., Processing of cues and contexts in the perception of voicing contrasts. *Proceedings of the Stockholm Speech Communication Seminar, Aug. 1-3, 1974*. Uppsala, Sweden: Almquist and Wiksell (in press).

TANNER, J. M., *Growth at Adolescence* (2nd ed.) Oxford: Blackwell Scientific Pub. (1962).

TENOLD, J. L. CROWELL, D. H., JONES, R. H., DANIEL, T. H., McPHERSON, D. F., POPPER, A. N., Cepstral and stationarity analyses of full-term and premature infants' cries. *J. acoust. Soc. Am.*, 56, 975-980 (1974).

TINGLEY, B. M., and ALLEN, G. D., Development of speech timing control in children. *Child Dev.*, 46, 186-194 (1975).

TONKOVA-YAMPOL 'SKAYA, R. V., Razvitie rechevoi intonatsii u detei pervykh dvukh let zhini (The development of speech intonation in children during the first two years of life). *Vop. Psikhiat.*, 14, 94-101 (1968). Also in C. A. Ferguson and D. A. Slobin (Eds.), *Studies of child Lang. Dev.*, New York: Holt, Rinehart, Winston, 128-138 (1973).

VAN OORDT, H. W. A., and DROST, H. A., Development of the frequency range in children. *Folia phoniat.*, 15, 289-298 (1963).

VUORENKOSKI, V., LIND, J., PARTANEN, T. J., LEJEUNE, J., LAFOURCADE, J., and WASZ-HOCKERT, O., Spectrographic analysis of cries from children with maladie du cri du chat. *Annls. Paediat. Fenn.*, 12, 174-180 (1966).

VUORENKOSKI, V., WASZ-HOCKERT, O., LIND, J., KOIVISTO, M., and PARTANEN, T. J., Training the auditory perception of some specific types of the abnormal pain cry in newborn and young infants. *Quart. Prog. Stat. Rept., Speech Trans. Lab.*, Royal Inst. Tech., Stockholm, No. 4, 37-48 (1971).

WASZ-HOCKERT, O., LIND, J., VUORENKOSKI, V., PARTANEN, T. J., and VALANNE, E., The infant cry: A spectrographic and auditory analysis (accompanied by a recording). *Clin. Dev. Med.*, No. 29. London: Spastics International Medical Publications and Heinemann Medical Books (1968).

ZLATIN, M. A., Development of the voicing contrast: A psychoacoustic study of voice onset time. Doctoral dissertation, Northwestern Univ. (1972).

Received October 28, 1975.
Accepted February 2, 1976.

APPENDIX A

Sources of data on fundamental frequency (f_0) of females, compiled according to the age of the subjects.

Age of Subjects	Source of Data
First day to 1 week	Flatau and Gutzman (1906); Ringel and Kluppel (1964); Sheppard and Lane (1968); Ostwald and Peltzman (1974); Prescott (1975); Tenold et al. (1974).
First week to 1 month	Sheppard and Lane (1968); Prescott (1975).
First month to 1 year	Sheppard and Lane (1968); Prescott (1975).
First year to second year	McGlone (1966).
Third year to sixth year	van Oordt and Drost (1963); Eguchi and Hirsh (1969).
Sixth year to ninth year	Fairbanks, Herbert, and Hammond (1949); van Oordt and Drost (1963); Eguchi and Hirsh (1969); McGlone and McGlone (1972).
Tenth year to thirteenth year	Duffy (1958); Eguchi and Hirsh (1969).
Fourteenth year to eighteenth year	Duffy (1958); Michel, Hollien, and Moore (1966); Hollien and Paul (1969).
Adulthood	Linke (1953); Snidecor (1951); Peterson and Barney (1952); Eguchi and Hirsh (1969); Boe and Rakotofiringa (1975).

APPENDIX B

Sources of data on fundamental frequency (f_0) of males, compiled according to the age of the subjects.

Age of Subjects	Source of data
First day to 1 week	Flatau and Gutzman (1906); Fairbanks (1942); Ringel and Kluppel (1964); Sheppard and Lane (1968); Ostwald and Peltzman (1974); Tenold et al. (1974); Prescott (1975).
First week to 1 month	Fairbanks (1942); Sheppard and Lane (1968); Prescott (1975).
First month to 1 year	Fairbanks (1942); Sheppard and Lane (1968); Prescott (1975).
First year to second year	McGlone (1966).
Third year to sixth year	van Oordt and Drost (1963); Eguchi and Hirsh (1969).
Sixth year to ninth year	Fairbanks, Wiley, and Lassman (1949); van Oordt and Drost (1963); Eguchi and Hirsh (1969).

Tenth year to thirteenth year	Curry (1940); Hollien and Malcik (1962); Hollien, Malcik, and Hollien (1965); Naidr, Zboril, and Sevcik (1965); Hollien and Malcik (1967); Eguchi and Hirsh (1969).
Fourteenth year to eighteenth year	Curry (1940); Hollien and Malcik (1962); Hollien, Malcik, and Hollien (1965); Naidr, Zboril, and Sevcik (1965); Hollien and Malcik (1967).
Adulthood	Peterson and Barney (1952); Eguchi and Hirsh (1969); Boe and Rakotofiringa (1975).

APPENDIX C

Chronological profile of changes in selected acoustic properties of speech.

Age of Subject (years)	Acoustic Property
Less than 1	Mean f_0 of newborn falls in range of 400-600 Hz. The mean f_0 increases until about four months of age, then stabilizes until the end of the first year.
1	Marked decrease in mean f_0 begins. By this age, seven distinct intonational patterns are present.
2	Distribution of VOT values is unimodal, with most values falling in the short lag range (VOT less than 30 msec).
3	Marked decrease in mean f_0 gives way to a more gradual decrease, which lasts until the onset of puberty. The mean f_0 at this age is approximately 300 Hz.
5	By this age, segment (consonant, vowel) durations are adjusted to phrase length and at least some aspects of phonetic context.
6	Bimodal distribution of VOT values is clearly present, but the overlapping of values for voiced and voiceless categories is greater than that for adults.
8	The variability of VOT values in stop production reaches an adultlike minimum.
10	The variability of f_0 values reaches an adultlike minimum.
11	Adultlike minima are reached for the variability of formant frequencies in vowel production and for the temporal patterns in phrases.
12	Pubescent voice change: mean f_0 drops markedly for males.

Vowel formant frequency characteristics of preadolescent males and females

Suzanne Bennett

University of Maryland, Department of Hearing and Speech Sciences, College Park, Maryland 20742
(Received 7 February 1980; accepted for publication 26 June 1980)

This report describes the vowel formant frequency characteristics (Fl–F4 of five vowels produced in a fixed phonetic context) of 42 seven and eight year old boys and girls and the relationship of vocal tract resonances to several indices of body size. Results showed that the vowel resonances of male children were consistently lower than those of females, and that the extent of the sexual differences varied as a function of formant number and vowel category. Averaged across all measured formants of all five vowels, the overall sexual distinction was approximately 10%. The range of differences extended from about 3% for F1 of /i/ to 16% for Fl of /æ/. Measures of body size were always significantly related to these children's formant frequencies (range in multiple r's -0.506 to -0.866). The origin of the sexual differences in vocal tract resonance characteristics is discussed with reference to differences in vocal tract size and articulatory behaviors.

PACS numbers: 43.70.Bk, 43.70.Ve

INTRODUCTION

It is known that listeners can accurately differentiate the recorded voices of men and women, and that these perceptions are related to acoustic variables reflecting sexual differences in overall head and neck size (Schwartz, 1968; Coleman, 1971; Lass et al., 1976). Since preadolescent boys and girls do not evidence the pronounced sexual differences in size seen among adults, it has been assumed that listeners would be unable to discern the sex of a child on the basis of speech recordings (Moses, 1954). However, several investigators have now shown that sexual characteristics are perceptually prominent in the voices of many children prior to the onset of puberty (Weinberg and Bennett, 1971; Marshall, 1972; Sachs et al., 1973; Bennett and Weinberg, 1979a, 1979b). Bennett and Weinberg (1979a, b) studied the acoustic cues which influenced listener judgments of child sex. They found that many of their 6 and 7 year old speakers showed sexual differences in format frequencies that were significantly related to listener judgments of sexual identity. However, formant frequency data for boys and girls were obtained from only one vowel.

There is a paucity of information about the vowel formant frequency characteristics of children in general and prepubertal males and females in particular. While several investigators (Potter and Steinberg, 1950; Peterson and Barney, 1952; Eguchi and Hirsh, 1969; Sachs et al., 1973; Kent and Forner, 1979) have studied the vowel productions of children, the data are limited because the number of subjects studied at any given age level has typically been small, the age of the subjects has not always been specified, and the corpus of speech samples has not been comparable from study to study.

Information about the vowel formant frequencies of male versus female children is especially lacking. For the most part, investigators have either combined the data for boys and girls with the assumption that there are no sexual differences prior to puberty (e.g., Eguchi and Hirsh, 1969), or they have included children in their study who may have already entered the pubertal stage of development (Sachs et al., 1973). As a result, we do not have sufficient acoustic data to describe the vowel productions of preadolescent speakers as a function of age and sex.

The data presented here, which represent the initial findings of a longitudinal study, describe the vowel formant frequency characteristics of 42 seven and eight year old boys and girls and the relationship of vocal tract resonances to several indices of body size.

I. METHOD

A. Subjects and recording procedures

The subjects were 42 normal speaking, normal hearing boys and girls between the ages of 7 years, 2 months and 8 years, 9 months. All were from monolingual homes and spoke the dialect common to Montgomery County, Maryland.

Speech recordings were made in a quiet room at an elementary school using a Nagra 4.2 tape recorder and a Sony Electret microphone (Model ECM-50). Each child was fitted with an adjustable head apparatus designed to hold the microphone at a fixed distance (15 cm) parallel to the lips.

Tape recordings were obtained of each child producing six vowels /i/, /I/, /ɛ/, /æ/, /u/, /ʌ/ in a meaningful word frame of dVd construction (deed, did, dead, etc.) embedded in the carrier phrase "I will say d__d again." The vowels /ɑ/ and /ɔ/ were omitted because most of the children did not differentiate these in their speech. The investigator produced the test words, one at a time from a random list of three of each of the words, and the child was asked to say each word in the carrier phrase using a comfortable level of effort.

B. Perceptual verification of vowel identifiability

Five listeners, experienced in phonetic transcription, evaluated the phonemic representativeness of each of these children's vowels. This procedure was used to help ensure that measured differences in formant frequencies were a reflection of talker differences and not variations in the phonemic identity of the vowel. A total of 606 test words in their carrier phrases were randomly assembled on listening tapes and presented to the listeners. Their task was to listen to each example and write the vowel heard on an answer sheet. The listeners chose from among eight vowels (/i/, /ɪ/, /ɛ/, /æ/, /ʌ/, /ɑ/, /ɔ/, /u/, /ʊ/) listed at the top of each response sheet. They were not told that only certain vowels would be spoken by the children.

The vowels produced were considered representative when four of the five listeners (80%) correctly identified the vowel intended by the speaker. Of the 606 examples evaluated by the listeners, 549 met the criterion established for acceptability. Hence, 549 vowels spoken by 19 females and 23 males were available for acoustic analysis.

C. Formant frequency analyses

Vowel formant frequencies were estimated directly from broadband (300 and 450 Hz bandwidth) spectrograms made with a Series 700 Sound Spectrograph (Voice Identification, Inc.). All measurements were made without knowledge of the sex of the speaker. The frequencies of the first four formants of each vowel were obtained by estimating the midpoints of the formant bands.

It was not possible to obtain reliable measurements from these children's /u/ vowels because $F2$ was changing throughout the /u/ vowels and $F3$ and $F4$ were often poorly defined. For these reasons, it was necessary to remove all /u/ vowels from the analysis.

Fifty-five spectrograms ($n = 11$ for each of five vowels) were selected at random from the total pool and remeasured by the author to obtain an estimate of measurement error. All repeated measurements included a redetermination of the midpoints of each of the formant bands; original and replicate measurements were obtained at approximately the same point within the vowel segments.

The measurement errors are summarized in Table I showing the mean differences and the standard deviation of the differences for original and repeat measurements. Across all vowels, the average remeasurement error was approximately 25 Hz (SD = 9.06 Hz). The theoretical error in measurement for these speakers' formant frequencies is probably larger because of the high fundamental frequencies associated with children's voices. However, Lindblom (1962) has shown that the error rarely exceeds $f_0/4$. Fundamental frequency data were not available for the present group of children. Based on the normative data of Eguchi and Hirsh (1969) showing that the average f_0 of 7 and 8 year olds is approximately 260 Hz, the hypothetical error for the present group of children was estimated to be ~65 Hz.

D. Physical measurements

Several measures of body size (standing height, sitting height, body weight, and neck circumference) were obtained from each of the children, with the subjects wearing street clothing and the shoes removed. Body weight was obtained using standard medical scales, while the remaining measures were obtained with a cloth tape measure. Standing height was defined as the distance from the floor to the highest point on the head (vertex). Estimates of sitting height were obtained while the subjects sat on a stool, with the measurement from the plane of the stool to the vertex. Neck circumference was measured at the approximate level of the thyroid cartilage, as determined by palpation.

II. RESULTS AND DISCUSSION

The means, standard deviations, and average sexual differences for the vowel formant frequencies are shown in Table II. Mean values for each of the formants were derived from at least two repetitions of the various vowels from each of 42 subjects. Not surprisingly, it was impossible to obtain a complete set of formant frequency values for every child. The number of speakers represented in any given mean formant frequency value varied between 13 and 22 in the case of males and between 14 and 18 for females (Table II).

The data in Table II provide clear indication that a sexual dimorphism in vocal tract resonance characteristics, and by inference vocal tract size, existed among the 7 and 8 year olds studied here. All measured formants of all five vowels were consistently lower in male children. Averaged across all of the vowels, the mean sexual difference was approximately 264 Hz. It may also be seen that the extent of the sexual differences varied as a function of the formant and the vowel. The range of mean differences extended from 12 Hz for $F1$ and /i/ to 582 Hz for $F4$ of /æ/.

A. Individual subject data

Figure 1 shows the distribution of points in the $F1-F2$ plane for individual males and females. As can be seen, these children's vowels are reasonably well separated on the basis of $F1$ and $F2$ measures. However, it was also not surprising to find that the formant frequencies of some representative vowels either fell outside of the appropriate vowel loop or within an area typical of another vowel. Several investigators (Potter and Steinberg, 1950; Peterson and Barney, 1952; Peterson, 1952) have noted that the phonetic identity of vowels

TABLE I. Measurement errors (Hz) observed for 7 and 8 year old male and female children's vowel formant frequencies.

| | /i/ | | /ɪ/ | | /ɛ/ | | /æ/ | | /ʌ/ | |
	$\bar{X}$ error	SD	$\bar{X}$ error	SD	$\bar{X}$ error	SD	$\bar{X}$ error	SD	$\bar{X}$ error	SD
$F1$	13.45	18.67	7.40	15.60	13.45	18.66	20.18	25.43	17.08	24.43
$F2$	37.00	28.66	18.50	19.50	27.00	24.12	30.36	34.92	17.15	19.29
$F3$	30.45	15.06	22.30	26.09	30.36	27.93	23.54	29.93	31.23	29.61
$F4$	33.64	34.92	18.50	26.16	37.00	17.44	40.36	34.92	28.46	26.83

TABLE II. Mean vowel formant frequency values obtained for 7 and 8 year old male and female children. Standard deviations are given in parentheses beside each of the mean values.

	/i/			/I/			/ɛ/		
	Males	Females	Diff.	Males	Females	Diff.	Males	Females	Diff.
$F1$	470 (43.41) ($n=22$)	482 (26.97) ($n=17$)	12	489 (40.37) ($n=19$)	511 (25.85) ($n=18$)	22	642 (52.17) ($n=19$)	717 (55.88) ($n=17$)	75
$F2$	3067 (196.48) ($n=22$)	3296 (148.79) ($n=17$)	229	2495 (171.59) ($n=19$)	2745 (138.80) ($n=17$)	250	2345 (170.64) ($n=19$)	2546 (134.92) ($n=17$)	201
$F3$	3624 (229.58) ($n=15$)	3917 (171.83) ($n=17$)	293	3532 (176.27) ($n=17$)	3793 (164.44) ($n=16$)	261	3507 (183.36) ($n=19$)	3823 (215.26) ($n=17$)	316
$F4$	4528 (243.78) ($n=17$)	4888 (282.00) ($n=15$)	360	4451 (202.09) ($n=15$)	4914 (263.70) ($n=14$)	463	4391 (196.97) ($n=14$)	4894 (229.18) ($n=14$)	503

	/æ/			/ʌ/		
	Males	Females	Diff.	Males	Females	Diff.
$F1$	878 (67.27) ($n=21$)	1020 (74.74) ($n=17$)	142	670 (67.92) ($n=21$)	760 (64.68) ($n=16$)	90
$F2$	2149 (136.38) ($n=21$)	2355 (105.68) ($n=17$)	206	1745 (191.47) ($n=19$)	1980 (126.50) ($n=16$)	235
$F3$	3331 (163.45) ($n=20$)	3639 (189.91) ($n=17$)	308	3429 (244.68) ($n=20$)	3737 (218.19) ($n=16$)	308
$F4$	4266 (233.82) ($n=13$)	4848 (245.25) ($n=16$)	582	4340 (236.11) ($n=19$)	4759 (266.16) ($n=14$)	419

sometimes cannot be uniquely specified on the basis of $F1$ and $F2$, especially when a variety of speakers is considered.

To illustrate the nature of the sexual differences among individual children's vowels, lines were drawn within each of the vowel loops at those frequencies which best separated (visually) the majority of male and female data points. The vertical lines were drawn at

points which best separated the two sexes on the basis of $F1$. Hence, examination of the number of points to the left and right of the vertical lines provides an indication of the extent of overlap/nonoverlap in $F1$ values. The horizontal lines were set at those frequencies which best separated most males and females on the basis of $F2$. The degree of separation in $F2$ values is indicated by the spread of data points above and below the horizontal lines. The upper right and lower left quadrants within each vowel loop denote the regions of nonoverlap in both $F1$ and $F2$ frequencies.

While there were areas where values for two sexes overlapped and instances where some children's formant frequencies fell in regions typical of the opposite sex, the majority of males and females clustered in separate regions within each of the vowel areas. With respect to $F1$ frequencies, the extent of overlap between the two sexes was least pronounced for the vowel /æ/, followed by /ɛ/ and /ʌ/, and most pronounced for /i/ and /I/. For example, 82% of the girls had $F1$ values for /æ/ that were >980 Hz, while 95% of the boys had values that were <980 Hz. Approximately 84% of the males and 82% of the females had $F1$ frequencies for /ɛ/ which were nonoverlapping. For the vowel /ʌ/, about 75% of the female data points fell above 700 Hz, while about 67% of the male values fell below 700 Hz.

Although there was separation in the $F1$ values of several boys' and girls' /i/ and /I/ vowels, the absolute frequency differences were often quite small (Fig. 1). In addition, the extent of overlap was somewhat more pronounced. Both of these factors are reflected in the mean data in Table II, where it can be seen that the average sexual distinctions were only 12 Hz for /i/ and 22 Hz for /I/. By contrast, the differences were 142, 75, and 90 Hz for /æ/, /ɛ/, and /ʌ/, respectively. Since the mean differences in $F1$ frequencies for /i/ and /I/ were within the hypothetical error (~65 Hz) as-

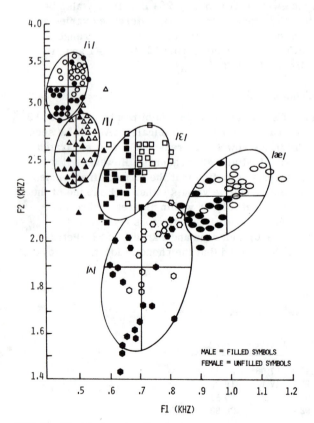

FIG. 1. $F1$–$F2$ plot of male and female children's vowels.

sociated with estimating these children's formant frequencies, the conclusion that a sexual dimorphism in $F1$ actually existed for the close front vowels must remain tentative. This was not a critical issue for the /æ/, /ɛ/, and /ʌ/ vowels because the mean sexual differences were always larger than both the theoretical error and the investigator measurement error.

With respect to $F2$ values, there was substantial sex separation across all five vowels (Fig. 1). For every vowel except /ʌ/, better than 84% of the boys and 82% of the girls had $F2$ values which fell in areas of nonoverlap. Although there was somewhat more overlap for the vowel /ʌ/, the $F2$ frequencies of 78% of the males and 69% of the females were clearly separated.

As noted, the upper right and lower left quadrants within each of the vowel loops in Fig. 1 designate the regions of nonoverlap in both $F1$ and $F2$. Here, it may be seen that most females clustered in the upper right portion of each vowel loop, while a majority of the males clustered in the lower left portion. For example, 13 of the 17 girls (76%) evidenced $F1$ and $F2$ frequencies for /æ/ which were >1000 and 2275 Hz, respectively, while 17 of the 20 males (85%) evidenced values which were <980 and 2260 Hz. For /ɛ/, about 69% of the boys and 72% of the girls were clearly separated on the basis of both $F1$ and $F2$. A larger degree of overlap occurred for the /i/, /I/, and /ʌ/ vowels. In the case of /i/ and /I/ $F1$ was the primary factor contributing to the overlap, while for /ʌ/ it was $F2$. However, even for these vowels 58%–65% of the male and female $F1$ and $F2$ values fell in separate regions within the various vowel loops.

Consistent differences were also found for these boys' and girls' $F3$ and $F4$ frequencies (Table II). Averaged across all of the vowels, the sexual difference in $F3$ was approximately 296 Hz, while for $F4$ it was 466 Hz. Again, most of the male and female data points were well separated, with better than 70% of the boys and girls having $F3$ and $F4$ values that fell in areas of nonoverlap.

B. Child versus adult sexual differences

It has been shown that the large majority of these 7 and 8 year olds evidenced a sexual dimorphism in vowel formant frequencies, and that the extent of the differences varied as a function of vowel category. Investigators who have studied the vowel productions of adults have also noted that the sexual distinctions are vowel- and formant-dependent. Fant (1973; 1975), who has provided the most extensive discussions on this topic, used formant scale factors (K-factors) to describe the percentage relationship of male and female formant frequencies. Using the formula $K_n\% = 100(F_n \text{ female}/F_n \text{ male} - 1)$ he determined that male/female differences were largest for $F2$ and $F3$ of the front vowels and $F1$ of /æ/, while the differences were smaller for $F1$ and $F2$ of the back vowels and $F1$ of the close front vowels. Fant (1975) later demonstrated the consistency of this phenomenon by showing that the pattern of sexual differences across the various vowels was similar for speakers of several different languages.

K-factors were calculated for the present group

of boys and girls to determine whether the pattern of sexual differences for children's vowels was similar to that reported for adults. The various formant scale factors for pre- and postadolescent speakers are graphed in Fig. 2. The formant frequency data of Peterson and Barney (1952) and Fant (1973) were used to derive K-factors for adult speakers.

The data in Fig. 2 illustrate the fact that while both age groups evidence a sexual dimorphism in vocal tract resonance characteristics, the magnitude of the difference is considerably less pronounced for children. Averaged across the lower three formants of all five vowels, the sexual distinction was about 19% for Peterson and Barney's (1952) English speakers and about 18% for Fant's (1973) Swedish speakers. In contrast, it was about 10% for these 7 and 8 year olds.

Fant (1973) has provided some anatomic data to show that although adult males and females differ with respect to both oral and pharyngeal cavity dimensions, the sexual distinction is largest for the pharynx. Although there is comparatively little information about the vocal tract dimensions of prepubertal males and females, there are some data to suggest that vocal tract differences among boys and girls do not necessarily mirror those seen in adults. For example, since Walker and Kowalski (1972) and Hunter and Garn (1972) have shown that mandibular length is highly similar among males and females prior to puberty, the two sexes probably do not differ markedly with respect to oral cavity size. There is some indication that boys

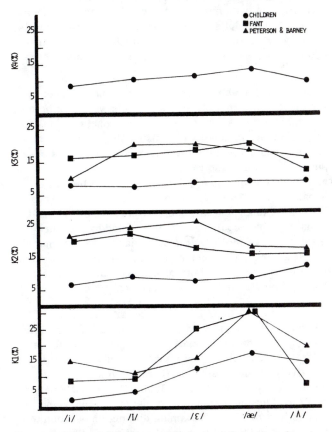

FIG. 2. Formant scale factors (K-factors) for pre- and postadolescent speakers (after Fant, 1973).

and girls differ with respect to pharynx length. Inspection of King's (1952) longitudinal cephalometric data shows that the portion of the pharynx extending from the most posterior part of the hard palate to the hyoid bone was consistently longer (2%–8%) in boys from the first through the tenth year. By age 16, this sexual difference was on the order of 13%. Assuming that the anatomic data cited above are generalizable to all males and females, it is likely that both the oral and pharyngeal cavities contribute to the overall sexual differences for adults, whereas for children it may only be the pharynx. This factor, coupled with the proportionately smaller sexual difference in pharynx size among children, may account for the overall 10% versus 19% sex difference seen here comparing children and adults. In this regard, it will be useful to determine whether the sexual distinction in children gradually widens as they progress through preadolescence and adolescence to eventually asymptote at the completion of puberty, or whether the difference remains relatively stable until the onset of pubescence. We are currently collecting longitudinal data on these children to try to answer this question.

Inspection of the $F1$ K-factors in Fig. 2 shows that the pattern of sexual differences across the five vowels was generally similar for children and adults. The one point of marked disagreement occurred for the /ʌ/ vowel from the Fant (1973) data, although there was also some discrepancy in the /i/ data for adults. As can be seen in Fig. 2, the scale factors for both age groups were usually small for the close front vowels (3% and 5% for children and 9%–15% for adults) and large for the open front vowel /æ/ (16% for children and about 30% for adults). Averaged across the five vowels, the mean $F1$ K-factor was approximately 10% for preadolescent speakers and 16% and 18% for postadolescent speakers.

We suggested above that since the sexual differences for these children's close front vowels were within the hypothetical measurement error, the conclusion that a sexual dimorphism actually existed should remain tentative. It is noteworthy that the mean differences observed for men's and women's /i/ and /I/ vowels (40 and 31 Hz, respectively, for Peterson and Barney's speakers and 22 and 40 Hz for Fant's speakers) were also quite small, and particularly because of the adult female values, could have been affected by measurement error as well. On the other hand, the fact that investigators have found these small sexual distinctions in both children and adults makes it equally plausible that the measured differences are real.

Assuming that the $F1$ frequencies are valid, it is interesting to consider why the sexual distinctions for both age groups were small for /i/ and /I/ and large for /æ/. Because /æ/ is typically produced with a relatively unconstricted vocal tract and a large mouth opening (Stevens and House, 1955), the acoustic output would reflect the dimensions of the entire tube, and as a result, provide for maximum distinction between the two sexes on the basis of vocal tract size. Yet, for both age groups the extent of the sexual differences in $F1$ of

/æ/ was larger than would be predicted on the basis of anatomic factors alone. Several investigators have suggested that sex-specific articulatory behaviors may have developed to further exhance the perceptual distinction between males and females (Mattingly, 1966; Sachs et al., 1973; Fant, 1975; Bennett and Weinberg, 1979a,b). For example, males might adopt a more pronounced degree of lip protrusion to effectively lengthen the vocal tract and bring about a further lowering of all formant frequencies. Although lip rounding is the most commonly cited example, it is known that most of the English vowels can be produced with a variety of other articulatory behaviors and still retain their phonemic identity (Stevens and House, 1955; House and Stevens, 1955). The /æ/ vowel is a particularly good candidate for displaying sex-dependent articulatory differences because it is the only one whose phonemic identity is relatively insensitive to large variations in the area of the mouth opening as well as area and location of the constriction (Stevens and House, 1955). Sexual differences in the width and height of the lip opening and/or amount of jaw opening during the production of /æ/ represent an additional factor to explain the large $F1$ scale factor because movement of $F1$ is sensitive to changes in the area of the mouth opening (Stevens and House, 1955; Lindblom and Sundberg, 1971). As suggested in a previous report (Bennett and Weinberg, 1979a,b), the lower $F1$ frequency of male speakers' /æ/ vowels may also reflect the fact that they used smaller mouth openings than females. Larynx lowering could also bring about a small reduction in $F1$ of /æ/ (Lindblom and Sundberg, 1971). In short, there are at least three factors (sexual differences in vocal tract size, size of the mouth opening, and vertical larynx adjustments) that could have helped create the large $F1$ K-factor for the /æ/ vowel.

As indicated, the smallest sexual differences in $F1$ occurred for /i/ and /I/. Fant (1960; 1973) has suggested that $F1$ of the close front vowels is largely dependent upon the tongue constriction and the pharynx. Given the assumption that males and females differ in terms of pharyngeal dimensions and the possibility that the distinction could be further enhanced by vertical laryngeal adjustments, one might expect the sexual differences for both children and adults to be large. Since they are not, it is probable that the narrow tongue constriction exerted the primary influence on $F1$. Stevens and House (1955) have shown that an identifiable /i/ requires a narrow tongue constriction near the front of the mouth, and that there is little opportunity for variation without changing the identity of the vowel. Although both /i/ and /I/ can be produced over a relatively large range of mouth openings and some variation in the location of the constriction, the frequency of $F1$ is largely unaffected as long as the constriction is relatively narrow. Since potential sexual differences in the size of the mouth opening or location of the constriction would not strongly influence $F1$ values, and since the influence of the pharynx is apparently diminished when the constriction is narrow, $F1$ sexual differences for /i/ and /I/ would be predictably small for both children and adults. The finding that the sexual distinctions, though small for both age groups, were largest for adults is most likely a result of the proportionately smaller sexual differences in pharynx size among boys and girls.

The $F2$ K-factors for children and adults may be examined in Fig. 2. The first factor worthy of note is that the vowel dependent sexual differences were not nearly as pronounced as those seen for $F1$ values. Averaged across the five vowels, the mean scale factor for adult $F2$ frequencies was approximately 21%, while for these 7 and 8 year olds it was about 10%. Male/female differences in pharyngeal dimensions were probably largely responsible for the sexual distinctions in $F2$ because the second formant of most of these vowels (particularly the high vowels) is related to a standing wave resonance of the pharynx (Fant, 1973). However, Fant (1979) has recently suggested that for children's /i/ vowels both the mouth and the pharynx may contribute equally to $F2$ and $F3$. It is also possible that sex-specific articulatory behaviors played a supplementary role. The Stevens and House (1955) articulatory data indicate that all of the vowels studied here (especially /i/ and /I/) can be produced with considerable variation in the size of the mouth opening, and that $F2$ frequencies are sensitive to such changes. It is also known that $F2$ values of most vowels are strongly influenced by vertical larynx adjustments (Lindblom and Sundberg, 1971).

Examination of the scale factors for $F3$ (Fig. 2) shows that although there was some discrepancy in the /i/ and /ʌ/ data for adults, the pattern of sexual differences across the various vowels was again similar for both age groups. For preadolescent speakers, the overall sexual distinction was approximately 8.5%, while for adults it was about 17%. Because reliable $F4$ data for adult vowels were unavailable, meaningful comparisons of the two age groups were not possible. The K-factors for these children's $F4$ frequencies (Fig. 2) averaged about 10%, and like the sexual differences observed for $F3$ values, probably occurred chiefly as a result of sexual differences in pharynx size. The potential influence of sex-specific articulatory behaviors on $F3$ values was probably small because variations in larynx height and size of the mouth opening do not have a pronounced effect on the frequency location of this formant (Lindblom and Sundberg, 1971; Stevens and House, 1955). However, there are data to indicate that larynx lowering has a somewhat stronger influence on $F4$ values (Lindblom and Sundberg, 1971).

C. Relationships between children's vowel formant frequencies and indices of body size

The present finding have been interpreted to suggest that overall differences in these children's formant frequencies occurred chiefly as a result of sexual differences in vocal tract size, but that sex-specific articulatory behaviors could have further enhanced the sexual distinction. Since direct estimates of these children's vocal tract dimensions were not possible, it seemed advantageous to determine whether more easily attainable indices of physical size such as sitting and standing height, body weight, and neck circumference were related to their vowel formant frequencies. It was reasoned that if such measures were strongly correlated with the

acoustic data there would be additional support for the inference that these boys and girls actually differed with respect to vocal tract size. It was also hoped that these measures could be used in conjunction with acoustic data to determine how changes in overall body size relate to the growth of the vocal tract as children progress from preadolescence through puberty.

Physical data obtained from these boys and girls are summarized in Table III. On the average, boys were approximately 7 cm taller and 4 kg heavier than girls. With respect to sitting height and neck circumference measures, the average sexual differences were approximately 4 and 1.50 cm, respectively. These findings are in agreement with data from the child development literature showing that the physical size of males is somewhat larger than that of the female prior to the onset of puberty (Nelson, 1975; Krogman, 1972).

Multiple correlation analyses were used to examine the relationship between the various physical measures and vowel formant frequencies. Separate analyses were completed for each formant of each vowel. In each analysis, the independent variables were the four indices of body size, while the dependent variable was the formant frequency value. The exact number of subjects included in each analysis varied from vowel to vowel because cases with missing values are automatically eliminated from all calculations for a particular vowel so that correlations could be based on the same universe of data.

One of the difficulties encountered in multiple regression is that if some or all of the independent variables are highly correlated with each other, the relative importance of individual variables, as determined by the partial regression coefficients, becomes difficult to assess (Kim and Kohout, 1975). Such a situation existed for the present analyses, i.e., all of the physical indices were significantly correlated with each other (range in R's $= 0.53-0.80$) and duplicated one another to some extent because each is measuring some aspect of body size. Because of these circumstances, the data were analyzed according to the percentage of the variance in formant frequency values accounted for by the various physical measures operating jointly as opposed to the singular contribution of each variable obtained via a stepwise solution.

The simple correlations between each of the measures of body size and the various vowel formants are shown in Table IV. Although the magnitude of the correlations varied as a function of the formant and the vowel, the vast majority (93%) were significant and ranged between

TABLE III. Physical measurements for 7 and 8 year old preadolescent children ($n = 42$).

	Boys Mean	Boys S.D.	Girls Mean	Girls S.D.
Standing height (cm)	132.63	6.20	125.81	5.13
Sitting height (cm)	70.16	3.18	66.53	3.12
Weight (kg)	30.76	5.68	26.61	4.09
Neck circumference (cm)	28.55	2.16	27.08	1.42

TABLE IV. Simple correlations between measures of body size and vowel formant frequencies.

		Sitting height	Standing height	Weight	Neck circumference
/i/	$F1$	−0.31	−0.41[a]	−0.12	−0.15
	$F2$	−0.75[a]	−0.64[a]	−0.61[a]	−0.63[a]
	$F3$	−0.66[a]	−0.55[a]	−0.51[a]	−0.43[a]
	$F4$	−0.77[a]	−0.68[a]	−0.63[a]	−0.60[a]
/I/	$F1$	−0.41[a]	−0.27	−0.06	−0.00
	$F2$	−0.78[a]	−0.61[a]	−0.65[a]	−0.69[a]
	$F3$	−0.67[a]	−0.75[a]	−0.69[a]	−0.53[a]
	$F4$	−0.77[a]	−0.67[a]	−0.55[a]	−0.49[a]
/ɛ/	$F1$	−0.56[a]	−0.53[a]	−0.58[a]	−0.48[a]
	$F2$	−0.61[a]	−0.54[a]	−0.61[a]	−0.59[a]
	$F3$	−0.66[a]	−0.67[a]	−0.69[a]	−0.64[a]
	$F4$	−0.69[a]	−0.66[a]	−0.74[a]	−0.70[a]
/æ/	$F1$	−0.53[a]	−0.46[a]	−0.43[a]	−0.40[a]
	$F2$	−0.72[a]	−0.63[a]	−0.61[a]	−0.71[a]
	$F3$	−0.68[a]	−0.70[a]	−0.66[a]	−0.61[a]
	$F4$	−0.53[a]	−0.52[a]	−0.47[a]	−0.42[a]
/ʌ/	$F1$	−0.48[a]	−0.44[a]	−0.44[a]	−0.46[a]
	$F2$	−0.55[a]	−0.61[a]	−0.56[a]	−0.58[a]
	$F3$	−0.59[a]	−0.71[a]	−0.61[a]	−0.55[a]
	$F4$	−0.58[a]	−0.57[a]	−0.64[a]	−0.69[a]

[a] $p \leq 0.01$.

−0.41 and −0.78. It is also important to note that all of the correlations were negative, indicating that an increase in any given physical measure was usually associated with a decrease in the formant frequency value. While it is recognized that these correlations are by no means an exact test of the relationship between formant frequencies and vocal tract length, the data suggest that the larger overall size of male children also results in a larger vocal tract. Additional evidence to support this inference may be found in the fact that estimates of standing or sitting height, which would encorporate potential sexual differences in neck length, were usually correlated most strongly with formant frequencies (Table IV).

Results of the multiple correlation analyses, summarized in Table V, illustrate the dynamic relationship between indices of body size and the various acoustic measures. All of the multiple R's were significant and varied between −0.506–0.866. Viewed in another way, the percentage of the variance in formant frequencies accounted for by the physical measures combined ranged from 26%–75%, depending upon formant number and vowel category. Averaged across all measured for-

mants of all five vowels, the percentage of common variance was about 49%.

Assuming that these multiple correlations are an indirect reflection of the relationship between sexual differences in vocal tract size (and especially pharynx size) and vowel formants, it was not surprising to find that the multiple R^2's were smallest for $F1$ of /i/ and /I/ (28% and 26%). As suggested previously, the first formant of these vowels is most strongly influenced by the narrow tongue constriction and only secondarily by vocal tract dimensions. Male/female differences in physical size were also poor predictors of $F1$ values for the remaining vowels (range in $R^2 = 30\%–37\%$ of the variance). This finding suggests that factors other than those related to physical size exerted a sizable influence on the first formant of these children's vowels. If females used larger mouth openings than males (or if males rounded the lips or lowered the larynx) during the production of /ɛ/, /æ/, and /ʌ/, the differences would be reflected in $F1$ values. As a result, the magnitude of the correlations would be reduced because a proportion of the variance in acoustic data occurred for reasons other than sexual differences in vocal tract size.

TABLE V. Multiple correlations between measures of body size and vowel formant frequencies.

	/i/ Multiple R	R^2		/I/ Multiple R	R^2		/ɛ/ Multiple R	R^2		/æ/ Multiple R	R^2		/ʌ/ Multiple R	R^2
$F1$	−0.525[a]	28%	$F1$	−0.506[a]	26%	$F1$	−0.607[a]	37%	$F1$	−0.545[a]	30%	$F1$	−0.543[a]	30%
$F2$	−0.794[a]	63%	$F2$	−0.866[a]	75%	$F2$	−0.669[a]	45%	$F2$	−0.816[a]	67%	$F2$	−0.668[a]	45%
$F3$	−0.668[a]	45%	$F3$	−0.795[a]	63%	$F3$	−0.734[a]	54%	$F3$	−0.750[a]	56%	$F3$	−0.722[a]	52%
$F4$	−0.798[a]	64%	$F4$	−0.780[a]	61%	$F4$	−0.777[a]	60%	$F4$	−0.564[a]	32%	$F4$	−0.738[a]	54%
	$n = 27$			$n = 26$			$n = 27$			$n = 28$			$n = 29$	

[a] $p \leq 0.01$.

Relationships among $F2$, $F3$, and $F4$ and the various physical measures were substantially stronger. As can be seen in Table V, the multiple R^2's ranged between 32% and 75%, with the majority falling between 45% and 63%. These findings lend support to earlier suggestions that a male/female distinction in vocal tract size was the primary factor responsible for sexual differences in the higher formants of these children's vowels.

III. SUMMARY AND CONCLUSIONS

The purpose of this investigation was to measure the vowel formant frequency characteristics of a large group of preadolescent boys and girls, and describe relations between formant frequencies and body size.

At this age (7–8 years) the sexual dimorphism in vowel formant frequencies is well defined in a large majority of children. Averaged across all measured formants of all five vowels, the overall sexual distinction was about 10%. The range of differences extended from about 3% for $F1$ of /i/ to about 16% for $F1$ of /æ/. These findings were interpreted to suggest that overall differences in children's formant frequencies occurred chiefly as a result of sexual differences in pharynx size, but that sex-specific articulatory behaviors could have further enhanced the sexual distinctions. In particular, males may have used smaller jaw openings, more lip rounding, and/or a lower larynx position than females.

Gross indices of body size (sitting and standing height, body weight, and neck circumference) were always significantly related to these children' formant frequencies, suggesting that the larger overall size of male children also results in a larger vocal tract. The multiple correlations ranged between −0.506 and −0.866, with the various physical measures accounting for between 26% and 75% of the total variance in formant data.

ACKNOWLEDGMENTS

This research was supported in part by Biomedical Research Grant No. RR-07042 to the University of Maryland, from the Division of Research Resources, National Institites of Health, Public Health Service, and in part by the General Research Board, University of Maryland.

Bennett, S., and Weinberg, B. (1979a). "Sexual Characteristics of Preadolescent Children's Voices," J. Acoust. Soc. Am. 65, 179–189.

Bennett, S., and Weinberg, B. (1979b). "Acoustic Correlates of Perceived Sexual Identity in Preadolescent Children's Voices," J. Acoust. Soc. Am. 66, 989–1000.

Coleman, R. (1971). "Male and Female Voice Quality and Its Relationship to Vowel Formant Frequency," J. Speech Hear. Res. 14, 565–577.

Eguchi, S., and Hirsh, I. (1969). "Development of Speech Sounds in Children," Acta Otolaryngol. Suppl., 257.

Fant, G. (1973). Speech Sounds and Features (MIT, Cambridge, MA).

Fant, G. (1975). "Non-Uniform Vowel Normalization," Speech Transmission Laboratory Quarterly Progress Status Report, Royal Institute of Technology, Stockholm, Sweden, 1–19.

Fant, G. (1979). "The Relations Between Area Functions and the Acoustic Signal," Paper presented at the 1979 International Congress of Phonnetic Sciences, Copenhagan.

House, A., and Stevens, K. (1955). "Auditory Testing of a Simplified Description of Vowel Articulation," J. Acoust. Soc. Am. 27, 882–887.

Hunter, W., and Garn, S. (1972). "Disproportionate Sexual Dimorphism In the Human Face," Am. J. Phys. Anthropol. 36, 133–138.

Kent, R., and Forner, L. (1979). "Developmental Study of Vowel Formant Frequencies in an Imitation Task," J. Acoust. Soc. Am. 65, 208–217.

Kim, J., and Kohout, F. (1975). "Multiple Regression Analysis; Subprogram Regression," in Statistical Package for the Social Sciences (McGraw–Hill, New York), 2nd ed.

King, E. (1952). "A Roentgenographic Study of Pharyngeal Growth," Angle Orthod., 22, 23–37.

Krogman, W. (1972). Child Growth (University of Michigan, Ann Arbor).

Lass, N., Waters, L., and Tyson, V. (1976). "Speaker Sex Identification from Voiced, Whispered, and Filtered Isolated Vowels," J. Acoust. Soc. Am. 59, 675–678.

Lindblom, B. (1962). "Accuracy and Limitations of Sonograph Measurements," in Proceedings of the Fourth International Congress of Phonetic Sciences (Mouton, The Hague, The Netherlands).

Lindblom, B., and Sundberg, J. (1971). "Acoustical Consequences of Lip, Tongue, Jaw and Larynx Movements," J. Acoust. Soc. Am. 50, 1166–1179.

Marshall, G. (1972). "Sex Typing of Speech of Prepubertal Children," Ph.D. dissertation, Louisiana State University.

Mattingly, I. (1966). "Speaker Variation and Vocal Tract Size," J. Acoust. Soc. Am. 39, 1219 (A).

Moses, P. (1954). The Voice of Neurosis (Grune & Stratton, New York).

Nelson, W. (1975). Textbook of Pediatrics (Saunders, Philadelphia).

Peterson, G. (1952). "The Information-Bearing Elements of Speech," J. Acoust. Soc. Am. 24, 629–637.

Peterson, G., and Barney, H. (1952). "Control Methods Used in the Study of Vowels," J. Acoust. Soc. Am. 24, 175–184.

Potter, R., and Steinberg, J. (1950). "Toward the Specification of Speech," J. Acoust. Soc. Am. 22, 807–820.

Sachs, J., Lieberman, P., and Erickson, D. (1973). "Anatomical and Cultural Determinants of Male and Female Speech," in Language Attitudes: Current Trends and Prospects, edited by R. Shuy and R. Fasold (Georgetown University, Washington, DC).

Schwartz, M. (1968). "Identification of Speaker Sex from Isolated Voiceless Fricatives," J. Acoust. Soc. Am. 43, 1178.

Stevens, K., and House, A. (1955). "Development of a Quantitative Description of Vowel Articulation," J. Acoust. Soc. Am. 27, 484–493.

Sundberg, J. (1970). "Formant Structure and Articulation of Spoken and Sung Vowels," Folia Phoniatr. 22, 28–48.

Walker, G., and Howalski, C., (1972). "On the Growth of the Mandible," Am. J. Phys. Anthropol. 36, 111–118.

Weinberg, B., and Bennett, S. (1971). "Speaker Sex Recognition of 5- and 6-Year Old Children's Voices," J. Acoust. Soc. Am. 50, 1210–1213.

Developmental study of vowel formant frequencies in an imitation task

R. D. Kent and L. L. Forner

Department of Communicative Disorders, University of Wisconsin, Madison, Wisconsin 53706

(Received 14 March 1978; revised 28 June 1978)

Imitations of ten synthesized vowels were recorded from 33 speakers including men, women, and children. The first three formant frequencies of the imitations were estimated from spectrograms and considered with respect to developmental patterns in vowel formant structure, uniform scale factors for vowel normalization, and formant variability. Strong linear effects were observed in the group data for imitations of most of the English vowels studied, and straight lines passing through the origin provided a satisfactory fit to linear $F_1 - F_2$ plots of the English vowel data. Logarithmic transformations of the formant frequencies helped substantially to equalize the dispersion of the group data for different vowels, but formant scale factors were observed to vary somewhat with both formant number and vowel identity. Variability of formant frequency was least for F_1 (s.d. of 60 Hz or less for English vowels of adult males) and about equal for F_2 and F_3 (s.d. of 100 Hz or less for English vowels of adult males).

PACS numbers: 43.70.Gr, 43.70.Bk, 43.70.Jt, 43.70.Ve

INTRODUCTION

A problem of long standing in acoustic phonetics is that of reconciling formant-frequency measurements of vowels with their phonetic equivalence. This problem was given classic portrayal by Peterson and Barney (1952) when they plotted the first and second formant-frequency measurements of ten vowels produced by 76 speakers, including men, women, and children (see Figs. 8 and 9 in their article). The vowel regions for the 76 talkers were characterized both by considerable spread of formant frequencies within a vowel category and frequent overlap of formant frequencies across vowel categories. Some 25 years later, the phonetic identification of vowels from the formant frequencies of a heterogeneous sample of speakers continues to be a research challenge (see, for example, the recent papers by Lennig and Hindle, 1977; Sroka, 1977; Broad and Wakita, 1977).

The normalization of formant frequencies for the purpose of demonstrating vowel equivalence has several possible complications. Fant (1966) noted that the vocal tracts of adult males differ from those of women and children in having a proportionately longer pharyngeal tube, and this anatomical disparity makes questionable the application of constant scale or correction factors. Another problem in the assignment of scale factors is that these factors may vary with vowel identity or with formant-frequency number (Fant, 1966). Even the data that have been used in the study of vowel normalization have been questioned because of possible dialectal differences among the speakers (Nordstrom and Lindblom, 1975; Lennig and Hindle, 1977). A number of solutions to the problem of vowel normalization have been proposed (Mol, 1963; Fujisaki and Kawashima, 1968; Gerstman, 1968; Nordstrom and Lindblom, 1975; Broad, 1976; Lennig and Hindle, 1977; Sroka, 1977), but for the most part these procedures have not been applied to a data base representing a specified wide range of speaker ages. For example, Peterson and Barney (1952) did not specify the ages of the children in their sample of speakers; nonetheless, their study remains one of the few sources of formant-frequency data for a large and heterogeneous set of talkers.

Furthermore, the available acoustic data on children's speech are not adequate to describe the details of developmental changes in the formant frequencies of different vowels. Although vowel formant frequencies for various ages of children have been reported (e.g., Eguchi and Hirsh, 1969), generalization and interpretation of the results is limited by the fact that the vowels were produced in varying phonetic contexts. Therefore, acoustic documentation of developmental changes in vowel production requires additional formant-frequency data for several age groups of children, preferably for isolated vowels or vowels embedded in a fixed phonetic context. It also is desirable to control for dialectal differences in vowel production, for these differences may confound the problem of vowel normalization.

This paper presents data on the imitation of 15 synthesized formant patterns representing five English vowels and ten other vowels chosen to sample the F_1-F_2-F_3 space. Synthesized vowels were used as stimuli because their acoustic characteristics could be specified exactly to satisfy the intended formant patterns and because control could be exercised over such factors as vowel duration, fundamental frequency contour, and diphthongization. The 33 speakers who served as subjects represented both sexes and ranged in age from 4 years to young adulthood. The chief purposes of this report are to (1) describe developmental variations in vowel formant frequencies, (2) evaluate possibilities for vowel normalization by uniform scaling factors, and (3) determine intersubject and intrasubject variability in the formant frequencies of vowel imitations. Another purpose of the experiment was to investigate vocal imitation as a developing sensorimotor skill, but this issue has been discussed in previous reports (Kent, 1978 and in press).

I. EXPERIMENTAL PROCEDURES

A. Subjects

The 33 speakers were grouped by age and sex as follows: five young adult men, four young adult women, five 12-year-old girls, five 6-year-old boys, five 6-

TABLE I. F_1, F_2, and F_3 frequencies (in Hz) of the synthetic vowel targets used in the limitation experiment.

		English vowels			
	[i]	[æ]	[ɑ]	[u]	[ɝ]
F_1	270	660	730	300	490
F_2	2290	1720	1090	870	1350
F_3	3010	2410	2440	2240	1690

		Arbitrary vowels			
	1	2	3	4	5
F_1	695	460	285	435	400
F_2	1400	1915	1580	855	1450
F_3	2425	2515	2625	2325	2300

year-old girls, three 4-year-old boys, and six 4-year-old girls. Actually, four 4-year-old boys participated in the study, but one boy was excluded from the analyses because his unusually high fundamental frequency resulted in strong formant-harmonic interactions in the spectrograms of his vowels. Because the primary purpose of this study was to obtain formant-frequency data for a variety of speakers, it was not considered essential to have an equal number of subjects in each group.

B. Stimuli

The ten synthesized vowels had formant-frequency ranges for F_1, F_2, and F_3 bounded roughly by the mean values that Peterson and Barney (1952) recorded for adult males' productions of the vowels [i u ɑ æ ɝ]. In fact, five of the synthesized vowels were modeled after Peterson and Barney's mean data for these English vowels. The other five vowels did not necessarily have a phonemic identity in English (most were variably labeled in a preliminary task of identification by phonetically trained listeners) and were selected because they gave a fairly uniform sampling of F_1-F_2-F_3 space. Because the stimuli presented for imitation were not necessarily English vowels, the subjects had to attend to the actual character of each vowel to make a satisfactory imitation. None of the subjects, even in the youngest age group, appeared to have any difficulty with this task. The first three formant frequencies of the stimuli are listed in Table I and depicted in Fig. 1.

The stimuli had a duration of 250 ms and were shaped with an amplitude rise–fall time of 30 ms. The fundamental frequency pattern was a linear ramp falling from 130 to 105 Hz. The vowels were synthesized with five formants but only the first three were variable in frequency (F_4 and F_5 were fixed at 3500 and 4500 Hz, respectively). The bandwidths of the five formants were, in ascending order of formant number, 50, 70, 110, 170, and 250 Hz. Because a series model (Klatt, 1972) was used in synthesizing the vowels, the relative formant amplitudes were determined by the formant frequencies.

A total of 50 synthetic vowel stimuli were presented for imitation, including five tokens of each vowel stim-

ulus. The stimuli were recorded in a quasi-random order, separated by a silent interval of approximately 12 s.

C. Instructions to subjects

The subjects were asked to say the same sounds that they would hear from a loudspeaker but they were informed that they should use their own natural voice pitch. With some coaching, even the youngest children understood this instruction. A short sample of the tape was played before the imitations were recorded to acquaint the subjects with the nature of the stimuli. One tape recorder was used for playback of the stimuli and another was used to record the subjects' imitations. The children were told they would be given candy or a toy at the end of the experiment.

D. Acoustic analysis

Formant frequencies of the vowel imitations were estimated from spectrograms made with a Kay Elemetrics 7029A Sona-Graph equipped with 45-, 300-, and 500-Hz analyzing filters and a frequency counter. For any given speaker, the spectrograms were made with the filter that yielded the optimum formant resolution. Narrowband section displays also were obtained. The formant frequencies were identified by locating the approximate center of formant bars on wideband (300 or 500 Hz) spectrograms or by fitting smooth curves to the narrowband (45 Hz) amplitude sections. Comparison of the two analyses was accomplished to arrive at a final estimate of the formant frequencies. All acoustic measurements were made by the first author. The reliability of measurement, determined for two groups of

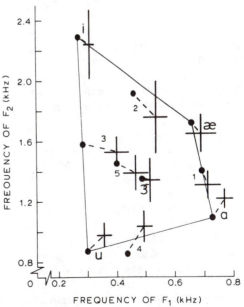

FIG. 1. F_1–F_2 plot showing ten imitation stimuli (filled circles) and the mean imitation responses of five men (crosses). The center of each cross indicates the mean F_1 and F_2 values for the vowel and the length of each arm represents 1 standard deviation (i.e., the horizontal arms are ±1 s.d. for F_1 and the vertical arms are ±1 s.d. for F_2). The stimuli represented are the English vowels [i u ɑ æ ɝ] and the arbitrary vowels 1–5.

speakers—adult males and 4-year-old children—was calculated for repeated formant-frequency measures for selected spectrograms. The standard deviation s_D of the measurement differences, the mean difference $\overline{D}$, and the standard error of the mean difference $s_{\overline{D}}$ were determined for the first three formant frequencies of 30 spectrograms for each group. The following formulas (Snedecor and Cochran, 1967) were used to compute s_D, $s_{\overline{D}}$, and a Student's t, the latter to determine if the mean differences were different from 0:

$$s_D = \left\{ \left[\frac{\sum\limits_{i}^{n} D_i^2 - \left(\sum\limits_{i}^{n} D_i\right)^2 / n}{n-1} \right]^{1/2} \right\} \quad ,$$

$$s_{\overline{D}} = s_D / n^{1/2} \quad ,$$

$$t = \overline{D} / s_{\overline{D}} , \quad \text{with } (n-1) \text{ d.f. } ,$$

where n is the number of remeasured spectrograms and D_i is the difference between any original and replicate measurement.

The sample mean difference, standard deviation of the differences, and standard error of the mean differences were as follows for the adult males: F_1; 13, 54, 11 Hz; F_2; 19, 63, 13 Hz; F_3; −8, 62, 13 Hz. For the 4-year-old children, the same statistics were: F_1; 15, 59, 11 Hz; F_2; −13, 68, 13 Hz; F_3; −6, 52, 10 Hz. None of the t values reached significance at the 0.10 level, indicating that the differences between replicate measurements were essentially randomly distributed around zero. Larger measurement errors are expected for the children than for the adults, given the age-dependent decline in fundamental frequency and the fact that the hypothetical error in the estimation of formant frequencies from spectrograms is equal to or greater than $f_0/4$ (Lindblom, 1972). The accuracy of formant-frequency measurement also was assessed by comparing the spectrographic measurements with measurements derived from a linear prediction analysis (Markel, 1971). The linear prediction analysis, which became available late in the study, was used to determine the formant frequencies for three of the 12-year-old girls. The statistics $\overline{D}$, s_D, and $s_{\overline{D}}$, computed with the formulas given above, were as follows for the comparison of spectrographic and linear prediction analyses for the first three formant frequencies; subject 12-a: F_1 (−4, 70, 11 Hz), F_2 (−2, 88, 13 Hz), F_3 (3, 81, 14 Hz); subject 12-b: F_1 (−17, 45, 6 Hz), F_2 (17, 96, 14 Hz), F_3 (−10, 81, 13 Hz); subject 12-c: F_1 (−5, 73, 9 Hz), F_2 (−34, 115, 16 Hz), F_3 (−58, 128, 19 Hz). These values are based on at least 90% of the imitations recorded for each subject; the remainder were eliminated from consideration, usually because the linear prediction analysis missed a formant or identified one spuriously. Of the nine t values, three were significant at the 0.05 level, with the LPC measures being lower in frequency than the spectrographic measures. These error estimates probably are liberal in that they include several sources of variability, including differences in the sampling points for the analysis as well as differences in the techniques of analysis. That is, although measures

for both analyses generally were made for the last half of a vowel segment, the measures did not apply to exactly the same instant within the vowel. Differences in sampling point can contribute to large differences in formant frequency whenever the productions are diphthongized, as sometimes happened with [æ], for example.

II. RESULTS AND DISCUSSION

A. Isovowel lines in linear F_1-F_2 and F_2-F_3 plots

The correspondence between ten imitation targets and the group means for imitations of these targets by adult males can be judged from the F_1-F_2 plot in Fig. 1. The F_1-F_2 values of the stimuli are represented by the filled circles and the F_1-F_2 means of the imitations are given by the intersections of the crossed lines. The horizontal and vertical lines that form each cross are ± one standard deviation for F_1 and F_2, respectively. Generally speaking, the F_1-F_2 means for the men subjects closely approximate the F_1-F_2 values of the stimuli. The major discrepancy between the targets and the imitation means is an overall shift in the vowel quadrilateral of the imitation responses to the right, in the direction of increased F_1 frequency.

The first two formant frequencies for imitations of the English vowels [i u ɑ æ] by all 33 subjects are shown in the scattergram of Fig. 2. Each point represents the mean of five imitations by one of the 33 speakers. Data for [ɝ] are not included because they overlapped extensively with the data for the other vowels. With the exception of the results for [æ], the points are arranged in elongated clusters oriented diagonally in the F_1-F_2 plane. Because it appeared that a straight line would fit the clusterings for [i u ɑ], straight-line regression was attempted using the method of least squares. The

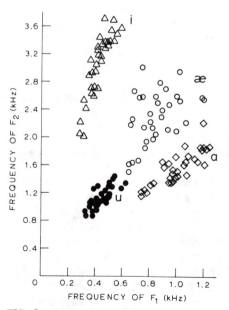

FIG. 2. Scattergram of the F_1 and F_2 frequencies for imitations of the English vowels [i u ɑ æ] by 33 men, women, and children. Each data point represents the mean for five imitations of the vowel by a given speaker.

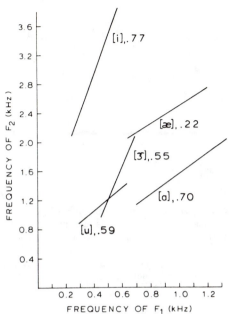

FIG. 3. Linear regression determined by the method of least squares for the F_1 and F_2 frequencies of imitations of the English vowels [i u ɑ æ ɝ] by the 33 speakers. The r^2 coefficient of determination is shown for each regression line.

results are depicted in Fig. 3, which shows the regression line determined for each vowel ([ɝ] included) as well as the r^2 coefficient of determination. With the exception of the result for [æ], the r^2 values are larger than 0.5, which means that the least-squares lines account for more than half of the variability for four of the five vowels. Thus, linear effects are substantial in the F_1–F_2 variability for four of the five vowels.

It was concluded in earlier reports based on partial analyses of the current data that straight lines through the origin provide a satisfactory fit to group means for each of the English vowels [i u ɑ æ ɝ] (Kent, 1978). To test this possibility statistically, a t test described by Snedecor and Cochran (1967) was used to evaluate the null hypothesis that a straight line determined for each English vowel passes through the origin. The formula for the test of significance is

$$t=(\overline{Y}-b\overline{X})/s_{y \cdot x}\left(1/n+\overline{X}^2\Big/\sum x^2\right)^{1/2}, \quad \text{with } (n-2)\,\text{d.f.}$$

where b is the least squares estimate of the slope β in the linear model

$$y=\alpha+\beta x+\epsilon:$$

$$b=\sum XY\Big/\sum X^2,$$

and $s_{y \cdot x}$ is the residual mean square,

$$s_{y \cdot x}=\left[Y^2-\left(\sum XY\right)^2\Big/\sum x^2\right]\Big/(n-1).$$

In these equations X is taken to be a F_1 value and Y is taken to be a F_2 value.

If a straight line through the origin is a satisfactory fit, then the linear model given above reduces to $y=\beta x$

$+\epsilon$, where β is the slope of the regression line and ϵ is a normally distributed random variable. None of the t values reached significance ($p>0.30$), so the null hypothesis that the lines pass through the origin cannot be rejected. The estimate of the slope β for each vowel is: [i], 7.11; [u], 2.48; [ɑ], 1.545; [æ], 2.65; and [ɝ], 2.79. These lines are shown together with the F_1–F_2 means for each age–sex group in Fig. 4. This result confirms Mol's (1963) suggestion that straight lines passing through the origin are a good approximation to the F_1–F_2 values for different vowels produced by a variety of speakers. Mol interpreted the lines passing through the origin as evidence for a principle of "axial growth," in which development of the vocal tract has a uniformity that is reflected by regular changes in the formant patterns of different vowels. Perhaps the most useful aspect of Mol's scheme is that it allows the vowel spaces of different speakers to be compared along fixed vectors in F_1–F_2 space, with an easy extrapolation for subjects who fall outside (longer or shorter vocal tracts) of an existing subject set. One area of application is the acoustic examination of vowels produced by persons with speech disorders, as the rays shown in Fig. 4 offer a quick, although approximate, test of the adequacy of a speaker's vowel F_1–F_2 patterns.

A scattergram of the F_2 and F_3 frequencies for imitations of the five English vowels is given in Fig. 5. As in Fig. 2, each point is the mean for five imitations of each vowel by one of the 33 speakers (except for vowel [ɝ] for which two of the 4-year-olds could not make a satisfactory phonemic production as judged by the investigators). Regression lines again were determined by the method of least squares, and the results are illustrated in Fig. 6. The r^2 coefficients of determina-

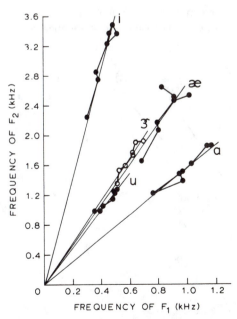

FIG. 4. F_1–F_2 regression lines for the English vowels [i u ɑ æ ɝ] according to the linear equation $Y=\beta x+\epsilon$. The straight lines, all of which pass through the origin, are determined with $b=\sum XY/\sum X^2$ as the estimate of the slope β, where X is an F_1 value and Y is an F_2 value.

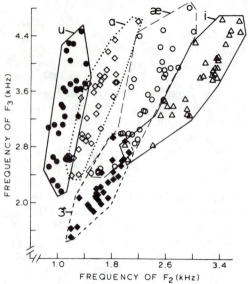

FIG. 5. Scattergram of the F_2 and F_3 frequencies for imitations of the English vowels [i u ɑ æ ɝ] by 33 men, women, and children. Each data point represents the mean for five imitations of the vowel by a given speaker.

tion are larger than 0.70 for each vowel except [u] (for which Fig. 5 shows a rather unsystematic variation in a narrow F_2 range). Thus, for four of the five vowels, the regression lines account for 70% or more of the variance in the group data. Calculation of the linear regression of F_3 on combined F_1 and F_2 resulted in small increases in the r^2 value (increments of 0.02 or less) except for vowels [u] and [æ], which had increments of 0.23 and 0.11, respectively. Thus, for the F_2–F_3 values, as with the F_1–F_2 values, linear effects are strong in the group formant data.

B. Formant scaling and logarithmic transformations

Attempts at vowel normalization by uniform scaling typically have involved the derivation of constant speaker-

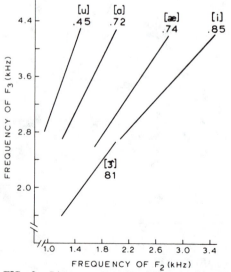

FIG. 6. Linear regression determined by the method of least squares for the F_2 and F_3 frequencies of imitations of the English vowels [i u ɑ æ ɝ] by the 33 speakers. The r^2 coefficient of determination is shown for each regression line.

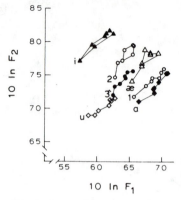

FIG. 7. Logarithmic transformations of the group F_1–F_2 means for imitations of the five English vowels and the two arbitrary vowels numbered 1, 2. The subject groups are men, women, 12-year-old girls, 6 year-old boys, 6-year-old girls, 4-year-old boys, and 4-year-old girls. Lines have been drawn to connect the mean data points for each vowel.

dependent scale factors that are used to transform the F_1 and F_2 frequencies (Fant, 1966). The success of a multiplicative scale factor rests upon a formant-frequency transformation that yields approximately equal dispersions for different vowels (Lennig and Hindle, 1977). Uniform scaling by multiplication may be regarded as a process of adding a speaker-dependent constant to logarithmically transformed F_1 and F_2 frequencies (Nearey, 1977). Thus, the potential success of uniform scaling procedures can be gauged by determining the extent to which vowel dispersion is equalized in a log-transformed F_1–F_2 space.

Figure 7 shows the log-transformed mean values of the F_1 and F_2 frequencies for the seven age–sex groups producing the English vowels [i u æ ɑ ɝ] and arbitrary vowels 1 and 2. Comparison of this log-transformed F_1–F_2 plot with the linear F_1–F_2 plot (Fig. 4) shows that the transformation does indeed make the vowel dispersions more nearly the same. For example, whereas the dispersion for [u] is markedly compressed relative to that for [i] in the linear F_1–F_2 plot, the dispersions for these two vowels are nearly equal in Fig. 7. The effect of the logarithmic transformation on the F_2 and F_3 frequencies is illustrated in Fig. 8. This log plot offers a somewhat equivalent dispersion for the five vowels, but the remaining differences probably are not negligible (for example, notice the compression for [ɝ] relative to [æ]).

These results with a logarithmic transformation of formant frequencies support Lennig and Hindle's (1977) conclusion that a logarithmic transformation can greatly reduce the differences in dispersion among vowels, although this transformation may not yield an exact equivalence of dispersion. The outcome perhaps is sufficiently satisfying to hold promise for uniform scaling factors, which will be considered again in the next section of this paper. Further work is needed to determine if the logarithmic transformation also serves to segregate the F_1–F_2 values by vowel category. This issue was considered by Lennig and Hindle (1977).

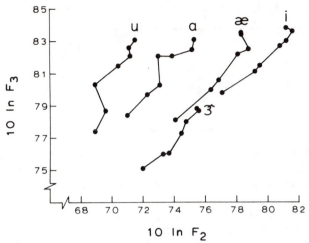

FIG. 8. Logarithmic transformations of the group F_2–F_3 means for imitations of the five English vowels [i u ɑ æ ɝ]. The subject groups are men, women, 12-year-old girls, 6-year-old boys, 6-year-old girls, 4-year-old boys, and 4-year-old girls. Lines have been drawn to connect the mean data points for each vowel.

Given the orderly arrangement of the vowels in the log F_2–F_3 plot of Fig. 8, it seemed useful to explore this graphical presentation with additional vowels. To reduce clutter in the graph, only the F_2–F_3 means for adult males and 4-year-olds, who represent the extremes of the F_2–F_3 data, were plotted. The resulting graph, shown in Fig. 9, illustrates the F_2–F_3 patterns for the five English vowels and the five arbitrary vowels 1–5. A straight line has been drawn to depict the pattern of differences between men (filled circles) and children (unfilled circles) within the plane. The nine nonretroflex vowels are arranged in a fairly systematic

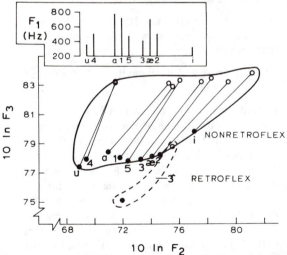

FIG. 9. Log F_2–F_3 plot of the means for adult males (filled circles) and 4-year-old children (unfilled circles) imitating the five English vowels and the five arbitrary vowels 1–5. The two mean data points for each vowel are connected by a line to show the orientation of the data in the plane. A closed curve has been drawn around the F_2–F_3 values for the nine nonretroflex vowels and another closed curve has been drawn around the data for the retroflex vowel [ɝ]. The inset shows the F_1 means for the adult males' imitations of the nine nonretroflex vowels.

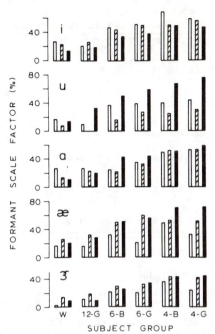

FIG. 10. Formant-frequency scale factors calculated for five English vowels produced by women, 12-year-old girls, 6-year-old boys, 6-year-old girls, 4-year-old boys, and 4-year-old girls, using the means for adult males as reference values. Within each group, the scale factors k_1, k_2, and k_3 (for the first three formants) are shown by the unfilled bar, striped bar, and filled bar, respectively.

fashion, with the log F_2 frequency increasing in the following order: rounded back vowels, unrounded back vowels, central vowels, low front vowels, and high front vowels. The log F_3 frequencies have a relatively small variation within the group of nonretroflex vowels, but, as expected, the log F_3 frequency for the retroflex [ɝ] is much lower in frequency than that for the nonretroflex vowels. These features make it appear that the vowel [ɝ] occupies a different level on the log F_2–F_3 plane than do the nonretroflex vowels (also see Broad and Wakita, 1977). The mean F_1 frequencies of the nine nonretroflex vowels produced by the adult males are shown in the inset graph of Fig. 8. The F_1 frequency undergoes two increasing–decreasing cycles when the vowels are arranged in ascending order of their F_2 frequencies.

C. Formant scale factors

To describe the developmental changes in the first three formant frequencies, formant scale factors were calculated according to Fant's (1966) method, using the formula

$$k_n = [(F_n / \mathrm{ref}_n) - 1] \times 100,$$

where k_n is the scale factor in percent, F_n is a formant-frequency value, ref_n is the reference value for a given formant, and n is the formant number. The formant scale factors k_1, k_2, and k_3 are graphed in Fig. 10, which shows results determined for six age–sex groups using the means for adult males as reference values. For each age–sex group, the magnitudes of the scale factors k_1, k_2, and k_3 are plotted in sequence as an un-

TABLE II. Intersubject standard deviations for the formant scale factors k_1, k_2, k_3 of the major age–sex groups. The mean formant frequencies of the adult males were used as reference values in the computations.

Age–sex group	[i]			[u]			[ɑ]			[æ]			[ɝ]		
	k_1	k_2	k_3	k_1	k_2	k_3	k_1	k_2	k_3	k_1	k_2	k_3	k_1	k_2	k_3
4-year-olds (male and female)	0.20	0.09	0.10	0.21	0.09	0.17	0.08	0.12	0.13	0.21	0.20	0.15	0.12	0.08	0.13
6-year-olds (females)	0.12	0.05	0.11	0.10	0.18	0.03	0.14	0.09	0.08	0.18	0.05	0.08	0.06	0.10	0.09
6-year-olds (males)	0.08	0.05	0.05	0.09	0.10	0.08	0.09	0.10	0.04	0.26	0.06	0.09	0.10	0.16	0.13
12-year-olds (females)	0.05	0.10	0.07	0.05	0.04	0.02	0.12	0.09	0.07	0.09	0.08	0.09	0.07	0.08	0.04
Adult females	0.08	0.06	0.02	0.07	0.09	0.01	0.01	0.05	0.04	0.14	0.06	0.01	0.02	0.08	0.03

filled bar, striped bar, and filled bar. Intersubject standard deviations for the scale factors are compiled by age–sex group in Table II. For [i], k_1 generally has the largest value and k_3 has the smallest value. For [u], k_3 usually has the largest magnitude and k_1 has the smallest. The three scale factors are more nearly equal for [ɑ] than for the other vowels, with k_3 tending to be larger than k_1 and k_2 for the younger subjects. For both [æ] and [ɝ], k_2 and k_3 generally are larger than k_1. These results support Fant's (1966) conclusion that formant scale factors are not uniform across vowels or formants, but the current data comparing men's and children's formants do not agree exactly with the patterns that Fant described in comparing women's and children's formants with men's. He reported that (1) k_1 and k_2 are low for rounded back vowels, (2) k_1 is low for any close or highly rounded vowel, and (3) k_1 is high for very open front or back vowels. For the current data, the largest values of k_1 tended to occur for [ɑ] and the high vowels [i] and [u], the largest values of k_2 were noted for the front vowels [i] and [æ], and the largest values of k_3 occurred for [u] and [æ]. The smallest k_1 values occurred for [ɝ], the smallest k_2 values for [u] and [ɝ], and the smallest k_3 values for [i] and [ɝ]. These results are similar in many respects to the scale factor patterns in Eguchi and Hirsh's (1969) data (see Kent, 1976, for the calculations). The differences between the current results and those derived by Fant (1966) from Peterson and Barney's (1952) vowel formant data can be summarized by ordering the vowels in *descending* magnitudes of k_1, k_2, and k_3. Fant's k_1 computations yield the series [æ] > [u] > [ɑ] > [i], whereas for the current data the order is [i] > [ɑ] > [u] > [æ] (based on the grouped children's data). Fant's k_2 results have the order [i] > [æ] ≃ [ɑ] ≃ [u], which is fairly close to the current ordering of [i] ≃ [æ] > [ɑ] > [u]. For k_3, Fant determined values that can be ordered as [u] > [æ] ≃ [ɑ] > [i], compared to the current ordering of [u] > [æ] > [ɑ] > [i]. Thus, the two sets of data are virtually reversed for k_1 values but are highly similar for k_2 and k_3 values. The disparities for k_1 are puzzling, and it is therefore interesting to note that the formant scale factors determined for Eguchi and Hirsh's (1969) data are in agreement with the current results in having the order [i] > [u] > [ɔ] > [æ] (they did not report data for [ɑ]).

Using double Helmholtz resonator theory and line analog measurements, Fant (1960) determined how vowel formant frequencies are affected by changes in the sizes of two resonator elements (double resonator theory) or lengths of vocal tract cavities (line analog). Of particular relevance to the present work are his calculations of the percentage increase in formant frequencies due to the removal of a section of 0.5-cm length from various parts of the line analog, which was a configurative analog in which successive sections of 0.5-cm axial length were represented by a series inductance and shunt capacitance. The calculations give some idea about the relative effects of shortening of the front cavity, back cavity, lip segment, tongue constriction segment, or larynx tube. The major cavity determinants of the first three formant frequencies were as follows for the vowels /i u ɑ/:

vowel /i/—F_1, back cavity and tongue constriction; F_2, back cavity; F_3, either front cavity plus tongue constriction or both front and back cavities;

vowel /u/—F_1, back cavity and lip section; F_2, both front and back cavities together with tongue constriction; F_3, front cavity;

vowel /ɑ/—F_1, front and back cavities; F_2 front and back cavities; F_3, front cavity.

Assuming that these associations can be generalized across age and sex differences of the vocal tract, then it is clear that both the front and back cavities figure in age–sex variations in formant structure. The fact that the F_1 scale factor is larger than the F_2 and F_3 factors in the comparison of women with men indicates that the primary vocal tract difference between the sexes is in the relative length of the back cavity, because Fant's results show that the F_1 frequency is largely dependent on the volume of this cavity. For the children, the relatively larger magnitude of the F_1 scale factor is maintained only for vowel /i/, for which the F_1 frequency is particularly sensitive to both the back cavity and the tongue pass. The greater magnitude of the F_2 scale factor for vowel /i/ than for /u/ and /ɑ/ in the women versus men comparison also agrees with a primary difference in back-cavity size. The rather small variations in the F_2 scale factor of vowel /u/ across age and

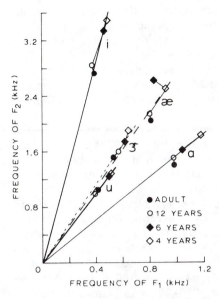

FIG. 11. Linear plot of the mean F_1–F_2 values for the five English vowels [i u ɑ æ ɝ] produced by four groups of female talkers: young adults, 12-year-olds, 6-year-olds, and 4-year-olds. The group means for each vowel have been fit by a straight line (drawn by eye) to pass through the origin. These isovowel lines virtually coincide with the lines determined mathematically in Fig. 4.

sex possibly is attributable to relatively small differences in tongue pass and symmetry of front and back cavities. The mostly parallel changes in the F_1 and F_2 scale factors of vowel /ɑ/ as a function of speaker age are explained by the mutual dependence of these formant frequencies on both front and back cavities. The regular increase in the F_3 scale factor moving from left to right in the figure probably reflects consistent differences across age–sex groups in the volume of the front cavity.

Given the possibility that adult males have a proportionately longer pharyngeal tube than women and children, it was decided to compute formant scale factors for the female subjects only, using the F_1, F_2, and F_3 means of the adult females as the reference values. As a preliminary step in judging the regularity of the females' data, the F_1 and F_2 means for the four female age groups were plotted in a linear graph for the five English vowels (Fig. 11). The four mean data points for each vowel then were fitted visually with straight lines passing through the origin. Comparison of these visually determined lines of fit with the mathematically determined lines of fit in Fig. 4 revealed that they virtually coincided for each vowel. The formant scale factors calculated for the female subjects and referenced to the adult women's means are displayed in the bar graphs of Fig. 12. The scale factors for the 12-year-old girls are difficult to interpret because their formant frequencies often were about equal to those of the adult women (Eguchi and Hirsh, 1969, reported a similar outcome). Essentially, the formant-scale patterns are like those noted earlier for six age–sex groups using the men's means as reference values (Fig. 10).

D. Formant variability

The variability of the F_1, F_2, and F_3 frequencies in vowel imitation is influenced by several factors, including the error of measurement (which varies with a speaker's fundamental frequency), the precision of a subject's vowel articulation, and the subject's familiarity with the imitation target. Because these factors are difficult to tease apart, the current report focuses on variability measures for the adult male subjects. The men are expected to have the smallest variability of formant frequencies for two major reasons: (1) they have the lowest fundamental frequencies of all the age-sex groups tested, so measurement error in the estimation of the formant frequencies should be minimal, and (2) the synthesized target vowels were modeled on data for adult male talkers, so that the men should be able to approach quite closely the actual formant frequencies of the stimuli (as shown in Fig. 1).

Formant variability was estimated by calculating the standard deviations for the F_1, F_2, and F_3 frequencies of the stimuli imitated five times each (i.e., the five English vowels and the arbitrary vowels 1–5). The standard deviations are plotted in Fig. 13 as two graphs, one showing the standard deviation for F_2 versus the standard deviation for F_1, and the other showing the standard deviation for F_3 versus the standard deviation for F_2. Each unfilled circle represents a pair of standard deviation values for five imitations of an English vowel by a given speaker, and each filled circle represents a pair of standard deviations for five imitations of an arbitrary vowel (vowels 1–5) by a given speaker. The two plots reveal that standard deviations calculated for the imitations of the English vowels do not exceed about 60 Hz for F_1 and about 100 Hz for both F_2 and F_3. Only data points for the arbitrary vowels (the filled cir-

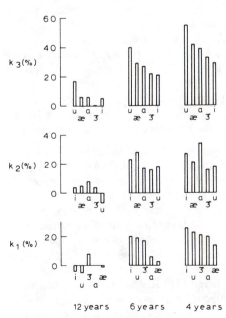

FIG. 12. Formant-frequency scale factors k_1, k_2, and k_3 (for the first three vowel formants) calculated for three age groups of female talkers with the means for adult women used as reference values. Results are shown for five English vowels.

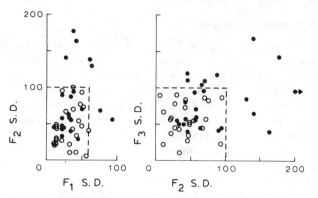

FIG. 13. Intrasubject standard deviations (in Hz) calculated for the formant frequencies of the adult males' imitations of the five English vowels [i u ɑ æ ɝ] and the five arbitrary vowels 1–5. The results are plotted as the F_2 s.d. *versus* the F_1 s.d. and the F_3 s.d. *versus* the F_2 s.d. The unfilled circles represent the production of one of the English vowels by a given subject, and the filled circles represent the production of one of the arbitrary vowels by a given subject. Notice that the standard deviations for the English vowels fall within the rectangles defined by F_1 s.d. ≤ 60 Hz, F_2 s.d. ≤ 100 Hz, and F_3 s.d. ≤ 100 Hz.

cles) fall outside these standard deviation limits. Similar results were observed for the other subject groups (Kent, 1978).

Figure 14 depicts developmental changes in the F_2 frequency of the vowels [i] and [u]. Each vertical line represents ±1 standard deviation around the mean (midpoint of the vertical line) computed for an individual subject. The data are grouped by age and sex along the abscissa. Progressing from left to right in the graph, the standard deviations tend to grow in magnitude, such that the values for the 4-year-olds are about twice those for the adult males. Some portion of this increase in the standard deviations as subject age decreases must be ascribed to age-dependent (or f_0-dependent, to put it more accurately) variations in measurement error. Apparently, intrasubject variability is not particularly large compared to intersubject variability within a given age–sex group. Frequently, the ±1 standard deviation lines for some subjects within a group do not even overlap. Thus, it appears that the intrasubject variability in F_2 frequency generally can be contained by the intersubject variability for speakers of the same age and sex.

The standard deviations calculated for the F_1 and F_2 frequencies of the adult males' imitations of the English vowels (and many of the arbitrary vowels) are roughly commensurate with the difference limens for formant frequency reported by Flanagan (1955). Similarly, Broad (1976) concluded that the standard deviations for the F_1 and F_2 frequencies in a task of vowel repetition were of about the same magnitude as these formant-frequency difference limens. Thus, for both the vowel imitation data reported here and the vowel repetition data reported by Broad, auditory resolution appears to be a major factor in the determination of articulatory precision in vowel production. However, this conclusion should be weighed with one caution. In the current study, formant variability occurred simultaneously for

all three of the measured formants, whereas Flanagan determined the formant-frequency difference limens for synthetic stimuli in which only one formant frequency was varied at a time. Possibly, if both the F_1 and F_2 frequencies were varied simultaneously, a different result might be obtained for the discrimination of changes in the formant frequencies. Nonetheless, it is striking that the standard deviations for the F_1 and F_2 frequencies of the imitations should be in the same range as the formant-frequency difference limens. This outcome means that both measurement error in the estimation of formant frequencies and articulatory error on the part of the speakers are reasonably small compared to the limitations imposed by the ear's resolution of formant frequency. As Fig. 13 illustrates, the five English vowels were reproduced by the five men subjects with a F_1 standard deviation of 11–60 Hz (compared to F_1 difference limens of 12–27 Hz in Flanagan's study) and with a F_2 standard deviation of 6–100 Hz (compared to F_2 difference limens of 20–90 Hz in Flanagan's study).

III. CONCLUSIONS

(1) Linear effects obtain in the formant-frequency data derived from imitations of vowel stimuli by a heterogeneous set of men, women, and children speakers.

(2) Straight lines passing through the origin provide a satisfactory first approximation to the F_1–F_2 data for men's, women's, and children's productions of the English vowels [i u ɑ æ ɝ].

(3) A logarithmic transformation of the formant frequencies of English vowels produced by men, women, and children helps to equalize the group dispersion for the vowels when the results are plotted in F_1–F_2 and F_2–F_3 planes.

(4) For comparisons of children's with men's formants, formant scale factors vary somewhat with formant and with vowel such that the F_1 scale factor tends to be largest for the high vowels, the F_2 scale factor tends to be

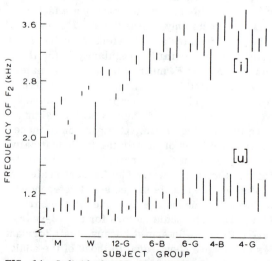

FIG. 14. Individual subject data, expressed as ±1 standard deviation bar, for the F_2 frequency of the vowels [i] and [u]. The midpoint of each bar is the individual subject mean. The age–sex groups are indicated along the horizontal axis.

largest for the front vowels plus [ɑ], and the F_3 scale factor tends to be largest for [u] and [æ]. Using either the means for adult males or adult females as reference values in computing formant scale factors for children does not alter the general pattern of the results for younger subjects.

(5) For adult males imitating English vowels, standard deviations are equal to or less than 60 Hz for F_1 and equal to or less than 100 Hz for F_2 and F_3. These limits on formant-frequency variability in vowel production correspond with published data on formant-frequency difference limens in vowel discrimination.

ACKNOWLEDGMENTS

This research was supported in part by NIH grants NS 12281 and NS 13274. The authors are grateful for the cooperation of the following persons who arranged for the participation of the children as subjects in the study: Rita Hibray, Director of the Salvation Army Day Care Center in Madison, Wisconsin; James Clark, Principal of the Oregon, Wisconsin Elementary School; and Edward Guziewski, Principal of the Oregon, Wisconsin Middle School. We also thank Denise Cariski for her help in the making of spectrograms and the recording of the imitations.

Broad, D. J. (1976). "Toward defining acoustic phonetic equivalence for vowels," Phonetica 33, 401–424.

Broad, D. J., and Wakita, H. (1977). "Piecewise-planar representation of vowel formant frequencies," J. Acoust. Soc. Am. 62, 1467–1473.

Eguchi, S., and Hirsh, I. J. (1969). "Development of speech sounds in children," Acta Otolaryngol. Suppl. 257.

Fant, G. (1960). Acoustical Theory of Speech Production ('s-Gravenhage, The Hague).

Fant, G. (1966). "A note on vocal tract size factors and non-uniform F-pattern scalings," Speech Transmission Lab. Q. Prog. Stat. Rep., R. Inst. Technol., Stockholm, No. 4, 22–30 (unpublished).

Flanagan, J. L. (1955). "A difference limen for vowel formant frequency," J. Acoust. Soc. Am. 27, 613–617.

Fujisaki, H., and Kawashima, T. (1968). "The roles of pitch and higher formants in the perception of vowels," IEEE Trans. Audio-Electro-acoust., AV-16, 73–77.

Gerstman, L. J. (1968). "Classification of self-normalized vowels," IEEE Trans. Audio-Electro-acoust. AV-16, 78–80.

Kent, R. D. (1976). "Anatomical and neuromuscular maturation of the speech mechanism: evidence from acoustic studies," J. Speech Hear. Res. 19, 421–447.

Kent, R. D. (1978). "Imitation of synthesized vowels by preschool children," J. Acoust. Soc. Am. 63, 1193–1198.

Kent, R. D. (in press). "The imitation of synthesized English and non-English vowels by children and adults," J. Psychol. Res.

Klatt, D. H. (1972). "Acoustical theory of terminal analog speech synthesis," Proc. IEEE Conf. Speech Commun. Process., Boston, Massachusetts (unpublished).

Lennig, M., and Hindle, D. (1977). "Uniform scaling as a method of vowel normalization," J. Acoust. Soc. Am. 62, S26(A).

Lindblom, B. (1972). "Comments on paper 15 (Development of speech sounds in children, by S. Eguchi and I. J. Hirsh)," in International Symposium on Speech Communication Ability and Profound Deafness, edited by G. Fant (Alexander Graham Bell Assoc. for the Deaf, Washington, D. C.).

Markel, J. D. (1971). "Formant trajectory estimation from a linear least-squares inverse filter formulation," SCRL Monograph No. 7, Speech Communication Research Lab., Santa Barbara, California (unpublished).

Mol, H. (1963). Fundamentals of Phonetics. Janua Linguarum, No. 26 (Mouton, The Hague).

Nearey, T. (1977). "Phonetic feature systems for vowels," Ph.D. dissertation, University of Conneticut (unpublished).

Nordström, P.-E., and Lindblom, B. (1975). "A normalization procedure for vowel formant data," paper presented at the 8th Intern. Congr. on Phonetic Sci., Leeds, England, Aug. 1975 (unpublished).

Peterson, G. E., and Barney, H. L. (1952). "Control methods used in a study of vowels," J. Acoust. Soc. Am. 25, 175–184.

Snedecor, G. W., and Cochran, W. G. (1967). Statistical Methods (Iowa State University, Ames).

Sroka, S. A. (1977). "Effects of various types of speaker normalization on an automatic vowel recognition scheme," J. Acoust. Soc. Am. 62, S63(A).

Acoustic features of infant vocalic utterances at 3, 6, and 9 months

Raymond D. Kent and Ann D. Murray

Boys Town Institute for Communication, Disorders in Children, Omaha, Nebraska 68131

(Received 13 October 1981; accepted for publication 4 May 1982)

Recordings were obtained of the comfort-state vocalizations of infants at 3, 6, and 9 months of age during a session of play and vocal interaction with the infant's mother and the experimenter. Acoustic analysis, primarily spectrography, was used to determine utterance durations, formant frequencies of vocalic utterances, patterns of f_0 frequency change during vocalizations, variations in source excitation of the vocal tract, and general properties of the utterances. Most utterances had durations of less than 400 ms although occasional sounds lasted 2 s or more. An increase in the ranges of both the $F1$ and $F2$ frequencies was observed across both periods of age increase, but the center of the F_1–F_2 plot for the group vowels appeared to change very little. Phonatory characteristics were at least generally compatible with published descriptions of infant cry. The f_0 frequency averaged 445 Hz for 3-month-olds, 450 Hz for 6-month-olds, and 415 Hz for 9-month-olds. As has been previously reported for infant cry, the vocalizations frequently were associated with tremor (vibrato), harmonic doubling, abrupt f_0 shift, vocal fry (or roll), and noise segments. Thus, from a strictly acoustic perspective, early cry and the later vocalizations of cooing and babbling appear to be vocal performances in continuity. Implications of the acoustic analyses are discussed for phonetic development and speech acquisition.

PACS numbers: 43.70.Bk, 43.70.Ve, 43.70.Yg

INTRODUCTION

Most studies of developing speech have applied linguistic methods of analysis, as though the child possesses an exotic language that is suitable for study by linguistic field methods. An alternative focus on the acoustic and anatomic/physiologic aspects of speech development takes less for granted than does the linguistic field study (see reviews by Kent, 1981, and Netsell, 1981). For example, this alternative focus immediately brings to the surface questions about the structural and neuromuscular capability of the infant and child. Although knowledge is far from complete in these areas, enough is known about them to pose anatomically and physiologically based hypotheses about early sound patterns. For instance, it is known that the infant's vocal tract is not simply a miniature of the adult's. In fact, in many respects, the infant's vocal tract is more like that of a lower primate than that of an adult human (Sloan, 1967; Wind, 1970; Lieberman *et al.*, 1971; Fletcher, 1973; Bosma, 1975; Laitman and Crelin, 1976; DuBrul, 1977; Sasaki *et al.*, 1977).

Compared to the adult, the infant has (1) an appreciably shorter vocal tract, (2) a relatively shorter pharyngeal cavity, (3) a relatively anterior tongue mass, (4) a gradual, rather than right-angle, bend of the oropharyngeal channel, (5) a high larynx position, and (6) approximation of the velopharynx and epiglottis (Fig. 1). To illustrate the consequences of such anatomic differences on sound production, it is sufficient to consider just the approximation of the velum and epiglottis (Fig. 2). Because of the engagement of laryngeal and velopharyngeal structures, the infant is an obligate nasal breather and an obligate nasal vocalizer. Separation of the velum and epiglottis apparently occurs by about 4–6 months (Sasaki *et al.*, 1977). At this time the child begins to produce what Oller (1978) calls "fully resonant nuclei," that is, nonnasal vowel sounds. Oller calls this period *the expansion*

stage of phonetic development. Although we do not want to overemphasize the anatomic determinants of sound patterns, such critical anatomic changes as disengagement of larynx and velopharynx should be carefully considered in explaining patterns of change in infant vocalizations. Kent (1981) has suggested how various anatomic changes may relate to stages of phonetic development described by Oller.

Despite the importance of a thorough knowledge of infant vocalizations for purposes ranging from early identification of developmental disorders to confirmation or disconfirmation of theories of language development, much has yet to be learned about the acoustic–phonetic properties of in-

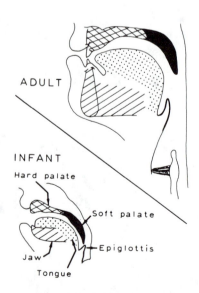

FIG. 1. Vocal tracts of adult and infant. Compared to the adult, the infant has a gradually sloping oropharyngeal channel, a short, broad oral cavity, a short pharynx, and an elevated larynx.

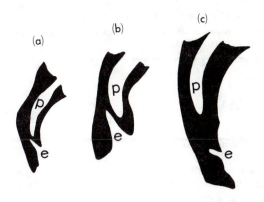

FIG. 2. Outline drawings of soft palate (p) and epiglottis (e) in infants at 2 mo. (a), 4 mo. (b), and 6 mo. (c) of age. Note separation of soft palate and epiglottis between 4 and 6 mo. (Redrawn from radiographs in Sasaki *et al.*, 1977.)

fant vocalizations. Although vocalization items are included on general developmental scales.(Knobloch *et al.*, 1966; Bayley, 1969; Fokes, 1971; Capute *et al.*, 1981), these scales permit only a gross characterization of infant sound production.

The purpose of the present study was to obtain some general acoustic descriptions of the utterances produced by 3-, 6-, and 9-month-old children. Of particular interest were durations, formant frequencies, intonation patterns, and age-typical acoustic features that might be useful in describing the developmental pattern of early sound production. We deal here with vocalic utterances (*vocants* in the terminology proposed by Martin, 1981), predominantly recorded during comfort state of the infant. Acoustic analysis of more consonantlike sounds, especially noise segments, is in progress. A primary goal of the research at this point is the development of an appropriate methodology for the acoustic–phonetic study of early utterances.

I. METHOD

A. Subjects

The 21 infants selected as subjects were within 20 days of one of the target ages—3, 6, or 9 months. One of the 9-month-olds exceeded this age criterion: she was 9 m, 29 d (9 months, 29 days) on the day of testing. The age range for each of the three ages was 2 m, 10 d–3 m, 12 d for 3-month-olds; 5 m, 25 d–6 m, 16 d for 6-month-olds; and 8 m, 24 d–9 m, 29 d for 9-month-olds. The sex ratio (girls to boys) was 3:4, 3:4, and 4:3 for the 3-, 6-, and 9-month-old groups, respectively.

All infants were without clinical history of postnatal illness, and the Bayley Scales of Infant Development were administered to the infant during the recording session to insure age-appropriate performance. Any child not meeting age-normal behavior (i.e., with MD1 or PD1 less than 85) was excluded from the study.

B. Recording

Subjects were videotaped and audiotaped while interacting with the mother and the investigators. Small toys were used to hold the infant's interest and to encourage vocalizations. The youngest infants were seated in an infant car seat or a high chair; older children were allowed to sit at a

small chair or to stand behind a small table. Audio recordings were made on either a Nagra IV-SJ or a TEAC A-3300SX and a high-quality microphone. For most recordings an Electro-Voice C0-90 condenser lapel microphone was attached to the collar of the infant's shirt. On a few occasions when the lapel microphone was not available, a Turner Model 2302 microphone was handheld within 20 cm of the infant's mouth. Recording sessions averaged about one hour in length. Appropriate steps were taken to insure the infant's comfort, as the focus of this study was on comfort-state vocalizations.

C. Acoustic analysis

Spectrograms were prepared with a Voice Identification Series 700 spectrograph. Generally, wideband (450 Hz) spectrograms were used for measurements of duration and for estimates of formant frequencies. Narrow-band (45 Hz) spectrograms were used for determination of fundamental frequency (f_0) and for examination of the harmonic structure of sounds. The intensity display function of a Kay Elemetrics Visi-Pitch Model 6187 was used for the measurement of durations of the entire recorded corpus, and the f_0 display function was used for corroborative estimates of fundamental frequency.

D. Acoustic feature coding

Several coding schemes have been proposed for the classification of infant utterances (Stark *et al.*, 1975; Oller *et al.*, 1976; Mavilya, 1969; Maskarinec *et al.*, 1981; Laufer, 1980). Some investigators have distinguished between speechlike and nonspeech utterances, partly because they believed that utterances perceived as speechlike help to shape the phonetic events in speech development. However, investigators have disagreed on the distinction between speechlike and nonspeech sounds. Maskarinec *et al.* (1981) were more liberal in defining speechlike sounds than was Mavilya (1969). Maskarinec *et al.* believed that data reported by Wasz-Hockert *et al.* (1968) show some of the sounds Mavilya would classify as nonspeech may, in fact, be precursors of later speech. Actually, the classification of speechlike sounds is highly impressionistic and it is possible that even nonspeech sounds help the infant learn to regulate the vocal structures. It seems advisable to define "speechlike" broadly if any definition is made for purposes of classification. Apparently, Maskarinec *et al.* classified a sound as speechlike if it "contained vowel or consonantlike qualities" (p. 269). However, it is questionable if reliable interjudge classifications can be made for sounds such as labial trills (raspberries), nasal snorts, glottal ejectives, hums, and nasal grunts. It is difficult to arrive at a satisfactory definition of vowel or consonant without consideration of linguistic function, or at least function in a syllable, which itself is difficult to define (Ladefoged, 1975; Shriberg and Kent, 1982). Recognition of vowels and consonants by judgments of auditory similarity to phonetic elements in natural languages also is a risky criterion, because of the large number of sounds to be considered in the world's languages. Given these difficulties, we used a very broad definition of "speechlike" that excluded primarily vegetative or reflexive sounds such as breathing noise, cough, or hiccough.

Because one of our goals was to evaluate the appropriateness of our acoustic–phonetic methodology within the limited recording time available in most clinical settings, we did not establish as a primary criterion the "representatives" of the recorded samples. Of course, this criterion is important and is being investigated longitudinally in a separate study. In this initial phase, we were concerned more with the applicability of our methods to a relatively large number of subjects in a standard setting than with the documentation of the representativeness of the sampled utterances across a variety of settings.

The coding system in Table I was developed for the purpose of acoustic categorization of the infant's utterances. The acoustic features were identified in a preliminary classification of spectrograms and were found to be suitable for coding nearly all of the spectrograms finally obtained. With multiple codings of a spectrogram, it was possible to make fairly detailed descriptions of an utterance. The three categories of intonation (rise, held, fall) were later expanded to a seven-category system, as explained in Sec. II, Results. The coding system in Table I was used for compiling an inventory of sound types, whether by individual infant or by age group. The details of the inventories are beyond the scope and purpose of the present paper, but the coding system is mentioned because (1) it was used in preliminary analysis of the utterances and (2) it offers an acoustically based alternative to other coding systems.

Acoustic features of special interest are illustrated by spectrograms. In the Appendix we give examples of classification. For instance, noise segments (Fig. A2) were distinguished from vocalic patterns by the appearance of aperiodic energy (except for modulation by voicing or trill) and the absence of a well-defined formant structure in wideband spectrograms and a well-defined harmonic structure in narrow-band spectrograms.

II. RESULTS AND DISCUSSION

A. Utterance duration

The durations of isolatable utterances (including either vowel-like or consonantlike elements) were determined with the intensity-display function of a Kay Elemetrics Visi-Pitch and associated storage oscilloscope. Durations were cumulated in 200-ms bins and then plotted as duration histograms for individual infants (Figs. 3–5). The great majority of utterance durations were less than 400 ms for all three age groups, but the histograms tend to assume a greater skewing to the right (larger durations) as age increases. In general, the infants' utterances tend to have about the same durations as syllables in adult speech, i.e., duration of 400 ms or less, although some utterances reached durations of 2 s or more. The histograms in Figs. 3–5 also show the number of vocalizations recorded for each infant, except for a small number of vocalizations that could not be effectively isolated for durational measurement. For example, short (less than 50 ms) repetitive grunts uttered at small intervals were excluded from analysis, as were some exceptionally long trills (5 s or

TABLE I. Coding table for acoustic features of infant vocalizations.

Vocalic (utterances with well-defined F pattern)

st - stationary
v - variant over time
    sl - slow change
    r - rapid change
na - noise alternation
nc - noise contamination
lf - low-frequency dominance of energy
F_n - measurable [formants
    through $n(n = 1, 2, 3, $ or $4)$]
sh - short, less than 100
m - mid-range, greater than
    100 ms, less than 500 ms
l - long, greater than 500 m
n - nasalization (suspected)

Phonation (for utterances with harmonic structure attributable to voicing)

L - level of f_0
    h - high, $f_0 > 600$ Hz
    m - mid, $200 < f_0 < 600$ Hz
    l - low, $f_0 < 200$ Hz
PP - phonatory pattern
    m - monotone
    sm - small f_0 variation
    mod - moderate f_0 variation
    l - large f_0 variation
    sl - slow f_0 variation
    r - rapid f_0 variation
    tr - tremor or vibrato
    bi - biphonation
    fry - fry or rough phonation
    int - interrupted
    ni - noise initiation
    nt - noise termination
    gl - glottalized
    br - breathy
    rise - rising intonation
    held - held or checked intonation
    fall - falling intonation

Noise segment (significant aperiodic component)

lf - low-frequency dominance
    (below 2 kHz)
mf - mid-frequency dominance
    (above 2 kHz but below 5 kHz)
hf - high-frequency dominance
    (above 5 kHz)
flat - uniform spread of energy
sh - short duration, < 50 ms
m - mid-range, $50 < d < 200$ ms
l - long, > 200 ms

more) from one 9-month-old subject.

B. Formant patterns of vocalic utterances

Formant patterns were determined for vocalic utterances, i.e., those having a well-defined formant structure either stationary or slowly varying in time. Special precautions were taken to avoid misinterpretation of harmonics as formants. For this purpose, it usually was sufficient to compare wideband and narrow-band spectrograms in estimating formant frequencies. An example is shown in Fig. 6 of wideband (top) and narrow-band (bottom) patterns for a vocalic

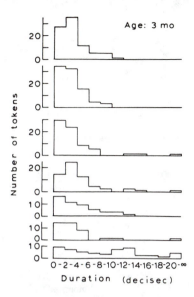

FIG. 3. Histograms of utterance durations of 3-month-olds. Number of occurrences is scaled on the ordinate for duration intervals of 200 ms, ranging from 0 to 2 s or more. A separate histogram is shown for each subject.

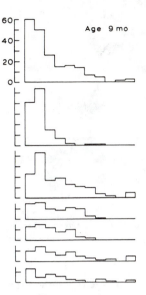

FIG. 5. Histograms of utterance durations of 9-month-olds. See axis label and caption of Fig. 3.

utterance from a 6-month-old child. Of particular importance is the fact that the formants evident in the wideband pattern at the top are composed of several harmonics, as shown by the narrow-band spectrogram at the bottom. So long as at least two laryngeal harmonics are associated with a formant, the risk of confusing harmonic energy with formant energy is minimized.

Although identification of formants can be difficult for spectrograms of infant vocalizations, formant-frequency estimation was accomplished with satisfactory reliability even for the utterances of 3-month-olds, some of which are illustrated in Fig. 7. The reliability of formant frequency estimation was determined by replicate measurement of 50 spectrograms to be 46 Hz for $F1$ and 50 Hz for $F2$. All formant frequencies were determined to the nearest 50 Hz. This rounding error seemed tolerable in view of the large bandwidths of infants' vowel formants.

F_1-F_2 plots for 3-, 6-, and 9-month-olds are depicted in

Figs. 8, 9, and 10, respectively. Each geometric symbol represents an individual infant in a given age group. For 3-month-olds, the ranges for F_1 and F_2 are approximately 0.5–1.5 kHz and 1.8–3.8 kHz, respectively. The corresponding ranges for the 6-month-olds are 0.5–1.7 and 1.6–3.8 kHz. The ranges for 9-month-olds are about 0.5–1.8 kHz for F_1 and 1.4–4.1 kHz for F_2. The ranges for both F_1 and F_2 increase somewhat with age across each interval. These increases are apparent in Fig. 10, which shows the individual data for 9-month-olds compared with envelopes that enclose nearly 100% of the data for the younger age groups (see Figs.

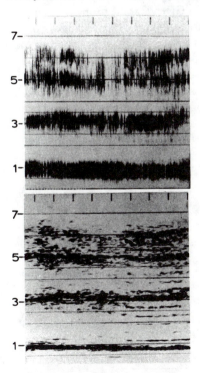

FIG. 6. Wideband (top) and narrow-band (bottom) spectrograms of infant's vocalic utterance. The first four formants have frequencies of about 0.8, 3.1, 5.0, and 6.0 kHz. In this and all following spectrograms, the numbers on the ordinate indicate frequency in kHz. The tics at the top margin of the spectrograms represent intervals of 100 ms.

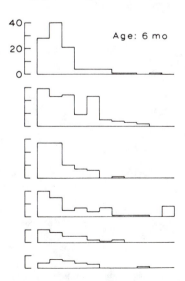

FIG. 4. Histograms of utterance durations of 6-month-olds. See axis label and caption of Fig. 3.

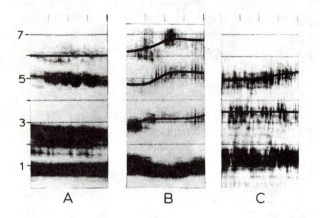

FIG. 7. Sample wideband spectrograms of utterances recorded from 3-month-old infants. The center frequency of the first three or four formants is highlighted in ink.

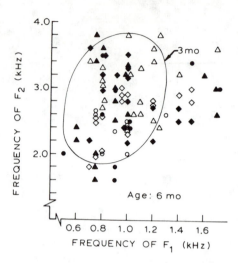

FIG. 9. $F1$-$F2$ plot of vocalic utterances produced by 6-month-olds. Closed line is redrawn from Fig. 8 to show $F1$-$F2$ region for 3-month-olds.

8 and 9 for derivation of the envelopes). Despite the extension of the F_1 and F_2 ranges, the majority of vocalic utterances produced by the 9-month-olds have about the same formant pattern as do the majority of utterances of the younger infants. The average vocalic utterance for all three age groups has a F_1 of about 0.9–1.0 kHz, a F_2 of about 3 kHz, and a F_3 of about 5 kHz.

The relationship of the formant frequencies for 3-month-olds to the vowel formant frequencies of older children and adults is depicted in Fig. 11. The heavy diagonal lines are isovowel lines derived from imitation experiments using computer-synthesized vowels as stimuli (Kent, 1979; Kent and Forner, 1979). The low-frequency end of each isovowel line represents the mean F_1-F_2 values for adult males and the high-frequency end indicates F_1-F_2 values for 4-year-old boys and girls. Given that the formant-frequency data for 3-month-olds are contained within extensions of the isovowel lines for vowels /i/ and /æ/, it is not surprising that phonemic inventories of early vowels have shown a preponderance of vowels transcribed as /ɛ/, /ɪ/, and /ʌ/ (Irwin, 1948). It appears that most vocalic utterances produced in the first 3 to 9 months of life are relatively mid-front or cen-

tral articulations when compared to the acoustic vowel space of older children and adults. Apparently, the F_1-F_2-F_3 pattern of 1, 3, and 5 kHz for the infants in this sample can be likened to the neutral, or *schwa*, vowel in adult speech (F_1-F_2-F_3 values of 0.5, 1.5, and 2.5 kHz for adult males).

C. Phonatory function

Generally, phonatory function was variable both within and across utterances. One form of this variability was in the regulation of f_0, which often varied within, as well as between, utterances. In addition, the mean f_0 within an utterance varied from vocalization to vocalization. The overall average f_0 was 445 Hz for 3-month-olds, 450 Hz for 6-month-olds, and 415 Hz for 9-month-olds. Generally, the individual mean f_0 of comfort-state vocalization fell between 350 and 500 Hz, a range which is also typical of published data on infant cry (Murry and Murry, 1980). This similarity of f_0 values indicates that cry and noncry vocalizations are similar in some aspects of laryngeal regulation and that some degree of continuity might be expected in the mean f_0 fre-

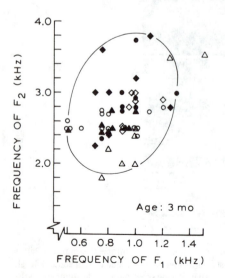

FIG. 8. $F1$-$F2$ plot of vocalic utterances produced by 3-month-olds. Closed line represents major region of $F1$-$F2$ values.

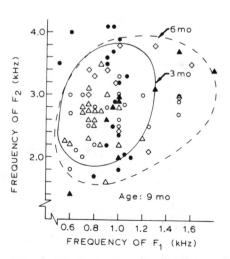

FIG. 10. $F1$-$F2$ plot of vocalic utterances produced by 9-month-olds. Closed lines are redrawn from Figs. 8 and 9 to show $F1$-$F2$ regions for 6- and 9-month-olds.

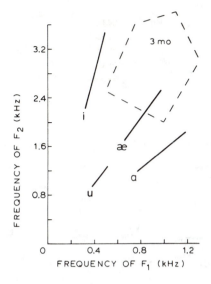

FIG. 11. $F1$-$F2$ region for 3-month-olds (area bounded by broken line) compared to isovowel lines for /i æ ɑ u/.

quency between early cry and later cooing and babbling.

Although the f_0 contour during vocalizations assumed a variety of shapes, some shapes occurred more frequently than others. As an estimate of the frequency of occurrence of the different intonation patterns, the f_0 patterns were categorized for approximately 100 vocalizations for each age group. The vocalizations selected satisfied three criteria: they had a well-defined F_1-F_2 pattern, a continuously phonated duration greater than 100 ms but less than 2 s, and a harmonic pattern discernible to at least the fifth harmonic in narrow-band spectrograms. Patterns with tremor or sudden f_0 shifts were accepted if aberrations did not obscure the overall or long-term pattern of f_0 change. We discarded vocalizations with abrupt f_0 shift, intervening noise segments, or other evidence of marked change in vocal fold activity that made simple characterization of intonation pattern impossible. It should be noted that many of these discarded phonatory patterns occurred frequently and were excluded not because they were considered to be rare, uninteresting events, but because we wanted to study potential predecessors of adultlike intonation patterns.

The seven simple f_0 shapes were falling–rising ($\smile$), flat ($-$), falling ($\backslash$), rising–falling ($\frown$), rising ($/$), double rising–falling ($\sim$), and complex, or a sequence of two or more basic shapes. These shapes determined from a preliminary analysis of f_0 shapes for a small set of data were found to be adequate for analysis of the larger sample. The frequency of occurrence for each intonation pattern is given in Table II.

For all three age groups, the three patterns of flat, falling, and rising–falling are predominant. When the percentage frequency of occurrence is averaged across age groups, these three patterns account for 31%, 24%, and 23%, respectively, of the total. The other f_0 patterns occurred much less frequently, and no confident conclusion can be reached about developmental trends in their usage. However, it is worth remarking that the rising and double rising–falling patterns were used quite frequently by some individuals. Nonetheless, for only one subject was the most frequently occurring f_0 pattern other than one of the three major categories listed above.

Many vocalizations could not be submitted to analysis of f_0-frequency pattern because of discontinuous or alternating modes of phonation (f_0 shift, noise, and other effects to be described). Figure 12 is an example of source variation in an utterance of a 6-month-old. The wideband spectrogram is shown at the top and the narrow-band spectrogram at the bottom. The utterance begins explosively (note the paired vertical striations at the extreme left in the wideband pattern) and then has a slightly rising f_0 with a mean value of about 400 Hz (this segment is identified by the letter a in the narrow-band pattern). At the point marked b, the harmonic pattern changes abruptly and the f_0 frequency suddenly increases to about 750 Hz. At point c, f_0 frequency begins to fall, and this falling portion is followed by a segment of aperiodic energy that begins at point d.

Laryngeal function in infant utterances frequently had characteristics seldom observed in normal adult speech. One of these characteristics was vocal tremor (vibrato), which is a slow modulation of vocal intensity, of f_0 frequency or, most commonly, of both intensity and frequency. Vocal tremor is one example of oscillatory behavior in neuromotor systems and is useful as a possible clinical sign of neurological disorder. Because the majority of normal infants at each age group in our sample exhibited at least some occasions of vocal tremor, tremor or vibrato itself cannot be indicative of developmental disorder. However, the frequency of tremor in Hz and its appearance in later stages of development eventually may be shown to be clinically important. The frequency of tremor was determined by inspection of narrow-band spectrograms or of Visi-Pitch displays for f_0 modulations in which at least three successive cycles of similar period were evident. The frequency of tremor was computed for as many cycles of modulation (beyond two) that were visible. Sample spectrograms of vocal tremor are shown in Fig. 13.

For 3-month-olds, the vocal-tremor frequency averaged 15 Hz and ranged from 10 to 20 Hz. The average and

TABLE II. Percentage frequency of occurrence of f_0 (intonation patterns in 100 selected vocalizations for each age group of subjects).

Age	$\smile$	$-$	$\backslash$	$\frown$	$/$	$\sim$	Complex
3 mo	1	29	24	32	4	9	2
6 mo	0	33	20	15	11	16	6
9 mo	0	31	27	21	12	2	8
mean	0	31	24	23	9	9	5

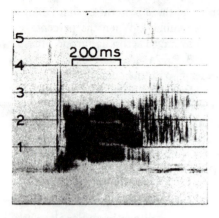

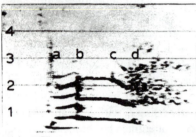

FIG. 12. Example of sound source variation shown in wideband (top) and narrow-band (bottom) spectrograms. See text for description.

range of vocal tremor for 6-month-olds were 15 and 9–20 Hz, respectively. Fewer instances of tremor were observed for 9-month-olds than for the younger infants, but three of these older subjects had occasional tremor, with a mean frequency of 18 Hz and a range of 12–25 Hz. It should be noted that some instances of slower tremor might have been missed because of the criterion of at least three cycles of modulation. However, a laxing of the criterion might have led to the inclusion of some f_0 variations not attributable to tremor, especially when the criterion of similar period was questionably satisfied.

Figures 14 and 15 show examples of a phonatory characteristic that occasionally was observed for most of the infants in each age group. This characteristic is an abrupt change in harmonic structure, sometimes appearing as a doubling of the harmonic pattern (that is, the insertion of a $1/2 f_0$ harmonic series) and sometimes appearing as an altered harmonic pattern bearing no simple relationship (especially halving or doubling) with the neighboring harmonic pattern(s). Harmonic doubling or double harmonic break has been described previously by Stark *et al.* (1975), Buhr and Keating (1977), Michelsson (1980), and Keating (1980). A similar, if not identical, characteristic has been noted in some speech pathologies, notably speech of the deaf (Monsen *et al.*, 1979) and laryngeal pathology (Kelman *et al.*, 1981). The appearance of the subharmonic series is associated with a perception of vocal roughness or harshness. The other form of abrupt harmonic change has been called shift (Michelsson, 1980) and has been reported previously for infant cry. Shift was defined by Stark *et al.* as a pitch break not attributable to halving or doubling of the f_0. The spectrograms in Figs. 14 (3-month-old samples) and 15 (6-month-old samples) give several examples of f_0 shift and harmonic doubling at the points marked by arrowheads. Infrequently,

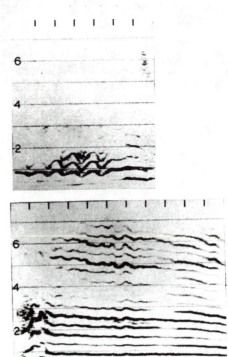

FIG. 13. Narrow-band spectrograms illustrating vocal tremor (vibrato) in infant vocalizations. The tremor is apparent as a rippling or modulation of the harmonics.

harmonic doubling would fade in and out of a spectrogram. Our observations, together with those of Keating (1980), indicate that many phonatory characteristics of early cry extend into the cooing and babbling period. That is, features such as f_0 shift and harmonic doubling are not unique to cry vocalizations but apply as well to some comfort-state sounds at later periods of development. Other types of phonatory patterns observed frequently in our sample of infants are illustrated in the Appendix.

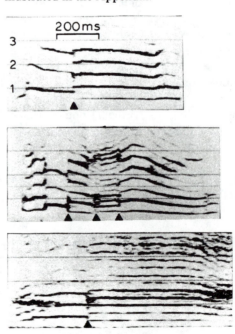

FIG. 14. Narrow-band spectrograms illustrating abrupt changes in harmonic pattern (filled arrowheads). Spectrograms are shown for three 3-month-olds.

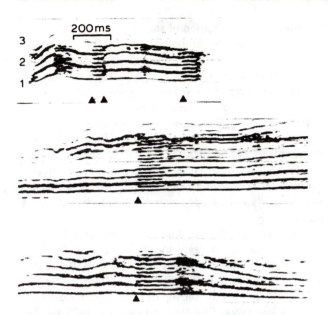

FIG. 15. Narrow-band spectrograms illustrating abrupt changes in harmonic pattern (filled arrowheads). Spectrograms are shown for three 6-month-olds.

III. GENERAL DISCUSSION

A. Acoustic features of early vocalizations

These acoustic data indicate that the typical vocalic utterance of the infants studied had an overall duration of 400 ms or less, a mean f_0 frequency within the range of 350–500 Hz, and was located in a formant space having as its center a $F1 = 1$ kHz, $F2 = 3$ kHz, and $F3 = 5$ kHz. The maximal range for the first two formant frequencies was 0.5–1.8 kHz for $F1$ and 1.4–4.1 kHz for $F2$. Excluding complex utterances with marked phonatory changes, the vocalizations usually assumed one of three intonation patterns: flat f_0, falling f_0, or rising–falling f_0. The phonatory patterns frequently were interrupted by intervals of tremor, abrupt f_0 shift, harmonic doubling, noise components, irregular vocal fold vibrations, or transient deviations from the overall f_0 contour. Some conspicuous fricativelike segments were observed, some of which contained spectral energy almost entirely above 6 kHz. Stoplike segments also were frequently heard and were associated with rapid formant transitions, stop gaps, or weak frictionalized segments.

The infants produced a variety of vocalic sounds, ranging from a sustained formant pattern to a rapidly changing formant pattern. If the apparent center of the acoustic vowel space is taken to be a central vowel with uniform cross-sectional area along the length of the tract, then the average length of the infant's vocal tract can be estimated by the odd-quarter wavelength relationship to be about 9 cm, compared to 17 cm for the average adult male.

Although the acoustic vowel space was observed to increase in its $F1$ and $F2$ dimensions across the age groups, it is risky to draw any major inferences about vowel development from these data. It is interesting that the center of the F_1-F_2 plot for these early vocal sounds does not change markedly across the 3 to 9 month period. Indeed, the center point of the three-formant acoustic space remained at about 1, 3, and

5 kHz across the 3 to 9 month age range. Some qualitative changes were noted, particularly in the quality of the vocalic sounds. More evidence of nasalization was observed for the 3-month-olds than for the older subjects (see the spectrogram in Appendix Fig. A1 for the presumed acoustic evidence of nasalization). This result is consistent with anatomic evidence that the velopharynx is markedly reshaped at about 3–5 months of age (Sasaki et al., 1977).

The formant-frequency ranges identified in the present study agree in at least a general way with previous formant data (Ringel and Kluppel, 1964; Lieberman et al., 1971; Colton and Steinschneider, 1980). For example, the mean values of the first three formant frequencies reported by Colton and Steinschneider for newborn infant cries were (a) for males, 1592, 3223, and 5337 Hz, and (b) for females, 1653, 3274, and 5368 Hz. Few data have been published on the formant-frequency changes that occur during the first year of life, but Buhr (1980), for example, showed for one infant a gradual expansion of vowel sounds along the $F1$ and $F2$ axes of the standard formant plot. The values he reported lie within the formant-frequency ranges reported here. Some variation in formant frequencies has been described even for different discomfort or distress sounds, such as cries versus fusses. Petrovich-Bartell et al. (in press) reported that cries, in comparison to fusses, had a lower $F2$ frequency and a larger F_1/F_2 ratio. This result was interpreted to mean that the oral constriction for vocalizations described as fusses is further from the glottis (more front vowel-like) than that for cries. Radiographic evidence of a relatively posterior constriction for cries was reported by Bosma et al. (1965).

Laryngeal features such as vocal tremor, f_0 shift, harmonic doubling, and breathiness may indicate that infant vocalizations are often unstable and are affected by nonlinearities that older speakers learn to avoid. Although vocalizations with a nearly invariant f_0 were frequently observed, the more common pattern was one of time-varying change, especially falling or rising–falling. Some of the time varying f_0 patterns may foreshadow intonational features of speech, with both rising and falling patterns in evidence at utterance terminations.

Conceivably, all three of the most frequently occurring intonation patterns might be classified as basically falling tones. Some of the f_0 patterns classified as flat had a very gradual fall with time, although the actual change in f_0 may not have been more than a few Hz over an interval of 200 ms or more. Because the f_0 change was slight and gradual, the flat category was used in preference to the falling category. The rising–falling patterns are really a subtype of the general class of falling patterns and are distinguished from the narrowly defined falling category by the inclusion of a rather long rising f_0 portion at the beginning of the utterance. If the falling, flat, and rising–falling patterns are considered together as members of a more general category of terminal F_0 fall, then almost 80% of the intonation patterns were of falling variety.

A preference for falling intonation has been reported by Wells et al., 1978 (cited by Cruttenden, 1981). Cruttenden summarized the Wells et al. (1978) work as showing that children generally use falling tones in their early one- and two-word utterances and apparently have to learn the special usage of rises. Crystal (1979) proposed a sequence of tonal development for early words in which falling patterns occur first, to be followed by contrasts of falling versus level, falling versus high rising, falling versus high falling, and so on. The preference for falling intonation exists as early as the 3-month-old period. None of the infants in the present study was observed to produce predominantly rising f_0 patterns, although a rising pattern was the second most frequently occurring (after falling pattern) for one 9-month-old. Delack and Fowlow (1978) reported that infants used different f_0-frequency contours depending on stimulus conditions. When infants were in the presence of the mother (as they were in the present study), a rise–fall contour predominated, a result consistent with the data presented here.

In terms of the underlying laryngeal physiology, a falling f_0 pattern is likely to occur because of a decline in subglottal pressure as the vocalization progresses. The fall also could be the result of a reduction of vocal fold length and tension as the adducting and tensing muscles of the larynx are relaxed at the end of a vocalization. In order for a distinct rising f_0 pattern to occur, there would have to be an increase at the end of the vocalization in vocal fold length/tension, or subglottal pressure, or both.

Some of the vocalization features observed in infants are similar to features described in the vocalizations of persons with deafness, laryngeal pathology, or neuromuscular dysfunction affecting the larynx (Monsen et al., 1979; Kelman, 1981; Kelman et al., 1981). For example, Kelman et al. (1981) offered two explanations for subharmonic components, which usually took the form of a $1/2 f_0$ series, observed in patients with abnormal vocal function:

(1) The f_0 abruptly is decreased by one octave, or

(2) The subharmonic components arise from a modulation of the vibratory pattern of the vocal folds. Kelman et al. (1981) note that such vibratory patterns occur in nonlinear systems, that is, systems characterized by restoring forces proportional to a power of displacement.

The importance of tremor to neuromotor dysfunction was discussed by Darley et al. (1975). With regard to static tremor, they wrote that "Abnormal tremor appears to be an accentuation in the amplitude with perhaps some slowing of the frequency of normal static tremor" (p. 225). Pathologic voice tremor in adults (aged 30–79 years) was reported by Brown and Simonson (1963) to have a frequency of 4–8 Hz. Thus the static voice tremor of adults falls below the frequency range (9–25 Hz) observed for infants in the present study.

B. Phonetic development during infancy

The description of continuities and discontinuities in development is related to, and in fact often leads to, the postulation of stages. Several stage descriptions of phonetic or vocalization development have been offered (Zlatin, 1975; Oller, 1978; Stark, 1979, 1981). Stark (1981) remarked that although there is general agreement about the nature and chronology of stages, questions remain about the actual identification of stages, particularly with respect to onset and offset. It appears that principles and criteria for the identification and discrimination of stages in phonetic development are similar to those proposed by Piaget (1952; 1960) for a stage theory of cognitive development. Four criteria in particular seem relevant to postulations of stages in phonetic development: invariant sequence, or constant order of succession; integration, or the blending of accomplishments in one stage into a following stage; consolidation, or a pattern of achievement and preparation between a given stage and its predecessor and successor; and equilibration, or variations in stability of behavior within and between stages. For a general review of these concepts, see the paper by Brainerd (1978) and the open peer commentaries published simultaneously.

However, the idea of stages is controversial. Lipsitt (1978) viewed stages as "gaps in our information as scientists, not gaps in the behavior of our subjects" (p. 194). Stage descriptions also have been criticized because they tend to obscure the presence of substantial behavioral variability within any given stage (Baldwin and Baldwin, 1978) and because the overall course of development reflects changes in interrelated components ("hardware" such as physical capacities and "software" such as the content and organization of processes and data structures), each of which has its own developmental course (Klahr, 1978).

We subscribe to a view of stages of phonetic development schematized in Fig. 16. This view recognizes an overlapping of behaviors across stages, such that some behaviors are integrated into a succeeding stage whereas other behaviors may persist into a succeeding stage only to fade or drop out. Thus development has aspects of both continuity and discontinuity. Stages must always be an abstract view of behavior, but they hold both conceptual and clinical utility and therefore are not likely to be abandoned.

The phonetic transcription studies of Irwin and Chen (Chen and Irwin, 1946; Irwin, 1947a, b, 1948; Irwin and Chen, 1946) indicated that most sounds uttered by a child before the eighth month of life are vowels. Because these data continue to be highly influential in accounts of speech development (cf. Mowrer, 1980), they warrant careful re-

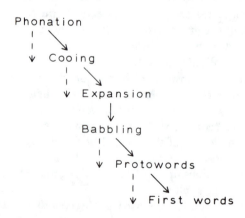

FIG. 16. Hypothesized stages in phonetic and lexical development in the first year of life. Continuity in performance is shown by a solid line, and lack of continuity by a broken line. The broken lines show that behaviors may persist into a succeeding stage but may drop out if they are not integrated into other behaviors at that stage. Thus transitions between stages are obscured because behavioral changes across stages are not immediate nor simultaneous. Most of the stages are based on Oller (1978) and Stark (1981).

examination, especially as acoustic data become available. Most of the early vowels are perceived as /ɛ/, /ɪ/, /ʌ/, or /ʊ/. The ratio of vowels to consonants declined from 4.5:1 at the 0–2 month stage, to 3.6:1 at the 2–4 month stage, to 2.8:1 at the 4–8 month stage. Across the same intervals, the proportion of total vowels accounted for by the three vowels /ɛ/, /ɪ/, and /ʌ/, declined from 95.8% to 81.8% to 77.7%. However, the vowel-to-consonant ratios should be interpreted in light of the fact that the predominant consonants were the glottal spirant /h/ and the glottal stop /ʔ/. Across the intervals noted above, these two glottal sounds accounted for the following proportions of total transcribed consonants: 87.1%, 75.3%, and 70.4%, respectively. Because infant vocalizations seem to be highly variable and unstable in laryngeal function, the high proportion of /h/ and /ʔ/ sounds might be more conservatively ascribed to alternate phonatory states used during vowel (or vowel-like) utterances than to genuine consonant production.

A major observation in the present study was documentation of several types of laryngeal behavior seldom observed in the older child or adult with normal speech. The infants in this study produced many vocalizations characterized by tremor (or vibrato), abrupt or rapid f_0 shifts, breathiness (noise contamination), and subharmonic components. All of these characteristics may be taken as evidence of instability of laryngeal control. To attribute these phonatory changes to consonant segments is a major, and at this point, unnecessary assumption about an infant's linguistic ability. Phonological analysis generally assumes segmentation of the utterance into phonemic or phonetic segments. But there is no guarantee that the "segments" an investigator hears really exist as control elements in the vocalization behavior of the child.

As an alternative to phonological analysis based on abstract linguistic units or categories (e.g., consonants, vowels, glides, and consonant clusters) one might describe vocalization behavior in terms of the observed or inferred *movements* of the articulatory structures. From the perspective of the neural control of behavior, there is no necessary reason to suppose that infant vocalization is regulated by linguistic units such as phonemes, or even by major phonetic categories such as consonants and vowels. What the linguist perceives as a CV syllable in an infant's babbling is a movement sequence, usually with concurrent phonation, in which one or more articulatory structures move from a position that constricts the vocal tract to one that does not constrict the vocal tract. The fact that most CV syllables are heard as stop + vowel syllables indicates that the initial constricted position is a complete obstruction, serving to shut off momentarily all air flow through the vocal tract. The fact that most babbling syllables are judged to be produced with single consonants rather than consonant clusters means that most sound patterns classified by the linguist as syllables are generated by single, one-directional articulatory movements rather than by multiple, sequential articulatory movements.

Early articulatory movements may bear important similarities to early movements of the limbs, fingers, and head. Some of these movements are one directional and functionally isolated from preceding and following movements, thus being similar to isolated monosyllabic utterances in cooing or babbling. In addition, the repetitive movement frequently observed for the limbs and fingers might be analogous to reduplication in babbling. Reduplicated utterances are motorically similar to rhythmical stereotypies, "The quite rapid, repetitious movement of the limbs, torso, and head that is common in human infants during the first year of life or so" (Thelen, 1981, p. 238). Many of these nonspeech rhythmical stereotypies reach their peak frequency of occurrence between 20 and 52 weeks of age, approximately the same time as the occurrence of reduplicated babbling. If early sounds are interpreted as their underlying movements, it may be possible to describe infant activity of various forms, vocal and nonvocal, in terms of general movement properties. Of course, the infant may differentiate his/her vocal behavior from other behaviors quite early, so that vocal behavior may assume unique motor properties within a few weeks.

It is likely that the emergence of phonetic contrasts can be understood in part from studies of the frequency of occurrence of early sound patterns in pre-word vocalizations, whether the data base is perceptually or acoustically derived. Our preference is for acoustic documentation, or at least acoustic confirmation of perceptually determined categories, in order that linguistic or general perceptual biases of the observer may be minimized. As Keating (1980) has remarked, early vowels may be "indeterminate" because they cannot be uniquely associated with a particular articulation (see also Lieberman, 1977; Kent, 1981). Keating states: "Which vowel is actually heard in a given utterance may be quite accidental, simply a function of whatever position these articulators [lips, larynx, and tongue] happen to be in" (p. 224). Martin (1981) also has cautioned on the use of nomenclature and phonetic symbols that are interpretable only within a mature linguistic system. He proposes that vowel-like and consonantlike sounds produced in the first few months of life be termed *vocants* and *closants*, respectively, and that any attempted phonetic transcription be enclosed in double square brackets, e.g., [[æ]]. With careful acoustic and phonetic description of a wide sampling of sounds produced by individual infants, it should be possible to establish the preferred categories or regions of sound production. Such preferences might be useful in testing hypotheses about continuity in sound development or the precursors of phonetic constrasts.

Even preferences as simple as front over back vowels and apical over dorsal consonants may provide some advantage in the learning of English sounds because front vowels and apical consonants predominate in frequency of occurrence (Dewey, 1923; Mines *et al.*, 1978). Front vowels account for about half of all vowel productions in adult English speech, and apical consonants account for about half of all consonant productions. Furthermore, it seems that front vowels and apical consonants share a relatively fronted position of the tongue body (Shriberg and Kent, in press). This shared articulatory feature is illustrated in Fig. 17, which shows tracings from lateral x rays of the front vowel /ɛ/ and the apical stop /d/. Aside from the expected and necessary differences in articulation of the apex, the overall tongue

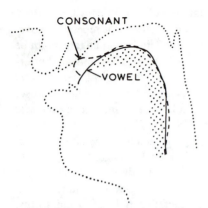

FIG. 17. Vocal-tract configurations for isolated production by an adult speaker of a front vowel /ε/ and production of an alveolar consonant in a neutral vowel context /d ʌ/. Note general similarity in position and shape of body, dorsum, and root of tongue.

shape and position is nearly congruent for the two sounds. In this sense, front vowels and apical consonants have an articulatory compatability. On the other hand, the dorsal consonants have a position of the tongue body that is more like a back rather than front vowel. Thus front vowels and apical consonants have in common a relatively anterior carriage of the tongue and high frequency of occurrence in English, whereas back vowels and dorsal consonants have in common a relatively posterior carriage of the tongue and a low frequency of occurrence.

Whereas a considerable amount has been written about the clinical implications of acoustic analysis of infant cry (see Wasz-Hockert et al., 1968; Lester and Zeskind, 1981; and the papers in Murry and Murry, 1980), relatively little has been written about similar implications for comfort-state vocalizations during the cooing and babbling stages. Nonetheless, preliminary guidelines and milestones are being proposed for clinical use in pediatrics and speech–language pathology (see, for example, Reilly, 1980). Some milestones require recognition of vocalization behaviors such as cooing, razzing, and babbling. Acoustic descriptions of these vocalization categories may aid in their reliable identification and clinical application.

ACKNOWLEDGMENTS

This research was supported by NIH (NINCDS) grant NS 16763. We thank Angela Wong and Mark McGovern for their assistance with recording procedures and the preparation of spectrograms. Ronald Netsell and Harold Bauer offered many valuable suggestions on an earlier draft of the manuscript. Carole Dugan patiently and efficiently brought the manuscript to its final typed form.

APPENDIX

Included here are spectrograms that illustrate major utterance types as features of special interest. Figure A1 shows wideband (top) and narrow-band (bottom) spectrograms of a 3-month-old's vocalic utterance that was judged to be nasalized. The acoustic evidence of nasalization is the reduction of energy in the $F2$ region co-occurring with strong low-frequency energy located at or below the $F1$ re-

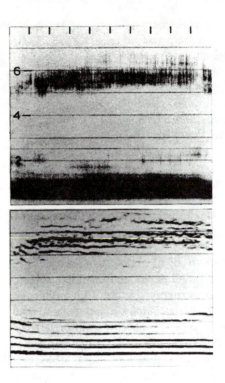

FIG. A1. Wideband (top) and narrow-band (bottom) spectrograms of a nasalized vocalic utterance produced by a 3-month-old infant.

gion. The energy centered around 500–600 Hz is thought to reflect the nasal formant, and the reduction of energy in the $F2$ region is thought to reflect the influence of antiresonances. Such strongly nasalized utterances were excluded from analyses of formant structure.

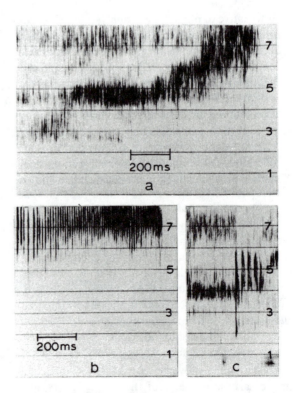

FIG. A2. Wideband spectrograms of infant sounds generated with an aperiodic energy source: (a) fricativelike sound with gradually changing spectrum, (b) trill or vibrant, (c) sequence of frication and trill.

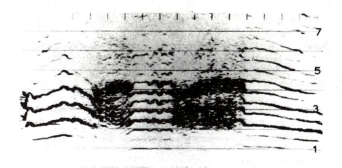

FIG. A3. Narrow-band spectrogram of infant vocalization produced with a complex phonatory pattern. Horizontal lines represent 1-kHz intervals, and tics at top represent 100-ms intervals.

Spectrograms in Fig. A2 depict consonantlike sounds associated with aperiodic energy sources, i.e., turbulence noise. Spectrogram (a) shows a complex fricative sound that gradually changed in its spectral properties from a relatively flat, diffuse noise to a more sharply tuned, high-frequency noise. Spectrogram (b) pertains to a sound judged to be labial trill. The noise energy, which is mostly above 6 kHz in frequency, is modulated by a trill frequency of about 75–80 Hz at its midsegment. Spectrogram (c) illustrates a sound that changed from fricativelike (continuous noise energy) to trill (modulated noise energy) having a trill frequency of about 30 Hz. Because the major energy in the infants' frication sounds frequently extended beyond the conventional bandwidth of 8 kHz used in spectrography, we are conducting a separate analysis of consonantlike sounds using a 16-kHz bandwidth.

Figure A3 presents a narrow-band spectrogram of a vocalization that changed repeatedly in its phonatory properties. The f_0 frequency sometimes changed quickly and markedly, for example, dropping from about 800 Hz to less than 200 Hz in 200 ms, or more than 3 Hz/ms. Tremor or vibrato also is evident for parts of this vocalization. Such rapid and dramatic changes in phonation were observed frequently.

Figure A4 represents a sound pattern perceived as a sequence of four CV syllables uttered in short succession. The subject was three months old. The f_0 contour is superimposed on the wideband spectrogram to show the "prosodic" character of the syllable sequence. Interestingly, the final syllable is marked prosodically by increased duration and an f_0 fall of about 200 Hz. Similar prosodic features character-

ize final stressed syllables in adult speech (Cooper and Sorenson, 1981). Thus a detailed analysis of tone patterns in cooing or babbling should recognize contextual or positional influences, which are neglected in the present study.

Baldwin, J. D., and Baldwin, J. L. (1978). "Open peer commentary on C. J. Brainerd's 'The stage question in cognitive developmental theory,' " Behav. Brain Sci. 1, 182–183.

Bayley, N. (1969). *Bayley Scales of Infant Development* (The Psychological Corporation, New York).

Bosma, J. F. (1965). "Anatomic and physiologic development of the speech apparatus," in *The Nervous System. Vol. 3: Human Communication and its Disorders*, edited by D. B. Tower (Raven, New York).

Bosma, J., Truby, H., and Lind, J. (1965). "Cry motions of the newborn infant," in *Newborn Infant Cry*, edited by J. Lind (Almqvist and Wiksells, Uppsala).

Brainerd, C. J. (1978). "The stage question in cognitive-developmental theory," Behav. Brain Sci. 1, 173–182.

Brown, J. R., and Simonson, J. (1963). "Organic voice tremor," Neurology 13, 520–525.

Buhr, R. D. (1980). "The emergence of vowels in an infant," J. Speech Hear. Res. 23, 73–94.

Buhr, R., and Keating, P. (1977). "Spectrographic effects of register shifts in speech production," J. Acoust. Soc. Am. 62, 525.

Capute, A. J., Palmer, F. B., Shapiro, B. K., Wachtel, R. C., and Accardo, P. J. (1981). "Early language development: clinical application of the language and auditory milestone scale," in *Language Behavior in Infancy and Early Childhood*, edited by R. E. Stark (Elsevier/North Holland, New York).

Chen, H. P., and Irwin, O. C. (1946). "Infant speech: vowel and consonant types," J. Speech Disord. 11, 27–29.

Colton, R. H., and Steinschneider, A. (1980). "Acoustic relationships of infant cries to the sudden infant death syndrome," in *Infant Communication: Cry and Early Speech*, edited by T. Murry and J. Murry (College-Hill, Houston, TX).

Cooper, W. E., and Sorenson, J. M. (1981). *Fundamental Frequency in Sentence Production* (Springer–Verlag, New York).

Cruttenden, A. (1981). "Falls and rises: meanings and universals," J. Linguist. 17, 77–91.

Crystal, D. (1979). "Prosodic development," in *Language Acquisition*, edited by P. Fletcher and M. Garmon (University of Cambridge, Cambridge, England).

Darley, F. L., Aronson, A. E., and Brown, J. R. (1975). *Motor Speech Disorders* (Saunders, Philadelphia).

Delack, J. B., and Fowlow, P. J. (1978). "The ontogenesis of differential vocalization: development of prosodic contrastivity during the first year of life," in *The Development of Communication*, edited by N. Waterson and C. Snow (Wiley, New York).

Dewey, G. (1923). *Relative Frequency of English Speech Sounds* (Harvard U. P., Cambridge, MA).

DuBrul, E. L. (1977). "Origin of the speech apparatus and its reconstruction in fossils," Brain Lang. 4, 365–381.

Fletcher, S. G. (1973). "Maturation of the speech mechanism," Folia Phoniat. 25, 161–172.

Fokes, J. (1971). "Developmental scale of language acquisition," in *Training the Developmentally Young*, edited by B. Stephens (John Day, New York).

Irwin, O. C. (1947a). "Infant speech: consonant sounds according to manner of articulation," J. Speech Disord. 12, 402–404.

Irwin, O. C. (1947b). "Infant speech: consonantal sounds according to place of articulation," J. Speech Disord. 12, 397–401.

Irwin, O. C. (1948). "Infant speech: development of vowel sounds," J. Speech Hear. Disord. 13, 31–34.

Irwin, O. C., and Chen, H. P. (1946). "Infant speech: vowel and consonant frequency," J. Speech Disord. 11, 123–125.

Keating, P. (1980). "Patterns of fundamental frequency and vocal registers," in *Infant Communication: Cry and Early Speech*, edited by T. Murry and J. Murry (College-Hill, Houston, TX).

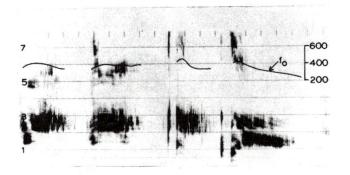

FIG. A4. Wideband spectrogram of syllable sequence produced by a 6-month-old infant. The f_0 frequency curve is superimposed on the spectrogram.

Kelman, A. W. (**1981**). "Vibratory pattern of the vocal folds," Folia Phoniat. **33**, 73–99.

Kelman, A. W., Gordon, M. T., Morton, F. M., and Simpson, I. C. (**1981**). "Comparison of methods for assessing vocal function," Folia Phoniat. **33**, 51–65.

Kent, R. D. (**1979**). "Isovowel lines for evaluating vowel formant structures in speech disorders," J. Speech Hear. Disord. **44**, 513–521.

Kent, R. D. (**1981**). "Articulatory-acoustic perspectives on speech development," in *Language Behavior in Infancy and Early Childhood*, edited by R. E. Stark (Elsevier/North Holland, New York).

Kent, R. D., and Forner, L. L. (**1979**). "A developmental study of vowel formant frequencies in an imitation task," J. Acoust. Soc. Am. **65**, 208–217.

Klahr, D. (**1978**). "Open peer commentary on C. J. Brainerd's 'The stage question in cognitive-developmental theory,' " Behav. Brain. Sci. **1**, 191–192.

Knobloch, H., Pasamanick, B., and Sherard, E. S., Jr. (**1966**). "A developmental screening inventory for infants," Pediat. **38**, Part II, 1095–1104.

Ladefoged, P. (**1975**). *A Course in Phonetics* (Harcourt, Brace and Jovanovich, New York).

Laitman, J. T., and Crelin, E. S. (**1976**). "Postnatal development of the basicranium and vocal tract region in man," in *Symposium on Development of the Basicranium*, edited by J. F. Bosma (DHEW Publication No. NIH 76-989, NIH, Bethesda, MD).

Laufer, M. Z. (**1980**). "Temporal regularity in prespeech," in *Infant Communication: Cry and Early Speech*, edited by T. Murry and J. Murry (College-Hill, Houston, TX).

Lester, B. M., and Zeskind, P. S. (**1981**). "A biobehavioral perspective on crying in early infancy," in *Theory and Research in Behavioral Pediatrics*, edited by H. E. Fitzgerald, B. M. Lester, and M. W. Yogman (Plenum, New York).

Lieberman, P. (**1977**). *Speech Physiology and Acoustic Phonetics: An Introduction* (MacMillan, New York).

Lieberman, P., Harris, K. S., Wolff, P., and Russell, L. H. (**1971**). "Newborn infant cry and nonhuman primate vocalization," J. Speech Hear. Res. **14**, 718–727.

Lipsitt, L. P. (**1978**). "Open peer commentary on C. J. Brainerd's 'The stage question in cognitive-developmental theory,' " Behav. Brain. Sci. **1**, 194.

Martin, J. A. M. (**1981**). *Voice, Speech, and Language in the Child; Development and Disorder. Disorders of Human Communication*, Vol. 4, edited by G. E. Arnold, F. Winckel, and B. D. Wyke (Springer–Verlag, New York).

Maskarinec, A. S., Cairns, G. F., Butterfield, E. C., and Weamer, D. K. (**1981**). "Longitudinal observations of individual infant's vocalizations," J. Speech Hear. Disord. **46**, 267–273.

Mavilya, M. P. (**1969**). "Spontaneous vocalization and babbling in hearing impaired infants," Unpublished doctoral dissertation, Columbia University (University Microfilms No. 70–12879).

Michelsson, K. (**1980**). "Cry characteristics in sound spectrographic cry analysis," in *Infant Communication: Cry and Early Speech*, edited by T. Murry and J. Murry (College-Hill, Houston, TX).

Mines, M., Hanson, B., and Shoup, J. (**1978**). "Frequency of occurrence of phonemes in conventional English," Lang. Speech **21**, 221–241.

Monsen, R. B., Engebretson, A. M., and Vemula, N. R. (**1979**). "Some effects of deafness on the generation of voice," J. Acoust. Soc. Am. **66**, 1680–1690.

Mowrer, D. E. (**1980**). "Phonological development during the first year of life," in *Speech and Language: Advances in Basic Research and Practice*, Vol. 4, edited by N. J. Lass (Academic, New York).

Murry, T., and Murry, J., Eds. (**1980**). *Infant Communication: Cry and Early Speech* (College-Hill, Houston, TX).

Netsell, R. (**1981**). "The acquisition of speech motor control: a perspective with directions for research," in *Language Behavior in Infancy and Early Childhood*, edited by R. E. Stark (Elsevier/North Holland, New York).

Oller, D. K. (**1978**). "Infant vocalizations and the development of speech," Allied Health Behav. Sci. **1**, 523–549.

Oller, D. K., Wieman, L. A., Doyle, W. J., and Ross, C. (**1976**). "Infant babbling and speech," J. Child Lang. **3**, 1–11.

Petrovich-Bartell, I., Cowan, N., and Morse, P. A. (in press). "Mothers' perceptions of infant distress vocalizations," J. Speech Hear. Res.

Piaget, J. (**1952**). *The Origins of Intelligence in Children* (Norton, New York).

Piaget, J. (**1960**). "The general problems of the psychobiological development of the child," in *Discussions on Child Development*, Vol. 4, edited by J. M. Tanner and B. Inhelder (Tavistock, London).

Reilly, A. P. (Ed.) (**1980**). *The Communication Game* (Johnson & Johnson Baby Products Co., printed in U.S.A.).

Ringel, R. L., and Kluppel, D. D. (**1964**). "Neonatal crying: a normative study," Folia Phoniat. **16**, 1–9.

Sasaki, C. T., Levine, P. A., Laitman, J. T., and Crelin, E. S. (**1977**). "Postnatal descent of the epiglottis in man," Arch. Otolaryngol. **103**, 169–171.

Shriberg, L. D., and Kent, R. D. (**1982**). *Clinical Phonetics* (Wiley, New York).

Sloan, R. F. (**1967**). "Neuronal histogenesis, maturation and organization related to speech development," J. Commun. Disord **1**, 1–15.

Stark, R. E. (**1979**). "Prespeech segmental feature development," in *Language Acquisition*, edited by P. Fletcher and M. Garom (Cambridge U. P., Cambridge).

Stark, R. E. (**1981**). "Stages of development in the first year of life," in *Child Phonology: Vol. I: Production*, edited by G. H. Yeni-Komshian, C. A. Ferguson, and J. Kavanagh (Academic, New York).

Stark, R. E., Rose, S. N., and McLagen, M. (**1975**). "Features of infant sounds: the first eight weeks of life," J. Child Lang. **2**, 205–222.

Thelen, E. (**1981**). "Rhythmical behavior in infancy: an ethological perspective," Dev. Psychol. **17**, 237–257.

Wasz-Hockert, O., Lind, J., Vuorenkoski, V., Partanen, T., and Valanne, E. (**1968**). "The infant cry," in *Clinics in Developmental Medicine 29* (Spastics International Medical Publications, Lavenham Press, England).

Wells, G., Montgomery, M., and MacLure, M. (**1978**). "The development of discourse: a report on work in progress," School of Education, University of Bristol. Cited by A. Cruttenden (1981), "Falls and rises: meanings and universals," J. Linguist. **17**, 77–91.

Wind, J. (**1970**). *On the Phylogeny and the Ontogeny of the Human Larynx* (Wolters–Noordhoff, Groningen, The Netherlands).

Zlatin, M. (**1975**). "Explorative mapping of the vocal tract and primitive syllabification in infancy: the first six months," Paper presented at the Annual Convention of the American Speech and Hearing Association, Washington, DC.

PART IV
Spectrography in Evaluation and Therapy

Spectrography has been used in many clinical investigations to specify acoustic clues to specific speech-language disorders. It has also served to verify the outcome of various types of therapy. Unfortunately it seldom has been used, on a day-to-day basis, to verify diagnosis or treatment of pathologies of speech. This is the result of several factors: the high cost of the spectrograph itself, clinicians' unfamiliarity with the technical aspects of spectrography, and lack of knowledge about how often and how readily spectrograms have been used successfully for diagnosis and appraisal.

Spectrography has been successfully used in the study of stuttering, neuromotor and aphasic disorders (Kent, Netsell, and Abbs, 1979; Kent and Rosenbek, 1983), misarticulation (Daniloff, Stephens, and Wilcox, 1980), and the speech of the deaf (Angelocci, Kopp, and Holbrook, 1964; Maki, Gustafson, Conklin, and Humphrey-Whitehead, 1981; Oller, Eilers, Bull, and Carner, 1985), to name just a few. Provided that segmentation methodology is well specified, spectrograms provide excellent means for temporal analysis of whole utterances, phrases, words, syllables, clusters, vowels, and subphonemic cues such as voice onset time, transition duration, and aspiration time. Similarly, accuracy of vocal tract shaping can be estimated from formant frequency measures of vocalic elements (Kent, 1979) and from noise spectra of obstruents. The integrity of velar-lingual-labial-vocal coordination can be inferred from the presence or absence, duration, or spectral properties of bursts, affrications, transitions, silent intervals, and the like. Indeed, the spectrograph is unique in providing — rapidly and reliably — a richly multidimensional array of time-locked cues.

The Sonagram is usually associated with demonstration of the articulatory features of speech, but this view is too limited. The glottal (or source) signal contributes significant components all its own, and these can be identified in appropriately prepared spectrograms. Therefore, Sonagrams can provide insight into vocal function as well.

Sonagrams are not the method of choice for quantifying the characteristics of phonation. Other widely available techniques provide better quantification of those spectral aspects of the voice signal that are widely accepted as indices of normality. But spectrograms often provide an excellent qualitative demonstration of the problems of voicing and they can be useful in grading the severity of dysphonia. A typical method for doing this is discussed by Yanagihara (1967). The other two articles in this section, Lebrun, Devreux, Rousseau, and Darimont (1982) and Rontal, Rontal, and Rolnick (1975), provide examples of how Sonagrams can be used to plan and guide vocal therapy.

Accurate measurement of spectrographic parameters may sometimes be laborious, and it is frequently impossible to do with the needed accuracy (Huggins, 1980). But there is an important place for the spectrograph in the laboratory and in the clinic, and there will continue to be, far into the forseeable future.

Readings

Articulatory Behavior

Huggins, A. W. F. (1980). Better spectrograms from children's speech: A research note. *Journal of Speech and Hearing Research, 23,* 19–27.

Kent, R. D. (1979). Isovowel lines for the evaluation of vowel formant structure in speech disorders. *Journal of Speech and Hearing Disorders, 44,* 513–521.

Kent, R. D., and Rosenbek, J. C. (1983). Acoustic patterns of apraxia of speech. *Journal of Speech and Hearing Research, 26,* 231–249.

Kent, R. D., Netsell, R., and Abbs, J. H. (1979). Acoustic characteristics of dysarthria associated with cerebellar disease. *Journal of Speech and Hearing Research, 22,* 627–648.

Daniloff, R. G., Wilcox, K., and Stephens, M. I. (1980). An acoustic-articulatory description of children's defective /s/ productions. *Journal of Communication Disorders, 13,* 347–363.

Oller, D. K., Eilers, R., Bull, D., and Carner, A. (1985). Prespeech vocalizations of a deaf infant: A comparison with normal metaphonological development. *Journal of Speech and Hearing Research, 28,* 47–63.

Angelocci, A. A., Kopp, G. A., and Holbrook, A. (1964). The vowel formants of deaf and normal-hearing eleven- to fourteen-year-old boys. *Journal of Speech and Hearing Disorders, 29,* 156–170.

Maki, J. E., Gustafson, M. S., Conklin, J. M., and Humphrey-Whitehead, B. K. (1981). The speech spectrographic display: Interpretation of visual patterns by hearing-impaired adults. *Journal of Speech and Hearing Disorders, 46,* 379–387.

Vocal Function

Yanagihara, N. (1967). Significance of harmonic changes and noise components in hoarseness. *Journal of Speech and Hearing Research, 10,* 531–541.

Lebrun, Y., Devreux, F., Rousseau, J.-J., and Darimont, P. (1982). Tremulous speech: A case report. *Folia Phoniatrica, 34,* 134–142.

Rontal, E., Rontal, M., and Rolnick, M. I. (1975). Objective evaluation of vocal pathology using voice spectrography. *Annals of Otology, Rhinology, and Laryngology, 84,* 662–672.

BETTER SPECTROGRAMS FROM CHILDREN'S SPEECH
A RESEARCH NOTE

A. W. F. HUGGINS

Massachusetts Institute of Technology, Cambridge

A major problem in the spectrographic analysis of children's speech is the poor resolution of formants, which is the result of the widely spaced harmonics of the high fundamental frequency. An attempt has been made to bypass this problem by exciting a child's vocal tract with an artificial larynx, using a fundamental frequency appropriate to a man. This method has promise for tracking formants in children's speech.

There are several problems in acoustic phonetics that could be answered at least partially if it were possible to get clear spectrograms from children's voices. Unfortunately, as anyone who has attempted a spectrographic study of children's speech must know, there are many obstacles in this path. Spectrograms of children's voices are often uninterpretable, even after successfully: (1) eliciting the desired utterance from the child, at a suitable rate and level and in a good acoustic environment; (2) recording it on tape at a sufficient signal-to-noise ratio, without the child turning away from the microphone, or hitting it, or laughing; (3) coaxing the spectrograph into yielding the desired spectrograms. There are several factors that contribute to this failure. The most obvious is the high fundamental frequency (f_o) typical of children's voices, as shown in the first three figures.

Figure 1 shows how the speech waveform as recorded by a microphone (bottom right) is built up. The volume velocity at the larynx has a line spectrum (bottom left), with progressively less energy in each harmonic of the fundamental as the number of the harmonic increases. The energy falls off at about 12dB/octave. The transfer function of the vocal tract (top left) then emphasizes some harmonics and de-emphasizes others. The radiation characteristic (top right) reflects the more efficient conversion of energy, from volume velocity to pressure, as frequency increases. The only source of information about the frequency of the formants (the peaks in the transfer function) is the relative amplitude of the harmonics of the fundamental. These relative amplitudes are affected both by the fundamental frequency and also by idiosyncratic peaks and valleys in the source function of individual speakers.

The confidence with which a formant frequency can be estimated is obviously greater when many harmonics of the fundamental fall within

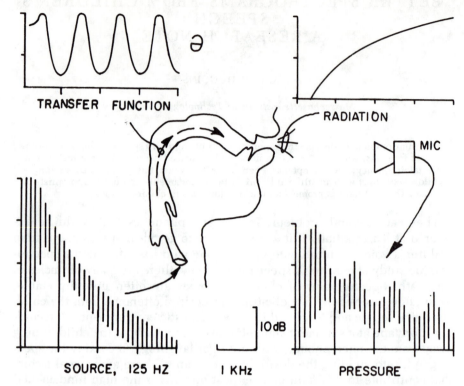

FIGURE 1. The spectrum of the speech waveform picked up by the microphone (bottom right) is built up from the spectrum of the energy injected at the larynx (bottom left), which is then shaped by the transfer function of the vocal tract (top left), and high-frequency-emphasized by the radiation characteristic, which reflects the more efficient conversion of volume velocity within the tract to pressure energy outside as frequency increases (top right).

the formant, than when only a few do. This is shown in Figure 2, where the top half shows an output spectrum generated synthetically with a fundamental of 125 Hz, and the bottom shows the same transfer function driven by a fundamental of 375 Hz. The dotted line shows the true transfer function, and the solid line shows erroneous estimates of the formants, such as might be assumed by attending to the intensity of the strongest harmonics only. In running speech of course, the fundamental frequency moves up and down, and the tops of the harmonics ride up and down, drawing out the spectral envelope of the transfer function. This is illustrated in Figure 3. At the left, a transfer function appropriate to the vowel /æ/ was swept by a fundamental that moved from 100 Hz to 133 Hz to 90 Hz, and at the right the same vowel was swept by a fundamental that moved from 300 Hz to 400 Hz to 270 Hz. Because these sounds were generated by a terminal analogue synthesizer (Klatt, 1972), the formant frequencies are exactly constant throughout which would never occur in natural speech.

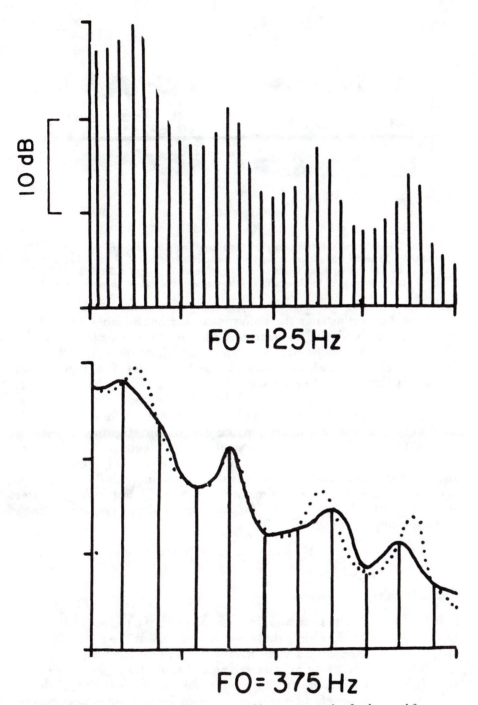

FIGURE 2. The *same* transfer function is excited by a source with a fundamental frequency of 125 Hz (top) and of 375 Hz (bottom). In the bottom half, the true transfer function is shown as a dotted line, and the solid line represents an erroneous transfer function that might easily result from over-literal reading of a spectrogram.

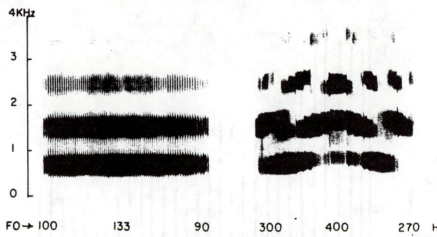

FIGURE 3. Broad-band spectrograms showing a fixed set of formants (*F1 = 600, F2 = 1500, F3 = 2400 Hz*) swept by a low frequency fundamental (left) from 100 Hz to 133 Hz to 90 Hz, and swept by a high frequency fundamental (right) from 300 Hz to 400 Hz to 270 Hz. The effect of wide separation of the harmonics of the fundamental can be seen on the right.

Figure 3 also illustrates the unfortunate, but unavoidable, conflict between the bandwidth of the analyzing filter of the spectrograph (usually 300 Hz for wide-band) and a high fundamental. At the left, with a low fundamental, the formants appear steady as F_o changes. The harmonics of the fundamental are close enough together that several harmonics fall within the passband of the filter. Individual harmonics would not be separated unless the bandwidth of the filter were narrowed, for example to 60 Hz. At the right of the figure, on the other hand, the fundamental is higher, and the harmonics are separated widely enough that even the wide band filter passes only one at a time, effectively generating a narrow-band spectrogram The accentuation of the individual harmonics of the fundamental makes the formants hard to read, although computer techniques have been suggested for estimating formant frequencies from harmonic amplitudes (Wolf, 1970).

METHOD

The Electrolarynx Technique

In this paper, we present a preliminary account of a technique that may permit some of the foregoing problems to be avoided. The technique consists of exciting the child's vocal tract with a fundamental appropriate to an adult male, by using an electrolarynx. Dunn (1961) used the same technique to measure formants for adult speakers, but applied to children it has the added benefit of giving much more detailed information about the formants than is normally available. The device we used was the Electrolarynx Model 5-A, which is a small handheld vibrator developed at Bell

Telephone Laboratories to allow laryngectomees to use the telephone (Barney, Haworth, and Dunn, 1959). The user places the electrolarynx against the thinnest and most rigid structure remaining above his larynx after his operation, to maximize the transfer of energy through the throat wall. A thumb switch controls the pitch, and vibration ceases when F_o falls below about 80 Hz (for the male-pitch model).*

Recordings were made of several children saying short phrases chosen to contain large formant movements, such as "a weed, a rock, a lamb." The subject first spoke the phrase normally, and then mouthed it with a closed glottis and with the electrolarynx pressed to the side of the pharynx, just above the glottis. An example of a nine-year old child saying "a weed" is shown in Figure 4. The natural utterance appears at the left, and the one produced with the electrolarynx at the right. The top spectrograms were made with the wide-band filter, and the bottom ones with the narrow-band filter. Several things stand out in this figure. First, the formants are quite clear in the top right quarter of the figure, although there seem to be too many present. The rate of speech is faster in the

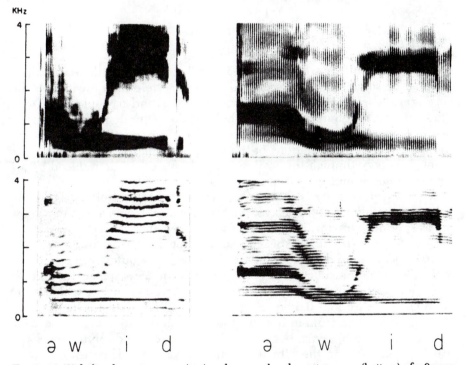

FIGURE 4. Wide band spectrograms (top) and narrow band spectrograms (bottom) of a 9-year old boy saying "a weed." At the left, the speech was normally voiced, and at the right the subject mouthed the words, while pressing the electrolarynx to the right side of his pharynx, just above the larynx.

*We are most grateful to Mr. Seaverns of New England Telephone for loaning us one of these devices.

natural utterance, and the narrow-band spectrograms make it obvious that the fundamental is about three times higher in the natural speech. The figure demonstrates that the technique can yield meaningful data with a child's speech.

As a further check, similar comparisons were made for an adult male, since formants are easier to measure in the speech of a male adult than a child. After some practice with the electrolarynx, the subject said nonsense phrases such as /abadaga/, /afaθašaša/, /alarawaya/, first spoken and then mouthed with the electrolarynx. Figure 5 shows two spectrograms of /alarawaya/, the natural one at the top, and the one made with the electrolarynx in the middle. At the bottom, tracings from the two spectrograms are superimposed, to show the similarity of the formant tracks. In general the match is close, and similar agreement was obtained from comparisons made on other utterances with the aid of Xerox transparencies. Note that the subject was trying to repeat the phrase as exactly as possible, so that the agreement found is probably as good as the technique will permit.

DISCUSSION

Future Directions

It should be obvious from the foregoing that there are still several problems to be solved before the electrolarynx can yield unequivocal results. In Figure 4 several extra formants can be seen, and it would be hard to know which to ignore without the help of the natural speech. The most likely source of the extra formants is leakage around the side of the vibrator, or the large vibrations of the throat wall that have to occur to get enough energy through the wall. Such leakages could be reduced by appropriate shielding.

A second possibility is that the spectrum of the electrolarynx may not fall off smoothly at 12 dB/octave, but may contain irregularities that show up as spurious formants. Of course as mentioned above, such irregularities may also occur in natural speech. No attempt was made to measure the source spectrum of the electrolarynx although this would clearly be desirable. Since the transducer was based on a telephone earpiece, the free air spectrum was probably close to that of the driving pulses, which were nominally square and 0.5 msec wide (Barney, Haworth, & Dunn, 1959). But the source spectrum in free air is not very informative of the spectrum injected into the pharynx, because the spectrum depends on the mechanical load imposed on the vibrator by the throat wall. This in turn varies with the pressure applied, and on the unknown transfer function of the tract wall. It would be appropriate, though beyond the scope of this preliminary study, to measure the injected spectrum directly. One possibility would be to measure the injected spectrum in the pharynx with a probe microphone, while the subject articulates a high front vowel, and another would be to make measurements with the vocal tract terminated in a tube

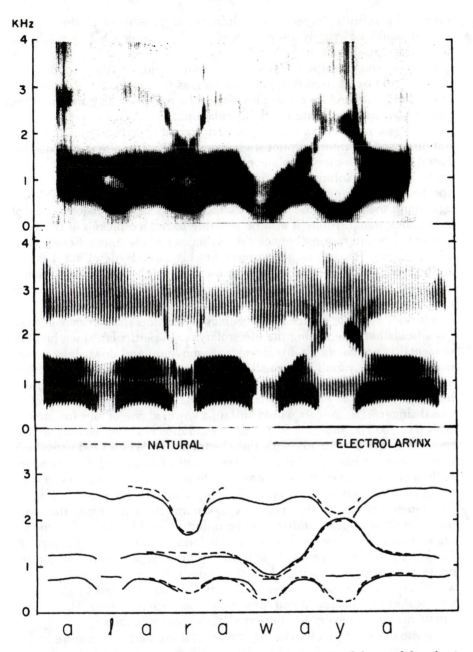

FIGURE 5. Natural and electrolarynx excited speech are compared for an adult male. A wide band spectrogram of /alarawaya/, spoken naturally, appears at the top. The version produced with the electrolarynx appears in the middle, and formant tracks traced from each of the above are superimposed in the bottom panel of the figure.

presenting infinite impedance.[1] Unfortunately, neither of these techniques could be widely used with children, although a few might be found who would not find them distressing.

Finally, even if false formants were introduced by the electrolarynx, these should be of fixed frequency as long as the fundamental frequency is held constant, and therefore they should be easy to distinguish from the moving formants associated with articulation.

There is a need for an electrolarynx designed specifically for the present purpose.[2] An informal pilot study suggested that an alternative design, based on a piezo-electric plate coupled to the throat through a liquid, might provide a solution. For one thing, this might permit control of the spectrum by shaping the driving pulses, and might also reduce the leakage round the edge of the vibrator, which seems to be a major source of extraneous signal. It might also be possible to reduce pickup of the leakage signal by interposing between the vibrator and the microphone a massive partition, into which the subject fits his face. Hyde (1968) has described such a device for separating the signals emanating from mouth and nose, but it is not clear that this solution could be used for young children.

A further possible source of inaccuracy is that the speaker may change his articulation when using the electrolarynx. In particular, since his fundamental is not changing, his larynx may move up and down less, which may reduce the variation normally present in the size of the pharyngeal cavity and in overall tract length. Sundberg (1975) encountered such problems when using an electrolarynx to study the vowel formants of a professional singer.[3] The subject would sustain a vowel at one of four fundamentals up to 700 Hz, and then freeze the articulation and stop voicing so that recordings could be made with the electrolarynx. When producing high front vowels at high fundamentals, the second formants shifted substantially when voicing stopped. The second formants of these vowels (/i e y/) are particularly sensitive to larynx height, which affects pharynx length. The remedy of having the speaker speak normally while using the electrolarynx, instead of mouthing, has the unfortunate side effect of introducing additional resonances due to the subglottal system, although work by Henke (1974) has suggested how these could be separated out by appropriate computer processing. A further possibility with natural speech[4] would be to drive the electrolarynx with a signal obtained by detecting the speaker's fundamental and dividing by (for example) four. This would simply accentuate every fourth period of the fundamental.

A quite different problem facing the general use of the procedure is that

---

[1] Flanagan, J. L. (personal communication).

[2] These comments were made in response to a question by G. C. W. Pols, who mentioned having done similar work.

[3] I am grateful to Janos Martony, whose question drew my attention to Sundberg's work.

[4] Crystal, T. H. (personal communication).

the electrolarynx can be quite frightening to small children. One of our three year old subjects needed half-an-hour's play with the electrolarynx, with the example of an older sister to follow, before she was willing to try speaking with it. Another would not try it even then. The recordings obtained from these children were not usable, because there was significant leakage of the electrolarynx signal around the edge of the vibrator. It is likely that the leakage could have been corrected, had we taken longer to familiarize the child, or spread the familiarization over several shorter sessions.

In conclusion, the technique of injecting an adult male's fundamental into a child's vocal tract seems feasible and promising, and worthy of further exploration.

ACKNOWLEDGMENT

This paper was presented at the 8th International Congress of Phonetic Sciences, Leeds, England, 17-23 August, 1975. The research was supported by NIH Grant No. NS 04332. I am grateful to Carolyn Chaney for help with making the recordings. Requests for reprints should be sent to A. W. F. Huggins, Bolt Beranek and Newman Inc., 50 Moulton Street, Cambridge, Massachusetts.

REFERENCES

BARNEY, H. L., HAWORTH, F. E., and DUNN, H. K., "An experimental transistorized artificial larynx." *Bell System Technical Journal,* **38**, 1337-1356 (1959).

DUNN, H. K., "Methods of measuring vowel formant bandwidths." *Journal of the Acoustical Society of America,* **33**, 1737-1746 (1961).

HENKE, W. L., "Signals from external accelerometers during phonation: attributes and their internal physical correlates." Research Laboratory of Electronics, Quarterly Progress Report **114**, 224-231, Massachusetts Institute of Technology (July 15, 1974).

HYDE, S. R., "Nose trumpet: apparatus for separating the oral and nasal outputs in speech." *Nature,* **219**, 763-765 (1968).

KLATT, D. H., "Acoustical theory of terminal analog speech synthesis." In *Proceedings of the 1972 IEEE Conference on Speech Communication and Processing,* **24-26**, 131-135 (April, 1972).

SUNDBERG, J., "Formant technique in a professional singer." *Acoustica,* **32**, 89-96 (1975).

WOLF, J. J., "Automatic analysis-by-synthesis of vowels." Research Laboratory of Electronics, Quarterly Progress Report **98**, 120-125, Massachusetts Institute of Technology (July 15, 1970).

Received July 26, 1978.
Accepted May 21, 1979.

ISOVOWEL LINES FOR THE EVALUATION OF VOWEL FORMANT STRUCTURE IN SPEECH DISORDERS

Ray D. Kent

Speech Motor Control Laboratories, Waisman Center
University of Wisconsin, Madison

This report describes a system of isovowel lines in the F_1-F_2 and F_2-F_3 planes and demonstrates how these linear approximations to vowel formant frequencies for a diverse sample of speakers can be used to evaluate the vowel formant structures of individuals with speech disorders. The application to disordered speech is illustrated with data for dysarthric adults, deaf adolescents, and young children with developmental errors of /ɝ/ production.

In the evaluation of many speech disorders, it is desirable to obtain quantitative physical information on vowel articulation. X-ray or acoustic analyses probably are the best alternatives for this purpose, but because x-ray methods present a radiation hazard, acoustic analysis has a premium attraction as a tool for vowel study. However, a frequently occurring difficulty in the acoustic analysis of vowels in disordered speech is the lack of suitable comparison data for normal speakers of the same sex and age. That is, because formant frequencies vary widely with sex and age (or more generally with size of the vocal tract) interpretation of acoustic data for the vowels of individual speakers often is problematic. Identifying a normal speaker whose vocal tract length exactly matches that of an individual with a speech disorder is challenging because of the difficulty of measuring the distance from glottis to lips. Recourse to published data for normal speakers is not always a satisfactory solution because of the large differences even within a given age-sex category. This problem is all the more serious with children because published data on children's vowels are not extensive.

This note describes a system of isovowel lines constructed from data obtained in a task of vowel imitation (Kent, 1978; Kent and Forner, 1979) and shows how these linear approximation criteria might be used to identify and interpret abnormalities in vowel formant structure. Formant-frequency data for vowels in selected speech disorders, primarily deafness and dysarthria, are used to illustrate the application of the isovowel lines. Basically, the isovowel lines allow a graphical evaluation of formant structure for any given speaker, regardless of age or sex.

THE SYSTEM OF ISOVOWEL LINES

For present purposes, an isovowel line (the term is borrowed from Broad, 1976) is a linear approximation to formant-frequency data for a heterogeneous group of speakers when the data are plotted in the F_1-F_2 plane (second-formant frequency versus first-formant frequency) or the F_2-F_3 plane (third-formant frequency versus second-formant frequency). Any stationary vowel is thus represented as a point in the F_1-F_2 plane and as another point in the F_2-F_3 plane. Isovowel lines can be determined if the aggregate points for a group of speakers can be fitted with a straight line that accounts for a sizeable portion of the group variance. The lines do not have to be straight, but it is more convenient if they are.

The formant-frequency data used to construct the isovowel lines were obtained from an experiment in which 33 speakers, including men, women, 12-year-old girls, six-year-old boys and girls, and four-year-old boys and girls imitated vowel sounds generated by a digital speech synthesizer (series arrangement of the modeled resonances). The procedures and results are described by Kent (1978) and Kent and Forner (1979). Mean F_1 and F_2 frequencies were determined for each speaker from five imitations of each of 10 vowels, including both English and non-English vocalic items. Straight lines then were fitted (both visually and by method of least squares) to the group data in the F_1-F_2 and F_2-F_3 planes. Coefficients of determination (R^2) associated with the lines of best fit for English vowels were used to evaluate the success of the linear approximations. (For details, see Kent and Forner, 1979).

Isovowel lines in the F_1-F_2 and F_2-F_3 planes are shown for the five English vowels /i u ɑ æ ɝ/ in Figure 1, a and b. The thick solid midportion of each line indicates the range of formant-frequency values for which normative data are available. The higher-frequency end of the thick solid line is defined by results for four-year-old children and the end nearer the origin of the graph is defined by results for adult males. The broken extensions of each isovowel line represent possible extrapolations to younger children (higher frequencies) and to adults with larger vocal tracts (lower frequencies). With some degree of accuracy, a portion of each line can be taken as the course of longitudinal F_1-F_2 or F_2-F_3 change for an average male or female. As a person matures and grows, his vocal tract lengthens and his vowel formants therefore become lower in frequency. The most pronounced lowering of the formants occurs during the active growing years of childhood and adolescence, but there is reason to believe that the progressive lowering of formant frequencies continues into old age. Anatomic studies (Israel, 1968, 1973) have revealed a symmetric craniofacial enlargement into the geriatric years, and a longitudinal acoustic study (Endres, Bambach, and Flösser, 1967) extending over a 15-year interval of adulthood evinced reductions in vowel formant frequencies. Of course, the two experimental results of craniofacial enlargement and lowering of vowel formant frequencies are thoroughly compatible. It may be concluded that as individuals mature and age, their vowel formant frequencies undergo a gradual

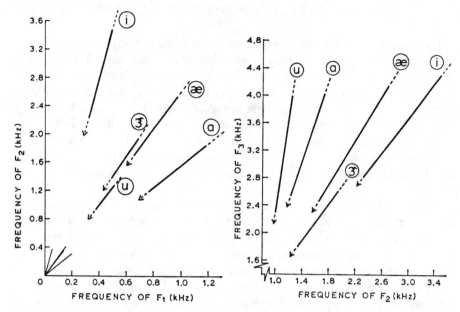

Figure 1. Isovowel lines for /i u ɑ æ ɝ/ in the F₁-F₂ (a) and F₂-F₃ (b) planes, based on data from Kent (1978) and Kent and Forner (1979). The solid midsegment of each line indicates the range of F₁-F₂ values for which normative data are available, and the broken lines show extrapolations to larger and smaller vocal tracts. Because each line in a intersects the origin, the lines are described by the linear equation $F_2 = b\ F_1$, where b has the following values: /i/, 7.11; /u/, 2.48; /ɑ/, 1.545; /æ/, 2.65; and /ɝ/, 2.79. The isovowel lines in b are described by the equation $F_3 = a + b\ F_2$, the more general form of the linear equation, in which a is the y-intercept and b is the slope of the line.

but persistent lowering. It is in this sense that an isovowel line is not only an approximation to the formant data for a cross-section of talkers, but also an acoustic life line of an average individual vocal tract.

The isovowel lines in the F₁-F₂ plane (Figure 1a) take the form of rays, or lines intersecting at the origin. Like linearity, this feature is a convenience and is not an a priori requirement of an isovowel system. However, the graphical simplicity of this result does have interesting implications, one of which is its interpretation as evidence for a principle of axial growth (Mol, 1963) which posits that growth of the vocal tract has uniform effects on vowel formant structure. Another implication is the relative ease with which the system can be applied to the evaluation of possibly deviant vowel formant structures, which is the subject of this report.

Confirmation that the isovowel lines provide a reasonable fit to formant-frequency data for speakers of both sexes and of different ages is shown in Figure 2. This illustration contains data for the vowels /i u ɑ æ/ reported by Peterson and Barney (1952) and by Kent (1978). The Peterson and Barney data for men, women, and children (three data points for each vowel) are represented by unfilled circles, and the Kent data for men, women, six-year-old children, and four-year-old children (four data points for each vowel) are depicted as filled circles. Generally, the data points fall on or close to the isovowel lines. For

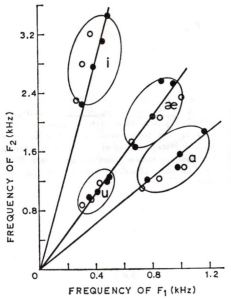

Figure 2. Isovowel lines for /i u ɑ æ/ in the F₁-F₂ plane, shown with mean data for normal speakers; unfilled circles: Peterson and Barney's (1952) means for men, women, and children; filled circles: Kent's (1978) means for men, women, six-year-old children, and four-year-old children.

both /i/ and /ɑ/, the data points from Peterson and Barney's study are displaced toward the axes from the isovowel lines, which can be interpreted to mean that these lines are conservative linear approximations (a desirable trait for many purposes).

THE ISOVOWEL SYSTEM AND THE IDENTIFICATION OF DEVIANT FORMANT STRUCTURES

The utility of an isovowel system can be demonstrated by showing that documented abnormalities of vowel formant structure are confirmed when the formant data are compared with the isovowel lines. One published source of apparently abnormal vowel formant patterns is Angelocci, Kopp, and Holbrook's (1964) comparative study of the vowel formants of normal-hearing and hearing-impaired boys aged 11 to 14 years. The vowels were produced in the context /h__d/, and the formant frequencies were estimated from spectrograms. The mean F₁ and F₂ frequencies for the vowels /i u ɑ/ are shown for the two groups of boys in Figure 3. The mean points have been connected by straight lines to depict the acoustic vowel triangles. The vowel positions for the normal-hearing boys (unfilled circles) fall close to the appropriate isovowel lines, but the vowel positions for the hearing-impaired boys (filled circles) are clearly displaced from these lines. Moreover, the abnormality of formant structures for the hearing-impaired subjects could be ascertained without knowledge of their sex and age. That is, because the vowel positions for /i u ɑ/ are distant from the isovowel lines, their abnormality is distinct from that feature alone, and sex-age identification is not required to establish formant abnormality.

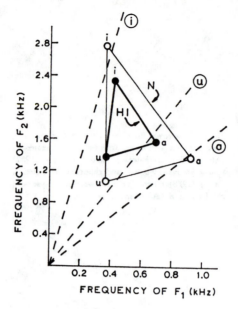

Figure 3. Angelocci et al's (1964) F₁F₂ data for vowels of normal-hearing (N) and hearing-impaired (HI) boys aged 11 to 14 years. Isovowel lines for the three vowels are shown for comparison. Note reduction of acoustic vowel triangle for hearing-impaired speakers and close fit of data for normal-hearing speakers by the isovowel lines.

Comparison of the two vowel triangles (or comparison of the vowel triangle for the hearing-impaired boys with the isovowel lines) shows that the subjects with hearing impairment have reduced ranges of both F_1 and F_2 frequencies (that is, a general centralization). F_1 for the high vowels /i/ and /u/ is perhaps closer to normal than are the other formant characteristics, indicating that the high tongue-jaw position for these vowels is preserved better than other vowel articulatory features.

Other data comparing normal-hearing and hearing-impaired speakers are shown in Figure 4, which is based on measurements reported by Monsen (1976). For the purpose of this illustration, two normal-hearing speakers (N1 and N2)

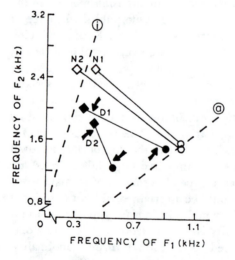

Figure 4. Sample data from Monsen (1976) for normal (N) and deaf (D) children's F₁F₂ values for /i/ and /a/. The normal data (open symbols) are closely fit by the isovowel lines, but the data for the deaf speakers (filled symbols) are not fit as well by these lines. In addition, when the points for the two vowels are connected by straight lines, the lines for the deaf speakers are rotated with respect to those for the normal speakers.

and two deaf speakers (D1 and D2) were selected arbitrarily from Monsen's data for formant plotting. The F_1-F_2 values for the vowels /i/ and /ɑ/ fall close to the appropriate isovowel lines for the two normal-hearing subjects, but the F_1-F_2 values for the deaf speakers do not span as great a distance in the plane, that is, centralization occurs. In addition, the lines connecting the points for /i/ and /ɑ/ do not have the same orientation for the normal and deaf speakers. For D1, the /i/-/ɑ/ line is rotated slightly counterclockwise with respect to the lines for N1 and N2. This rotation reflects a relatively greater compression of the range for F_2 than for F_1. For D2, the opposite rotation, clockwise relative to the lines for N1 and N2, results because of a relatively greater restriction of F_1 than of F_2. Although the abnormality in vowel formant patterns for D1 and D2 is evident from comparison with the isovowel lines alone, it is helpful to have additional lines, like those shown for N1 and N2, to make a fuller interpretation of the data. However, the primary point to be made here is that extreme centralization, like that for D2, is apparent with only the isovowel lines available for comparison. The fact that the two deaf speakers have lower formant frequency values than the normal speakers may indicate that the former have somewhat larger vocal tracts (a possibility that confounds the interpretation of absolute or non-normalized formant frequencies).

Another example of vowel formant assessment for individuals with a speech disorder is shown in Figure 5. The filled circles represent the F_1-F_2 values of the vowels /i u ɑ æ/ obtained for four speakers with ataxic dysarthria. The sample of speakers included two males and two females, making for a considerable range of formant frequency values. Isovowel lines offered a quick means of evaluating the adequacy of the vowel formant structures because the

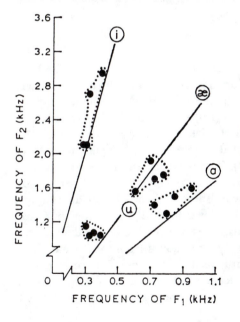

Figure 5. F1-F2 data for four speakers with ataxic dysarthria, compared to isovowel lines for /i u ɑ æ/. The data for the dysarthrics (two males and two females) fall on or close to the isovowel lines, indicating that vowel formant structure is normal for these speakers.

lines are applicable to data for both sexes. The F_1-F_2 coordinate points in Figure 5 are aligned fairly closely with the isovowel lines, so it may be concluded that the ataxic vowels had nearly normal formant structures and that the ranges of both F_1 and F_2 frequencies were adequate for English vowels. Perceptual evaluation confirmed the conclusion of acceptable vowel production.

Normal and error productions for the retroflex /ɝ/ are shown in Figure 6

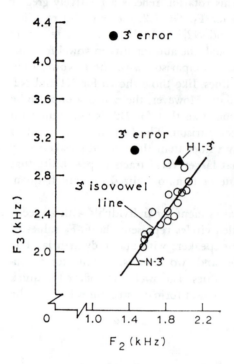

Figure 6. Normal and error productions of /ɝ/ represented in the F_2-F_3 plane and compared with the isovowel line for this vowel. The circles are results for acceptable (unfilled symbols) and unacceptable (filled symbols) productions by four- and six-year-old children (Kent and Forner, 1979), and the triangles are results for productions by normal-hearing boys (unfilled symbols) and hearing-impaired boys (filled symbols), both aged 11 to 14 year (Angelocci et al, 1964).

to demonstrate the importance of isovowel lines in the F_2-F_3 plane. The F_2-F_3 coordinate points for normal /ɝ/ productions are shown by the unfilled circles for four- and six-year-old children (Kent and Forner, 1979), and by the unfilled triangle for normal 11 to 14-year-old boys (Angelocci et al, 1964). Errors in /ɝ/ production are depicted by the filled circles for two four-year-olds (Kent, 1978; Kent and Forner, 1979) and by the filled triangle for hearing-impaired 11 to 14-year-old boys (Angelocci et al, 1964). The isovowel line is a satisfactory fit to the normal results. The error sounds represented by filled circles are distinguished easily from both the isovowel line and the normal data points. These error productions are characterized by a lower F_2 and a higher F_3 frequency compared to normal productions. The error production by the hearing-impaired boys (filled triangle) is not really far removed from the isovowel line, but the abnormality of formant pattern is readily apparent when compared to the F_2-F_3 point for normal boys (unfilled triangle). That is, the hearing-impaired boys have both higher F_2 and F_3 frequencies. This result illustrates a general caution to be observed in any application of isovowel lines: results for any given single vowel should be considered with respect to results for other vowels (to establish the speaker's vowel region in the plane) or with respect to the expected location of the speaker's formant values on the isovowel line (for example, the F_2-F_3 values for the hearing-impaired boys aged 11 to 14 years fall near the values obtained for four-year-old children). Another helpful procedure is to use both the F_1-F_2 and F_2-F_3 planes when considering individual vowel data.

CAVEATS AND CONCLUSION

This note describes a simple graphical system for the evaluation of vowel formant structures and demonstrates that certain abnormalities in formant structure are in fact registered with the isovowel lines. Further work is needed to demonstrate generalizability of the isovowel system and to establish limits or regions of acceptable vowel production. Research on both issues is in progress. With respect to the need for regions of acceptable formant frequency values, one approach is to define angles of scatter for normal production (see Kent, 1978, for preliminary angle data). However, the isovowel lines, even without these refinements, have potential value for general description of vowel production (as shown in Figures 3, 4, 5, and 6) and for documenting acoustic change in vowel production subsequent to management or treatment. With regard to the latter, isovowel lines have the capability for illustrating improvement (or lack of it) in vowel production even when the average formant frequencies change with vocal tract growth (say over a five-year span of late childhood). Another possible application lies in the visual feedback of acoustic information. Formant frequencies for vowels could be displayed together with isovowel lines to give a subject general feedback about his vowel acoustic space. If the isovowel lines really can be generalized across speaker age and sex, then one system of lines could be used for all subjects.

ACKNOWLEDGMENTS

This work was supported by NIH grants NS 12281 and NS 13274. Requests for reprints should be addressed to the author at Boys Town Institute for Communication Disorders in Children, 555 North 30th Street, Omaha, Nebraska 68131.

REFERENCES

Angelocci, A. A., Kopp, G. A., and Holbrook, A., The vowel formants of deaf and normal-hearing eleven to fourteen year old boys. *J. Speech Hearing Dis.*, 29, 156–170 (1964).

Broad, D. J., Toward defining acoustic phonetic equivalence for vowels. *Phonetica*, 33, 401–424 (1976).

Endres, W., Bambach, W., and Flosser, G., Voice spectrograms as a function of age, voice disguise and voice imitation. *J. Acoust. Soc. Am.*, 49, 1842–1848 (1967).

Israel, H., Continuing growth in the human cranial skeleton. *Arch. Oral Biol.*, 13, 133–137 (1968).

Israel, H., Age factor and the pattern of change in craniofacial structures. *Am. J. Phys. Anthropol.*, 39, 111–128 (1973).

KENT, R. D., Imitation of synthesized vowels by preschool children. *J. Acoust. Soc. Am.*, **63**, 1193–1198 (1978).

KENT, R. D., and FORNER, L. L., A developmental study of vowel formant frequencies in an imitation task. *J. Acoust. Soc. Am.*, **65**, 208–217 (1979).

MOL, H., *Fundamentals of Phonetics. Janua Linguarum, No. 26.* The Hague: Mouton (1963).

MONSEN, R. B., Normal and reduced phonological space: The production of English vowels by deaf adolescents. *J. Phonetics*, **4**, 189–198 (1976).

PETERSON, G. E., and BARNEY, H. L., Control methods in a study of the vowels. *J. Acoust. Soc. Am.*, **24**, 175–185 (1952).

Received September 28, 1978.
Accepted May 22, 1979.

ACOUSTIC PATTERNS OF APRAXIA OF SPEECH

R. D. KENT*
Boys Town Institute, Omaha, Nebraska

JOHN C. ROSENBEK
Veterans Administration Hospital, Madison, Wisconsin

Apraxia of speech (or verbal apraxia) is a controversial disorder, considered by some to be an impairment of the motor programming of speech. Because the disorder is characterized by "higher order" errors such as metathesis and segment addition as well as by errors of apparent dyscoordination of articulation, it seems to reflect a relatively high level of damage to the nervous system. This report presents acoustic descriptions of the speech of seven persons diagnosed as having apraxia of speech but without severe aphasic impairment, especially agrammatism. The acoustic results indicate a variety of segmental and prosodic abnormalities, including slow speaking rate with prolongations of transitions, steady states, and intersyllable pauses; reduced intensity variation across syllables; slow and inaccurate movements of the articulators; incoordination of voicing with other articulations; initiation difficulties; and errors of selection or sequencing of segments. These error patterns are discussed with respect to a theory of motor control based on spatial-temporal schemata. In addition, consideration is given to the controversy about phonologic versus motor programming impairment in apraxia of speech.

Controversies about nosology and neuropathology notwithstanding (Buckingham, 1979; Geschwind, 1975; Martin, 1974; Mlcoch & Noll, 1980), a fairly large literature has developed around the disorder commonly called apraxia of speech or verbal apraxia. A general definition that conforms to most clinical reports of this disorder was given by Rosenbek and Wertz in 1976 (cited by Rosenbek, 1980):

> Apraxia of speech is a sensorimotor speech disorder resulting from brain damage. Symptoms are impaired volitional production of normal articulation and prosody. The articulation and prosodic disturbances do not result from muscle weakness or slowness. Rather, they result from inhibition or impairment of CNS programming of skilled oral movements. (p. 239)

This definition is consistent with the original use of the term *apraxia* by Steinthal in 1871 (cited by Roy, 1978) to describe various neuropathological conditions that result in an inability to execute purposive, voluntary movements in the absence of motor paralysis, ataxia, or dementia.

Many characteristics of the disorder have been described, but Johns and LaPointe (1976) listed the following three as the most clinically salient (see also LaPointe, 1975):

1. a predominance of articulatory substitution errors, including some additive substitutions of consonant clusters for singleton consonants
2. initiation difficulty, characterized by stops and restarts and phoneme, syllable, and whole-word repetitions
3. variability of error pattern on repeated trials of the same word.

*Currently affiliated with the University of Wisconsin–Madison.

Shewan (1980) commented that (a) the hierarchy of difficulty for phonetic sequences increases in the order of vowels, singleton consonants, and consonant clusters; (b) the feature most vulnerable to errors is place of articulation; (c) phonemic substitutions are the predominant type of error; and (d) errors increase with increasing syllable length of utterance.

The inference that apraxia of speech is a motor programming or sequencing disorder seems to rest most heavily on the observations that (a) errors are predominantly substitutions (as opposed to omissions or distortions), (b) initiation difficulties are common, (c) the error pattern is highly variable, (d) place of articulation is more frequently in error than manner of articulation, and (e) error rate varies with phonetic complexity. Mlcoch and Noll cited as evidence of preprogramming errors in apraxic speech two types of speech errors: anticipatory sequencing errors, including metathesis and errors of coarticulation; and errors of temporal incoordination.

However, Buckingham has criticized the vagueness of some terms (e.g., *programming, incoordination, initiation, selection,* and *sequence*) used in describing apraxia of speech especially as they relate to concepts of motor programming or seriation. Terms such as *programming, incoordination,* and *variability* probably can be defined more explicitly than they have been so far in the literature on apraxia of speech. One reason these terms have not been defined as carefully as they might be is that they usually are intended as motoric descriptions but are tested against rather abstract levels of speech and language behavior, such as substitution errors. Apraxia of speech often has been studied by perceptual techniques, which do not permit the examination of the details of articulatory movements or their acoustic consequences.

These details may prove critical to a full understanding of the disorder.

This study sought to determine:

1. if the utterances of apraxic subjects are lengthened in comparison to the utterances of normal-speaking subjects

and, if so:

2. whether differential lengthening effects exist as a function of the segmental properties or the syllabic length of utterances
3. whether apraxic and normal speech are distinguished by nondurational aspects of prosody, such as relative syllable intensity or F_0-frequency contour
4. if spectrograms show evidence of phonetic (subphonemic) errors in apraxic speech
5. the degree to which acoustic patterns of apraxic speech confirm perceptually based descriptions of the disorder.

These five objectives were selected because they are within the scope of an acoustic study and because they should lead to a refined description of the segmental and prosodic features of the disorder.

METHOD

Acoustic characteristics were identified in wide-band (300 Hz) and narrow-band (45 Hz) spectrograms, with frequency ranges and time intervals of either 80–8000 Hz and 2.4 sec (conventional) or 40–4000 Hz and 4.8 sec (expanded time scale). Additional acoustic data were obtained with the intensity and F_0-frequency display functions of a Kay Elemetrics Visi-Pitch Model 6187. Because little has been published on the acoustic features of apraxic speech, this study was directed broadly to identify and describe the acoustic correlates of articulatory disturbances in this disorder. Details of the procedures are discussed most effectively as the results are presented. The primary test words on which the acoustic analyses were based are listed in the Appendix. These items are used routinely in the examination for apraxia of speech. The speech tasks also included conversation, picture description, and reading a paragraph. Except for the paragraph reading task, all test words were elicited by imitation.

Subjects

The seven male subjects studied were chosen from a larger group of 31 patients with apraxia of speech seen at the Madison, Wisconsin, Veterans Administration Hospital between 1977 and 1980. They were chosen because apraxia of speech was unquestionably their major communication deficit. Each had suffered a single cerebrovascular accident involving the left hemisphere. Descriptive data on age, education, handedness, etiology, site of lesion and condition of the extremities, and time post-CVA appear in Table 1. Side, type of lesion, and condition of the extremities were determined at neurological examination. One subject (#7) was judged to have a "foreign accent" dysprosody and has been described elsewhere (Kent & Rosenbek, 1982).

Speech-language diagnoses were made by a panel of three speech-language pathologists, experienced in diagnosing and treating the neuropathologies of speech and language. The judges independently evaluated each patient's performance on an extensive standard speech sample requiring imitative, spontaneous, and reading responses (Wertz & Rosenbek, 1971), on the *Porch Index of Communicative Ability* (PICA) (Porch, 1967), and on the *Token Test* (DeRenzi & Vignolo, 1962).

To be called apraxic, each patient's spontaneous and imitative speech had to have similar types and numbers of errors and to show these characteristics:

1. effortful trial-and-error groping articulatory movements and attempts at self-correction
2. dysprosody unrelieved by extended periods of normal rhythm, stress, and intonation
3. error inconsistency on repeated productions of the same utterance elicited nontherapeutically (patient was instructed to repeat polysyllabic words several times without being encouraged to slow down or to plan and without being told how well he was doing)
4. obvious difficulty in initiating utterances.

To rule out Broca's aphasia (as defined by the *Boston Diagnostic Aphasia Examination* profile), each patient's spontaneous speech was judged by the same three speech-language pathologists according to four of the Boston exam's speech production scales (Goodglass &

TABLE 1. Descriptive data for the seven apraxic subjects chosen for study.

Subject	Age	Education	Handedness	Etiology	Side of lesion	Condition of extremities	Time post-CVA
1	57	12	L	Thromboembolic	Left hemisphere	Transient hemiplegia; chronic sensory impairment	2
2	65	8	R	Thrombolic	Left hemisphere	Transient hemiplegia	3
3	52	11	R	Thromboembolic	Left hemisphere	Moderate chronic hemiplegia	3.6
4	63	12	R	Embolic	Left hemisphere	Transient hemiplegia	2
5	55	12	R	Thromboembolic	Left hemisphere	Mild chronic hemiplegia	3.5
6	56	8	R	Embolic	Left hemisphere	Transient hemiplegia; chronic sensory impairment	1.5
7	44	8	R	Embolic	Left hemisphere	Moderate chronic hemiplegia	1

Kaplan, 1972). All patients had impaired articulatory agility and melodic line (score of 1, 2, and 3), but their phrase length and grammatical form were toward normal (scores of 6 and 7). In other words, they were not agrammatic, which is the cardinal characteristic of the Broca's aphasic speaker (Mohr, Pessing, Finkelstein, Funkenstein, Duncan, & Davis, 1978). And although all had some coexisting aphasia, they had scores at or above the tenth percentile for normal men on the *Token Test* (Wertz & Lenne, Note 1). We recognize that what we have called apraxia of speech might be called Broca's aphasia or motor aphasia by others, but whatever name is given to this disorder, the most important issue is to describe the features of speech or language impairment because it is these features that permit generalization from the subject sample. Not all patients had received CT scans, and although radiographic localization of the site of the lesion would have been interesting, such localization was not a purpose of this study.

Control (normal-speaking) subjects for each task were at least seven men aged between 25 and 50 years.

RESULTS

Speaking Rate and Speech Rhythm

All seven apraxic subjects had slow speaking rates compared to the seven normally speaking controls. For example, when total durations were compared for four sentences (Table 2), the apraxic productions without exception exceeded criterion values determined by the normal speakers' means plus two standard deviations ($\bar{x}$ + 2 SD). To illustrate with the sentence *Please put the*

TABLE 2. Sentence durations (in sec) for normal speakers (n = 10) and apraxic speakers 1–7.

The valuable watch was missing

Normal	Apraxic						
$\bar{x}$ = 2.24	1	2	3	4	5	6	7
SD = .28	6.0	7.6	15.2	3.2	3.2	15.2	6.8

In the summer they sell vegetables

Normal	Apraxic						
$\bar{x}$ = 2.12	1	2	3	4	5	6	7
SD = .27	5.6	8.8	18.0	3.6	2.8	7.6	6.0

The shipwreck washed up on the shore

Normal	Apraxic						
$\bar{x}$ = 2.4	1	2	3	4	5	6	7
SD = .33	4.0	8.0	16.0	3.2	4.0	12.8	–[a]

Please put the groceries in the refrigerator

Normal	Apraxic						
$\bar{x}$ = 2.0	1	2	3	4	5	6	7
SD = .25	8.2	12.8	15.2	4.8	5.6	8.0	8.4

[a]Not measured because of word-ordering errors.

groceries in the refrigerator, the criterion value for the normal speakers was 2.5 sec ($\bar{x}$ of 2.0 sec and SD of .25 sec), and the sentence durations for the apraxic subjects ranged from 4.8 to 15.2 sec.

The slowed rate during polysyllabic words, phrases, or sentences usually took one of two forms, which we have termed *articulatory prolongation* and *syllable segregation* (Kent & Rosenbek, 1982). The two forms are illustrated with representative samples in Figure 1, which shows spectrograms of the word *refrigerator* spoken by a normal speaker (a) and by two subjects with apraxia of speech (b and c). Because the apraxic productions were extremely lengthened relative to the normal production, only the final three syllables of the apraxic utterances are shown, for convenience of scale.

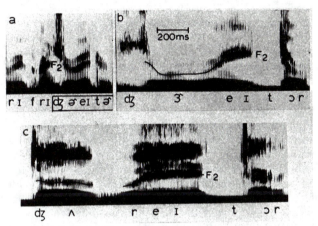

FIGURE 1. Spectrograms of the word *refrigerator* as spoken in sentence context by a normal speaker (a) and by two apraxic speakers (b and c). The pattern in (b) illustrates *articulatory prolongation* and the pattern in (c) illustrates *syllable segregation*. Unless noted otherwise, all spectrograms are conventional wide-band (300 Hz).

The apraxic pattern in Figure 1-b is an example of *articulatory prolongation*, which is defined as a lengthening of steady-state segments and the intervening transitions. In this example [ɝ] was over 300 msec in duration and was followed by a transitional segment of almost 200 msec in duration. The pattern of articulatory prolongation gives the impression of a general slowing of all movements within monosyllabic or polysyllabic utterances, without conspicuous interruptions (pauses) at syllable boundaries.

Figure 1-c is an example of *syllable segregation*, a pattern of temporally separated or isolated syllables (sometimes called "scanning" speech). This pattern differs from that of articulatory prolongation in that syllable segregation has conspicuous intervals between the lengthened syllables. The intervals sometimes show continuity of voicing, but in many if not most instances, voicing ceases during the intersyllabic break. Syllable dissociation gives the impression that speech is uttered on a syllable-by-syllable basis, with lengthy intervals between syllables for the preparation of the next portion of the utterance.

Articulatory prolongation and syllable segregation are observational terms, and we do not mean to suggest that they are fundamentally different expressions of an apraxic disorder. Conceivably, both patterns result from a basic disturbance of speech organization. In any case, they appear to represent the most frequently occurring patterns of severely slowed speaking rate and abnormal rhythm.

Although most measured durations were long compared to those for normal speakers, the utterance durations were highly variable across apraxic subjects, and these speakers varied with respect to the factors that contributed to utterance lengthening. The variability is attributable to the two patterns of lengthening described above and to differences in the perceived severity of the disorder. Intersubject differences in syllabic patterning are depicted in Figure 2 for the word *gingerbread*. The rectangles represent the durations of the syllabic nuclei associated with the vowels /ɪ/, /ɚ/, and /ɛ/. The filled rectangles labeled "N" show the mean results for normal speakers. Figure 2 illustrates the overall lengthening of the syllabic sequences for the apraxic subjects and also shows how some apraxic subjects deviated from the relative nuclei durations observed for normal speakers. For example, whereas normal speakers produced the unstressed syllable nucleus for /ɚ/ with a much shorter duration than that for the stressed syllable containing the vowel /ɛ/, apraxic subjects 1, 5, and 6 do not show the expected syllabic reduction for unstressed /ɚ/. The result for apraxic subject 3 is a rather extreme example of syllable segregation (note the long intervals between syllabic nuclei). Apraxic subject 2, on the other hand, evidenced articulatory prolongation (the durations of syllabic nuclei are proportionately long compared to the intervals between syllabic nuclei).

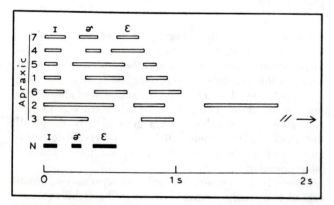

FIGURE 2. Durations of syllable nuclei and their intervals for the word *gingerbread* produced by seven apraxic speakers. Mean results for seven normal speakers are shown for comparison. The overall duration for apraxic subject 3 was too long to be shown on this time scale.

Additional data for utterance syllabic patterns are given in Table 3. The table shows the durations of syllabic nuclei for the first six syllables of the sentence *In the summer they sell vegetables*. For all but one apraxic

TABLE 3. Durations (in msec) of syllabic nuclei for normal and apraxic productions of the sentence, *In the summer they sell vegetables* (results tabled for first 6 syllables). Vowel symbols identify syllabic nuclei.

Apraxic subjects	Vowel nuclei					
	/ɪ/	/ə/	/ʌ/	/ɚ/	/eɪ/	/ɛ/
1	320*	320*	144*	352*	448*	448*
2	352*	640*	256*	640*	512*	640*
3	416*	160*	320*	64*	288*	352*•
4	96*	72	176*	144*	288*	256*
5	64	64	96	216*	224*	336*
6	384*	224*	160*	208*	416*	416*
7	192*	160*	128*	272*	192*	288*
Mean for apraxic subjects	261*	234*	183*	271*	338*	391*
Mean for normal subjects	61	63	85	143	123	119
Mean + 2 SD for normal subjects	99	73	125	199	191	179

*Exceeds mean for normal speakers by 2 SD.

subject (#5), the durations of the syllabic nuclei almost always exceeded the criterion value of mean + 2 SD for the normal speakers.

The lengthening of syllabic nuclei by the apraxic speakers also is apparent in the mean data. The mean durations for apraxic subjects were as much as four or more times as long as those for normal speakers. Furthermore, the apraxic subjects often had durations of syllable nuclei for normally unstressed vowels that were unusually long by either absolute or relative standards. For example, for the apraxic subjects the mean duration of the syllable nucleus for the word *the* was 234 msec, compared to only 63 msec for the normal speakers. For the apraxic speakers this nucleus was about .7 as long as the nucleus for the stressed tense vowel in *they*. For the normal speakers the nucleus for *the* was about half as long as that for *they*. In other words, the normal speakers tended to show greater relative differences between the durations of unstressed and stressed vowels.

In view of the consistent lengthening of utterances (especially multisyllabic words or sentences) by the apraxic subjects, we next determined segment durations for vowels (Figure 3) and consonants (Figure 4) in selected test words. In each of these figures, the mean segment durations for the apraxic subjects (AS) are plotted against the mean segment durations for the normal subjects (NS). Segments are identified by phonetic symbols, large symbols for segments in long utterances (multisyllabic words or phrases) and small symbols for segments in short utterances (isolated monosyllables). All the symbols in Figure 3 lie above the $x = y$ diagonal, indicating consistently longer vowel durations for the apraxic speakers. Moreover, the larger phonetic symbols lie farther from the $x = y$ diagonal than do the small symbols. Nearly all the small phonetic symbols lie in the region between the $x = y$ diagonal and the dashed diagonal, whereas the large phonetic symbols lie almost entirely above the dashed diagonal. Thus, vowel

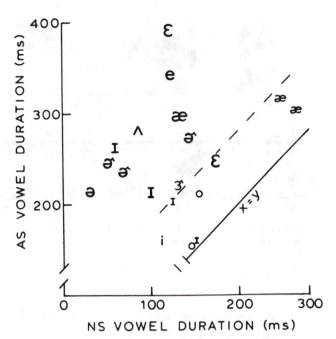

FIGURE 3. Vowel segment durations for apraxic speakers (AS) plotted against those for normal speakers (NS). Small phonetic symbols represent vowels in monosyllabic words, and large phonetic symbols represent vowels in longer words. The dashed diagonal nearly separates the apraxic data for the two symbol rises, indicating longer durations for vowels produced in the longer words.

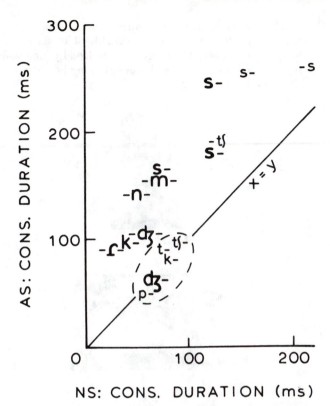

FIGURE 4. Consonant segment durations for apraxic speakers (AS) plotted against those for normal speakers (NS). Small phonetic symbols represent consonants in monosyllabic words, and large phonetic symbols represent consonants in longer words. Position of consonant in word is shown by positions of dashes; e.g., s- is word initial, -s- is word medial, and -s is word final. Dashed line encloses segment symbols for which no group difference emerges.

lengthening for the apraxic subjects increased as syllabic length of utterance increased.

Figure 4 shows consonant segments identified by large phonetic symbols for multisyllabic contexts and small phonetic symbols for isolated monosyllables. A dash is used to specify segment position, e.g., s- indicates a word-initial /s/, -s represents a word-final /s/, and -s- denotes an utterance-medial /s/. Word-initial stops and affricates in monosyllables did not differ in duration between normal and apraxic speakers. However, fricative /s/ in monosyllables, affricate /tʃ/ in final-monosyllable position, and nearly all consonants in multisyllabic utterances assumed greater durations for apraxic than for normal speakers. The lengthening for consonants in multisyllabic utterances was observed for stops, fricatives, affricates, and nasals.

Figure 5 isolates the first word from the sentence *Please put the groceries in the refrigerator* to illustrate articulatory prolongation within a syllable. Of particular interest are the rate of change and the duration of transition of the second formant (F_2) frequency during the [pli] sequence in *please*. Compared to the normal pattern in Figure 5-a, the apraxic patterns in Figures 5-b and 5-c had slower rates of F_2 increase and longer F_2 transitions. Thus, the underlying articulation was slower for the apraxic subjects. The duration of the final fricative segments also illustrates the effects of articulatory prolongation: The segments for the apraxic subjects were four to five times as long as those for the normal speaker. In fact, the normal speaker produced the entire phonetic

sequence for *please* within the time that the apraxic subject in Figure 5-c produced only the final fricative.

An example of extreme lengthening of a polysyllabic word by an apraxic speaker is given in Figure 6. This figure shows normal and apraxic productions of the word *responsibility*, displayed on a 4.8-sec, 4-kHz spectrogram. The apraxic pattern is about four times as long as the normal pattern. In the spectrogram for the apraxic speaker, virtually every phonetic segment is lengthened, including the frication segment for [s], the stop closure for [p], the nasal murmur for [n], and the vocalic nucleus for the unstressed [ɪ].

Lengthening of segments and pauses in apraxic productions was not confined to the tasks of reading or word repetition but also occurred during conversation and verbal formulation tasks. For example, in a picture description task, several of the apraxic subjects had prolonged segments on *cookies*, a word which seemed to represent articulatory obstacles to most of the apraxic speakers. Examples of apraxic productions of this word are shown in Figure 7. The top pattern shows marked lengthening, especially of the final syllable, and voicing abnormalities (note the long voicing lag for the initial [k] and the failure of voicing to carry into the final fricative). For the production shown at the bottom of Figure 7, the speaker nearly uttered the entire word on the first attempt but faltered on the last syllable. The second attempt was successful but was characterized by long voicing lags for [k] phones and a greatly lengthened vowel [i] in the final syllable.

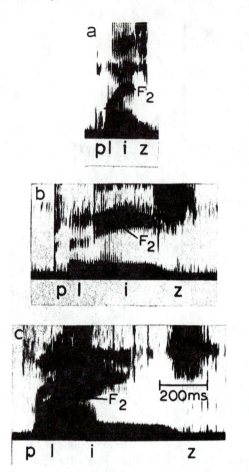

FIGURE 5. Spectrograms of the word *please* produced in sentence context by a normal speaker (a) and by two apraxic speakers (b and c). Note the long durations for formant transition in (b) and (c).

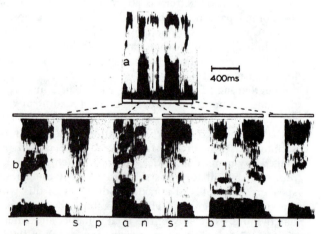

FIGURE 6. Expanded time-scale spectrograms (4-kHz rather than 8-kHz frequency range) of the word *responsibility* uttered in isolation by a normal talker (a) and an apraxic speaker (b).

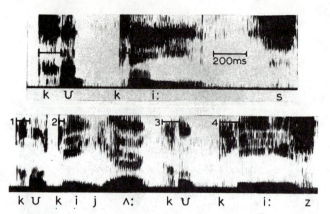

FIGURE 7. Spectrograms of the word *cookies* spoken in a picture description task by two apraxic subjects. Note segment prolongations (especially for vowel [i]) and segregation of syllables. The bracketed intervals are voice onset times for [k] which often are abnormally long.

Other Prosodic Abnormalities: Intensity Envelope and F_0 Contour

Relative peak intensity across syllables was measured using the Kay Elemetrics Visi-Pitch. It was hypothesized that the slowing of speaking rate described above would be associated with other prosodic abnormalities. Among the expected abnormalities was a flattening of the intensity envelope across a syllabic sequence. We expected relatively little intensity variation from syllable to syllable, largely because of the absence of normal syllable reduction (Figures 1 and 2).

To test for the hypothesized flattening of the intensity envelope, the peak intensities were measured for individual syllables in each of the four test sentences cited in Table 2. The intensity values were expressed relative to the most intense syllable in each sentence, so that all syllables except the reference syllable were assigned negative intensity levels in dB, e.g., $-11, 0, -8, -5, -7$ for a five-syllable sequence in which the second syllable was the most intense. The intensity values for the syllables in each test sentence were averaged for each speaker. For sentence productions having little intensity variation from syllable to syllable, the mean result was a small negative number (in the range of -1 to -3 dB for many apraxic productions). On the other hand, for sentence productions having large intensity fluctuations, the mean result was a larger negative number (-3 to -7 dB for most productions by normal speakers). The differences between apraxic and normal speakers were tested by Wilcoxon's test for rankings of unpaired measurements (Snedecor & Cochran, 1967, p. 130). Significant differences were noted for the two sentences *Please put the groceries in the refrigerator* ($p < .01$) and *The valuable watch was missing* ($p < .05$).

Figure 8 shows relative intensities, averaged across subjects for each of the two groups, for the two sentences on which significant differences were observed. The peak intensity is shown here only for the normally tonic syllable in words of two syllables or more. In general,

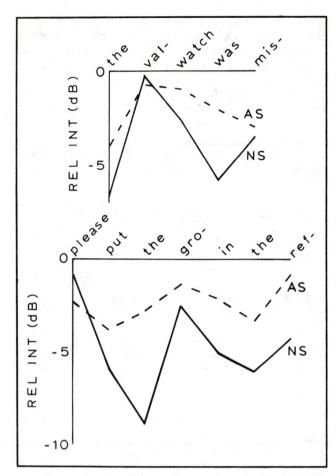

FIGURE 8. Relative peak intensities for words produced in two sentences by apraxic speakers (AS) and normal speakers (NS). Mean data are shown for each group. The sentences are *The valuable watch is missing* and *Please put the groceries in the refrigerator.*

the normal and apraxic speakers gave greatest intensity to the same syllables in each sentence (*val-* in *The valuable watch . . .* and *please, gro-,* and *re-* in *Please put the . . .*). The major difference was that the apraxic subjects showed less variation in relative peak intensity across syllables. Thus, *the* in *Please put the . . .* has nearly the same average relative intensity as *please, gro-,* or *re.* In contrast, the normal speakers produced *the* with about 8 dB less intensity than the most intense syllable, *please.* The results conform to the expectation that the apraxic speakers would display a flattening of the intensity envelope across a syllabic sequence.

To describe further this tendency toward reduced intensity variation across syllables, the average relative intensity was computed for the *least* intense syllable in each test sentence. Essentially, this derived value is an index of the degree of intensity reduction for unstressed syllables in the sentences. Because syllabic intensity peaks were not always reliably identifiable for each syllable in multisyllabic words like *valuable*, only the tonic syllable was used in such words. The mean relative peak intensities for apraxic subjects (first value) and normal subjects (second value) were as follows:

In the summer . . .	(−4.4 dB; −6.5 dB)
The valuable watch . . .	(−5.6 dB; −7.3 dB)
The shipwreck washed . . .	(−5.0 dB; −7.0 dB)
Please put the groceries . . .	(−5.0 dB; −9.3 dB)

The mean intensity reduction was consistently smaller for the apraxic speakers than for the normal speakers. In practical terms, this means that normally reduced syllables, especially function words like *the, in, on,* and *was,* are relatively more intense in apraxic speech than in normal speech.

The third major element of prosody, the F_0-frequency contour, was analyzed by means of the Visi-Pitch F_0 display and narrow-band spectrograms. Values of F_0 were determined for the midpoints of words or syllables in sentence productions. Because the speakers varied greatly in utterance duration and in mean F_0 level, the data were normalized in time and F_0 frequency as shown in Figure 9. The data for apraxic subject 7 are not shown because he was judged to have a "foreign-accent" dysprosody, which was associated acoustically with an unusual F_0 contour. Each numeral at the top of the graph represents a sampling point during the sentence *In the summer they sell vegetables.* The alphabet letters designate the results for individual apraxic subjects. Even after percentage transformation of the F_0 values, the results are quite variable across subjects. Despite the large individual differences in the overall pattern, all six apraxic speakers showed sentence-terminal fall, as did all normal speakers. Apparently, this prosodic feature is highly robust, because it was preserved in the F_0 pattern

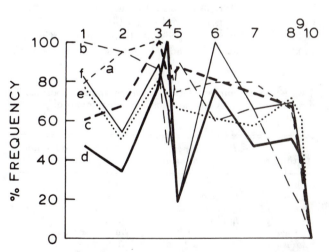

FIGURE 9. Normalized fundamental frequencies for selected time points in the sentence *They sell vegetables in the summer.* The letters represent apraxic speakers and their total sentence durations as follows (in order of increasing duration):

a) A2, 2.8 sec	d) A5, 7.6 sec
b) A4, 3.6 sec	e) A6, 8.8 sec
c) A1, 5.6 sec	f) A3, 18.0 sec.

The sampling points are (1) midpoint of diphthong /eɪ/; (2) midpoint of vowel /ɛ/; (3, 4, and 5) vowel midpoints for /ɛ/, /ə/, /ə/ in *vegetables;* (6) vowel midpoint for /ɪ/; (7) vowel midpoint for /ə/; (8, 9, 10) vowel midpoint for /ʌ/, nasal murmur for /m/, and vowel midpoint for /ɚ/ in *summer.*

even for the slowest apraxic speaker (pattern f, for which the total sentence duration was 18 sec).

The F_0-frequency patterns for other sentences were similar to those in Figure 9 in showing substantial interspeaker variability but preservation of terminal fall. The interspeaker variability precluded other generalizations about the prosodic regulation of F_0. The large interspeaker variability was not unique to the apraxic speakers, given that the normal speakers also varied from one another.

Segmental Errors: General Patterns

Segmental errors such as substitutions additions, and omissions have received considerable attention in perceptual descriptions of apraxia of speech, but few acoustic descriptions have been published. These errors are of particular interest in relation to theories that apraxia of speech represents a disorder in the selection, retrieval, or seriation of phonemic or phonetic units. One indication that apraxia of speech is a disorder of segment sequencing is that substitutions often are sequential errors. LaPointe and Johns (1975) reported that 7% of the substitution errors observed for their sample of 13 apraxic speakers were sequential errors and that anticipatory errors outnumbered reiterative errors by a ratio of 6:1.

Some examples of the segmental errors made by the apraxic speakers in this study are listed in Table 4. These errors involve units having the size of phonemes or phonetic segments, and the errors include omissions, additions, and substitutions. This list is not intended to be exhaustive but only to show that such perceptually conspicuous errors occurred rather frequently.

The speakers in the present study were particularly prone to errors on [l] and [r]. Both sounds were occa-

sionally omitted, and one was sometimes substituted for the other. Acoustic illustration of r/l substitution is given in Figure 10. A spectrogram of a normal speaker's production of the word *please* is shown in Figure 10-a, and spectrograms for two apraxic productions are shown in Figures 10-b and 10-c. The lines labeled with the numerals 2 and 3 highlight the second and third formants in each pattern. The apraxic productions differed from the normal pattern for [l] in having a close spacing of F_2 and F_3 and a much more gradual rate of F_2 frequency change, as would be expected for [r].

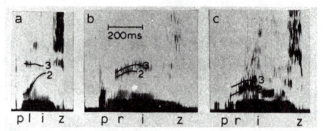

FIGURE 10. Spectrograms of the word *please* produced in sentence context by a normal speaker (a) and two apraxic speakers (b and c). The numerals identify the second and third formants. The apraxic utterances were perceived to be produced with r/l substitutions.

Apraxic error patterns for the word *tornado* are depicted in Figure 11. Pattern A shows a production by a normal speaker. Pattern B was lengthened and contained d/t and r/ɾ substitution errors. The leading voice bar (prevoicing) for [d] indicates a timing or coordination error in that vocal fold vibration significantly preceded the release of the stop. Pattern C shows an apparent anticipatory error, or, alternatively, a mistiming of the segmental commands for [d] and [o]. The spectrogram shows that the formant pattern for the first [o] was essentially a replica for that of the final [o]. Although nearly all segments were lengthened, two that stand out are the nasal murmur for [n] and the stop gap for [d]. Pattern D was segmentally correct insofar as no substitution errors were made, but the utterance was prolonged (about three times as long as the normal production in A).

More complex errors are shown in Figure 12. Figure 12, upper spectrogram, shows the initial attempt of one speaker to say the word *responsibility*. The error sequence transcribed [j u r s] has the following features identified by numerals in the spectrogram: 1) lengthy prevoiced interval, 2) a glidelike initial phonetic segment, 3) a prolonged vowel segment, 4) a relatively brief transitional segment perceived as [r], and 5) a final [s] segment. After this error, the subject restarted the word with a phonemically correct first syllable. Figure 12, lower spectrogram, is a spectrogram of an apraxic speaker's attempted production of *zoo* [z u]. Some features of error are as follows: 1) the leading portion of the initial fricative was voiceless, 2) voicing began at the point marked by the arrow, 3) a brief [ʊ]-like vowel was produced, and 4) production ceased and a new attempt was begun. The second attempt was still in error since

TABLE 4. Seriation or selection errors in apractic speech. The errors involve omissions, additions, or substitutions of phonetic segments.

Intended utterance		Error production
Orthographic	Phonemic	
dishes	/d ɪ ʃ ə z/	/d r ɪ ʃ ə z
jab	/d ʒ æ b/	/g æ b/
please	/p l i z/	/p r i z/
pleasingly	/p l i z ɪ ŋ l ɪ/	/r i z ɪ ŋ r ɪ/
Nebraska	/n ɛ b r æ s k ə/	/n ɛ b r æ s ə/
television	/t ɛ l ə v ɪ ʒ ə n/	/t ɛ l ə v ɪ z ə n/
several	/s ɛ v ɚ ə l/	/ʃ ɛ v r o/
tornado	/t ɔ r n e ɪ d o/	/t ɔ r n e o d o/
wreck	/r ɛ k/	/w ɛ k/
groceries	/g r o ʊ ʃ ɚ i z/	/g o ʊ ʃ ɚ i z/
twelve	/t w ɛ l v/	/t w ɛ l v z/
sixteen	/s ɪ k s t i n/	/s ɪ s t i n/
impossibility	/ɪ m p a s ə b ɪ l ɪ t ɪ/	/ɪ m p a s ə b u l t l ɪ/
washed up	/w ɔ ʃ t ʌ p/	/w ɔ ʃ ʌ p t/
shush	/ʃ ʌ ʃ/	/ʃ ʌ s/
judge	/d ʒ ʌ d ʒ/	/g d ʒ ʌ z/
vegetables	/v ɛ d ʒ t ə b ə l z/	/v ɛ d ʒ t ɚ b ɛ l z/
drinking	/d r ɪ ŋ k ɪ ŋ/	/d r ʌ ŋ k ɪ n/
vacation	/v e k e ɪ ʃ ə n/	/v e f e ɪ k ʃ ə n/

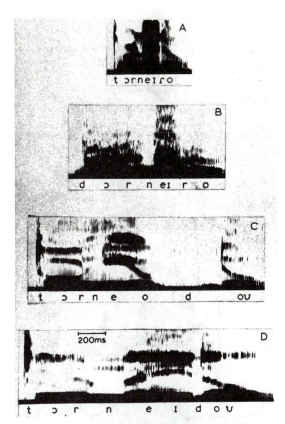

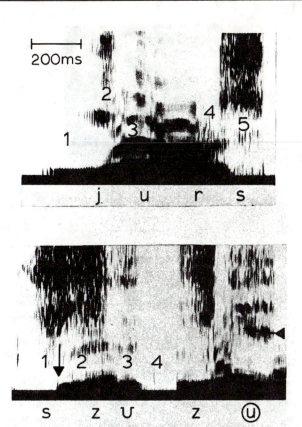

FIGURE 11. Spectrograms of the word *tornado* produced in isolation by a normal speaker (a) and by three apraxic speakers (b, c, d). The apraxic patterns illustrate a variety of errors of sequencing, timing, and coordination.

FIGURE 12. Shown in the upper spectrogram is a false start (initiation error) on the first syllable of the word *responsibility*. The numerals identify the following segments: 1) lengthy prevoiced interval, 2) glidelike initial phonetic segment, 3) prolonged vowel, 4) brief transition, and 5) final [s]. The lower spectrogram shows apraxic errors in the recitation of the monosyllable [zu]: 1) voiceless portion of initial fricative, 2) voiced portion of initial fricative, 3) brief vowel, 4) pause before a new attempt at the syllable is made. Line with arrowhead at extreme right indicates the second formant, which is inappropriately high in frequency for the intended vowel [u].

the vowel was more like [i] than [u] (note the inappropriate high-frequency second formant). The spectrograms in Figure 12 illustrate the articulatory groping often described in apraxia of speech. The subject may make multiple errors, and the resulting sequence can be acoustically complex.

Initiation difficulties often took the form of part-word repetitions or "false" start vocal behavior, as illustrated in Figure 13 for one apraxic speaker who had marked difficulty in this area. The top of this figure is an oscilloscope display of an intensity-by-time plot (derived from the Kay Elemetrics Visi-Pitch). At the bottom is a wide-band spectrogram focusing on the repetitions visible in the intensity-by-time plot as four brief, relatively weak pulses surrounded by word-duration maxima of longer durations. The wide-band spectrogram shows that the repetitions (interval bounded by the arrow) consisted of a few glottal cycles and ranged in duration about 80–140 msec. The F_1-F_2 pattern was quite consistent throughout the repetitions and was also consistent with the pattern that began the following word. However, there appears to have been a gradual lowering of F_3 frequency through the repetitions and into the word. We did not examine this behavior in detail, but this example points up one potentially interesting form of analysis. If the formant structure gradually changed during the repetitions until it converged on the formant structure of the

"fluent" word, then we have evidence of purposive or goal-directed articulatory modifications during the interval of repetitions or false starts. Analyses of this sort would help to tell us if the disfluent character of apraxic speech represents a systematic convergence on an articulatory goal rather than a haphazard groping from syllable to syllable.

Voicing Errors

Because neuromotor control of the larynx and of the oral articulators are presumed to be relatively independent, the relative timing between voicing and stop or fricative articulations is a good focus for an inspection of coordination errors. Such errors did indeed occur, although they were inconsistent. Examples are given in Tables 5 and 6 and Figures 14, 15, and 16.

Table 5 shows voice onset times for single tokens of syllable-initial stops in CVC utterances (*peep, tote, coke,* and *gag*). Data are not shown for apraxic subject 7 be-

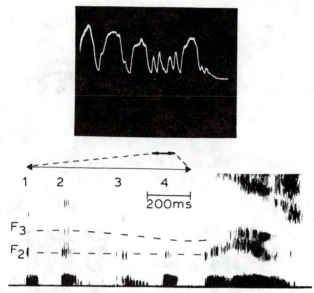

FIGURE 13. Intensity-by-time display (top) and spectrogram showing initiation difficulty in the interval marked by arrows. The four brief vocalic repetitions had weak intensity maxima compared to surrounding syllables and a gradual adjustment in formant pattern (note F_2 and F_3).

cause he had occasional lack of voicing for an entire word. The results for apraxic subjects 1–6 are quite variable, with VOT ranges of 24–128 msec for /p/, 32–176 msec for /t/, 52–128 msec for /k/, and −136 to 256 msec for /g/. The mean data for apraxic speakers are quite close to the mean results for normal speakers, and especially for the voiceless stops the voice onset time for an apraxic subject rarely exceeded the criterion of mean + 2 SD for the normal group. Hence, for these particular simple stop + vowel + stop syllables, voicing control was not markedly impaired in the apraxic subjects, although the results for /g/ indicate that voiced stops might be more deviant than voiceless stops.

Voice onset time for word-initial /d/ is illustrated in Figure 14 for one normal speaker (a) and three apraxic speakers (b, c, d). As is shown by the interval marked by the arrows, these three apraxic subjects had a substantial

TABLE 5. Voice onset time (VOT) for syllable-initial stops in CVC utterances produced by normal speakers (NS) and apraxic speakers A1–A6. All values in msec.

Subject	Stop			
	/p/	/t/	/k/	/g/
A1	48	176*	88	136*
A2	128*	104	128*	256*
A3	40	56	72	72
A4	24	80	52	−136*
A5	56	80	96	44
A6	24	32	60	−76
Mean, AS	53	88	83	49
NS Mean (SD)	56 (30)	74 (160)	78 (15)	11 (38)

*Exceeds mean for normal speaker by 2 SD.

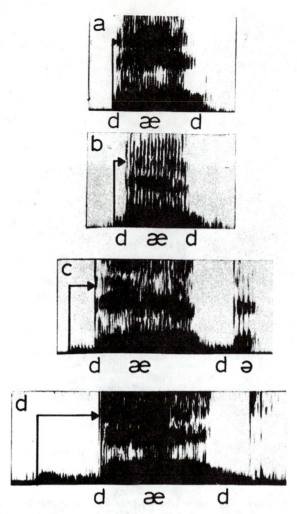

FIGURE 14. Spectrogram of the word *dad* [d æ d] produced by a normal talker (a) and three apraxic speakers (b, c, d). The interval marked by arrows is prevoiced. The three apraxic productions are characterized by an unusually long prevoiced interval, up to nearly 250 msec in (d).

voicing lead. In fact, for the result in d, the onset of voicing preceded articulatory release of the stop by almost 250 msec. The spectrogram in part b shows about 40 msec of voicing lead. This large range of voicing leads illustrates that apraxic subjects can differ greatly from one another. A similar conclusion was reached by Itoh, Sasanuma, Tatsumi, and Kobayashi (1979). Although all our apraxic subjects seemed to have difficulties with control of timing and coordination, the acoustic manifestations of the control problems varied from individual to individual. For this reason, it may be unwise to represent the behavior of a sample of apraxic subjects by reporting only a group mean.

Figure 15 illustrates the general type of evidence of voicing incoordination for fricatives. The spectrogram is for an apraxic speaker's attempted production of the isolated word *shush* [ʃ ʌ ʃ]. The production was disfluent [ʃ ə ʃ ʌ ʃ], with a barely audible schwa [ə] in the initial part-word attempt. The interesting feature is the relative

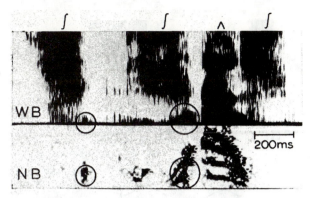

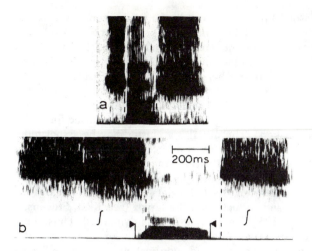

FIGURE 15. Incoordination of voicing in an apraxic production of the word *shush*. WB = wide-band (300 Hz) spectrogram, NB = narrow-band (45 Hz) spectrogram. Smaller circles to the left side of figure enclose acoustic evidence of very brief vowel in a false start. Larger circles to the right show onset of voicing during the final portion of the initial voiceless fricative. (See text for details.)

FIGURE 16. Normal (a) and apraxic (b) productions of the word *shush* [ʃ ʌ ʃ]. The solid and dashed lines in (b) show a timing or coordination error between the voiced segment for the vowel and the frication noise for the surrounding [ʃ] segments. (See text for explanations.)

timing of [ʃ] frication and the onset of voicing. The circles in the whole-word production show the evidence of incoordination: voicing began before the frication segment ended. Voicing is evident in the wide-band spectrogram as the low-frequency voice bar (upper larger circle) and in the narrow-band spectrogram as harmonic structure (lower large circle). The smaller circles in the part-word production indicate similar features, but the overlap between voicing and frication was not as marked for this portion of the utterance.

A similar incoordination of voicing and frication is obvious in Figure 16. For the apraxic production of [ʃ ʌ ʃ] in part b, the onset of voicing (indicated by the leftmost vertical line with attached arrowhead) preceded the end of frication (leftmost broken line). In the normal production (part a), the onset of voicing very closely followed the end of frication. In addition, for the apraxic production, the offset of voicing (rightmost vertical line with attached arrowhead) preceded the onset of frication (rightmost broken line) for the final [ʃ]. The incoordination of both voice onset and voice offset may indicate that the entire voiced segment for the vowel was shifted

in time relative to the voiceless consonant frame. Such temporal shifts between vowel and consonant features are of potential interest with respect to the theory that vowels and consonants are specified in parallel by a speech motor executive (Ohman, 1967; Perkell, 1969).

Voice onset times for the fricatives /z/ and /s/ are compiled in Table 6. Shown for each fricative is the voice onset time (VOT) and the duration of frication (FD). A completely voiceless segment has a VOT equal to FD. A segment that is continuously voiced has a VOT = 0. The frication segment is partially voiced if VOT < FD and the frication segment is followed by a voiceless interval (delayed onset of voicing) when VOT > FD.

The results for initial /z/ in *zoos* indicate that voicing commenced during the frication period for apraxic speakers 1, 2, 3, and 6. Apraxic speaker 4 produced a fully voiced /z/, and apraxic speaker 5 produced a fully voiceless initial fricative. In comparison, the normal speakers produced /z/ with a slight voicing lead or a slight voicing lag; their data averaged out to a voicing

TABLE 6. Voice onset time (VOT) and frication duration (FD), both in msec, for word-initial /z/ or /s/. When VOT = FD, the frication segment is voiceless; when VOT = 0, the frication segment is fully voiced; when VOT < FD, the frication segment is partially voiced; and when VOT > FD, a voiceless interval follows the end of frication. (VOT is measured relative to the onset of frication.)

Subject[a]	/z/ - zoos		/s/ - sis		/s/ - several		/s/ - snowman	
	VOT	FD	VOT	FD	VOT	FD	VOT	FD
A1	88	296	216	204	260	228	248	168
A2	232	424	480	440	456	456	332	304
A3	84	96	236	192	252	192	388	180
A4	0	144	152	152	128	112	148	136
A5	32	32	412	412	232	232	208	176
A6	84	220	256	256	264	252	252	124
Ax̄	87	202	292	276	265	245	263	181
Nx̄	−19	106	162	144	142	120	161	119

[a]A = apraxia; N = normal.

lead of 19 msec. The results for /s/ show an essentially normal VOT-FD relationship (except for obvious lengthening) for the words *sis* and *several*. The VOT-FD difference was close to 20 msec for both words and for both groups of speakers, indicating that initial /s/ tends to be followed by a short null (silent) segment before voicing begins. The silent segment is larger for /s/ in *snowman* (82 msec for apraxic speakers and 42 msec for normal speakers). The initial /sn/ cluster may be associated with a longer silent interval because the transition from /s/ to /n/ requires the performance of two relatively sluggish articulations: opening of the velopharynx (see Björk, 1961, and Nylen, 1961, for data on velopharyngeal dynamics) and adduction of the larynx (see Klatt, Stevens, & Mead, 1968, for relevant data on dynamics). Thus, the /sn/ cluster is an interesting situation for assessment of articulatory dynamics and coordination.

The data in Table 6 show that differences between apraxic and normal speakers occur with respect to (a) overall segment durations, (b) voice onset time for initial /z/, and (c) voice onset time for initial /sn/ cluster. The apraxic subjects' difficulty with /z/ may reflect an impairment in the coordination of gestures that should be simultaneous (i.e., onset of frication and onset of voicing). These results may be useful in specifying phonetic sequences that are most sensitive to apraxic disturbances, but obviously these data only begin to scratch the surface.

Vowel Errors

Although some earlier reports have concentrated more on substitution errors than distortion errors of vowels, the spectrograms show that both kinds of errors may occur frequently, presumably because of a general inaccuracy in articulatory positioning for vowels. When the error in positioning is large, the examiner will hear a vowel substitution. When the error is small, the examiner is more likely to hear a normal vowel or a vowel distortion; that is, the acoustic change is not sufficient to place the sound in another phoneme category.

Because our apraxic subjects frequently had errors of prolongation or transitionalizing (to use Trost and Canter's term, 1974), it does not seem sufficient to say that vowel errors in apraxia of speech are mainly substitutions. Even when a substitution was heard, as in the case of the word *church*, illustrated in Figure 17-a, the error pattern shows more than a simple substitution. The target vowel /ɝ/ was replaced by a complex vocalic nucleus transcribed phonetically as /ɔ ɪ ə/ (a diphthong with a schwa offglide). Moreover, the onglide portion of the diphthong was about 160 msec in duration, which is as long as the entire diphthong would be in normal speech. To describe this error only as a vowel substitution neglects the deviance in temporal pattern. Another example of vowel error is given in Figure 17-b, a spectrogram of one apraxic speaker's production of the final four syllables of the word *refrigerator*. For the first three syllables shown, the formant patterns had very little vowel

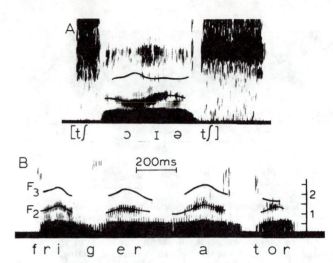

FIGURE 17. Vowel errors in apraxic productions of the words *church* (a) and *refrigerator* (b). (See text for discussion of formant patterns.)

differentiation (compare with the patterns in Figure 1). This speaker tended to use a neutral vowel (actually more of a central diphthong) in place of other vowels. Given the fact that the substituted sound was quite long, up to 300 msec or so, the centralization did not seem to result from unstressing or reduction. Moreover, the formant patterns of these centralized vocalic segments are dynamic, that is, they change over time. To describe these vowel errors simply as substitutions would ignore their complex dynamic structure.

One method of assessing the adequacy of vowel production is to compare the F_1-F_2 values of the vowels against a system of isovowel lines (Kent, 1979; Kent, Netsell, & Abbs, 1979). The isovowel lines represented best fits to the F_1-F_2 data for a heterogeneous group of normal speakers, including men, women, and children. Isovowel lines for vowels /i/, /æ/, /ɑ/, and /u/ are drawn in Figure 18. The geometric symbols in the figure represent the F_1-F_2 values for productions for vowels by apraxic speakers. Comparison of apraxic data with the isovowel lines shows that the apraxic subjects have a satisfactory overall range of F_1-F_2 values for the English vowel system. However, some individual productions were extremely deviant in F_1-F_2 pattern (e.g., the one /u/ attempt that falls directly on the isovowel line for /i/), and some group results have unusually large F_1-F_2 ranges (as for vowels /i/ and /ɪ/).

DISCUSSION

Taking into account the various apraxic errors documented acoustically in this report, a composite description of an apraxic speaker is as follows:

1. slow speaking rate with prolongations of transitions and steady states as well as intersyllable pauses
2. restricted variation in relative peak intensity across syllables
3. slow and inaccurate movements of the articulators to spatial targets for both consonants and vowels

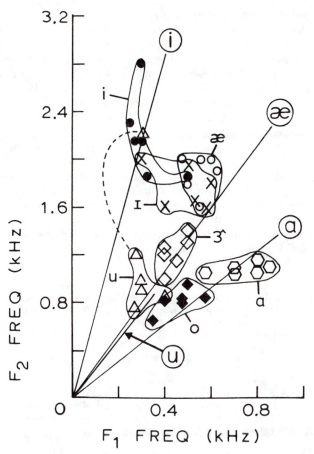

FIGURE 18. Vowels of six apraxic subjects shown in F_1-F_2 plot with isovowel lines for normal productions of [i u a æ].

4. frequent mistiming or dyscoordination of voicing with other articulations
5. occasional errors of segment selection or sequencing including intrusion, metathesis, and omission
6. initiation difficulties often characterized by false starts and restarts
7. complex sound sequences associated with prolongations, interruptions, and inappropriate phonetic variations.

Speaking Rate, Timing Errors, and Related Prosodic Disturbances

For the present sample of apraxic speakers, one of the most striking and consistent abnormalities was a slow speaking rate, characterized by prolonged transitions, steady states, and pauses. The slow rate probably contributes significantly to the perceptual impression of apraxic speech as effortful and groping. Furthermore, slow rate may be predisposing to increased timing error—that is, errors in the timing of individual movements—given that slow speakers have larger timing errors than fast speakers (see Kent & Forner, 1980, for a review of the evidence). In fact, Newell, Hoshizaki, and Carlton (1979) concluded that the timing accuracy of normal limb movements deteriorated when the velocity fell below a certain limit (about 15 cm/sec, which is similar to some velocities in speech).

The measurements of vowel and consonant segment duration (Figures 3 and 4) show that excessive lengthening is likely to occur in utterances of longer syllabic length. In this respect, lengthening is similar to other apraxic errors (Shewan, 1980). Increased syllabic or phonetic complexity apparently affects most if not all dimensions of apraxic disturbances. Accordingly, manipulation of the variable of complexity is important for diagnosis and for assessing the effects of management. If the complexity or length of an utterance does in fact affect all types of apraxic errors, this fact of symptomatologic unity has implications for a theoretical understanding of the disorder.

The lengthened formant transition times (Figures 1, 5, 7, and 11) frequently observed in this sample of apraxic subjects indicate a slowness of articulatory movements. This inference agrees with a report by Itoh et al. (1980) describing an apraxic patient who had reduced articulatory velocities compared to a normal speaker. On the other hand, DiSimoni and Darley (1977) concluded from their measurements of /p/ segment duration in one apraxic subject that "while the overall rate of speech measured in words or syllables per second may be slower, the rate of movement of the articulators in the intrasyllabic condition appears to be more rapid in apraxia than in normal speech" (p. 263).

This conclusion, apparently based on the assumption that a shorter segmental duration of /p/ reflects a more rapid articulatory movement, was questioned by Itoh et al. (1980), who cited data to the effect that the velocity of lip movement may decrease even as syllabic duration shortens. However, there is a more fundamental difficulty with DiSimoni and Darley's conclusion. They measured /p/ duration in VCV utterances as the interval "from the point on the tracing at which oscillation of the signal due to vocal cord activity for the initial vowel ceased, to the point at which it began to the final vowel" (p. 260). Hence, what they actually measured was the interval of voicelessness and not the stop gap for /p/. This distinction is especially important in view of the possibility demonstrated herein that apraxic speakers may have discoordinations between laryngeal and supralaryngeal movements. The conservative interpretation of DiSimoni and Darley's data is that the apraxic speaker had shorter intervals of voicelessness than their normal speaker. The interval measured by DiSimoni and Darley is not directly related to the rates of movement of the oral articulators.

Ryalls (1981) reported spectrographic measurements of duration and vowel formant frequencies for 11 "motor aphasics" who had verified lesions in the fronto-rolandic portion of the left hemisphere. The durations of five vowel segments, two words, and one sentence tended to be longer for the aphasic than for the control subjects.

The slowed speaking rate in our sample of apraxic subjects was accompanied by other prosodic abnormalities. The most consistent of these was a reduction of the intensity variation across syllables in a syllabic sequence. Thus, in the more severe instances of the disorder, syllables were lengthened, sometimes with a complete neutralization of expected durational contrasts (e.g., stressed vs. unstressed vowels), and also were produced with a rather uniform intensity envelope. As a result, the prosodic contrast between syllables was diminished. The F_0-frequency pattern was less reliably affected by the disorder, but the large intersubject variability precluded confident conclusions. Terminal falling F_0 contour was preserved even by the most severely apraxic speaker, who had sentence durations of up to nine times those for normal controls and long pauses between syllables. Similarly, Danly, deVilliers, and Cooper (Note 2) reported a dissociation of the control of timing and F_0 frequency in Broca's aphasics. Their three subjects preserved both the terminal falling F_0 contour and the declination of F_0 peaks during an utterance but failed to show utterance-final lengthening.

Either terminal F_0 fall is a highly robust characteristic of linguistic organization, resistant to all but devastating neural lesions, or it is governed by predictable physiologic mechanisms. Such mechanisms could include relaxation of vocal fold tension in preparation for inspiration or a drop in subglottal air pressure at the end of an utterance. Terminal F_0 fall does not necessarily carry sophisticated linguistic intent, since it frequently is observed on the last word of a recited list (which is why "dummy" words are sometimes placed at the ends of recitation lists used in phonetic studies).

Phonological vs. Motoric Perspectives on Apraxia of Speech

Identification of a phonological deficit is not an easy matter. Several authors have suggested that the articulatory errors in apraxic speech represent phonological simplifications. Formal investigation of this hypothesis has been conducted with distinctive feature and markedness analyses (Klich, Ireland, & Weidner, 1979; Marquardt, Reinhart, & Peterson, 1979). Klich and his colleagues concluded that in terms of markedness theory, articulatory substitutions in apraxic speech have much in common with the articulatory substitutions in children's speech. In view of this similarity, Klich et al. suggested that phonemic regression occurs in apraxia of speech. However, Marquardt et al. questioned the developmental regression hypothesis because "there are observable differences between children and apractic speakers in the errors produced" (p. 493).

A difficulty in studying apraxia of speech is that the perceived nature of the disorder can vary with the methods used to study it. Klich et al. (1979) concluded from their distinctive feature and markedness analyses that "apraxia of speech as a phonological disorder is manifested by changes in the binary specifications and markedness of distinctive features" (p. 468). However, this interpretation runs a risk of confusing methods of analysis with the conclusions of that analysis. The mere fact that distinctive features can be used to describe apparent substitution errors does not necessarily mean that the errors are evidence of a phonological disorder in-

volving feature errors. Klich et al. stated that the "distinctive features most susceptible to both +/− and markedness changes are closely associated with laryngeal control, overall constriction in the vocal tract, and configuration of that constriction" (p. 468). But the gross classification of voicing errors as voiced/voiceless or voiceless/voiced substitutions (or as +/− or −/+ changes in a voicing feature) can easily overlook motoric errors in the coordination of voicing with other articulations. The description of apraxic errors as phonological errors based on distinctive feature analyses is valid only if the articulatory changes are completely and sufficiently described as feature errors—that is, if the errors are in fact genuine substitutions, for example, voiced sound occurring in place of its voiceless cognate.

Pertinent here is a comment by DeRenzi, Pieczuro, and Vignolo (1966), concerning the difficulty of interpreting voicing errors:

It is hard to decide if the substitution of voiced consonantal sounds (e.g., b, v, g) by the corresponding voiceless consonants (p, f, k, respectively) is due to the wrong choice of phonemes . . . or to lack of synergy of the vocal cord with the muscles of articulation. (p. 55)

In the same vein, Ryalls (1981) remarked:

In listening to the speech output of aphasia patients, there is no a priori reason for assuming that an error that we perceive as listeners as phonemic substitution indeed resulted from an error in the patient's phonemic selection process. (p. 55)

(For similar remarks on this issue, see Blumstein, Cooper, Zurif, & Carmazza, 1977).

Some writers (e.g., Shewan, 1980) implicitly or explicitly link phonetic and articulatory errors, on the one hand, and phonemic and phonological errors, on the other. However, this assumption immediately denies allophonic sensitivity to the phonology and any aspect of primary goal or item selection to the articulatory control system. If one were to apply the same argument to the study of sequencing errors in normal speech, then all such errors would perforce be called "phonological," implying that most normal speakers have transient disturbances in their phonological systems. However, many explanations of such common errors invoke not phonological but motor or execution explanations (Keller, 1979; Kent, 1976).

Shewan (1980) noted that the interpretation of apraxia as an impairment of motor speech sequencing has been questioned because of reports demonstrating the influence of linguistic variables on the verbal performance of apraxic subjects. Papers cited supporting such linguistic influence include Deal and Darley (1972), Martin and Rigrodsky (1974), Tonkovich and Marquardt (1977), and Dunlop and Marquardt (1977). However, just because certain "linguistic" variables can be shown to influence the performance of apraxic subjects, it does not follow logically that apraxia is a linguistic (phonological) rather than a motor disorder. Because linguistic variables often are associated with motor variables, it is quite possible for manipulation of a linguistic factor to result in some change in a corresponding motor factor. For example, manipulations of utterance complexity or length, stress pattern, or frequency of occurrence can have fairly direct effects on motor control, particularly in view of theories that speech motor control is accomplished largely through the preparation of motor programs. It is not at all unexpected that motor programs for speech would be sensitive to linguistic variables such as morphological complexity, length of utterance, stress pattern, or frequency of occurrence. It also should be noted that linguistic variables have been shown to influence the performance of stutterers (St. Louis, 1979), but it does not then necessarily follow that stuttering is a phonological disorder.

Some writers take the presence of phonemic substitution errors to be prima facie evidence of "an impairment in phonological selection or an incorrect underlying phonological representation" (Shewan, 1980, p. 72). The latter interpretation probably can be discounted because apraxic errors usually are highly variable, and therefore do not seem to reflect the systematic effects to be expected from a phonological representation (whether normal or abnormal). However, even the first alternative, that of an impairment in phonological selection, does not necessarily apply, because we probably have to allow the motor control system a role in selection and seriation.

It appears that the apraxic error patterns identified in the present study—errors in sequencing, timing, coordination, initiation, and vocal-tract shaping—are as effectively described and explained as errors in motor organization and execution as errors of phonology. At least some of the errors do not seem to fall in the domain of phonology because as the term is commonly understood, phonology is not intended to explain the details of timing and coordination in speech. These matters are best attributed to mechanisms of motor control. We do not claim that apraxia of speech is only a motor impairment, but simply argue that published reports on this disorder rarely have applied methods appropriate to its investigation as a motor disorder. Although analysis of substitution errors in apraxia of speech can be revealing, such an analysis addresses only part of this speech disorder. Thus, a distinctive feature analysis of the substitution errors in apraxia of speech not only forces on the data the abstractness of the feature descriptions but also neglects other aspects of the disorder that ultimately might fit with the apparent substitutions in a unified explanation of the speech impairment. Apraxia of speech usually has been interpreted as either a phonological impairment or a motor programming impairment. The preferred interpretation is the one that explains more fully the various features of the disorder. It may be necessary to consider both types of impairment as coexisting factors.

Aspects of Motor Programming Disturbance in Apraxia of Speech

Sequencing is a central component of skilled motor behavior. Locke (1978, p. 112) remarked that sequencing "determines the goal-directed aspects of the action system" and that sequenced behavior "occurs at each level of neurological performance, and is a constituent of the central program at each level of organization." Canter, Burns, and Trost (Note 3), cited by Buckingham (1979), distinguished between the sequential ordering of phonemes and "transitionalizing" between phonemes. Thus, one might conceive of two major types of disorders in temporal organization: disorders of sequential ordering and disorders of sequential flow. A similar distinction has been suggested for speech acquisition using the terms *sequencing errors* and *phasing errors* (Kent, 1983). An error of sequential order is an apparent error in assembly or retrieval of a phonetic sequence, most commonly realized as a substitution of one phonetic segment for another. This kind of error might be classified by some authors as a phonological error because it presumably involves errors in phoneme-sized units or segments. The other kind of error, a transitionalizing or phasing error, is a case of mistiming or dyscoordination of the component articulations for a given sound or a given transition between sounds. Prime examples are the instances of voice onset and offset errors (Figures 14, 15, and 16), in which vocal fold vibration is not properly timed with respect to the supralaryngeal articulation.

Sequencing errors and phasing errors, together with errors of articulatory positioning, may function primarily as broad descriptive categories for many of the deviant speech behaviors reported on apraxia of speech. Furthermore, the combined use of these categories can address behaviors at both phonological and motoric levels of analysis, if necessary. For example, sequencing errors could be used to include all errors of phone or phoneme size, including substitutions. Phasing errors would include all errors apparently involving faulty coordination or timing of component articulatory gestures. An argument can be made for the division of sequencing errors into (a) actual sequential errors such as prepositioning and (b) substitution errors that do not represent serial confusions of elements in an utterance.

In agreement with Locke (1978), whom we quoted earlier with respect to sequencing functions in skilled motor behavior, we believe that sequencing is imposed at several levels of neural control. Therefore, the terms *sequencing* and *phasing* are intended to distinguish only two major classes of temporal control functions. Sequencing functions themselves are preceded by other related functions that might be disturbed in apraxia of speech. For example, errors might occur in what Lashley (1951) called the "priming of expressive units," a mechanism that arouses and selects the appropriate units, which are as yet unordered. Errors in priming could account for some intrusion errors, for example, /d r˘ɪ ʃ ə z/ for *dishes* and /t w ɛ l v z/ for *twelve* in Table 4.

The lengthening of segments and the errors in control of relative segment duration could be ascribed either to errors at a high level of motor programming or to unreliable reafferent information concerning the timing of movements. The first explanation supposes that the basic temporal plan of movement organization is deficient.

The second explanation supposes that when normal reafference is not available, movements and postures are prolonged, possibly in an attempt to gather the required sensory information by which the antecedent motor program can be evaluated.

The apparent difficulties that apraxic speakers have with both positioning and response sequencing of the articulators might be explained at least in part by a theory of the motor control of speech in which (a) temporal schemata (time plans of movement) help to control the sequencing of movements and (b) spatial targets are defined by a space coordinate system of the vocal tract. That is, spatio-temporal schemata, or abstract goals in space and time, for speech articulation are learned and stored and individual motor programs are specified from these schemata. Semjen (1977) discussed this idea as it applies to motor control generally, and Paillard (1960) remarked on how the disintegration of schemata might result in apraxic disorders in which the subject cannot plan an ordered motor sequence.

One attraction of a spatio-temporal (or motor) schema in accounting for skilled motor performance (of which speech is one example) is that the schema is a generalization by which various factors such as current conditions, past experience, and desired outcome are considered in formulating response specifications for a particular—even novel—motor performance (Schmidt, 1975). In the case of apraxia of speech, the subject might retain effective nonverbal movement control (e.g., for swallowing, tongue protrusion, and lip pursing) over the articulators, but experience faulty control for speech because of deterioration of the spatio-temporal schemata that subserve phonetic performance.

Some general properties of a space coordinate system of the vocal tract have been discussed by MacNeilage (1970) and Sussman (1972). MacNeilage envisaged the space coordinate system as part of a target-based model in which phonological input is translated into a series of spatial target specifications. The targets "would result in a series of demands on a motor system control mechanism to generate movement command patterns which would allow the articulators to reach the specified targets in the required order" (MacNeilage, 1970, p. 189). A schema model of speech production might use targets defined within a space coordinate system as part of the information by which response specifications are generated. The inaccuracies of place of production described in apraxia of speech might be taken to mean either that the subject's access to the space coordinate system is impaired or that the spatio-temporal schema cannot reliably use the spatial information in generating response specifications. Perhaps slowness of speech movements and prolongations of articulatory postures also are partly attributable to difficulties in retrieving and evaluating information about spatial targets.

Rosenbek, Wertz, and Darley (1973) reported that apraxic patients have depressed performance on tests of oral form identification, tasks that presumably require integration of kinesthetic and tactile information. In considering this deficit and the preference of verbal apraxics for the alveolar place of articulation in consonant substitutions, Klich et al. (1979) proposed that:

> place errors in apraxia of speech may be attributed to breakdowns in processes needed to use the space coordinate system for speech ... [and that when] ... such a breakdown occurs, speakers with apraxia of speech apparently restrict their articulatory activity to the more stable alveolar position. (p. 465)

Initiation errors in verbal apraxia could reflect a general failure of the schema to specify motor commands, given the intended motor responses, the current state of the articulators, and motor experience in meeting similar demands. Substitution errors, and perhaps even some intrusion errors, may represent a sort of default motor execution in which preference is given to the most well-established schema. Schemata for alveolars should be especially well established by virtue of the high frequency of occurrence of alveolar sounds in English. Klich et al. (1979) observed a greater frequency of occurrence of substitutions in the initial word position. They suggested that the word-position asymmetry in substitutions is related to the contextual sensitivity of initial consonants:

> For example, production of an initial consonant usually involves simultaneous articulatory adjustments for that consonant and for succeeding sounds (Ohman, 1966; Kent and Moll, 1969) whereas production of word-final postvocalic consonants requires no anticipation of other speech sounds (MacNeilage and DeClerk, 1969). Since initial consonants therefore are accompanied by more complex encoding requirements, they may be associated with relatively more phonetic information. (Klich et al., 1979, p. 464)

Putting a schema perspective on this argument, one might suggest that the generation of response specifications is more complex for initial than for medial or final consonants.

If schema also are used to evaluate a motor performance in terms of comparing the actual performance with the intended action (e.g., Schmidt's, 1975, recognition schema), a schema theory of speech production might explain why persons with apraxia of speech sometimes have difficulty in correcting their errors, even though they seem to be aware of them (Deal & Darley, 1972). That is, a deterioration of schema could affect not only the generation of response specifications to perform an intended sequence, but also the derivation of error information to be used in correcting or adjusting the response specifications for future attempts. Locke (1978) summarized the role of reafferent input in motor control as follows:

> Current thinking suggests that it functions as a regulating system that compares the results achieved with an antecedent plan and allows for the generation of an error signal and compensation in the case of mismatch. (p. 113)

The major factors to be considered in the regulation of motor performance are explicit in Roy's (1978) model of motor skill performance, which was partly based on considerations of apractic errors in movement control. Similar aspects of movement control seem to be involved in speech, so Roy's model may be relevant to understanding apraxia of speech, particularly if this disorder is conceptualized as an impairment of motor programming. At the top of Roy's hierarchical model is a goal selector, which, as its name implies, selects the goal for an action, particularly when the action is not habitual. The goal selector and a subdominant sequencer comprise the planning component of the model. The sequencer makes decisions about sequential order through both a cognitive and a perceptual component. The cognitive component is responsible for decisions about the sequential activities of several effectors, whereas the perceptual component provides the visual-spatial (and perhaps other sensory) information needed for decision processes. Thus, Roy's model predicts that the sequencer will be impaired in function if either the cognitive or perceptual component is disrupted. The lower levels of the model are formed by movement subroutines and the individual movements (units) of which the subroutines are composed. The subroutines and units together are called the executive component of the model, which also includes a programmer.

Roy assigned to feedback important motor control functions. One form of feedback, considered similar to knowledge of results, informs the planner about the consequences of executing a given movement sequence. Another form of feedback, similar to knowledge of performance, informs the sequencer "whether the individual movements were executed in the proper sequence and in the proper spatial framework" (p. 204). A third form of feedback is kinesthetic and is used to exercise fine control over the individual movements within a sequence. Roy suggested that disruption of this type of feedback gives an ataxic quality to the movements. Interestingly, some features described in the present report for apraxic speech resemble characteristics of ataxic dysarthria described by Kent et al. (1979).

CONCLUSION

Apraxia of speech is a complex disorder that results in a variety of abnormalities in the segmental and prosodic structure of speech. The disorder is controversial because of uncertainties in nomenclature, pathophysiology, and symptomatology. The present report has focused only on the third of these areas and has attempted to present a set of acoustic measures that might be helpful in constructing an acoustic profile of the disorder. The acoustic method offers two primary advantages over perceptual description: a greater degree of quantification and a greater sensitivity to some aspects of deviant speech production. Many of the acoustic observations confirm and extend earlier perceptually based descriptions of the disorder. For example, perceptual studies have shown that apraxic subjects tend to make more phonetic errors as syllabic complexity (length) increases. The present acoustic results indicate a similar pattern for segment durations: The individual durations of consonant and vowel segments tend to increase as syllabic length increases.

It is probably unwise at this point to conceptualize apraxia of speech as being exclusively a phonological or motor programming disorder. Although a variety of segmental errors can be identified by perceptual methods, the full range of more subtle errors in articulatory control has yet to be determined. In addition, prosodic abnormalities such as slow rate (prolonged segments and pauses) may be more central to the disorder than previously supposed. The present results are taken as evidence that much more descriptive work—phonological, physiological, and acoustic—needs to be done before definitive statements can be issued on the nature of apraxia of speech and how it differs from other neuropathologies of speech and language.

ACKNOWLEDGMENTS

This research was supported in part by grants from the National Institute of Neurologic and Communicative Disorders and Stroke. We thank the editorial staff for constructive suggestions on the manuscript.

REFERENCE NOTES

1. WERTZ, R. T., & LENNE, M. *Measurements of input and output.* Social Rehabilitation Services Final Report, Washington, DC, 1974.
2. DANLY, M., DEVILLIERS, J. G., & COOPER, W. E. *The control of speech prosody in Broca's aphasia.* Paper presented to the 97th Meeting of the Acoustical Society of America, Cambridge, MA, 1979.
3. CANTER, G., BURNS, M., & TROST, J. *Differential phonemic behavior in anterior and posterior aphasic syndromes.* Paper presented at the 13th Annual Meeting of the Academy of Aphasia, Victoria, BC, 1975.

REFERENCES

BJÖRK, L. Velopharyngeal function in connected speech: Studies using tomography and cineradiography synchronized with speech spectrography. *Acta Radiologica,* 1961, *202* (Suppl.).

BLUMSTEIN, S. E., COOPER, W. E., ZURIF, E. B., & CARMAZZA, A. The perception and production of voice-onset time in aphasia. *Neuropsychologia,* 1977, *15,* 371-383.

BUCKINGHAM, H. W. Explanation in apraxia with consequences for the concept of apraxia of speech. *Brain & Language,* 1979, *8,* 202-226.

DEAL, J. L., & DARLEY, F. L. The influence of linguistic and situational variables on phonemic accuracy in apraxia of speech. *Journal of Speech and Hearing Research,* 1972, *15,* 639-653.

DERENZI, E., PIECZURO, A., & VIGNOLO, L. A. Oral apraxia and aphasia. *Cortex,* 1966, *2,* 50-73.

DERENZI, E., & VIGNOLO, L. A. The Token Test: A sensitive test to detect receptive disturbances in aphasics. *Brain,* 1962, *95,* 556-578.

DISIMONI, F. G., & DARLEY, F. L. Effect on phoneme duration control of three utterance-length conditions in an apractic patient. *Journal of Speech and Hearing Disorders,* 1977, *42,* 257-264.

DUNLOP, J., & MARQUARDT, T. Linguistic and articulatory aspects of single word production in apraxia of speech. *Cortex*, 1977, *13*, 17-39.

GESCHWIND, N. The apraxias: Neural mechanisms of disorders of learned movement. *American Scientist*, 1975, *63*, 188-195.

GOODGLASS, H., & KAPLAN, E. *The assessment of aphasia and related disorders.* Philadelphia: Lea & Febiger, 1972.

ITOH, M., SASANUMA, S., TATSUMI, I., & KOBAYASHI, Y. Voice onset time characteristics of apraxia of speech. In *Annual Bulletin No. 13* (pp. 123-132). Tokyo: Research Institute of Logopedics and Phoniatrics, University of Tokyo, 1979.

JOHNS, D. F., & LAPOINTE, L. L. Neurogenic disorders of output processing: Apraxia of speech. In H. Whitaker & H. A. Whitaker (Eds.), *Studies in neurolinguistics* (Vol. 1). New York: Academic Press, 1976.

KELLER, E. Planning and execution in speech production. *Montreal Working Papers in Linguistics, 13.* Montreal: Universite du Quebec a Montreal and Centre de Reeducation du Language et de Recherche Neuropsychologique, 1979.

KENT, R. D. Models of speech production. In N. J. Lass (Ed.), *Contemporary issues in experimental phonetics.* New York: Academic Press, 1976.

KENT, R. D. Isovowel lines for evaluating vowel formant structures in speech disorders. *Journal of Speech and Hearing Disorders*, 1979, *44*, 513-521.

KENT, R. D. Segmental organization of speech. In P. F. MacNeilage (Ed.), *The production of speech.* New York: Springer-Verlag, 1983.

KENT, R. D., & FORNER, L. L. Speech segment durations in sentence recitations by children and adults. *Journal of Phonetics*, 1980, *8*, 157-168.

KENT, R. D., & MOLL, K. L. Vocal-tract characteristics of the stop cognates. *Journal of the Acoustical Society of America*, 1969, *46*, 1549-1555.

KENT, R. D., NETSELL, R., & ABBS, J. H. Acoustic characteristics of dysarthria associated with cerebellar disease. *Journal of Speech and Hearing Research*, 1979, *22*, 627-648.

KENT, R. D., & ROSENBEK, J. C. Prosodic disturbance and neurologic lesion. *Brain & Language*, 1982, *15*, 259-291.

KLATT, D. H., STEVENS, K. N., & MEAD, J. Studies of articulatory activity and airflow during speech. In A. Bouhuys (Ed.), *Sound production in man. Annals of the New York Academy of Sciences*, 1968, *155*, 1-381.

KLICH, R. J., IRELAND, J. V., & WEIDNER, W. E. Articulatory and phonological aspects of consonant substitutions in apraxia of speech. *Cortex*, 1979, *15*, 451-470.

LAPOINTE, L. L. Neurologic abnormalities affecting speech. In D. B. Tower (Ed.), *The nervous system. Vol. 3. Human communication and its disorders* (E. L. Eagles, Vol. ed.). New York: Raven Press, 1975.

LAPOINTE, L. L., & JOHNS, D. F. Some phonemic characteristics in apraxia of speech. *Journal of Communication Disorders*, 1975, *8*, 259-269.

LASHLEY, K. S. The problem of serial order in behavior. In L. A. Jeffress (Ed.), *Cerebral mechanisms in behavior.* New York: Wiley, 1951.

LOCKE, S. Motor programming and language behavior. In G. A. Miller & E. Lenneberg (Eds.), *Psychology and biology of language and thought.* New York: Academic Press, 1978.

MACNEILAGE, P. F. Motor control of serial ordering of speech. *Psychological Review*, 1970, *3*, 182-196.

MACNEILAGE, P. F., & DECLERK, J. L. On the motor control of coarticulation in CVC monosyllables. *Journal of the Acoustical Society of America*, 1969, *45*, 1217-1233.

MARQUARDT, T. P., REINHART, J. B., & PETERSON, H. A. Markedness analysis of phonemic substitution errors in apraxia of speech. *Journal of Communication Disorders*, 1979, *12*, 481-494.

MARTIN, A. D. Some objections to the term apraxia of speech. *Journal of Speech and Hearing Disorders*, 1974, *39*, 53-64.

MARTIN, A. D., & RIGRODSKY, S. An investigation of phonological impairment in aphasia. I. *Cortex*, 1974, *10*, 317-328.

MLCOCH, A. G., & NOLL, J. D. Speech production models as related to the concept of apraxia of speech. In N. J. Lass (Ed.), *Speech and language: Advances in basic research and practice* (Vol. 4). New York: Academic Press, 1980.

MOHR, J. P., PESSING, M. S., FINKELSTEIN, S., FUNKENSTEIN, H. H., DUNCAN. G. W., & DAVIS, K. R. Broca aphasia: Pathologic and clinical. *Neurology*, 1978, *28*, 311-324.

NEWELL, K. M., HOSHIZAKI, L. E. F., & CARLTON, M. J. Movement time and velocity as determinants of movement timing accuracy. *Journal of Motor Behavior*, 1979, *11*, 49-58.

NYLEN, B. O. Cleft palate and speech. *Acta Radiologica*, 1961, *203* (Suppl.).

OHMAN, S. E. G. Coarticulations in VCV utterances: Spectrographic measurements. *Journal of the Acoustical Society of America*, 1966, *39*, 151-168.

OHMAN, S. E. G. Numerical model of coarticulation. *Journal of the Acoustical Society of America*, 1967, *41*, 310-320.

PAILLARD, J. The patterning of skilled movements. In J. Field, H. W. Magoun, & V. E. Hall (Eds.), *Handbook of physiology. Section I. Neurophysiology* (Vol. 3). Washington, DC: American Physiological Society, 1960.

PERKELL, J. S. *Physiology of speech production: Results and implications of a quantitative cineradiographic study* (Research Monograph No. 53). Cambridge: MIT Press, 1969.

PORCH, B. E. *The Porch Index of Communicative Ability.* Palo Alto, CA: Counselling Psychologists Press, 1967.

ROSENBEK, J. Apraxia of speech—Relationship to stuttering. *Journal of Fluency Disorders*, 1980, *5*, 233-253.

ROSENBEK, J. C., WERTZ, R. T., & DARLEY, F. L. Oral sensation and perception in apraxia of speech and aphasia. *Journal of Speech and Hearing Research*, 1973, *16*, 22-36.

ROY, E. A. Apraxia: A new look at an old syndrome. *Journal of Human Movement Studies*, 1978, *4*, 191-210.

RYALLS, J. H. Motor aphasia: Acoustic correlates of phonetic disintegration in vowels. *Neuropsychologia*, 1981, *19*, 365-374.

SCHMIDT, R. A. A schema theory of discrete motor learning. *Psychological Review*, 1975, *82*, 225-240.

SEMJEN, A. From motor learning to sensorimotor skill acquisition. *Journal of Human Movement Studies*, 1977, *3*, 182-191.

SHEWAN, C. M. Phonological processing in Broca's aphasics. *Brain & Language*, 1980, *10*, 71-88.

SNEDECOR, G. W., & COCHRAN, W. G. *Statistical methods* (6th ed.). Ames, IA: Iowa State University Press, 1967.

ST. LOUIS, D. O. Linguistic and motor aspects of stuttering. In N. J. Lass (Ed.), *Speech and language: Advances in basic research and practice* (Vol. 1). New York: Academic Press, 1979.

SUSSMAN, H. M. What the tongue tells the brain. *Psychological Bulletin*, 1972, *77*, 262-272.

TONKOVICH, J. D., & MARQUARDT, T. P. The effects of stress and melodic intonation on apraxia of speech. In R. H. Brookshire (Ed.), *Clinical aphasiology: Proceedings of the Conference, 1977.* Minneapolis, MN: BRK Publishers, 1977.

TROST, J., & CANTER, G. J. Apraxia of speech in patients with Broca's aphasia: A study of phoneme production accuracy and error patterns. *Brain & Language*, 1974, *1*, 63-80.

WERTZ, R. T., & ROSENBEK, J. C. Appraising apraxia of speech. *Journal of the Colorado Speech and Hearing Association*, 1971, *5*, 18-36.

Received April 23, 1981
Accepted July 15, 1982

Requests for reprints should be sent to John C. Rosenbek, Chief, Speech Pathology and Audiology, William S. Middleton Memorial VA Hospital, 2500 Overlook Terrace, Madison, WI 53705.

APPENDIX

Test words and sentences for eliciting apraxic errors (primarily from a larger list in F. L. Darley, A. E. Aronson, and J. R. Brown, *Motor Speech Disorders,* Philadelphia: W. B. Saunders, 1975, p. 97).

Longer Words and Phrases

snowman	catastrophe
several	impossibility
tornado	statistical analysis
gingerbread	Methodist Episcopal Church
artillery	

Sentences

The valuable watch was missing.
In the summer they sell vegetables.
The shipwreck washed up on the shore.
Please put the groceries in the refrigerator.

Monosyllables

mom	mine	lull
bib	shush	roar
peep	sis	fife
tote	zoos	coke
dad	church	gag

ACOUSTIC CHARACTERISTICS OF DYSARTHRIA ASSOCIATED WITH CEREBELLAR DISEASE

RAY D. KENT, RONALD NETSELL, *and* JAMES H. ABBS

University of Wisconsin–Madison

The speech of five individuals with cerebellar disease and ataxic dysarthria was studied with acoustic analyses of CVC words, words of varying syllabic structure (stem, stem plus suffix, stem plus two suffixes), simple sentences, the Rainbow Passage, and conversation. The most consistent and marked abnormalities observed in spectrograms were alterations of the normal timing pattern, with prolongation of a variety of segments and a tendency toward equalized syllable durations. Vowel formant structure in the CVC words was judged to be essentially normal except for transitional segments. The greater the severity of the dysarthria, the greater the number of segments lengthened and the degree of lengthening of individual segments. The ataxic subjects were inconsistent in durational adjustments of the stem syllable as the number of syllables in a word was varied and generally made smaller reductions than normal subjects as suffixes were added. Disturbances of syllable timing frequently were accompanied by abnormal contours of fundamental frequency, particularly monotone and syllable-falling patterns. These dysprosodic aspects of ataxic dysarthria are discussed in relation to cerebellar function in motor control.

The cerebellum in the adult weighs about 140 grams, which amounts to about 10 percent of the total brain weight (Minckler, 1972; Elliott, 1963). In vertebrate comparisons, the cerebellum has its greatest relative weight in primates and man, "the animals with the greatest need for synergic control in their highly skilled activities" (Elliott, 1963, p. 268). By gross anatomy, the cerebellum is made up of (1) an expansive cortex overlying the thin, branching convolutions of the folia, (2) the large, paired dentate nuclei, (3) a group of small paired nuclei (fastigial, globose, and emboliform), and (4) the white matter of the *corpus medullare*. The cerebellum attaches to the brain stem by means of three peduncles, the superior, middle, and inferior. Evolutionary stages have been linked with cerebellar structure according to three regions: archicerebellum (primarily vestibular inflow), paleocerebellum (spinal and tectal inflow), and neocerebellum (cerebral and olivary inflow). See Larsell (1947) for a discussion of these regions and their functional significance. Histological descriptions have been reviewed by Ito (1968) and Eccles (1969). Of primary interest to speech is the neocerebellum, which consists of most of the vermis in the middle lobe and all of the hemispheres except for minor regions (declive, uvula, and tonsils). Of course, this is the part of the organ to appear latest in the evolutionary series.

The cerebellar hemisphere has access to corticospinal and corticobulbar information via the pontine nucleus and inferior olive. The output from the hemisphere originates in the dentate nucleus and travels through the ventrolateral nucleus of the thalamus to reach the motor area of the cerebrum. The other principle efferent discharge is to the motoneurone pool. By virtue of these efferent pathways, the cerebellum is in a highly advantageous position to coordinate motor behavior, having both peripheral and central connections in the motor system. Moreover, there is substantial evidence that the cerebellum is involved in the alpha-gamma regulation of motor control (Granit, Holmgren and Merton, 1955; Calma and Kidd, 1959; manni et al, 1964; Denny-Brown and Gilman, 1965; Gilman, 1970; Brooks, 1972).

Depending on the location and possibly the size of a cerebellar lesion, the clinical signs in humans may include hypotonia, dyssynergia, dysmetria, static or postural tremor, intention tremor, ataxia of gait and falling to the side of the lesion, and nystagmus. Dyssynergia may be manifest as a number of movement abnormalities, including delay in starting and stopping movements, rebound phenomenon, dysdiadochokinesia, a decomposition of movement and speech, and slurring dysarthria (Lance and McLeod, 1975).

The most extensive description of dysarthria in cerebellar disease was provided by Brown, Darley, and Aronson (1970), who identified clusters of deviant perceptual dimensions in the speech of 30 individuals with ataxic dysarthria. The ten perceptual dimensions determined to be most important in characterizing the speech patterns were organized as three clusters: articulatory inaccuracy, prosodic excess, and phonatory-prosodic insufficiency. Articulatory inaccuracy, comprises the dimensions of imprecise consonants, irregular articulatory breakdown, and distorted vowels, was attributed to errors of individual movements and dysrhythmia of repetitive movements. Prosodic excess, based on the four dimensions of excess and equal stress, prolonged phonemes, prolonged intervals, and slow rate, was interpreted to be the consequence of slow individual movements and slow repetitive movements. Phonatory-prosodic insufficiency, incorporating the dimensions of monopitch, monoloudness, and harsh voice, was related to the presence of hypotonia. Articulatory-acoustic correlates for many of these perceptual dimensions were described by Kent and Netsell (1975) in a case study that included acoustic and cinefluorographic analyses of ataxic dysarthria. Among the motor irregularities were slow movements, prolonged articulatory settings for vowels and consonants, errors of direction and range in articulatory movements, and reduction of overall articulatory mobility. Among the acoustic characteristics were monotone with occasional instances of sweeping changes in fundamental frequency, lengthened vowel and consonant segments, lengthened formant transition durations, and frictionalization of stop gaps.

Kornhuber (1977, p. 32) comments on the cerebellum's role in speech production as follows.

> Cerebellar lesions result in a slow, hesitant or dysarthric speech which agrees with other cerebellar motor symptoms, such as dysmetria, adiodochokinesia, and lack of

coordination of fast movements. The cerebellum seems to be a device for the generation and adjustment of fast movements that are too quick to be regulated continuously by outer (such as visual) stimuli and that therefore must be preprogrammed and adjusted by motor learning. In addition, the cerebellum seems to contain a mechanism for holding those positions reached by the fast movements and for the temporal coordination of quick successive series of movements. . . .

The loci of cerebellar lesions most likely to result in dysarthria are not entirely clear, but a recent report by Lechtenberg and Gilman (1978) points strongly to the left cerebellar hemisphere's involvement. Dysarthria was noted in 54% (22 of 41) of patients with left-hemisphere disease, whereas a speech disorder was present in only 15% (7 of 47) of patients with right-hemisphere disease and 6% (2 of 34) of patients with vermal disease. Moreover, the extent of cerebellar damage did not bear an obvious relationship to the occurrence of dysarthria. Given the vast documentation of laterality effects on cerebral–cortical functions, particularly speech, and the ample connections between individual cerebral and cerebellar hemispheres, Lechtenberg and Gilman were not surprised that laterality should be a factor in cerebellar functions. Furthermore, the authors speculated that because cerebrocerebellar connections are primarily contralateral, the left cerebellar hemisphere interacts more with the right than the left cerebral cortex. Given that processing of melodies has been linked with the nondominant (usually right) hemisphere of the cerebrum, Lechtenberg and Gilman suggested that the dysprosody of ataxic dysarthria reflects a disturbance between the right cerebral hemisphere, with its melodic processing abilities, and the left cerebellar hemisphere. By this reasoning, damage to the left hemisphere of the cerebellum is expected to result in a speech disorder characterized by prosodic abnormalities.

This report presents the acoustic results from a physiological and acoustic study of individuals with cerebellar disease and ataxic dysarthria. From the foregoing review of studies of this speech disorder, it is clear that dysprosody is of special interest. Therefore, a major objective of the acoustic method was to describe dysprosodic aspects of ataxic dysarthria, including any deviations in intonational patterns, syllable durations, and timing adjustments in various speech tasks.

PROCEDURES

Subjects

Five individuals with ataxic dysarthria participated in the study. These subjects are identified as A1–A5. Brief descriptions follow.

A1 was a 57-year-old male with spinocerebellar degeneration. The neurological exam disclosed a generalized, symmetrical hypotonia except for tight heel cords which may have been due to spasticity of the gastrocnemius and soleus muscles. This subject also had gaze nystagmus with ocular dysmetria, a broad-based gait, and a mild ataxic dysarthria.

A2, a 59-year-old female with ideopathic cerebellar degeneration, was judged to have diffuse cerebellar disease affecting the midline and hemispheres. Neurologic signs included gaze nystagmus, dysmetria, and intention tremor in upper and lower extremities. She had ataxic dysarthria of moderate severity.

A3 was a 65-year-old woman with cerebellar degeneration of unknown origin. Neurologic examination revealed an ataxic gait, moderate hypotonia of the extremities, bilateral past pointing to the right, intention tremor of the arms and legs, poor execution of rapid alternating movements, and a scanning type of speech. Her dysarthria was judged to be of moderate severity.

A4, a 59-year-old male, was diagnosed as having ideopathic cerebellar degeneration. He had a mild generalized hypotonia and was nonambulatory. Other characteristics were nystagmus; intention tremor of the head, neck and upper extremities; dysmetria of the upper and lower limbs, and a severe ataxic dysarthria.

A5 was a 62-year-old woman with hereditary (Friedreich's) ataxia. She was nonambulatory and had a moderate-to-severe ataxic dysarthria. It should be noted that Friedreich's ataxia frequently involves the spinocerebellar tracts, posterior columns, pyramidal tracts and peripheral nerves. Thus, this subject cannot be readily grouped with the other four subjects, who had a more restricted cerebellar or spinocerebellar degeneration.

The judgments of severity of dysarthria were agreed on by the three authors, who heard samples of conversational speech and reading.

Data for normal speakers were obtained for six to 10 males and females ranging in age from 22 to 40 years. A minimum of six subjects was used for the overall speech sample but 10 subjects were included for all parts but one.

Speech Sample and Measurements

The subjects were asked to recite each of six sentences five times, following auditory presentation of the sentence by tape recording and visual display on a large card. Listed after each sentence below are the segment durations that were of primary interest in acoustic analysis.

> *Buy Bobby a puppy:* diphthong [aɪ], vowel [ɑ], voice onset time for [p], vowel [ʌ] stop gap for [p], and vowel [ɪ]
> *I saw you hit the cat:* frication for [s], vowel [ə], voice onset time for [k], vowel [æ]
> *The box is blue and red:* vowel [ɑ], stop gap for [k], combined noise segment for [ks], voice onset time for [bl] cluster, formant transition for [rɛ]
> *I took a spoon and a dish:* voice onset time for [t], vowel [ʊ], vowel [ə], frication for [s], stop gap for [p], vowel [u], vowel [ɪ], and frication for [ʃ].
> *Please buy me that cute little dog:* voice onset time for [pl], diphthong [aɪ], voice onset time for [k], and vowel [ɔ].
> *The sunlight strikes raindrops in the air:* frication for [s], syllables [sʌn] and [laɪt], frication for initial [s] of *strikes*, stop gap for [t], voice onset time for [tr], syllable nucleus [raɪ], stop gap for [k], combined noise segment for [ks], syllables [reɪn] and [drɑps].

For each vowel, diphthong and syllable duration above, the measurement included the formant transitions surrounding the vocalic element.

The speech sample also included CVC syllables constructed from the vowels [i æ ɑ u ʌ] in a /d_d/ context. These syllables were repeated five times in succession and were used to study vowel formant structure, vowel duration, and CV and VC formant transitions.

One token of each of the words in Table 1 was recorded in the frame

TABLE 1. List of words used to study adjustment of base-word (stem) duration as a function of the number of syllables in a word.

Base word (stem)	Two-syllable word	Three-syllable word
law	lawful	lawfully
please	pleasing	pleasingly
sad	sadden	saddening
sleep	sleeping	sleepingly
truth	truthful	truthfully
wake	wakeful	wakefully
work	workman	Workmanship
werck (reck)	reckless	recklessly

"Say _____ again." The listed items were built around eight base words, or stems, to which suffixes were added to create words of two and three syllables. These words were used to examine adjustments in base-word duration to changing syllabic patterns. Only six normal speakers were run on this portion of the speech sample.

Finally, recordings were made of [pɑ] syllable trains, counting 1 to 20, and at least three minutes of conversation.

Equipment

Tape recordings were made with a Shure Model 5335B microphone and a Pioneer Model CT-F8282 cassette tape deck, or, in the case of Subjects A3 and A5, with a Sony Model TC 520CS cassette recorder. Spectrograms were produced with a Kay Elemetrics Model 7029A Sona-Graph equipped with a scale magnifier/frequency counter.

Segment durations were obtained by measuring to the nearest 0.25 mm the spectrogram intervals of interest and converting the linear measures to time values in msec. Measurement reliability for the bulk of the speech sample used in this study has been determined for a variety of speakers, representing various ages and both sexes. For over 90% of the measured segments, the agreement between replicate values was within 7 msec, or about 1 mm of linear measure on a spectrogram.

RESULTS

Vowel Formant Frequencies

The first and second formant (F_1 and F_2) frequencies were measured for the midvowel portions of the symmetric CVC syllables, made up of the vowels /i u æ ɑ ʌ/ in a /d_d/ frame. Each syllable was repeated five times, and the principle formant frequency measurements were derived from the third token. (Because A4 diphthongized vowel /u/ in the CVCs, measures of formant frequencies for /u/ were obtained from the sentence materials for this speaker only.) Inspection of the spectrograms showed little variation in formant structure among the five tokens for a given vowel. All vowels were judged perceptually by the experimenters to have been adequately produced (phonemic criterion), although most of the syllables of the ataxic subjects appeared lengthened. The vowels of the ataxics are shown together with isovowel lines for normal speakers (Kent and Forner, in press) in the F_1-F_2 plane of Figure 1. No conspicuous abnormalities of formant structure were observed in the ataxic vowels. Ranges of the F_1 and F_2 frequencies seemed appropriate. For example, for male speakers A1 and A4, the F_1 frequency range was 300 to 800 Hz and 300 to 750 Hz, respectively, and the F_2 frequency range was 1050

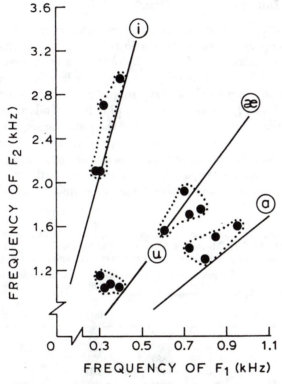

FIGURE 1. First and second formant frequencies of the vowel /i u ɑ æ/ produced by the ataxic subjects compared with isovowel lines for normal speakers (Kent and Forner, in press). Note correspondence between data points for the ataxic subjects and linear approximations to results for normal speakers.

to 2100 Hz and 1300 to 2100 Hz, respectively. For female subjects A2 and A3, the F_1 frequency range was 400 to 950 Hz and 425 to 850 Hz, respectively, and the F_2 frequency range was 1075 to 2950 Hz and 750 to 2700 Hz, respectively. These ranges compare closely with vowel formant frequencies for normal speakers as shown in the illustration. In fact, about the only distinguishing characteristics between the CVC syllables of the ataxic and normal subjects were that the ataxics had longer syllable durations (up to 532 msec), occasionally longer voice onset times for /d/ (up to 46 msec, compared to a maximum of about 10 msec for normals), and longer formant transitions (sometimes in excess of 80 msec, whereas transition durations for normals rarely exceeded 40 to 50 msec). Thus, timing abnormalities for ataxics were common whereas vowel formant structure was generally normal. But it should be acknowledged that the long syllable durations and long formant transitions mean that the ataxic subjects had considerable time to reach vowel target positions. Vowel errors could increase with longer utterances and faster rates.

Mean Segment Durations

Because analysis of individual data was considered more appropriate than a pooled or group analysis for the ataxic subjects, we calculated individual means and standard deviations for the five tokens of a given item. We regarded a mean duration for an ataxic subject to be significantly different from the duration for normal subjects if the ataxic subject's value was equal to or greater than the group mean for normal speakers plus two standard deviations. This criterion of significance was applied to all of the phonetic segment data derived from the sentence recitations. Data are compiled in Tables 2 through 6 for a variety of segments.

Tables 2 and 3 contain mean segment durations for the words *box* (from *The box is blue and red*) and *strikes* (from *The sunlight strikes raindrops in*

TABLE 2. Mean segment durations in the word *box*, based on five tokens, for five ataxic dysarthrics (subjects A1-A5). Means for a group of normal speakers, as well as their means plus two standard deviations, are shown for comparison. All values are in msec.

Subject	Segment		
	[ɑ]	[k] closure	[ks] frication
A1	279°	67	97
A2	253°	103°	150°
A3	288°	95°	144°
A4	445°	170°	135°
A5	386°	163°	262°
Normals			
Mean	182	58	88
Mean + 2 SD	212	80	99

°Segment duration for ataxic subject exceeds mean for normals by 2 *SD*

TABLE 3. Mean segment durations in the word *strikes*, based on five tokens, for five ataxic dysarthrics (subjects A1-A5). Means for a group of normal speakers, as well as their means plus two standard deviations, are shown for comparison. All values are in msec.

	Segment					
Subject	[s] frication	[t] closure	[t] VOT	[rɑɪ] nucleus	[k] closure	[ks] frication
A1	122°	76°	31	185°	49	114
A2	147°	80°	19	246°	38	151°
A3	163°	116°	26	242°	84	203°
A4	91	88°	64°	357°	105°	94
A5	154°	64°	64°	285°	122°	177°
Normals						
Mean	73	35	32	124	42	83
Mean + 2 *SD*	107	45	37	162	66	119

°Segment duration for ataxic subject exceeds mean for normals by 2 *SD*

the air). In Table 2, the segment durations are defined as follows: [ɑ] vowel nucleus including formant transitions; [k] closure or stop gap; and [ks] combined frication. All five ataxic subjects have significantly longer durations than the normal speakers for the [ɑ] nucleus in *box* and the [t] closure and [rɑɪ] nucleus in *strikes*. Four of the ataxics also have longer durations for the [k] closure and [ks] frication in *box* and for the initial [s] in *strikes*. Only the most severely involved ataxic subjects, A4 and A5, show significant lengthening of [t] voice onset time and [ks] frication in *strikes*. The least severe ataxic, A1, had some durations that approached the group mean values for normals even though he exhibited significant lengthening on four of the nine segments shown in Tables 2 and 3. By contrast, A5 had significantly longer durations than the normal speakers for all nine of the segments, and A2, A3, and A4 had significantly longer durations for seven of the nine.

The differences in total word duration between ataxic and normal subjects were quite large. For the word *strikes*, the mean word durations of 578, 681, 833, 799, and 854 msec for subjects A1-A5 compare with a normal group mean of only 389 msec (mean + 2 SD = 536). To determine if the initial [st] cluster, the [rɑɪ] nucleus, and the final [ks] cluster were proportionately lengthened by the ataxics, proportions of the total word duration were calculated for each of these three. The values for ataxics generally were comparable to those for the normal subjects. Subject A5, for example, who had the longest overall word durations, had proportions of 0.32, 0.33, and 0.35 for the initial voiceless cluster, nucleus, and final cluster, respectively. The mean values for normals were 0.36, 0.32, and 0.32. Similarities in proportionate duration also were seen for the word *box*. Thus, it appeared that the effect of the ataxic dysarthria was a uniform lengthening of the consonant clusters and nucleus portions of the words.

Mean segment durations derived from the sentence *I saw you hit the cat* (which contains no clusters) are given in Table 4. All the ataxic subjects show

TABLE 4. Mean segment durations in the sentence *We saw you hit the cat*, based on five tokens, for five ataxic dysarthrics (Subjects A1-A5). Means for a group of normal speakers, as well as their means plus two standard deviations, are shown for comparison. All values are in msec.

	Segment			
Subject	[s] frication	[ə]	[k] VOT	[æ]
A1	154*	104*	51	297*
A2	156*	104*	67	200*
A3	95*	110*	85*	256*
A4	347*	305*	64	372*
A5	206*	64*	118*	375*
Normals				
Mean	125	38	61	192
Mean + 2 *SD*	154	64	73	232

*Segment duration for ataxic subject equals or exceeds mean for normals plus 2 *SD*

significant lengthening of [ə] in *the*, and four of the subjects significantly lengthened the [s] in *saw* and the [æ] in *cat*. The voice onset time for [k] was significantly longer than normal only for subjects A2 and A5. Extreme lengthening of the segments (and pause) in the phrase *I saw* is illustrated in Figure 2 for subject A4.

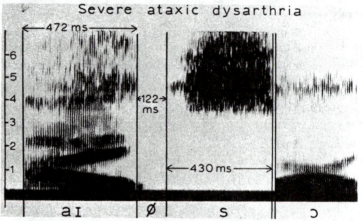

FIGURE 2. Broad-band spectrogram for subject A4's production of the words *I saw*. A marked lengthening of all segments occurs.

The most striking difference between normals and ataxics occurs for the lax central vowel [ə]. With the exception of A5 (the only subject with Friedreich's ataxia), the ataxic subjects exceeded the mean for normals by three standard deviations or more. Spectrograms illustrating the lengthening of [ə] are shown in Figure 3. The spectrograms show the words *the cat* for a normal speaker (top), mild ataxic A1 (center), and severe ataxic A4 (bottom). For subject A4, the duration of [ə] almost equals that of the stressed vowel [æ].

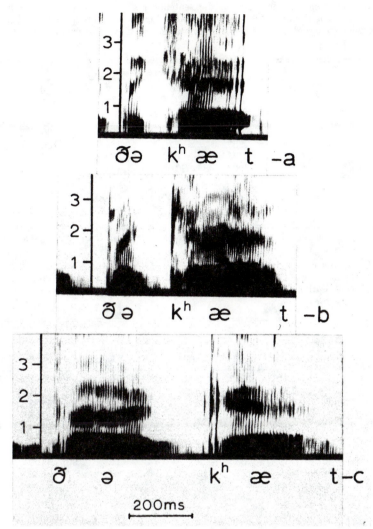

FIGURE 3. Broad-band spectrograms of the phrase *the cat* produced by a normal speaker in (a), a mild ataxic speaker, A1, in (b), and a severe ataxic speaker, A4, in (c). Note lengthening of vowel [ə] in *the* in the ataxic productions.

Mean segment durations for the sentence *Buy Bobby a puppy* (which is loaded with bilabial consonants) are given in Table 5. In general, the ataxic subjects do not show consistent lengthening by the significance criterion for these segments. However, for the vowels [ɑ] in *Bobby* and [ʌ] in *puppy*, four of the five ataxic subjects have durations that exceed the criterion. Only one subject had a significantly lengthened duration for the closure of the second [p] in *puppy*.

A large number of segments is considered in Table 6, which applies to the sentence *I took a spoon and a dish*. Segment durations significantly lengthened by at least four of the five ataxics are the following.

TABLE 5. Mean segment durations in the sentence *Buy Bobby a puppy*, based on five tokens, for five ataxic dysarthrics (Subjects A1-A5). Means for a group of normal speakers, as well as their means plus two standard deviations, are shown for comparison. All values are in msec.

			Segment			
Subject	[ɑɪ]	[ɑ]	[p] VOT	[ʌ]	[p] closure	[ɪ]
A1	200	160	43	149*	54	163
A2	300*	201*	94*	96	106	142
A3	254	225*	27	120*	106	173
A4	322*	277*	60*	323*	114	202*
A5	448*	290*	110*	179*	149*	242*
Normals						
Mean	214	148	36	78	78	135
Mean + 2 SD	300	186	46	108	116	201

*Segment duration for ataxic subject equals or exceeds mean for normals plus 2 SD

TABLE 6. Mean segment durations in the sentence *I took at spoon and a dish*, based on five tokens, for five ataxic dysarthrics (Subjects A1 to A5). Means for a group of normal speakers, as well as their means plus two standard deviations, are shown for comparison. All values are in msec.

				Segment					
Subject	[t] VOT	[ʊ]	[ə]	[s] frication	[p] closure	[p] VOT	[u]	[ɪ]	[ʃ] frication
A1	37	134*	119*	77	128*	16	199	232*	150
A2	48	139*	149*	161*	140*	–	204	204	117
A3	30	142*	146*	129*	134*	14	210	215*	250*
A4	49	229*	266*	176*	145*	49*	266	323*	133
A5	74*	91*	115*	197*	151*	20	239	249*	190
Normals									
Mean	40	52	63	90	74	19	190	169	176
Mean + 2 SD	62	64	109	128	96	37	276	215	242

*Segment duration for ataxic subject equals or exceeds mean for normals plus 2 SD

(1) The lax vowel [ʊ] in *took*.
(2) the lax vowel [ə] in *a*.
(3) The [s] frication in *spoon*.
(4) The closure for [p] in *spoon*.
(5) The lax vowel [ɪ] in *dish*.

The marked lengthening of the lax vowels stands in contrast to the normal or only slightly lengthened duration of the tense vowel [u] in *spoon*. In agreement with the data in earlier tables, voice onset time values for the ataxics rarely exceeded normal values; in fact, some ataxics had shorter voice onset times than the mean for normal speakers. Both the [s] frication and the [p] closure in *spoon* are markedly longer for ataxics than normals, although the final [ʃ] in *dish* is significantly lengthened by only one ataxic.

Given the extreme prolongation of lax vowels by the ataxics, it was of interest to define a measure for the relative comparison of tense and lax vowels in a given phrase or sentence. These comparisons were made using the ratio of the duration of a lax vowel to the duration of a tense vowel. Sample results are shown in Table 7. In almost every instance, the lax-tense vowel ratio was sig-

TABLE 7. Vowel duration ratios formed by dividing the duration of a normally short or lax vowel by the duration of a long or tense vowel. Results are shown for five ataxic dysarthrics and a group (mean score) of normals.

	Vowel duration ratios		
Subject	the cat [ə] : [æ]	took . . . spoon [ʊ] : [u]	a spoon [ə] : [u]
A1	0.35	0.65*	0.60*
A2	0.44*	0.67*	0.70*
A3	0.53*	0.70*	0.73*
A4	0.81*	0.89*	1.00*
A5	0.17	0.38	0.48
Normals	0.22	0.30	0.34
(SD)	(0.08)	(0.09)	(0.09)

*Ratio for ataxic subject exceeds mean for normal subject by 2 SD

nificantly greater for the four ataxic subjects A1 to A4 than for the normal speakers. A5 behaves somewhat differently. Moreover, the duration ratios increase with severity of the dysarthria, that is, in the order A1, A2, A3, A4. For A4, the ratio either approaches or reaches unity, indicating that the normal durational difference between tense and lax vowels is nearly neutralized (also see Figure 3).

Variability of Segment Durations

The precision or reliability of motor control can be gauged from the size of the intrasubject standard deviations for segment durations. However, this matter has to be approached with some caution because it is possible that the variability of segment duration varies with mean duration. In other words, fast talkers (those with short segment durations) tend to be less variable than slow talkers (among whom we can number most dysarthrics). The relationship between variability of segment duration and mean duration is not really well established but some data on this point are available (Lehiste, 1972; Klatt, 1974; Kent and Forner, 1977). The caution to be observed is simply that precision of durational control may vary with mean duration even in normal talkers; therefore, dysarthrics with large means and variances of segment durations to some extent may be following a general principle of speech motor control.

Because lax vowel segments were especially lengthened by the ataxic dysarthrics, these sounds are interesting for an initial look into segment variability. The relevant data are compiled in Table 8. Although the ataxic subjects generally have larger standard deviations than the normal speakers,

TABLE 8. Intraindividual variability in the segment durations of lax vowels. The values for ataxic subjects A1-A5 are standard deviations in msec and the values for normal subjects are standard deviation ranges in msec.

Subject	[ʌ] (puppy)	[ʊ] (took)	[ə] (took a)	[ɪ] (dish)	[ə] (a cat)
			Segment		
A1	18	15	20	10	18
A2	11	19	14	24	5
A3	6	14	23	12	15
A4	18	34	40	18	5
A5	55	26	23	18	18
Normals	5–10	4–11	4–17	8–14	3–10

the differences in variability are not great considering the fact that the ataxics often had mean segment durations four to seven times those for normal speakers (Tables 4, 5, and 6). Furthermore, the ataxic speakers occasionally were capable of extremely fine durational control for some very long segments. For example, the mean duration of A4's [ə] in *the cat* was 305 msec with a standard deviation of 5 msec. The normal group's mean duration for this vowel was only 38 msec and the intrasubject standard deviations ranged from 3 to 10 msec. On a relative basis, A4 actually was more precise than the normal speakers, for his coefficient of variability (mean divided by standard deviation) was about 0.02 whereas that for the normal talkers, based on the group mean and smallest intrasubject standard deviation, is about 0.08. Nonetheless, one should not lose sight of the fact that some lax vowel durations were highly variable for ataxic speakers, for example, A4 and A5.

Given that the variance of segment durations may depend on mean duration, it is useful to compare the variability data for normal and ataxic subjects on a graph that relates the intrasubject standard deviation for segment duration with the subject's mean duration. This plot is shown in Figure 4 for data on closure duration for [p] and [k] consonants in the sentence recitations. Results for normal speakers are represented by filled circles and results for ataxics are depicted by unfilled circles. Although a rare data point for an ataxic subject falls within or close to the rectangle bounding the points for normal speakers, the preponderance of the data points for ataxics are displaced toward the right, the top, or both. It is noteworthy that some ataxic stop closures of long duration, 130 msec or greater, are associated with intrasubject standard deviations within the normal range of about 3 to 15 msec. On the other hand, some of the results for ataxic subjects fall within the range of normal means but exceed the normal range of standard deviations. The results in this figure, like those in Table 8, indicate that although ataxic speakers are not necessarily more variable in segment durations than normals, they often are, especially in severe forms of ataxia.

The part of the speech sample that used base words plus one or two suffixes (for example, *please, pleasing,* and *pleasingly*) was included to determine if

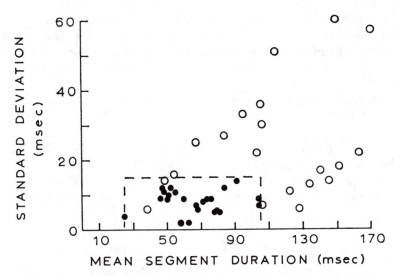

FIGURE 4. Intrasubject standard deviation plotted against mean segment duration for [p] and [k] stop gaps of normal (filled circles) and ataxic (unfilled circles) speakers. The mean and standard deviation ranges for normals are enclosed by broken lines.

and how the ataxic subjects adjusted syllable duration to the number of syllables in a word. Studies have shown that normal speakers make systematic adjustments in base-word duration as the number of syllables in a word is varied (Lehiste, 1972). That is, base word duration decreases as the number of syllables increases from one to three (in a word series like please-pleasing-pleasingly).

For the eight series of suffixing base words in this study, normal speakers adjusted base-word duration in the predicted manner. The average duration of base-word syllables in two-syllable and three-syllable words was 0.86 and 0.78, respectively, of the average duration in the one-syllable utterance. The range of proportions was 0.84 to 0.88 for two syllable words and 0.76 to 0.80 for three-syllable words.

The ataxic subjects A1 to A4 (data for A5 are not available for this part of the study) exhibited inconsistent reductions in syllable duration of the base word as the number of syllables in the words was increased. Whereas the normal speakers never showed an increase in base-word duration between one-syllable and three-syllable words, such a result frequently was observed in the data for ataxic subjects A1, A2, and A4. The base-word duration in three-syllable words spoken by the ataxic subjects was, on the average, 0.94 of that for single-syllable productions, with a range of 0.85 to 1.02 (compared to the normal range of 0.76-0.80). The degree of reduction in base-word duration with increases in syllabicity was not clearly related to the severity of the dysarthria. The most severely dysarthric speaker, A4, had an average base-word reduction of almost 10% between one- and three-syllable words, and subjects A1, judged mild in severity, and A2, judged moderate in severity, showed no consistent reductions. In summary, when faced with a speech task that normally results in systematic reductions of syllable duration, the ataxic subjects showed inconsistent reductions, small reductions, and even some instances of lengthening.

Spectrograms were made of conversational speech samples for several reasons but primarily to ascertain if the effects observed in word and sentence recitations also occurred in conversational speaking. Because conversation is intrinsically idiosyncratic, it was not possible to obtain suitable group measures for the conversational samples. In this section, sample spectrograms are presented to illustrate the characteristics of ataxic conversational speech.

Figure 5 shows a spectrogram of a conversational sample from A1 who was

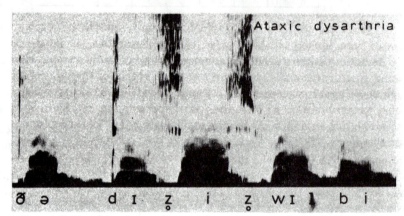

FIGURE 5. Broad-band spectrogram of a conversational sample from subject A1, showing scanning speech. The phrase in the spectrogram is "the disease will be."

saying that doctors informed him that as he grows older, "the worse the disease will be." Observe that the five syllables in the final words of this phrase tend toward equal duration and to be rather regularly separated in time. Of particular interest in this regard are the four syllabic nuclei [ɪ], [i], [ɪ], and [i] in *disease will be*, which present a strongly measured pattern. The perceptual impression of this sample was one of scanning or singsong speech.

Durational and intonational features are shown in a narrow-band (45 Hz) spectrogram of a sample from A2 in Figure 6. The subject was referring in her conversation to a friend who was visiting her while on "vacation from Chicago." In this spectrogram, the scanning type of speech is evident as (1) syllable nuclei of limited variation in duration, (2) wide and regular spacing between syllable nuclei, and (3) a generally flat f_0 contour except for the final two syllables. The flatness of the f_0 contour can be judged from the fact that the harmonics parallel the 500 Hz frequency lines drawn on the spectrogram.

Scanning speech is illustrated again for subjects A1 and A2 in Figure 7,

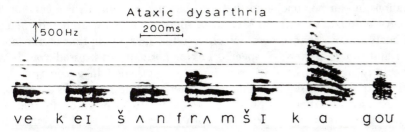

FIGURE 6. Narrow-band spectrogram of a conversational sample from subject A2, showing scanning speech. The phrase in the spectrogram is "vacation from Chicago."

which contains narrow-band (45 Hz) spectrograms for "the disease will be" spoken by A1 and "cocktail before dinner" spoken by A2. These spectrograms show the two most commonly observed f_o contours for subjects A1, A2, A3, and A4. The top pattern is one in which f_o usually falls within each syllable, almost as though each syllable carries its own declarative (or falling) intonation. The bottom pattern is one of monotone or rather flat f_o contour. Generally, scanning speech was associated with one or the other of these f_o contours, although occasional f_o sweeps (see Kent and Netsell, 1975) or intervals of vocal fry also were observed. Finally, the lower spectrogram in Figure 7 (subject A2) is another example of the marked segregation of syllable nuclei in scanning speech.

DISCUSSION

General Acoustic Characteristics of Ataxic Dysarthria

Because a large number of the measured durations of segments in the ataxic speech samples exceeded those for normal speech by two standard

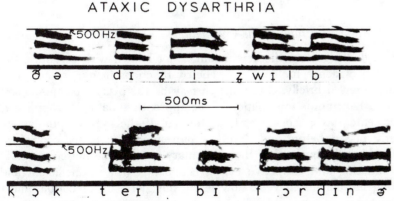

FIGURE 7. Narrow-band spectrograms for subjects A1 and A2, showing two common types f_o contour in ataxic dysarthria: syllable-falling (top) and flat (bottom). The phrases in the spectrograms are "the disease will be" and "cocktail before dinner."

deviations, it can be concluded that lengthening of segments is a fundamental property of ataxic dysarthria. Moreover, some segments were lengthened proportionately more than others, which resulted in a disruption of the normal stress and timing pattern of speech. Lax or normally unstressed vowels were particularly likely to be disproportionately lengthened in ataxic speech. Increased variability of segment duration sometimes but not always accompanied the increased duration of phonetic segments. It is noteworthy that some lengthened segments were produced with a surprisingly small intraindividual variability in repeated tokens of an utterance. The ataxic speakers also did not make normal adjustments of the syllable duration of the stem as suffixing syllables were added to it to make longer words. Individuals judged to have a greater severity of ataxic dysarthria usually had longer segment durations and a greater number of lengthened segments than did individuals with a less severe dysarthria. In the most severe forms, segment durations were as much as seven times the segment durations recorded for normals. Increasing severity of the dysarthria was marked by increased durations of all segments, including some, like voice onset time, that were of normal duration in the speech of less severe dysarthrics. Measurements of segment duration thus appeared to reflect the severity of the ataxic dysarthria.

In contrast to the duration measures, measures of formant frequency for vowels in CVC syllables were normal. This is not to say that vowel distortions do not occur in ataxic dysarthria, particularly when these elements are produced in connected speech. However, when sufficient time was available, the ataxic speakers were capable of reaching the appropriate vowel targets. Abnormalities of formant structure in ataxic speech were noted more frequently for dynamic than static features; for example, compared to the normal speakers, the ataxic speakers often had longer transition durations associated with CV and VC combinations and reduced rates of formant frequency change for some glide and diphthong segments. Thus, as indicated above, timing control is a major problem in ataxic dysarthria.

General Motor Functions of the Celebellum

Although the role of the cerebellum is not known with certainty, there is substantial evidence for certain cerebellar functions in motor control. These will be reviewed briefly. One function may be the biasing of muscle spindles to insure that spindle information of the appropriate nature is supplied to the higher centers as a movement is performed. If the muscle spindles are not properly biased before and during a movement, the motor control system will not be fully apprised of the momentary state of the musculature. Therefore, initiating and corrective neural commands will be inefficient and the resulting movements may be slow in starting, jerky in execution, and often misdirected.

Another function may be the integration and interpretation of afferent information. Konorski (1967) stressed this function in describing the cerebellum as a "true kinesthetic receptive surface informing the brain about the movements performed by the subject and their character" (p. 516). Obviously, if such a receptive surface were damaged, movement control would be impaired.

A third possible function of the cerebellum in motor performance is to exercise a revisory control over the commands issued by the motor cortex. This function has been described by Ito (1970) and Eccles (1973). Eccles suggested that the commands from the motor cortex are imprecise and provisional, requiring for their refinement the continuous action of cerebellar loops. Thus, the higher centers may depend on the cerebellum and its connections to modify grossly formed neural instructions. Presumably, if the cerebellum is damaged and its revisory control is weakened or eliminated, then the higher centers would continue to issue rather gross patterns of motor commands. Whereas these gross patterns may suffice for a rough shaping of movement, they would lack the finesse needed for movements finely graded in time and position.

Boylls (1975) presented a theory of cerebellar function in locomotion that emphasized "a muscle linkage principle." This principle is based on the idea that aggregates of muscles, rather than individual muscles, are the most primitive, independently controllable effectors. At some level of control, these aggregates are constrained to act as a unit, and it is in this unitary activity that the aggregate becomes a "linkage." Given this view of motor control, Boylls proposed that the role of the cerebellum then must be explained by specifying those parameters of motor control that (1) define multijoint adjustments in the actions of many muscles, and (2) portray the linkage constraints among the muscles. This conception gives the cerebellum a different status than simply being a high-speed computer that has limited memory for recently completed movements and little or no predictive capability. Boylls argued that the olivocerebellar system acts holistically to program locomotor acts as linkages of movements, including some movements that are not under execution. The "spino-olivo cerebellar system tunes the structure of locomotor muscle linkages" (p. 185) and the anterior lobe computes structural prescriptions that are constrained in parallel with the spinal constraints on limb coordination. By this reasoning, the spino-olivo-cerebellar system is responsible for integration of motor acts, that is, "for developing cohesion between the separate pieces of a performance however they might be dispersed in time" (p. 195). The anterior lobe has a planning capability that is freed from mandatory specification of individual muscle participation. This abstract representation of movement, being unbound to particular sets of effectors, gives the cerebellum a flexible, coordinative power over the regulation of movement. Damage to a system with this capability would be expected to have consequences on more than isolated movements in a motor act; indeed, the entire act or sequence of movements should be disturbed and there should be evidence of a breakdown in the temporal relationships of movements.

Ataxic Dysarthria in Relation to Cerebellar Motor Control

Whereas many dysarthrias are characterized by the dysprosody of slow rate, ataxic dysarthria is distinguished by a slow speaking rate that assumes a peculiar pattern called scanning, staccato, singsong, or measured. Despite occasional misarticulations and interruptions in the flow of speech, ataxic dysarthria conveys an impression of underlying regularity. This investigation indicates that this regularity may be derived in part from a tendency toward uniform syllable durations, brought about chiefly by the lengthening of normally brief segments such as unstressed vowels, lax vowels, and consonants in clusters. Because normal speech contains a variety of syllable durations, the reduced range of syllable durations in ataxic speech is striking by comparison. The homogeneity of syllable duration becomes all the more striking when coupled with monotone or syllable-falling intonation contours. The intonational properties of ataxic speech often reduce contrasts between and among syllables. That is, when syllables have nearly the same duration and f_o contour, it is unlikely that any one syllable will stand out as being either tonic or reduced.

Perhaps the current data, especially for subjects A1-A4, can best be summarized as demonstrating that ataxic subjects do not reduce syllables when it is appropriate to do so. Syllable reduction requires a flexible and responsive capacity for sequencing of complex motor instructions, and it is in this area that ataxics are challenged. In ataxic dysarthria, there is a slowing of motor patterns but also a disturbance of the normal relative temporal relationships among the syllables within phrases and, to a lesser extent, the phonetic segments within syllables. The problem in part may be a difficulty in making transitional movements in a movement sequence.

The study of neuromotor speech disorders is complicated by the probable interaction of motor impairment and motor control compensations in response to that impairment. That is, the speech behavior of individuals with lesions of the nervous system has some characteristics that are directly related to the lesion's interference with motor control and other characteristics that are related to voluntary or involuntary compensations that may partially correct for the motor disturbance. It is often extremely difficult to tease apart the various consequences of a neural lesion, and the current data are no exception. The acoustic characteristics described herein should be taken not so much as a description of what the cerebellum does in regulating speech, but rather as a description of what the speech motor control system can do in the face of damage to the cerebellum. Thus, ataxic dysarthria is not transparent to the role of the cerebellum in speech, and interpretations of the cerebellum's participation have to be made cautiously.

One particular difficulty in this respect is that a person with a neuromotor speech disorder may alter, voluntarily or involuntarily, the high-level motor programming of speech. We imagine that motor programs for speech are stored in a buffer, or motor program memory. To some extent, the individual speaker can select the amount of information that is prepared for storage in this buffer. Presumably, the neurologically intact adult speaker can store a large amount of information, covering perhaps several syllables of the intended utterance (see, for example, Kozhevnikov and Chistovich, 1965). However, an individual with motor impairment may find it advantageous to store less motor control information at any given time. Instead of preparing motor programs for several syllables, the dysarthric individual may prepare programs for three syllables, two syllables, or even one syllable. In the extreme instance of single-syllable preplanning, the speaker probably cannot help but neglect the many forms of sequential dependencies that are present in normal speech. With a single-syllable preparation, each syllable becomes a unit unto itself and is not integrated within a larger span of syllables (stress group). One consequence of this motor strategy would be a degeneration of the normal prosody into a stereotypic syllable intonation, such as the syllable-falling or monotone f_0 contour noted for our ataxic subjects. Hence, a change in high-level motor programming conceivably could result in some characteristics of ataxic dysarthria.

In making this suggestion, we adopt Sternberg et al's (in press) notion that the motor executive conducts a self-terminating sequential search of a non-shrinking buffer (motor program memory) to retrieve subprograms as needed. An individual whose sequencing ability is slowed by a neuromotor disorder very likely discovers that reducing the buffer size is helpful in organizing and retrieving the motor programs for speech.

Thus, it is not readily apparent if the scanning character of ataxic dysarthria is a direct consequence of the cerebellum's failure to perform its normal role of integrating movements (or linkages of movements) or if it reflects a change in high-level motor strategy from a multiple-syllable motor memory to a single-syllable motor memory. However, because the ataxic subjects did show some adjustment of base-word duration as syllables were added to the base, it appears that motor programming is not strictly performed on single syllables. Perhaps the requirements for durational adjustments are properly laid down by the motor executive, but the cerebellum, because of its loss of abstract, flexible, and coordinative motor prescriptions, cannot reliably assign the appropriate timing patterns to the speech musculature.

Our summary conception is based on the view that the cerebellum, through the inhibitory actions of its Purkinje cells on target neurones, shapes the efferent outflow to provide fine revisions of a basic motor program generated by a motor executive (cerebrum). When the cerebellum's short-loop revisory function is handicapped by disease, the motor control system is forced to rely on longer loops to control movement. Consequently, segment durations in speech are increased to allow time for the longer loops to operate. With this alteration of strategy, there is a disproportionate increase in the duration of segments that normally are brief, such as unstressed vowels, lax vowels, word-medial consonants, consonants in clusters, and intersyllable pauses. A conspicuous dysprosody, scanning speech, results from the tendency toward equalized syllable durations and dissociated syllables. The intonational pattern of utterances also is affected by this change in syllabic organization, with a tendency toward monotone or a degeneration of the intonation contour into syllable-bound, rather than phrase-bound, patterns. In addition, segmental errors or misarticulations are likely because of improper biasing of muscle spindles and perhaps even through misinterpretation of afference. Correct articulation is possible through labored efforts at movement control exercised in a rather inflexible pattern of syllable durations, so that in the extreme case, syllable durations are nearly uniform. Apparently, there is a delay in the effective contraction of muscles, but the cause of this delay is not immediately clear. Physiological studies of these subjects are in progress and may reveal the relative roles played by reduced strength, a phasic motor recruitment problem, reduced gamma bias of the muscle spindles, cocontraction of muscle groups, increased loop delay of motor regulation, and voluntary slowing.

We conclude with remarks on the clinical application of acoustic phonetic data. At this point, we think that these data are useful for two general purposes. First, if it can be demonstrated that some acoustic phonetic segments are affected more than others by a neuromuscular disorder, then this information is relevant to the design of a speech sample that is maximally sensitive to the disorder in question. The data presented in the present report should be useful in constructing a speech sample and set of measurements that are highly sensitive to cerebellar ataxia. With further work along this line with other dysarthrias, it eventually should be possible to characterize each of these disorders with respect to its phonetic sensitivity, that is, its peculiar effects on selected acoustic-phonetic segments. The second application concerns assessing the effects of speech therapy, medication, surgery, or other intervention. If, as the present data indicate, some fairly simple acoustic measures provide a sensitive index of speech production ability, then these measures may be the basis for an index of improvement. Changes resulting from a therapeutic method might be determined earlier and more reliably by acoustic than by solely perceptual means. The quantification of change in speech behavior afforded by acoustic analysis also may help to satisfy the demand for accountability. In working toward this goal, it is desirable to demonstrate that certain acoustic measures relate to the perceived severity of the dysarthria. We hope that the data in this report are a useful step in this direction.

ACKNOWLEDGMENTS

This research was supported in part by Public Health Service Research Grant NS-13274 from the National Institute of Neurological and Communicative Disorders and Stroke. We are grateful to Dr. Frederic Darley of the Mayo Clinic for his cooperation in the identification of subjects for this study and to Dr. Gerald Zimmerman of the University of Iowa for his comments on the manuscript. Requests for reprints should be addressed to the first author, Boys Town Institute, Communication Disorders for Children, 555 North 30th St., Omaha, Nebraska 68131.

REFERENCES

BOYLLS, C., A theory of cerebellar function with application to locomotion. II. The relation of anterior lobe climbing fiber function to locomotor behavior in the cat. COINS Technical Rept. 76-1, Computer and information Sciences, Univ. of Massachusetts at Amherst (1975).

BROOKS, V., Some new experiments on cerebellar motor control. In J. Cordeau and P. Gloor (Eds.), *EEG Supplement No. 31, Recent Contributions to Neurophysiology.*

BROWN, J., DARLEY, F., and ARONSON, A., Ataxic dysarthia. *Int. J. Neurol.,* 7, 302-318 (1970).

CALMA, I., and KIDD, G., The action of the anterior lobe of the cerebellum on alpha motoneurones. *J. Physiol., Lond.,* 149, 626-652 (1959).

DENNY-BROWN, D., and GILMAN, S., Depression of gamma innervation by cerebellectomy. *Trans. Am. Neurol. Assoc.,* 90, 96-101 (1965).

ECCLES, J., The dynamic loop hypothesis of movement control. In K. N. Leibovic (Ed.), *Information Processing in the Nervous System.* New York: Springer-Verlag (1969).

ECCLES, J., A re-evaluation of cerebellar function in man. In J. Desmedt (Ed.), *New Developments in Electromyography and Clinical Neurophysiology.* Vol. 3. Basel: Karger (1973).

ELLIOTT, H., *Textbook of Neuroanatomy.* Philadelphia: Lippincott (1963).

GILMAN, S., The nature of cerebellar dyssynergia. In D. Williams (Ed.), *Modern Trends in Neurology.* Vol. 5, pp. 60-79. London: Butterworths (1970).

GRANIT, R., HOLMGREN, B., and MERTON, P., The two routes for excitation of muscle and their subservience to the cerebellum. *J. Physiol., Lond.,* 130, 213-224 (1955).

ITO, M., Neurophysiological aspects of the cerebellar motor control system. *Int. J. Neurol.,* 7, 162-176 (1970).

KENT, R., and NETSELL, R., A case study of an ataxic dysarthric: cineradiographic and spectrographic observations. *J. Speech Hearing Dis.,* 40, 115-134 (1975).

KENT, R., and FORNER, L., A development study of speech production: data on vowel imitation and sentence recitation. Paper presented at the 94th Meeting of the Acoustical Society of America, Miami Beach, Florida (1977).

KLATT, D., The duration of [s] in English words. *J. Speech Hearing Res.,* 17, 51-73 (1974).

KONORSKI, J., Integrative Activity of the Brain. Chicago: Univ. of Chicago Press (1967).

KORNHUBER, H., A reconsideration of the cortical and subcortical mechanisms involved in speech and aphasia. In J. Desmedt (Ed.), Language and Hemispheric Specialization in Man: Cerebral ERPs. Progress in Clinical Neurophysiology. Vol. 3, pp. 28-35 (1977).

KOZHEVNIKOV, V., and CHISTOVICH, L., *Rech: Artikulyatsiya i Vospriyatiye* (Moscow-Leningrad, 1965). Trans. *Speech: Articulation and Perception.* Washington, D.C.: Joint Publication Research Service, No. 30, 543 (1965).

LANCE, J., and McLEOD, J., *Physiological Approach to Clinical Neurology,* 2nd ed. London: Butterworths (1975).

LARSELL: The development of the cerebellum in man in relation to its comparative anatomy. *J. Comp. Neurol.,* 87, 85-129 (1947).

LECHTENBERG, R., and GILMAN, S., Speech disorders in cerebellar disease *Ann Neurol.,* 3, 285-290 (1978).

LEHISTE, I., The timing of utterances and linguistic boundaries. *J. acoust. Soc. Am.,* 51, 2018-2024 (1972).

MANNI, E., HENATSCH, H., HENATSCH, E-M., and DOW, R., Localization of facilitatory and inhibitory sites in and around the cerebellar nuclei affecting limb posture, alpha and gamma motoneurons. *J. Neurophysiol.,* 27, 210-227 (1964).

MINCKLER, T., Growth, biometrics, and aging. In J. Minckler (Ed.), *Introduction to Neuroscience,* pp. 139-150. St. Louis: Mosby (1972).

STERNBERG, S., MONSELL, S., KNOLL, R., and WRIGHT, C., The latency and duration of rapid movement sequences: comparisons of speech and typewriting. In G. Stelmach (Ed.), *Information Processing in Motor Control and Learning.* New York: Academic Press (in press).

Received September 26, 1978.
Accepted December 8, 1978.

AN ACOUSTIC–ARTICULATORY DESCRIPTION OF CHILDREN'S DEFECTIVE /s/ PRODUCTIONS*

RAYMOND G. DANILOFF

Department of Communication Sciences and Disorders, University of Vermont

KIM WILCOX

Department of Audiology and Speech Sciences, Purdue University

M. IRENE STEPHENS

Department of Communication Disorders, Northern Illinois University

The /s/ productions of six /s/-defective children and two normal controls were subjected to spectrographic analysis. Articulatorily, two of the children were dentalizers, two had lateral emission of friction, and two were of an "other" type. Results show for normals an /s/ spectrum which is compact (5–11 kHz), powerful, and dominated by strong, sharp spectral peaks at 6 and 10 kHz. Their spectra were context sensitive. Dental subjects showed flatter, less peaked, higher frequency (6–12 kHz), and less intense noise spectrum, which was not so context sensitive. Lateral /s/ subjects showed a broad 4−9 or 4−10 kHz spectrum characterized by somewhat smaller, more numerous peaks, and a lower cutoff frequency (about 4kHz) than for normals. The "other" /s/ defectives varied very widely, so that no consistent pattern emerged. The acoustic data are then discussed in terms of the articulation of varieties of friction noise.

Introduction

In a preliminary report, Stephens and Daniloff (1979) speculated that subpopulations of /s/ misarticulating children might display archetypal spectral patterns for their /s/ approximations. The present study is an extension of their results, including a survey of the acoustic and physiological literature pertaining to strident fricative articulation.

Physiology of /s/ Production

X-ray films (Carney and Moll, 1971; Perkell, 1969; Subtelny, Oya, and Subtelny, 1972; Bladon and Nolan, 1977; Eckerdahl and Elert, 1977), and palatography (Fujimura et al., 1969, 1973; Hardcastle, 1975, Wolfe et al., 1976; Hasegawa et al., 1978, 1979) provide direct data concerning the size and shape of the articulatory constriction for /s/. Other methods, such as aerodynamics (Scully, 1971), and acoustics (Stevens, 1971), provide indirect estimates of

Address correspondence to: Dr. Raymond G. Daniloff, Department of Communication Sciences and Disorders, University of Vermont, Burlington, VT 05405.

*This work was supported in part by NINCDS Research Grant 1RO1N515069 to Northern Illinois University and by the Purdue Research Foundation XR Grant XR0314.

constriction size and shape. The Subtelny et al. (1972) data indicate that /s/ is produced with a very close, tight, precise position of the mandible and tongue tip. In addition, the oral dorsum of the tongue (including tip and blade) is quite precisely positioned, funneling the airstream into a tapering tube which terminates at a tight, precise, groove constriction at or just beyond the alveolar ridge eminence. Indeed, as Chomsky and Halle (1968) note, /s/ is a 'distributed' segment, one whose articulatory constriction occupies considerable *length* along the vocal tract. The critical alveolar groove for /s/ is roughly 9 mm wide, 4.2 mm long, and 1.2 mm thick, with a cross-sectional area of about 1/2 cm² and volume of about 50 mm³ (Subtelny et al., 1972, Stevens, 1971. and Hasegawa et al., 1979).

/s/ Spectrum

The acoustic spectrum for adult male /s/ friction noise reveals intense spectral peaks in the 4–8 kHz region with substantial, continuous acoustic power throughout this roughly 4 kHz-wide band of frequencies (Hughes and Halle, 1956). Despite Strevens (1960) claim that /s/ spectrum peaks are irregularly spaced with greater than 1000 Hz separation, Heinz and Stevens (1961) and Hasegawa (1976) have shown that the adult /s/ spectrum is minimally characterized by two major resonance peaks and one antiresonance. Resonance peaks one and two for adult males are at about 4.5 kHz and nearly 8 kHz, with the antiresonance about ½ octave below peak 1, suppressing low-frequency energy so strongly that on a normal wideband spectrogram, there is little visible spectral energy below 4kHz. Sample values from Hasegawa's (1976) /s/ spectrographic data for adult males and females and Stephens and Daniloff's (1979) data for children are shown in Table 1.

Notice that females' noise spectra are shifted upward substantially from that of males, by about 1000 Hz or more for peak 1 and 1100 Hz for peak 2. This upward shift reflects the smaller overall dimensions of the female vocal tract. For children, we would expect even higher peak /s/ frequencies, and indeed, they appear to exceed that for women by 500 and 1000 Hz for peaks 1 and 2, respectively. The range of frequencies over which substantial acoustic power is

TABLE 1
Sample Spectral Data for /s/ for Men, Women, and Children

	Peak 1 Hz	BW1 Hz	Peak 2 Hz	BW2 Hz	Relative Intensity, re: vowel
male	4800	700	7900	2400	−3 to −5 dB
female	6000	800	9000	——	−3 to −5 dB
children	6500	1000	10000	——	−3 to −5 dB

seen for /s/ is 4–10 kHz for males, 5–12 kHz for females, and about 5–12+ kHz for children. Typically, /s/ friction noise is about −3 to −5 dB less intense than the peak level of adjacent vowels.

All articulatory descriptions of /s/ emphasize the longitudinal tongue dorsum groove, which narrows to a tight, tube-like constriction at and/or just beyond the alveolar ridge. Propelled by intraoral air pressure, the air stream is accelerated and exceeds the critical Reynolds Number, and at the tube orifice it deaccelerates turbulently, radiating noise vibration. In addition, the turbulent air jet in its outward passage strikes lips and teeth, and creates a "spoiler" or "edge" noise in addition to the jet turbulence noise. The composite noise is resonated by the small lip cavity anterior to the constriction, yielding an intense, compact (4−5 kHz bandwidth) high-frequency noise spectrum with two, and generally more, prominent spectral peaks. This combination of acoustic features produced by two sources of turbulence noise reflects the distinctive feature of "stridency" (Jakobson, Fant, Halle, 1951).

Articulatory Variation

Both Heffner (1969) and Ladefoged (1975) emphasize that strident, /s/-like sounds can be articulated in several alternative ways. For optimum stridency, a long, tapering conduit feeding into a groove constriction with teeth/lips projecting into the turbulent jet stream beyond the groove opening are needed. If the gradually tapering cavity posterior to the groove is absent, or tapers very rapidly, or if the groove is replaced by a thinner, tighter, broader slit, the resultant will be a less optimally strident, weaker, and more "mellow" noise whose time waveform is less random (Jakobson, Fant, Halle, 1951). Among the alternative articulations of /s/, Heffner (1969) mentions that, optimally, the tongue tip may be raised to form a groove slit at the alveolar ridge; or, the tip may be lowered and a groove slit formed between alveolar ridge and tongue dorsum, as seen in Eckerdahl and Elert (1977). If the tongue tip is curled retroflexively upward, a somewhat broader, more open slit between alveolar ridge and tongue surface is formed. Or if the tongue tip is retracted to make a post-alveolar constriction, as in some Semitic languages, a broader, less groove-like slit is formed. The broader and tighter slit and the more abruptly tapering oral channel for the retroflex, retracted, and tip-depressed versions yield less hissy, less optimally strident friction noise, which is oftentimes much less intense as well. Furthermore, if the tongue tip is pressed against the teeth or between them, the broader, tighter, less groove-like constriction again yields a less optimally strident sound, and the secondary obstacle-source of noise generation is missing. In any case, dentalization, retroflexion, or retraction-palatalization yield a less optimally strident noise, one whose spectrum is shifted beyond the 4−10 kHz region and displays fewer prominent peaks.

/s/ Misarticulation as Approximation

In general, disorders of /s/ articulation may involve apparent omission of /s/, substitution of another sound such as [t] for /s/, or a nonsatisfactory substandard "approximation" of /s/. The approximations, often called 'distortions,' usually preserve the features +[friction], +[continuant], even if the spectral shape of the noise is inappropriate. The great majority of /s/ misarticulating children produce, in some phonetic contexts, substandard approximations. In this study we will focus on these approximations. The approximations fall into three operational classes. For the dentalized /s/, i.e., /s/ → [s̪], the tongue tip is advanced and pressed against the incisors, where the tip can be readily seen through the opening between upper and lower incisors, in most cases, protruding between them. The alveolar groove slit is replaced with a tight, broad abrupt constriction which produces a relatively weak, flat, high-frequency noise, which often sounds high pitched. In rare cases, dentalization may result in production of the dental fricative /θ/ as an error response for /s/, i.e., /s/ → [θ]. This is indeed rare, since a true [θ] has very low intensity, whereas the approximation [s̪] is generally more intense.

A second distortion of /s/, and much less common, is the unilateral /s/, i.e., /s/ → [sˡ]. Here, the tight, central apical groove is replaced by a much broader, more open, lateral slit through which air escapes noisily over the side of the tongue blade. The resulting noise is lower pitched, occasionally marked with saliva trills, and though not easily detected visually, except for a somewhat more open than the usual mandible, the resulting noise is unmistakable in quality. The third common class of /s/ approximations we choose to call "other." The "other" category is defined primarily by exclusion criteria; that is, the obvious dentalization or lateralization described above is absent. The quality of the distorted, "other" [s] can range from high to low pitch across subjects, and even within a subject, successive productions of [s] can vary considerably in perceptual quality. We suspect that the children use their tongue blade or retroflexed tongue tip to produce not a long groove slit, but a broad, narrow slit which tapers sharply into the slit-like constriction. Clearly, palatographic data would be ideal to delineate the obvious subtypes of /s/ misarticulation contained within the "other" category.

Procedures

Eight children ranging in age from 6.5 to 8.5 yr of age, mean of 7.5 yr, served as subjects. These subjects were older than the 5.5-yr olds studied in Stephens and Daniloff (1979). The older children were chosen because, by the first or second grade, the children with /s/ errors are likely to be maintainers, who would not "outgrow" the error pattern spontaneously. The Stephens and Daniloff (1977) speech samples, therefore, were used as confirmatory back-up data, and in essence were confirmed by analyses performed on the present subjects, except for somewhat differing pole-frequency characteristics for the younger children's data.

Two of the eight children were normally articulating controls. The six /s/ misarticulators, with otherwise normal speech, hearing, and language, were each diagnosed as being /s/-defective from conversational speech samples and confirmed by the Templin Darley Screening Test of Articulation. These children, selected from a larger population of /s/-defective children, were chosen by the school speech clinician as being "optimal," or "ideal" examples of three classes of /s/ formation: [lateralizers] [sˡ], [dentalizers] [s̠], and [others] [s̠]. Using a Sony ECM 50 electret microphone which was set in a headband and connected to a Nagra IV recorder, recordings were made of each child as he repeated a list of 40 sentences containing /s/-words in a variety of phonetic contexts. The children's live productions were judged correct or incorrect by an experienced speech and language pathologist who faced him/her at a distance of 3 ft. All items judged incorrect, and matched sample /s/ words of the control subjects were analyzed on a Voiceprint 700 Spectrograph using a 450-Hz filter. In addition, sample utterances were slow-played at 7½ ips re: 15½ ips recording speed, on the Voiceprint, to determine the upper bandwidth of the children's /s/ approximations. All frequency cross sections were made with a flat reproduction setting, with the exception of Subject JS, a dentalizer whose productions were so low in amplitude in many cases that they could be visualized on sections only if reproduced with the high emphasis setting. The resulting spectrograms were inspected and sorted into subtypes by the first two authors. Sample spectrograms for each subtype which best illustrated the variety of friction noises produced by normal and /s/-defective children are shown in Figures 1–8. The spectrograms, from top to bottom, represent the most-to-least frequently occurring spectral patterns for each child, and are selected to show the full range of friction noise diversity. The top most panel in each figure is the most frequently occurring spectral pattern, with the second, and on occasion the third panels being less frequent, but substantial in number. The bottom three or four panels reflect infrequently occurring varieties of /s/ approximations. Table 2 lists the spectral characteristics of the first two /s/ tokens shown in Figures 1–8, these two tokens being taken as representative of the subjects' /s/ productions. The /s/-vowel ratios, in decibels, are an average over eight representative tokens for each subject. Also shown are the frequencies of major spectral peaks below 8 kHz, the friction noise duration (also an average over eight representative tokens), and the overall noise bandwidth, arbitrarily defined as the range of frequencies with noise energy not less than −12 dB re: the largest spectrum peak. In general, the data for younger children, taken from Stephens and Daniloff (1979), parallels the results for these older children.

TABLE 2

Spectral Characteristics of Friction Noise Spectra for Typical Tokens (see panels 1 and 2) Shown in Figures 1–8. Also Shown are Certain Average Data Based on 8 "Typical" Friction-Noise Tokens

Subject	Item	Largest Spectral Peaks (0–8 KHz) Arranged from Greatest to Least Amplitude		Duration msec	Ave. Duration msec	Consonant to Vowel Ratios (CV) in dB	Average C/V ratio dB	Noise Bandwidth Hz
		I	II		(8 tokens)		(8 tokens)	
JR_N	store	6500	4875	138	(115 msec)	−2	(−3.5)	4100+
	mister	6250	4250	112		−3		3000
GD_N	soup	7125	5750	212	(130 msec)	−2	(−1.5)	3700+
	sue	6750	7400	208		+7		2700+
JS_D	sue	5100	7125	150	(150 msec)	−14	(−13.6)	4125
	Wilson	6175–7100	5250	212		−18		4000
RR_D	seal	6875	6300	160	(137 msec)	−7	(−8.0)	1825
	sad	6775	—	155		−8		1675
SP_L	Wilson	5625	6575/7250	162	(189 msec)	−7	(−3.0)	4960
	soup	3750	6500	200		−10		N.A.
JN_L	store	6250	7150	180	(155 msec)	−2	(−2.8)	2875
	sun	6700	4850	138		+2		4200
LV_O	store	4375	5318	125	(110 msec)	0	(−2.0)	1850
	soup	4750	7625	150		−3		650
RM_O	soup	6375	7000	138	(125 msec)	−11	(−10.0)	1800
	mister	7250	6375	112		−19		2750

Results

Figures 1 and 2 display sample cross-sections for the normal control subjects, JR and GD. From the top of each figure in descending order, panels 1 and 2 for both subjects account for more than ⅔ *of all productions*. Panels 3–4 are examples of /s/ spectra, in order of increasing rarity, which sounded normal, but presented atypical spectral shape. Concentrating on panels 1 and 2, the normal child's /s/ spectra show little or no energy below 4000 Hz, but strong, continuous energy from roughly 5–12 kHz (as shown by spectrograms made from half-speed tape recordings). The normal 0.1–8 kHz spectrograms show large spectral peaks in the 4–5 kHz and 6–7 kHz region, and slow play shows another peak in the 10–11 kHz regions. There may be as few as two or as many as three major (high amplitude) peaks in the 4–8 kHz band, but overall, the largest spectral peaks are in the 6–7 kHz and 9–11 kHz frequency region. For the normals, the relative amplitude of the /s/ noise re: adjacent vowels was about −2 to −3 dB, in accordance with Hasegawa's results for adults, indicative of an acoustically powerful friction. Also, the duration of the /s/-noise was about 130–150 msec, which agrees well with previous findings (Klatt, 1971; Schwartz, 1969, 1970) and underscores the similarities to normal adult /s/ productions. In the 4–8 kHz

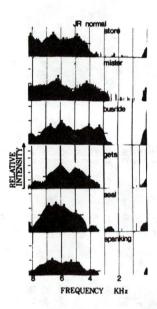

Fig. 1.   Spectrographic sections of /s/ for normal subject JR. From top, panels range from most to least frequent type of friction noise spectrum. Dots indicate noise peaks, cross-lines mark − 12 dB bandwidth.

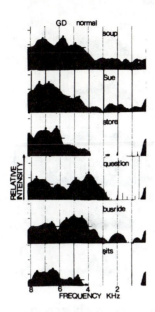

Fig. 2. Spectrographic sections of /s/ for normal subject GD. From top, panels range from most to least frequent type of friction noise spectrum. Dots indicate noise peaks, cross-lines mark −12 dB bandwidth.

region visible on these sections, the noise bandwidth, arbitrarily defined as that range of spectral energy no more than 12 dB re peak spectral level, was 3–4 kHz wide, indicative of a strong concentration of energy in the 5–11 kHz band, as shown on slow-play spectrograms. The less frequently occurring normal /s/ tokens for subject JR are more strongly bandlimited, and in 3 of 4 cases, display less prominent, closer-spaced peaks (panels 3, 5, 6). For subject GD, certain spectra were flatter (panels 4, 5, 6) and the lower noise cutoff frequency varied widely from about 6 kHz (panel 3) to 3500 Hz (panel 4). The spectra of normal childrens' /s/ shows wide coarticulatory variations dependent upon vowel and consonant. In general, rounded vowels and consonants lower the /s/ spectra, and front vowels and apical consonants (t, n) raise spectral frequencies of /s/ noise.

Dental /s/

A characteristic of both dental and lateral misarticulations is that the noise spectra show less coarticulation. This reduction of context sensitivity was not expected, but can be seen in the sections of Figures 3 and 4. Broadband slow-play spectrograms of the dental subjects' tokens revealed visible energy out to 13–14 kHz on occasions, a spectrum of greater width and higher frequency

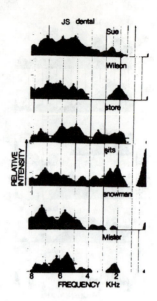

Fig. 3.   Spectrographic sections of /s/ for dentalizing subject JS. From top, panels range from most to least frequent type of friction noise spectrum. Dots indicate noise peaks, cross-lines mark −12 dB bandwidth.

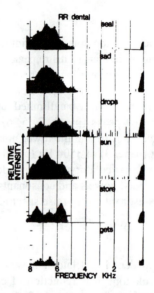

Fig. 4.   Spectrographic sections of /s/ for dentalizing subject RR. From top, panels range from most to least frequent type of friction noise spectrum. Dots indicate noise peaks, cross-lines mark −12 dB bandwidth.

than that for normal /s/. The reader should be aware that the spectrograms for subject JS could only be made with the high emphasis setting of the Voiceprint. Under flat reproduction/analysis conditions the spectral sections were blank. Indeed, the consonant vowel ratio for interdental /s/ averages −7 dB for RR and −16 dB for JS. The interdental [s̪] can be weak indeed, in cases little stronger than the dental /θ/. Panels 1 and 2, going from top to bottom, in Figures 3 and 4, account for more than ¾ of all tokens produced by the dental subjects. RR's spectra show significant energy only above 6 kHz for all samples displayed. His most typical exemplars show a peak at about 7 kHz, and another shown at about 11 kHz. Most [s̪] productions of subject JS displayed low-level energy from 2-5 or 2-6 kHz, slightly more from 5-8 kHz with slow-play spectrograms revealing low-level energy from 5-12 or 5-13 kHz. In contrast with normal /s/, most [s̪] tokens displayed either a slightly weaker, much higher frequency spectrum, or a very weak, flat spectrum which spanned a vary wide bandwidth. These data fit in good part the description of the distinctive feature "mellow" described by Jakobson, Fant, and Halle (1951).

Lateralized /s/

[s^l], the lateralized fricative, has an unmistakable, low-pitched "hushing" quality. Inspection of sections reveals (see Figures 5 and 6) spectra extending from 3 or 4 kHz to 7 or 8 kHz, and occasionally to 9 kHz. The friction noise is of substantial intensity with a consonant to vowel ratio of about 0 and −8 dB for these two subjects. Subjects JN and SP reflect two strongly differing patterns of [s^l] noise. SP shows, in panels 1 and 2, a weak, flat spectrum extending from about 3.5 kHz to about 7 kHz, with further, less frequently occurring examples, panels 3−6, showing a more peaked, more strongly bandlimited (panels 3, 5, 6) spectrum with a lowest peak at about 4 kHz or less. Clearly, this subject's noise differs from that of subject JN. Subject JN shows a strong consistent spectrum extending from 4 to about 10 kHz, as shown by slow-played spectrograms. Panels 1 and 2, with samples of [s^l] accounting for more than ¾ of his productions, shown moderately strong spectral peaks, with the lowest peak between 4−5 kHz. Other of his productions are flatter (panels 3, 5) or more bandlimited (panel 6). Both lateralizers clearly manifest lateral emission, but one has low-level "hushy" noise, and the other higher level, higher pitched, "hushy" noise. A major characteristic of lateralizers' noise spectra is noise ranging from mid to high intensity with a wide bandwidth in the 4−12 kHz region marked by modest spectral peaks. The lowest spectral peak, which is often quite strong, is at or below 4 kHz. As compared with normal subjects, [s^l] spectra cover a wider and lower range of frequencies, and are flatter, and generally of lesser or equal intensity.

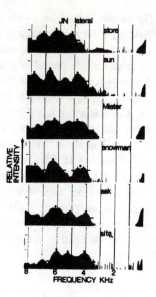

Fig. 5. Spectrographic sections of /s/ for lateralizing subject JN. From top, panels range from most to least frequent type of friction noise spectrum. Dots indicate noise peaks, crosslines mark −12 dB bandwidth.

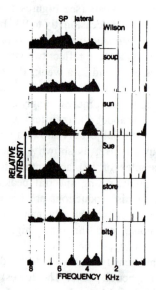

Fig. 6. Spectrographic sections of /s/ for lateralizing subject SP. From top, panels range from most to least frequent type of friction noise spectrum. Dots indicate noise peaks, cross-lines mark −12 dB bandwidth.

"Other" Misarticulated /s/

These subjects display neither tongue between teeth, nor open mandible, nor does one hear the peculiar lateral emission quality. By default, the "other" category of misarticulatiors might be called "retracted." The friction noises they produce vary *widely* between subjects, and within a subject. They are strongly context sensitive in that differing phonetic contexts elicit widely varying friction spectra. The noises vary widely in perceptual quality, ranging from mellow to very hissy. For example, subject LV displays fairly intense spectra (CV ratio -2 dB) which show strong spectral peaks, with a noise bandwidth ranging from 4–5 kHz to a little over 11 kHz. Perceptually, his [s̲] sounded like a very high frequency /s/. On the other hand, subject RM has a weak (CV ratio -10 dB) hissy noise of modest bandwidth, generally 5–6 kHz to -8 or 9 kHz with modest peaks. Certain of his less frequent tokens are very weak (panels 4, 5, 6), and one (panel 6) shows energy only at 3–4 kHz. Indeed, the "other" subjects are difficult to judge perceptually because of their articulatory lability, at times producing friction noise of near-acceptable quality.

Analysis by Synthesis

Tape-recorded samples of the subjects' speech, in connection with another study, were subjected to analysis by synthesis. Using a PDP-11/34 system, words containing /s/ were played at ½ recorded speed through a 0–5 kHz filterbank, digitized and stored, yielding a 0–10 kHz spectral window. Using an analysis-by-synthesis schema implemented by Hasegawa (1976) the spectral patterns of /s/ for normal and defective children were explored. The AS routine permitted the experimenter to control the center frequencies and bandwidths of up to 4 poles and 2 zeroes, and to construct a synthetic spectrum to fit the actual spectrum of the friction noise. Goodness of fit was estimated as the RMS error between actual and synthetic spectral envelopes. Using a 2–3 dB RMS or less error criterion for goodness of fit, the experimenter succeeded in producing 2 pole 1 zero synthetic tokens of /s/ which fit the normal, and dentalizing subjects' "typical" productions quite well. For the lateralizing subject, a few of the typical noise spectra could be fit with a 2 pole 1 zero spectrum, but other lateralized typical tokens could be fit well with a 1 pole 1 zero model. Analyses of the misarticulating category of "other" were not even attempted because of the wide variability.

This preliminary work suggests that the children's noises, at least for some defective exemplars, display *two* important spectral peaks below 10 kHz, coupled with an antiresonance below the peaks, lending confidence to our analysis of typical normal and dentalized /s/ productions as well as a few of the typical lateralized productions.

Discussion

The most powerful impression gained from these data is the large inter- and intrasubject variability evident within each misarticulating group, as well as the normal group. Indeed, Hughes and Halle (1956) emphasized the variability in fricative spectra for different speakers and contexts.

However, each subject does exhibit a range of archtypical spectral shapes from which individual deviations occur. From Figures 1 through 8 it can be seen that certain subjects exhibit more variability than others (e.g., contrast GD-normal and RR-dental) across phonetic contexts. In general, it can be said that the normal subjects exhibit as much or more contextual variability as any of the pathological groups. Subtelny et al. (1972) and Bladon and Nolan (1971) agree that the major coarticulatory influences on /s/ production are not manifested in changes of tongue blade or tip positions. Rather, Subtelny et al. (1972) suggest that the tongue body and lips are strongly affected by phonetic context during /s/ production. The reason for this is the necessity of a relatively precise positioning of the blade and/or tip of the tongue for creation of the longitudinal slit present in correct /s/ production. Given the wide range of variability in the normal /s/ spectra seen in this study, it would seem that the nonconstrained articulators are

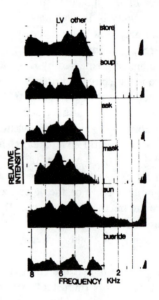

Fig. 7.   Spectrographic sections of /s/ for ''other'' subject, LV. From top, panels range from most to least frequent type of friction noise spectrum. Dots indicate noise peaks, cross-lines mark −12 dB bandwidth.

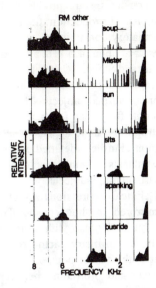

Fig. 8.   Spectrographic sections of /s/ for "other" subject, RM. From top, panels range from most to least frequent type of friction noise spectrum. Dots indicate noise peaks, cross-lines mark −12 dB bandwidth.

indeed exercising their freedom to move. In addition, it would appear that the critical slit constriction must be undergoing some important changes. For although articulation of the /s/ constriction is relatively stable, small perturbations of the type barely noticeable on two-dimensional X-rays may impart major changes to the acoustic spectra. These changes are partly due to alterations in the direction of the airstream past the incisors, and changes in the size of the anterior cavity (Stevens, 1971).

Although the two lateralizers and two dentalizers presented here also evidenced some contextual variability, they represent far less fluctuation than their normal articulatory peers. In the case of the dentalizers, their tongue tip must be in contact with the incisors or protruding through the incisal opening. Hence, the location of the sound source is defined by a tight slit constriction at an immobile articulator (the incisors); in most cases, the only free parameter of consequence is the size of the anterior cavity, which is solely dependent upon lip displacement. Therefore, major changes in the spectra would not be expected. In the case of the lateralized /s/ producers, the sound source is not a narrow groove but rather a broad opening which directs the airstream over the lateral margin of the tongue and past the lateral teeth. Given the relatively large distribution of the constriction, small change in its exact configuration appear to have minor effects on the overall acoustic spectra produced. It seems then, that rather than an increase in variability of production, the misarticulating groups are more consistent, due to articulatory constraints.

Resonance peaks at about 4.5 kHz and nearly 8 kHz have been seen for /s/ in adult males (Heinz and Stevens, 1969; Hasegawa, 1976). Given the shorter vocal tract in children, we would expect to see these values shifted significantly upward in the spectra for our normal subjects. Investigation of Table 2 shows that for JR and GD the first pole frequency for their /s/ spectra is raised to 6−7 kHz, and on half-speed spectrograms, there appears a second major peak in the spectrum in the 11 kHz region. Further, detailed investigation of ½ speed recordings in an analysis-by-synthesis schema should help define the entire /s/ spectra for normal and misarticulating subjects.

A number of clinical impressions associated with the subtypes of /s/ misarticulators are mirrored in the acoustic data. The acoustic characteristic of low-frequency ''hushy'' noise with saliva trills make the lateralizer easy to identify. That is, the primary factor for classification is auditory. For the dentalizer, though, the visual component is equally important. Typically, the tongue tip is broad and protruding between the teeth and some productions become flat and greatly weakened spectrally, more closely approximating the /θ/. This combination of visual and auditory factors has resulted in the traditional clinical judgment of ''θ/s substitution''. However, since the spectra more often include prominent peaks and show substantial intensity, the acoustic product is less like the normal /θ/. Thus, in many cases it is not accurate to describe such a production grossly as a ''θ/s substitution'' (Stephens, 1976). The wide variability in the acoustic displays associated with the ''other'' subtype of /s/ misarticulation is matched by clinical descriptions. The very general term ''distortion'' is used and applied to a wide range of children's approximations. These children are also often described as inconsistent—some productions being judged acceptable—but clinician agreement on specific instances of production is poor.

Summary

/s/ is unusual in several respects. It occurs frequently in speech, carries a high information load, is resistant to confusion with other sounds (Miller and Nicely, 1955), and occupies a valuable distinctive slot in the sound pattern of English. But in terms of speaker control and monitoring, /s/ is highly vulnerable. It occurs late developmentally (Sander, 1972), is misarticulated often (Winitz, 1969), is disrupted by adventitious hearing loss (Binnie and Daniloff, 1980), is badly distorted in deaf speech (Hudgins and Numbers, 1942), and is easily disrupted by oral anesthesia (Daniloff, Bishop, and Ringel, 1977).

/s/ appears to have a wide range of permissible acoustic allophonic variants, as shown in this study and the work of Hughes and Halle (1956). The powerful, compact, peaky, "strident" spectra of /s/ can tolerate substantial shifts in upper and lower cutoff frequency, and the frequency, and amplitude of major spectral peaks. Distortions of /s/ preserve the features +[friction] +[continuant], even if [stridency] and [place] are lost or altered. Thus, despite the high demands placed upon powers of articulatory control and feedback monitoring for /s/ production, the listener compensates for the acute physiological context and control sensitivity for /s/ by accepting a wide range of allophonic variants as acceptable allophones. And what is more, if the distortions are severe, several major class features of /s/ are preserved, assisting the listener's interpretation of the distortion.

References

Binnie, C., and Daniloff, R. G. (1980). Phonetic disintegration in a five year old following sudden hearing loss. Submitted to *J. Speech Hear. Dis*.

Bladon, R. A. W., and Nolan, F. J. (1977). A video-fluorographic investigation of tip and blade alveolars in English. *J. Phonetics* 5:185–93.

Carney, P. J., and Moll, K. L. (1971). A cineradiographic investigation of fricative consonant-vowel coarticulation. *Phonetica* 23:193–202.

Chomsky, N., and Halle, M. (1968). *The Sound Pattern of English*. New York: Harper and Row.

Daniloff, R. G., Bishop, M., and Ringel, R. (1977). Alteration of children's articulation by application of oral anesthesia. *J. Phonetics* 5:285–298.

Eckerdahl, O., and Elert, C. C. (1977). Tomographic xeroradiographic registration of the front oral cavity at the pronunciation of the *s* sound. Publication No. 11, Umea University, Umea, Sweden.

Fujimura, O., Kiritani, S., and Ishida, H. (1969). Digitally controlled dynamic radiography. *Ann. Bull., Res. Inst. Logopedics Phoniatrics* (Univ. of Tokyo) 3:135.

Fujimura, O., Tatsumi, I. F., and Kagaya, R. (1973). Computational processing of palatographic patterns. *J. Phonetics* 1:47–54.

Hardcastle, W. J. (1975). Some aspects of speech production under controlled conditions of oral anesthesia and auditory masking. *J. Phonetics* 3:197–214.

Hasegawa, A. (1976). Some perceptual consequences of fricative coarticulation. Ph.D. dissertation Purdue University.

Hasegawa, A., Christensen, J. M., Fletcher, S. G., and McCutcheon, M. J. (1978). Articulatory and acoustic properties of /s,z/ consonants produced by esophageal speakers. Paper, 95th Meeting of the Acoustical Society of America, Providence, Rhode Island.

Hasegawa, A., Christensen, J. M., McCutcheon, M., and Fletcher, S. (1979). Articulatory properties of /s/ in selected consonant clusters. Paper submitted to 98th Meeting of Acoustic Society of America, Salt Lake City, Utah.

Heffner, R-M. S. (1969). *General Phonetics*. Madison, Wisconsin: University of Wisconsin Press.

Heinz, J. M., and Stevens, K. N. (1961). On the properties of voiceless fricative consonants. *J. Acoust. Soc. Amer.* 33:589–596.

Hudgins. C. V., and Numbers, F. C. (1942). An investigation of the intelligibility of the speech of deaf and normal subjects. *Genet. Psychol. Monogr.* 25:289–392.

Hughes, G. W., and Halle, M. (1956). Spectral properties of fricative consonants. *J. Acoust. Soc. Amer.* 28:303–310.

Jakobson, R., Fant, C. G. M., and Halle, M. (1951). *Preliminaries to Speech Analysis. The Distinctive Features and Their Correlates*. Cambridge, Massachusetts: MIT Press.

Klatt, D. (1971). On predicting the duration of the phonetic segment /s/ in English. *Prog. Rep. Res. Lab. Elec. Eng.* 103:111–126.

Ladefoged, P. (1975). *A Course in Phonetics.* New York: Harper and Row.

Miller, G. A., and Nicely, P. E. (1955). Perceptual confusions among consonants. *J. Acoust. Soc. Amer.* 27:338–352.

Perkell, J. S. (1969). *Physiology of Speech Production: Results and Implications of a Quantitative Cineradiographic Study.* Cambridge, Massachusetts: MIT Press.

Sander, E. (1972). When are speech sounds learned? *J. Speech Hear. Disord.* 37:55–64.

Schwartz, M. (1968). Identification of speaker sex from isolated, voiceless fricatives. *J. Acoust. Soc. Amer.* 43:1178–1179.

Schwartz, M. (1969). Influence of vowel environment upon the duration of /s/ and /š/. *J. Acoust. Soc. Amer.* 46:480.

Schwartz, M. (1970). Duration of /s/ and /š/—plosive blends. *J. Acoust. Soc. Amer.* 47:1143–1144.

Scully, C. (1971). A comparison of /s/ and /z/ for an English speaker. *Lang. Speech* 14:187–200.

Stephens, M. I. (1976). A longitudinal study of /s/ misarticulators. Paper, Annual Meeting of the American Speech and Hearing Association, Houston, Texas, November.

Stephens, M. I., and Daniloff, R. G. (1977). A methodological study of factors affecting the judgment of misarticulated /s/. *J. Commun. Disord.* 10:207–220.

Stephens, M. I., and Daniloff, R. G. (1979). Spectral characteristics of /s/ misarticulating children. Paper, Conference Proceedings, 97th Annual Meeting, Acoustical Society of America, Cambridge, Massachusetts.

Stevens, K. N. (1971). Airflow and turbulence noise for fricative and stop consonants: static considerations. *J. Acoust. Soc. Amer.* 50:1180–1192.

Strevens, P. (1960). Spectra of fricative noise in human speech. *Lang. Speech* 3:32–49.

Subtelny, J. D., Oya, N., and Subtelny, J. D. (1972). Cineradiographic study of sibilants. *Folia Phoniatrica* 24:30–50.

Winitz, H. (1969). *Articulatory Acquisition and Behavior.* New York: Appleton-Century-Crofts.

Wolfe, M. B., McCutcheon, M. J., Hasegawa, A., and Fletcher, S. G. (1976). Linguapalatal contact characteristics during /s/ production. 91st Meeting Acoustical Society of America, *J. Acoust. Soc. Amer.,* Suppl. 1, Vol. 59:S85.

PRESPEECH VOCALIZATIONS OF A DEAF INFANT: A COMPARISON WITH NORMAL METAPHONOLOGICAL DEVELOPMENT

D. KIMBROUGH OLLER   REBECCA E. EILERS   DALE H. BULL
University of Miami Mailman Center for Child Development, Miami, FL

ARLENE EARLEY CARNEY
University of Illinois at Urbana

A comparative study of the speech-like vocalizations of a deaf infant and a group of 11 hearing infants was conducted in order to examine the role of auditory experience in the development of the phonological and metaphonological capacity. Results indicated that from 8 to 13 months of age, the deaf subject differed strikingly from hearing infants of comparable age. She produced no repetitive canonical babbling, whereas all the hearing infants produced many canonical syllables. The topography of the deaf infant's vocalizations resembled that of 4–6-month-old (i.e., Expansion stage) hearing infants. Detailed comparisons of the proportion of production of various metaphonologically defined categories by the deaf infant and Expansion stage hearing infants demonstrated many similarities in vocalization, although possible differences were noted. It is concluded that hearing impairment notably affects vocalization development by the end of the first year of life, if not earlier. Spectrographic displays illustrate the categories of infant sounds produced by the deaf and hearing infants.

In the second half-year of life, normal infants produce babbling sounds that are so speech-like as to be commonly mistaken for meaningful utterances. The syllables that occur most often in babbling also occur commonly in early meaningful speech (see Cruttenden, 1970; Menyuk, 1968; Oller, Wieman, Doyle, & Ross, 1975) and appear to constitute the inventory of universal syllables of mature natural languages. General similarity in the kinds of sounds produced during prespeech development has been documented in infants of all language backgrounds that have been studied, including English, Chinese, French, Dutch, Swiss-German, Yucatec, Japanese, Spanish, Arabic, and Norwegian (Atkinson-King, MacWhinney, & Stoel-Gammon, 1970; de Boysson-Bardies, Sagart, & Bacri, 1981; Eady, 1980; Elbers, 1981; Enstrom, 1976; Huber, 1970; Murai, 1963; Nakazima, 1962; Oller & Eilers, 1982; Olney & Scholnick, 1976; Preston, Yeni-Komshian, & Port, 1967; Vanvik, 1971).

Given evidence of universal patterns of vocalization development during the first year of life, questions arise concerning the relative role of audition and maturation in the emergence of the phonological capacity. Is babbling and/or prebabbling a maturational phenomenon independent of external auditory stimulation, or does it involve systematic accommodation to environmental sounds? By studying the vocalization development of severely hearing-impaired infants and comparing this development to that of hearing infants, one view of the role of audition can be obtained. To the extent that a deaf infant vocalizes like a hearing infant, the sounds of both can be assumed to be independent of auditory input. To the extent that the infants systematically differ, the vocalizations of the hearing infant can be assumed to involve imitation or some other form of adaptation to environmental sounds. Comparative research on deaf and hearing infants constitutes a "natural experiment."

Of course, all natural experiments have disadvantages. Deaf and hearing babies may be (intentionally or unintentionally) treated differently. Deaf babies often have handicaps in addition to deafness. Deafness is rarely, if ever, complete, and early amplification may provide important auditory stimulation to the deaf infant. It is usually not possible (and it might be viewed as unethical) to obtain vocalization samples from deaf infants who have not had amplification because it is believed that amplification should be provided as soon as deafness is diagnosed. A final problem with the comparison of deaf and hearing infant vocalizations results from the fact that deaf babies are not easily found.

In spite of the difficulties of the natural experiment, vocalizations of deaf infants are widely viewed as important for understanding the role of audition in infant sounds. Continued interest in the sounds of deaf infants seems justified since it appears impossible to determine the effects of hearing on infant sounds through controlled laboratory experimentation.

Research evidence on three deaf infants compared with a single hearing infant (Mavilya, 1969) and on one deaf infant compared with four hearing infants (Maskarinec, Cairns, Butterfield, & Weamer, 1981) suggests that deaf infants, unlike hearing infants, may not increase the amount of speech-like vocalizing across the first year of life. Quantity of vocal output, however, does not directly address the issue of whether or not the content of infant babbling is systematically influenced by auditory experience. To evaluate the specific effects of audition on prespeech development, it is necessary to consider the kinds of vocalizations produced by deaf and hearing infants. Lenneberg, Rebelsky, and Nichols (1965) and Lenneberg (1967) implied that deaf and hearing infant vocalizations are similar in the first half-year but differ by the second half-year. Gilbert (1982) expressed concern that these studies were based only on data from a deaf infant whose vocalizations were described superficially within a linguistically uninteresting context. He similarly expressed skepticism concerning discussions of deaf babbling by Whetnall and Fry (1964) and Fry (1966) and claimed their view was "unsubstantiated by any research evidence" (p. 514). Gilbert concluded that the traditional beliefs about the vocal sounds produced by deaf infants are not documented empirically.

Gilbert expressed particular concern over the widely held, but unproven, belief (often expressed with citations to Lenneberg and colleagues) that deaf infants "babble" and do so at the same age as normal infants. Ambiguous use of the term *babbling* may have contributed to the confusion apparent in the literature. Sometimes *babbling* is used in a nontechnical sense to refer to many prespeech infant vocalizations, whereas other times it is used in a technical sense to refer specifically to canonical syllabic forms (those obeying timing restrictions of natural languages). Although occasional canonical syllables may occur early in life, repetitive canonical babbling is a phenomenon of the second half-year in hearing babies. It seems unlikely that Lenneberg's deaf infant produced canonical babbling, since the infant had not yet reached the mean age of onset for the canonical stage in hearing infants (approximately 7 months).

Similarly, Mavilya (1969) provided transcriptional data on three deaf infants, suggesting that these infants produced canonical[1] babbling at 4–6 months (well before the mean age of onset for such sounds in hearing infants). It appears, however, that Mavilya's conclusions were based on transcriptional conventions that made no distinction between canonical (i.e., involving syllabic timing patterns of natural languages) and "marginal" sequences (involving inappropriately timed patterns). Stark (personal communication, April 1980), after reviewing some of Mavilya's tapes, has offered the opinion that some of the transcribed babbling sequences may indeed be marginal in timing. It is, thus, unclear to what extent the vocalizations of the deaf infants in the Mavilya study may have been similar to those of hearing infants of similar precanonical age.

Smith and Stoel-Gammon (1977) also have suggested that there is a similarity between the kinds of vocalizations produced by *moderately-to-profoundly* hearing-impaired infants and those produced by hearing infants in the first year of life. In this study, hearing-impaired infants, at about 6 months of age, shifted from a tendency to produce predominantly dorsal (back) consonant-like elements to producing predominantly coronal and labial (front) elements. In addition, the hearing-impaired infants showed a tendency to avoid low and back vowels. Both the back-to-front shift and the avoidance of low and back vowels are tendencies of normally hearing infants. Combined data for four infants suggested the presence of reduplicated canonical babbling during the second half-year of life. Interpretation of this finding is especially

difficult, however, since two of the four infants were not severely impaired (Stoel-Gammon, personal communication, 1983), but rather showed mild-to-moderate conductive loss due to bilateral atresia.

It may be that the appearance of canonical syllable production is possible with certain auditory deficits, especially if the loss is mild-to-moderate and the cochlea is intact and distortion free. Striking differences in the kinds of prelinguistic vocalizations produced by hearing-impaired and hearing babies may not occur, then, unless the impaired babies are severely-to-profoundly deaf.

The literature on prespeech vocalizations leaves a number of questions regarding comparative vocal development in hearing and deaf babies unanswered. Do deaf babies produce vocalizations that differ in kind from those of hearing babies at any time across the first year of life? More specifically, do deaf babies produce canonical syllabic vocalizations during the first year? Further, do noncanonical speech-like vocalizations of deaf infants resemble or differ broadly from those of hearing infants?

The present study is based on tape-recorded sampling of vocalizations of a profoundly deaf but otherwise intact infant. By comparing her vocalizations with those of both age-matched and stage-matched hearing babies, it is possible to provide information on the important unresolved issues concerning the role of audition in infant vocalizations.

METHODS

Subjects

Deaf subject. The deaf subject was initially referred to the Mailman Center for Child Development for an audiological evaluation and genetic work-up at age 3½ months. The subject was a Caucasian girl from a middle-class family. The infant's mother had been previously diagnosed as presenting Waardenburg's syndrome (Konigsmark & Gorlin, 1976) with characteristic laterally displaced medial canthi, flat nasal root, and a unilateral profound sensorineural hearing loss.

Upon physical examination, the subject was described as a normocephalic, alert infant with widening of the nasal bridge, laterally displaced medial canthi, and blue eyes with no heterochromia. The infant did not respond to any auditory stimuli during the medical examination. The diagnosis was Waardenburg's syndrome with no accompanying motor or intellectual impairment.

The infant was tested audiologically using behavioral observation techniques. No startle responses, eye widening, limb movement, arousal, or rudimentary localization responses could be elicited with a variety of noise bands, warble tones, and noisemakers, even at levels of 100 dB SPL. Impedance testing yielded normal tympanograms with absent stapedial reflexes bilaterally for pure tones and broadband noise at levels of 115 dB SPL. These results were consistent with parental observation of the infant's total lack of interest in and response to environmental auditory stimuli.

---

[1]Mavilya also uses the term *canonical* but apparently in a manner substantially different from that intended here.

Essentially identical audiological test results were obtained when the infant was tested both at 5 and 7 months of age. The subject could not be conditioned to respond to auditory stimuli with Visually Reinforced Audiometric techniques at levels of 100 dB SPL in a soundfield condition. Brainstem evoked response testing revealed no responses to high-frequency click stimuli (2.4–7.4 kHz) presented at 90 dB HL through headphones to individual ears or through a speaker. This pattern was consistent with the presence of a profound, sensorineural hearing loss bilaterally, with any residual hearing probably limited to the low-frequency range. Brainstem testing was repeated with stimuli presented through the speaker while the infant was fitted with a powerful body-model hearing aid in either cap. Changes in wave morphology were noted at 50–60 dB HL, indicating that the prognosis for receiving some benefit from amplification was favorable.

At age 7 months, the subject was fitted with a pseudo-binaural body-model hearing aid that had input to two ears (Oticon P15P). Aided responses to monitored live voice stimuli, bands of noise, and warble tones averaged 65–70 dB HL in soundfield. The infant's mother received extensive counseling from an audiologist regarding appropriate auditory and visual stimulation, care of the hearing aid, and overall infant development. The infant was brought to the Mailman Center several times a month between the ages of 7 and 9 months for preliminary intervention (involving elicitation of vocalizations and gestures), and at 9 months the subject began receiving such intervention and stimulation on a weekly basis. These sessions continued on a weekly basis throughout this study.

The subject is now 5 years old and is enrolled in special classes for the deaf. Recent evaluations have confirmed the original diagnosis of profound bilateral hearing impairment and normal intelligence. In spite of speech and language intervention for over 4 years, she remains extremely speech and language delayed.

The subject provided an excellent opportunity to evaluate the role of hearing impairment in early vocalizations because of her lack of handicaps other than deafness. However, the fact that amplification was begun before tape recordings of vocalizations were made suggests caution in interpretation. Similarities that might occur between the deaf baby's sounds and those of hearing babies could be attributable either to common auditory experience or to other common maturational or experiential patterns. The strongest evidence of effects of audition on infant vocalizations would be differences in the vocalization development of deaf and hearing infants.

Hearing subjects. Tape recordings of vocalizations of 11 normally hearing infants were collected during a 3-year longitudinal study on speech development in normal English- and Spanish-learning infants. Six infants (4 girls, 2 boys) were from primarily English-speaking homes and 5 (3 girls, 2 boys) were from Spanish-speaking homes. Several studies comparing vocalizations of these infants have shown marked similarities in vocalization development between Spanish and English learners (Eilers,

Oller, & Benito-Garcia, 1984; Oller & Eilers, 1982; Thevenin, Eilers, Oller, & Bull, 1983). In spite of extensive attempts to demonstrate differences between the two language groups during the first year of life, no concrete differences have been isolated. Consequently, in the data presented, results from Spanish-learning and English-learning babies are pooled.

All infants were healthy and showed no indications of handicapping conditions. All came from middle-class homes. Hearing screening was conducted periodically for all the normal infants using a visually reinforced technique. Whenever one of the infants proved unresponsive, a tympanometric evaluation was conducted by an audiologist. If warranted, an appropriate medical referral was made and the infant was retaped after normal auditory responses were obtained.

Recordings

All the infants in the study participated in recording sessions in which at least one parent and one experimenter were present. High-fidelity equipment was used in a sound-attenuated chamber. The environment of the recording included two features that might influence vocalization: (a) Since infants often vocalize while playing, the infants were given quiet, age-appropriate toys to manipulate. (b) Since infants often vocalize socially, the experimenter engaged the child in face-to-face interaction.

An effort was made to provide similar vocalization models to all subjects. Little, if any, imitation was noted, however. The duration of each session was about 30 min, although sessions were terminated and rescheduled when a baby was fussy or sleepy.

The available recordings of the 11 hearing babies were periodic (averaging more than one per month per child) across the first year of life. The deaf baby was seen for recording on four occasions, at 8, 11, 12, and 13 months of age.

The tape recordings of the deaf baby were all coded according to procedures to be described below. In addition, two samples from each of the 11 hearing babies were also coded. Samples for this special coding were chosen on the basis of prespeech stage matching with the deaf infant's samples. Two precanonical stage recordings were selected for each hearing infant, one from an early precanonical period (4–5 months) and the second from a late precanonical period (5–6 months). In addition, comparison of the deaf baby's vocalizations with those of age-matched hearing babies was made by employing previous transcriptional data (Oller & Eilers, 1982) involving the same sample of hearing infants at 11–13 months of age. Table 1 provides the subjects' demographic data and the number of utterances considered in all samples.

Tape Coding

In order to provide a linguistically significant account of the vocalizations of infants, it is necessary to adopt a

TABLE 1. Demographic data and number of utterances (n) categorized in all samples.

Hearing subjects	Canonical sample age	n	Late precanonical sample age	n	Early precanonical sample age	n	Sex	Language background
1	11	54	6	56	5	65	M	Spanish
2	13	41	6	53	5	70	F	Spanish
3	13	43	5	66	4	53	F	English
4	10	61	6	70	5	64	F	Spanish
5	10	52	6	54	5	70	F	English
6	11	56	6	39	5	57	F	Spanish
7	11	48	6	54	5	55	F	English
8	13	33	6	53	5	51	M	Spanish
9	13	54	6	59	6	64	M	English
10	10	46	6	52	6	69	M	English
11	12	68	6	50	5	52	F	English

Deaf subject	All precanonical samples 1 age	n	2 age	n	3 age	n	4 age	n	Sex	Language background
12	8	76	11	62	12	75	13	90	F	English

Note. Age is given in months.

broad view of phonetic description. Once the infant has reached the canonical stage, when babbled utterances obey the timing constraints of syllables in natural languages, it is appropriate to apply segmental phonetic transcription systems to the canonical syllables. Prior to the canonical stage, however, much of the content of infant sounds cannot be appropriately described with either traditional segmental or suprasegmental terminology because these systems require all sounds to fit within the narrow confines of mature concrete phonological units.

Linguistically meaningful description of precanonical vocalizations can be obtained by employing a metaphonological level of description to supplement standard segmental and suprasegmental transcriptional systems. The metaphonological system specifies how general acoustic and articulatory parameters (pitch, voice quality, resonance, intensity, timing) are manipulated to generate well-formed units of any mature phonology. Metaphonology defines linguistically universal constructs such as syllabic structure, syllable nucleus, syllable margin, vocalicness, formant transition, suprasegmental contour, normal phonation, and so on. Such constructs constitute the underlying fabric of the concrete segmental and prosodic elements of all mature phonologies. Linguistic sound systems can be most usefully distinguished from other kinds of sound systems (e.g., birdsong, monkey vocal systems, human infant cry, etc.) by noting that basic constructs (e.g., syllabic structure, formant transition, etc.) are defined differently (if at all) in each system. The speech-like quality of a given sound is defined by the extent to which that sound obeys the specific requirements of metaphonological constructs.

Since all vocal sounds (regardless of speech-like quality) can be described in terms of acoustic parameters that can in turn be referenced to metaphonological constructs,

it is possible in a metaphonological framework to address the extent to which infant sounds (or any other kind of sounds) approximate mature speech sounds, even when the infant sounds are acoustically very different from adult speech. Similarly, in comparing sounds produced by deaf and hearing babies, metaphonological descriptions offer the potential for broadly assessing differences and similarities in vocal outputs.

The descriptive system employed in the present study involves 18 vocal categories defined by reference to metaphonological constructs (see Oller, 1980, and Results below for definitions). When adult listeners judge that an infant consistently produces any of these metaphonologically defined categories, it can be said that the infant has demonstrated a mastery of some metaphonologically significant construct. Most of the categories described in the present study have been widely seen in early infant vocalizations (Oller, 1980; Smith & Oller, 1980; Stark, 1980; Zlatin-Laufer, 1975). The study approach allows for the possibility of capturing unexpected categories that might occur. One advantage of this coding system is that it is featurally oriented so that an utterance can be characterized by several different features simultaneously. A particular utterance might, for example, be characterized as possessing a Fully Resonant nucleus (i.e., a nucleus obeying the metaphonological requirement of vocalicness and indicating utilization of the vocal tract's potential as a variable resonator), a Raspberry (i.e., a bilabial or labiolingual trill or vibrant), a Marginal transition (longer than 120 ms) between the Raspberry and the nucleus, and Squeal quality (high pitch, tense voice) during a portion of the nucleus.

Canonical stage vocalizations of the hearing infants were transcribed segmentally in a previous study (Oller & Eilers, 1982) by two phonetically trained observers. All precanonical stage recordings were coded by two observers using the metaphonologically oriented scheme. The observers first worked independently and later conferred on each utterance. If one observer could convince the other of an error in judgment, a change in the coding of the mistaken judge would be made. However, in most cases of disagreement, two separate judgments were entered for analysis, reflecting the ambiguity inherent in some infant vocalizations.

Two judges worked together similarly to categorize precanonical vocalizations of the deaf and hearing infants. The judges knew which child was involved in each categorization session due to parent and experimenter comments (often naming the child) on the tapes.

Judgment reliabilty for the precanonical tapes was assessed in two ways. First, the disagreements were recorded and data were analyzed to yield a proportion of agreement score on each utterance category investigated within the metaphonological perspective (mean agreement = 81%). Agreement data are presented in Table 2. In addition, after all data were collected, one taped session was selected at random to be categorized a second time. This tape was recorded using the same procedure and submitted to a reanalysis to compare with the original. The absolute intrajudge agreement on the two codings of the same tape for Transcriber 1 was 86% and for Transcriber 2, 88%. The average discrepancy in the proportion of utterances given a particular featural description from the first to the second coding was just over 1% (mean discrepancy across all features analyzed), and the average proportion of disagreement between the two judges across all features was between 1% and 2%.

TABLE 2. Interjudge reliability on precanonical stage features and utterance types.

Feature or utterance type	n	% Agreed
Clicks	20	100%
Ingressive-Egressive Sequences	40	98
Syllabic kx/x	33	97
Normal Phonation	1,053	96
Whisper	19	95
Raspberries	70	93
Quasi-resonant Nuclei	949	93
Syllabic ts/s	21	90
Fully Resonant Nuclei	706	90
Squeals	122	88
Glottal Stop Sequences	103	81
Glottal Fricative Sequences	123	81
Growls	109	80
Canonical Babbles	32	78
Yells	25	68
Trills	8	63
Marginal Babbles	37	59
Intermittent Voice	38	Unavailable[a]
		$\bar{x}$ = 81%

[a]This feature was considered only after the feature was noticed in review of Subject 10's samples. A single observer then went back to all previous tapes and coded them for that feature alone.

Analysis Instrumentation

Spectrographic analyses were produced by a Kay Digital Sona-Graph (7800) using filter widths appropriate to the characteristics of the specific features to be analyzed and the fundamental frequency of the utterance. Spectrographic analyses were used for two purposes: to provide figures illustrative of frequently occurring vocalization types and to help interpret ambiguous or difficult to categorize auditory preceptions.

RESULTS AND DISCUSSION

Canonical Babbling

The critical questions to be addressed in this study concern the degree of similarity or difference between deaf and hearing infants' prespeech vocalizations. First, does the deaf infant produce canonical syllables? And second, are precanonical vocalizations similar in deaf and hearing infants? To address the former question we compared the deaf baby's performance with age-matched hearing infants. The 11 hearing babies of the present sample all produced canonical babbling repetitively and frequently by age 10 months. A single (approximately 30-min) tape-recorded sampling of vocalizations of each of the 11 hearing infants at ages 11–13 months (Oller & Eilers, 1982) yielded an average of 83 canonical syllables per child, with a range of 36–139. Furthermore, all additional normal infants for whom we have reliable records evidenced canonical babbling by 10 months. The relative uniformity of the onset of this developmental event is emphasized by the fact that canonical babbling usually begins at 7–8 months in both normal and Down's syndrome infants (Smith & Oller, 1981).

In contrast to the hearing babies, the deaf baby did not produce repetitive canonical forms. She produced only two exemplars of canonical syllables through four recordings (8–13 months). These two occurrences cannot be taken to indicate canonical stage of development, because such utterances occur occasionally in isolation in precanonical periods beginning with the Gooing stage in hearing infants (2–3 months). Not only was the age-appropriate canonical pattern absent from any of the four samples for the deaf baby, but also the mother and the clinicians working with the child confirmed that the baby did not and had not produced repetitive canonical babbling at any time before or during the sampling period.

The nature of canonical syllables in 9-to-11-month-old hearing infants is exemplified in Figures 1a–1c. Important features to note are the regularity of syllable timing (see 1a, showing a reduplicated babble in narrow-band analysis) and the brevity of formant transitions (120 ms or less in 1b and 1c)[2].

---

[2]Formant frequencies and transition durations are often difficult to assess in infant utterances due to high $F0$ (see Fant, 1966). The problem can be combatted in part by using very wide-band spectrographic analysis. A 600-Hz filter bandwidth was sufficient to resolve formants in Figures 1b and 1c. Transition duration can be determined with substantial accuracy in these cases using $F1$ in Figure 1b and using both $F1$ and $F2$ in Figure 1c.

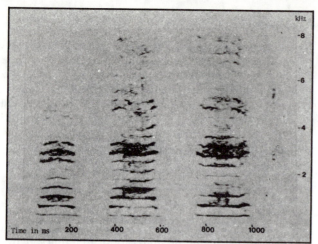

FIGURE 1a. Canonical babble, [tʌtʌtʌtʰ], produced by Subject 1 (hearing) at 9 months, analyzed with a 45-Hz filter.

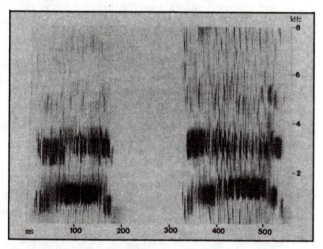

FIGURE 1b. Canonical babble, first two syllables from utterance pictured in Figure 1a, produced by Subject 1 (hearing) at 9 months, analyzed with a 600-Hz filter. Note $F1$ transitions (<120 ms).

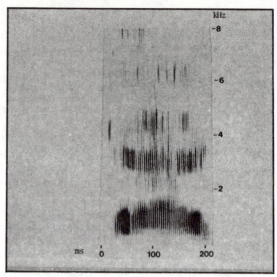

FIGURE 1c. Canonical babble, [tat], second syllable of a reduplicated sequence, produced by Subject 2 (hearing) at 9 months, analyzed with a 600-Hz filter. Note both $F1$ and $F2$ transitions (<120 ms).

Precanonical Vocalizations

The following data represent a comparison of precanonical stage vocalizations of the deaf and hearing infants. The intersession variability in precanonical category usage apparent in these data tends to cloud the issue of possible differences between deaf and hearing infants. Although some of the deaf infant's samples showed a higher occurrence of a given vocal feature than for any of the hearing subject samples, it was also true that some vocal features occurred much more frequently in some hearing infants than in others. Aside from the apparent differences to be noted below, the preponderance of Expansion stage vocalizations showed notable featural similarity in the deaf infant and the hearing infants. It is not possible, based on existing evidence, to determine the extent to which this similarity may be the result of intervention with the deaf infant or more general organismic similarities of deaf and hearing babies.

Nucleic elements. Syllable nuclei of natural languages are normally vowels with identifiable formant structures. When produced in isolation, such formant patterns can be identified as potential vowels and can be said to possess a particular "vowel quality." The nuclei of early infant vocalizations, on the other hand, often involve formant or resonance patterns that lack full vowel quality as judged by mature listeners. Although the acoustic and articulatory characteristics of such nuclei are still under investigation, it appears that the perceived nonvocalicness is attributable in part to the intense low-frequency (below 1500 Hz or so) energies in such utterances relative to limited high-frequency formant energies. Such a pattern of vocalization has been described as "Quasi-resonant" (or partially resonant) (Oller, 1980), because the relatively closed vocal posture involved in production of the sound fails to take advantage of the substantial potential of the

The study provides, then, a clarification of the issues raised in the writings of Lenneberg et al. (1965) and referred to in Gilbert's (1982) review. At least for this deaf baby, it is not true that normal canonical babbling occurred during the first year of life. The baby appeared to be more like younger hearing infants in vocalization topography. At the same time, given rather large individual and intersession differences in infant vocal patterning, it was not possible to assert with confidence that the deaf baby's vocalizations were different or indistinguishable from those of younger (precanonical) hearing babies. In order to obtain a more general view of the possible similarity or difference in the deaf and hearing infant vocalizations, a comparison was made between the vocalizations of the deaf subject and those of younger hearing infants in an early and a late precanonical stage of development. Both the early and late samples of the deaf and hearing babies were from the Expansion stage (Oller, 1980).

vocal tract to serve as a resonator. In addition, nasalization and consequent nasal antiresonances are commonly involved in Quasi-resonant infant sounds. Infants also produce "Fully Resonant" adult-like vocalic sounds, which involve substantial high-frequency energies. The idea of a Fully Resonant sound corresponds roughly to the notion, "potential vowel in a natural language." Quasi-resonant sounds are those vocal nuclei that would be judged inappropriate as vowels, apparently due to their lack of sufficiently identifiable high resonances, nasalization, or some combination of these.

A spectrographic representation of a sound (from the deaf infant) judged to be a Quasi-resonant nucleus is presented in Figure 2a. Note that low-frequency energies are relatively intense compared to those at higher frequency. Figure 2b contains a double Quasi-resonant sequence (bisyllabic) from one of the hearing babies. Here, the predominance of low-frequency energies is so great as to impede the identification of any higher frequency formant.[3] Figure 2c presents a bisyllabic utterance from the deaf baby. The two judges felt uncertain whether to call the first nucleus Quasi-resonant or Fully Resonant. Note that in the first portion of the utterance (ending at about 250 ms), formant information at 1500 Hz and above is comparable in intensity to that of the lower resonance. The second nucleus (beyond about 350 ms) shows a more clearly Quasi-resonant pattern, in which the lowest formant energy (1200–1500 Hz or below) is considerably more intense than higher formant energies.

Figures 2d and 2e show Fully Resonant sounds (with more well-defined higher formants) from the deaf infant and one of the hearing infants, respectively. The noisiness of the utterance in 2e is attributable to a hoarse, breathy vocal quality.

Figure 3 shows the proportion of utterances in each sample with Quasi-resonant or Fully Resonant nuclei for the hearing babies at each of the two developmental levels (early and late precanonical) and for the deaf baby in each of the four samples. The hearing babies show, as predicted, a tendency to produce relatively fewer Quasi-resonants and relatively more Fully Resonants in the later sample. This trend is predictable since hearing babies tend to vocalize in a more speech-like manner across the first year; furthermore, mature speech involves primarily Fully Resonant nuclei.

On the whole the four samples from the deaf baby appear to be similar to those of the hearing babies in the proportion of production of these sounds. Nevertheless, the deaf baby shows no tendency to increase her proportion of Fully Resonant sounds across the sampled time frame, but rather shows a trend toward fewer Fully Resonant nuclei with age. This may be due either to differences in vocal development in deaf and hearing babies or to intersession differences for the deaf subject.

Amplitude features. Figure 4 shows the proportions of Yell (distinct from Cry) and Whisper occurring in the samples. Hearing babies produce Yells and Whispers during precanonical vocalization, but as can be seen, there are large intersession variations in the proportion of usage. In a typical recorded sample, there may be no evidence of either Yells or Whispers. When they do occur, they tend to do so in clusters, suggesting a systematic exploration by the infant of the amplitude dimension (Oller, 1980; Zlatin-Laufer, 1975). Considering all Yells produced in the entire data corpus, over half came from 2 of the 26 recordings (Subject 9, late sample, and Subject 10, late sample). Similarly, over half the Whispers came from two recordings (Subject 6, late, and Subject 7, early). The deaf child's samples contained very few Yells or Whispers, a pattern similar to several of the hearing children.

Pitch and voice quality features. Squeals and Growls, categories that appear to be involved in infant exploration of high and low pitches, are shown spectrographically in Figures 5a, 5b, and 5c. Data on Squeals and Growls for the deaf subject and the hearing subjects are shown in

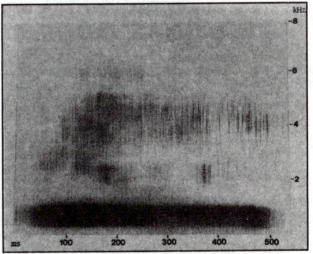

FIGURE 2a. Quasi-resonant nucleus produced by Subject 12 (deaf) at 12 months, analyzed with a 600-Hz filter.

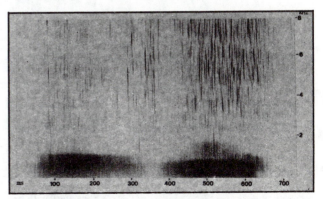

FIGURE 2b. Quasi-resonant nuclei produced by Subject 7 (hearing) at 6 months, analyzed with a 600-Hz filter.

---

[3]The low-frequency energy bands in the figures showing Quasi-resonant sounds are resonance peaks, and not merely voice bars, as indicated by narrow-band analyses that show multiple harmonics contributing to the bands represented in the wide-band displays.

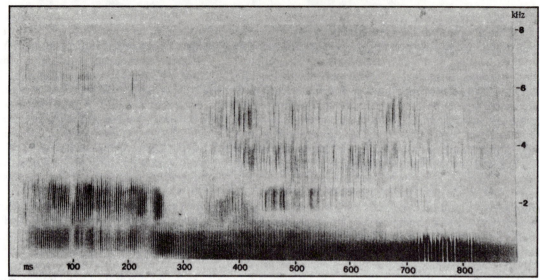

FIGURE 2c. Quasi-resonant nuclei produced by Subject 12 (deaf) at 11 months, analyzed with a 600-Hz filter. Nucleus 1 (centered near the 100-ms mark) was judged ambiguous as to resonance.

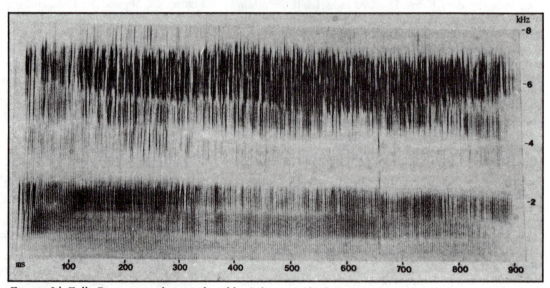

FIGURE 2d. Fully Resonant nucleus produced by Subject 12 (deaf) at 8 months, analyzed with a 600-Hz filter.

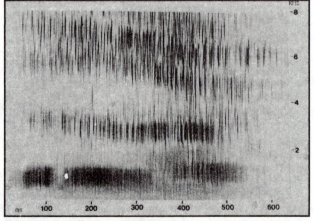

FIGURE 2e. Fully Resonant sequence produced by Subject 5 (hearing), with breathy, hoarse voice, at 6 months, analyzed with a 600-Hz filter.

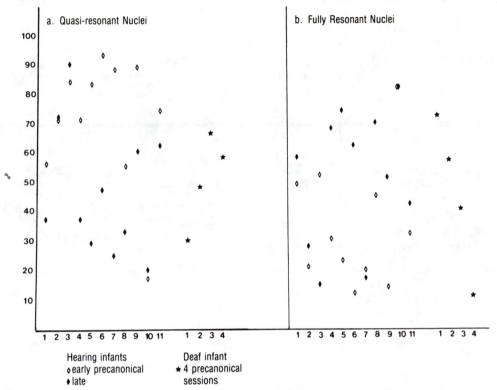

FIGURE 3. Proportions of utterances produced by hearing infants in early and late precanonical stages and by a deaf infant in the precanonical stage showing (a) Quasi-resonant nuclei and (b) Fully Resonant nuclei.

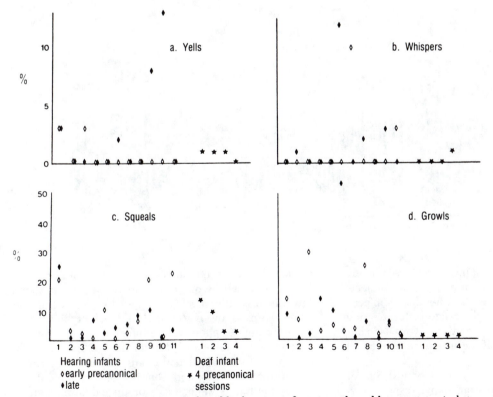

FIGURE 4. Proportions of utterances produced by hearing infants in early and late precanonical stages and by a deaf infant in the precanonical stage showing the features of (a) Yells, (b) Whispers, (c) Squeals, and (d) Growls.

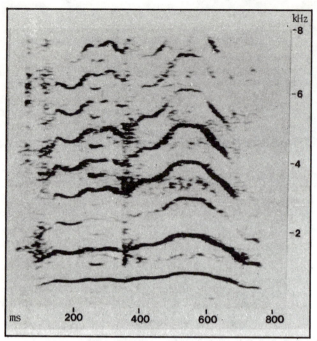

FIGURE 5a. Squeal produced by Subject 12 (deaf) at 11 months, analyzed with a 45-Hz filter. Note high *F0*.

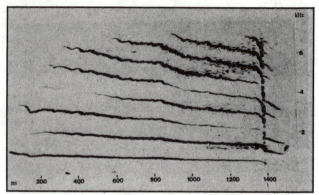

FIGURE 5b. Squeal produced by Subject 9 (hearing) at 5 months, analyzed with a 45-Hz filter.

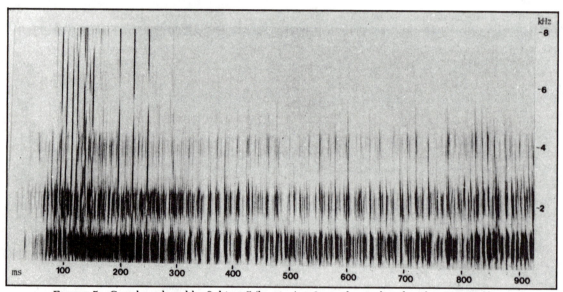

FIGURE 5c. Growl produced by Subject 5 (hearing) at 6 months, analyzed with a 600-Hz filter.

Figure 4. The deaf infant did not produce Growls in any session, a pattern similar to that for two hearing subjects (9 and 11) in two sessions each. The deaf subject's Squeals show a scatter within the range of the hearing group. Subject 6 shows a high proportion of Growls in her late session, wherein over half the utterances produced showed this feature.

Figures 5a and 5b show displays of a typical Squeal from the deaf baby and a hearing baby, respectively. Fundamental frequency in these utterances reaches or surpasses 1000 Hz (over twice the value expected for normal phonation in infants at these ages). In Figure 5c a Growl produced by one of the hearing babies is shown. Pitch in this utterance (as judged by glottal pulsation pattern) dips as low as 100 Hz (less than half the expected value for normal phonation in infants).

Phonation pattern and glottal features. Spectrographic examples of normal phonation are shown in Figures 2a–2e, presenting Fully and Quasi-resonant elements. Infants sometimes systematically produce different patterns of amplitude fluctuation during normal phonation. Fluctuation is sometimes achieved in a controlled regular fashion. One of the hearing babies produced many utterances with this regular Intermittent Voice (in which voicing is continuous but amplitude fluctuates regularly) in both samples. Figures 6a and 6b illustrate Machine Gun Voice. Figure 6a, from a hearing infant, shows four distinct amplitude peaks beyond the 300-ms mark. These peaks do not correspond to perceived syllabic nuclei, presumably because their duration is insufficient. The

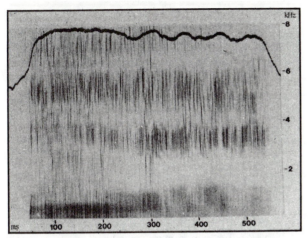

FIGURE 6a. Fully resonant sound with Intermittent Voice produced by Subject 10 (hearing) at 6 months, analyzed with a 600-Hz filter. Note amplitude variations.

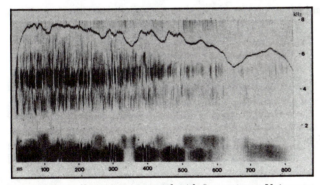

FIGURE 6b. Fully Resonant sound with Intermittent Voice produced by Subject 12 (deaf) at 12 months, analyzed with a 600-Hz filter. Note amplitude variations.

deaf baby's pattern in 6b similarly shows rapid rises and falls in amplitude that are not perceived as syllabic. The auditory impression is that the phonation pattern is broken in a rapid staccato fashion. Voicing does not cease entirely during these breaks (the pattern is similar in this regard to the "glottal catch," or "stød," of Danish), and the chunks of higher intensity voice between the breaks are too short (as little as 25 ms) to have syllabic status.

The distribution of production of Intermittent Voice and Normal Phonation is presented in Figure 7. As before, the deaf infant falls within the range of the hearing group. Hearing subject 10, however, differs drastically from the other infants in both samples.

Sometimes infants produce interruptions of voice with Glottal Stops or Glottal Fricatives (h-like consonants), and not uncommonly these interruptions occur at intervals consistent with syllabic timing. Figure 8 shows a Glottal Stop Sequence from the deaf infant. The two nuclei, both of sufficient duration to function as syllables in mature speech, are separated by a 175-ms glottal stop. Note that the first syllable also begins with a glottal fricative [h].

Although the deaf baby's samples are unremarkable in their proportions of sequences involving glottal fricatives (see Figure 7), the second of four samples from the deaf infant showed the largest proportion of Glottal Stop Sequences (see Figure 7) of any of the samples. It may be that the deaf baby's second sample just happened to be one in which she was focused on Glottal Stop Sequences, not unlike the phenomenon of Subject 6's focus on Growls in her later sample. Alternatively, recent unpublished data on other deaf babies (from our own laboratory and as seen by Ling-Phillips, personal communication, December 1981, and Stoel-Gammon, personal communication, 1983) have suggested the possibility that deaf babies may, in general, produce relatively large proportions of this particular feature. The reason is unclear at this time, but the matter is being explored further.

Clicks. A suction stop or Click produced by one of the hearing babies is pictured in Figure 9. Like many other sounds types, these occur primarily in clusters. Of all clicks in the 26 tapes, 40% occurred in a single sample from Subject 7 (see Figure 10). Eighteen of the samples (including the four from the deaf baby) yielded no clicks.

Trills and vibrants. Raspberries (labial or labiolingual trills and/or vibrants) are one of the most salient utterance types of infancy. Figures 11a–11c show trilled and vibrant Raspberries from two of the hearing infants and the deaf infant. Figure 11a, in the portion from 1000 to 1400 ms, illustrates relative regularity of vertical noise striations (occurring at 20–25-ms intervals), a pattern typical of trills. Note that between 200 and 600 ms no trilling occurs, as evidenced by irregular striations. This vibrant Raspberry pattern is also seen in Figures 11b and 11c.

The deaf baby produced no trills in our samples (see Figure 10), but neither did most of the hearing babies. Subject 5 produced half the trills in a single sample. The deaf baby's sample of vibrant Raspberries is also unremarkable (see Figure 10). Nearly half the Raspberries were produced by Subject 7 in two samples.

Airstream direction. Ingressive-Egressive Sequences can be interpreted to represent exploration of the airstream mechanism. Figure 12 shows a narrow-band (45 Hz) display of a sequence from Subject 7 (who produced nearly half the Ingressive-Egressive Sequences in one sample) with a typical fundamental frequency (about 400 Hz) egress first, followed by a much higher fundamental frequency (nearly 1000 Hz) ingress. The deaf baby and 5 of the hearing babies produced no such sequences (see Figure 10).

Timing of articulations. The development of the canonical syllabic forms of speech involves several steps. One is the appearance of widespread Fully Resonant nuclei. Another is the production of such nuclei adjacent

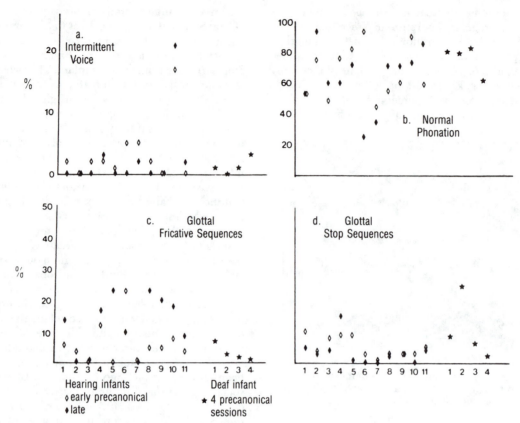

FIGURE 7. Proportions of utterances produced by hearing infants in the early and late precanonical stages and by a deaf infant in the precanonical stage having (a) Intermittent Voice, (b) Normal Phonation, (c) Glottal Fricatives, and (d) Glottal Stops.

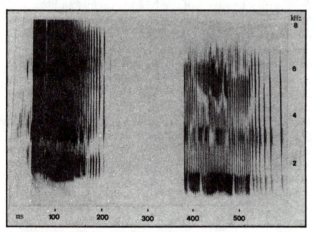

FIGURE 8. Glottal Stop Sequence, [haʔə], produced by Subject 12 (deaf) at 8 months, analyzed with a 600-Hz filter.

to consonant-like elements. Prior to the Canonical stage, these sequences of consonant-like elements and Fully Resonant nuclei occur with extremely variable transition times, usually greater than acceptable for canonical syllables, and often involving voice breaks during the transitions. Marginal Babbles result from over-long transitions. Figure 13a shows a Marginal Babble from the deaf baby.

Note that the Fully Resonant nucleus at the beginning involves a long-duration (around 160 ms) transition (visible especially in the falling second formant). The noisy element at the end of the utterance is a vibrant Raspberry. Figure 13b shows a Marginal Babble from a hearing subject. It begins in this case with a voiced labial stop and moves into a Fully Resonant sound through a second formant transition of over 200-ms duration.

Given the variability of duration of transitions during precanonical babbling, it is not surprising that some of the primitive syllables of this period would have canonical timing. However, none of those occurring in the taped samples used here were in the repetitive or reduplicated form of Figure 1a. Figure 14 plots the distributions of usage of both Marginal and Canonical syllables. Marginal syllables (those considered too long to be canonical) were judged to occur about twice as often as Canonical syllables. Of the 26 recordings, 7 showed no Marginal syllables, whereas 14 showed no Canonicals. Of the 11 hearing babies, 9 produced some Canonical syllables. In spite of an absence of reduplicated babbling, all 9 produced more Canonical syllables in the second (later) than in the first sample, indicating perhaps a precursor development to the Canonical stage. In contrast, the deaf baby produced only two Canonical utterances, both in the first of her four samples. This same sample also yielded the highest proportion of Marginal Babbling in the entire

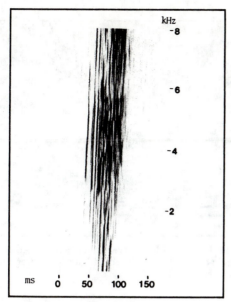

FIGURE 9. Click (suction stop) produced by Subject 7 (hearing) at 6 months, analyzed with a 600-Hz filter.

corpus. At the same time the absolute difference between her Marginal Babbling proportion (14%) and that of some

of the hearing children (12%, 9% . . . .) is not great.

Syllabic friction sounds. The extreme individuality of certain samples is well demonstrated in the occurrence of Syllabic Fricative/Affricate sounds. Figure 15a shows two [s]-like sounds (from Subject 7), the second of which is ingressive. Figure 15b shows a sequence of two syllabic [kx]-like sounds (velar affricate) produced by the deaf baby. Both kinds of sounds are relatively rare in hearing babies, as can be seen in Figure 14. Virtually all the examples of each type occurred in a single sample. Had it not been for Subject 7's later sample, we might have been tempted to speculate that the occurrence of syllabic fricative/affricate sounds was a sign of hearing impairment. The data, however, impose greater caution.

CONCLUSIONS

An intriguing footnote to this work is found in the observation that a relatively high proportion of any particular vocal type in a particular session will unlikely have diagnostic value, since large intersession differences occurred in the sample of hearing infants. A single hearing infant accounted for much of the spread in distributions reported here. Subject 7 produced samples with the largest proportions of Syllabic Fricatives/Affricates,

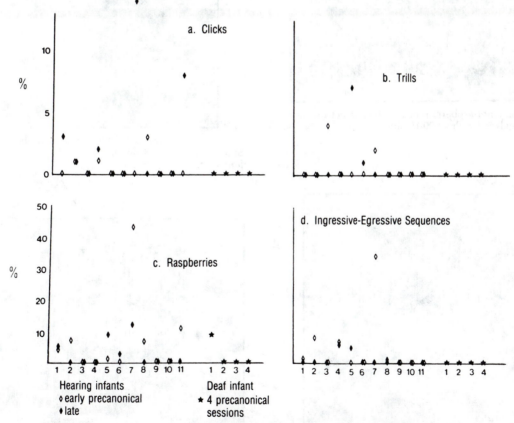

FIGURE 10. Proportions of utterances, produced by hearing infants in early and late precanonical stages and by a deaf infant in the precanonical stage, that were (a) Clicks, (b) Trills, (c) Raspberries, and (d) Ingressive-Egressive sequences.

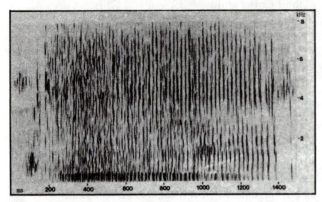

FIGURE 11a. Combination of vibrant and trilled Raspberry produced by Subject 5 (hearing) at 6 months, analyzed with a 300-Hz filter.

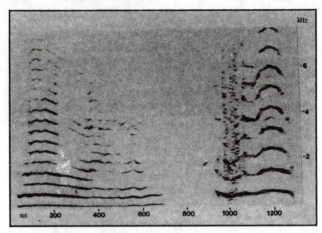

FIGURE 12. Ingressive-Egressive sequence produced by Subject 7 (hearing) at 5 months, analyzed with a 45-Hz filter. Note high $F0$ of ingressive nucleus.

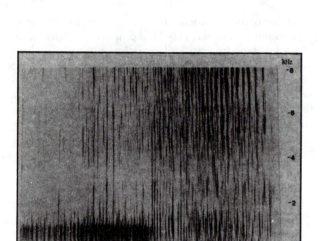

FIGURE 11b. Vibrant Raspberry produced by Subject 7 (hearing) at 6 months, analyzed with a 600-Hz filter.

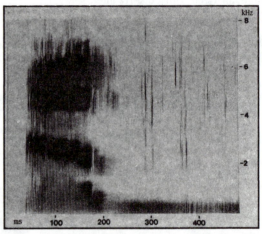

FIGURE 13a. Marginal Babble, vibrant Raspberry produced by Subject 12 (deaf) at 8 months, analyzed with a 600-Hz filter. Note long $F2$ transition (>120 ms).

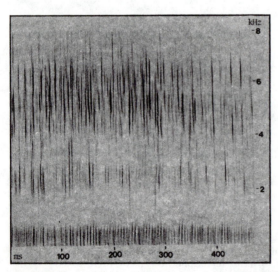

FIGURE 11c. Vibrant Raspberry produced by Subject 12 (deaf) at 8 months, analyzed with a 600-Hz filter.

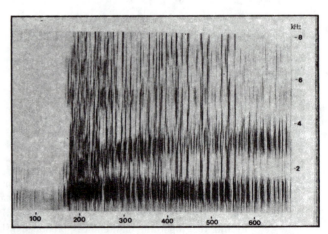

FIGURE 13b. Marginal Babble produced by Subject 5 (hearing) at 6 months, analyzed with a 600-Hz filter. Note voiced labial stop and long $F2$ transition (>200 ms).

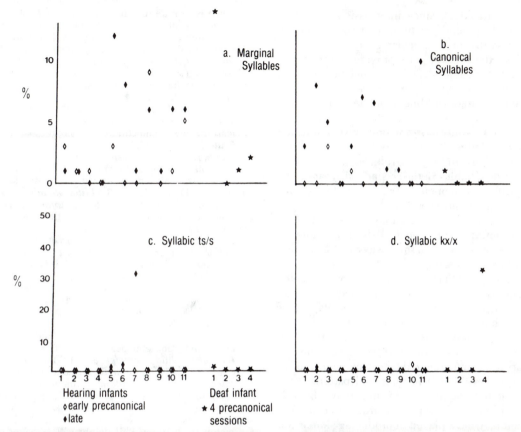

FIGURE 14. Proportions of utterances produced by hearing infants in early and late precanonical stages and by a deaf infant in the precanonical stage with (a) marginal syllables, (b) canonical syllables, (c) syllabic ts/s, and (d) syllabic kx/x.

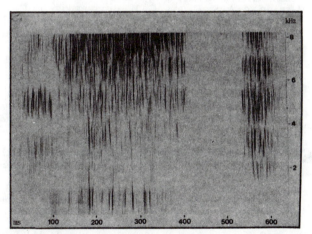

FIGURE 15a. Coronal (alveolar) syllabic fricative sequence with the second segment ingressive, produced by Subject 7 (hearing) at 6 months, analyzed with a 600-Hz filter.

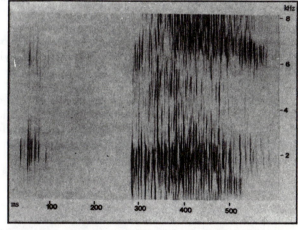

FIGURE 15b. Velar syllabic affricate sequence produced by Subject 12 (deaf) at 13 months, analyzed with a 600-Hz filter.

Clicks, Ingressive-Egressive Sequences, and Raspberries. She showed a greater inclination than any other baby in the sample to focus on particular features. She was also the first baby in the sample to acquire meaningful words, and was far ahead of the other babies in vocabulary development at 20 months.

The deaf infant also showed a tendency for individual session focus. Such tendencies are important because they seem to reflect a child's interest in vocal behavior and perhaps even the extent of a child's phonological talent. But the same tendency poses problems for our interest in demonstrating the possible unique features of vocalizations of the deaf, since intersession variability makes it difficult to identify patterns that pertain specifically to an individual or a particular group.

Nevertheless, the present work provides clear indication that profound deafness can have a notable effect on vocalization development in the first year of life. The absence of reduplicated babbling in the deaf baby during the sampling period suggests that she was unlike any hearing infant in the study or in any previously published work, to our knowledge. It is worth pointing out also that even though previous studies have referred to a paucity of vocalization in deaf babies in the second half-year of life, we found no difficulty in obtaining a full sample from this deaf baby on each of four occasions.

The comparison of the vocalizations of the deaf infant with those of younger (precanonical) hearing babies is somewhat more ambiguous. In some ways, the deaf infant seems much like the hearing babies in that she produces Raspberries, Squeals, Quasi- and Fully Resonant nuclei, Marginal Babbles, and Glottal Stop Sequences. The auditory-based descriptions and spectrographic displays show these vocalizations to be very similar in form to those of hearing babies. On the whole, the proportion of occurrence of various features in the deaf baby's repertoire is also unremarkable compared to the hearing sample. Such similarities may result from maturational patterns common to deaf and hearing infants. It is uncertain what role the limited auditory experience (with amplification) of the deaf infant may have played in producing similarities of vocal pattern with hearing infants.

The study raises the following questions warranting future research with additional deaf infants:

1. Do deaf infants tend to produce a lower rather than higher proportion of Fully Resonant sounds near the end of the first year of life, whereas the hearing babies show an opposite tendency?

2. Do deaf infants produce relatively high proportions of Glottal Stop Sequences, Marginal Syllables, and Syllabic Velar Fricative/Affricates during multiple samples across the first year?

The study of other profoundly deaf infants, within a metaphonological framework, in relation to age- and stage-matched hearing peers should provide answers to these and other questions regarding the role of auditory experience in vocalization development.

ACKNOWLEDGMENTS

This work was supported by NIMH Grant No. MH 30634 to the authors, the Rita and Jerome Cohen Tactual Speech Project, and the Mailman Foundation.

REFERENCES

ATKINSON-KING, K. B., MACWHINNEY, B., & STOEL-GAMMON, C. (1970). An experiment in the recognition of babbling. *Papers and Reports on Child Language Development* (Stanford University), *1*, 71–76.

DE BOYSSON-BARDIES, B., SAGART, L., & BACRI, N. (1981). Phonetic analysis of late babbling: A case study of a French child. *Journal of Child Language, 8*, 511–524.

CRUTTENDEN, A. (1970). A phonetic study of babbling. *British Journal of Disorders of Communication, 5*, 110–118.

EADY, S. J. (1980). *The onset of language-specific patterning in infant vocalizations.* Unpublished master's thesis, University of Ottawa, Ottawa, Canada.

EILERS, R. E., OLLER, D. K., & BENITO-GARCIA, C. R. (1984). The acquisition of voicing contrasts in Spanish and English learning infants and children: A longitudinal study. *Journal of Child Language, 11*, 313–336.

ELBERS, L. (1981). *Operating principles in repetitive babbling: A cognitive continuity approach.* Psychologisch Laboratorium, Rijks Universiteit Utrecht, The Netherlands.

ENSTROM, D. H. (1976). *Babbling sounds of Swiss-German infants: A phonetic and spectrographic analysis.* Paper presented at the Annual Convention of the American Speech and Hearing Association, Houston.

FANT, C. (1966). A note on vocal tract size factors and non-uniform F-pattern scalings. *Speech Transmission Laboratory: Quarterly Progress Report* (Royal Institute of Technology, Stockholm), *4*, 22–30.

FRY, D. B. (1966). The development of the phonological system in the normal and the deaf child. In F. Smith & G. A. Miller (Eds.), *The genesis of language: A psycholinguistic approach.* Cambridge, MA: MIT Press.

GILBERT, J. H. V. (1982). Babbling and the deaf child: A commentary on Lenneberg et al. (1965) and Lenneberg (1967). *Journal of Child Language, 9*, 511–515.

HUBER, H. (1970). *A preliminary comparison of English and Yucatec infant vocalization at nine months.* Papers from the sixth regional meeting of the Chicago Linguistic Society, Chicago.

KONIGSMARK, B. W., & GORLIN, R. J. (1976). *Genetic and metabolic deafness.* Philadelphia: W. B. Saunders.

LENNEBERG, E. H. (1967). *Biological foundations of language.* New York: Wiley.

LENNEBERG, E. H., REBELSKY, G. F., & NICHOLS, I. A. (1965). The vocalizations of infants born to deaf and to hearing parents. *Human Development, 8*, 23–37.

MASKARINEC, A. S., CAIRNS, G. F., BUTTERFIELD, E. C., & WEAMER, D. K. (1981). Longitudinal observations of individual infant's vocalizations. *Journal of Speech and Hearing Disorders, 46*, 267–273.

MAVILYA, M. P. (1969). *Spontaneous vocalization and babbling in hearing impaired infants.* Doctoral dissertation, Columbia University. (University Microfilms No. 70-12879)

MENYUK, P. (1968). The role of distinctive features in children's acquisition of phonology. *Journal of Speech and Hearing Research, 11*, 138–146.

MURAI, J. (1963). The sounds of infants: Their phonemicization and symbolization. *Studia Phonologica, 3*, 18–34.

NAKAZIMA, S. A. (1962). A comparative study of the speech developments of Japanese and American English in childhood. *Studia Phonologica, 2*, 27–46.

OLLER, D. K. (1980). The emergence of the sounds of speech in infancy. In G. Yeni-Komshian, J. Kavanagh, & C. Ferguson (Eds.), *Child phonology: Vol. 1* (pp. 93–112). New York: Academic Press.

OLLER, D. K., & EILERS, R. E. (1982). Similarities of babbling in Spanish and English learning babies. *Journal of Child Language, 9*, 565–577.

OLLER, D. K., WIEMAN, L. A., DOYLE, W., & ROSS, C. (1975). Infant babbling and speech. *Journal of Child Language, 3*, 1–11.

OLNEY, R. L., & SCHOLNICK, E. K. (1976). Adult judgments of age and linguistic differences in infant vocalization. *Journal of Child Language, 3*, 145–156.

PRESTON, M. S., YENI-KOMSHIAN, G., & PORT, R. (1967). Voicing in initial stop consonants produced by children in the prelinguistic period from different language communities. *Johns Hopkins University School of Medicine, Annual Report of*

Neurocommunications LAB, 2, 305–323.

SMITH, B., & OLLER, D. K. (1981). A comparative study of premeaningful vocalizations produced by normal and Down's syndrome infants. *Journal of Speech and Hearing Disorders, 46,* 46–52.

SMITH, B., & STOEL-GAMMON, C. (1977). Speech production: Segmental phonology. In *An investigation of certain relationships between hearing impairment and language disability* (Prog. Rep. No. 5, Research Contract No. NIH-NICHD-N01-HD-3-2793). Seattle: University of Washington.

STARK, R. E. (1980). Stages of speech development in the first year of life. In G. Yeni-Komshian, J. Kavanagh, & C. Ferguson (Eds.), *Child phonology: Vol. 1* (pp. 73–90). New York: Academic Press.

THEVENIN, D., EILERS, R. E., OLLER, D. K., & BULL, D. H. (1983). *Monolingual and bilingual adult's perception of infant babbling.* Paper presented at the biannual meeting of the Society for Research in Child Development, Detroit.

VANVIK, A. (1971). The phonetic-phonemic development of a Norwegian child. *Norsk Tidsskrift for Sprogvidenskap* (Oslo), *24.*

WHETNALL, E., & FRY, D. B. (1964). *The deaf child.* London: Heinemann.

ZLATIN-LAUFER, M. A. (1975). *Preliminary descriptive model of infant vocalization during the first 24 weeks: Primitive syllabification and phonetic exploratory behavior* (Final Report, Project No. 3-3014, Grant NE-6-00-3-0077). Washington, DC: National Institute of Education.

Received May 5, 1983
Accepted August 8, 1984

Requests for reprints should be sent to D. Kimbrough Oller, Mailman Center for Child Development, University of Miami, P.O. Box 016820, Miami, FL 33101.

The Vowel Formants of Deaf and Normal-Hearing Eleven- to Fourteen-Year-Old Boys

ANGELO A. ANGELOCCI

GEORGE A. KOPP

ANTHONY HOLBROOK

Although the sound spectrograph has been utilized by a number of investigators (Peterson and Barney, 1952; Fairbanks, *et al.*, 1961; Holbrook and Fairbanks, 1962) in the study of normal speakers, the application of this instrument to the study of the speech of the deaf has not been extensive. One such study was undertaken by Morley (1949), in which the characteristics of consonant distortion were examined and related to the intelligibility of deaf speech. By examination of broad band spectrograms, he was able to discover what consonants were most distorted and found that these agreed with the judgments of listeners as to the least intelligible consonants. A further use of spectrographic information was made in a pilot study by Watson (1961) in which the spectra of the speech sounds of normal speakers were compared with the audiograms of deafened adults in order to predict what sounds would be correctly interpreted. The results indicated that the consonant prediction was slightly better than that of the vowel, and that hearing for the first two formants seemed of more significance than hearing for all three formants. Clearly there is a need for more information relating the acoustical characteristics of deaf speech to those of normal speech, which would contribute to our knowledge of teaching speech to the deaf.

It was the purpose of the study reported here to analyze and compare the vowel formants of the deaf and normal-hearing eleven- to fourteen-year-old boys. Previous research (Potter *et al.*, 1947, Ch. 7) has indicated that the first three formants contribute the greatest part of vowel information. Consequently, the frequencies and amplitudes of the fundamental and first three formants of ten General American vowels were the main concern of

Angelo A. Angelocci (Ph.D., Wayne State University, 1962) is Assistant Professor of Speech, Western Washington State College. George A. Kopp (Ph.D., University of Wisconsin, 1933) is Professor of Speech, Wayne State University. Anthony Holbrook (Ph.D., University of Illinois, 1958) is Assistant Professor of Speech, Wayne State University. This article is based on a Ph.D. dissertation completed under the direction of Dr. George A. Kopp. The research was supported, in part, by a grant from the Office of Vocational Rehabilitation, Department of Health, Education, and Welfare.

this study. It was of further interest to compare the acoustic output of both groups with the auditory perception of that output by normal-hearing listeners. By this means it was hoped that some indication would be given as to the direction in which training and teaching of vowels to the deaf should proceed.

Procedures

Selection of Subjects. Two groups of eighteen subjects each were used for the collection of speech samples. The normal-hearing subjects were drawn from the Birmingham, Michigan public schools. Criteria for the selection of these subjects were: no dialectal or clinical speech problems; no obvious hearing problem; a history of General American speech in the home; male; and eleven to fourteen years old. The deaf subjects were drawn from the Detroit Day School for the Deaf. Criteria for the selection of these subjects were: General American speech in the home; an average of 60-dB or more hearing loss over the frequencies of 250, 500, 1000, 2000, and 4000 cps; male; and eleven to fourteen years old.

Collection of Samples. The ten vowels /i/, /ɪ/, /ɛ/, /æ/, /ɑ/, /ɔ/, /ʊ/, /u/, /ʌ/, and /ɝ/ were selected for analysis. It was felt that a more normal production of these vowels would be secured if they were placed in real words and within sentences. The h-d environment suggested by Potter and Steinberg (1950) was utilized, and to insure internal consistency in the production of the intended vowel, the h-d word was included as the third word of four successive rhyming words in each sentence similar to the procedure of Holbrook and Fairbanks (1962). For example: the sentence for the vowel /i/ was as follows: I will say weed, feed, heed, deed, end. In order to familiarize the subjects with the recording procedure, four sample sentences were composed using dipthongs in place of vowels.

Immediately prior to the recording of the subjects, the 14 sentences were shown to them on a sheet of paper. One of the sample sentences was read aloud by the experimenter and the subjects were asked to read the remaining sentences aloud. When vowels were mispronounced, a list of rhyming words not used in the test sentences was presented to the subjects for pronunciation until it was established that the pronunciation of all vowels was correct as they perceived them. No attempt was made to instruct the subjects with respect to rate of utterance, excepting those subjects whose rates were obviously too fast for accurate articulation.

The subjects were seated in front of the microphone and the fourteen sentences were then presented separately on 4″ x 6″ cards at five-second intervals. The four sample sentences were always presented first in order to assure that the subjects understood the task. The ten experimental sentences were presented in a different random order for each subject. In the event of a reading error or inconsistency in the rhyming words within a sentence, the card was placed at the end of the order for repetition. The entire procedure was recorded in a two-room, sound-treated recording studio located in each school, by means of an Ampex 351 tape recorder, operated at 15 ips and an Electro-Voice cardioid 666 microphone.

Spectrographic Measurements. A Western Electric Sound Spectrograph was used for the acoustical analysis of the vowels. This instrument has a full scale frequency range of 3500 cps. The frequency calibration of this apparatus was accomplished by the method and equipment described by Fairbanks and others (1961), with the exception that for this study the fundamental of the calibrating tone was 100 cps; while the amplitude calibration followed the pattern described by Holbrook and Fairbanks (1962).

Prior to the analysis of the experimental words, the recording gain of the sound spectrograph was established. This level was held constant throughout the analysis period by means of a constant voltage one KC pure tone presented to the sound spectrograph. The reproduce amplifier attenuator was set at an appropriate level and this position was varied only when the amplitude of a formant was below the resolving power of the original attenuator setting.

Analysis of Vowels. The tape recordings were played on the original recording apparatus, and the playback gain was adjusted to peak at 0 dB for the experimental word in each sentence. On the sound spectrograph, the combination of a 45 cps bandwidth and no shaping (NS) frequency response was used. This adjustment of the machine produced a fairly flat portrayal of the speech signal. Immediately after the speech signal was recorded, a calibration tone was recorded at a point adjacent to the vowel sample and sectioned simultaneously with it.

After each conventional spectrogram was made, but before it was removed from the instrument, the display was inspected and the section points located. Section points were located at the initial occurrence of the steady state of formants as far removed from the effects of the /d/ as possible. The spectrogram was then removed and the amplitude section made. When each section was completed it was examined to determine if all of the formants to be measured were resolved. In the event that a given formant could not be located, the section was reanalyzed with an increase of 6, 12, and sometimes 18 dB of gain above the reference setting in the reproduce amplifier of the sound spectrograph. It was not possible to locate Formant Three for two of the normal-hearing subjects on the vowel /u/ even when the additional gain revealed the noise level of the recordings.

On all of the sections, frequency and amplitude measures were made for the fundamental and three lowest formants. In the two instances where Formant Three could not be located, the mean frequency of Formant Three of the other subjects was assigned to them for statistical purposes, and the amplitude was given as the base line of the section.

The peak component of the vowel envelope was chosen as representative of the formant frequency. In the event that two peak components were of equal amplitude, a point midway between the two components was defined as the formant frequency. Upon determination of a given formant frequency the obtained value was rounded to the nearest five cps.

Amplitude measures were made from a template constructed in the manner outlined by Holbrook and Fairbanks (1962). The amplitude was estimated to the nearest one dB using the plastic template. The formant amplitude was defined as the amplitude of the strongest component expressed in dB re the baseline of the section.

In the selection of the formants, those of the normal-hearing subjects were located with relatively less difficulty than those of the deaf. There were several reasons for this. First, the deaf subject's production of the vowels was at times so distorted that a vowel identification was impossible. Second, the characteristics of deaf speech itself, such as excessive aspiration, nasality, and hoarseness, interfered with clearly defined formant peaks. Third, there was a scarcity of acoustical studies of deaf speech for reference purposes. With both the normal-hearing and the deaf subjects it was in some instances not possible to differentiate the fundamental frequency from Formant One frequency; Formant One from Formant Two; and Formant Two from Formant Three. When this occurred, the same frequency was assigned to the two formants in question.

Identification of Samples. Dubbings of the original samples were made for presentation to judges for identification. This was accomplished by playing the samples on the original recording equipment which was connected to an Ampex 400A recorder by means of a line containing a presenter switch. The h-d word was dubbed from each sentence by use of the presenter switch, which, when depressed, allowed this word to be re-recorded. The presenter switch was designed to eliminate any transient effect. After the h-d words were dubbed, they were cut apart into 360 separate segments—180 for the deaf and 180 for

the normal-hearing subjects. The words for each group were then randomly spliced into two continuous stimulus tapes with a five-second interval following each word. An additional five h-d words, which were not analyzed in the experiment, were placed at the beginning of each tape for listener accommodation. Thirty-four students enrolled in a freshman speech class were used as judges. They were given answer sheets at the top of which were typed the ten experimental words. Instructions were given requiring the judges to write one of the ten words for each utterance heard. The tapes were presented at approximately 70-dB sound pressure level on the original recording equipment accompanied by a McIntosh 60 amplifier and an Electro-Voice Regal III speaker. The tape with normal-hearing subjects was presented first, and it was followed immediately by the tape with deaf subjects.

Results

The mean frequencies and amplitudes of the fundamental and first three formants of the normal-hearing and deaf subjects are found in Table 1. These values are plotted graphically in Figure 1.

Fundamental Frequency. It may be seen in Figure 1 that the mean fundamental frequency (F_0) for deaf subjects was considerably higher for all vowels than for normal-hearing subjects. For all vowels pooled, the mean fundamental frequency was 193 cps for the normal-hearing and 236 cps for the deaf, a difference of 1.7 tones. In the upper left-hand corner of Figure 1, the vowel /i/ yielded the greatest difference between the mean fundamental

TABLE 1. Mean frequencies and amplitudes of the fundamental and first three formants of vowels for normal-hearing (N) and deaf (D) subjects. Frequencies in cps and amplitudes in dB re baseline of section.

Item		F_0	A_0	F_1	A_1	F_2	A_2	F_3	A_3
/i/	N	199	46	262	47	2776	25	3251	24
	D	254	45	421	45	2325	29	3099	24
/ɪ/	N	191	44	410	46	2300	31	2974	25
	D	245	42	447	45	2173	30	3091	23
/ɛ/	N	189	43	606	44	2079	35	2908	25
	D	214	38	536	43	1946	34	3019	26
/æ/	N	187	44	588	45	2231	33	2961	25
	D	234	39	609	44	1799	34	2966	23
/ɑ/	N	188	45	917	41	1376	38	2705	23
	D	230	40	694	44	1576	34	2825	23
/ɔ/	N	189	44	762	43	1067	39	2750	20
	D	223	37	681	44	1177	39	2805	25
/ʊ/	N	194	43	500	47	1216	29	2791	14
	D	242	45	484	45	1563	30	2798	20
/u/	N	204	44	363	47	1061	22	2757	7
	D	248	46	364	47	1377	23	2748	15
/ʌ/	N	195	45	671	43	1427	33	2813	19
	D	227	39	682	45	1433	34	2793	25
/ɝ/	N	194	44	396	46	1459	28	1909	29
	D	241	43	463	46	1946	28	2948	21

frequencies for the two groups, where F_0 for the normal-hearing was 199 cps and for the deaf 254 cps. The vowel reflecting the least difference between the mean fundamental frequencies was /ɛ/, with the F_0 for the normal-hearing being 189 cps and for the deaf 214 cps.

Examination of the mean fundamental frequency of the vowels for the normal-hearing revealed that it followed a definite pattern related to the nature of the production of the vowels. Starting in the upper left-hand corner of Figure 1, with /i/ at 199 cps, the fundamental decreases steadily to /æ/ at 187 cps. On the right of Figure 1, the fundamental frequency increases from /ɑ/ at 188 cps to /u/ at 204 cps. Examining the fundamental frequency of the deaf and progressing from /i/ to /æ/ on Figure 1, it can be seen that /æ/ did not follow the normal progression, since it was higher, rather than lower than /ɛ/. Moving up from /ɑ/ to /u/, it can be seen that /ɔ/ did not follow the pattern set by the normal subjects for the back vowels. With the above two exceptions, however, the deaf followed the same pattern as the normal-hearing except at higher mean frequencies. This phonemic variation in fundamental frequency was also observed by Black (1949) and House and Fairbanks (1953).

In addition to exhibiting a higher mean fundamental frequency, the deaf also exhibited a far wider range of mean frequencies. The range of means for the normal-hearing subjects was 187 to 204 cps; for the deaf subjects it was 214 to 254 cps. The range of fundamental frequencies for individual subjects was 85 to 280 cps for the normal-hearing and 100 to 350 cps for the deaf. These ranges reflect the fact that in both groups physiological changes were taking place that affected the fundamental frequency. It appears that some of the subjects exhibited preadolescent fundamental frequencies, while others had fundamental frequencies characteristic of the postadolescent period.

Amplitude of the Fundamental. The group differences observed above with respect to fundamental frequency were found also in the amplitude of the fundamental (A_0). In general, A_0 for the deaf was lower than A_0 for the

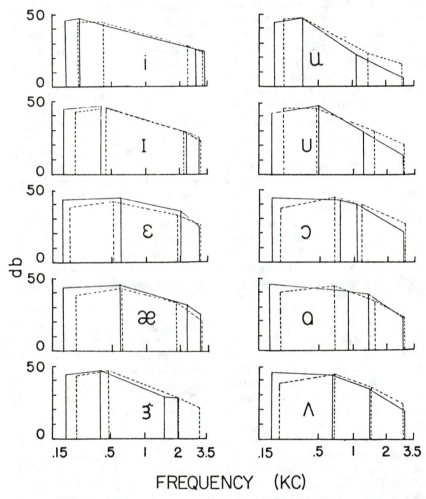

Figure 1. Mean frequencies and amplitudes of the fundamental and first three formants of vowels. Solid lines indicate normal-hearing subjects. Dotted lines indicate deaf subjects.

normal-hearing. For all vowels pooled, the mean A_0 was 44 dB for the normal-hearing, and 41 dB for the deaf. The greatest difference was for the vowel /ɔ/, whose mean was 44 dB for the normal-hearing, and 37 dB for the deaf, a mean difference of 7 dB. There was a greater range of A_0 means for the deaf than for the normal-hearing, as was the case for F_0. The range of individual A_0 values for the normal-hearing subjects was 37 to 50 dB; while for the deaf it was 23 to 51 dB. The inadequate monitoring system of the deaf appears to be reflected in that their A_0 range was more than twice that of the normal-hearing subjects.

Formant One Frequency. Immediately to the right of the fundamental in Figure 1 may be seen the ordinates representing Formant One. The means of Formant One frequency (F_1) for the deaf are higher than for the normal-hearing for the vowels /i/, /ɪ/, /æ/, /u/, /ʌ/, and /ɝ/ and lower for the vowels /ɛ/, /ɑ/, /ɔ/, and /ʊ/. As may be seen in Figure 1, with the exception of /i/, and /ɝ/, F_0 and F_1 are closer together for the deaf than for the normal-hearing. The phonemic pattern of F_1 reported by previous investigators (Fairbanks *et al.*, 1961; Potter *et al.*, 1947, Ch. 7) was followed by both groups in this study. That is, F_1 rose in frequency as it progressed from /i/ to /ɑ/, where it reached its maximum frequency position, and then it lowered in frequency as it progressed from /ɑ/ to /u/. The exception to this pattern is seen in F_1 of /æ/ for the normal-hearing subjects. As may be seen in Figure 1, F_1 of /æ/ is to the left of F_1 of /ɛ/ rather than to the right as would be expected from previous research. The range of the means

of F_1 for the vowels of the normal-hearing was 655 cps while that for the deaf was only 330 cps. The movement of the means of F_1 for the normal-hearing was greater than for the deaf by 325 cps. Although the F_0 means for the deaf showed a greater range of values than for the normal-hearing, the reverse is true for F_1.

Formant One Amplitude. In Figure 1 it may be seen that the means of Formant One amplitude (A_1) for the normal-hearing were higher for the front vowels /i/, /ɪ/, /ɛ/, and /æ/ than for the deaf. They were equal to or lower than the deaf for the back and neutral vowels /ɑ/, /ɔ/, /u/, /ʌ/, and /ɝ/. The exception was /ʊ/ in which A_1 was higher for the normal-hearing than for the deaf. The range of A_1 means for the normal-hearing was 41 to 47 dB; for the deaf it was 43 to 47 dB. It is of interest to note that the ranges of the means of the vowels of F_1 and A_1 were greater for the normal-hearing than for the deaf. This finding suggests that the vowels of the deaf are apt to be less well differentiated than those of the normal-hearing.

With respect to the slope of the spectrum between A_0 and A_1, A_1 for the deaf was equal to or higher than A_0 for all vowels. A_1 for the normal-hearing had a similar pattern except for the vowels /ɑ/, /ɔ/, and /ʌ/.

Formant Two Frequency. The pattern of Formant Two frequency (F_2) which may be seen in Figure 1 reveals that F_2 for the deaf was lower than for the normal-hearing for the front vowels /i/, /ɪ/, /ɛ/, and /æ/; F_2 for the deaf was higher than for the normal-hearing for the back and neutral vowels /ɑ/, /ɔ/, /ʊ/, /u/, /ʌ/, and /ɝ/.

For the normal-hearing the means of F_2 proceeded from a high frequency position for /i/ of 2776 cps to a low frequency position for /u/ of 1061 cps in a gradually descending order for each vowel execpt /æ/ and /ʊ/. The obtained F_2 postion of /ʊ/ was expected on the basis of previous investigations. It is apparent that F_1 and F_2 for /æ/, as spoken by the normal-hearing subjects of this study, are both out of line when compared with previous research.

The expected pattern of the means of F_2 was generally followed for the deaf with the exception of /u/ which was in a relatively higher position than would be expected. F_2 means covered a wider range of frequencies than F_1 means for both groups. The range of F_2 means for the normal-hearing subjects for the vowels was 1715 cps, while the comparable figure for the deaf was 1148 cps. As was the case with F_1, the range of the means of F_2 was greater for the normal-hearing than for the deaf.

Formant Two Amplitude. The means of the Formant Two amplitudes (A_2) for both groups did not show a pattern as a function of the vowels. A_2 means were equal to or higher for the deaf than for the normal-hearing for vowels /i/, /æ/, /ɔ/, /ʊ/, /u/, /ʌ/, and /ɝ/. They were lower for the vowels /ɪ/, /ɛ/, and /ɑ/. Both groups had the greatest amplitude for /ɔ/ with a mean A_2 of 39 dB. The range of A_2 means was 22 to 39 dB for the normal-hearing and 23 to 39 dB for the deaf. Generally it might be stated that the close vowels had a steeper A_1/A_2 slope than the open vowels, and for all vowels A_2 had a lower amplitude than A_1 for both groups.

Formant Three Frequency. The ordinate seen on the extreme right of each vowel portrayal in Figure 1 represents the Formant Three frequency (F_3) position. It may be seen that F_3 for the deaf was higher than for the normal-hearing for all vowels except /i/, /u/, and /ʌ/. By far the greatest group difference in the position of F_3 was for the vowel /ɝ/ in which the normal-hearing had a F_3 of 1909 cps and the deaf 2948 cps. The position of F_3 offered less information with respect to vowel differentiation than did F_1 and F_2. The normal-hearing had a high F_3 of 3251 cps for /i/. This dropped 277 cps to /ɪ/ with a frequency of 2974 cps, and remained fairly constant through /u/ which had a frequency of 2757 cps. F_3 then dropped 848 cps to /ɝ/ which had a frequency of 1909 cps. Other investigators (Fairbanks *et al*, 1961; Potter *et al.*, 1947, Ch. 7) have reported similar findings. In contrast, F_3 for the deaf did not follow the pattern reported above. Between /i/ at 3099 cps and /ɪ/ at 3091 cps, there was a drop of only 8 cps. In the transition from /u/ at 2748 cps to /ɝ/ at 2948 cps there was a 200 cps increase rather than the expected decrease of approximately 800 to 1000 cps. There was a difference of 1342 cps between /i/ and /ɝ/ for the normal-hearing; while for the deaf this difference was only 151 cps. A possible explanation of this great difference between the groups may be the difficulty encountered by the deaf in the production of the /ɝ/ sound. The usual result is perceived as something other than /ɝ/. A more detailed analysis of the perception of the vowels is to be found under the discussion of vowel intelligibility.

Formant Three Amplitude. The

means of Formant Three amplitudes (A_3) revealed little difference either between groups or within each group for the front vowels. The range of means for the normal-hearing subjects for the front vowels was from 24 to 25 dB; for the deaf this range was from 23 to 26 dB. In contrast, the back and neutral vowel range of means was from 7 to 29 dB for the normal-hearing; for the deaf it was 15 to 25 dB. The normal-hearing had a steeper A_2/A_3 slope than the deaf for vowels /ɛ/, /ɑ/, /ɔ/, /ʊ/, /u/, and /ʌ/. The deaf had a steeper A_2/A_3 slope than the normal-hearing for the vowels /i/, /ɪ/, /æ/, and /ɝ/. The steepest A_2/A_3 slope for both groups was found with the vowel /ɔ/ in which the deaf had a 14-dB slope, and the normal-hearing had a 19-dB slope.

Vowel Identification. The stimulus tapes which were prepared for identification purposes were presented to 34 college students who were instructed to write the words they heard spoken. Since there were 18 samples of each vowel and 34 judges, the total possible

identification score for each vowel was 612. In Tables 2 and 3, the identification matrices allow a comparison of perceived vowels with intended vowels. The normal-hearing subjects represented in Table 2 had an overall vowel identifiability of 81%; while the overall figure for the vowels of the deaf, shown in Table 3, was only 32%. While there was a high agreement between the intended and perceived vowels for the normal-hearing subjects, there was nevertheless some scatter indicating misidentifications. In contrast, the identification of the vowels of the deaf revealed such a scattered distribution that in all instances except /ɑ/ and /ʌ/ the vowels were misidentified as every other vowel by some of the judges. For the normal-hearing subjects the individual vowels ranged in correct identification from 603 or 98.5% for the vowel /i/ to 294 or 48% for the vowel /æ/. As was mentioned above in the discussion of the position of F_1 and F_2 for the normal-hearing subjects for the vowel /æ/, both of these formants appeared to be

TABLE 2. Identification matrix of vowels of normal-hearing speakers. Total possible identifications equals 612.

Intended Vowel	Perceived Vowel /i/	/ɪ/	/ɛ/	/æ/	/ɑ/	/ɔ/	/ʊ/	/u/	/ʌ/	/ɝ/
/i/	603	3	6							
/ɪ/		572	32	3		1		3	1	
/ɛ/	1	77	497	29	2				1	5
/æ/		43	259	294	9				1	6
/ɑ/			1	14	420	145	1		30	1
/ɔ/				2	174	416			18	2
/ʊ/					2		536	38	22	14
/u/					2	2	24	578	4	2
/ʌ/				1	74	33	26	3	472	3
/ɝ/		2	2					5	5	598
Totals	604	697	797	343	683	597	587	627	554	631

out of line when compared with previous research. Since the formant positions for /æ/ were not in their expected positions, it is not surprising that this vowel was misidentified 52% of the time. The formant positions for /æ/ were close to those of /ɛ/ and indeed, /æ/ was perceived as /ɛ/ 259 times.

For the deaf subjects, the most correctly identified vowel was /u/ at 282 or 46%; while the least correctly identified vowel was /ɝ/ at 129 or 21%. The most highly identified vowel for the deaf had a smaller percentage of correct identification than the least identified vowel for the normal-hearing. The poor intelligibility of /ɝ/ among the deaf subjects appeared to be a function of the positions of F_2 and F_3. These formants were in areas usually associated with front vowels. It is not surprising that /ɝ/ was misidentified as a front vowel 45% of the time.

The order of the vowels of the deaf from the most identified to the least identified was as follows: /u/, /i/, /ɛ/, /ɔ/, /ʊ/, /æ/, /ɪ/, /ɑ/, /ʌ/, and /ɝ/. The order of the vowels for the normal-hearing was as follows: /i/, /ɝ/, /u/, /ɪ/, /ʊ/, /ɛ/, /ʌ/, /ɑ/, /ɔ/, and /æ/. In general, each vowel was most often misidentified as its adjacent vowel, but this was not always the same adjacent vowel for both groups. Regardless of the intended vowel, the judges perceived /ɛ/ more frequently than any other vowel for both the deaf and normal-hearing.

Frequencies of Formants One and Two: A coordinate plot of F_1 and F_2 for all vowel samples of the deaf is presented in Figure 2. The enclosed areas indicate the scatter of F_1 and F_2 for each vowel. It is immediately apparent from this figure that there is considerable overlapping of the vowel areas. In fact, each vowel enclosure overlaps into the area of every other vowel. This graphic portrayal could have been predicted from the information in Table 3. Since the vowels were frequently misidentified, one would expect the F_1/F_2 scatter to be rather extensive, and that many of the points would fall into areas normally associated with other vowels. In contrast, Figure 3, representing the F_1/F_2 scatter

TABLE 3. Identification matrix of vowels of deaf speakers. Total possible identifications equals 612.

Intended Vowel	Perceived Vowel									
	/i/	/ɪ/	/ɛ/	/æ/	/ɑ/	/ɔ/	/ʊ/	/u/	/ʌ/	/ɝ/
/i/	239	161	64	20	3	11	22	32	25	35
/ɪ/	49	183	109	29	9	19	46	26	63	79
/ɛ/	9	37	212	135	36	52	5	9	64	53
/æ/	3	23	129	197	69	44	15	5	76	51
/ɑ/		2	67	121	158	97	11	11	103	42
/ɔ/	7	16	17	79	117	208	26	51	41	50
/ʊ/	20	47	39	11	27	14	205	120	62	67
/u/	11	26	12	11	11	5	165	282	24	65
/ʌ/		23	79	91	110	95	18	7	141	48
/ɝ/	75	64	99	39	16	22	73	59	36	129
Totals	413	582	827	733	556	567	586	602	635	619

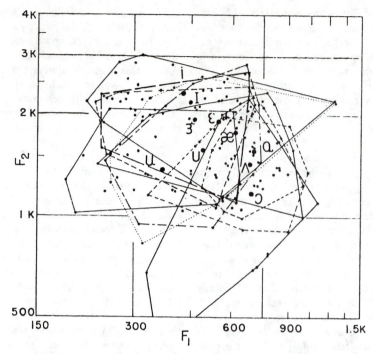

Figure 2. Frequencies (F₁ and F₂) of Formants One and Two for individual vowel samples of deaf subject. Means shown by large dots.

for the normal-hearing shows some overlapping of the vowel areas but not to the extent seen in Figure 2. Some overlapping of adjacent vowel areas was also shown by Peterson and Barney (1952) and Fairbanks *et al.* (1961).

In spite of the extensive overlapping of the vowel areas of the deaf, the means do show a tendency to follow the vowel progression as presented by other investigaors (Fairbanks *et al.*, 1961; Holbrook and Fairbanks, 1962; Peterson and Barney, 1952). The progression of the means of the normal-hearing approximated the expected pattern with the exception of /æ/. This deviation of /æ/ from the usual pattern is yet another indication that the subjects were not producing an ac-

ceptable /æ/ sound. It will be recalled that /æ/ was misidentified as /ɛ/ 259 times. Holbrook and Fairbanks (1962) reported a similar tendency for the vowel /æ/. Their subjects were midwestern young adult males while the subjects of this study were midwestern preadolescent and adolescent males. These data suggest that young midwesterners are not discriminating well in their production of /æ/ and /ɛ/.

A direct comparison of Figures 2 and 3 reveals that the means of both F₁ and F₂ for the deaf occupy a far more limited range of frequencies than do the normal-hearing. On the other hand, the large vowel enclosures of the deaf suggest a high degree of inaccuracy in the placement of the artic-

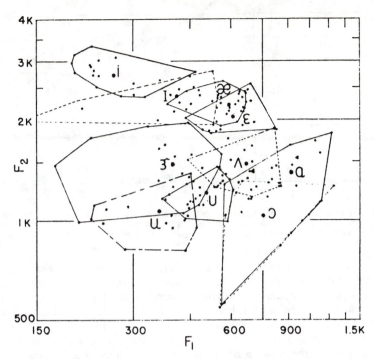

Figure 3. Frequencies (F₁ and F₂) of Formants One and Two for individual vowel samples of normal-hearing subjects. Means shown by large dots.

ulators when producing the vowels. The enclosures for the vowels of the normal-hearing are considerably smaller suggesting far more accuracy in this respect.

In the lower right-hand corner of Figure 3, the extensive overlapping of the /ɑ/ and /ɔ/ areas is also reflected in the identification data seen in Table 2. In this instance /ɑ/ was perceived as /ɔ/ 145 times; while /ɔ/ was perceived as /ɑ/ 174 times.

The enclosed vowel areas in Figures 4 and 5 indicate the scatter of F₁ and F₂ of the vowels spoken by the deaf and normal-hearing subjects that were identified correctly by at least 75% of the judges. For example, vowel /i/ was identified correctly by at least 75% of the judges for only four deaf subjects; therefore, in Figure 4, the enclosed vowel area of /i/ represents the F₁/F₂ coordinate plot of these four subjects. Hereafter, the phrase *identified* vowels will indicate those vowels correctly identified by at least 75% of the judges. Table 4 gives the mean values of Formants One and Two and the number of identified vowels for deaf and normal-hearing subjects. While Figure 4 reflects a considerably reduced number of identified vowels as spoken by the deaf subjects, identified vowels as spoken by the normal-hearing subjects and presented in Figure 5, were only slightly less than the total sample. A

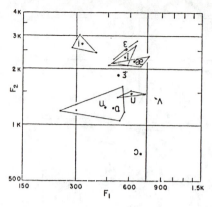

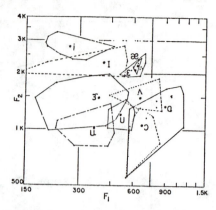

Figure 4. Frequencies (F₁ and F₂) of Formants One and Two for *identified* vowels of deaf subjects. *Identified* vowel means shown by large dots.

Figure 5. Frequencies (F₁ and F₂) of Formants One and Two for *identified* vowels of normal-hearing subjects. *Identified* vowel means shown by large dots.

direct comparison of Figures 4 and 5 reveals that the positions of the vowels for the deaf are considerably different from those of the normal-hearing. Again, with the exception of the vowel /æ/, the progression for the normal-hearing follows the usual pattern. In contrast, the vowels of the deaf reveal an unusual pattern.

The most identified vowel of the deaf was /u/ with a score of five. The least identified vowels of the deaf were /ɑ/, /ɔ/, and /ɝ/, each with a score of one. The least identified vowel for the normal-hearing was /æ/ with a score of five. The most identified vowels of the normal-hearing were /i/, /u/, and /ɝ/, each having a score of 18. This means that these three vowels as produced by all 18 subjects were identified by 75% or more of the judges. Figure 4 presents a paradox in that one would expect the frequency positions of F₁ and F₂ for the identified vowels to fall

TABLE 4. Mean values of Formants One and Two and the N of *identified* vowels for deaf and normal-hearing subjects. Values in cps.

Vowels	Deaf F₁	F₂	N	Normal-hearing F₁	F₂	N
/i/	323	2716	4	262	2776	18
/ɪ/	567	2273	3	410	2303	17
/ɛ/	570	2532	3	614	2106	12
/æ/	640	2168	3	629	2231	5
/ɑ/	485	1225	1	898	1391	11
/ɔ/	700	700	1	674	1057	7
/ʊ/	617	1458	3	507	1216	15
/u/	437	1238	5	363	1061	18
/ʌ/	833	1390	2	657	1481	13
/ɝ/	520	1835	1	396	1459	18

within rather narrow limits and in the usual pattern. It is obvious from an examination of Figure 4 that the positions and patterns of F_1 and F_2 of the identified vowels of the deaf do not satisfy these criteria. A possible explanation may be that the judges received cues from the transitions and/or other formants, which enabled them to make the identifications.

Conclusions

Some of the conclusions which may be drawn from this study are as follows: There are a number of differences between the two groups for the fundamental and Formants One, Two, and Three in both frequency and amplitude. The distortion of the fundamental and formant values was reflected in the relatively poor identification scores of the deaf subjects. The extensive overlapping of the vowel areas of the deaf children of this study indicates that they are missing the acoustical vowel targets. It is reasonable to assume that they are not placing their articulators accurately enough to meet this criterion.

The means of fundamental frequency and amplitude for the deaf covered a wider range than the same measures for the normal-hearing. In contrast, the range of the mean frequencies and amplitudes of the three formants was greater for the normal-hearing than for the deaf. This would suggest that for the statistically average subject at least, the deaf child attempts to achieve vowel differentiation by varying fundamental frequency and amplitude of the voice relatively more than the frequency and amplitude of the formants. In physiological terms, he is achieving vowel differentiation by excessive laryngeal variations with only minimal articulatory variations.

Summary

Ten vowels in an h-d environment were placed in sentences and recorded by 18 deaf and 18 normal-hearing boys, all General American speakers, between the ages of 11 and 14 years. Spectrographic measures of frequency and amplitude of the fundamental and first three formants were taken. Examination of means revealed: (a) the deaf had higher mean fundamental frequencies for all vowels; (b) mean ranges of fundamental frequencies and amplitudes were greater for the deaf; (c) mean ranges of first three formant frequencies and amplitudes were greater for the normal-hearing.

College students judged the h-d words. Overall identifiability of vowels for normal hearing was 81%; for the deaf 32%. Coordinate Formant One/Formant Two frequency plots showed the complete overlapping of vowel areas of the deaf.

It was concluded that the deaf did not have clearly defined articulatory vowel target areas. In effect, vowels were seldom accurately spoken by the deaf.

References

BLACK, J. W., Natural frequency, duration, and intensity of vowels in reading. *J. Speech Hearing Dis.*, 14, 1949, 216-221.

FAIRBANKS, G., and GRUBB, PATTI M., A psychophysical investigation of vowel formants. *J. Speech Hearing Res.*, 4, 1961, 203-220.

HOLBROOK, A., and FAIRBANKS, G., Diphthong formants and their movements. *J. Speech Hearing Res.*, 5, 1962, 38-58.

House, A. S., and Fairbanks, G., The influence of consonant environment upon the secondary acoustical characteristics of vowels. *J. acoust. Soc. Amer.*, 25, 1953, 105-113.

Morley, D. E., An analysis by sound spectrograph of intelligibility variations of consonant sounds spoken by deaf persons. (Ph.D. dissertation, University of Michigan), 1949, 98-111.

Peterson, G. E., and Barney, H. L., Control methods used in a study of the vowels. *J. acoust. Soc. Amer.*, 24, 1952, 175-184.

Potter, R. K., Kopp, G. A., and Green, Harriet C., *Visible Speech*. New York: D. Van Nostrand Company, Inc., 1947.

Potter, R. K., and Steinberg, J. C., Toward the specification of speech. *J. acoust. Soc. Amer.*, 22, 1950, 807-820.

Watson, T. J., The use of residual hearing in the education of deaf children. *Volta Review*, 63, 1961, 385-392.

THE SPEECH SPECTROGRAPHIC DISPLAY: INTERPRETATION OF VISUAL PATTERNS BY HEARING-IMPAIRED ADULTS

JEAN E. MAKI   MARIANNE STREFF GUSTAFSON
JOHN M. CONKLIN   BRENDA K. HUMPHREY-WHITEHEAD
National Technical Institute for the Deaf
Rochester, New York

If visual speech training aids are to be used effectively, it is important to assess whether hearing-impaired speakers can accurately interpret visual patterns and arrive at correct conclusions concerning the accuracy of speech production. In this investigation with the Speech Spectrographic Display (SSD), a pattern interpretation task was given to 10 hearing-impaired adults. Subjects viewed selected SSD patterns from hearing-impaired speakers, evaluated the accuracy of speech production, and identified the SSD visual features that were used in the evaluation. In general, results showed that subjects could use SSD patterns to evaluate speech production. For those pattern interpretation errors that occurred most were related either to phonetic/orthographic confusions or to misconceptions concerning production of speech.

For many hearing-impaired speakers, improper control of respiration, phonation and/or articulation has a negative effect on the intelligibility of speech. Speech production errors of hearing-impaired speakers have been documented by Hudgins and Numbers (1942), Angelloci, Kopp and Holbrook (1964), Nober (1967), Markides (1970), Smith (1975), Monsen (1974, 1976), and others. In an effort to assist hearing-impaired speakers in the correction of these and other speech production errors, many speech training aids have been developed.

One of the most recent developments is the *Speech Spectrographic Display* (Stewart, Larkin & Houde, 1976). This instrument provides visual displays in real-time that reflect the frequency, intensity and temporal characteristics of the acoustic signal. In an effort to define the potential applications of the *Speech Spectrographic Display* (SSD), preliminary research involved visual identification of distinctive display characteristics. Results of this research showed that hearing-impaired subjects can distinguish between the visual patterns of most consonants and vowels produced by a normal-hearing speaker (Maki, 1977).

Hearing-impaired speakers often experience difficulty with several aspects of speech production simultaneously; hence, it is possible that their SSD patterns would be more difficult to evaluate than those obtained from normal-hearing speakers. It is critical therefore, to determine if patterns from hearing-impaired speakers can be interpreted accurately. If hearing-impaired subjects can use the SSD to distinguish correct from incorrect productions, the usefulness of the instrument as a speech training aid would be supported.

Thus, the purpose of this investigation was to determine if hearing-impaired subjects could evaluate the speech production of other hearing-impaired speakers using visual features from the SSD patterns. Specifically, the intent was to investigate whether hearing-impaired subjects could (1) use SSD patterns to identify the better of two productions and (2) specify the correct visual display characteristics which are associated with selected articulatory events.

METHOD

Subjects

The only selection criteria for subjects was that they be hearing-impaired adults who were familiar with interpretation of SSD patterns. Ten subjects completed the display interpretation task. As part of a concurrent investigation, all had received approximately 30 hours of speech therapy which involved use of the SSD. As a result, all had used the instrument and were familiar with display characteristics. Although the subjects had used the SSD in therapy to evaluate their own speech, none had been trained for the specific task of evaluating patterns from other hearing-impaired speakers. The mean age of the group was 20 years, two months and it contained five male and five female subjects. The mean pure tone average was 103.5 dB HTL (ANSI, 1969) and the mean rating of speech intelligibility was 1.8 indicating poor speech production skills (Johnson, 1976).

Test Stimuli

The speech samples were obtained from four severely to profoundly hearing-impaired speakers. Speech and hearing characteristics for each speaker can be found in Appendix A.

The samples, taken from pre- and post-therapy recordings, were selected using the following criteria: (1) the pre-therapy production demonstrated one or more of eight selected articulatory errors which have been documented in past research with hearing-impaired speakers; (2) the corresponding post-therapy production was judged auditorally to be more accurate than the pretherapy production, and (3) the pre/post difference in production was visually discernible on the SSD. With respect to the last criterion, pattern distinctiveness data (Maki, 1977) were used to prevent selection of speech sample pairs which would not be distinctive on the SSD, such as plosives differing in place of production.

Six sets of one and two-word utterances were selected to demonstrate consonant and vowel errors common to hearing-impaired speakers. The specific error types are listed in Appendix B. In order to specify the pre/post changes in the utterances, the taped samples were played to three speech-language pathologists. Each listener was given a list of the intended utterances and asked to phonetically transcribe the productions. Transcriptions are presented in the figures and in Appendix B.

Each speech sample was played from a cassette tape recorder, (Wollensak, Model 2532) into a Speech Spectrographic Display, (Spectraphonics, Model 1) using a trace duration of 1.5 seconds and a 450 Hz bandwidth. Using a 35 mm camera with 55 mm macro close-up lens, each pattern was photographed according to specifications found in Kodak Pamphlet AC-10 (1977). The resultant photographs are shown in Figures 1 through 6. In Figures 2, 4 and 6, note that several non-test sounds were transcribed, but did not appear in the visual displays. With a dynamic range of 30 dB, it is assumed that the lower-intensity /h/, /p/, /θ/ and /s/ were outside the range of the instrument. Although the intensity of /s/ is high for normal-hearing speakers, the /s/ productions of this hearing-impaired speaker were apparently too low for detection by the instrument.

Test Procedures

During individual testing, subjects were shown the photographs of each set of pre/post SSD patterns in randomized order. The subjects were told the intended utterance and asked to choose the "better" production of selected articulatory targets, e.g., "Which is the better /t/?" They were then asked to give reasons for their choice. In all questioning, subjects were encouraged to report any observations about the displays and interpret them relative to speech production. During each test session, the experimenter asked the questions and noted subject responses. For all test sessions, the speech pathologist currently working with each student was present to insure that responses were accurately understood by the investigator. Subject responses were tallied to determine the percentage of correct identifications of the "better" productions and the percentage of observations which reflected accurate understanding of the display characteristics as they relate to speech production.

RESULTS

Subjects achieved an average score of 90% correct in identifying which SSD patterns contained the better productions. To support their decisions, subjects reported a total of 118 visual characteristics which they used in distinguishing the improved productions. An analysis of the 118 observations showed that 88.1% were the correct visual features for identifying improved speech production. Subject responses, presented below, are organized according to speech error type. To assist in identifying the visual features on the displays, the approximate locations are provided using the time scale in each figure. These values appear in parentheses after each visual feature along with the number of subjects who made that observation. It should be noted that although eight error types were tested directly, subjects spontaneously identified three additional errors resulting in a total of 11 speech error types.

Consonant omission. Figure 1 shows the SSD patterns from the pre (a) and post-therapy (b) productions of "tease her" spoken by Speaker CF. For accurate production of /z/, 6 subjects chose Figure 1b as correct, indicating the presence of "air" (600-825 msec, 5 subjects) and voicing (600-650 msec, 4 subjects) as reasons for their choice. Figure 1a was chosen as correct by 4 subjects who identified /z/ as the dark area between the first and second formants (200-350 msec).

Consonant substitution/voicing error. In Figure 1, 9 subjects identified 1b as having the correct /t/ in the production "tease her". Observations in support of that decision included the plosive release (25 msec, 7 subjects) and no voicing (6 subjects). One subject chose Figure 1a as correct stating that it had a /t/ whereas Figure 1b did not.

Consonant substitution/manner of production error. Figure 2 shows productions of "hammer" spoken by Speaker PM at the beginning (a) and end (b) of therapy. All subjects identified 2b as correct, reasoning that /m/ is "joined" in Figure 2b (500-900 msec), but stops in Figure 2a (700 msec, 9 subjects). One subject stated that "two m's is longer" and, therefore, Figure 2b is correct.

Consonant substitution/combined voicing and manner errors. Figures 3a and b show pre and posttherapy productions of "I see" spoken by Speaker DK. For the /s/ production, 9 subjects identified 3b as correct, selecting the presence of "air" (425-675 msec, 8 subjects) and no voicing (425-675 msec, 4 subjects) as reasons for their choice. One subject simply noted that there was no /s/ in Figure 3a. Another subject chose Figure 3a as correct stating that the sound in 3b was /ʃ/.

Vowel centralization. Figure 3 also illustrates a change in vowel production for /i/. All subjects identified Figure 3b as having the better /i/ production since there was greater separation between the first and second formants (680-1500 msec, 10 subjects) and the second and third formants came closer together (2 subjects).

Vowel diphthongization. With respect to Figure 3, 5 subjects also commented that although better than Figure 3a, the /i/ production in Figure 3b still was not good enough because of the slow separation of the first two formants (4 subjects) and because the separation was not great enough (1 subject). Since diphthongization was not

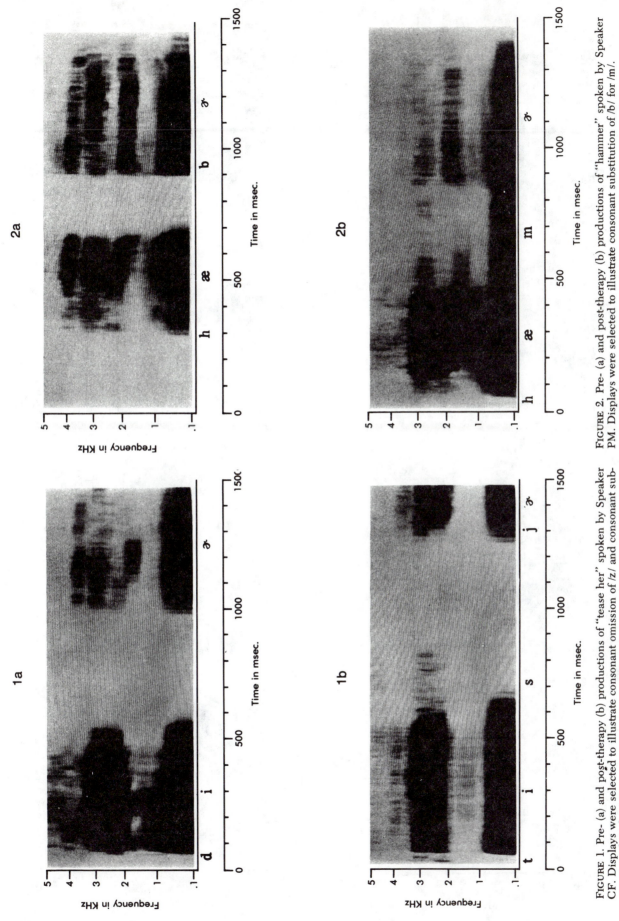

FIGURE 1. Pre- (a) and post-therapy (b) productions of "tease her" spoken by Speaker CF. Displays were selected to illustrate consonant omission of /z/ and consonant substitution of /d/ for /t/.

FIGURE 2. Pre- (a) and post-therapy (b) productions of "hammer" spoken by Speaker PM. Displays were selected to illustrate consonant substitution of /b/ for /m/.

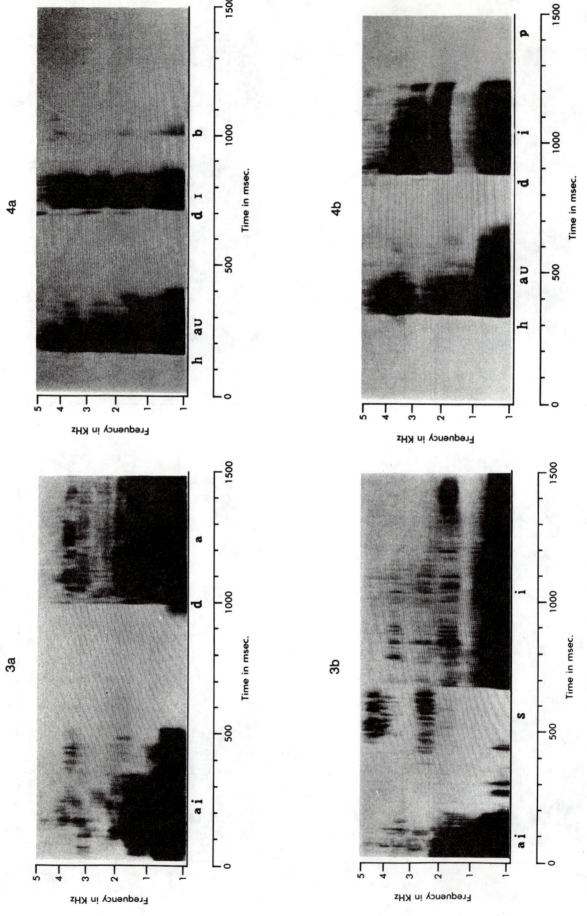

FIGURE 3. Pre- (a) and post-therapy (b) productions of "I see" spoken by Speaker DK. Displays were selected to illustrate consonant substitution of /d/ and /s/ and vowel centralization.

FIGURE 4. Pre- (a) and post-therapy (b) productions of "how deep" spoken by Speaker JL. Displays were selected to illustrate vowel substitution of /ɪ/ for /i/.

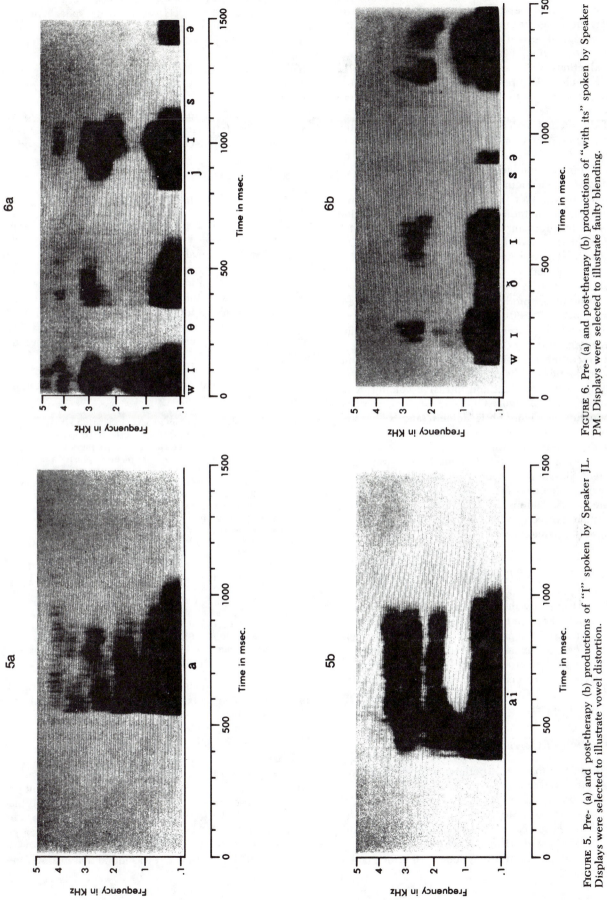

FIGURE 5. Pre- (a) and post-therapy (b) productions of "I" spoken by Speaker JL. Displays were selected to illustrate vowel distortion.

FIGURE 6. Pre- (a) and post-therapy (b) productions of "with its" spoken by Speaker PM. Displays were selected to illustrate faulty blending.

questioned directly in this test set, these responses were not calculated in the percent correct identification score; however, the observations were included in calculating the percentage of correct observations.

Vowel substitution. Figures 4a and b show the pre/post productions of "how deep" spoken by Speaker JL. All subjects chose Figure 4b as the correct production of /i/. Reasons given included separation of the first and second formants (880-1250 msec, 9 subjects), the closeness of the second and third formants (5 subjects), the relatively longer duration of the vowel in Figure 4b (2 subjects), and the fact that the third formant could not be seen in Figure 4a (1 subject).

Vowel distortion. Figure 5a and b show productions of "I" spoken by Speaker JL. Nine subjects chose Figure 5b as correct, basing their decision on clearer separation of the first two formants (525-1000 msec, 9 subjects), separation of the second and third formants (600-1000 msec, 3 subjects), and longer duration of the vowel in Figure 5b (1 subject).

Duration. In Figure 5b, 3 subjects spontaneously indicated that although production of /ai/ was better, there was "too much /i/" (650-1000 msec) for a good /ai/ production. These responses were included in calculating the percentage of correct responses.

Faulty blending and intrusive voicing. Figures 6a and b show productions of "with its" spoken by Speaker PM, illustrating faulty blending and intrusive voicing. Nine of the subjects chose Figure 6b as correct, reasoning that the production in Figure 6b is "joined" and is "cut up" in Figure 6a. One subject chose Figure 6a as correct, making the observation that the words were separate, but then stating that the words should be separate and not joined. Six subjects spontaneously inquired about the intrusive voicing occurring between "with" and "its" in Figure 6a (350-600 msec). Since intrusive voicing was not questioned directly, this was not included in the calculation of the percent correct identification score.

DISCUSSION

Results of this study showed that subjects were able to use visual patterns from the SSD to evaluate a variety of articulatory errors. In completing this task, subjects identified the specific visual features which they used to evaluate the speech productions. Results of this study are discussed with respect to error types, the associated visual features, and correct versus incorrect interpretation of those features.

Identification of Correct Productions

With respect to the first experimental question of this study, it was found that subjects identified the better of two productions with 90% accuracy. Subjects used SSD patterns to evaluate a variety of error types common to hearing-impaired speakers. These included: sound omission; consonant substitution; vowel substitution, diphthongization, and distortion; durational errors; faulty

blending; and intrusive voicing. Thus, it is evident that hearing-impaired subjects can evaluate speech production accuracy for a variety of articulatory targets using only information provided by the SSD patterns. This is remarkable since even the "better" productions did not have the clearly defined visual characteristics of speech patterns produced by normal-hearing speakers. Apparently, those visual features critical for accurate evaluation of speech production were distinguishable to the subjects. The following section summarizes those visual features which subjects used to evaluate speech production.

Visual Display Characteristics

As subjects in this study identified the 11 error types, they made a total of 118 observations concerning the visual display. An analysis of these observations resulted in a list of 9 basic types of visual information which subjects used in evaluating the speech samples. In general, the types of visual information was based on frequency and temporal characteristics of the speech samples. Of the observations which subjects made, recall that 88.1% were correct interpretations relative to speech production.

Correct interpretations. The following visual characteristics were identified and used correctly in judging accuracy of production:

1. high frequency random energy, indicating either frication (Figures 1 & 3) or plosive release (Figure 1);
2. appropriately timed onset of low frequency periodic energy, indicating voiced or voiceless plosive production (Figure 1);
3. presence or absence of continuous low frequency energy, indicating nasal or voiced plosive production, respectively (Figure 2);
4. relative position of first and second formants, indicating correct vowel production (Figures 3 & 4);
5. relative position of second and third formants, indicating correct vowel production (Figures 3 & 4);
6. change in formant position over time, indicating vowel diphthongization or diphthong production (Figures 3 & 5);
7. distance between onset and offset of acoustic features, indicating duration (Figures 4 & 5);
8. appropriate continuation of acoustic energy, indicating blending (Figure 6); and
9. inappropriate low frequency periodic energy, indicating intrusive voicing (Figure 6).

Given the general nature of the visual characteristics previously listed, it is expected that subjects would be able to use the SSD in obtaining feedback concerning errors other than those tested in this investigation, provided they were similar error types. For example, since SSD patterns distinguished /m/ and /b/, they would also be effective in distinguishing /n/ and /d/ as well as /ŋ/ and /g/. In another speech sample, change in formant position was used to evaluate /ai/. Thus, it is expected that the SSD could be used to evaluate other diphthongs as well.

Although the SSD could be used to distinguish a variety of articulatory patterns, it was found that misinterpretations of visual information do occur. This is particularly true if individual subjects have misconceptions similar to those discussed below.

Incorrect Interpretations. Errors which subjects made while interpreting the displays were one of three types. First, subjects did not understand how the orthographic/fingerspelled representation of English related to the acoustic representation displayed in the SSD patterns. Second, subjects had misconceptions about the segmental and transitional aspects of speech production. Third, subjects made errors that were simply incorrect interpretations of the visual information.

Errors related to orthographic versus acoustic representations of English were found when subjects evaluated Figures 1a, 2b and 5b. For the word "tease" in Figure 1a, 4 subjects incorrectly identified the /z/ as occurring between 200 and 350 msec on the display. Upon further questioning, subjects proceeded to identify the next segment (350-575 msec) as the "second 'e'" at the end of the word. The additional noise in the spectrum, appearing between the first and second formants, apparently caused confusion and presented a difficult segmentation problem. If subjects applied the appropriate pronunciation rule, they would have known that the final "e" had no acoustic representation and this interpretation error should not have occurred. Another error of this type can be found in Figure 2b for the word "hammer". One subject identified Figure 2b as correct, reasoning that "two m's is longer". It appears that he was relating the orthographic "mm" and the acoustic /m/ inappropriately, i.e., suggesting that duration of production was related to the number of times a letter appeared in the written word. The third error of this type occurred for Figure 5b for the production of /ai/. For this pattern, three subjects stated that Figure 5b was correct because there was a separation between formants 2 and 3. Although a correct observation, this visual characteristic is not related to production of /ai/. It is, however, an appropriate visual feature for production of /ɪ/. It is speculated that subjects made this error because the orthographic "I" represents both sounds, and subjects were not clear on the acoustic differences.

The second error type related to subjects' misconceptions concerning segmental and transitional aspects of speech production. There were two errors of this type which are related to Figures 5 and 6. For the production of /ai/ in Figure 5b, two subjects relied on overall vowel duration as a cue to accuracy of production. In making this error, subjects demonstrated that they did not have an accurate understanding of vowel dynamics. Specifically, they were not aware that although internal timing of diphthongs is critical, the overall vowel duration can vary without changing perception of the vowel. The second error occurred for the production of "with its" in Figure 6. When evaluating this pair, one subject stated that words should not be joined as in Figure 6b. Thus, her perception concerning speech production was that words were isolated productions, produced without blending.

There were three miscellaneous errors which appeared to be solely inaccurate interpretations of the display. The first of these occurred for the production of /t/ in Figure 1. One subject identified Figure 1a as having the correct /t/ and assigned no significance to the visual characteristics of /t/ found in Figure 1b. The second error occurred for the production of /s/ in Figure 3. One subject identified the fricative production in Figure 3b as /ʃ/, thus concluding that Figure 3a must contain the correct production. The third error occurred for production of /i/ in Figure 4a. One subject stated that he could not see the third formant. This observation was considered inappropriate for distinguishing the better production of this set.

It is interesting to note that most interpretation errors were related to other misconceptions concerning either pronunciation or the dynamics of speech production. Since misconceptions could lead to development of incorrect speech production patterns, it is important that they be identified and corrected. Use of a procedure similar to the one used in this study might facilitate the identification, and subsequent correction, of false concepts concerning speech production.

Clinical Implications

This study provides basic information concerning display interpretation skills of hearing-impaired adults, plus an overview of the types of articulatory errors which present distinctive contrasts on the SSD. There are several conclusions which can be drawn from this study relative to clinical application of the SSD with hearing-impaired adults.

In general, hearing-impaired subjects were able to interpret the SSD patterns in order to evaluate speech production accuracy. This was true for many types of articulatory errors. With respect to clinical application, these results suggest that the SSD could be used as a source of feedback when correcting many of the speech production errors common to hearing-impaired speakers.

Since subjects could interpret the patterns accurately, it is clear that there would be little need to depend on verbal feedback from the instructor. This is considered an advantage since subjects can evaluate directly the results of articulatory changes, attempting to associate those changes with internal feedback. Thus, the student is actively involved in self-evaluation using external feedback when evaluation of speech using internal feedback, i.e., auditory, kinesthetic and tactile, may not be possible. Since pattern interpretation errors did occur, it is possible for subjects to receive inaccurate information from the display which has the potential of reinforcing incorrect productions. Therefore, it is concluded that total reliance cannot be placed on the instrument.

The results of this study indicate that the SSD can be used by hearing-impaired adults to evaluate speech production accurately. Applied in the clinical setting, this capability could assist the student in understanding the task, and would allow him to take an active role in evaluating his own speech. Since pattern interpretation errors do occur, it is necessary that the instructor provide feedback, when needed, to evaluate complex patterns or correct misconceptions which cause interpretation errors. It is believed that combining the instructor's feedback with the Speech Spectrographic Display, would provide hearing-impaired adults with the optimal condition for developing and/or refining speech production skills.

ACKNOWLEDGMENT

This work was conducted in the course of an agreement with the Department of Health, Education and Welfare.

REFERENCES

AMERICAN NATIONAL STANDARDS INSTITUTE Specifications for audiometers ANSI S3.6-1969. New York: American National Standards Institute, 1970.

ANGELLOCCI, A., KOPP, G., & HOLBROOK, A. The vowel formants of deaf and normal-hearing eleven to fourteen-year-old boys. *Journal of Speech and Hearing Disorders*, 1964, *29*, 156-170.

HUDGINS, C., & NUMBERS, F. An investigation of the intelligibility of the speech of the deaf. *Genetic Psychology Monographs*, 1942, *25*, 189-392.

JOHNSON, D. Communication characteristics of a young deaf adult population: Techniques for evaluating their communication skills. *American Annals of the Deaf*, 1976, *121*, 409-423.

KODAK PUBLICATION AC-10, Photographing Television Images, Rochester, New York, 1977.

MAKI, J. Visual discrimination and identification of spectrographic patterns by hearing-impaired adults. Paper presented to the American Speech and Hearing Association, Chicago, 1977.

MARKIDES, A. The speech of deaf and partially-hearing children with special reference to factors affecting intelligibility. *British Journal of Disorders of Communication*, 1970, *5*, 126-140.

MONSEN, R. Durational aspects of vowel production in the speech of deaf children. *Journal of Speech and Hearing Research*, 1974, *17*, 386-398.

MONSEN, R. Second formant transitions of selected consonant-vowel combinations in the speech of deaf and normal-hearing children. *Journal of Speech and Hearing Research*, 1976, *19*, 279-289.

NOBER, E. Articulation of the deaf. *Exceptional Children*, 1967, *33*, 611-621.

SMITH, C. Residual hearing and speech production in children. *Journal of Speech and Hearing Research*, 1975, *18*, 795-811.

STEWART, L., LARKIN, W., & HOUDE, R. A real-time sound spectrograph with implications for speech training for the deaf. Paper presented to the IEEE International Conference on Acoustics, Speech and Signal Processing, Philadelphia, 1976.

Received October 1, 1979
Accepted October 23, 1980

Requests for reprints should be addressed to Jean E. Maki, Speech and Hearing Clinic, Andrews University, Berrien Springs, Michigan 49104.

APPENDIX A

Age, sex, hearing loss and percent articulation error for speakers who supplied the pre- and posttherapy speech samples used to obtain visual patterns shown in Figures 1 - 6.

Figures	Speaker	Age (yrs-mos)	Sex	Hearing Loss[1]		Percent Articulation Error[2]
				Right	Left	
1	CF	21-9	F	112	113	41.0
2 & 6	PM	25-2	F	92	88	51.0
3	DK	20-9	M	103	102	70.0
4 & 5	JL	21-0	M	105	100	81.0

[1] 3-frequency pure tone average at 500, 1000 and 2000 Hz.
[2] Total percent articulation error as obtained on the *Fisher-Logemann Test of Articulation*.

APPENDIX B

Information for each figure includes the intended utterance, pre- and posttherapy transcriptions from three auditors, speech error types illustrated in each figure, and the visual characteristics related to accurate production of the intended targets.

Utterance	Phonetic Transcriptions		Speech Error Types and Related SSD Visual Characteristics Indicating Correct Production*
Figure 1	PRE:	A. /di jɚ/	1. Consonant omission: -/z
		B. /di ɚ/	/z/ - high frequency random energy; low frequency periodic energy and/or appropriate duration relative to preceding vowel
"tease her"		C. /di ɚ/	
	POST:	A. /tis jɚ/	2. Consonant substitution/voicing: d/t
		B. /tis jɚ/	/t/ - delay in low frequency periodic energy after plosive burst
		C. /diz jɚ/	
Figure 2	PRE:	A. /hæ-bɚ/	3. Consonant substitution/manner: b/m
		B. /hæ-b _/	/m/ - low frequency periodic energy continuous with adjacent sounds; no visual features to indicate cessation of voicing associated with plosive production
"hammer"		C. /hæm-bɛ/	
	POST:	A. /hæ-mɚ/	
		B. /hæ-mɚ/	
		C. /hæ-mɚ/	
Figure 3	PRE:	A. /ai d₊u-ɚ/	4. Consonant substitution/manner and voicing: d/s
		B. /ai da/	/s/ - high frequency random energy with no low frequency energy
"I see"		C. /ai da/	5. Vowel centralization: a/i
	POST:	A. /ai si/	/i/ - separation between low frequency periodic energy (voicing and first formant) and mid-high frequency energy band (second formant)
		B. /a si/	6. Vowel diphthongization
		C. /ai si/	non-diphthongized /i/ - rapid formant shift from preceding phonetic segment to target vowel
Figure 4	PRE:	A. /hau dIp-I/	7. Vowel substitution: I/i
		B. /hau dIb-ə/	/i/ - separation between first and second formants; minimal separation between second and third formants.
"how deep"		C. /hau dIb/	
	POST:	A. /hau dip/	
		B. /hau dip/	
		C. /hau dip/	
Figure 5	PRE:	A. /a/	8. Vowel distortion: a/ai
		B. /ha/	/ai/ - downward frequency shift for first formant with concurrent upward shift of second formant; duration of /a/ is longer than /i/ with smooth transition between components of the diphthong
"I"		C. /a/	
	POST:	A. /ai/	9. Duration - length of second component, /i/, is incorrect for production of the diphthong
		B. /ai/	
		C. /hai/	
Figure 6	PRE:	A. /wɪð-I jɪts-ə/	10. Faulty blending
		B. /wɪθ-ə ɪs-ə/	For correct production - continuous energy between phonetic segments where appropriate
"with its"		C. /wɪθ-ə jɪθ-ə/	11. Intrusive voicing
	POST:	A. /wɪð ɪts-ə/	For correct production - absence of extraneous low frequency energy between sounds
		B. /wɪð ɪs-ə/	
		C. /wɪθz#/	

*This list should not be considered all-inclusive. It is expected that individual speakers will require additional or different cues depending on error type, phonetic context, etc.

SIGNIFICANCE OF HARMONIC CHANGES AND NOISE COMPONENTS IN HOARSENESS

NAOAKI YANAGIHARA

The Institute of Laryngology and Voice Disorders, Los Angeles, California

Acoustic Analysis and synthesis of hoarseness by sound spectrography suggests that the acoustic properties of hoarseness are mainly determined by the interactions of the following three factors: 1) noise components in the main formant of each vowel, 2) high frequency noise components above 3000 Hz, and 3) the loss of high frequency harmonic components. These three findings are more pronounced in the vowels /ɑ/, /ɛ/, and /i/ than in /u/ and /ɔ/. With the progression of the severity of hoarseness, these three abnormal patterns become more prominent and exaggerated. On the basis of these findings, a classification of four types of hoarseness was presented using sonagram tracings.

Hoarseness, the cardinal symptom of laryngeal diseases, is often a sign of extralaryngeal involvement as well. Considerable emphasis has been placed on this symptom (Jackson and Jackson, 1937; Frank, 1940; von Leden, 1958; Palmer, 1959) and several approaches, including acoustic, cinematographic, aerodynamic, and electrophysiologic have been utilized to explore the mechanism and pathologic physiology of hoarse voice production. However, the evaluation of hoarseness—the estimation of the degree and quality of hoarseness—has been made chiefly on the basis of the clinician's subjective perception. This practice has led to the creation of confusing terms to describe similar changes of vocal quality. Among the terms are included: *harsh, husky, breathy, rough, rasping,* and *strident.* Their exact definition, however, has been a matter of debate and discussion. Little is known about the acoustical properties of these variations of pathologic voices and the related dysfunction of the larynx.

In this report the changes of harmonic components (changes in overtone structure) and the additional noise components in hoarse voices are discussed on the basis of two experimental studies—sound spectrographic analysis and synthesis of hoarseness.

ANALYSIS OF HOARSENESS

Method

The hoarse voice samples were recorded on magnetic tape using a dynamic microphone (FP-1, Sony). The voice was recorded at a distance of 20 cm from the microphone.

Five vowels /u, ɔ, ɑ, ɛ, i/ were selected. The subject was instructed to phonate the five vowels: (1) gliding from /u/ to /i/ and (2) sustaining each vowel for several seconds. These utterances were carried out in the most comfortable manner with no restriction imposed on pitch or loudness.

The recordings of the entire series of vowels produced by 167 patients with hoarseness were subjected to perceptual evaluation of the degree of hoarseness. The judges were three otolaryngologists with ample clinical experience. They rated each subject as having a slight, moderate, or severe degree of hoarseness.

From the total number of 167 cases, 10 with each degree of hoarseness—slight, moderate, and severe—were selected with the following two precautions: (1) In each case, all three judges agreed on the degree of hoarseness, (2) Sex and age distribution were as similar as possible among the three groups. The selected cases included 16 male and 14 female subjects ranging in age from 18 to 60 years. Sonagrams of the entire series of vowels were made under constant conditions using a narrow band filter (45 Hz). Sections were taken at the approximate midpoint of the vowels /u/, /ɑ/, and /ɛ/. The fundamental frequency of voice was measured at these points. The average value of the fundamental frequencies of these three vowels was taken to be the fundamental frequency of comfortable phonation.

Results

Figure 1 illustrates the sonagrams of the sustained vowels /u/, /ɑ/, and /ɛ/ phonated by a normal female subject at a fundamental frequency of 250 Hz. Compared with these normal patterns, the sonagrams of the vowels /u/, /ɑ/, and /ɛ/ phonated by a very hoarse female patient at fundamental frequency of 210 Hz (Figure 2) indicate three distinctive features: (1) There is strong

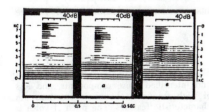

FIGURE 1. Sonagrams and sections of a normal female voice. The pitch of the voice is approximately 250 Hz (C¹).

noise energy above 5000 Hz in the vowels /ɑ/ and /ɛ/, (2) The harmonic structures between 1000 Hz and 3000 Hz in /ɑ/ (2nd and 3rd formants) and between 2000 Hz and 3000 Hz in /ɛ/ (2nd and 3rd formants) are almost completely replaced by noise components, and (3) In the pattern of the vowel /u/, there is scarcely any structural change in the harmonic components and no remarkable noise component.

Throughout the observation of these 30 cases, the noise components represent pertinent findings of hoarseness. The range and energy of the noise com-

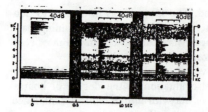

FIGURE 2. Sonagrams and sections of hoarse voice of a female patient with hyperplastic laryngitis. The pitch of voice is around 210 Hz (a). The additional noise components, and change of harmonic components are clearly shown. Note that these factors differ from vowel to vowel.

ponents vary with the perceptual degree of hoarseness, and they are more evident in the vowels /ɑ/, /ɛ/, and /i/ than in the vowels /u/ and /ɔ/.

In slight hoarseness the noise components are limited to the main formant ranges in these five vowels, especially to the second and third formants, and there is no remarkable noise component in the high frequency range. Figure 3 illustrates these findings by a representative sonagram. With the progression

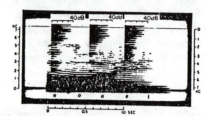

FIGURE 3. Sonagram and sections of slight hoarseness in a female patient. Noise components are limited within main formants of vowels. The pitch of voice is approximately 210 Hz (a). Clinical diagnosis is acute laryngitis, and acoustic diagnosis is hoarseness Type I.

of hoarseness, the energy of the noise components in the formant ranges (mainly 2nd and 3rd formants) are intensified and predominate over the harmonic components. Simultaneously, noise components in the high frequency range increase in energy and expand in range. Finally, the harmonic structure in the formant ranges (mainly 2nd and 3rd formants) are completely replaced by the noise components. These findings are clearly demonstrated in the sonagram of severe hoarseness (Figure 4).

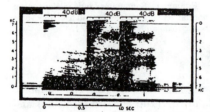

FIGURE 4. Sonagram and sections of severe hoarseness in a female patient. Expanded and intensified noise components, and loss of high frequency harmonic structure are characteristic features. The pitch of voice is approximately 210 Hz (a). Clinical diagnosis is cordal cancer, and acoustic diagnosis is hoarseness Type IV.

The following classification of hoarseness is suggested:

Type I: The regular harmonic components are mixed with the noise component chiefly in the formant region of the vowels.

Type II: The noise components in the second formants of /ɛ/ and /i/ predominate over the harmonic components, and slight additional noise components appear in the high frequency region above 3000 Hz in the vowels /ε/ and /i/.

Type III: The second formants of /ε/ and /i/ are totally replaced by noise components, and the additional noise components above 3000 Hz further intensify their energy and expand their range.

Type IV: The second formants of /ɑ/, /ε/, and /i/ are replaced by noise components, and even the first formants of all vowels often lose their periodic components which are supplemented by noise components. In addition, more intensified high frequency additional noise components are seen.

Table 1 summarizes the perceptual degree of hoarseness, the sound spectrographic type, and the age, sex, fundamental frequency, and clinical diagnosis of each subject. The correlation coefficient between the spectrographic type and judge-perceived degree of hoarseness was found to be 0.65 at the 0.01 significance level.

TABLE 1. Acoustic classification of hoarseness on the basis of four spectrographic types, related to perceived hoarseness, age, sex, fundamental frequency and clinical diagnosis of 30 patients. (M = Male, F = Female, FF = Fundamental Frequency, * = FF not determined.)

No.	Spectrographic Type	Perceptual Degree	Age	Sex	F. F. in Hz	Clinical Diagnosis
1		Slight	18	F	214	Acute Laryngitis
2		Slight	55	M	143	Chronic Laryngitis
3	Type I	Slight	34	F	214	Acute Laryngitis
4		Slight	23	F	286	Acute Laryngitis
5		Slight	54	M	150	Papilloma of Larynx
6		Slight	46	M	143	Vocal Nodules
7		Slight	37	F	286	Paralysis of Vocal Cord
8		Slight	60	M	164	Vocal Cord Cancer
9		Slight	49	F	178	Chronic Laryngitis
10		Slight	29	M	143	Vocal Nodules
11		Moderate	31	F	178	Chronic Laryngitis
12	Type II	Moderate	36	M	143	Chronic Laryngitis
13		Moderate	49	M	128	Chronic Laryngitis
14		Moderate	37	F	286	Paralysis of Vocal Cord
15		Moderate	39	M	150	Paralysis of Vocalis Muscle
16		Moderate	63	F	200	Vocal Cord Cancer
17		Moderate	39	M	107	Hyperplastic Laryngitis
18		Moderate	31	F	214	Hyperplastic Laryngitis
19		Moderate	64	M	143	Vocal Cord Cancer
20		Moderate	36	M	118	Paralysis of Vocal Cord
21	Type III	Severe	34	F	286	Vocal Nodules
22		Severe	51	M	143	Hyperplastic Laryngitis
23		Severe	37	F	214	Paralysis of Vocal Cord
24		Severe	40	F	178	Vocal Cord Polyp
25		Severe	48	F	214	Vocal Cord Cancer
26		Severe	40	M	143	Paralysis of Vocal Cord
27	Type IV	Severe	62	M	*	Vocal Cord Cancer
28		Severe	59	M	*	Atrophic Laryngitis
29		Severe	55	M	107	Paralysis of Vocal Cord
30		Severe	45	F	143	Hyperplastic Laryngitis

These results suggest: (1) the noise components and changes of harmonic structures are significant factors related to the perceptual degree of hoarseness, and (2) there is a positive correlation between the perceptual degree of hoarseness and the hoarseness type defined by the sound spectrogram. The schematic presentation of the sound spectrographic classification of hoarseness is shown in Figure 5.

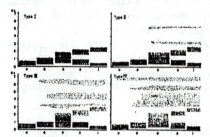

FIGURE 5. Schematic presentation of sonagrams of four degrees of hoarseness. Step by step increment of noise components and loss of high frequency harmonic components are shown. These findings are more evident in vowels /ɑ/, /ɛ/, and /i/ than /u/ and /ɔ/.

Qualitative analysis of the sound spectrograms of hoarseness revealed that the vowels /u/, /ɑ/, and /ɛ/ or /i/ provided most of the essential information regarding the classification of hoarseness. For this reason, more detailed analysis was made on the sections of vowels /u/, /ɑ/, and /ɛ/ in order to know the extent of variation in the range of noise components among each type of hoarseness.

Table 2 gives the ranges of noise components derived from the measurements of the sections of these three representative vowels. The lower and upper frequencies of each range were determined from the section pattern of each vowel. Then the average frequencies at the lower and upper limit of each range were computed. These ranges show considerable intersubject and sex-linked variabilities. These variabilities in frequency are estimated at less than ± 200 Hz in the first three formant ranges and less than ± 400 Hz in the high frequency noise ranges.

SYNTHESIS OF HOARSENESS

Method

The significance of additional noise components and changes in the harmonic structure revealed by the sound spectrographic analysis was supplemented by a synthetic study. An outline of the method is illustrated in Figure 6. The synthesized hoarseness was prepared from a normal male voice and band-pass filtered noise, recorded at constant intensity level. As shown by Figure 6, a tape recorder (A) was used for the reproduction of the normal vowels /u/, /ɑ/, and /ɛ/, and a similar tape recorder (B) for the reproduction of the full band noise. Filtered noise and nonfiltered or low pass filtered vowels were recorded on each channel of the endless loop tape and reproduced by a two-

TABLE 2. Common ranges of noise components and their relation to the first three formants.

Type I

	F₁	F₂	F₃	High Frequency Noise
u	200 ←————————→ 700 Hz			
a	300 ←————————→ 1700			
ε	200 ↔ 700	1600 ←————————→ 2600		

Type II

	F₁	F₂	F₃	High Frequency Noise
u	200 ←————————→ 800 Hz			
a	300 ←————————→ 1500	2800 ↔ 3700		
ε	200 ↔ 600	1800 ←————————→ 2800		3100 ↔ 4100 5700 ↔ 6300

Type III

	F₁	F₂	F₃	High Frequency Noise
u	200 ←————————→ 900 Hz			
a	400 ←————————→ 1600	2400 ↔ 3500		4400 ↔ 4800 5500 ←——→
ε	200 ↔ 900	2000 ←————————→ 3000		3500 ↔ 4300 5200 ←——→

Type IV

	F₁	F₂	F₃	High Frequency Noise
u	200 ←————————→ 1200 Hz			
a	400 ←————————→ 1600	2000 ↔ 3600		3900 ↔ 4600 5600 ←——→
ε	200 ↔ 900	1400 ←————————→ 3000		3200 ↔ 4400 5100 ←——→

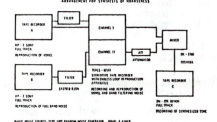

FIGURE 6. Schematic diagram showing the method of synthesis of hoarseness.

TABLE 3. Agreement among judges measured by reliability coefficient.

Judge	2	3	4	5	6
No. 1	0.81	0.82	0.84	0.79	0.86
2		0.81	0.63	0.45	0.73
3			0.73	0.94	0.84
4				0.93	0.79
5					0.53

Average interjudge agreement = 0.77

channel tape recorder. The output of each channel of this tape recorder was fed to another tape recorder (C) through the mixer. Before mixing, the intensity level of band-filtered noise was attenuated to a predetermined value

TABLE 4. The significance of noise components in the formant ranges is shown by synthesis of hoarseness. Relative intensity of each constituent of synthetized tone: Vowel /ɑ/ 0 dB; 600-1700 Hz band noise: —10 dB; 2400-3400 Hz band noise: —25 dB. Vowel /ɛ/ 0 dB; 300-600 Hz band noise: —25 dB; 1700-2400 Hz band noise: —25 dB. Vowel /u/ 0 dB; 212-1200 Hz band noise: —15 dB.

No.	Structure of Test Tone	Rating
1	Vowel e	0.2
2	Vowel e +300-600 Hz B.N.	1.1
3	Vowel e +300-600 Hz B.N. +1700-2400 B.N.	2.2
4	Vowel a	0.3
5	Vowel a +600-1700 Hz B.N.	1.8
6	Vowel a +600-1700 Hz B.N. +2400-3400 Hz B.N.	3.8
7	Vowel u	0
8	Vowel u +212-1200 Hz B.N.	2.0

that caused listeners to perceive hoarseness in the mixed tone. Thus the relative intensity levels of each vowel and the corresponding band noise were kept constant at the final stage of the synthesis; they are shown in Tables 4, 5, and 6.

TABLE 5. Significance of the energy loss of high-frequency harmonic components. Low-pass filtering of each vowel is abbreviated as L.P. and intensity of L.P. vowel is kept at 0 dB. The relative intensity of band-pass noise is constant throughout the experiment.

No.	Structure of Test Tone	Rating
1	Vowel e +300-600 Hz B.N. +1700-2400 Hz B.N.	2.2
2	2400 Hz L.P. e +300-600 Hz B.N. +1700-2400 Hz B.N.	2.8
3	2400 Hz L.P. e +300-600 Hz B.N. +1700-3400 Hz B.N.	2.5
4	1700 Hz L.P. e +300-600 Hz B.N. +1700-2400 Hz B.N.	3.2
5	1700 Hz L.P. e +300-600 Hz B.N. +1700-3400 Hz B.N.	3.5
6	Vowel a +600-1700 Hz B.N.	1.8
7	1200 Hz L.P. a +600-1700 Hz B.N.	4.1
8	1200 Hz L.P. a +600-1700 Hz B.N. +2400-3400 Hz B.N.	4.5
9	Vowel u +212-1200 Hz B.N.	2.0
10	1200 Hz L.P. u +212-1200 Hz B.N.	3.0

The quality and degree of hoarseness of synthetic sounds—vowel—band noise mixtures—were judged by several listeners in a sound proof room. For this purpose, the tape was cut into short segments, four sec in duration of sound,

TABLE 6. Significance of expansion of high frequency additional noise. Relative intensity of low pass filtered noise is —10 dB, and —25 dB in case of /ɛ/ and /ɑ/ respectively. The band noise of 3400-4800 Hz in case of /u/ is —25 dB.

No.	Structure of Test Tone	Rating
1	1700 Hz L.P. e +300-600 +1700-3400 Hz B.N. + 6800 Hz L.P.N.	4.4
2	1700 Hz L.P. e +300-600 +1700-3400 Hz B.N. +4800 Hz L.P.N.	4.4
3	1200 Hz L.P. a +600-1700 +3400-4800 Hz B.N.	4.5
4	1200 Hz L.P. a +600-1700 Hz B.N. +3400 Hz L.P.N.	4.8
5	1200 Hz L.P. a +600-1700 Hz B.N. +4800 Hz L.P.N.	4.3
6	1200 Hz L.P. u +212-1200 Hz B.N. +3400-4800 B.N.	4.7

and spliced in random order with four sec intervals. Six otolaryngologists served as listeners. They were instructed to listen to a series of test tones and attempt to give one of the following six ratings to each test tone whenever it was judged to be a hoarse voice. If the test tone appeared to be an artificial hoarse voice, instruction was given to place a check mark beside the tone. The ratings were: (0) normal voice, (1) very slightly hoarse, (2) slightly hoarse, (3) moderately hoarse, (4) very hoarse, and (5) extremely hoarse. The degree of hoarseness of each test tone was expressed by averaging the ratings given by the six listeners.

Results

Interjudge agreement on the hoarseness rating was tested by calculating the reliability coefficient (McNemar, 1962, pp. 145-148). The coefficient was obtained by correlating each judge's rating for each tone with the rating by the five other judges. These correlations are given in Table 3. The average coefficient of 0.77 demonstrated that the interjudge agreement was close enough to permit the use of averaged rating scores as indicators of the listener's responses.

Sound spectrograms of all the test tones were made to see the result of the synthesis and to correlate the acoustic structure of each test tone with the corresponding judgment of the listeners.

Tables 4, 5, and 6 show the results of this experiment. Any test tones which were checked by any one of the listeners as "artificial" were excluded from these tables.

The significance of the noise components in the formant ranges is shown in Table 4. When the band-filtered noise intrudes on the formant range, the sound is perceived as a very slight or slight hoarseness. In the case of vowels /ɑ/ and /ɛ/, mixing of the band-filtered noise into the second formant region results in an increase of the degree of hoarseness.

In Table 5, the effect of elimination of high frequency harmonics of vowels on the perceptual hoarseness is shown. Even if the relative intensity of the noise components and the harmonic components remain unchanged, the loss of high frequency harmonics results in an increase of the degree of perceived hoarseness. When the elimination includes the second formants of these vowels, an advance in the degree of perceived hoarseness results.

In the case of severe hoarseness, an expansion of the additional noise component is an outstanding feature. In order to reproduce this feature, band-pass noise and low-pass noise were superimposed on the low-pass vowel-band filtered noise mixtures. Table 6 shows the effect of this procedure. All test tones of this group are perceived as either very hoarse or extremely hoarse.

Figures 7 and 8 illustrate the sonagrams and sections of synthesized hoarseness of the vowel /ɛ/. Their schematic drawing is given in Figure 9, which shows step-by-step increase of the perceptual degree of hoarseness and the corresponding acoustical structure changes.

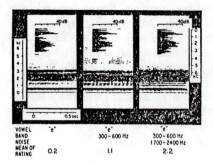

FIGURE 7. Sonagrams of composed hoarseness of vowel /ɛ/—mild hoarseness.

VOWEL	"e"	"e"	"e"
BAND			
NOISE		300~600 Hz	300~600 Hz
			1700~2400 Hz
MEAN OF RATING	0.2	1.1	2.2

FIGURE 8. Sonagrams of composed hoarseness of vowel /ɛ/—moderate to severe hoarseness.

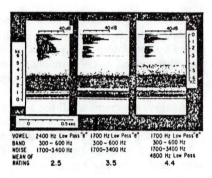

VOWEL	2400 Hz Low Pass "e"	1700 Hz Low Pass "e"	1700 Hz Low Pass "e"
BAND	300~600 Hz	300~600 Hz	300~600 Hz
NOISE	1700~3400 Hz	1700~3400 Hz	1700~3400 Hz
			4800 Hz Low Pass
MEAN OF RATING	2.5	3.5	4.4

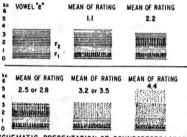

SCHEMATIC PRESENTATION OF SOUNDSPECTROGRAPH
OF SYNTHESIZED HOARSENESS AND ITS MEAN OF RATING

FIGURE 9. Schematic drawing of the sonagrams of synthesized hoarseness. Step by step rise of the degree of perceptual hoarseness and corresponding acoustical structure changes of vowel sound are shown.

DISCUSSION

The major acoustic factors relating to hoarseness consist of (1) noise components, and (2) loss of harmonic components. As to the noise components, the intensity and range differ from vowel to vowel and also vary with the degree of hoarseness. Generally, the noise element is much more evident in the vowels /ɑ/, /ɛ/, and /i/ than in the vowels /u/ and /ɔ/. The present study reveals that the noise components appear in the formant ranges, especially in the second and third formant ranges at the initial stage of hoarseness. With the progression of hoarseness, the noise components predominate the harmonic structures in the second and third formant ranges. Parallel with these findings, noise components become manifest in the frequency range above 3000 Hz. Noise components above 3000 Hz intensify their energy and widen their range.

Classification of degrees of hoarseness is found to be clinically useful in the following two respects: (1) The degree of hoarseness can be numerically expressed; and (2) the objective acoustic degree of hoarseness based on this method closely agrees with subjective, perceived degree of hoarseness.

Previous studies (Moore, 1957; Isshiki and von Leden, 1964; and Flanagan, 1958) suggest the importance of noise components and the loss of high frequency harmonic components in hoarseness. Noise components may originate from the turbulent air flow due to incomplete closure of the glottis during vibratory cycle, or irregular vibratory attitudes of the glottis. Loss of high frequency harmonic components may be attributable to the incomplete or shorter closing phase during vibratory cycles. For the objective evaluation of hoarseness associated with different laryngeal pathologies, more detailed study of the sound spectrogram of hoarseness is required. The time-frequency resolution of the sound spectrogram depends on the width of filter band. The sound spectrogram traced through a narrow band filter gives better frequency resolution. However, the details in variation in noise and harmonic component as a function of time cannot be demonstrated. Studies of cycle to cycle spectrum change in hoarseness with the use of wide band filter settings will provide additional information on noise components and harmonic changes. However, it should be emphasized that the quality of hoarse voice is not entirely dependent upon the noise components and changes in harmonic structure mentioned above. There is another aspect of hoarseness, the aperiodicity of the fundamental frequency. On the basis of accurate measurements of high speed motion pictures of the pathologic larynx, von Leden, Moore, and Timcke (1960) concluded that the most common observation in the pathologic condition is a strong tendency for frequent and rapid changes in the regularity of the vibratory pattern. Dunker and Schlosshauer (1961) reached the same conclusion after high speed film analysis. Investigations on rapid changes or cycle to cycle variations of periodic components, including perturbation of pitch, are needed in order to reach a more satisfactory understanding of this problem.

This research was supported by Public Health Service Research Grant No. NB 04430-04 from the National Institute of Neurologic Diseases and Blindness.

REFERENCES

DUNKER, E., and SCHLOSSHAUER, B., Unregelmässige Stimmlippenschwingungen bei Funktionellen Stimmstörungen. Z. Laryng. Rhinol., 40, 919-934 (1961).

FLANAGAN, J. L., Some properties of the glottal sound source. J. Speech Hearing Res., 1, 99-116 (1958).

FRANK, D. I., Hoarseness—a new classification and a brief report of four interesting cases. Laryngoscope, 50, 472-478 (1940).

ISSHIKI, N., and VON LEDEN, H., Hoarseness—aerodynamic studies. *Arch. Otolaryng.*, 80, 206-213 (1964).

JACKSON, C., and JACKSON, C. L., *The Larynx and its Diseases*. Phila.: W. B. Saunders (1937).

MOORE, P., Voice disorders associated with organic abnormalities. *Handbook of Speech Pathology*, New York: Appleton-Century-Crofts (1957).

McNEMAR, Q., *Psychological Statistics*. New York: Wiley (1962).

PALMER, J. M., Hoarseness in laryngeal pathology, a review of the literature. *Laryngoscope*, 61, 500-516 (1959).

VON LEDEN, H., The clinical significance of hoarseness and related voice disorders. *Lancet*, 78, 50-53 (1958).

VON LEDEN, H., MOORE, P., and TIMCKE, R., Laryngeal vibrations: measurement of the glottic wave. Part III, The pathologic larynx. *Arch. Otolaryng.*, 71, 16-35 (1960).

Received for publication September 1966

Tremulous Speech

A Case Report

Yvan Lebrun, Françoise Devreux, Jean-Jacques Rousseau, Philippe Darimont

Vrije Universiteit Brussel, Belgium; Fondation Universitaire Luxembourgeoise, Arlon, Belgium; Centre Hospitalier de Ste Ode, Baconfoy-Tenneville, Belgium

While much has been written on essential tremor, few authors have sought to document the speech disorders which this affection may entail. It therefore seems worthwhile reporting a case of essential tremor involving tremulant speech.

The patient is a right-handed French-speaking male who was born in 1897. In his early twenties he started to have intention tremor in the upper limbs. At first the tremor was slight and did not interfere much with everyday activities. It increased with time, however, and eventually the patient became unable to write legibly or to perform actions requiring much accuracy. In recent years the tremor became so severe as to incapacitate the patient from performing such plain actions as washing, shaving, or lifting a full glass to his lips. In prehension tasks, the tremulation typically increases as the hand draws nearer to the object (movement tremor with terminal crescendo). At times, the shaking is so intense as to remind one of the jerky movements of dyskinetic patients. The left upper limb is even more affected than the right one. When the patient is requested to write or to draw, he tries to reduce the trembling of the right hand by immobilizing his right forearm with his left hand, which then does not shake. For some years the tremor has been affecting the speech organs as well. When the patient protrudes his tongue on request, one can see that it is trembling, as is his lower jaw. When the tongue reposes in the mouth, no tremulation is visible. At rest there is no velar tremor either. The velum can be seen trembling, however, when the patient utters a protracted /a/ with open mouth. During speech, there is a slight but constant head nodding of limited amplitude, which is superimposed on the head movements accompanying and stressing what is being said. During speech the lateral aspects of the neck are trembling, too. Conversely, at rest there are slight tremulations of the peribuccal musculature, which are not visible, or at least are masked, when the patient talks. There is minimal tremor in hands and arms during spontaneous movements accompanying speech.

Although the patient underwent several complete medical examinations in the course of time, no neurological symptom other than the tremor could ever be observed. When

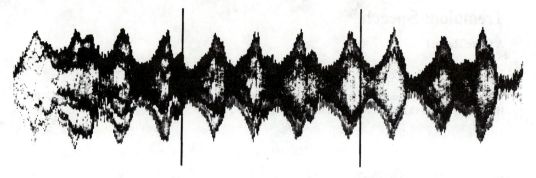

Fig. 1. Oscillographic recording of protracted /i/. The oscillogram shows 3 successive seconds. The frequency of the voice tremulation is 4 cycles/s.

seen for the last time in 1981, the patient, although he was 84 years old, was found to be intellectually alert, to be talkative and to move about normally. Apart from the tremor, no pyramidal, extrapyramidal or cerebellar deficit could be detected. The EEG was normal. There was increased emotivity, however, the patient being prone to weep when his incapacitation was examined or simply talked about.

In the past, various medications were used with a view to alleviating the tremor, but none proved efficient. As there was no other case of tremor among the patient's relatives, it was concluded that this was an instance of sporadic essential intention tremor of the irregular (dyskinetic) type. As was to be expected, the patient's delivery is tremulant and his voice quavers. Oscillographic analysis of protracted vowels spoken by the patient (fig. 1) indicates that voice tremulation has a fairly constant frequency of 4 cycles/s. The same periodicity could be recorded electromyographically in the upper limbs during voluntary contraction (postural and movement tremor). A frequency of 4 cycles corresponds to the lower end of the frequency range observed by *Brown and Simonson* [1963] in organic voice tremor.

Voice tremulation comprises intensity as well as pitch fluctuations as figures 1 and 2 show. Intensity is represented by vertical deflections in figure 1, and pitch by horizontal lines in the lower part of figure 2. In addition to these fairly regular variations, there were erratic vocal breaks to a lower pitch and voice arrests in the patient's speech production. A vocal break to a lower pitch is a sudden and short drop of fundamental frequency. Such a drop occurred during the last low phase shown in figure 2. Three vocal breaks of one octave each (i.e., the fundamental frequency was each time reduced by half) can be seen in figure 3, which is a high-speed oscillographic recording of part of a prolonged /a/.

A voice arrest, on the other hand, is a sudden interruption in voice production during a voiced sound. Such an arrest occurred during the final /ã/ in *convenablement* (fig. 7) and during the /u:/ in *vous* (fig. 8). In connected speech there were also sudden increases in fundamental frequency. Such a tonal rise occurred on the /ã/ of *employé* (fig. 4), on the

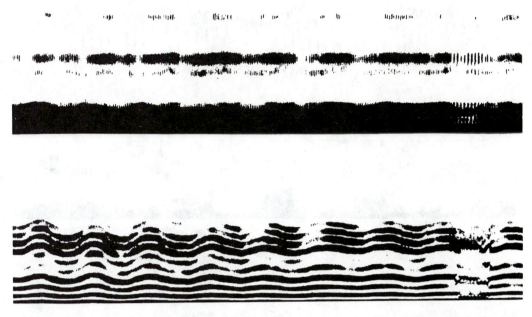

Fig. 2. Sonagraphic recording of protracted /a/. The sonagram below (narrow-band analysis) clearly shows the pitch fluctuations. The total duration of the recording being slightly less than 2.4 s, 9 periods are visible. The upper part of the recording (wide-band analysis) reveals a vocal break of one octave during the last low phase.

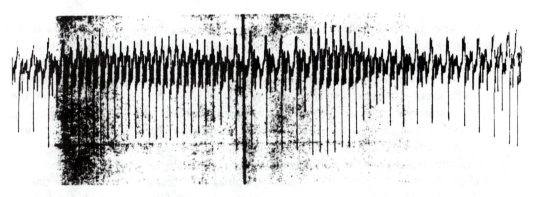

Fig. 3. High-speed oscillographic recording of protracted /a/. Each maximal deflection corresponds to a vocal wave. Three times (left extremity, middle, and right end of the picture) there occurred a vocal break of one octave: the pitch was suddenly reduced by half.

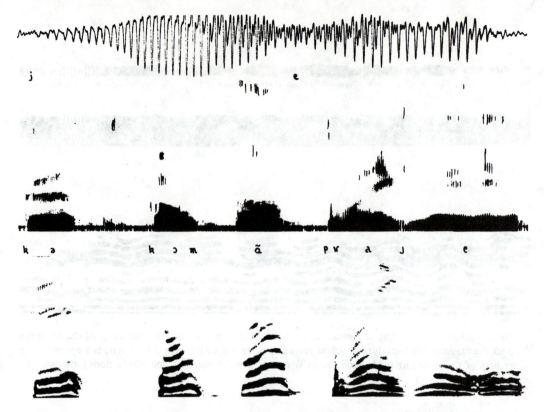

Fig. 4. Sonagraphic recording of the phrase *que comme employé* and oscillogram of the last vowel. As is often the case in informal French, the last word was pronounced as /ãpwaje/.

/ɛ/ of *nervosité* (fig. 5), and on the /a/ of *attendez* (fig. 6).

What is the pathophysiology of the vocal anomalies? Voice tremulation is most probably due to rhythmic fluctuations in the contraction of expiratory chest muscles (progressive contraction) and of laryngeal muscles (isometric contraction).

In an attempt to ascertain the part played by the chest musculature in vocal tremor, *Hachinski* et al. [1975] studied 3 patients fluoroscopically. They found that 'while the patient held her breath, the diaphragm did not move. Towards the end of inspiration slight irregular up-and-down jerky movements occurred synchronous with the interruption of breathing. During expiration, phonation (aaah) and speech, the interruption of the normally smooth downward movement of the diaphragm became increasingly pronounced.' This description is puzzling, as it has been established that during speech the diaphragm generally relaxes at the beginning of the utterance [*Draper* et al., 1960; *Lebrun*, 1966a] and moves upward while the subject speaks [*Jeanmart* et al., 1971]. It is therefore

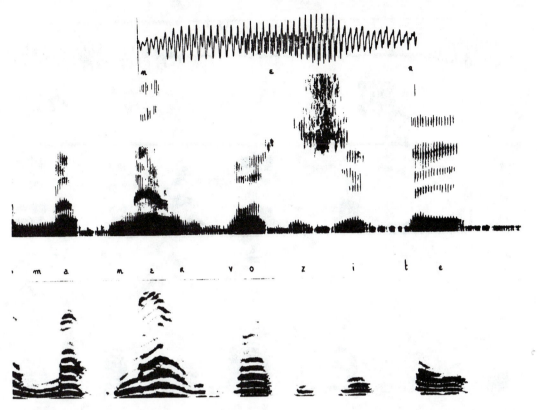

Fig. 5. Sonagraphic recording of the phrase *(de) ma nervosité* and oscillogram of the first syllable of the third word.

strange that *Hachinski* et al. [1975] should have observed a 'downward movement of the diaphragm' during speech. In all likelihood, the diaphragm, because it is generally relaxed in speech, is not affected by the intention tremor when the subject talks, and therefore is not responsible for voice tremulation. In fact, the muscles which have been found to control the expiratory air pressure during speech are the external and internal intercostals [*Draper* et al. 1960; *Lebrun,* 1966b] and most probably they cause the intensity and pitch fluctuations that are characteristic of voice tremulation.

The tremor may also account for the unsteadiness of the timbre of some vowels. As may be seen in the upper part of figure 4, the final /e/ in *employé*[1] had not only altering intensity but also changing quality (the intensity is depicted by the vertical deflections, and the timbre by the form or cast of the wave). Probably the oral muscles could not keep a stable articulatory position to insure a steady timbre. In fact, during the production of a protracted /a/ the tremor in the oral

[1]   Which the patient pronounced /apwaje/. This is a common pronunciation in informal French.

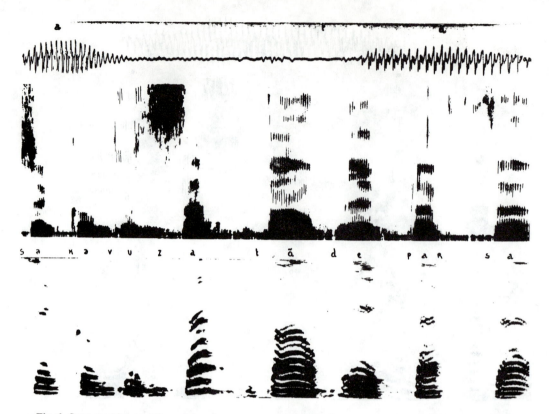

Fig. 6. Sonagraphic recording of the phrase *ce que vous entendez par çà* and oscillogram of the first two syllables of the fourth word. The first syllable of this word was denasalized, so that the target word *entendez* sounded like *attendez*.

structures was visible to the naked eye. It is reflected in the variability of the cast of the waves in figure 3.

Voice breaks, especially those consisting in a drop of one octave, can also be observed in voice mutation and in dysphonia [*Lebrun and Hasquin,* 1971]. The pathogenesis of such breaks remains to be discovered.

In their book on *Motor Speech Disorders,* *Darley* et al. [1975] seem to imply that in tremulous speech voice arrests are due to hyperadduction of the vocal folds. While it is perfectly plausible that voice stoppages are caused by spasmodic closures of the glottis, it

may equally well be that at least some of the disruptions in voice production result from the reverse phenomenon, namely from a sudden slackening of the vocal muscles. The sonagraphic recording of the vocal arrest in /ã/ (fig. 7) and in /u:/ (fig. 8) supports the latter hypothesis: if the interruption in voice production had been due to hyperadduction of the vocal folds (as is commonly the case in glottal catch), the beginning of the second part of the vowel (immediately after the stoppage) would have been more abrupt, and the sonagram would have shown a sort of spike corresponding to the forceful opening of the

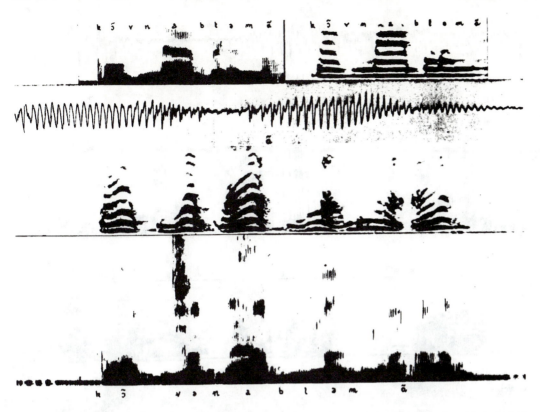

Fig. 7. Sonagraphic recording of the word *convenablement* as spoken by the patient (below) and by a normal speaker (above), and oscillogram of the final vowel of the word as articulated by the patient (middle). The patient's narrow-band and wide-band sonagrams as well as the oscillogram reveal a voice arrest during the final vowel /ã/. In addition, the narrow-band sonagram indicates that there occurred a tonal rise on the third vowel, /a/. From the comparison of the normal sonagrams with those of the patient it may be seen that the patient's articulation was twice as slow as normal delivery (the time scale is the same for all four sonagrams).

glottis at the end of the spasm. Instead, the two sonagrams show what the Germans call *weicher Einsatz* [*Krech,* 1968], i.e. smooth, gradual resumption of voice production. It may therefore be that in our patient voice arrests, or at least some of them, are caused by a momentary decrease in laryngeal muscle tension rather than by a laryngospasm. It follows that since voice stoppage resulting from a laryngospasm is 'the cardinal symptom of spastic dysphonia' [*Aronson* et al., 1968],

there may be less resemblance between essential voice tremor and spastic dysphonia than has sometimes been assumed. While voice arrests do not appear to have been (all) caused by sudden hyperadduction of the vocal folds, sudden increases in fundamental frequency were most probably brought about by sudden increases in the contraction of the laryngeal and/or thoracic musculature. It is perhaps of some significance that one of these tonal rises was accompanied by denasaliza-

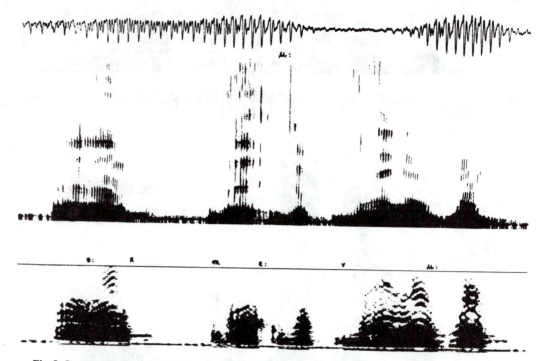

Fig. 8. Sonagraphic recording of the phrase *dormez-vous* as sung by the patient, and oscillogram of the last vowel.

tion of the vowel: /ã/ became /a/, so that the target word *entendez* sounded like the word *attendez* (fig. 6). In all probability, the laryngeal (and/or thoracic) clonus was accompanied by a sudden contraction of the velum resulting in the substitution of /a/ for /ã/. Similarly, some jerk of the tongue may have caused the deletion of the first consonant and the substitution of /ə/ for /ɔ/ in the sung phrase *dormez-vous?* (fig. 8).

The patient's mean fundamental frequency during prolongation of vowels was 150 cycles/s. The present case thus does not verify the assumption made by *Aronson* et al. [1968] that in essential voice tremor there is nearly always excessively low pitch. Also, in contradiction to the expectation of *Aronson*

et al., voice arrests did not occur at regular intervals, nor did they coincide with points of highest pitch.

In addition to being quavering, the patient's delivery is slow. His articulation rate is approximately half that of normal speakers. This reduction is due to the fact that speech sounds tend to last longer; moreover, there are often short pauses between successive syllables or between words which form a phrase and are normally uttered uninterruptedly. Figure 7 shows a sonagraphic recording of the word *convenablement* as spoken by the patient (below) and by a normal speaker (above). The time scale is the same in both cases. It may be seen that the patient took twice as long to say the word. In figures 5 and 6, on the other hand, the pauses between the successive syllables of the word *nervosité* and of the word *entendez* are clearly visible. The tremor may account for this slow scanning speech.

Essential tremor is a monosymptomatic affection appearing as a familial disorder or – as in the present case – sporadically. Although it is a benign condition, it can be a considerable nuisance. It often has an adverse effect on manual skills. When the speech organs are affected, the voice becomes tremulant; in addition there may be slow, scanning speech, as in the patient described above. Such quavering speech, while remaining intelligible, has a whimpering quality which may at times become exasperating.

Various drugs have been used in an effort to control essential tremor. So far propranolol has been found to be among the most efficient. Other medications may be tried in the future. The analysis provided in the present paper offers objective criteria by which to judge the efficacy of treatment in patients with essential tremulous speech.

Résumé

La parole d'un patient atteint de tremblement essentiel a été étudiée. Une analyse oscillographique et sonagraphique des trémulations de la voix, des chutes de la fréquence fondamentale et des arrêts dans la production de la voix a été réalisée. La pathogénie des phénomènes est discutée.

Zusammenfassung

Die Sprache eines Patienten mit essentiellem Tremor wurde untersucht. Das Zittern der Stimme, die Stimmbrüche und die Unterbrechungen der Stimmgebung wurden oszillographisch und sonagraphisch analysiert. Die Pathogenese dieser Erscheinungen wird diskutiert.

References

Aronson, A.; Brown, J.; Litin, A.; Pearson, J.: Spastic dysphonia II. Comparison with essential (voice) tremor and other neurologic or psychogenic dysphonias. J. Speech Hear. Disorders *33:* 219–231 (1968).

Brown, J.; Simonson, Y.: Organic voice tremor. Neurology *13:* 520–525 (1963).

Darley, F.; Aronson, A.; Brown, J.: Motor speech disorders (Saunders, Philadelphia 1975).

Draper, M.; Ladefoged, P.; Whitteridge, D.: Expiratory pressures and air flow during speech. Br. med. J. *ii:* 1837–1843 (1960).

Hachinski, V.; Thomsen, I.; Buch, N.: The nature of primary vocal tremor. Can. J. neurol. Sci. *2:* 195–198 (1975).

Jeanmart, L.; Lebrun, Y.; Jorissen, E.; Hasquin, J.: Etude cinéradiographique des mouvements diaphragmatiques dans l'acte de parole. Röntgenblätter, Berl. *24:* 514–517 (1971).

Lebrun, Y.: Sur l'activité du diaphragme au cours de la phonation. Linguistique *2:* 71–78 (1966a).

Lebrun, Y.: Sur l'activité des muscles thoraco-abdominaux pendant la phonation. Folia phoniat. *18:* 354–368 (1966b).

Lebrun, Y.; Hasquin, J.: Variations in vocal wave duration. Lar. Otol. *85:* 43–56 (1971).

Received: May 24, 1981
Accepted: June 2, 1981

Prof. Dr. Yvan Lebrun, Neurolinguïstiek,
Gebouw F/R₃, Faculteit Geneeskunde,
Vrije Universiteit Brussel, Laarbeeklaan, 103,
B–1090 Brussel (Belgium)

OBJECTIVE EVALUATION OF VOCAL PATHOLOGY
USING VOICE SPECTROGRAPHY

Eugene Rontal, M.D.

Michael Rontal, M.D.   Michael I. Rolnick, Ph.D.

Southfield, Michigan

SUMMARY — Permanent objective evaluation of vocal changes associated with laryngeal pathology is a goal which has been difficult for the laryngologist and speech pathologist to attain. Most attempts at achieving objective records have focused on direct visual examination of the larynx using techniques such as high speed photography, x-ray studies or histologic sectioning. However, the important subjective qualities of the voice are difficult to translate into objective visual patterns. In order to produce these patterns, certain individual components of the voice (i.e., breathiness, periodicity and formant structure) must be analyzed. Recently, modifications of the sound spectrograph have enabled the clinician to objectively visualize these components. The patterns produced by the spectrograph may be applied to a variety of clinical situations. For example, the technique aids greatly in determining the success or failure of medical and surgical management for vocal cord lesions. Secondly, voice spectrography can readily show improvements or deficiencies in vocal rehabilitation for functional dysphonia. Lastly, this method provides an objective, permanent record of the voice which may be useful from a medicolegal standpoint. Sound spectrographic analysis of vocal pathology is an important diagnostic tool for the clinician. Its future use should be encouraged as a more precise aid in the evaluation of the voice.

Permanent objective evaluation of vocal changes associated with laryngeal pathology is a goal which has been difficult for the laryngologist and speech pathologist to attain. Most attempts at achieving objective records are focused on direct visual examination of the larynx, using techniques such as high speed photography, x-ray studies, or histologic sectioning. However, the subjective qualities of the voice are difficult to translate into objective visual patterns. In order to produce these patterns, the individual components of the voice must be analyzed.

Clinical modifications in voice spectrographic analysis have allowed adequate visualization of these components. Once these patterns are formalized, they can be applied to a variety of clinical situations. Although attempts have been made in the past to use spectrography in the evaluation of certain types of hoarseness, direct clinical application to voice problems has been a recent development. This paper is a presentation of our use of spectrography in a clinical situation for evaluation of vocal rehabilitation, surgical treatment and medical management of a variety of vocal cord disorders.

DESCRIPTION OF VOICE SPECTROGRAPHY

The voice spectrograph is not a new method of voice analysis. Potter et al[1] first developed this technique at the Bell Telephone laboratories in the 1940's. Spectrography has been a useful tool in voice research since its first development.[2-6] It differs from a visible speech translator in that an actual graphic analysis of the speech pattern rather than a display in a cathode ray tube is produced. The graphic display is known as a spectrogram.

Presented at the meeting of the American Broncho-Esophagological Association, Atlanta, Georgia, April 7-8, 1975.

Iwata and Von Leden[7] have discussed the use of spectrograms in the study of laryngeal disease. They suggested that different laryngeal diseases might yield different spectrographic characteristics. Cooper[8] reported spectrographic analysis as a tool to describe and compare fundamental frequencies and hoarseness in dysphonic patients before and after vocal rehabilitation. Isskiki et al[9] have presented a classification system for hoarseness using spectrograms. Rontal et al[4] pointed out the usefulness of spectrographic analysis as a clinical tool in evaluation of the voice following Teflon®* paste injection of paralyzed vocal cords. In spite of these contributions to the literature, few laryngologists or speech pathologists are utilizing this important, objective method of voice analysis.

Sound spectrography, through a series of filters, presents a picture of the intensity, frequency and duration characteristics of the voice. These characteristics are translated into an electrical impulse represented by an electrical stylus which prints out the pattern on a rotating paper graph. Either steady state vowels such as "ah" or "ee" or spoken words and sentences can be evaluated by this technique. Depending on the information desired, a number of different patterns can be elucidated. A trained individual may then "read" the spectrograms produced and view the phonatory, articulatory and resonance qualities of the human voice.

The technique called "voice printing" has confused the clinical application of voice spectrography. The voice print is a form of voice spectrogram used to identify individuals for criminal purposes, based on vocal characteristics of their spoken words. The voice spectrograph, on the other hand, analyzes the specific components of the voice by relating acoustic energy to physiology, so that vocal function can be assessed.

The sound spectrogram best analyzes steady state vowels for the purpose of evaluation of phonatory characteristics.

The patient is asked to produce a vowel in front of the input microphone for a period of 2.4 seconds. A recording is made on a special tape loop in the spectrograph. This sample is then repeated many times and analyzed through a series of filters. The analysis can be performed in approximately three minutes. Broad band spectrograms are made for the analysis of phonation and can be kept permanently in a patient's file. A spectrographic analysis of phonatory characteristics is performed at periodic intervals so that changes during treatment can be monitored.

SPECTROGRAPHIC CHARACTERISTICS OF THE NORMAL VOICE

In order to adequately understand voice spectrography, the normal physiology of voice production at the level of the glottis must be understood.[10,11] This physiologic sound production is then related to the graphic display on the spectrogram. Sound is the alternate compression and rarefaction of air molecules. Subglottic air, trapped in the trachea by the closed vocal cords, is compressed by the accessory muscles of respiration. As the pressure beneath the glottis increases, the vocal cords are separated, allowing the escape of the compressed air. When subglottic pressure falls, the vocal cords cannot be held open. They move back passively by their intrinsic tension. The subglottic pressure can then build to produce another wave of compressed air. The result is a train of compressions and rarefactions and the result is sound.

The sound spectrogram will show the various physiologic characteristics of the normal voice. In this range of normality, there are certain definable differences, such as different characteristics between a male and a female voice, the characteristics of trained singers, the whisper voice and vocal fatigue.

In the analysis of the spectrographic characteristics of the normal voice,

---

* E.I. DuPont de Nemours and Co., Wilmington, Delaware.

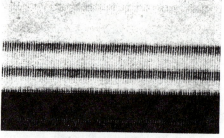

Fig. 1. Spectrogram of a normal male "ah" vowel produced by an individual with no vocal pathology. Regular, periodic vertical striations indicate synchronous vocal cord movements with no irregularity of the vibratory pattern. The horizontal bars going across the pattern are formants and represent frequency regions of energy selectively amplified by the resonating cavities. The top half of the spectrogram is relatively clear, indicating that no excessive breathiness exists.

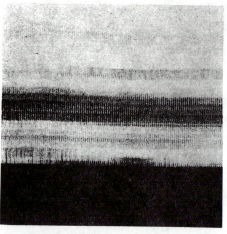

Fig. 2. "Ah" vowel produced by a female speaker. Normal periodicity of vocal cord movement is seen by the regularly spaced vertical lines. These vertical lines differ from the male voice in Figure 1 inasmuch as they are closer together. This is due to the higher pitched voice. The horizontal bars or formants are typical of the female voice. A lack of breathiness in the upper half of the spectrogram indicates good closure of the vocal cords.

phonatory samples are made from steady state vowels. Because of interference from articulatory characteristics, spoken words are less apt to give reproducible, analyzable data. The patterns visible on the spectrogram are evaluated in terms of acoustic parameters (Fig. 1).

Periodicity of vocal cord movement is a measure of the regularity of the opening and closing of the vocal cords. It is translated on the spectrogram as the vertical striations seen (Fig. 1). The synchronous, periodic opening and closing of the vocal cords in a normal voice will produce a corresponding regularity in the vertical striations seen. While periodicity is measured by the pattern of individual vertical striations, certain pitch characteristics of the voice can be observed in the closeness of the vertical striations on the spectrogram.

The spectrogram also measures the formants of the normal voice. These formants are the horizontal bars represented as the darker bands on the spectrogram (Fig. 1). These bars or formants relate to the size and shape of the resonating cavities of the vocal tract. Formants will shift position during connected speech and with each sound being produced. On the spectrogram, clear

and adequate formant structure is dependent upon a good resonating system and a lack of breathiness, as well as normal periodicity of vocal cord movement.

Differences between the male and female voice are demonstrable on the spectrogram (Fig. 2). In the female voice, the fundamental pitch is generally higher. Subsequently, the rapid vibrations of the vocal cords are represented by closer vertical striations. The remainder of the spectrographic characteristics are usually the same. A child's voice closely parallels the female voice in fundamental pitch and resonance characteristics. Until vocal changes associated with pubescence occur, both the male and female child will exhibit a similar spectrographic pattern.

The singing voice differs from the spoken voice. Vocal cord closure is too rapid to distinguish individual striations on the pattern produced (Fig. 3). The extra formant structure present is indicative of a finely tuned vocal mechan-

Fig. 3. A trained singer singing an "ah" vowel at a very high pitch. The vertical lines are blurred together although they make up the actual spectrogram. Extra formant structure can be seen at different frequency regions on the spectrogram. The wavy characteristic relates to tremulo so often found in the trained singing voice.

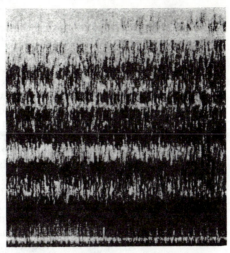

Fig. 4. Whispered vocal quality showing no evidence of vocal cord movement. Only frictional, random noise is present, caused by escape of air through a partially opened glottis. This glottal fricative sound can be produced in isolation, resulting in a whispered voice or with phonation resulting in a breathy vocal quality. The formant structure can be seen occurring due to the fact that the glottal fricative sound is being resonated by the resonating cavities.

ism. This is one of the distinguishing features of the voice that is trained, or voice involved in the singing act. The regular wavy motion to the formant structure is indicative of the vibrato commonly heard in a singer's voice.

Other variations of the normal voice can produce distinct changes on a spectrogram. A whispered voice with no vocal cord movement shows a distinct pattern (Fig. 4). The excessive energy throughout the pattern is created by air escaping through a constricted, partially open glottis. Frequency is represented in the vertical axis of the spectrogram from 0 to 8,000 Hz. When the whispered or breathy voice is produced, energy is present in the highest frequency regions of the spectrogram. Further, vocal fatigue will also be indicated as a normal variant in a voice spectrogram (Fig. 5). Cords which are able to move in a regular, periodic manner may suddenly go into an aperiodic, low-pitched tone with subsequent return to a normal voice. This can occur in a normal individual's phonatory pattern at some time during the speaking day, when the vocal cords are fatigued or mucus rests upon them.

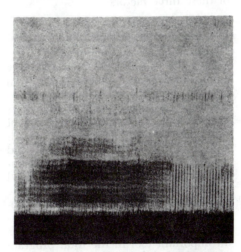

Fig. 5. Example of a normal speaker producing an aperiodic voice due to mucus on the vocal cords. No laryngeal pathology is present. This is a normal occurence that can take place at different times during the speaking day. This type of pattern can also be caused by vocal fatigue. The spectrograph is capable of picking up and portraying these normal variations of the voice.

The sound spectrograph was designed to show a graphic representation of the energy involved in the phonatory act. Consideration of the spectrographic characteristics of the normal voice show what is occurring on a physiologic basis. An extension of this would then allow an observation of the acoustic end result of various dysphonic or pathological problems. in doing so, certain characteristics can be identified as representing specific spectrographic aspects of dysphonia. In order to evaluate the voice adequately, each parameter of the spectrogram must be analyzed: 1) aperiodicity or loss of regular vocal cord closure is observed; 2) breathiness or increase in energy in the high frequency regions of the spectrogram is also evaluated; and 3) a breakdown in the formant or energy resonance of the voice must also be analyzed. Individual abnormalities or combinations of abnormal conditions would create spectrograms characteristic of vocal cord pathology. Correction of vocal cord problems will be reflected by an improvement in the abnormalities of each of these three factors.

USES OF VOICE SPECTROGRAPHY IN THE EVALUATION OF VOCAL REHABILITATION

Both organic and functional disturbances of the vocal cords are frequently amenable to vocal rehabilitation. An objective description of the acoustic end result of the vocal cord pathology is important to the subsequent treatment program. Spectrographic analysis allows both the speech pathologist and the patient to be aware of ongoing improvement in the voice. Vocal cord nodules, vocal paralyses, hyperkinetic dysphonia and dysphonia plica ventricularis are just a few examples of disorders in which the spectrograph was an important tool in the total program of vocal rehabilitation.

The presence of vocal nodules prevents adequate movement of the vocal cords with a subsequent aperiodic breathy voice. Some patients with these nodules will respond well to vocal hygiene and rehabilitation. This is especially true in children. The objective

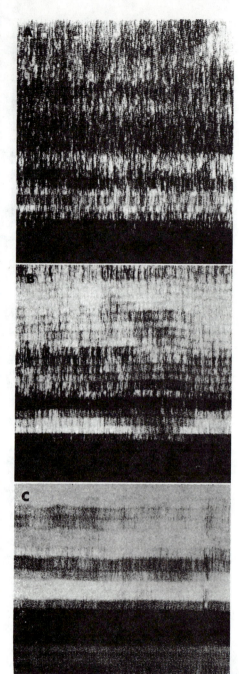

Fig. 6. Three spectrograms A, B and C, in serial order showing improvement in dysphonia related to the resolution of vocal cord nodules. As the nodules reduce in size one can see a lessening of the breathiness, better periodicity of vocal cord movement, and more distinct formant structure.

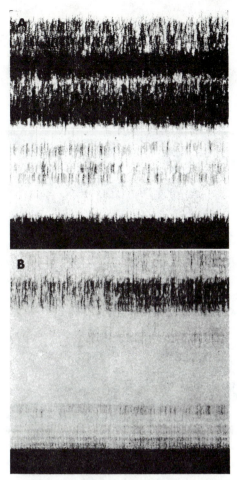

Fig. 7. Improvement in the voice of a patient with unilateral vocal cord paralysis (A). While the post treatment spectrogram (B) is obviously improved with the reduction in high frequency breathiness, and noticeably more adequate periodicity of vocal cord movement, continued problems are still evident. There is a continuation of high frequency breathiness indicating that complete closure of vocal cords is not possible due to remaining problems.

measurement of change in the voice during the process of vocal rehabilitation can be accurately assessed by the voice spectrogram. Therefore, one may be able to see the exact progression of events in correction of the vocal pathology. Serial spectrograms made at different stages in treatment can clearly show a decrease in dysphonic characteristics (Fig. 6).

Vocal cord paralysis shows most of the abnormal spectrographic characteristics of the voice. There is evidence of aperiodicity, breakdown of formant structure and breathiness. Vocal rehabilitation programs related to this condition involve improvement of each of these abnormal components of the voice. The spectrogram allows observation of the change in the voice following treatment. Both vocal rehabilitation and surgical correction of vocal cord paralysis have been used. In the vocal rehabilitation program, the voice spectrogram can evaluate the efficacy of the treatment technique. This type of program generally involves forced adduction exercises. The documentation of the improvement through spectrographic analysis makes a meaningful visual presentation to the referring laryngologist, speech pathologist and the patient (Fig. 7). Lack of resolution of high frequency energy indicative of continued breathiness will aid in the clinical consideration of vocal cord injection.

Vocal rehabilitation is the prime modality of treatment is functional dysphonias. Hyperkinetic dysphonia and dysphonia plica ventricularis are common examples of this type of vocal disorder. In hyperkinetic dysphonia, there is an incoordination of vocal cord movement. This is commonly associated with stressful situations or prolonged vocal strain. With spectrography, the before and after treatment progress of the patient is made visible (Fig. 8). Treatment generally involves hypofunctional voice use with specific attention to decreased vocal strain.

Dysphonia plica ventricularis is another example of a functional neuromuscular vocal disorder which can be treated effectively by vocal rehabilitation. In this situation, the false vocal cords meet in the midline before the true cords. This is clearly demonstrable on indirect laryngoscopy. The dysphonic characteristics of the voice in

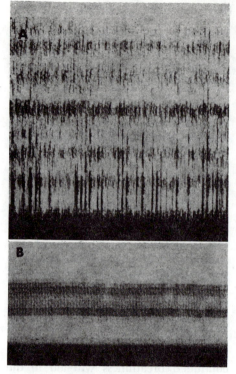

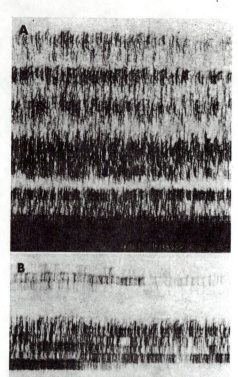

Fig. 8. Dramatic improvement in the voice of a patient with hyperkinetic dysphonia. A severely dysphonic voice with very little evidence of periodic vocal cord movement (A) was vastly improved through the use of a hypofunctional approach to voice production. The post treatment spectrogram (B) shows marked improvement in periodicity. All of the breathiness has cleared due to more adequate vocal fold closure.

Fig. 9. Patient wtih dysphonia ventricularis (A) exhibits a much improved voice after a hypofunctional approach to treatment. A major acoustic characteristic that has been eliminated in the post-treatment spectrogram (B) is the excessive breathiness found throughout the pretreatment pattern.

dysphonia plica ventricularis are related to an attempt by the false vocal cords to participate in the phonatory act (Fig. 9). There is an extreme amount of breathiness throughout the pattern, represented by high frequency energy. The formant structure is hidden within the breathiness which is caused by the escape of air through an apparently tense and nonactive pair of vocal cords. Vocal rehabilitation involves the use of the hypofunctional approach to voice production. With the emergence of formant structure and the decrease in breathiness as indicated by the post-treatment spectrogram, voice use is encouraged. As can be seen in each of

these examples, the voice spectrograph is extremely useful in demonstrating objective changes in voice, related to the vocal rehabilitation program.

EVALUATION OF SURGICAL PROCEDURES OF THE LARYNX

Voice spectrography is useful in evaluation of certain surgical procedures of the larynx. Vocal cord injection, conservative laryngeal operations for carcinoma of the larynx and evaluation of pre- and postoperative vocal cord stripping procedures have all been successfully evaluated by the use of voice spectrograms. The objective evidence

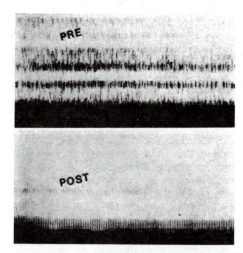

Fig. 10. Pre- and postspectrograms of a patient who underwent Teflon® paste injection for unilateral vocal cord paralysis. The postsurgical spectrogram shows an essentially normal voice with none of the aperiodicity, breathiness or formant breakdown noted in the presurgical example.

indicated by spectrographic analysis is useful both in the management of the patient in the clinical situation, and in the professional evaluation of the voice by both the laryngologist and speech pathologist.

As mentioned previously, vocal cord paralysis can be treated by vocal rehabilitation. However, many of these patients are amenable to vocal cord injection with dramatic results. Widely displaced cords in the intermediate position or vocal cords paralyzed in the paramedian position with breathiness are all subjects for potential vocal cord injection. The voice spectrogram has been advocated in the evaluation of vocal cord injections with Teflon.®[4] This is becoming increasingly useful in the proper evaluation of the pre- and post operative voice (Fig. 10). As mentioned previously, the abnormalities of aperiodicity, breakdown of formant structure and breathiness are all seen in vocal cord paralysis. Their correction by vocal cord injection is dramatic when pre- and postoperative spectrograms are compared. Persistent abnormalities of the spectrogram can give information

to the laryngologist and help him decide whether a second injection may be necessary.

Voice spectrography is also useful in evaluation of the voice associated with the various types of glottic reconstruction following vertical hemilaryngectomy. Vertical hemilaryngectomy has been advocated as an excellent means of removal of carcinoma of the true cord with sparing of the voice. Excessive breathiness and hoarseness following this procedure has prompted a variety of laryngoplasties to be advocated as a means of reconstructing tissue opposite to the normally mobile cord in an attempt to achieve glottic closure. Although several techniques have been advocated, there is no uniform opinion as to which is the best. An evaluation of these techniques by spectrography is helpful on an objective basis to decide which technique is most efficacious in the improvement of the voice following this surgical procedure. In a limited series, we have compared the results of sternohyoid muscle grafts to the use of hemilaryngectomy alone without laryngoplasty. The spectrograms when analyzed are compared with the normal voice. The objective evidence produced by the spectrograms would indicate that there is no improvement by laryngoplasty in the long-term follow-up of these individuals. However, it must be emphasized that only large studies with long-term follow-ups can be adequately used to produce a final statement on this problem.

Lastly, vocal cord nodules and polyps are frequent inciting etiologies responsible for many vocal cord strippings. The pre- and postoperative voice attained has not until this time been adequately evaluated. Frequently, hoarseness persists after vocal cord stripping. An objective evaluation of the pre- and postoperative voice is essential for the laryngologist to adequately evaluate his patients. Frequently, the ability to produce a spectrogram and show the patient that though the voice has not returned to normal levels but has been dramatically improved is extremely im-

Fig. 11. Pre- and postsurgical example of phonation related to vocal cord stripping for bilateral nodules. The presurgical example (A) shows noticeable evidence of breathings and aperiodicity of vocal cord movement. The postsurgical example (B) reflects an essentially normal voice with no evidence of dysfunction.

portant in the postoperative management of these individuals (Fig. 11). Again, the objective evidence of vocal cord change cannot be overemphasized as an essential component in the adequate evaluation of laryngeal surgical candidates.

EVALUATION OF MEDICAL MANAGEMENT OF VOCAL CORD LESIONS

The voice spectrogram will in the future have significant use in the evaluation of medical treatment for certain illnesses causing laryngeal disorders. Both hypothyroidism and myasthenia gravis have distinct vocal cord changes associated with their respective metabolic disturbances. Improvement in the

_____
* Roche Laboratories, Nutley, New Jersey

metabolic condition is frequently associated with marked improvement in the voice. The changes subjectively seen in the treatment program will actually be demonstrable based on objective changes seen in the spectrogram. It is further hoped that in the future the end point in the so-called Tensilon®* test for myasthenia gravis may be indicated more readily by close evaluation of the voice spectrogram. An improvement in periodicity in patients with myasthenia gravis could be an objective indication of improvement with injected Tensilon.® This may help establish the diagnosis of myasthenia gravis. Further studies will be needed for complete evaluation of this technique.

Further, the objective determination of the voice is of vital interest from a medicolegal standpoint. A quality tape recording can be a great asset in assessing the exact nature of the voice. The accompanying spectrogram produced from this tape will give increasing objective evidence of the laryngeal disorders described by the clinician. Just as the audiogram helps in evaluating the pre- and postoperative condition of the ear, so too the spectrogram will help in evaluating the pre- and postoperative condition of the voice. As the legal implications of laryngeal surgery become more and more important, the voice spectrogram will have increased usage.

LIMITATIONS OF VOICE SPECTROGRAPHY

As in any other objective technique, the limitations of voice spectrography should be well understood. The exact quantification of spectrogram measurements is not feasible. It is the visual qualitative change of pattern in the parameters of the voice on the spectrogram rather than the actual measureable degree of change in formant structure, periodicity or breathiness, that is the significant aspect of voice spectrography. The spectrogram as such produces a clinically usable objective evaluation of the voice.

To date, spectrograms cannot differentiate between different types of vocal cord lesions. Vocal cord nodules do not produce acoustic characteristics different from a contact granuloma. Furthermore, dysphonic characteristics, as indicated on a spectrogram, cannot indicate the existence or nonexistence of a malignant lesion. It is important to remember that many types of vocal cord pathologies yield similar resultant acoustic characteristics as seen on the spectrogram.

Spectrograms should not be used in place of indirect laryngoscopy to determine whether or not lesions have been resolved. Spectrograms are not a substitute for direct or indirect observation of the larynx. It should be emphasized that voice evaluation by spectrography should not be used as a substitute for good clinical acumen. Again, the final judgements of vocal conditions should be an evaluation of all the parameters available to the clinician and not on the basis of a single test.

————

Request for reprints should be sent to Eugene Rontal, M.D., 21700 Northwestern Hwy., Tower 14, Suite 545, Southfield, Mich. 48075.

ACKNOWLEDGMENT—The authors acknowledge the assistance of Mrs. Sydnor Gilbreath for her generous support of these research activities through the Gilbreath Voice Analysis Laboratory, Speech and Language Pathology Department, William Beaumont Hospital, Royal Oak, Michigan. Technical assistance was given by the Audio-Visual Department at William Beaumont Hospital.

REFERENCES

1. Potter R, Kopp G, Green H: *Visible Speech.* New York, D. Van Nostrand Company, Inc., 1947

2. Arnold GE: Vocal rehabilitation of paralytic dysphonia: IX Technique of intracordal injection. Arch Otolaryngol 76:358-368

3. Rolnick MI, Hoops HR: Plosive phoneme duration as a function of palato — pharyngeal adequacy. Cleft Palate J 8:65-76, 1971

4. Rontal E, Rontal M, Rolnick MI: The use of spectrograms in the evaluation of vocal cord injection. Laryngoscope 85:47-56, 1975

5. Yanagihara N: Significance of harmonic changes and noise components in hoarseness. J Speech Hearing Res 10:531-541, 1967

6. Holbrook A, Fairbanks G: Diphthong formants and their movements. J Speech Hearing Res 5:38-58, 1962

7. Iwata S, Von Leden H: Voice prints in laryngeal disease. Arch Otolaryngol 91:346-351, 1970

8. Cooper M: Spectrographic analysis of fundamental frequency and hoarseness before and after vocal rehabilitation. J Speech Hearing Disord 39:286-297, 1974

9. Isshiki N, Yanagihara N, Morimoto M: Approach to the objective diagnosis of hoarseness. Folia Phoniatr (Basel) 18: 183-192, 1964

10. Koyama T, Kawasaki M, Ogura JH: Mechanics of voice production, regulation of vocal intensity. Laryngoscope 79:337-354, 1969

11. Timcke R, Von Leden H, Moore P: Laryngeal vibrations; measurement of the glottic wave. Part I. The normal vibratory cycle. Arch Otolaryngol 68:1-19, 1958

Permissions

Part I: Basics and Beginnings

The Sound Spectrograph (pp. 3–33). Reprinted with permission from *The Journal of the Acoustical Society of America*, Vol. 18, pp. 19–49, (1946). © 1946 American Institute of Physics.

Accuracy and Limitations of Sona-Graph Measurements (pp. 34–46). Reprinted with permission from *Proceedings of the Fourth International Congress of Phonetic Sciences*, Mouton De Gruyter & Co., pp. 188–202, 1962.

Sound Spectrography (pp. 47–66). Reprinted with permission from *Proceedings of the Fourth International Congress of Phonetic Sciences*, Mouton De Gruyter & Co., pp. 14–33, 1962.

Parameter Relationships in the Portrayal of Signals With Sound Spectrograph Techniques (pp. 67–72). Reprinted with permission from *Journal of Speech and Hearing Disorders*, Vol. 17, pp. 427–432, 1952. © 1952 the American Speech-Language-Hearing Association, Rockville, Maryland.

Part II: Spectrographic Characteristics of Normal Speech

The Spectra of Vowels (pp. 75–95). Reprinted with permission from *The Sounds of Speech Communication*, written by J.M. Pickett, Austin, TX: PRO-ED Inc., Chap. 4, pp. 57–78, (1980).

Consonant Features, Glides, and Stops (pp. 96–112). Reprinted with permission from *The Sounds of Speech Communication*, written by J.M. Pickett, Austin, TX: PRO-ED Inc., Chap. 6, pp. 103–120, (1980).

Consonant: Nasal, Stop, and Fricative Manners of Articulation (pp. 113–123). Reprinted with permission from *The Sounds of Speech Communication*, written by J.M. Pickett, Austin, TX: PRO-ED Inc., Chap. 7, pp. 121–132, (1980).

Control Methods Used in a Study of the Vowels (pp. 124–133). Reprinted with permission from *The Journal of the Acoustic Society of America*, Vol. 24, pp. 175–184, (1952). © 1952 American Institute of Physics.

Duration of Syllable Nuclei in English (pp. 134–144). Reprinted with permission from *The Journal of the Acoustic Society of America*, Vol. 32, pp. 693–703, (1960). © 1960 American Institute of Physics.

Speech Wave Analysis (pp. 145–178). Reprinted with permission from *Acoustic Theory of Speech Production*, written by Dr. Gunnar Fant, Mouton De Gruyter & Co., 1970.

Stops in CV-Syllables (pp. 179–215). Reprinted with permission from *Speech Transmission Labs Quarterly Progress Reports*, written by Dr. Gunnar Fant, Royal Institute of Technology, Stockholm, Sweden, Vol. 41, (1969).

Acoustic Properties of Stop Consonants (pp. 216–225). Reprinted with permission from *The Journal of the Acoustic Society of America*, Vol. 29, pp. 107–116, (1957). © 1957 American Institute of Physics.

Voice Onset Time, Frication, and Aspiration in Word-Initial Consonant Clusters (pp. 226–246). Reprinted with permission from *Journal of Speech and Hearing Research*, Vol. 18, No. 4, pp. 686–706, 1975. © 1975 the American Speech-Language-Hearing Association, Rockville, Maryland.

A Cross-Language Study of Voicing in Initial Stops: Acoustical Measurements (pp. 247–285). Reprinted with permission from *Word*, Vol. 20, No. 3, pp. 384–422, (1964).

Transitions, Glides, and Diphthongs (pp. 286–295). Reprinted with permission from *The Journal of the Acoustic Society of America*, Vol. 33, pp. 268–277, (1961). © 1961 American Institute of Physics.

Acoustic Characteristics of English /w, r, l/ Spoken Correctly by Young Children and Adults (pp. 296–303). Reprinted with permission from *The Journal of the Acoustic Society of America,* Vol. 57, pp. 462–469, (1975). © 1975 American Institute of Physics.

Part III: Speech Sound Development

Development of Speech Sounds in Children (pp. 307–356). Reprinted with permission from *Acta Oto-Laryngologica,* written by S. Eguchi and I.J. Hirsh, Suppl. 257, pp. 5–48, (1969).

Anatomical and Neuromuscular Maturation of the Speech Mechanism: Evidence From Acoustic Studies (pp. 357–383). Reprinted with permission from *Journal of Speech and Hearing Research,* Vol. 19, No. 3, pp. 421–447, 1976. © 1976 the American Speech-Language-Hearing Association, Rockville, Maryland.

Vowel Formant Frequency Characteristics of Preadolescent Males and Females (pp. 384–391). Reprinted with permission from *The Journal of the Acoustic Society of America,* Vol. 69, pp. 231–238, (1981). © 1981 American Institute of Physics.

Developmental Study of Vowel Formant Frequencies in an Imitation Task (pp. 392–401). Reprinted with permission from *The Journal of the Acoustic Society of America,* Vol. 65, pp. 208–217, (1979). © 1979 American Institute of Physics.

Acoustic Features of Infant Vocalic Utterances at 3, 6, and 9 Months (pp. 402–414). Reprinted with permission from *The Journal of the Acoustic Society of America,* Vol. 72, pp. 353–365, (1982). © 1982 American Institute of Physics.

Part IV: Spectrography in Evaluation and Therapy

Better Spectrograms From Children's Speech: A Research Note (pp. 417–425). Reprinted with permission from *Journal of Speech and Hearing Research,* Vol. 23, No. 1, pp. 19–27, 1980. © 1980 the American Speech-Language-Hearing Association, Rockville, Maryland.

Isovowel Lines for the Evaluation of Vowel Formant Structure in Speech Disorders (pp. 417–425). Reprinted with permission from *Journal of Speech and Hearing Disorders,* Vol. 44, No. 4, pp. 513–521, 1979. © 1979 the American Speech-Language-Hearing Association, Rockville, Maryland.

Acoustic Patterns of Apraxia of Speech (pp. 435–453). Reprinted with permission from *Journal of Speech and Hearing Research,* Vol. 26, pp. 231–249, 1983. © 1983 the American Speech-Language-Hearing Association, Rockville, Maryland.

Acoustic Characteristics of Dysarthria Associated with Cerebellar Disease (pp. 454–475). Reprinted with permission from *Journal of Speech and Hearing Research,* Vol. 22, pp. 627–648, 1979. © 1979 the American Speech-Language-Hearing Association, Rockville, Maryland.

An Acoustic-Articulatory Description of Children's Defective /s/ Production (pp. 476–492). Reprinted with permission of the publisher from "An Acoustic-Articulatory Description of Children's Defective /s/ Productions", by R. Daniloff, K. Wilcox and M.I. Stephens, *Journal of Communication Disorders,* Vol. 13, pp. 347–363, (1980). © by Elsevier Science Publishing Co., Inc.

Prespeech Vocalizations of a Deaf Infant: A Comparison With Normal Metaphonological Development (pp. 493–509). Reprinted with permission from *Journal of Speech and Hearing Research,* Vol. 28, pp. 47–63, 1985. © 1985 the American Speech-Language-Hearing Association, Rockville, Maryland.

The Vowel Formants of Deaf and Normal-Hearing Eleven- to Fourteen-Year-Old Boys (pp. 510–524). Reprinted with permission from *Journal of Speech and Hearing Disorders,* Vol. 29, No. 2, pp. 156–170, 1964. © 1964 the American Speech-Language-Hearing Association, Rockville, Maryland.

The Speech Spectrographic Display: Interpretation of Visual Patterns by Hearing-Impaired Adults (pp. 525–533). Reprinted with permission from *Journal of Speech and Hearing Disorders,* Vol. 46, pp. 379–387, 1981. © 1981 the American Speech-Language-Hearing Association, Rockville, Maryland.

Significance of Harmonic Changes and Noise Components in Hoarseness (pp. 534–544). Reprinted with permission from *Journal of Speech and Hearing Research,* Vol. 10, pp. 531–541, 1967. © 1967 the American Speech-Language-Hearing Association, Rockville, Maryland.

Tremulous Speech: A Case Report (pp. 545–553). Reprinted with permission from *Folia Phoniatrica,* written by Y. Lebrun, F. Devreus, J.J. Rousseau and P. Darimont, S. Karger AG. Basel, Vol. 34, pp. 134–142, (1982).

Objective Evaluation of Vocal Pathology Using Voice Spectrography (pp. 554–563). Reprinted with permission from *Annals of Otology, Rhinology and Laryngology,* written by E. Rontal, M. Rontal and M.I. Rolnick, Vol. 84, pp. 662–671, (1975).